T0213700

Lecture Notes in Computer Science 9784

Commenced Publication in 1973
Founding and Former Series Editors:
Gerhard Goos, Juris Hartmanis, and Jan van Leeuwen

Editorial Board

David Hutchison
Lancaster University, Lancaster, UK
Takeo Kanade
Carnegie Mellon University, Pittsburgh, PA, USA
Josef Kittler
University of Surrey, Guildford, UK
Jon M. Kleinberg
Cornell University, Ithaca, NY, USA
Friedemann Mattern
ETH Zurich, Zürich, Switzerland
John C. Mitchell
Stanford University, Stanford, CA, USA
Moni Naor
Weizmann Institute of Science, Rehovot, Israel
C. Pandu Rangan
Indian Institute of Technology, Madras, India
Bernhard Steffen
TU Dortmund University, Dortmund, Germany
Demetri Terzopoulos
University of California, Los Angeles, CA, USA
Doug Tygar
University of California, Berkeley, CA, USA
Gerhard Weikum
Max Planck Institute for Informatics, Saarbrücken, Germany

More information about this series at http://www.springer.com/series/7409

Yu Wang · Ge Yu
Yanyong Zhang · Zhu Han
Guoren Wang (Eds.)

Big Data Computing and Communications

Second International Conference, BigCom 2016
Shenyang, China, July 29–31, 2016
Proceedings

 Springer

Editors
Yu Wang
Department of Computer Science
University of N. Carolina at Charlotte
Charlotte, NC
USA

Ge Yu
College of Information Science
  and Engineering
Northeastern University
Shenyang, Liaoning
China

Yanyong Zhang
Department of Electrical & Computer
  Engineering
Rutgers University
Piscataway, NJ
USA

Zhu Han
Department of Electrical & Computer
  Engineering
University of Houston
Houston, TX
USA

Guoren Wang
College of Information Science
  and Engineering
Northeastern University
Shenyang, Liaoning
China

ISSN 0302-9743   ISSN 1611-3349 (electronic)
Lecture Notes in Computer Science
ISBN 978-3-319-42552-8   ISBN 978-3-319-42553-5 (eBook)
DOI 10.1007/978-3-319-42553-5

Library of Congress Control Number: 2016944343

LNCS Sublibrary: SL3 – Information Systems and Applications, incl. Internet/Web, and HCI

© Springer International Publishing Switzerland 2016
This work is subject to copyright. All rights are reserved by the Publisher, whether the whole or part of the material is concerned, specifically the rights of translation, reprinting, reuse of illustrations, recitation, broadcasting, reproduction on microfilms or in any other physical way, and transmission or information storage and retrieval, electronic adaptation, computer software, or by similar or dissimilar methodology now known or hereafter developed.
The use of general descriptive names, registered names, trademarks, service marks, etc. in this publication does not imply, even in the absence of a specific statement, that such names are exempt from the relevant protective laws and regulations and therefore free for general use.
The publisher, the authors and the editors are safe to assume that the advice and information in this book are believed to be true and accurate at the date of publication. Neither the publisher nor the authors or the editors give a warranty, express or implied, with respect to the material contained herein or for any errors or omissions that may have been made.

Printed on acid-free paper

This Springer imprint is published by Springer Nature
The registered company is Springer International Publishing AG Switzerland

Preface

It is a great pleasure for us to welcome you to the proceedings of the Second International Conference on Big Data Computing and Communication (BigCom 2016), which was held in Shenyang, China. BigCom is an international symposium dedicated to addressing the challenges emerging from big data-related computing and networking. This year, we were fortunate to receive many excellent papers covering a diverse set of research topics related to big data computing and communication. The event brought together numerous delegates from around the globe to discuss the latest advances in this vibrant and constantly evolving field.

BigCom 2016 received more than 90 submissions from Australia, Brazil, Canada, China, Finland, Hong Kong, Japan, Korea, Taiwan, and USA, out of which 39 were selected for publication as regular papers with an acceptance rate of 43 %. Most submissions received two or more peer reviews from our Technical Program Committee and external reviewers. We were only able to accept papers that received broad support from the reviewers. The final technical program included three excellent keynote speeches (by Prof. Lixin Gao, Prof. Jianzhong Li, and Prof. Yunhao Liu) and ten technical sessions. We would like to thank our Program Committee members as well as external reviewers, consisting of eminent researchers, whose dedication and hard work made the selection of papers for the proceedings possible.

We also wish to thank everyone who contributed to the quality and success of BigCom 2016, from all the authors to all the student volunteers. We particularly appreciate the guidance and support from the Steering Committee chair, Prof. Xiang-Yang Li. Special thanks also go to the three track Chairs, Lan Zhang, Chenren Xu, and Lei Zou, for their outstanding job in handling the review process, to the publication co-chairs, Zenghua Zhao, Fan Li, and Yingjian Liu, for collecting the final versions of all accepted papers, and to the publicity co-chairs, Dan Tao, Yuanfang Chen, and Yao Liu, for promoting the conference and attracting great submissions. We would like to thank our local organizing team Lan Yao and Zhibin Zhao for their great job organizing the local arrangements and making the stay of every conference attendee a pleasant and memorable one. We also thank the other members of the Organizing Committee for their help and support. Finally, we thank Northeastern University (China) for its support and for contributing student volunteers, and Tsinghua University Press, Springer LNCS, Beijing University of Posts and Telecommunications, Ocean University of China, University of Science and Technology of China, Audaque Data Technology Ltd., Neusoft, Qihoo360, ZTE, and CERNET for their grants in supporting the conference.

In addition to the stimulating program of the conference, Shenyang, with its tourist attractions and the diversity and quality of its cuisine, is an unforgettable place to visit. Shenyang is the provincial capital and largest city of Liaoning Province, as well as the largest city in northeast China. In the 17th century, Shenyang was conquered by the Manchu people and briefly used as the capital of the Qing dynasty. We hope you enjoy the technical program and have a great time in Shenyang.

June 2016

Yu Wang
Ge Yu
Yanyong Zhang
Zhu Han
Guoren Wang

Organization

Honorary Chair

Jinkuan Wang   Northeastern University, China

General Co-chairs

Ge Yu   Northeastern University, China
Yu Wang   University of North Carolina at Charlotte, USA

TPC Co-chairs

Yanyong Zhang   Rutgers University, USA
Zhu Han   University of Houston, USA
Guoren Wang   Northeastern University, China

TPC Track Chairs

Lei Zou   Peking University, China
Chenren Xu   Peking University, China
Lan Zhang   Tsinghua University, China

Local Co-chairs

Zhibin Zhao   Northeastern University, China
Lan Yao   Northeastern University, China

Poster/Demo Co-chairs

Ye Yuan   Northeastern University, China
Chunhong Zhang   Beijing University of Posts and Telecommunications, China

Workshop Co-chairs

Lanchao Liu   Cisco, USA
Mengshu Hou   University of Electronic Science and Technology, China

Industry Co-chairs

Xu Zhang	Beijing University of Posts and Telecommunications, China
Dazhe Zhao	Northeastern University, China
Jiahao Wang	University of Electronic Science and Technology, China

Publicity Co-chairs

Dan Tao	Beijing Jiaotong University, China
Yuanfang Chen	Pierre and Marie Curie University, France
Yao Liu	University of South Florida, USA

Publication Co-chairs

Zenghua Zhao	Tianjin University, China
Fan Li	Beijing Institute of Technology, China
Yingjian Liu	Ocean University of China, China

Finance Co-chairs

Lan Yao	Northeastern University, China
Hongli Xu	University of Science and Technology of China, China
Xufei Mao	Tsinghua University, China
Shaojie Tang	University of Texas at Dallas, USA

Web Chair

Lan Yao	Northeastern University, China

Program Committee

Shlomo Argamon	Illinois Institute of Technology, USA
Ashwin Ashok	Carnegie Mellon University, USA
Gautam Bhanage	WINLAB, Rutgers University, USA
Cheng Bo	University of North Carolina at Charlotte, USA
Jiannong Cao	Hong Kong Polytechnic University, SAR China
Marcelo Carvalho	Universidade de Brasilia, Brazil
Guihai Chen	Shanghai Jiaotong University, China
Hanhua Chen	Huazhong University of Science and Technology, China
Thang Dinh	Virginia Commonwealth University, USA
Wei Dong	Zhejiang University, China
Xiaoyong Du	Renmin University, China

Amr El Abbadi	University of California, Santa Barbara, USA
Hong Gao	Harbin Institute of Technology, China
Wei Gao	University of Tennessee, USA
Yong Ge	University of North Carolina at Charlotte, USA
Deke Guo	National University of Defense Technology, China
Junze Han	Illinois Institute of Technology, USA
Zhu Han	University of Houston, USA
Bonghee Hong	Pusan National University, South Korea
Liang Hong	Wuhan University, China
Xia Hu	Texas A&M University, USA
Bo Ji	Temple University, USA
Taeho Jung	Illinois Institute of Technology, USA
Seungwoo Kang	Korea Tech, South Korea
Salil Kanhere	The University of New South Wales, Australia
Donghyun Kim	North Carolina Central University, USA
Gene Moo Lee	University of Texas at Austin, USA
Fan Li	Beijing Institute of Technology, China
Zhanhuai Li	Northwestern Polytechnic University, China
Xin Li	Nanjing University, China
Xiang Lian	University of Texas Rio Grande Valley, USA
Chengfei Liu	Swinburne University of Technology, Australia
Chuanren Liu	Rutgers Business School, USA
Ke Liu	National Natural Science Foundation of China, China
Kebin Liu	Tsinghua University, China
Hongbo Liu	Indiana University-Purdue University Indianapolis, USA
Lanchao Liu	Cisco Inc., USA
Yan Liu	Concordia University, Canada
Junzhou Luo	Southeast University, China
Xufei Mao	Tsinghua University, China
Xin Miao	Tsinghua University, China
Yi Mu	University of Wollongong, Australia
Nam Tuan Nguyen	Schlumberger, USA
Nam Nguyen	Towson University, USA
Xia Ning	Indiana University-Purdue University Indianapolis, USA
M. Tamer Ozsu	University of Waterloo, Canada
Peng Peng	Peking University, China
Feng Qian	Indiana University, USA
Christine Reilly	University of Texas Rio Grande Valley, USA
Walid Saad	Virginia Tech, USA
Dola Saha	Rutgers University, USA
Sherif Sakr	National ICT Australia (NICTA), ATP lab, Sydney, Australia
Ganesh Ram Santhanam	Iowa State University, USA
Jungtaek Seo	National Security Research Institute, South Korea

Shuo Shang	China University of Petroleum, China
Stephan Sigg	Aalto University, Finland
Junggab Son	North Carolina Central University, USA
Guozhen Tan	Dalian University of Technology, China
Shaojie Tang	University of Texas at Dallas, USA
Dan Tao	Beijing Jiao Tong University, China
Yongxin Tong	Beihang University, China
Hoang Nguyen Tran	Kyung Hee University, South Korea
Hanli Wang	Tong Ji University, China
Guoren Wang	Northeastern University, China
Jie Wang	University of Massachusetts Lowell, USA
Jiliang Wang	Tsinghua University, China
Xinbing Wang	Shanghai Jiaotong University, China
Ka-Chun Wong	University of Toronto, Canada
Yongwei Wu	Tsinghua University, China
Zhenyu Wu	NEC Laboratories America Inc., USA
Yong Xiao	University of Houston, USA
Hui Xiong	Rutgers University, USA
Chenren Xu	Peking University, USA
Xiaochun Yang	Northeastern University, China
Jie Yang	Florida State University, USA
Panlong Yang	University of Science and Technology of China, China
Zheng Yang	Tsinghua University, China
Lan Yao	Northeastern University, China
Seongwook Youn	Korea National University of Transportation, South Korea
Ge Yu	Northeastern University, China
Xu Yu	Chinese University of Hong Kong, SAR China
Zhiwen Yu	Northwestern Polytechnical University, China
Chunhong Zhang	Beijing University of Posts and Telecommunications, China
Lan Zhang	Tsinghua University, China
Xu Zhang	Beijing University of Posts and Telecommunications, China
Yanyong Zhang	Rutgers University, USA
Huiqun Zhao	Northern Technology University, China
Jumin Zhao	Taiyuan University of Technology, China
Zenghua Zhao	Tianjin University, China
Zhibin Zhao	Northeastern University, China
Weiguo Zheng	The Chinese University of Hong Kong, SAR China
Aoying Zhou	East China Normal University, China
Xiangmin Zhou	RMIT University, Australia
Shiai Zhu	MCRLab, University of Ottawa, Canada
Lei Zou	Peking University, China

Additional Reviewers

Chen, Linlin
Choi, Yun-Sik
Du, Haohua
Erte, Pan
Fan, Zhang
Gao, Jun
Georgiou, Theodore
Hou, Jiahui
Hu, Yiqing
Hussain, Rasheed
Jia, Zhenhua
Jian, Xuesi
Kumbhkar, Ratnesh
Li, Feng

Li, Kai
Li, Sugang
Li, Ting
Li, Yingyu
Lin, Changfu
Liu, Xin
Liu, Xiruo
Lu, Xinjiang
Men, Hao
Mi, Xianghang
Mukherjee, Shreyasee
Niu, Xing
Nguyen, Hung
Qian, Jianwei

Sagari, Shweta
Sai, Mounika
Su, Kai
Tan, Hailun
Velasco, Yesenia
Wang, Wenbo
Wang, Zhitao
Xie, Jin
Yan, Shankai
Zhang, Jiao
Zhang, Jin
Zhang, Yanru
Zhao, Yi
Zou, Rui

Contents

Smart Phone and Sensing Application

Sensor Networks and RFID

Machine Learning and Algorithm

Architecture and Applications

Routing and Resource Management

Security and Privacy

Signal Processing and Pattern Recognition

Social Networks and Recommendation

Best Paper Candidate

Similarity Search Algorithm over Data Supply Chain Based on Key Points

Peng Li[1]($\boxtimes$), Hong Luo[1], Yan Sun[1], and Xin-Ming Li[2]

[1] Department of Computer Science,
Beijing University of Posts and Telecommunication,
Beijing 100876, China
`lipeng1106,luoh,sunyan@bupt.edu.cn`
[2] Science and Technology on Beijing Complex Electronic System Simulation
Laboratory, Academy of Equipment, Beijing 100876, China
`13911729321@163.com`

Abstract. In this paper, we target at similarity search among data supply chains, which plays essential role in optimizing the chain and extending its value. This problem is very challenging for application-oriented data supply chains because the high complexity of data supply chain makes the computation of similarity extremely complex and inefficiency. In this paper, we propose a feature space representation model based on key points, which can extract the key features from sub-sequences of the original data supply chain and simplify the original data supply chain into a feature vector form. Then, we formulate the similarity computation of key points based on the multi-scale features. Further, we propose an improved hierarchical clustering algorithm for similarity search over data supply chains. The main idea is to separate sub-sequences into disjoint groups such that each-group meets one specific clustering criteria, and thus the cluster containing the query object is the similarity search result. The experimental results show that the proposed approach is both effective and efficient for data supply chain retrieval.

Keywords: Data supply chain · Similarity search · Feature space · Hierarchical clustering

1 Introduction

Data trade markets enable data to flow freely for the benefit of the whole organizations. A data supply chain is constructed when data is created, transformed, combined with other data, and exported to next user [1]. A lot of efforts have been made on developing novel similarity search algorithms among data supply chains due to its promising applications. For example, similarity query identifies those data supply chains whose structure evolved similarly to a specific one. It is not only offering users the best candidates of data supply chains to optimize the products, but also helps finding the potential consumers of their data and extending its value.

© Springer International Publishing Switzerland 2016
Y. Wang et al. (Eds.): BigCom 2016, LNCS 9784, pp. 3–12, 2016.
DOI: 10.1007/978-3-319-42553-5_1

Cluster analysis [2,3] is an important technique in data mining and data analysis, so it can be used in similarity search of data supply chain. However, there are few studies of similarity search of data supply chain. For example, Iwashita et al. [4] propose a method of determining the optimal number of clusters. Ghassempour et al. [5] propose an approach based on Hidden Markov Models (HMMs), where we first map each trajectory into an HMM, then define a suitable distance between HMMs and finally proceed to cluster the HMMs with a method based on a distance matrix. However, this method does not consider errors incurred. Those approaches generally cluster original data supply chains, its efficiency degrades rapidly with the increase of number of node. And all of them don't distinguish the difference between global similarity and local similarity, results may not be reasonable in practical.

In this paper, we design a Similarity Search System for Data Supply Chain (SSS-DSC). The challenges include: (1) how to replace the original data supply chains and remain the intrinsic feature for improving the searching efficiency; (2) how to formulate the distance for measuring the closeness of the corresponding unequal data supply chain.

To tackle the above challenges, a novel feature space representation model based on key points is proposed. We firstly seek and extract key points reflecting the changed application purpose. Using these key points, the original data supply chains can be partitioned into a number of sub-sequences. Then, we extract the feature of each sub-sequence and construct a feature space to represent the original DSC. In order to tackle previously low precision of a distance measure for unequal data supply chains, we further develop a novel similarity computation algorithm with multi-dimensional features. Sub-sequences are characterized in multi-dimensional feature vectors form. For features in different dimensions, we calculate the distances of each pair of sub-sequence by different distance formula and integrate different value with linear weights. Our algorithm reaches the most similar results according to specific criteria, which performs sub-sequence matching and sub-sequence searching. Sub-sequence searching means that the query pattern may be comprised between any nodes in the candidate sequence. We conduct simulation experiments and the experimental results show that the proposed approach can condenses the original data supply chains by applying a feature extraction technique whose query performance outperforming the existing algorithms by at least 20 %.

2   Problem Definition

Data supply chain is treated as an object in this paper; it consists of plentiful dynamic time-seried data. In order to provide a convenient expression, we give some definitions as follows.

Definition 1 (Data Supply Chain Set). *A set of data supply chains, denoted by $\sum = \{S_1, S_2, ..., S_n\}$, where n is the serial number of data supply chain.*

Definition 2 (Data Supply Chain). *Given a data supply chain S, which consists of a data sequence ordered by the generation time. A data supply chain is denoted by $S = \{d_1, d_2, ..., d_n\}$, where $d_{t_i}(t_0 < t_i < t_n)$ is a instance of data generated at t_i.*

Definition 3 (Sub-Sequence). *Given a data supply chain S of length n, a sub-sequence of S is a sampling of length m $(m \leq n)$ of contiguous positions from S, that is $\beta = \{d_{t_p}, ..., d_{t_{p+m-1}}\}(1 \leq p \leq n - m + 1)$.*

Definition 4 (Segment Feature). *Consider a data supply chain S that has been segmented into k sub-sequences $\{\beta_1, \beta_2, ..., \beta_k\}$, SF_i is a triple of feature vector of the ith sub-sequence β_i.*

$$SF_i = (ARS_i, AP_i, DES_i) \tag{1}$$

Here, ARS_i is the feature vector representing association rules set of β_i; AP_i is the feature vector of the application purpose; DES_i is the feature vectors representing its evolution.

Definition 5 (Distance). *Given two segment features SF_1 and SF_2 representing β_1 and β_2 respectively, the distance between β_1 and β_2 is given by:*

$$\begin{aligned} D(\beta_1, \beta_2) = & w_1 * d_1(ARS_1, ARS_2) + w_2 * d_2(AP_1, AP_2) \\ & + w_3 * d_3(DES_1, DES_2) \end{aligned} \tag{2}$$

where $d_i()$ is the distance of each feature vector and $w_i(1 \leq i \leq 3)$ is the weight associated with a specific attribute. The summation of all weights is 1.

Definition 6 (Similarity Calculation). *Given a reference data supply chain or sub-sequence of chain Q and its segment feature SF_q, a set of data supply chains $\sum$, a user specified distance threshold ε, a similarity search retrieves all data supply chains $S_i \in \Sigma$ such that*

$$D(SF_q, SF_j) \leq \varepsilon \tag{3}$$

where $\varepsilon > 0$. If Eq. 3 is established, it is say that Q and sub-sequence β_j of S_i are similar to the case of the ε boundary.

The similarity search basic problem can be stated as follows: given a set of objects, find the most similar ones to a given query object.

3 Overview of SSS-DSC

A similarity search process for data supply chain consists of three phases that are described hereafter:

(1) Feature exaction and modeling: this is the core of system. Here, we propose a novel Feature Space Representation Model based on Key Points (FSRM-KP). FSRM-KP firstly seeks and extracts the key points for each data supply

chain, then divides each chain into a set of sub-sequence using these points (also called boundary point). Then, several features can be extracted from sub-sequence such as Association Rule Sets (ARS), Application Purpose (AP) and Data Evolution Sequence (DES). As a result, we construct a feature space for each sub-sequence and describe the original data supply chains according to the feature space model. By this way, the storage of each chain is shrunk significantly.

(2) Similarity measure based on multi-dimensional features: we design a similarity measurement algorithm based on feature space model. Feature spaces are divided into three classes feature: Association Rule Sets, Application Purpose and Data Evolution Sequence. By dividing the feature spaces into the above classes, we calculate distances of each pair of sub-sequence features using the available NLP (Natural Language Processing) APIs and edit distance techniques. Further, we get the pair-wise distance of sub-sequence by integrating different distance value with linear weights.

(3) Nearest neighbor classification: finally, a hierarchical clustering algorithm for data supply chains is proposed. Since the proposed FSRM-KP presents features of sub-sequence, we choose those as a new specific clustering criteria. The proposed clustering algorithm processes the transformed sub-sequences and outputs the similarity search result.

4   Similarity Search for Data Supply Chains

This section discusses the core algorithms and calculations in the SSS-DSC.

4.1   Feature Space Representation Model Based on Key Points

In order to reduce computation time and improve the search efficiency, the data supply chains must be reduced in complexity. Hence, we propose a feature space representation model based on key points. The basic idea of FSRM-KP provides the oscillation behavior of a data supply chain that has been transformed into a feature space by linear segments. This representation, however, depends on a number of points chosen in the segmentation process. Demonstrating a data supply chain by one feature may not be sufficient to describe actual oscillation trends. To solve this, we extract several features from sub-sequence such as association rules sets, application purpose and data evolution sequence and extend the solutions to a multi-dimensional approach. Each sub-sequence includes three feature vectors. We use frequent pattern mining algorithm [6] as the basic algorithm and add the temporal constraints to discover correlation among multiple data nodes and get association rules set. By adding the sequential constraint and the time factor, the algorithm achieves more precise mining and shorter computation. Using the PROV, the standard provenance technology, we get the attribute arguments which depicts the actions performed on data and the entities being responsible for those actions. Each PROV record, which contains identity information, activity, occurring time, and consumer demand, is stored in the PROV database. Therefore, we can extract consumer purpose and data evolution sequence from it. Data evolution sequence is composed of data and the operations associated with the data. Formally, a sub-sequence is defined as a triple. Furthermore, a data supply chain is represented by a matrix M (consisting of N segments and three features).

Let $S \in \sum$ denote a data supply chain and SF denote segment feature of sub-sequence. The feature space model transforming algorithm based on key points is shown as Algorithm 1.

Algorithm 1. Feature Space Model Transforming Algorithm based on Key Points

---

Input: S
Output: $SF_1, SF_2, ... , SF_n$ // n is the number of segments of all data supply chains
　1: Seek and extract key points from S; // the point reflecting the data supply chain's changed application purpose
　2: Segment S into n sections $\{\beta_1, \beta_2, ..., \beta_n\}$ using these key points ;
　3: **for** each sub-sequence $\in$ S **do**
　4:　　extract association rules set, application purpose and data evolution sequence from sub-sequence;
　5:　　construct the feature space for sub-sequence $SF = (ARS, P, DES)$;
　6: **end for**
　7: return $SF_1, SF_2, ... , SF_n$;

4.2　Similarity Computation Based on Multi-scale Features

In the previous section we demonstrated how to computationally reduce the complexity of a data supply chain, representing it by the major turning points and feature space. This transformation is obviously required for the searched candidate sequences. Similarity measuré can efficiently support similarity search, which directly influence the shape of the clusters, the next step is to define the distance function. The use of multi-dimensional features causes the problem of measuring the similarity between two data supply chains becoming measuring the distance between the two data supply chains of feature vector. For this reason, a suitable similarity measurement algorithm based on it should be given. The comparison between two data supply chains is done in two basic steps. First of all, the data supply chains of features relative to each scale are compared, using the different distance function defined before. The proposed FSRM-KP supports several kinds of distance functions, in our implementation, we distinguish features in different dimensions and those distance is usually measured by different distance formula.

4.2.1　Similarity Measurement Method for Association Rules Set

ARS is a set of association rules which can describe the correlation among multiple data nodes of region. It can be described as:

$$ARS = (AR_1, AR_2, ..., AR_n) \tag{4}$$

where AR_i is a association rule with support S.

Definition 7 (Sub-Sequence). *Let ARS_1 and ARS_2 denote different associ-ation rules set respectively, $ARS_1 \neq \oslash$, $ARS_2 \neq \oslash$, the distance between ARS_1 and ARS_2 is given by:*

$$d(ARS_1, ARS_2) = \frac{|ARS_1 \cap ARS_2|}{|ARS_1 \cup ARS_2|} \tag{5}$$

where $|ARS|$ denotes the number of association rules set.

4.2.2 Similarity Measurement Method for Application Purpose

Comparing application purpose (AP) helps us with computing a more accurate similarity ranking. All AP attributes are text based that including information such as consumer demand and the objective of data analysis. According to its characteristics, the measure similarity task is done through available NLP APIs. By using third party NLP APIs that adding semantic annotation or tagging to data supply chain of texts, we can extract a topic/key word from each one. To perform this task many potential NLP web APIs have been looked into and tested. They include Wikimeta [7], OpenCalais [8], Pingar [9], AlchemyAPI [10] and Semantria [11]. In many cases the NLP service may not be able to return a correct topic name for a given text. To obtain a larger number of topic names multiple NLP services are used in conjunction. OpenCalais allows for 50,000 API calls a day and 4 calls per second as part of the free license. AlchemyAPI provides up to 30,000 API calls a day for research purposes. Once all application purpose features are established, we will try to find commonality among the obtained topics to compute the distance value between each sub-sequence and a given one.

4.2.3 Similarity Measurement Method for Data Evolution Sequence

To determine the similarity of two data evolution sequences, an approximate symbol matching algorithm based on edit distance [12] is used. Its main idea is: the more similarity between two data evolution sequences, the minimum number of data transformation operations required to transform one data evo-lution sequence into the other. Data transformation operation can be weight by an arbitrary weight function that assigns each data transformation oper-ation a numeric value. The sequence distance is a numeric value that repre-senting the sum weight of data transformation operations which is required to equalize two data evolution sequences. Let S and T denote two data evolution sequences, $O_{sum} = \{O_1, O_2, ..., O_n\}$ denotes a set of data transformation oper-ations sequence transforming S into T, $t(O_i)$ denotes a weight of data trans-formation operation. Given $T(O_{sum}) = \sum_{i=1}^{k} t(O_i)$, the sequence distance $d(S, T)$ between S and T is then defined as:

$$d(S, T) = min\{T(O_{sum}) | O_{sum} \text{ is a set of transformation of } S \text{ into } T\} \tag{6}$$

In the final step, different distance values are integrated with linear weights. The weight assignment is based on the distance values. We assign a more weight for the smaller value of feature, which avoid each feature vector affect the final results dramatically.

4.3   Hierarchical Clustering Algorithm for DSC

Up to this point, data supply chains are expressed in terms of feature space model and distance measure formula is defined. In order to provide more accurate results, we proposed a hierarchical clustering algorithm for data supply chains, which differentiates global similarity and local similarity of data supply chains and performs sub-sequence matching and sub-sequence searching. The algorithm can improve the efficiency while keep the accuracy at the same time. The basic idea of the algorithm is: Firstly, the original data supply chains is divided into a set of sub-sequences represented by feature model; Then, each sub-sequence is called as a cluster. According to the above mentioned similarity measure approach, the distances between each cluster are measured. We separate sub-sequences into disjoint groups such that the same-group of sub-sequences meets a specific clustering criteria. The cluster which the query object lies within is the similarity search results.

Let $\sum$ denote a set of data supply chains, Q denotes a reference data supply chain or sub-sequence of chain, C_i denotes the ith cluster, ε denotes a user specified distance threshold, $C_{results}$ denotes the cluster including the query object of sub-sequence and the most similar ones. The algorithm of a hierarchical clustering algorithm for data supply chains is shown as Algorithm 2.

Algorithm 2. A Hierarchical Clustering Algorithm for Data Supply Chains

---

Input: $Q, \sum, \varepsilon$
Output: $C_{results}$
 1: **for** each $S \in \sum$ **do**
 2:    $\{SF_1, SF_2, ..., SF_n\} \leftarrow FSRM - KP(S)$;
 3:    $C_i \leftarrow SF_i$ // C_i indicates a cluster ;
 4: **end for**
 5: **repeat**
 6:    Compute the distances between each pair of clusters by using similarity measure approach;
 7:    find the most similar clusters C_i and C_j , where C_i and C_j coming from different data supply chain;
 8:    merge them into one cluster and update the center of the generated cluster;
 9: **until** the distances between each pair of clusters is beyond the ε specified by the user
10: return $C_{results}$;

---

5   Experiments and Analysis

5.1   Experimental Setup

We run our experiments on Window 7 operating system. The configurations of computer are Inter Core i5-3200M 2.5 GHz processors, 2 GB memory and 500 GB hard drive. To the best of our knowledge there are seldom authoritative datasets and reported approaches can clustering analysis for data supply chains. Hence, the experiments are conducted on synthetic datasets to evaluate the performance of the proposed approach. The number of classes is 10 in the datasets. All data supply chains are labeled according to the class they belonging to. We compare a Hierarchical Clustering Algorithm for Data Supply Chains (HCA-DSC) with a Dictionary-Based Compression for Long Time-Series Similarity (DBC-TSS) [13] from query accuracy and time.

5.2   Query Accuracy

In order to evaluate the accuracy of the proposed approach, regarding N, the total number of data supply chains is set equal to 30 and 50, whereas the average length M of data supply chains ranges from 20 to 50. Figure 1 shows the query accuracy for M using HCA-DSC and the DBC-TSS methods respectively.

Figure 1 presents the query accuracy for varying dimensionality when the total number of data supply chains is set equal to 30. The main observation is that the query accuracy ranges from 52 % to 85.75 %. Although the DBC-TSS can present ideal results, its accuracy degrades rapidly with the increase of the dimensionality and the lowest error rate is achieved at high dimensionality. Query accuracy of HCA-DSC performs better than DBC-TSS because it reduces the storage requirements, it potentially allows an efficient implementation of similarity measurement and it improves the quality of similarity search results.

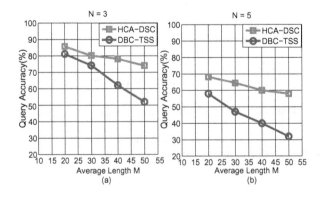

Fig. 1. Query accuracy comparison (Color figure online)

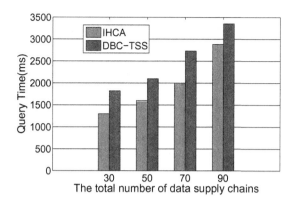

Fig. 2. Query time comparison (Color figure online)

5.3 Query Time

In order to evaluate the query performance, we provide results for two algorithms, namely the HCA-DSC and the DBC-TSS. Regarding N, the total number of data supply chains is set equal to 30, 50, 70 and 90. Figure 2 shows the query time.

In Fig. 2, the query performance of HCA-DSC and the DBC-TSS is presented with respect to the number of data supply chains that is searched. The main observation is that when the total numbers of data supply chains increases, the corresponding query time decreases. The reason is that, searching a database for the most similar object (data supply chains) to a given one, the above mentioned algorithms have to compare a query object to every object in a database in order to find the most similar one. These approaches become prohibitive, when the reference database is extremely large. The efficiency of which is affected by the number of objects in the database, since a distance measure is calculated for measuring the closeness of the corresponding objects.

6   Conclusion

In this paper, we focus on a novel data supply chains similarity search problem. We firstly develop a feature space representation model based on key points, which can greatly reduces complex structures and the storage requirements. In addition, to measure the pair-wise distances of sub-sequences of data supply chains with high efficiency, we define a novel similarity measure based on multi-scale features. Lastly, we propose a hierarchical clustering algorithm for data supply chains, which improves the quality of the similarity search results by identifying the most similar sub-sequences to a given query.

In our future work, we intend to establish a model of data supply chain performance evaluation based on multi-dimension evaluation index, which makes clear the operation performance of data supply chain, reduces operating costs, further improves the competitive advantage.

Acknowledgment. This work is partly supported by the National Natural Science Foundation of China under Grant 61272520, 61370196, 61532012.

References

1. Groth, P.: Transparency and reliability in the data supply chain. IEEE Internet Comput. **17**(2), 69–71 (2013)
2. Ozturk, C., Hancer, E., Karaboga, D.: Dynamic clustering with improved binary artificial bee colony algorithm. Appl. Soft Comput. **28**, 69–80 (2015)
3. Hatamlou, A.: Black hole: a new heuristic optimization approach for data clustering. Inf. Sci. **222**, 175–184 (2013)
4. Iwashita, T., Hochin, T., Nomiya, H.: Optimal number of clusters for fast similarity search of time series considering transformations. In: 2014 IIAI 3rd International Conference on Advanced Applied Informatics (IIAIAAI), pp. 711–717. IEEE (2014)
5. Ghassempour, S., Girosi, F., Maeder, A.: Clustering multivariate time series using hidden Markov models. Int. J. Environ. Res. Public Health **11**(3), 2741–2763 (2014)
6. Huang, Y.-S., Yu, K.-M., Zhou, L.-W., Hsu, C.-H., Liu, S.-H.: Accelerating parallel frequent itemset mining on graphics processors with sorting. In: Hsu, C.-H., Li, X., Shi, X., Zheng, R. (eds.) NPC 2013. LNCS, vol. 8147, pp. 245–256. Springer, Heidelberg (2013)
7. Wikimeta (2013). http://wikimeta.com/
8. OpenCalais (2013). http://www.opencalais.com/
9. Pingar (2013). http://www.pingar.com/
10. AlchemyAPI (2013). http://www.alchemyapi.com/
11. Semantria (2013). http://semantria.com/
12. Backurs, A., Indyk, P.: Edit distance cannot be computed in strongly subquadratic time (unless SETH is false). In: Proceedings of the Forty-Seventh Annual ACM on Symposium on Theory of Computing, pp. 51–58. ACM (2015)
13. Lang, W., Morse, M., Patel, J.M.: Dictionary-based compression for long time-series similarity. IEEE Trans. Knowl. Data Eng. **22**(11), 1609–1622 (2010)

Privacy-Preserving Strategyproof Auction Mechanisms for Resource Allocation in Wireless Communications

Yu-E Sun[1,3], He Huang[2,3(✉)], Xiang-Yang Li[3], Yang Du[3], Miaomiao Tian[3],
Hongli Xu[3], and Mingjun Xiao[3]

[1] School of Urban Rail Transportation, Soochow University, Suzhou, China
[2] School of Computer Science and Technology, Soochow University, Suzhou, China
huangh@suda.edu.cn
[3] School of Computer Science and Technology,
University of Science and Technology of China, Hefei, China

Abstract. In recent years, auction theory has been extensively studied and many state-of-art solutions have been proposed aiming at allocating scarce resources (*e.g.* spectrum resources in wireless communications). Unfortunately, most of these studies assume that the auctioneer is always trustworthy in the sealed-bid auctions, which is not always true in a more realistic scenario. On the other hand, performance guarantee, such as social efficiency maximization, is also crucial for auction mechanism design. Therefore, the goal of this work is to design a series of strategyproof and privacy preserving auction mechanisms that maximize the social efficiency. To make the designed auction model more general, we allow the bidders to express their preferences about multiple items, which is often regarded as the *multi-unit auction*. As computing an optimal allocation in multi-unit auction is NP-hard, we design a set of near optimal allocation mechanisms with privacy preserving separately for: (1) The auction aims at identical multi-items trading; and (2) The auction aims at distinct multi-items trading, which is also known as combinatorial auction. To the best of our knowledge, we are the first to design strategyproof multi-unit auction mechanisms with privacy preserving, which maximize the social efficiency at the same time. The evaluation results corroborate our theoretical analysis, and show that our proposed methods achieve low computation and communication complexity.

Keywords: Approximation mechanism · Multi-unit auction · Privacy preserving · Social efficiency · Strategyproof

1 Introduction

Auction serves as a preeminent way to allocate resources to multiple bidders, especially for the scarce resources in wireless communications (such as *the computing resources in cloud* [14], *spectrum licenses* [7,8,21], *cellular networks* [6],

© Springer International Publishing Switzerland 2016
Y. Wang et al. (Eds.): BigCom 2016, LNCS 9784, pp. 13–26, 2016.
DOI: 10.1007/978-3-319-42553-5_2

CRNs [19,20], and *etc.*) due to its fairness and efficiency [1,11]. Strategyproof-ness (*a.k.a truthfulness*) is regarded as one of the key objectives in the auction mechanism design, which means that the optimal strategies for bidders is to bid their *true valuations* of the items for sale. Most of the auction mechanisms are designed to charge each winner the minimum bid value, by which he can win the auction, to ensure the strategyproofness of bidders. Unfortunately, the auctioneer may not always be trustworthy. Once the true valuation of each bidder is revealed to an untrustworthy auctioneer, he may take advantage of this to maximize his own profits.

To solve the above challenge, the bid values should be hidden in the whole procedure of the auction. Thus, protecting the privacy of bids should be regarded as an attractive objective in the design of auction mechanisms. In recent years, some researchers have dedicated their efforts in the auction mechanism design with privacy preserving. For instance, in [2,10], the authors design some mechanisms to protect the bid value in the first price and the second price sealed-bid auctions. Huang *et al.* [9] propose a strategyproof and bid privacy preserving auction mechanism for spectrum allocation. Pan *et al.* [15,16] also give a secure combinatorial spectrum auction by using homomorphic encryption to deal with the untrustworthy auctioneer. However, none of these auction mechanisms with privacy preserving provides any performance guarantee on *social efficiency, i.e.* the total bid value of winners, which is a standard and critical auction metric [4,13].

In this paper, we focus on the privacy preserving and strategyproof auction mechanism design for resource allocation, which can maximize the social efficiency at the same time. Observe that most of the existing auction mechanisms fail to take the multiple items trading into consideration. Nevertheless, bidders may often express their preferences for a specified number of items or some specified bundles of items, instead of individual item. This kind of auction is called by the *multi-unit auction*. There are two cases in multi-unit auction: the items sold in the market are *identical* or *distinct*. In this work, we will propose two auction mechanisms to deal with the identical condition and the distinct condition. In our design for identical items, the demand of each bidder is a fixed number of items, which is inseparable. The auction for distinct items is also known as *combinatorial auction*. In a combinatorial auction, all the bidders can bid for bundles of items rather than individual items [3]. Thus, the combinatorial auctions enable bidders to express their preferences in a more meaningful way. In both auction models, the bid values of bidders are private information. Except that, which items that each bidder wants to buy is also a sensitive information in the combinatorial auction. This is because if the auctioneer knows that how many bidders are interested in each item, he may raise the price in future auctions to maximize his own profit. Besides, the auctioneer needs to know each winner's demand to finish the auction. Therefore, except for protecting the bid values of bidders in both auction models, we also need to protect the *combination items* that each loser wants to buy in the combinatorial auction.

The multi-unit auction mechanism design with consideration of social efficiency maximization issue is NP-hard [17]. Many efficient approximation algorithms have been proposed for both the Identical items Auction model (*i.e.* IA model) and Combinatorial Auctions model (*i.e.* CA model). For example, there are a polynomial time approximation scheme (PTAS), which is suitable for the IA auction model, and an approximation algorithm with an approximation factor of $\sqrt{h}$ that has been proved tight for the combinatorial auctions. Thus, our work in this paper is not to design approximation algorithms that improve the performance of the existing studies, but is to design mechanisms with privacy preserving, based on these existing approximation mechanisms.

However, the computation burden which relies on the bid values of bidders is too heavy in the existing approximation algorithms with good performance guarantee. Thus, the task of designing privacy preserving auction mechanisms with performance guarantee is highly challenging. To tackle this, we introduce an agent into our auction model, who is a *semi-trusted* third party, and he can help the auctioneer to decide the winners and compute their charges. In our design, the auctioneer generates a public key and a secret key of Paillier's homomorphic cryptosystem. Bidders encrypt their bids by using the public key. Then, the agent performs homomorphic computation on the ciphertexts, adds random numbers, and sends the results to the auctioneer for making allocation decision and computing payment of winners. By this design, the privacy is protected without affecting the correctness of the auctions.

Although there exists a PTAS for the IA model, it is considered as a very challenging work to design a privacy preserving version of PTAS. To this end, we propose a privacy preserving bid mechanism with an approximation factor of 2. For the combinatorial auction, we give a privacy preserving version of the auction mechanism proposed in [5], which has an approximation factor of $\sqrt{h}$. We prove that our new method for combinatorial auction can protect both the bid value of all bidders and the items each loser wants to buy. To the best of our knowledge, the auction mechanisms presented in this paper are the first strategyproof and privacy preserving multi-unit auction mechanisms with social efficiency performance guarantee.

2   Preliminaries

2.1   Auction Model

We consider a sealed-bid auction, in which there exist an auctioneer, a set of bidders, and an agent. At the beginning of the auction, all bidders first encrypt their bids by using the public key generated from the agent, and then submit their encrypted bids to the auctioneer. Next, the auctioneer allocates the items to the bidders, and decides the charges for the winners after communicating with the agent. We assume that the agent is a *semi-trusted* third party, who is curious about the bid values of bidders, but will not collude with the auctioneer.

We study two auction models in this paper: the Identical items Auction model (*e.g.* IA model) and the distinct items auction model (*a.k.a* Combinatorial

Auction model, CA model). In the IA model, we assume that there exist a set of identical items denoted as $\mathcal{I} = \{I_1, I_2, \ldots, I_h\}$, and m bidders denoted by $\mathcal{B} = \{1, 2, \ldots, m\}$ in the market. Each bidder i is only interested in a fixed number of items, denoted by N_i, and is willing to pay *no more than* v_i for all of them. In the CA model, the items in the market are distinct, and each bidder $i \in \mathcal{B}$ wants to buy the items in a specified subset $c_i \subseteq \mathcal{I}$. Note that both in the IA model and the CA model, the demand of each bidder is inseparable, which means that bidder i will get all the items that he wants to buy if he wins.

2.2   Auction Goals

Our primary goal is to design a strategyproof auction mechanism which can maximize the social efficiency. We define the *social efficiency* of an auction as the total bid values of the winning bidders. Suppose b_i, v_i, p_i, are the bid value, true valuation, and the payment of bidder i for all the items he want to buy, respectively. Then, the utility of bidder i is defined as

$$u_i = \begin{cases} v_i - p_i \text{ if bidder } i \text{ wins the auction} \\ 0 \qquad \text{otherwise} \end{cases} \tag{1}$$

Strategyproofness is often regarded as one of the most crucial properties of auction mechanisms. We say an auction is strategyproof if bidding truthfully is the *dominant strategy* for each bidder. Therefore, we need to prove that for each bidder i, u_i is maximized when $b_i = v_i$ to ensure the strategyproofness of bidders. It has been proved by Myerson that an auction is strategyproof if and only if the following two conditions hold:

- **Bid-monotone Constraint:** The items allocation mechanism is bid-monotone, which means that, when bidder i wins the auction by bidding b_i, he will always win by bidding $b_i' > b_i$.
- **Critical Value Constraint:** The charge from a winner i is his critical value, *i.e.*, the minimum bid that he will win the auction.

Following this direction, we design the strategyproof auction mechanisms satisfying the above-mentioned characteristics.

The privacy goals of our auction mechanisms are as follows:

- In the IA model, we protect the bid values of bidders, which means that all bids from bidders are blind to both the auctioneer and the agent.
- In the CA model, neither the auctioneer nor the agent knows the true bid values of bidders, as well as which items that each loser wants to get.

3   IAMP: Identical Items Auction Mechanism Design with Privacy Preservation

In this section, we design a strategyproof mechanism IAMP for Identical items Auction model (IA model), which achieves an approximately optimal social efficiency and supports privacy preservation. Our auction mechanism mainly consists of three steps: bidding, allocation and payment calculation.

3.1   Bidding

Before running the auction, the agent first generates an encryption key EK and a decryption key DK of Paillier's cryptosystem. Then, he publishes EK as a public key, and keeps DK in private. We assume that the parameter n is of 1024-bit length in this work. Each bidder i encrypts his bid b_i to $E(b_i)$, and sends $(E(b_i), N_i)$ to the auctioneer, where N_i is the number of items that he wants to buy.

3.2   Allocation Mechanism

After receiving the encrypted bids from the bidders, the auctioneer needs to make the winner decision aiming at maximizing the social efficiency. We can prove that the social efficiency maximization problem can be reduced to the Knapsack problem, which is a well known NP-hard problem.

To address this NP hardness, a Polynomial Time Approximation Scheme (PTAS) was proposed in [12] for knapsack problem, which is also suitable for our model. Besides, it has been proven that this PTAS is bid-monotone, which implies that there exists a strategyproof auction mechanism. Unfortunately, it is really a hard work to design a bid privacy preservation version based on this mechanism. There is a large computation and comparison overload in this PTAS based on dynamic programming. Therefore, we build our privacy preserving method on the top of another approximation algorithm which can approximate the optimal allocation within a factor of 2.

Next, we will show the detail of our allocation mechanism with privacy preserving. Following the approximation algorithm above, we need to sort the per-unit bid values of bidders to decide the winners. To solve this with privacy preserving, bidders first encrypt their bids by using the Encryption Key (EK) of the agent, and submit the encrypted bids to the auctioneer. Then, the auctioneer masks them by using two random values $\delta_1 \in \mathbb{Z}_{2^{\gamma_1}}$ and $\delta_2 \in \mathbb{Z}_{2^{\gamma_2}}$ as $\delta_1 b_i + \delta_2 N_i$. Note that the range $[1, 2^{\gamma_1}]$ and $[1, 2^{\gamma_2}]$ for δ_1 and δ_2 should be chosen based on the consideration of the correctness of modular operations: $\delta_1 b_i + \delta_2 N_i$ should be smaller than the modulo used in Paillier's system. Since the agent has the decryption key, he can compute and sort $\delta_1 \frac{b_i}{N_i} + \delta_2$ in the non-increasing order without access any true bid values of bidders.

Furthermore, the auctioneer also maps the true ID of bidders by using a permutation before sending $\{E(\delta_1 b_i + \delta_2 N_i), N_i\}_{i \in \mathcal{B}}$ to the agent. Thus, the agent cannot map the masked bids $\{\delta_1 b_i + \delta_2 N_i\}_{i \in \mathcal{B}}$ to bidders either. With the sorted per-unit bids, the agent can find the bidders with top $k-1$ per-unit bids and the bidder with k-th per-unit bid. After the agent sends the permutated ID of bidders with top k per-unit bids to the auctioneer, the auctioneer can compute the encrypted bid sum of bidders with top $k-1$ per-unit bids. Since the agent has the decryption key, the auctioneer then randomly chooses two integers δ_3 and δ_4 to hide the true value of $E(\sum_{i=1}^{k-1} b_{\sigma(i)})$ and $E(b_{\sigma(k)})$, and communicates with the agent to decide the winning bidders. The detail of our allocation mechanism with privacy preserving is depicted in Algorithm 1.

Algorithm 1. Allocation mechanism for identical items model

1: The auctioneer randomly picks two integers $\delta_1 \in \mathbb{Z}_{2^{1012}}$, $\delta_2 \in \mathbb{Z}_{2^{1022}}$, and executes the homomorphic operation:

$$E(\delta_1 b_i + \delta_2 N_i) = E(b_i)^{\delta_1} E(\delta_2 N_i).$$

2: Then, the auctioneer maps the ID of bidders by using permutation $\pi : \mathbb{Z}_m \rightarrow \mathbb{Z}_m$, and sends $\{E(\delta_1 b_i + \delta_2 N_i), N_i, \pi(i)\}_{i \in \mathcal{B}}$ to the agent.
3: The agent decrypts $E(\delta_1 b_i + \delta_2 N_i)$ by using his private key $DK = (\lambda, \mu)$, then computes $\delta_1 \frac{b_i}{N_i} + \delta_2$ and sorts b_i / N_i in non-increasing order.
4: The agent finds the critical bidder $\sigma(k)$ by computing:

$$\sum_{i=1}^{k-1} N_{\sigma(i)} \leq h \leq \sum_{i=1}^{k} N_{\sigma(i)}.$$

5: To decide the winners, the agent sends $(\{\sigma(i)\}_{i<k}, \sigma(k))$ to the auctioneer, where $\{\sigma(i)\}_{i<k}$ is out of order.
6: The auctioneer randomly picks two integers $\delta_3 \in \mathbb{Z}_{2^{1012}}$, $\delta_4 \in \mathbb{Z}_{2^{1022}}$, computes the following and sends the result back to the agent.

$$E(\delta_3 \sum_{i=1}^{k-1} b_{\sigma(i)} + \delta_4) = (\prod_{i=1}^{k-1} E(b_{\sigma(i)}))^{\delta_3} E(\delta_4)$$

$$E(\delta_3 b_{\sigma(k)} + \delta_4) = E(b_{\sigma(k)})^{\delta_3} E(\delta_4)$$

7: After receiving the ciphertexts, the agent decrypts them , and sends $\{\sigma(i)\}_{i<k}$ to the auctioneer if $\sum_{i=1}^{k-1} b_{\sigma(i)} \geq b_{\sigma(k)}$; otherwise, he sends $\sigma(k)$ to the auctioneer.
8: The auctioneer chooses the bidders that the agent sends to him as winners, and sets other bidders as losers.

Then, we will show that our allocation mechanism for identical items auction model is bid monotone.

Lemma 1. *The proposed allocation mechanism is bid-monotone, which means that if bidder $\sigma(i)$ wins by bidding $b_{\sigma(i)}$, he will always win by bidding $b'_{\sigma(i)} > b_{\sigma(i)}$.*

Proof. Due to page limits, the proof is referred to [18].

3.3   Payment Calculation Mechanism

It has been proved that an auction is strategyproof if and only if its winner determination mechanism is bid monotone and it always charges each winner its critical value. We have proved that our allocation mechanism is bid-monotone, which indicates that there exists a critical value for each winner. Hence, the objective of this step is to compute the critical values of winners with privacy preserving.

Since our allocation mechanism is bid monotone, there must exist some intervals denoted by $[L_i, U_i]$, which satisfies that bidder $\sigma(i)$ wins the auction as long as his per-unit bid value is larger than the L_i-th per-unit bid value in the sorted bid list and always loses if his per-unit bid value is less than the U_i-th per-unit bid value. We say $[L_i^*, U_i^*]$ is the critical interval of winner $\sigma(i)$ if $L_i^* = U_i^* - 1$. It is not hard to get that i is the lower bound of L_i^*, and f is the upper bound of U_i^* which satisfies:

$$\sum_{i=1}^{f-1} N_{\sigma(i)} \leq h \leq \sum_{i=1}^{f} N_{\sigma(i)} \tag{2}$$

Obviously, the critical value of each winner $\sigma(i)$ is less than the L_i^*-th bid value, while larger than the U_i^*-th bid value. In order to find the critical value of each winner, we first compute their critical intervals. As shown in Algorithm 2, we use binary search to compute the critical interval for each winner $\sigma(i)$. In each round of the binary search, we set the per-unit bid of bidder $\sigma(i)$ being equal to the per-unit bid of the M-th bidder in the sorted list, and then compare the bid sum of new top $k-1$ bids and the k-th bid, to check whether $\sigma(i)$ with the new bid value will win or not. This can be done since the auctioneer can compute the encrypted value $E(b_{\sigma(M)}N_{\sigma(i)})$, which is equal to $E(b_{\sigma(i)}N_{\sigma(M)})$, and further, the auctioneer can get the encrypted values of $E(\sum_{j=1}^{k-1} b_{\sigma(j)*}N_{\sigma(M)})$ and $E(b_{\sigma(k)*}N_{\sigma(M)})$ through homomorphic operations. With these encrypted values, the agent can check whether bidder $\sigma(i)$ win or not, by decrypting and comparing the values $\sum_{j=1}^{k-1} b_{\sigma(j)*}$ and $b_{\sigma(k)*}$. Then, the agent can get the new boundary of binary search, until he finds the critical interval of bidder $\sigma(i)$.

After getting the critical interval of each winner, we compute the critical values for them. For the case that winner $\sigma(i)$ is the new k-th bidder, and his per-unit bid value is smaller than the L_i^*-th, but larger than the U_i^*-th per-unit bid value in the sorted list, we compute the critical value $p_{\sigma(i)}$ of winner $\sigma(i)$ as follow:

$$p_{\sigma(i)} = \max\left(\sum_{j=1}^{k-1} b_{\sigma(j)*}, \frac{b_{\sigma(U_i^*)}N_{\sigma(i)}}{N_{\sigma(U_i^*)}}\right)$$

In the other case, the critical value of winner $\sigma(i)$ is

$$p_{i'} = \max\left(b_{\sigma(k)*} + b_{\sigma(i)} - \sum_{j=1}^{k-1} b_{\sigma(j)*}, \frac{b_{\sigma(U_i^*)}N_{\sigma(i)}}{N_{\sigma(U_i^*)}}\right)$$

Assume that $s_1 = \sum_{j=1}^{k-1} b_{\sigma(j)*}$, and $s_2 = b_{\sigma(U_i^*)}N_{\sigma(i)}$, $s_3 = b_{\sigma(k)*} + b_{\sigma(i)}$. The details of our payment calculation mechanism with privacy preservation are described in Algorithm 3.

We have proved that our allocation mechanism is bid monotone, and we charge each winner its critical value, thus we can also get that:

Theorem 1. *The auction mechanism we proposed is strategyproof.*

Since the goal of this work is to design strategyproof auction mechanism with privacy preserving, we will show that the proposed IAMP protects the true bid values of bidders in the next subsection.

Algorithm 2. Compute the critical interval for winner $\sigma(i)$

1: The agent first computes the interval of the binary search $[i, f]$, and sets $L = i$, $U = f$ at the beginning. Then, he sets $M = \lfloor (U + L)/2 \rfloor$.

2: The agent sends the IDs $(\{\sigma(j)^*\}_{j<k}, \sigma(M), \sigma(k)^*)$ to the auctioneer, where $\{\sigma(j)^*\}_{j<k}$ is out of order, $\sigma(j)^*)$ and $\sigma(k)^*)$ are the new bidders with the j-th and k-th per-unit bid value when $\sigma(i)$ bids $\frac{b_{\sigma(M)} N_{\sigma(i)}}{N_{\sigma(M)}}$, respectively.

3: The auctioneer first sets the bid of bidder $\sigma(i)$ in this round of binary search by setting $E(b_{\sigma(i)} N_{\sigma(M)})$ as:

$$E(b_{\sigma(i)} N_{\sigma(M)}) = E(b_{\sigma(M)})^{N_{\sigma(i)}}.$$

4: Then, he randomly chooses two integers $\delta_{M,1} \in \mathbb{Z}_{2^{1012}}$, $\delta_{M,2} \in \mathbb{Z}_{2^{1022}}$, computes the follows and sends the results back to the agent.

$$E(\delta_{M,2} N_{\sigma(M)} + \delta_{M,1} \sum_{j=0}^{k-1} b_{\sigma(j)^*} N_{\sigma(M)}) = E(\delta_{M,2} N_{\sigma(M)}) E(b_{\sigma(k)^*})^{N_{\sigma(M)} \delta_{M,1}}$$

5: The agent decrypts the ciphertexts he received and checks bidder $\sigma(i)$ win or not by bidding $\frac{b_{\sigma(M)} N_{\sigma(i)}}{N_{\sigma(M)}}$, then he executes the following operation.

6: **if** $\sigma(i)$ wins by bidding $\frac{b_{\sigma(M)} N_{\sigma(i)}}{N_{\sigma(M)}}$ **then**

7:     The agent sets $L = M$, and $M = \lfloor (U + L)/2 \rfloor$;

8: **else**

9:     The agent sets $U = M$, and $M = \lfloor (U + L)/2 \rfloor$;

10: Repeat step 2 $\sim$ 8 until $U = L + 1$.

11: The agent sets $U_i^* = U$, and $L_i^* = L$, then $[L_i^*, U_i^*]$ is the critical interval of winner $\sigma(i)$.

3.4   Security Analysis

The most important target of our auction mechanism is to protect the bid values of bidders. There are two central parties in our mechanism, including the auctioneer and the agent. In the following, we will show that the bid values of bidders are blind for both the auctioneer and the agent.

Theorem 2. *Our auction mechanism for identical items guarantees the bid privacy preserving.*

Proof. Due to page limits, the proof is referred to [18].

Algorithm 3. Payment calculation for winner $\sigma(i)$

1: **if** $\sigma(i) = \sigma(k)^*$ **then**
2:    The auctioneer randomly chooses two integers $\delta_5 \in \mathbb{Z}_{2^{1012}}$, $\delta_6 \in \mathbb{Z}_{2^{1022}}$, computes the follows and sends the results to the agent.

$$E(\delta_6 + \delta_5 s_1) = E(\delta_6)(\prod_{j=0}^{k-1} E(b_{\sigma(j)^*}))^{\delta_5}$$

$$E(\delta_6 N_{\sigma(U_i^*)} + \delta_5 s_2) = E(\delta_6 N_{\sigma(U_i^*)}) E(b_{\sigma(U_i^*)})^{\delta_5 N_{\sigma(i)}}$$

3:    The agent computes and sends $p'_{\sigma(i)}$ to the auctioneer, where

$$p'_{\sigma(i)} = \max(\delta_6 + \delta_5 s_1, \delta_6 + \delta_5 s_2 / N_{\sigma(U_i^*)}).$$

4: **else**
5:    The auctioneer randomly chooses two integers $\delta_5 \in \mathbb{Z}_{2^{1012}}$, $\delta_6, \delta_7 \in \mathbb{Z}_{2^{1022}}$, computes the follows and sends the results to the agent.

$$E(\delta_6 + \delta_5 s_3) = E(\delta_6)(E(b_{\sigma(k)^*})E(b_{\sigma(i)}))^{\delta_5}$$

$$E(\delta_6 N_{\sigma(U_i^*)} + \delta_5(s_2 + s_1 N_{\sigma(U_i^*)}))$$
$$= E(\delta_6 N_{\sigma(U_i^*)})(E(b_{\sigma(U_i^*)})E(\prod_{j=0}^{k-1} E(b_{\sigma(j)^*})))^{\delta_5 N_{\sigma(i)}}$$

$$E(\delta_7 + \delta_5 s_1) = E(\delta_7)E(\prod_{j=0}^{k-1} E(b_{\sigma(j)^*}))^{\delta_5}$$

6:    After receiving the ciphertext, the agent computes $p'_{\sigma(i)}$ and sends it to the auctioneer, where

$$p'_{\sigma(i)} = \max(\delta_6 - \delta_7 + \delta_5(s_3 - s_1), \delta_6 - \delta_7 + \delta_5 s_2 / N_{\sigma(U_i^*)}).$$

7: The auctioneer sets the payment of winner i' is $p_{i'}$, where

$$p_{i'} = (p'_{i'} - \delta_6 + \delta_7)/\delta_5.$$

4   CAMP: Combinatorial Auction Mechanism Design with Privacy Preservation

4.1   Bidding

Similar to the bidding process in IAMP, the agent first generates encryption and decryption keys of Paillier's cryptosystem, and publishes his encryption key. Then, each bidder encrypts $b_i/\sqrt{|c_i|}$ by using the encryption key of the agent and sends the results to the auctioneer. However, every bidder not only wants to protect his bid in our combinatorial auction model (CA model), but also wants to hide the items that he wants to buy if he loses in the auction. Thus, each bidder will also encrypt the set of items that he wants to buy. Let $X_i = \{x_{i,1}, x_{i,2}, \ldots, x_{i,h}\}$ be the demand vector of bidder i, where $x_{i,j} = 1$ if $I_j \in c_i$, $x_{i,j} = 0$ otherwise. For each $x_{i,j} \in X_i$, bidder i generates a random integer r and encrypts $x_{i,j}$ by using the encryption key of the agent. Finally, bidder i sends $(E(b_i/\sqrt{|c_i|}), E(X_i))$ to the auctioneer, where $E(X_i) = \{E(x_{i,1}), E(x_{i,2}), \ldots, E(x_{i,h})\}$.

4.2 Allocation Mechanism

After receiving the encrypted bids and demands from the bidders, the auctioneer chooses a set of bidders as winners if the social efficiency is maximized. It has been proven in [5] that the social efficiency maximization problem in the combinatorial auction is NP hard, and the upper bound of approximation ratios of polynomial time algorithms is $\sqrt{h}$.

Dong *et al.* propose an auction mechanism with a greedy allocation mechanism in [5], which can approximate the optimal one within a factor of $\sqrt{h}$. We will briefly describe it below:

- First, a normalized bid $\frac{b_i}{\sqrt{|c_i|}}$ for each bid b_i is calculated, and then the bidders are sorted according to the non-increasing order of the normalized bids.
- Finally, the greedy allocation mechanism examines every bidder in the sorted list sequentially, and grants the bidder only if his demand does not overlap with all the demands of the previously granted bidders.
- Assume $l(i)$ is the first bidder following i in the sorted list that has been denied but have been granted were it not for the presence of i. Then, the bidder i pays zero if his bid is denied or $l(i)$ does not exist; otherwise, he pays $\sqrt{|c_i|} * n_{l(i)}$, where $n_{l(i)}$ is the normalized bid of bidder $l(i)$.

Following the combinatorial auction mechanism stated above, only two operations rely on the true bid values of bidders: sorting the bidders according to their normalized bids and computing the payment for each winner i by using the normalized bid of $l(i)$. Thus, we can use the similar way as what we did in IAMP to protect the bid privacy of bidders. However, the agent needs to know the demand vectors of all the bidders to check if they are overlapping with each other in combinatorial auction. Therefore, the most challenging issue of designing privacy preserving combinatorial auction mechanism is to protect the demand of losers. To deal with this challenge, we encrypt the demand vector of bidders. More specifically, we confuse the ID of bidders and the ID of items by separately using permutations $\pi_1 : \mathbb{Z}_m \to \mathbb{Z}_m$ and $\pi_2 : \mathbb{Z}_h \to \mathbb{Z}_h$, before the auctioneer send the demand vectors to the agent. With the confused information and decryption key, the agent can also get the overlapping information of bidders, but can hardly map them to the true demands of losers. On the other hand, the auctioneer only gets the encrypted demand vectors and the auction result, he has no idea with the demand of each loser either. Then, the demand privacy of losers are protected. The detail of our allocation mechanism with privacy preserving is shown in Algorithm 4.

Algorithm 4. Allocation mechanism for combinatorial auction

1: The auctioneer randomly picks two integers $\delta_1 \in \mathbb{Z}_{2^{1012}}$, $\delta_2 \in \mathbb{Z}_{2^{1022}}$, and executes the following homomorphic operation, then he sends $\{\pi_1(i), E(\delta_1 \frac{b_i}{\sqrt{|c_i|}} + \delta_2), \{E(x_{i,j}), \pi_2(j)\}_{I_j \in \mathcal{I}}\}_{i \in \mathcal{B}}$ to the agent.

$$E(\delta_1 \frac{b_i}{\sqrt{|c_i|}} + \delta_2) = E(\frac{b_i}{\sqrt{|c_i|}})^{\delta_1} E(\delta_2)$$

2: The agent decrypts the set of bids $\{E(\delta_1 \frac{b_i}{\sqrt{|c_i|}} + \delta_2)\}_{i \in \mathcal{B}}$ by using his private key, and reorder them in descending order.
3: The agent decrypts the demand of bidders, and computes the winners as follows:
4: Set $W = \mathcal{B}$
5: **for** $i = 1$ to m **do**
6:     Set $j = 1$
7:     **while** $j \leq h$ and $\sigma(i) \in W$ **do**
8:         **if** $x_{\sigma(i),j} = 1$ and $\sum_{k=1}^{i-1} x_{\sigma(k),j} \geq 1$ **then**
9:             Set $W = W \setminus \{\sigma(i)\}$
10:        Set $j = j + 1$
11: The agent sends the set W of winners to the auctioneer.

4.3   Payment Calculation Mechanism

Recall that an auction is strategyproof if and only if it is bid-monotone and always charges each winner its critical value. For each winner i in the greedy allocation mechanism, his normalized bid is larger than the normalized bid of $l(i)$. Thus, $n_{l(i)} * \sqrt{|c_i|}$ is the critical value of winner i if $l(i)$ exist. Otherwise, the critical value of winner i is zero. Our payment calculation mechanism is shown in Algorithm 5.

Algorithm 5. Payment calculation for combinatorial auction

1: For each winner $i \in W$, the agent first finds $l(i)$ and then computes p_i' as follows:

$$p_i' = \begin{cases} \delta_1 \frac{b_{l(i)}}{\sqrt{|c_{l(i)}|}} + \delta_2 & \text{if } l(i) \text{ exist} \\ 0 & \text{otherwise} \end{cases}$$

2: The agent sends the set $\{p_i', X_i, \pi(i)\}_{i \in W}$ to the auctioneer.
3: The auctioneer computes the payment for each winner as follows:

$$p_i = \max(\sqrt{|c_i|}(p_i' - \delta_2)/\delta_1, 0).$$

Theorem 3. *Our combinatorial auction mechanism protects the demand c_i of each loser i.*

Proof. Due to page limits, the proof is referred to [18].

Theorem 4. *Our combinatorial auction mechanism guarantees the bid privacy preserving.*

Proof. Due to page limits, the proof is referred to [18].

5   Simulation Results

We evaluate the computation and communication overhead of our approximation algorithms with privacy preserving. Since computation overhead is dominated by the auctioneer and the agent in both auction models, we do not plot the bidders' computation overhead. As shown in Fig. 1, the auctioneer spends more time in the identical auction model than in the combinatorial auction model. This is because auctioneer spends most of his time in computing the payment of winners. However, we can easily find them in the combinatorial auction model.

The run time of each bidder is roughly 30 ms in the identical auction model. However, bidders need to encrypt their bids and demand in the combinatorial auction model. Thus, the run time of the agent or a bidder is related to the number of items in the combinatorial auction. Our simulation results show that the run time of each bidder is roughly 180 ms in CAMP when $h = 5$, and the run time of the agent is much more than that in IAMP.

In the evaluation, we set n to be of 1024-bit length. Figure 1c shows the communication overhead of our auction mechanisms with privacy preserving. We find that the communication overhead of CAMP is much higher than that of IAMP. The main reason is that bidders only encrypt their bids in the identical auction, but encrypt both their bids and demands in the combinatorial auction.

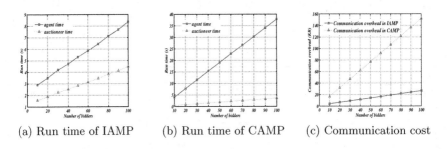

(a) Run time of IAMP   (b) Run time of CAMP   (c) Communication cost

Fig. 1. Computation and communication overhead when $h = 5$

6   Conclusion

In this paper, we proposed the first strategyproof and privacy preserving multi-unit auction mechanisms that maximize the social efficiency. We study two cases for multi-unit auction, where the items in the market are identical and distinct.

Under these two cases, the optimal item allocation problem is NP hard to solve. Thus, we designed secure and near optimal allocation mechanisms for them, which have the approximation factors of 2 and $\sqrt{h}$, respectively. Further, we also computed the critical payment with privacy preserving for each winner, and theoretically proved the properties of our auction mechanisms, such as strategyproofness, privacy preserving and approximation factor. Our evaluation results demonstrated that our protocols not only achieve good social efficiency, but also perform well at computation and communication.

Acknowledgements. This work is partially supported by National Natural Science Foundation of China (NSFC) under Grant No. 61572342, No. 61303206, Natural Science Foundation of Jiangsu Province under Grant No. BK20151240, China Postdoctoral Science Foundation under Grant No. 2015M580470. Any opinions, findings, conclusions, or recommendations expressed in this paper are those of author(s) and do not necessarily reflect the views of the funding agencies (NSFC).

References

1. Chen, D., Yin, S., Zhang, Q., Liu, M., Li, S.: Mining spectrum usage data: a large-scale spectrum measurement study. In: ACM Mobicom 2009, pp. 13–24 (2009)
2. Chung, Y.F., Huang, K.H., Lee, H.H., Lai, F., Chen, T.S.: Bidder-anonymous English auction scheme with privacy and public verifiability. J. Syst. Softw. **81**(1), 113–119 (2008)
3. Cramton, P., Shoham, Y., Steinberg, R.: Combinatorial Auctions, vol. 475. MIT Press, Cambridge (2006)
4. Dobzinski, S., Nisan, N., Schapira, M.: Approximation algorithms for combinatorial auctions with complement-free bidders. In: Proceedings of the Thirty-Seventh Annual ACM Symposium on Theory of Computing (STOC), pp. 610–618 (2005)
5. Dong, M., Sun, G., Wang, X., Zhang, Q.: Combinatorial auction with time-frequency flexibility in cognitive radio networks. In: IEEE INFOCOM 2012, pp. 2282–2290 (2012)
6. Dong, W., Rallapalli, S., Jana, R., Qiu, L., Ramakrishnan, K., Razoumov, L., Zhang, Y., Cho, T.W.: iDEAL: incentivized dynamic cellular offloading via auctions. IEEE/ACM Trans. Netw. (TON) **22**(4), 1271–1284 (2014)
7. Gopinathan, A., Li, Z.: Strategyproof auctions for balancing social welfare and fairness in secondary spectrum markets. In: IEEE INFOCOM 2011, pp. 3020–3028 (2011)
8. Huang, H., Sun, Y.-E., Li, X.-Y., Chen, Z., Yang, W., Xu, H.: Near-optimal truthful spectrum auction mechanisms with spatial and temporal reuse in wireless networks. In: ACM MobiHoc 2013, pp. 237–240 (2013)
9. Huang, Q., Tao, Y., Wu, F.: Spring: a strategy-proof and privacy preserving spectrum auction mechanism. In: IEEE INFOCOM 2013, pp. 827–835 (2013)
10. Kikuchi, H.: (M+1)st-price auction protocol. IEICE Trans. Fundam. Electron. Commun. Comput. Sci. **85**(3), 676–683 (2002)
11. Krishna, V.: Auction Theory. Academic Press, San Diego (2009)
12. Lai, K., Goemans, M.X.: The knapsack problem, fully polynomial time approximation schemes (FPTAS) (2006). Accessed 3 Nov 2012

13. Lehmann, D., Oćallaghan, L., Shoham, Y.: Truth revelation in approximately efficient combinatorial auctions. J. ACM (JACM) **49**(5), 577–602 (2002)
14. Lin, W.-Y., Lin, G.-Y., Wei, H.-Y.: Dynamic auction mechanism for cloud resource allocation. In: 10th IEEE/ACM International Conference on Cluster, Cloud and Grid Computing (CCGrid), pp. 591–592 (2010)
15. Pan, M., Li, H., Li, P., Fang, Y.: Dealing with the untrustworthy auctioneer in combinatorial spectrum auctions. In: IEEE GLOBECOM 2011, pp. 1–5 (2011)
16. Pan, M., Zhu, X., Fang, Y.: Using homomorphic encryption to secure the combinatorial spectrum auction without the trustworthy auctioneer. Wirel. Netw. **18**(2), 113–128 (2012)
17. Rothkopf, M.H., Pekeč, A., Harstad, R.M.: Computationally manageable combinational auctions. Manag. Sci. **44**(8), 1131–1147 (1998)
18. Sun, Y.-E., Huang, H., Li, X.-Y., et al.: Privacy-preserving strategyproof auction mechanisms for resource allocation in wireless communications. Technical report, Soochow University, June 2016. http://home.ustc.edu.cn/~huang83/bigcom.pdf
19. Wang, X., Huang, L., Xu, H., Huang, H.: Truthful auction for resource allocation in cooperative cognitive radio networks. In: IEEE ICCCN 2015, pp. 1–8 (2015)
20. Wang, X., Li, Z., Xu, P., Xu, Y., Gao, X., Chen, H.-H.: Spectrum sharing in cognitive radio networks an auction-based approach. IEEE Trans. Syst. Man Cybern. Part B Cybern. **40**(3), 587–596 (2010)
21. Zhou, X., Gandhi, S., Suri, S., Zheng, H.: eBay in the Sky: strategy-proof wireless spectrum auctions. In: ACM Mobicom 2008, pp. 2–13 (2008)

Cost Optimal Resource Provisioning for Live Video Forwarding Across Video Data Centers

Yihong Gao[1,2(✉)], Huadong Ma[1,2], Wu Liu[1,2], and Shui Yu[2]

[1] Beijing Key Lab of Intelligent Telecommunications Software and Multimedia,
Beijing University of Posts and Telecommunications, Beijing 100876, China
hii_gao@hotmail.com, {mhd,liuwu}@bupt.edu.cn
[2] School of Information Technology, Deakin University,
Melbourne, VIC 3125, Australia
shui.yu@deakin.edu.au

Abstract. Live video forwarding for IP cameras has become a popular service in video data centers. In the forwarding service, requests of end users from different regions arrive in real-time to gain live video streams of IP cameras from inter-connected video data centers. A fundamental scheduling problem is how to assign resources with the global optimal resource cost and forwarding delay to forward live video streams. We introduce the resource provisioning cost as the combination of media server cost, connection bandwidth cost, and forwarding delay cost. In this paper, a multi-objective resource provisioning ($MORP$) approach is proposed to deal with the online inter-datacenter resource provisioning problem. The approach aims at minimizing the resource provisioning cost during live video forwarding. It adaptively allocates media servers in appropriate video data centers and connects the chosen media servers together to provide system scalability and connectivity. Different from previous works, $MORP$ takes both resource capacity and diversity (e.g. location and price) into consideration during live video forwarding. Finally, the experimental results show that $MORP$ approach not only cuts the resource provisioning cost of 3 % to 10 % comparing to the bench mark approach, but also shortens the resource provisioning delay.

Keywords: Video surveillance as a service · Video data center · Live video forwarding · Resource provisioning

1 Introduction

Recent geo-distributed video data centers (VDCs) can collect massive IP camera streams from real-world to power the *Video Surveillance as a Service* (*VSaaS*)—a live video analysis and forwarding service for globalized end users [1–3]. For example, travelers from anyplace can remotely access to the IP cameras around the scenic spots to plan their tours. Generally, VDCs are situated in diverse places and connected by high capacity networks [1], which provides virtual machines (VMs) as media servers to forward live video streams for end users. Since there are usually more than one VDCs around arrival end user, a scalable online resource provisioning plan is very important for VDCs to decide which VDC to provide media

© Springer International Publishing Switzerland 2016
Y. Wang et al. (Eds.): BigCom 2016, LNCS 9784, pp. 27–38, 2016.
DOI: 10.1007/978-3-319-42553-5_3

server for the end user. Moreover, as VDCs charge different prices for both media servers and bandwidths [4–7], and provide different forwarding delay to the end user which can be evaluated as delay cost [10], the scheduler must decide how to select media servers from VDC candidates to minimize the resource provisioning cost. However, commercial video forwarding services in the above VDCs do not consider any cost evaluation details. To this end, we evaluate resource provisioning cost as the combination of the forwarding delay cost, the media server cost, and the connection bandwidth cost. Furthermore, the main challenge is to assign media servers for each arrival end user in real-time, and build up network connections among media servers and IP cameras for video streams forwarding to achieve global optimal resource provisioning cost.

Existing resource provisioning solutions are deployed in three different video services: video delivery service, interactive video forwarding service, and live video forwarding service. However, all these solutions have the follow drawbacks which must be strengthened in *VSaaS*. First, most cloud-assistant solutions of video delivery service are offline, and use P2P or Server-Client structure [8,9]. Nonetheless, offline approaches need all request information before scheduling. For the interactive video forwarding service, media servers are deployed between any two communicating users [10–13]. Lack of media server sharing, the resource provisioning of interactive forwarding service is costly. Furthermore, for the live video forwarding service, video stream is usually transmitted through a forwarding tree which consists of media servers and video sources [14–16]. However, the proposed resource provisioning approaches for live video forwarding cannot give full consideration to system scalability and resource diversity (e.g. resource location and price). Finally, some existing online resource provisioning approaches across VDCs are based on some unreasonable assumptions. For example, the proposed approaches of [8,15] suppose the number of media servers is not scalable to serve arrival requests and the requests can be denied. Therefore, all the existed approaches only aim at maximizing the throughput of the system. In conclusion, previous works cannot optimize the resource usage and system scalability during real-time video forwarding.

In this paper, we propose Multi-Objective Resource Provisioning *(MORP)*— an online resource provisioning approach on virtualization platform, to provide the minimum resource provisioning cost for *VSaaS*. In the approach, a forwarding tree is exploited to forward live video streams from IP cameras to end users simultaneously. Different from previous works [14–16], we not only take the capacity of media server into consideration, but also combine the resource locations, prices, and forwarding delay as optimality criterion. As a result, our approach can adaptively provide or remove media servers from VDCs and dynamically construct the forwarding trees for end users. More important, to efficiently organize the runtime media servers, we formulate our scheduling problem as a cost optimized Steiner tree problem. However, it is too complicated to select the media servers and network connections together in an online system. To support the large system scalability and connectivity, we convert our problem into two traditional *NP-hard* problems with service capacity and resource diversity constraints: *Facility*

Location (FL) and *Steiner Tree* (ST) problems. An online iterative algorithm is utilized to deal with the *FL* problem, which selects a proper media server among VDCs to provide resource scalability. To support the connectivity, *MORP* further establishes a forwarding path to connect the chosen media server to the forwarding tree with the minimum cost by an online *ST* algorithm. The evaluations demonstrate that the proposed approach can obviously cut the resource provisioning cost of VDCs and largely reduce the computation delay of resource scheduling. The main contributions of our work are as follows:

- We propose to exploit the resource capacity and diversity to formulate the resource provisioning problem, which can be addressed by an online multi-objective optimization algorithm.
- The proposed approach not only has the less time complexity $(O(|F|\log(|F|)))$ comparing to the traditional *Greedy* approach $(O(2^{|F|}))$, but also achieves lower resource provisioning cost.
- The comprehensive evaluations on a built real-world scenario demonstrate the effectiveness and efficiency of our approach.

The rest of this paper is organized as follows. Section 2 describes the system model and the problem formulation. In Sect. 3, we present our resource provisioning approach to solve the optimization problem. Section 4 shows the evaluation of our approach. Finally, we conclude our work in Sect. 5.

2 System Model

2.1 System Overview

The system is shown in Fig. 1, which consists of four components: End users, Web server, VDCs, and IP cameras. End users access to the web server of *VSaaS* to require their IP camera streams. Web server receives each end user's request and runs a scheduler to generate a scheduling plan based on the resource usage of VDCs. When a request arrives at the web server, the scheduler redirects the

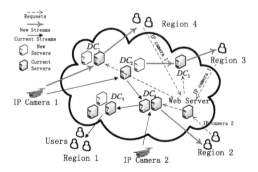

Fig. 1. A system overview for live video forwarding across VDCs

Table 1. Parameters and definitions

Parameters	Definitions
F, U, S	Sets of VDCs, IP cameras and end users respectively
L_u^u, L_u^s	End user location and IP camera location of end user u
Cap^*	The number of the requests can be simultaneously handled by one media server
pr_v^s	Media server leasing price at video data center v
pr_v^b	Network bandwidth price at video data center v
d_{ij}	Forwarding delay between participant i and j
C_v	Media server cost to open a media server at VDC v
C_{ij}	Bandwidth cost from participant i to j
x_{ij}	An indicator to describe whether the edge from participant i to j is chosen
y_{uv}	An indicator to describe whether a media server is opened for u in v
$Path_{v,v',e}$	The chosen path which consists of the selected media servers and connections
$\{Path(T_s, v)\}$	Set of all possible forwarding paths from chosen media server to IP camera s

request to an appropriate media server in a certain VDC, and builds up a forwarding path for end user. Media servers are managed by geo-distributed VDCs from different Cloud Service Providers (CSPs). VDCs are connected by networks which exchange millions of data streams [7]. Media servers can access IP cameras to gain live video streams or exchange streams from one another. The chosen media server gets the required video stream from the IP camera or other media server based on the scheduling plan. Furthermore, the most frequently utilized parameters are shown in Table 1. The critical issues are presented as follows.

User Arrival Model. Suppose m end users sequentially access k IP cameras during time period T, and no more than one end users arrive at each time. Let $D = \{D_1, D_2, \ldots, D_m\}$ be a set of end user requests. End user request is represented by $D_u = \{L_u^u, L_u^s\} \in D$, which is a location pair of end user $u \in \{1, 2, \ldots, m\}$.

Resource Usage Model. Suppose that there are n VDCs around end users. VDCs provide the media servers with the maximum capacity Cap^* to end users. Each VDC $v \in \{1, 2, \ldots, n\}$ has the server leasing price pr_v^s. When idle capacities run out, scheduler can open media server and build up new connections to get live video streams. Note that the connection between any two media servers in the same VDC is not charged by CSPs. Therefore, denote pr_v^b as the network bandwidth price for the connection from VDC v to any other VDC.

Video Forwarding Delay. We define the sets of the participants as F for VDCs, S for IP cameras, and U for end users. Usually, $|U|$ and $|S|$ are much larger than $|F|$. Then, we denote d_{sv} as the forwarding delay between IP camera $s \in S$ and VDC $v \in F$. Denote d_{uv} as the forwarding delay from the media server of VDC v to end user $u \in U$, and $d_{vv'}$ as the delay between any two media servers of VDC v and v'. Finally, we denote d_{min} as the minimum forwarding delay between any two participants in the same location.

2.2   Problem Formulation

We utilize a directed acyclic graph $G = \{V, E\}$ to describe the topology of the inter-connected participants. V is the vertex set of graph G, and $F \subseteq V$, $U \subseteq V$ and $S \subseteq V$, respectively. E is the edge set of graph G. An edge in E means there is a connection between two vertices for stream forwarding. Then, a spanning tree $T_s = \{V^*, E^*\}$ is utilized as a forwarding tree that consists of IP camera s, end users and inter-connected media servers for live video forwarding. The scheduler needs to select VDCs and edges from V and E to construct V^* and E^*. For example, Fig. 2 illustrates a forwarding tree: The numbered cycles are media servers in numbered VDC, the cycle with s is IP camera s, and the squares represent end users. $C_v = pr_v^s$ denotes media server cost to open a media server at VDC v. $C_{uv} = B \times pr_v^b$ represents bandwidth cost from the data center v to end user u, in which B is the bandwidth to forward one video stream. Similarly, $C_e = B \times pr_v^b$ denotes the bandwidth cost of edge $e = \{v, v'\}$ and $C_{vv} = 0$.

Let x_{ij} be an indicator to describe whether edge from participant i to j is chosen: $x_{ij} = 1$ when edge $\{i, j\}$ is selected. Otherwise, $x_{ij} = 0$. Particularly, we denote $x_{vv'}$ for each end user u as x_e^u, if $e = \{v, v'\} \in E$ and $v, v' \in F$. When $x_{vv'} = 1$ and the capacity of the media servers in v' is taken up by arrival requests and media servers, the media server in VDC v and edge $e = \{v, v'\}$ can't transmit live video streams for other participants. Therefore, new media server in v' and additional connections are needed, which means x_e^u must be set to 1 for the end user u. Otherwise, set x_e^u to be 0. For new media servers, we have an indicator y_{uv} as follows: Set $y_{uv} = 1$ means VDC v opens a media server to serve the request of end user u. Otherwise, $y_{uv} = 0$.

Assuming that the sequence of requests within time period T is known, the offline resource provisioning cost is formulated as follows:

$$Cost(U) = Cost_B + Cost_D + Cost_S. \qquad (1)$$

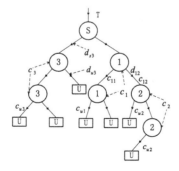

Fig. 2. Forwarding tree of live video stream for inter-datacenter network

Let resource provisioning cost $Cost(U)$ is the sum of the total bandwidth cost $Cost_B$, the total delay cost $Cost_D$, and the total media server cost $Cost_S$. The offline solution must determine how to assign media servers, and connect the relays to forward video streams from IP cameras at the same time. However, this problem is too complicated to be well solved in polynomial time as shown in [17]. Therefore, we convert the problem into two parts: Find a proper media server for arrival end user to provide scalability (*Facility Location problem*); Connect it to the forwarding tree of the IP camera to provide connectivity (*Steiner Tree problem*). Both problems are typical *NP-hard* problems with approximate optimal solutions. The cost function can be rewritten as follows:

$$Cost(U) = Cost_{FL} + Cost_{ST}, \tag{2}$$

$$Cost_{FL} = \sum_{u \in U} \sum_{v \in F} x_{uv} f_{uv} + \gamma \sum_{u \in U} \sum_{v \in F} y_{uv} C_v, \tag{3}$$

$$Cost_{ST} = \alpha \sum_{u \in U} \sum_{e \in E} x_e^u C_e + \beta (\sum_{u \in U} \sum_{e \in E} x_e^u d_e +$$
$$\sum_{s \in S} \sum_{v \in F} x_{sv} d_{sv}) + \gamma \sum_{u \in U} \sum_{v' \in F} y_{uv'} C_{v'}, \tag{4}$$

$$f_{uv} = \alpha C_{uv} + \beta d_{uv}. \tag{5}$$

Finally, parameters α, β, and γ are positive constants to denote the weight of each type of cost. Then the objective function of the offline resource provisioning problem is as follows:

$$\min Cost(U),$$
$$subject\ to:$$
$$Path_{v,v',e} \subseteq \{Path(T_s, v)\}. \tag{6}$$

Note that there is only one edge from the chosen media server to the end user u at each time, and at most one connection from IP camera s to the chosen media server of v. Generally, the system requires no more than 1 new media server (if possible) to serve arrival request of u, and scheduler can add media servers as relays to help to forward video stream for the end user u. In Constraint (6), we define $Path_{v,v',e}$ as the chosen path consisting of the selected media servers and connections. $\{Path(T_s, v)\}$ is a set which contains all possible paths from the chosen media server to IP camera s. $Path_{v,v',e}$ must belong to $\{Path(T_s, v)\}$ to support the connectivity. Since the traditional online algorithms are not scalable as shown in [17], we design a novel online algorithm to deal with this new problem.

3   Online Resource Provisioning Approach

In this section, we propose our online resource provisioning approach, which is shown in Fig. 3.

3.1   Scalable Algorithm for Online VM Provisioning

We use a primal-dual method to design an online VM provisioning algorithm to improve the system scalability. The VM provisioning algorithm aims at minimizing $Cost_{FL}$ for each arrival end user. Therefore, we have following primal problem definition:

$$\min \sum_{u \in U} \sum_{v \in F} x_{uv} f_{uv} + \gamma \sum_{u \in U} \sum_{v \in F} y_{uv} C_v,$$

subject to:

$$\sum_{u \in U} Cap^* y_{uv} \geq \sum_{u \in U} x_{uv}, \ for \ any \ v \in F. \tag{7}$$

Constraint (7) means the total capacities of the VM cluster must be larger than the number of end users. Then we use a relaxation method to get its dual problem, which is defined as follows:

$$\max \sum_{u \in U} z_u, \tag{8}$$

subject to:

$$z_u \leq \frac{1}{|F|} \sum_{v \in F} g_{uv}, \ for \ any \ u \in U, \tag{9}$$

$$g_{uv} = f_{uv} + \gamma C_v / Cap^*. \tag{10}$$

Inspired by the algorithms proposed in [8,15], we first get the optimal fractional online provisioning plan in Algorithm 1. We replace C_v with C_v^*. If there are idle capacities in VDC v, C_v^* is set to be 0 which means there is a VM that can be employed to serve the arrival end user. Otherwise, $C_v^* = C_v$ which means opening a VM for arrival end user. Then a random rounding method is utilized in Algorithm 1 to get the optimal integer scheduling plan. The time complexity of the algorithm is $O(|F| \log |F|)$.

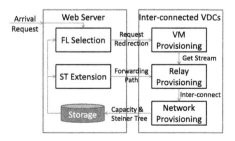

Fig. 3. Online resource provisioning for each arrival request

---

Algorithm 1. Online FL Algorithm

Input: $G = (V, E)$, D_u, d_{ij}, pr_i^s, and pr_i^b;
Output: Fractional x_{uv} vector;
1: For arrival request of u, get the IP camera location L_u^s and end user location L_u^u.
2: **while** $\sum_{v \in F} x_{uv} < 1$ **do**
3:    For each $v \in F$: $x_{uv} = x_{uv}(1 + 1/g_{uv}) + 1/|F|g_{uv}$.
4:    $z_u = z_u + 1$.
5: **end while**
6: For each set $v \in F$, choose $2 \ln n$ independently random variables $X(v, i)$ uniformly at random in the interval $[0, 1]$.
7: For each set s, let $\Theta(v) = \min_{i=1}^{2 \ln n} X(v, i)$.
8: Take the candidate v with the minimum cost if $\Theta(v) \leq x_{uv}$.

Algorithm 2. Online Steiner Tree Algorithm

Input: $G = (V, E)$, D_u, d_{ij}, pr_i^s, and pr_i^b;
Output: Proper ST_s;
1: **for all** $s \in S$ **do**
2:    $ST_s = s$
3: **end for**
4: **while** Request of u arrives to require stream s **do**
5:    Get chosen VM from *Algorithm 1*.
6:    **if** There is new VM opened in v **then**
7:        $ST_s \leftarrow ST_s \bigcup \{(v, u)\} \bigcup Spath(v, ST_s)$.
8:    **end if**
9:    Assign v to the arrival u.
10: **end while**
11: Release the idle VMs, and adjust each forwarding path.

3.2 Online Algorithm for Forwarding Tree Adjustment

Scheduler must connect the chosen VM to current forwarding tree to get the live video stream. Algorithm 2 is proposed to adaptively adjust the forwarding tree to provide system connectivity. In our algorithm, the scheduler firstly sets the required IP camera as the root of the forwarding tree. When a request of an end user arrives, the scheduler uses Algorithm 1 to select the proper VM among VDCs at first. Then the chosen VM is connected to current forwarding tree with the cheapest resource provisioning cost. Our algorithm finally returns a forwarding tree ST_s connecting all arrival end users and VMs together. We denote $Spath(v, ST_s)$ as the forwarding path with the minimum resource provisioning cost between chosen VM and forwarding tree ST_s. Furthermore, the time complexity of our algorithm is also $O(|F| \log |F|)$.

4 Performance Evaluation

4.1 Experiment Setup

We set up an inter-datacenter topology $G\{V, E\}$: VDCs can build up connections to any participants in the topology, IP cameras and end users only connect to VDCs. The topology has 50 vertices which are the real cities in China. Among the vertices, we select 15 vertices as VDCs, and 35 vertices as the locations of end users as well as IP cameras. VM in each VDC is employed as a media server which can serve 50 end user requests simultaneously. According to our observation, most IP camera bitrates are ranged from $300\,Kpbs$ to $800\,Kpbs$.

Table 2. VM Prices ($yuan/h$) and Bandwidth Prices ($yuan/Mbps/h$)

Shenyang	Beijing	Tianjin	Xian	Qingdao
0.67 & 1.08	0.88 & 0.8	0.56 & 0.868	0.67 & 1.08	0.792 & 0.72
Zhengzhou	Nanjing	Shanghai	Hangzhou	Wuhan
0.67 & 0.744	0.56 & 0.868	0.67 & 0.868	0.88 & 0.8	0.67 & 1.08
Changsha	Fuzhou	Shenzhen	Hongkong	Chengdu
0.88 & 0.8	0.56 & 0.868	0.88 & 0.8	0.456 & 1.0	0.67 & 1.08

VM and bandwidth prices of VDCs are shown in Table 2, which take the reference to the resource charges of *Amazon, Aliyun,* and *Google* [4–6]. To evaluate video forwarding delay, we multiply the average forwarding delay by the distance of the edge to get the delay of each edge, which is ranged from 10 ms to 70 ms. We also set the delay between any two participants in the same regions as $d_{min} = 0.01$.

We compare our approach to the other two state-of-the-arts: *Greedy Scheduling* approach [15] and *Nearest Available* approach, which are widely utilized in video delivery service. *Greedy Scheduling* approach, which is employed as a bench mark approach, exhaustively explores all the possibilities to build up the forwarding path from forwarding tree to end user with the minimum resource provisioning cost. Thus, its time complexity is $O(2^{|F|})$. For the *Nearest Available* approach, it first selects the nearest media server to the arrival end user. Then, the chosen media server is directly connected to the required IP camera to get live video stream. Then, its time complexity is $O(|F|)$. When the capacities of the media servers run out, new media server is added in both approaches. We randomly choose L_u^u and L_u^s for each request at each time. End user arrival process is a *Poisson Process*. We use the following parameters to evaluate the performance: cumulative total cost C_{total}, cumulative media server cost C_{VM}, cumulative bandwidth cost C_B, and cumulative delay cost $C_D = \beta \times Delay$.

4.2   Performance Comparison

The experimental results are given to show the resource provisioning cost of the three approaches in Figs. 4, 5, and 6. To evaluate the influence of the delay cost, we give two different delay charges based on the different values of parameter β, *i.e.*, 1 and 0.03 respectively. $\beta = 1$ leads to the delay cost is obviously larger than VM cost and bandwidth cost. That is to say the delay cost is the dominant cost during resource provisioning. When β is decreased to 0.03, the delay cost for one edge is nearly the same with the VM cost to add one media server and the bandwidth cost to forward one video stream. Note that we set parameter α and γ to be 1 according to the resource charges of commercial CSPs in the real-world.

The cumulative VM cost, bandwidth cost, and delay cost under different β are given by Figs. 4 and 5. According to the experimental results, our approach can obviously reduce the total cost not only by controlling the dominant cost,

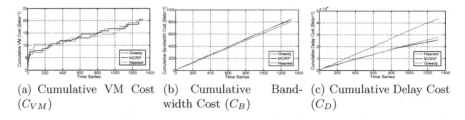

(a) Cumulative VM Cost (C_{VM}) (b) Cumulative Band-width Cost (C_B) (c) Cumulative Delay Cost (C_D)

Fig. 4. Experimental results for $\beta = 1$ (Color figure online)

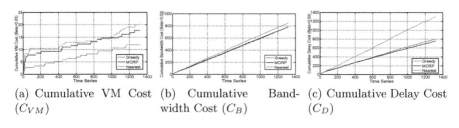

(a) Cumulative VM Cost (C_{VM}) (b) Cumulative Band-width Cost (C_B) (c) Cumulative Delay Cost (C_D)

Fig. 5. Experimental results for $\beta = 0.03$ (Color figure online)

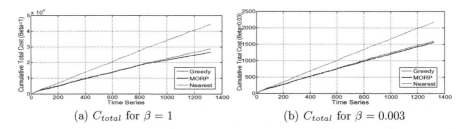

(a) C_{total} for $\beta = 1$ (b) C_{total} for $\beta = 0.003$

Fig. 6. Cumulative total cost under different β (Color figure online)

but also by achieving tradeoffs among similar types of cost. When β is set to be 1, the C_D is the dominant cost. Our approach has the minimum delay cost which leads to the minimum cumulative total cost as shown in Fig. 4(c). At the same time, C_{VM} and C_B are similar to the values of the other two approaches, which are shown in Fig. 4(a, b). When $\beta = 0.03$, the average delay cost for one connection is nearly the same with the cost for one VM or one live video stream. Although we get a little higher C_{VM} than *Greedy* approach and *Nearest Available* approach given in Fig. 5(a), we maintain less C_B and much less C_D as shown in Fig. 5(b, c). Therefore, our approach is with the minimum C_{Total} comparing with the other two approaches as shown in Fig. 6(a, b) when $\beta = 1$ and 0.03. Furthermore, we averagely cut the total cost of 3 % to 10 % comparing to the *Greedy* approach, and the computation time of our approach also significantly faster than the *Greedy* approach. The *Greedy* approach needs a few seconds to get the scheduling plan, but our approach just needs a few milliseconds, which is nearly as faster as the *Nearest* approach. The *Nearest* approach has the shortest computation time among the three approaches, but has higher resource provisioning cost. When more VDCs are involved into the forwarding service, the computational advantage of our approach is more obvious.

5 Conclusion

In this paper, we propose a multi-objective optimization approach for online resource provisioning across VDCs in *VSaaS*. We give a full consideration on the resource capacity and diversity of the system. The resource provisioning problem is formulated as an online cost optimized Steiner tree problem. VM cost, bandwidth cost, and delay cost are combined to evaluate the resource provisioning cost. To efficiently optimize the problem in a simplified method, we convert the problem into the combination of *FL* and *ST* problems. To deal with these two *NP-hard* problems, we provide online approximate optimal solutions. The experimental results show that the proposed approach is effective and efficient, which obviously cuts the resource cost during resource provisioning and shorten the computational delay of the scheduling plan.

Acknowledgements. The research reported in this paper is supported by the National Natural Science Foundation of China under Grant No. 61332005 and No. 61190114; The Cosponsored Project of Beijing Committee of Education; The Beijing Training Project for the Leading Talents in S&T (ljrc 201502).

References

1. Mega Eyes. http://qqy.fjii.com/
2. Liu, W., Mei, T., Zhang, Y., Che, C., Luo, J.: Multi-task deep visual-semantic embedding for video thumbnail selection. In: Proceedings of IEEE CVPR, pp. 3707–3715 (2015)
3. Gao, Y., Ma, H.D., Zhang, H., Yang, X., Cao, N.: Minimizing resource cost for camera stream scheduling in video data center. In: Proceedings of IEEE CloudCom, pp. 210–217 (2015)
4. Amazon EC2. https://aws.amazon.com/ec2
5. Aliyun. https://ecs-buy.aliyun.com
6. Google Cloud Platform. https://cloud.google.com
7. Adhikari, V.K., Jain, S., Chen, Y., Zhang, Z.: Vivisecting YouTube: an active measurement study. In: Proceedings of IEEE INFOCOM, pp. 2521–2525 (2012)
8. Hao, F., Kodialam, M., Lakshman, T., Mukherjee, S.: Online allocation of virtual machines in a distributed cloud. In: Proceedings of IEEE INFOCOM, pp. 10–18 (2014)
9. Hu, M., Luo, J., Wang, Y., Veeravalli, B.: Practical resource provisioning and caching with dynamic resilience for cloud-based content distribution networks. IEEE Trans. Parallel Distrib. Syst. **25**(8), 2169–2179 (2014)
10. Jiao, L., Li, J., Du, W., Fu, X.: Multi-objective data placement for multi-cloud socially aware services. In: Proceedings of IEEE INFOCOM, pp. 28–36 (2014)
11. Wang, Z., Li, B., Sun, L., Zhu, W., Yang, S.: Dispersing instant social video service across multiple clouds. IEEE Trans. Parallel Distrib. Syst. **99**, 1–14 (2015)

12. Nishida, H., Nguyen, T.: Optimal client-server assignment for internet distributed systems. IEEE Trans. Parallel Distrib. Syst. **24**(3), 565–575 (2013)
13. Zheng, H., Tang, X.: The server provisioning problem for continuous distributed interactive application. IEEE Trans. Parallel Distrib. Syst. **27**(1), 271–285 (2016)
14. Wang, F., Liu, J., Chen, M.: CALMS: cloud-assisted live media streaming for globalized demands with time/region diversities. In: Proceedings of IEEE INFOCOM, pp. 199–207 (2012)
15. Liao, J., Chou, P., Yuan, C., Hu, Y., Zhu, W.: Online allocation of communication and computation resources for real-time multimedia services. IEEE Trans. Multimedia **15**(3), 670–683 (2013)
16. Mukerjee, M.K., Naylor, D., Jiang, J., Han, D., Seshan, S., Zhang, H.: Practical, real-time, centralized control for CDN-based live video delivery. In: Proceedings of ACM SIGCOMM, pp. 311–324 (2015)
17. San Felice, M.C., Williamson, D.P., Lee, O.: The online connected facility location problem. In: Pardo, A., Viola, A. (eds.) LATIN 2014. LNCS, vol. 8392, pp. 574–585. Springer, Heidelberg (2014)

Research and Application of Fast Multi-label SVM Classification Algorithm Using Approximate Extreme Points

Zhongwei Sun[1], Zhongwen Guo[1(✉)], Mingxing Jiang[2], Xi Wang[1],
and Chao Liu[1]

[1] Department of Computer Science and Technology, Ocean University of China,
Qingdao, China
guozhw@ouc.edu.cn
[2] Department of Computer Foundation, Ocean University of China,
Qingdao, China
jiangmx@ouc.edu.cn

Abstract. In Large-Scale of Multi-label classification framework, applications of Non-linear kernel support vector machines (SVMs) classification algorithm are restricted by the problem of excessive training time. Hence, we propose Approximate Extreme Points Multi-label Support Vector Machine (AEMLSVM) classification algorithm to solve this problem. The first step of AEMLSVM classification algorithm is using approximate extreme points method to extract the training subsets, called the representative sets, from training dataset. Then SVM is trained from the representative sets. In addition, the AEMLSVM classification algorithm also can adopt Cost-Sensitive method to deal with the imbalanced data issue. Experiment results from three Large-Scale public datasets show that AEMLSVM classification algorithm can substantially shorten training time greatly and obtain a similar result compared with the traditional Multi-label SVM classification algorithm. It also exceeds existing fast Multi-label SVM classification algorithm in both training time and effectiveness. Besides, AEMLSVM classification algorithm has advantages in the classification time.

Keywords: Support vector machine · Multi-label classification · Extreme points · Imbalanced data

1 Introduction

Multi-label classification is a typical supervised learning issue, in which each individual example is represented by an instance. However, every instance can be possibly linked to several labels, thus the labels are no longer mutually exclusive [1]. Researchers have proposed many Multi-label classification methods, for example, methods based on problem transformation strategy, methods based on SVM, methods based on neural network, methods based on decision tree

© Springer International Publishing Switzerland 2016
Y. Wang et al. (Eds.): BigCom 2016, LNCS 9784, pp. 39–52, 2016.
DOI: 10.1007/978-3-319-42553-5_4

and methods based on K-nearest neighbor (KNN) [7]. These methods have been successfully applied in the field of text categorization [2], automatic image and video annotation [3], bioinformatics prediction [4], music emotion categorization [5], etc. However, many current Multi-label classification methods cannot work efficiently in Large-Scale datasets. The main restriction is the excessive training time, which is especially obvious in SVM.

Traditional SVM [6] is a widely used machine learning method which can only solve Single-Instance Single-Label classification problem. But, improved SVM algorithm like Rank-SVM [8] algorithm can work on Multi-label classification. Because Non-linear dataset is very universal in Multi-label datasets, Non-linear kernel is required to attain a better effect in classification. This further restricts the use of the SVM algorithm in Large-Scale datasets.

Besides, an unavoidable problem in Multi-label classification algorithm is that most Multi-label datasets are imbalanced dataset [9], which affects the classification algorithm results.

In this paper, we combine Binary Relevance (BR) problem transformation strategy with binary Approximate Extreme Points SVM (AESVM) [11] classification algorithm to construct a new Multi-label classification algorithm (AEMLSVM). It can be used to solve the problem of Multi-label SVM classification algorithm used in Large-Scale datasets. AEMLSVM classification algorithm utilizes approximate extreme points method to extract representative sets from training dataset, and Cost-Sensitive method to solve the imbalanced data problem. Results from experiment on three public datasets show that AEMLSVM classification algorithm proposed in this paper has the shortest training time compared with other algorithms which all use Binary Relevance (BR) problem transformation strategy, such as ML-LIBSVM [10], ML-CVM [12], and ML-BVM [13]. Meanwhile, AEMLSVM classification algorithm has a similar performance compared with ML-LIBSVM classification algorithm among five evaluation metrics, which surpass ML-CVM and ML-BVM classification algorithm. Additionally, AEMLSVM classification algorithm has advantages in classification time.

The rest of this paper is organized as follows. In the second part, related work is introduced; the newly proposed AEMLSVM classification algorithm is given in the third part; the forth part is the experiment result and analysis; the last part is conclusion.

2   Related Work

In the past few decades, Many Multi-label classification algorithms have been proposed and applied in many fields. This chapter is the introduction of several present Multi-label classification algorithms.

The kind of Multi-label classification algorithm based on problem transformation strategy is to joint problem transformation trick and present binary classification methods to accomplish Multi-label classification. Problem transformation trick includes binary relevance (BR) or One-Versus-Rest (OVR) [14], One-Versus-One (OVO) and label powerset (LP) [7], etc. The BR or OVR trick transforms the Multi-label classification issue into multiple binary classification issues, one for each label. Then, these classifiers are assembled into an entire Multi-label classification algorithm by using a proper threshold function. In [32], the BR or OVR trick has three main problems. First of all, since it is assumed that the labels are independent, the correlations and interdependencies between labels are ignored. Secondly, it causes the imbalanced data issue. For every Sub-dataset, negative instances tend to outnumber positives instances. Lastly, as the number of labels increases, the imbalanced data issue will further exacerbate and the number of Sub-classifiers will further increase. Despite these problems, the BR or OVR technique is simple and practical, and the dataset can be reversed. In [33], the main advantages of BR are emphasized. Firstly, compared with other methods, the BR or OVR trick not only has low computational complexity but also scales linearly with the quantity of labels. Additionally, due to the independence of labels, the addition and removal of labels will not affect other label classification models, which allows BR to be applied to an evolutionary or dynamic scenario and provides opportunities for parallel execution. To summarize, this paper employs the most famous BR or OVR problem transformation method to implement Multi-label classification.

Clare and *King* [15] propose a C4.5-type Multi-label classification algorithm, which realizes Multi-label classification by modifying the entropy calculation formula and allowing leaves of decision tree to be a label set. Multi-label Back-Propagation neural networks (BP-MLL) [21] classification algorithm introduces a new empirical loss function considering the characteristic of Multi-label learning, which makes BP-MLL be applied in Multi-label classification and consequently leads to a Large-Scale unconstrained optimization problem. ML-KNN [3] classification algorithm estimates label prior and conditional probabilities, through the use of discrete binary Bayesian rule for each label independently. However, these algorithms are suitable for small scale datasets.

Rank-SVM [8] utilizes the extension of Multiple-class SVM and the minimized ranking loss to accomplish Multi-label classification, which leads to an extremely complex quadratic programming problem. *Xu* [16] reduces the computation complexity in Multi-label classification by adding zero label as an benchmark to separate relevant and irrelevant label in SVM. Although such two Rank-SVM classification algorithms can be solved by FW [17,18] method, the training of these two methods is quite Time-Consuming. To tackle this problem, *Xu* [19] proposes the Multi-label classification algorithm Rank-CVM by employing core vector machine (CVM [12]). Rank-CVM can speed up the training efficiency to some extent, however, causes a reduction in classification accuracy. *Xu* [20] adds zero label as Benchmark label in Rank-CVM [19] to separate relevant and irrelevant label, which can reduce computation complexity. Both Rank-CVM Multi-label classification algorithms can be solved by FW [17,18] method.

Imbalanced data issue will impact on all kinds of classification algorithms, which has been detailed in [22]. Many strategies are proposed and applied to solve this problem. And these strategies have got good effects. They can be classified into three mainstream methods: Re-sampling method [22], Instance-Based method [23] and Cost-Sensitive method [24]. AEMLSVM classification algorithm utilizes Cost-Sensitive method to solve imbalanced data problem.

In conclusion, although many Multi-label classification algorithms have been proposed and applied, they still have restrictions in the use of Large-Scale Multi-label datasets, especially algorithms based on SVM. AEMLSVM classification algorithm can solve this problem efficiently, which can substantially reduce training time as well as obtain a similar classification result compared with the ML-LIBSVM classification algorithm. Additionally, it also solves the problem of imbalanced data efficiently by adopting the Cost-Sensitive method.

3   Fast Multi-label SVM Classification Algorithm Using Approximate Extreme Points

In this section, we will briefly review binary support vector machine (SVM) and binary approximate extreme points support vector machine (AESVM). Then the improvement of binary approximate extreme points support vector machine (AESVM) will be introduced in detail. After that, we will design and implement fast multi-label support vector machine (SVM) classification algorithm using approximate extreme points (AEMLSVM). Finally, we will analyze the complexity of the AEMLSVM classification algorithm.

3.1   Improvement of Binary Approximate Extreme Points SVM

In this subsection, we will firstly introduce the optimization of binary SVM and binary approximate extreme points SVM (AESVM). To adapt to the imbalanced data situation of training dataset, we revise the binary approximate extreme points SVM (AESVM).

Assume a two label dataset including N data vectors, $\boldsymbol{X} = \{\boldsymbol{x}_i : \boldsymbol{x}_i \in R^D, i = 1, 2, ..., N\}$, and the corresponding target labels $\boldsymbol{Y} = \{y_i : y_i \in [-1, 1], i = 1, 2, ..., N\}$. The binary SVM primal optimization problem can be transformed into the following unconstrained optimization problem [31]:

$$\underset{\boldsymbol{w}, b}{min} F_1(\boldsymbol{w}, b) = \frac{1}{2}\|\boldsymbol{w}\|^2 + \frac{C}{N}\sum_{i=1}^{N} l(\boldsymbol{w}, b, \Phi(\boldsymbol{x}_i)) \qquad (1)$$

where $l(\boldsymbol{w}, b, \Phi(\boldsymbol{x}_i)) = max\{0, 1 - y_i(\boldsymbol{w}^T\Phi(\boldsymbol{x}_i) + b)\}, \forall \boldsymbol{x}_i \in \boldsymbol{X}$ and $\Phi : R^D \longrightarrow H, b \in R$, and $\boldsymbol{w} \in H$, a Hilbert space.

Here $l(\boldsymbol{w}, b, \Phi(\boldsymbol{x}_i))$ is hinge loss of training example $\boldsymbol{x}_i$. $\|\boldsymbol{w}\|^2$ reflects the complexity of the model [6]. Parameter C is designed to balance the model complexity and the sum of losses of the training dataset. The punishment parameter C is divided by N has been widely used [25]. Based on these formulas, we can analyze the scaling of C with N [26]. The training time complexity of the SVM algorithm using Non-linear kernels is typically quadratic in the size of the training dataset [27]. Although binary SVM has excellent classification results, the training time is excessive when faced with Large-Scale dataset. *Nandan et al.* [11] proposes a binary approximate extreme points SVM (AESVM) classification algorithm. The algorithm utilizes the approximate extreme points method to choose the representative sets of the training dataset. They run the binary SVM algorithm on the representative sets. The primal optimization problem of binary approximate extreme points SVM (AESVM) can be transformed into the following unconstrained optimization problem [11]:

$$\min_{w,b} F_2(w,b) = \frac{1}{2}\|w\|^2 + \frac{C}{N}\sum_{t=1}^{M}\beta_t l(w,b,\Phi(x_t)), \tag{2}$$

where $l(w,b,\Phi(x_t)) = max\{0, 1 - y_t(w^T\Phi(x_t) + b)\}, \forall x_t \in X^*$ and $\Phi : R^D \longrightarrow H, b \in R$ and $w \in H$, a Hilbert space.

M is the size of X^* which is a representative set of X. β_t is related with the approximate extreme points method. In [11], *Nandan* proves that the AESVM classification algorithm can realize a similar classification result with the traditional SVM classification algorithm under the situation of improving training speed by setting a small value of ε. To obtain the representative set, *Nandan* proposes the DeriveRS algorithm based on approximate extreme points technology. Its time complexity is linear.

The Large-Scale Multi-label datasets cause the imbalanced data problems, which will affect the results of classification algorithms. To solve the mentioned problem, we transform the binary approximate extreme points SVM's primal optimization problem into the following unconstrained optimization problem:

$$\min_{w,b} F_3(w,b) = \frac{1}{2}\|w\|^2 + \frac{C}{N}\sum_{t=1}^{M}\beta_t \tau_t l(w,b,\Phi(x_t)), \tag{3}$$

where $l(w,b,\Phi(x_t)) = max\{0, 1 - y_t(w^T\Phi(x_t) + b)\}, \forall x_t \in X^*$ and $\Phi : R^D \longrightarrow H, b \in R$ and $w \in H$, a Hilbert space.

Here τ_t is the amplification coefficient to solve the imbalanced data problem.

$$\tau_t = \frac{1 + y_t}{2}R + \frac{1 - y_t}{2} \tag{4}$$

$$R = \frac{n}{p\alpha} \tag{5}$$

R is the level of imbalanced dataset. n is the quantity of negative examples of training dataset. p is the quantity of positive examples of training dataset. α is a positive integer constant $(0 < \alpha < \frac{n}{p})$.

The improvement of the binary approximate extreme points SVM can adapt to the imbalanced data situation of training dataset and improve the classification result. It worth noting that an improper R will lead to negative effect on classification results.

3.2 AEMLSVM Algorithm

The Approximate Extreme Points Multi-label SVM (AEMLSVM) classification algorithm proposed in this paper utilizes the Binary Relevance (BR) problem transformation strategy. It transforms a Multi-label dataset into K binary

---

$Y = AEMLSVM(S, x, P, V, k)$

Input : S *The Multi-label training set*
            $\{(x_1, Y_1), (x_2, Y_2), \cdots , (x_N, Y_N)\}$,
    x *The test example $x \in X$,*
    P *Maximum size of subset after first level of*
            segregation.
    V *Maximum size of subset after second level*
            of segregation.
    k *The number of labels.*

Output: Y The set predicted labels of $x(Y \in y)$;

begin

   For Multi-label training set
   $S = \{(x_1, Y_1), (x_2, Y_2), \cdots , (x_N, Y_N)\}$,
   Decompose Multi-label training set S into k
   independent binary training subsets using Binary
   Relevance method. i.e.,$S_1, S_2, \cdots , S_k$.

for *each binary training subset $S_i (i = 1, 2, \cdots , k)$* **do**
   Compute the representative set using $[S_i^*, \beta_i] = ImpDeriveRS(S_i, P, V)$;
   Train an LIBSVM classifier using $f_i = SVMTrain(S_i^*, \beta_i)$ Based on
   Non-linear kernel, using the formulation (2)
end

Obtain the label set of a test example x,
return $Y = \{i | f_i(x) > 0\}(i = 1, 2, \cdots , k)$;

Algorithm 1. AEMLSVM

dataset. K is the quantity of labels. Each binary dataset is composed by positive and negative examples of specific label. The quantity of examples in each binary dataset is equal to that in Multi-label dataset. Then we improve the DeriveRS algorithm in [11] and propose ImpDeriveRS algorithm to obtain each binary dataset's representative set. Finally, we use improved LIBSVM algorithm in [10] to process the representative sets. After that, we acquire K binary classifiers and integrate the K classifiers to realize fast Multi-label classification. We use LIBSVM because it well realizes the SMO algorithm [28]. The AEMLSVM algorithm has two Sub-algorithm based on whether considering about imbalanced data, the AEMLSVM and AEMLSVM-IMBL. Basing on the introduction above, we expect that the AEMLSVM algorithm with Non-linear kernels can adapt to the Large-Scale Multi-label classification datasets. It will reduce training time and have nearly the same results with that of ML-LIBSVM algorithm.

The pseudocode of AEMLSVM algorithm is shown in Algorithm 1. The pseudocode of AEMLSVM-IMBL algorithm is shown in Algorithm 2. In Algorithms 1 and 2, S_i^* represents a representative set of the training subset S_i. β_i is a constant associated with the approximate extreme points method. f_i is the ith label prediction model of the representative set S_i^*. $f_i(x)$ is the ith label predicted value of test example x. R_i is the level of the imbalanced representative set S_i^*.

$Y = AEMLSVM - IMBL(S, x, P, V, k, \alpha)$

Input : S The Multi-label training set
$\{(x_1, Y_1), (x_2, Y_2), \cdots, (x_N, Y_N)\}$,

$\quad x$ The test example $x \in X$,

$\quad P$ Maximum size of subset after first level of
$\qquad$ segregation.

$\quad V$ Maximum size of subset after second level
$\qquad$ of segregation.

$\quad k$ The number of labels.

$\quad \alpha$ The constants of positive integer.

Output: Y The set predicted labels of $x(Y \in y)$;

begin

For Multi-label training set
$S = \{(x_1, Y_1), (x_2, Y_2), \cdots, (x_N, Y_N)\}$,
Decompose Multi-label training set S into k
independent binary training subsets using Binary
Relevance method. i.e.,$S_1, S_2, \cdots, S_k$.

for each binary training subset $S_i(i = 1, 2, \cdots, k)$ **do**

$\quad$ Compute the representative set using $[S_i^*, \beta_i] = ImpDeriveRS(S_i, P, V)$;
$\quad$ Compute the imbalanced level of S_i^* dataset using ;
$\quad$ a) The number of negative instances n_i;
$\quad$ b) The number of positive instances p_i;
$\quad$ c) Compute $R_i = \frac{n_i}{p_i \alpha}$ using the formulation (5);
$\quad$ Train an LIBSVM classifier using $f_i = SVMTrain(S_i^*, \beta_i, R_i)$ Based on
$\quad$ Non-linear kernel, using the formulation (3)

end

Obtain the label set of a test example x,

return $Y = \{i | f_i(x) > 0\}(i = 1, 2, \cdots, k)$;

Algorithm 2. AEMLSVM-IMBL

3.3   Complexity Analysis of AEMLSVM

Standard SVM training has $O(m^3)$ time complexity and $O(m^2)$ space complexity, where m is the size of training dataset [12]. AEMLSVM has $O(km)$ time complexity in computing the representative set. Because of using SMO algorithm [28] to optimizing SVM, the training time complexity is between $O(km)$ and $O(km^{2.2})$ and the space complexity is $O(km)$, where k represents the number of labels. By reducing the training dataset size, AEMLSVM algorithm realizes faster training, meanwhile can also improve the classification speed.

4   Experiments

In this section, we compare our AEMLSVM classification algorithm with three existing Multi-label classification algorithms including ML-LIBSVM, ML-CVM and ML-BVM experimentally. Before presenting our experimental results, we briefly introduce three existing Multi-label classification methods, three public Large-Scale Multi-label datasets and five performance evaluation metrics.

Table 1. A description of datasets

Dataset	Training instances	Testing instances	Features	Labels
Mediamill(exp1)	30993	12914	120	101
Siam-competition2007	21519	7077	30438	22
Rcvlv2(topics;full sets)	23149	12000	47236	103

4.1 Three Existing Multi-label Methods and Three Large-Scale Multi-label Datasets

In this paper, we selected three existing Multi-label classification methods: ML-LIBSVM, ML-CVM and ML-BVM, which will be compared with our AEMLSVM experimentally. These three methods and our AEMLSVM all use Binary Relevance (BR) problem transformation strategy to transform Multi-label dataset into multiple binary data subsets. Their differences lie in processing method of binary data subsets. We collected three public Large-Scale Multi-label datasets to conduct the experiment. The datasets are downloaded from LIBSVM's website [29]. The scale and attribute of datasets are in the Table 1.

4.2 Performance Evaluation Metrics

The performance evaluation of Multi-label classification is more complicated than that of traditional Single-Label setting because multiple labels can be assigned to each example simultaneously. A number of specific evaluation metrics of Multi-label classification have been proposed [3,7,19,30]. We choose the Widely-Used evaluation metrics: Hamming Loss, One-Error, Coverage, Ranking Loss and Average-Precision, as in [30]. Briefly, in Multi-label classification algorithms, it is hoped to obtain a larger value for the Average-Precision, and smaller values for the other four evaluation metrics.

4.3 Experimental Setup and Analysis of Experimental Results

In our experiment, the RBF kernel $K(x,y) = exp(-\gamma\|x - y\|_2^2)$ is tested for our AEMLSVM, ML-LIBSVM, ML-CVM and ML-BVM, where γ and $\| \cdot \|_2$ denote the kernel scale factor and the Euclidean distance respectively. In order to obtain the optimal representation set, we set three parameters in AEMLSVM algorithm: P, V and ε. At the same time, we set e as a parameter that represents the allowable termination criterion and $C^*(C^* = C/N)$ as a parameter that represents loss function in these five Multi-label classification algorithms. To ensure the fairness and rationality of the experimental results, we set the same parameter for the same dataset. However, the parameter of different datasets will be changed. The experiments are conducted on the same Lenovo desktop, with 4 GB memory, I5-4690 processor, 3.5 GHz frequency.

In order to obtain the optimal representation set from mediamill(exp1) dataset, we set parameter P = 500, V = 300 and $\varepsilon = 0.065$. At the same time,

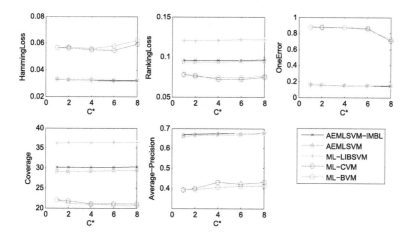

Fig. 1. Data comparison of five evaluation metrics (Color figure online)

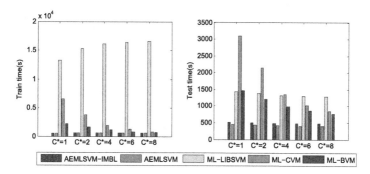

Fig. 2. Comparison of training time and classifying time (Color figure online)

we set parameter e = 1.95e-5 and C* = 1, 2, 4, 6, 8 respectively in these five Multi-label classification algorithms. By setting the above parameters, Figs. 1 and 2 show the experimental results of five different Multi-label classification algorithms in mediamill(exp1) dataset.

The data in Fig. 1 indicate that compared with ML-LIBSVM classification algorithm, the values of Hamming Loss and One-Error increased by 0.1 % and 1.4 % respectively at most, the value of Average-Precision decreased by 1.4 % at most in AEMLSVM classification algorithm. Its values of Coverage and Ranking Loss were also superior to ML-LIBSVM classification algorithm. All above fully explain that the classification result of AEMLSVM classification algorithm was similar to ML-LIBSVM classification algorithm, and the values of Hamming Loss, One-Error and Average-Precision in AEMLSVM classification algorithm were superior to these values in ML-CVM and ML-BVM classification algorithm. Meanwhile, we can conclude from Fig. 2 that the training time and classifying time of AEMLSVM classification algorithm was the shortest, especially its training time was only 1/24 of ML-LIBSVM classification algorithm. In the internal comparison of AEMLSVM classification algorithm, the values of

Hamming Loss, One-Error and Average-Precision in AEMLSVM-IMBL classification algorithm were superior to AEMLSVM classification algorithm, the values of Coverage and Ranking Loss of AEMLSVM-IMBL classification algorithm were inferior to AEMLSVM classification algorithm. But AEMLSVM-IMBL classification algorithm spent more 2 % of the training time than AEMLSVM classification algorithm.

In order to obtain optimal representative set from Siam-competition2007 dataset, we set P = 100, V = 80 and ε = 0.835. At the same time, we set parameter e = 9.5e-5 and C* = 1, 2, 4, 6, 8 respectively in these five multi label classification algorithms. By setting the above parameters, Figs. 3 and 4 show the experimental results of five different Multi-label classification algorithms in Siam-competition2007 dataset.

The data in Fig. 3 indicate that compared with ML-LIBSVM classification algorithm, the values of Hamming Loss, Ranking Loss, Coverage and One-Error increased by 0.74 %, 0.92 %, 0.2255 % and 4.81 % respectively at most, the value of Average-Precision decreased by 3.6 % at most in AEMLSVM classification algorithm. All above explain that the classification result of AEMLSVM classification algorithm was similar to ML-LIBSVM classification algorithm, and the values of the results in AEMLSVM classification algorithm were superior to these values in ML-CVM and ML-BVM classification algorithm. Meanwhile, we can conclude from Fig. 4 that the training time of AEMLSVM classification algorithm was the shortest, only 1/4 of ML-LIBSVM classification algorithm. In the internal comparison of algorithm classification AEMLSVM, the values of the five evaluating metrics in AEMLSVM-IMBL classification algorithm were all superior to AEMLSVM classification algorithm. But AEMLSVM-IMBL classification algorithm spent more 10 % of the training time than AEMLSVM classification algorithm.

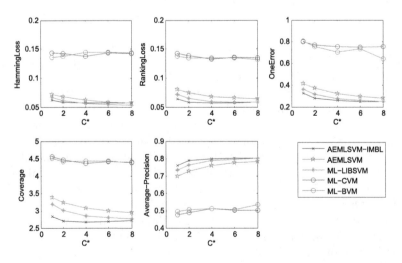

Fig. 3. Data comparison of five evaluation metrics (Color figure online)

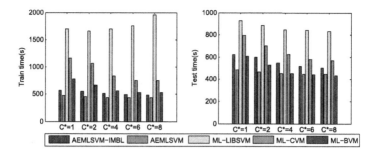

Fig. 4. Comparison of training time and classifying time (Color figure online)

In order to obtain optimal representative set from rcv1v2 dataset, we set P = 120, V = 82 and ε = 1.54. At the same time, We set parameter e = 2.65e-4 and C* = 1, 2, 4, 6, 8 respectively. By setting the above parameters, Figs. 5 and 6 show the experimental results of five different Multi-label classification algorithms in Siam-competition2007 dataset.

The data in Fig. 5 indicate that compared with ML-LIBSVM classification algorithm, the values of Hamming Loss, Ranking Loss, Coverage and One-Error increased by 0.53 %, 0.09 %, 0.1726 and 1.4 % respectively at most, the value of Average-Precision decreased by 4.3 % at most in AEMLSVM classification algorithm. All above explain that the classification result of AEMLSVM classification algorithm was similar to ML-LIBSVM classification algorithm, and the values of the results in AEMLSVM classification algorithm were superior to these values in ML-CVM and ML-BVM classification algorithm. Meanwhile, we can conclude from Fig. 6 that the training time of AEMLSVM classification algorithm is the shortest, only 1/6 of ML-LIBSVM classification algorithm. In the

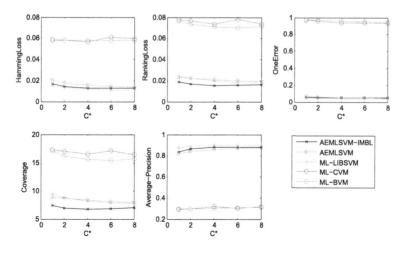

Fig. 5. Data comparison of five evaluation metrics (Color figure online)

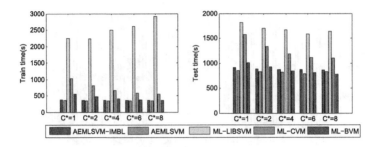

Fig. 6. Comparison of training time and classifying time (Color figure online)

internal comparison of AEMLSVM classification algorithm, the values of the five evaluating metrics in AEMLSVM-IMBL classification algorithm were all superior to AEMLSVM classification algorithm. But AEMLSVM-IMBL classification algorithm spent more 8 % of the training time than AEMLSVM classification algorithm.

In summary, the experimental results show that the result of AEMLSVM classification algorithm is similar to ML-LIBSVM classification algorithm, and superior to ML-CVM and ML-BVM classification algorithm, as far as the five evaluating metrics is concerned. At the same time, AEMLSVM classification algorithm also reduces the training time and classifying time. We have obtained better classification results and adapt it to the imbalanced data by improving the algorithm.

5   Conclusion

Aiming to solve the excessive training time problem, a fast Multi-label SVM classification algorithm (AEMLSVM) is propsed. Meanwhile, it is improved by adopting Cost-Sensitive method to deal with imbalanced data problem. These have greatly improved the applicability of this algorithm used in Large-Scale Multi-label datasets. Results from experiment show that AEMLSVM classification algorithm can improve the training and classification speed obviously and obtain similar classification effects compared with ML-LIBSVM classification algorithm. It is superior to ML-CVM and ML-BVM classification algorithm. Our further work is to find out the correlations among labels to improve the classification accuracy.

Acknowledgments. This work is supported by the National Natural Science Foundation of China (NSFC) under the grant number 61170258, 61103196, 61379127, 61379128, 61572448 and by the Shandong Provincial Natural Science Foundation of China under the grant number ZR2014JL043.

References

1. Tsoumakas, G., Katakis, I., Vlahavas, I.: Mining multi-label data. In: Maimon, O., Rokach, L. (eds.) Data Mining and Knowledge Discovery Handbook, pp. 667–685. Springer, US (2009)
2. Brucker, F., Benites, F., Sapozhnikova, E.: Multi-label classification and extracting predicted class hierarchies. Pattern Recogn. **44**(3), 724–738 (2011)
3. Zhang, M.L., Zhou, Z.H.: ML-KNN: a lazy learning approach to multi-label learning. Pattern Recogn. **40**(7), 2038–2048 (2007)
4. Chou, K.C., Shen, H.B.: Cell-PLoc 2.0: an improved package of web-servers for predicting subcellular localization of proteins in various organisms. Nat. Sci. **02**(10), 1090–1103 (2010)
5. Trohidis, K., Tsoumakas, G., Kalliris, G., et al.: Multi-label classification of music into emotions. In: ISMIR, vol. 8, pp. 325–330 (2008)
6. Cortes, C., Vapnik, V.: Support-vector networks. Mach. Learn. **20**(3), 273–297 (1995)
7. Gibaja, E., Ventura, S.: A tutorial on multi-label learning. ACM Comput. Surv. **47**(3), 1–38 (2015)
8. Elisseeff, A., Weston, J.: A kernel method for multi-labelled classification. In: Advances in Neural Information Processing Systems, pp. 681–687 (2001)
9. Tahir, M.A., Kittler, J., Bouridane, A.: Multi-label classification using heterogeneous ensemble of multi-label classifiers. Pattern Recogn. Lett. **33**(5), 513–523 (2012)
10. Chang, C.C., Lin, C.J.: LIBSVM: a library for support vector machines. ACM Trans. Intell. Syst. Technol. (TIST) **2**(3), 27 (2011)
11. Nandan, M., Khargonekar, P.P., Talathi, S.S.: Fast SVM training using approximate extreme points. J. Mach. Learn. Res. **15**(1), 59–98 (2014)
12. Tsang, I.W., Cs., U.H.J.T., Cheung, H.M., Nello, C.U.H.: Core vector machines: fast SVM training on very large data sets. J. Mach. Learn. Res. **6**(1), 363–392 (2010)
13. Tsang, I.W., Kocsor, A., Kwok, J.T.: Simpler core vector machines with enclosing balls. In: Proceedings of the 24th International Conference on Machine Learning, pp. 911–918. ACM (2007)
14. Boutell, M.R., Luo, J., Shen, X., et al.: Learning multi-label scene classification. Pattern Recogn. **37**(9), 1757–1771 (2004)
15. Clare, A.J., King, R.D.: Knowledge discovery in multi-label phenotype data. In: Siebes, A., De Raedt, L. (eds.) PKDD 2001. LNCS (LNAI), vol. 2168, p. 42. Springer, Heidelberg (2001)
16. Xu, J.: An efficient multi-label support vector machine with a zero label. Expert Syst. Appl. **39**(5), 4796–4804 (2012)
17. Gulat, J., Marcotte, P.: Some comments on Wolfe's away step. Math. Program. **35**(1), 110–119 (1986)
18. Frank, M., Wolfe, P.: An algorithm for quadratic programming. Naval Res. Logistics Q. **3**(1–2), 95–110 (1956)
19. Xu, J.: Fast multi-label core vector machine. Pattern Recogn. **46**(3), 885–898 (2013)
20. Xu, J.: Multi-label core vector machine with a zero label. Pattern Recogn. **47**(7), 2542–2557 (2014)
21. Zhang, M.L., Zhou, Z.H.: Multi-label neural networks with applications to functional genomics and text categorization. IEEE Trans. Knowl. Data Eng. **18**(10), 1338–1351 (2006)

22. He, H., Garcia, E.A.: Learning from imbalanced data. IEEE Trans. Knowl. Data Eng. **21**(9), 1263–1284 (2009)
23. Li, Y., Zhang, X.: Improving k nearest neighbor with exemplar generalization for imbalanced classification. In: Cao, L., Huang, J.Z., Srivastava, J. (eds.) PAKDD 2011, Part II. LNCS, vol. 6635, pp. 321–332. Springer, Heidelberg (2011)
24. Sun, Y., Kamel, M.S., Wong, A.K.C., et al.: Cost-sensitive boosting for classification of imbalanced data. Pattern Recogn. **40**(12), 3358–3378 (2007)
25. Joachims, T., Yu, C.N.J.: Sparse kernel SVMs via cutting-plane training. Mach. Learn. **76**(2–3), 179–193 (2009)
26. Joachims, T.: Training linear SVMs in linear time. In: Proceedings of the 12th ACM SIGKDD International Conference on Knowledge Discovery and Data Mining, pp. 217–226. ACM (2006)
27. Shalev-Shwartz, S., Srebro, N.: SVM optimization: inverse dependence on training set size. In: Proceedings of the 25th International Conference on Machine Learning, pp. 928–935. ACM (2008)
28. Platt, J.C.: Fast training of support vector machines using sequential minimal optimization. In: Advances in Kernel Methods, pp. 185–208 (1999)
29. LIBSVM datasets. https://www.csie.ntu.edu.tw/cjlin/libsvmtools/datasets/
30. Schapire, R.E., Singer, Y.: BoosTexter: a boosting-based system for text categorization. Mach. Learn. **39**(2), 135–168 (2000)
31. Shalev-Shwartz, S., Singer, Y., Srebro, N., et al.: Pegasos: primal estimated subgradient solver for SVM. Math. Program. **127**(1), 3–30 (2011)
32. Zhou, Z.H., Zhang, M.L., Huang, S.J., et al.: Multi-instance multi-label learning. Artif. Intell. **176**(1), 2291–2320 (2012)
33. Read, J.: Advances in multi-label classification (2011)

Database and Big Data

Determining the Topic Hashtags for Chinese Microblogs Based on 5W Model

Zhibin Zhao$^{(\boxtimes)}$, Jiahong Sun, Zhenyu Mao, Shi Feng, and Yubin Bao

School of Computer Science and Engineering, Northeastern University,
3-11 Wenhua Road, Heping District, Shenyang 110819, China
{zhaozhibin,fengshi,baoyubin}@cse.neu.edu.cn,
{348493118,1554221782}@qq.com

Abstract. A hashtag is an important metadata in microblogs and used to mark topics or index messages. With topic-related hashatags microblogs are well grouped, and users can retrieve the microblogs efficiently and then follow the interested conversations. At the same time, microblogging service providers can leverage hashtags to classify the massive microblogs for building high-level applications such as event detection and tracking, sentiment analysis, and opinion mining. However, statistics show that hashtags are absent from most of the microblogs. In this paper, we summarize the similarities between microblogs and short-message-style news, and then propose an algorithm named 5WTAG for detecting microblog topics based on the model of five Ws(When, Where, Who, What, hoW). Since five-W(5W) attributes are the core components in event description, it is guaranteed theoretically that 5WTAG can extract the semantical topic from a microblogs properly. We introduce the detailed procedure of the algorithm 5WTAG in this paper including microblog segmentation and candidate hashtag construction. We propose a novel method of recommendation computing for ranking candidate hashtags, which combines syntax analysis and semantic analysis, and observes the distribution law of human-annotated topic tags. We conduct comprehensive experiments to verify the semantical correctness and completeness of the candidate hashtags as well as the accuracy of recommendation using the real data from Sina Weibo.

Keywords: Hashtag · Microblogs · Topic detection · Short message news · 5W model

1 Introduction

Hashtags are the most important metadata in microblogging systems. They are used to mark individual messages as relevant to a particular group, topic or "channel". According to Twitter, a hashtag, prefixed with the symbol "#", is a word or an acronym used to describe a tweet in order for people to easily follow a conversation [1]. In Sina Weibo, a hashtag is defined more explicitly as the keywords that can represent the topics of a microblog(also called Weibo).

© Springer International Publishing Switzerland 2016
Y. Wang et al. (Eds.): BigCom 2016, LNCS 9784, pp. 55–67, 2016.
DOI: 10.1007/978-3-319-42553-5_5

As defined by Twitter and Sina Weibo, a hashtag is the topic of a microblog. It plays a very important role in microblog system: (1) Hashtags help to accelerate the retrieval for topic-specific microblogs and also promote its precision. Given hashtags, users can find and follow the interested conversations easily; (2) Hashtags help to classify microblogs in a more accurate and efficient way. Fine-grained topic-oriented classification for microblogs is a significant prerequisite for event detection, sentiment analysis and opinion mining.

Despite the great importance of hashtags in microblogging systems, its generation totally relies on the freewill participation of users up to now. So, in order to encourage and help users to tag their tweets, Twitter released a detailed user guide [1] to explain how to choose and mark a topic hashtag. Similarly, Sina Weibo tries to provide a more friendly and convenient interface so as to guide users to propose a hashtag for every microblog. Unfortunately, the great effort does not lead to satisfactory results. Liu et al. [2] measured over 0.2 million tweets and found that only around 23 % of them have at least one #hashtag in each. The situation is worse in Sina Weibo. We measured 840,593 Weiboes and found that only 108,714 of them, as low as 12.9 %, have at least one artificial tag in each. This becomes a large obstacle to retrieving and leveraging these microblogs.

In this paper, we aim at generating a topic hashtag for individual microblogs automatically and propose a novel algorithm named 5WTAG. There are three contributions in our work.

☐ According to the analysis of the similarity between microblogs and short-message-style news in content and structure, we propose to model microblogs with five Ws. Since answering the five-W problems can describe the event completely and correctly, it is more rational to use five-W model to express the semantics hidden in microblogs.

☐ We propose a complete solution to extract possible topic tags from Chinese microblogs. We discuss the two ways to segment a microblog and analyse their effect on the construction of candidate topic hashtags.

☐ We introduce a quantitative method for computing the recommendation of a candidate topic tag, in which semantic completeness and correctness, importance of content and location, and statistical distribution of artificial hashtags are all considered. For each of the considerations, we explain how it is measured and impacts the recommendation of a candidate topic tag.

Section 2 summarizes the related work in topic detection and tracking(TDT), especially some up-to-date research progress on topic-oriented microblog analysis problems. In Sect. 3 we introduce the 5 W model and why and how it can be employed to model microblogs. Section 4 provides the detailed procedure of the algorithm 5WTAG. The performance evaluation is reported in Sect. 5. Finally, we conclude in Sect. 6.

2   Related Work

TDT (Topic Detection and Tracking) is always a hot topic in academic community. In the field of topic detection, most of the initial studies focus on text stream or massive document set, and mainly use the techniques of document clustering [3,4]. Document clustering has two primary technical issues: (1) how the documents are modeled, and (2) how the similarities among the documents are measured. These two issues are closely related, and have effect on the clustering results as well as the topic detection results. Zhang et al. summarize several classical document representation models and similarity calculation methods in paper [5]. In recent years, topic models are receiving extensive attention. Xu et al. introduce the topic models and how the similarity is calculated under these models in detail in [6]. Topic tracking based on microblogs are also receiving popularity. In this field, an concerned topic is given, and the task of a tracking system is to classify in a supplied list of stories as either on-topic or off-topic [7–10]. Topic tracking sets its goals to restore the development of a specific event even though the key point of the event shifts with time. Although the work in this paper belongs to the same research field as the work mentioned above, they are quite different in essence: the 5WTAG algorithm aims at detecting topic from individual text, such as a piece of tweet or Sina Weibo. To this end, semantic analysis along with syntactic analysis and empirical statistics, instead of clustering technologies, are employed for topic hashtag construction and recommendation calculation.

The huge volume of microblogs carrying sentiments necessitates automatic sentiment analysis techniques, which assist users in summarizing public opinions. Most research work in microblog-oriented sentiment analysis are based on existing hashtags [2,11–14]. For example, in [2] Liu et al. conduct a comprehensive study on the problem of entity-centric(such as celebrities and brands) topic-oriented opinion summarization in twitter. In order to produce opinion summaries and remarkable insight behind the opinions in accordance with some certain entities and topics, they first have to mine topics from tweets. Topic detection in [2] is totally based on existing human-annotated semantic tags in tweets. Specifically, they integrate the human-annotated #hashtags as weakly supervised information into topic modeling algorithms to obtain better interpretation and representation for similarity calculation. Then, they run the Affinity Propagation clustering algorithm to group #hashtags into coherent topics. Obviously, the above-mentioned work is quite different from the work described in this paper, where we aim at mining topics from the untagged microblogs.

3   Modeling Chinese Microblogs with Five Ws

In this section, we summarize the similarity between a short-message-style news and a microblog, which is the theoretical foundation to model a microblog with five Ws. Then, we show how we map each of the words in microblog to an attribute in five Ws and formalize microblogs using 5 W model.

3.1   Similarity of Microblogs and Short-Message-Style News

The five-W model has been attributed to Thomas Wilson, who was a English rhetorician and introduced the method in his discussion of the "seven circumstances" of medieval rhetoric [15]. Nowadays, it is often mentioned in journalism and refers to five interrogative words: Who, What, When, Where and hoW (Sometimes six Ws with Why added). They are exactly the reporters' questions of which the answers are considered basic in information-gathering. To be specific, a report can only be considered complete if it answers these questions starting with an interrogative word [16]: Who did that? What was involved? When did it take place? Where did it take place? and hoW did it happen?

Each question above should have a factual answer. Importantly, none of these five questions can be answered with a simple "yes" or "no". So, we define 5 W as {"When", "Where", "Who", "What", "hoW"}.

Microblogs are quite similar to short-message-style news in two aspects: (1) They both center on event description [17,18], and (2) They are both organized in the structure of "Inverted Pyramid"[19].

3.2   Mapping Chinese Microblogs to Five Ws

According to the analysis above, we can conclude that a Chinese microblog, such as a Sina Weibo, can be considered as a piece of short-message-style news. It inspires us that we can use the 5 W model to describe the event hidden in the microblog. Let $< w, h >$ represents a piece of Chinese microblog. w is its content, and h is its topic hashtag. Next, we will introduce how we map each of the notional words in w to the attribute of X in 5W({"When", "Where", "Who", "What", "hoW"}). Here we take a piece of microblog as an example.

Assume w ="shiyuefen, Beijing, Shanghai, Gangzhou, Shenzhen fangjia shang zhang 20 %, Wenzhou tongbi xiajiang. duoshu goufangzhe yuqi yixian chengshi fangjia hui jixu shangzhang". (In the past October, housing price rose 20 % in Beijing, Shanghai, Guangzhou, ShenZhen, while in Wenzhou it fell. Most homebuyers forecast that in first-tier cities housing price will keep rising)".

Definition 1. *"When" is the set of words that refer to time, festivals, and Chinese solar terms in microblogs;*

In w, When = {"shiyuefen(October)"}.

Definition 2. *"Where" is the set of the words that refer to geographical nouns in microblogs;*

In w, where = {"Beijing", "Shanghai", "Gangzhou", "Shenzhen", "Wenzhou"}.

Definition 3. *"Who" is the set of the words that refer to the name of a person, a group of people or an institute.*

In w, Who = {"goufangzhe(homebuyer)"}.

Definition 4. *"What" is the set of the words that refer to the things or abstract concepts in microblogs. Of particular note it also includes some proper nouns such as movie or television products, music products, novels, PC games, and commodities and trade markers;*

In w, What $= \{$ "fangjia(housing price)" $\}$.

Definition 5. *"hoW" is the set of the words that refer to actions or states of being in microblogs;*

In w, hoW $= \{$ "shangzhang(rise)", "xiajiang(fall)", "chixu(keep)", "yuqi(fore-cast)" $\}$.

Let $\Psi_y(x)$ represent the set of words contained in the text x and classified to the attribute y. According to the Definition 1 to 5, the 5 W model of the microblog $< w, null >$ can be illustrated as the Formula (1).

$$\Psi_{5W}(w) = \bigcup_{X \in 5W} \Psi_X(w) \tag{1}$$

We implement the mapping relation from part-of-speech annotations in ICT-CLAS2013 to the attribute X in five Ws. We list it in Table 1.

Table 1. Mapping the part-of-speech annotations to five Ws

$X =$	Annotations in ICTCLAS2013
When	/t;
Where	/ns, /nd, /s;
Who	/nr, /nt, /r;
What	/nz, /n(except /ns, /nd, /nr, /nt, /nz);
How	/v, /vn;

4   The Description of the Algorithm 5WTAG

5WTAG is designed to be integrated into the micrblogging services and run online on the client side. The input of 5WTAG is the microblog released by a user, and the output is a list of recommended hashtags as well as the corresponding recommendation evaluations. Firstly, we segment the microblog into several clauses and extract candidate topic hashtags from each of the clauses. Then, recommendation evaluation module will assign a recommendation to every candidate hashtag according to several considerations.

4.1 Exatracting the Candidate Hashtags

In order to construct candidate topic hashtags for a given microblog, we have to segment the microblog into several clauses. Each clause has relatively complete semantics and will contribute to one candidate hashtags. We have two categories of punctuations worthy of consideration as separators: (1) Terminal Punctuations, namely period, question mark, exclamation mark and semicolon; and (2) Pause Punctuations, including comma and all the terminal punctuations.

Assume that $< w, h >$ is a microblog. After segmentation, it can also be denoted as $<< s_1, s_2, ...s_l >, h >$, where $< s_1, s_2, ...s_l >$ is the sequence of clauses. Let d be any 5 W word in s_i. Then, any word d in w can be denoted as the Formula (2).

$$d =< \text{str}(d), \Psi_{5W}(d), ssid, loc > \qquad (2)$$

$\text{str}(d)$ is the content of d. $\Psi_{5W}(d)$ is the category of five Ws that d belongs to, i.e. $\Psi_{5W}(d) \in 5W$. $ssid$ is the sequence number of the clause s_i by which d is contained. loc is the index of d in w.

In order to guarantee the correctness of semantics as more as possible, we follow two rules in our work when constructing the candidate topic hashtags:

Rule 1. *All the words that compose the same candidate topic hashtag should come from the same clause.*

Rule 2. *All the words should be in the same order in candidate hashtag as they are in the corresponding clause.*

We use h^* to denote a candidate topic hashtag. According to the Rules 1 and 2, we can illustrate h^* as the Formula (3).

$$h^* =< d_1, d_2, ..., d_m > \quad \text{s.t.} \quad \forall d_i, \forall d_j$$
$$\begin{cases} d_i.ssid = d_j.ssid \\ d_i \prec d_j \Leftrightarrow d_i.loc < d_j.loc \end{cases} \qquad (3)$$

4.2 Recommendation Computation

In this subsection, we evaluate each of the obtained candidate topic hashtags on the basis of several parameters, namely semantical completeness and correctness, probability of occurrences for the 5 W presentation mode, keywords density, and the location of the clause from which the candidate hashtag comes.

(1) Semantical Completeness of a Candidate Topic Hashtag

The semantical completeness defines that to what extent a candidate topic hashtag can represent the whole event. In order to quantify the semantical completeness, we introduce the concept of hashtag presentation mode.

Definition 6. *"Hashtag Presentation Mode" is the union of categories that a hashtag owns according to the Formula (1). We use $M(h^*)$ to denote the presentation mode of $h^* =< d_1, d_2, ..., d_m >$. It can be calculated with (4).*

$$M(h^*) = \{\Psi_{5W}(d_1), \Psi_{5W}(d_2), ..., \Psi_{5W}(d_m)\} \qquad (4)$$

Since five 5Ws are the core elements for event description, the more 5 W attributes that a candidate topic hashtag contains in its presentation mode, the more details it can tell about the event. Therefore, we can conclude that the semantical completeness of h^* is proportional to the cardinality of $M(h^*)$.

(2) Semantical Correctness of a Candidate Topic Hashtag

The remarkable character of natural language is that the words which are logically relevant are often closer to each other. This provides us an effective approach to determine the correctness of a candidate hashtag. We define the Average Word Interval $\bar{\lambda}$ for the candidate hashtag $h^* =< d_1, d_2, ..., d_m >$. $\bar{\lambda}$ can be calculated by the Formula (5).

$$\bar{\lambda} = \frac{\sum_{i=1}^{m-1} (d_{i+1}.loc - d_i.loc - length(d_i))}{m} \tag{5}$$

The correctness of a candidate hashtag is inversely proportional to $\bar{\lambda}$. In other words, the more widely the 5 W words in h^* scatters in the corresponding clause, the worse semantical correctness h^* may have.

(3) Probability of Occurrences of the 5W Presentation Mode

As we discussed above, from the viewpoint of semantical completeness, more 5 W attributes in a hashtag presentation mode mean more details about the event. However, artificial hashtags show an opposite phenomenon: not all the attributes in five 5Ws necessarily contribute to the final presentation mode of every artificial topic hashtags. Actually, according to our statistics on the 11,008 human-annotated hashtags, only about 1.2 % of total contain at least 4 attributes of five Ws in their presentation mode. Furthermore, according to the presentation rate of each attribute, we can calculate the probability of occurrences for 5 W presentation mode of h^* with the Formula (6).

$$p(M(h^*)) = \prod_{X \in M(h^*)} p(X) \prod_{X \notin M(h^*)} (1 - p(X)) \tag{6}$$

$p(X)$ is the presentation rate of the attribute X, and can be measured with artificial hashtags. All values of $p(X)$ are all less than 0.5. Thus, Formula (6) will give a higher score to the shorter and simpler hashtags. It is exactly consistent with the tendency of simplification in human-annotated hashtags.

(4) Importance of a Candidate Topic Hashtag

When people describe an event, it is common that they may repeat some special words. Based on this ground truth, we conclude that the importance of a candidate hashtag is proportional to the Keyword Density [20] of the words it contains.

Let ρ_{h^*} denote the importance of the candidate hashtag $h^* =< d_1, d_2, ..., d_m >$, and ρ_{d_i} denote Keyword Density of the word d_i in h^*. Obviously, ρ_{h^*} is the continued product of multiple ρ_{d_i}s as is depicted in the Formula (7).

$$\rho_{h^*} = \prod_{d_i \in h^*} \rho_{d_i} = \prod_{d_i \in h^*} \frac{count(d_i|w)}{\sum\limits_{\forall d \in w} count(d|w)} \tag{7}$$

$count(x|y)$ is the frequency of occurrences of the word x in the text y.

(5) Location of the Clause Corresponding to a Candidate Hashtag

Due to the limitation of characters, microblogs and SM news are usually structured in the form of inverted pyramid, i.e. the most important information is placed first within a text, and decreasing importance of information in subsequent paragraphs. So, we can determine the importance of a candidate hashtag according to its source clauses location within the microblog.

For a candidate hashtag $h^* = <d_1, d_2, ..., d_m>$, its location is defined as being the same as that of its source clause, i.e. $h^*.ssid = d_i.ssid(d_i \in h^*)$.

So far, we have analyzed all the factors that have influence on the recommendation of a candidate hashtag. The Formula (8) is the general score function for evaluating the recommendation of h^*, taking all the factors into consideration.

$$S(h^*) = |M(h^*)| * \frac{1}{\lambda} * p(M(h^*)) * \rho_{h^*} * \frac{1}{h^*.ssid} \tag{8}$$

Note that some microblogs may have titles at the very beginning. A title can be regarded as the first clause of a microblog. The candidate hashtag derived from the title has the location of 0 in the microblog, i.e. $h^*.ssid = 0$, or say $S(h^*) \sim \infty$. Therefore, candidate hashtags extracted from titles will rank highest.

4.3   Compressing OverLength Candidate Hashtags

Due to the directly proportional relation between the completeness of a candidate topic hashtag and its recommendation, longer candidate hashtags may defeat the shorter ones. However, long candidate hashtags are not advantageous in the classification and retrieval of microblogs. Moreover, they are not in accord with the characteristics of shortness and simpleness of human-annotated hashtags. So, we set a threshold to limit the length of a automatically-annotated hashtags. In this paper, we make use of the statistical result from artificial hashtags, and set the length threshold T as $\lceil \mu + \sigma \rceil = 10$. Next, we introduce two strategies for compressing the hashtags with the length larger than T.

Method 1 *Length-Based Compression. The basic idea of this method is to remove the longest words from h^* iteratively until it meets the requirement of length constraint. The advantage of this method is the simpleness in implementation and the efficiency in execution. The weakness is that this method neglects the semantic of words and may decrease the semantical correctness of h^*.*

Method 2 *Semantic-Based Compression. The basic idea of this method is to remove all the words of one attribute in five Ws once time so as to shorten the length of h^*. Considering the statistical result based on empirical data, we should remove the words of "Where" first, then of the others successively in the order of attribute presentation rate. Compared with the former method, the latter takes the semantic of words into consideration, but it may weaken the completeness of h^*, and lead to the failure of h^* in event description.*

5   Experiment Evaluation

5.1   Experimental Data Set and Methodology

In this section, we present the evaluation results on the real microblog data set collected from Sina Weibo. Table 2 is the details of the experimental data set.

In our experiments, two methods are implemented: 5WTAG-P(Period) and 5WTAG-C(Comma). The former uses termination punctuations as the separators to split the microblogs, while the latter uses pause punctuations to do that. Besides, we regard the data set of artificial hashtags as our baseline. We verify the 5WTAG algorithm in three aspects: the semantical correctness, the quality of recommendation, the semantical correctness comparison on the two compression strategies for overlength topic hashatags.

Table 2. Description of experimental data set

Categories	Number
Total microblogs	840,593
Microblogs with at least one hashtags	108,714
Total distinct artificial hashtags	11,008

5.2   Experimental Results

Semantical Correctness Evaluation. We evaluate the semantical correctness of a candidate hashtag in two aspects: (1) whether the candidate topic hashtag is semantically understandable to users, and (2) whether the candidate topic hashtag is the accurate abstract of its source clause. Theoretically, the semantical correctness evaluation can only be conducted by man. However, in order to promote the efficiency, we partially adopt automatic evaluation of machine. For that sake, we propose two principles: (1) If a candidate hashtag contains only one 5 W word, it is semantically correct, and (2) If the average word interval of a candidate hashtag is 0, it is semantically correct.

We sample randomly 1,000 microblogs from our data set and construct candidate hashtags for each of them using 5WTAG-P and 5WTAG-C, respectively. Table 3 is the result of semantical correctness evaluation.

Table 3. The Result of semantical correctness evaluation

Method	5WTAG-P	5WTAG-C
Number of candidate hashtags	2566	4218
semantical correctness	42.1 %	69.7 %

Table 3 shows that 5WTAG-C performs better than 5WTAG-P in the semantical correctness of candidate hashtags. 5WTAG-C segments a microblog into finer-grained clauses, which results in more candidate topic hashtags than 5WTAG-P. 5WTAG-C can effectively resolve long sentences with multiple semantics, and thus it can avoid semantics confusion better than 5WTAG-P. Essentially, the user's arbitrary and ill-formed usage of punctuation in microblogs is the predominant reason that makes 5WTAG-C more advantageous in semantical correctness. However, more candidate hashtags possibly mean worse semantical completeness. In order to validate our prediction, we further test the cardinality of hashtag mode as well as the length of 5WTAG-C, 5WTAG-P and human-annotated hashtags. Figure 1 illustrates the result.

From Fig. 1(a), we can see that most of human-anotated hashtags are relatively short. Comparatively, 5WTAG-P is more inclined to create longer candidate hashtags. This is the result of the larger-grained segmentation of microblogs with termination punctuations. Figure 1(b) reflects the semantical completeness of artificial, 5WTAG-C and 5WTAG-P hashtags. X-axis is the number of attributes contained in candidate topic hashtags, i.e. the cardinality of hashtag mode. Figure 1(b) can exactly explain the phenomenon in Fig. 1(a) that human-annotated hashtags are relatively shorter and simpler in most cases. The reason is that most microbloggers are more willing to use one or two keywords to represent the whole event. Besides, due to the different granularities of microblog segmentation, 5WTAG-C creates more candidate hashtags with single attribute of presentation mode, while 5WTAG-P creates more combination hashtags with multiple 5 W attributes.

Recommendation Quality Evaluation. We conduct the recommendation quality evaluation based on 500 pieces of microblogs sampled randomly from the data set. For each of the microblog, we use 5WTAG-C and 5WTAG-P to create candidate topic hashtags, from which we manually choose the most satisfying

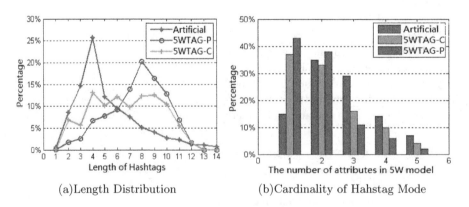

(a)Length Distribution   (b)Cardinality of Hahstag Mode

Fig. 1. Comparison on artificial, 5WTAG-P, and 5WTAG-C hashtags (Color figure online)

Table 4. The result of recommendation quality evaluation

Methods	Accuracy
5WTAG-P	64.8%
5WTAG-C	45.1%

candidate as its topic. Afterwards, we run the recommendation function so as to assign recommendation score for each of the candidate topic hashtags. Next, we examine whether the artificial hashtag is the same as the candidate hashtag that ranks highest according to the recommendation function. If they are the same, recommendation function is considered accurate. Table 4 shows the result.

Table 4 shows that 5WTAG-P performs better than 5WTAG-C in recommendation quality. The reason is that the candidate hashtags created by 5WTAG-C are often too simple to describe the whole event. When 5WTAG-C segments microblogs in a finer-grained way, it breaks the overall semantics of microblog at the same time. Topic-related words are scattered into more clauses, which means that every single candidate hashtags may lost some of key details about the event. So, it leads to more failure in recommendation accuracy.

According to experiments above, we can conclude that 5WTAG-C performs better in the semantical correctness, while 5WTAG-P is better in the semantical completeness and recommendation accuracy.

Compression Method Evaluation. In the third experiment, we test the performance of two methods for compressing overlength hashtags. We choose 500 hashtags which are generated by 5WTAG-P manually so as to guarantee the semantical correctness of these hashtags. Each of the 500 hashtags contains over ten Chinese characters, and their topic are uniformly distributed in multiple social fields, namely sports, politics, economy, entertainment, culture and military. Then we run the two compressing methods and examine whether a compressed hashtag still convey the main idea of the microblog. If it does, it is still semantically correct. Table 5 is the result.

Table 5. Evaluation result on different compression methods

Pruning strategies	Semantical correctness
Length-based	40%
"When"-based	78%
"Where"-based	72%
"Who"-based	51%
"hoW"-based	40%
"What"-based	30%

Table 5 shows that the semantical correctness of length-based compression method drops dramatically. It is because this method totally ignores the semantics of words. When the words that are vital to semantics presentation are removed, the whole topic hashtag may be no longer understandable to people. Among semantic-based compression methods, the semantical correctness of "What"-based pruning method drops most. The reason is "What"-related words are the most necessary elements in event description. The result in this experiment is consistent with the statistics from empirical data: the importance of "What"-related words gives them more opportunities to be in topic hashtags. The experiment result in Table 5 suggests that if we have to shorten a candidate topic hashtag, we should adopt a hybrid compression method: pruning the longest words successively in the attribute order of "Where", "When", "hoW", "What" and "Who" until the candidate hashtag meets the length constraint.

6   Conclusion and Future Work

In this paper, we propose to model Chinese microblogs with 5 W model. The concept of Five Ws comes from journalism and represents five questions, the answers of which are considered as the basic elements for event description. We reveal the justification to model microblogs with 5 W model by comparing the similarity between microblogs and short-message-style news. We introduce the detailed procedure of the algorithm 5WTAG, including segmenting a microblog, extracting candidate topic hashtags and recommendation evaluation.

There are several applications based on 5WTAG are in the plan of our near future work. For example, when a public event happens, many witnesses on spot may release microblogs describing the same event. These microblogs are possibly different in writing or added with individual comments, but they are quite similar in five Ws. We can merge them and detect the public events at the first time. Besides, it can be applied to identifying Internet rumors.

Acknowledgments. Supported by the National Natural Science Foundation of China under Grant No. 61173027, the Northeastern University Fundamental Research Funds for the Central Universities under Grant Nos. N150404012 and N140404006.

References

1. http://support.twitter.com/articles/49309-what-are-hashtagssymbols
2. Liu, X.H., Meng, X.F., Wei, F.R.: Entity-centric topic-oriented opinion summarization in Twitter. In: Proceedings of the Eighteenth Annual ACM Conference on Knowledge Discovery and Data Mining, pp. 379–387. ACM Press (2012)
3. Yap, I., Loh, H.T., Shen, L., Liu, Y.: Topic detection using MFSs. In: Ali, M., Dapoigny, R. (eds.) IEA/AIE 2006. LNCS (LNAI), vol. 4031, pp. 342–352. Springer, Heidelberg (2006)
4. Seo, Y.-W., Sycara, K.: Text clustering for topic detection. Technical report CMU-RI-TR-04-03, Robotics Institute, Pittsburgh, PA, January 2004

5. Wang, T., Zhang, X.Y.: Research of technologies on topic detection and tracking. J. Front. Comput. Sci. Technol. **261**(3), 347–357 (2009). Higher Education Press, Beijing

6. Wang, H.F., Xu, G.: The development of topic models in natural language processing. Chin. J. Comput. **34**(8), 1423–1436 (2011). Science Press, Beijing

7. Chen, F., Brants, T.: A system for new event detection. In: Proceedings of the 26th Annual International ACM Conferenceon Research and Development in Information Retrieval, pp. 330–337. ACM Press, New York (2003)

8. Zhai, C.X., Mei, Q.Z.: Discovering evolutionary theme patterns from text: an exploration oftemporal text mining. In: Proceedings of the Eleventh Annual ACM Conference on Knowledge Discovery and Data Mining, pp. 198–207. ACM Press, New York (2005)

9. Peng, P.C., Nallapati, R., Feng, A.: Event threading within news topics. In: Proceedings of the Thirteenth ACM Conference of Information and Knowledge Management, pp. 446–453. ACM Press (2004)

10. Hong, Y., Zhang, Y., Liu, T., et al.: Topic detection and tracking review. J. Chin. Inf. Process. **21**(6), 77–79 (2007)

11. Lee, L., Pang, B.: Opinion mining and sentiment analysis. Found. Trends Inf. Retrieval **2**, 1–135 (2008)

12. Rappoport, A., Davidov, D., Tsur, O.: Enhanced sentiment learning using Twitter hashtags and smileys. In: Proceedings of the 23rd International Conference on Computational Linguistics, pp. 241–249. Tsinghua University Press, Beijing (2010)

13. Zhou, M., Jiang, L., Yu, M.: Target-dependent Twitter sentiment classification. In: Proceedings of the 49th Annual Meeting of the Association for Computational Linguistics: Human Language Technologies, pp. 151–160. The Association for Computer Linguistics, Stroudsburg (2011)

14. Liu, X., Wang, X., Wei, F.: Topic sentiment analysis in twitter: a graph-based hashtag sentiment classification approach. In: Proceedings of the 20th ACM Conference on Information and Knowledge Management, pp. 151–160. ACM Press (2011)

15. Wilson, T., Boss, J., et al.: The arte of rhetorique (1998)

16. http://www.owenspencerthomas.com/journalism/

17. Mei, Q.Z., Jiang, Y.L., Lin, C.X.D.: Context comparison of bursty events in web search and online media. In: Proceedings of the 2010 Conference on Empirical Methods in Natural Language Processing, pp. 1077–1087 (2010)

18. Java, A., Song, X., Finin, T., Tseng, B.: Why we Twitter: an analysis of a microblogging community. In: Zhang, H., Spiliopoulou, M., Mobasher, B., Giles, C.L., McCallum, A., Nasraoui, O., Srivastava, J., Yen, J. (eds.) WebKDD 2007. LNCS, vol. 5439, pp. 118–138. Springer, Heidelberg (2009)

19. Blake, K.: Inverted pyramid story format. http://kelab.tamu.edu/spb_encyclopedia

20. Yamaguchi, M., Kise, K., Mizuno, H.: On the use of density distribution of keywords for automated generation of hypertext links from arbitrary parts of documents, document analysis and recognition. In: Proceedings of the Fifth International Conference on Document Analysis and Recognition, pp. 301–304. IEEE Computer Society, Washington (1999)

HMVR-tree: A Multi-version R-tree Based on HBase for Concurrent Access

Shan Huang, Botao Wang$^{(\boxtimes)}$, Shizhuo Deng, Kaili Zhao, Guoren Wang,
and Ge Yu

School of Computer Science and Engineering, Northeastern University, Shenyang
110819, Liaoning, China
huangshan.neu@gmail.com, wangbotao@cse.neu.edu.cn,
dengshizhuo@gmail.com, 1335888327@qq.com,
wanggr@mail.neu.edu.cn, yuge@mail.neu.edu.cn

Abstract. With the development of cloud computing, more and more large scale multi-dimensional data are stored on cloud platforms. Multi-dimensional index is an efficient technique to support processing data efficiently. Designing a multi-dimensional index which supports multi-user concurrent access efficiently has become a challenging problem. In this paper, we propose a multi-version R-tree based on HBase (HMVR-tree) to support multiple concurrent access. HMVR-tree maintains the newest version of tree while keeping all the old versions of the nodes for efficient concurrent update and query access to different nodes. The evaluation results show that MHVR-tree has good scalability and has much higher update throughput and the same level query throughput compared to the original R-tree on HBase.

Keywords: HBase · R-tree · Concurrent access · Multi-version

1 Introduction

More and more large scale multi-dimensional data are stored to cloud platforms in recent years. As one key technique of processing large scale data, multi-dimensional index that supports multi-user concurrent access on the cloud platform efficiently has become a challenging problem.

Key-value stores such as Bigtable [4] and HBase [1] have been proven to process millions of updates while being fault-tolerant and highly available, but they cannot support multi-dimensional access natively. Recent work [6,7,9,11,12] has studied on building multi-dimensional indices on HBase, but there is little consideration about concurrent access to the indices. MD-HBase [8] used space-filling curve technique to transform multi-dimensional space into one dimension, but it is inefficient for queries with high dimensional data. Different from space-filling curve technique, R-tree [5] is built based on space partition technique. Synchronization mechanisms are needed to support concurrent access to R-tree, which are the main causes of inefficiency.

© Springer International Publishing Switzerland 2016
Y. Wang et al. (Eds.): BigCom 2016, LNCS 9784, pp. 68–77, 2016.
DOI: 10.1007/978-3-319-42553-5_6

For this challenge, this paper designs new access mechanisms for R-tree on cloud platform which allow multiple users accessing R-tree nodes concurrently and implements a multi-version R-tree based on HBase (HMVR-tree). HMVR-tree maintains the newest version of tree while keeping all the old versions of nodes. HMVR-tree also provides efficient concurrent update and query access to different nodes. HMVR-tree is evaluated with synthetic data and the result shows that it has good scalability.

The remainder of this paper is organized as follows. Section 2 briefly introduces HBase and R-tree. Section 3 describes HMVR-tree framework with related algorithms. Section 4 evaluates HMVR-tree with synthetic data and Sect. 5 concludes the paper.

2   Preliminaries

2.1   HBase

HBase [1] is an open source, distributed, versioned non-relational database. HBase uses HDFS (Hadoop Distributed File System) [3] as its underlying storage file system and provides random, realtime read/write access to large scale data on clusters of commodity machines. HBase supports high throughput while being fault-tolerant and highly available.

Figure 1 shows the structure of HBase table. An HBase table consists of many rows. Each row is addressed uniquely by one *key* and is composite of one or more columns. Each column may contain multiple versions, with each distinct *value* contained in a separate *cell*. The columns are grouped into several *families*. A column can be uniquely identified by *family* : *qualifier*. The number of columns has no limitations. It is free of cost to store NULLs where there is no value in the column for HBase. HBase also provides split and compact algorithms to keep its good scalability.

In HBase, ZooKeeper [2] is used to provide distributed lock service. HBase provides lock mechanisms to make sure one row can be modified by only one client at the same time. HBase supports the following three atomic operations.

$$put(rowkey, family, qualifier, value); \qquad (1)$$

$$get(rowkey, family, qualifier); \qquad (2)$$

$$increase(rowkey, family, qualifier, amount); \qquad (3)$$

put operation updates the specific column in one row with *value*. *get* operation acquires data in the specific column of one row. *increase* operation increases the *value* of the specific column with *amount* value.

Figure 1 also shows the scan sequence of HBase. HBase starts to scan the cells in the next column until all cells in this column are scanned. Similarly, it starts to scan the next row after all the columns in this row are scanned. The scan operations are performed on the server side and filter mechanism is provided to reduce the cost of scanning unnecessary cells.

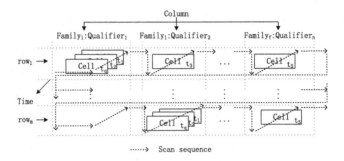

Fig. 1. HBase table structure and scan sequence

2.2 R-tree

R-tree [5] is a data structure based on B^+ tree [10], which is a popular data structure for multi-dimensional data organization. In R-tree, multi-dimensional objects are represented by minimum bounding rectangles (MBRs). Each node of R-tree corresponds to the MBR that bounds its children nodes. The entries of the children are generally stored in a page of the filesystem, so the number of entries in one node is generally fixed. R-tree can support efficient multi-dimensional queries that benefit from high efficient pruning ability.

3 HMVR-tree

In order to support concurrent access to R-tree, synchronization mechanisms must be provided. During data insertion, because the child nodes may be split, new entries are possible to be added to the parent. Thus, other update and query operations cannot be executed until it completes execution. This is the main cause of inefficiency. To solve this problem, we design new mechanisms for HMVR-tree.

3.1 Basic Idea

Update Operations. There are three kinds of update operations, data insertion, data deletion and data update. HMVR-tree treats update and delete operations as special insert operation. This means the update and delete operations are treated as insert objects with marks. During the execution of update operation, HMVR-tree maintains the newest version of tree while keeping all the old versions of the nodes except the MBRs of the entries. HMVR-tree executes split procedure in a lazy way, which means that the split procedure may not be executed immediately when it is needed to be split. The version of one node changes if and only if it splits. The update operation uses write version to search down the tree and maintains the read versions if the node can be correctly accessed by queries. HMVR-tree maintains relationship of timestamps and versions periodically.

Query Operations. The query operations use read versions to search down the tree. Before the processing of each query, one unique timestamp is assigned to the query. The query operation uses the assigned timestamp to find the newest version to query for spatial queries. For a spatio-temporal query, mapping relationship is used to find the root entries in the query time range and the query is decomposed to multiple sub-queries and then be processed.

3.2 Data Structure

Figure 2 shows the logic view and storage view of HMVR-tree. There are four tables in HMVR-tree.

(1) **Metadata table.** Metadata table stores the metadata of HMVR-tree. In this table, there is only one family named "Meta". The "RV" and "WV" columns store the read and write version of the entire HMVR-tree respectively. The "NodeIDs" column stores the current allocated rowkeys in node table.

(2) **Version conversion table.** Version conversion table stores mapping relationships among timestamps and versions. The "TimeStamp" column stores the allocated timestamp and the "Conversions" family stores the mapping relationships. In the "Conversions" family, $qualifier$ stores the timestamp and $value$ stores the corresponding version.

(3) **Root information table.** Root information table stores root nodes information. In the "Meta" family, the "RV" and "WV" columns store the read version and write version of the root node respectively. The "RootID" column stores the current root node ID in node table and the "RootCol" column stores the current $qualifier$ of root node entry stores in the "RootIDs" family. In the "RootIDs" family, $qualifier$ of each column stores the version of HMVR-tree and $value$ stores the corresponding root entry.

(4) **Node table.** Node table stores all the nodes of HMVR-tree. The "Meta" family stores the metadata of the node such as the column allocated in this

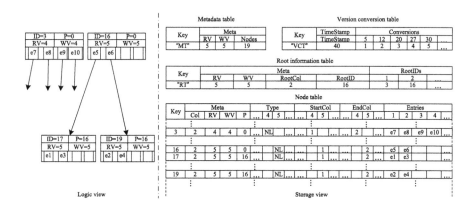

Fig. 2. Logic view and storage view of HMVR-tree

Algorithm 1. Insertion

Input: *o*: multi-dimensional object;
1 **insert(Object o)**
2   rootRow= *get*("RT", "Meta", "RootID");
3   version =*get*("MT", "Meta", "WV");
4   *insertInternal*(rootRow, o, version);

Algorithm 2. insertInternal

Input: *nodeID*: ID of the node in R-tree;
        o: multi-dimensional object;
        version: the version of the node;
1 **insertInternal(long nodeID, Object o, long version)**
2   type = *get*(nodeID, "Type", version);
3   **if** *type!=LEAF* **then**
4   start = *get*(nodeID, "StartCol", version);
5   end = *get*(nodeID, "EndCol", version);
6   entries = *getEntries*(nodeID, "Entries", start, end);
7   entry = *minExtend*(entries, o);
8   entry.extend(o);
9   *put*(nodeID, "Entries", entry.col, entry);
10   *insertInternal*(entry.nodeID, o, version);
11   **else**
12   col=*increase*(nodeID, "Meta", "Col", 1);
13   *put*("Entries", col, o);
14   *increase*(node, "Meta", "EndCol", 1);
15   *split*(nodeID, version);

---

row (in "Col"), read version (in "RV"), write version (in "WV") and parent node ID (in "P"). The "Type" family stores versions of the node and the corresponding node type. The "Start" family stores versions of the node and the corresponding start column in the "Entries" family. Similarly the "End" family stores the versions and the corresponding end column. The entries of one node are stored in the "Entries" column.

We use little-endian coded row key instead of default big-endian coded row key. Thus, consecutive integers are mapped to inconsecutive integers. This optimization reduces the data skews among different region servers and accelerates data processing efficiency.

We store the opposite values of the versions to make newer versions are accessed earlier. During data insertion, the newest versions of entries are accessed frequently. During query processing, newer versions of entries are accessed more frequently in most cases because the users often pay more attention to events that recently happened. So storing the opposite values accelerates processing efficiency of HMVR-tree.

Algorithm 3. split

Input: *nodeID*: ID of the node in R-tree;
       version: the version of the node;

1 **split(long nodeID, long version)**
2   start = *get*(nodeID, "StartCol", version);
3   end = *get*(nodeID, "EndCol", version);
4   if *end - start < CAPACITY* then
5   return;
6   else
7   *increase*("MT", "Meta", "WV", 1);
8   *increase*(nodeID, "Meta", "WV", 1);
9   entries = *getEntries*(nodeID, "Entries", start, end);
10   *rtreesplit*(entries, group1, group2);
11   nodeID1=*increase*("MT", "Meta", "Rows", 1);
12   nodeID2=*increase*("MT", "Meta", "Rows", 1);
13   *addEntriesToNode*(nodeID1, group1);
14   *addEntriesToNode*(nodeID2, group2);
15   entry1=*calculateMBR*(group1);
16   entry2=*calculateMBR*(group2);
17   parentID = *get*(nodeID, "Meta", "P");
18   *addEntriesToNode*(parentID, {entry1, entry2});
19   *increase*("MT", "Meta", "RV", 1);
20   *increase*(nodeID, "Meta", "RV", 1);
21   *split*(parentID, version);

3.3 Insertion Algorithm

The insertion algorithm of HMVR-tree is shown in Algorithm 1. First the root node ID is got from root information table (Line 1). Then the version of HMVR-tree is got from metadata table (Line 2). Last **insertInternal** algorithm is called to insert multi-dimensional object into HMVR-tree (Line 3).

    insertInternal algorithm is shown in Algorithm 2. The node type is got according to the version (Line 2). If the node is not a leaf node, it needs to search for the minimum extended entry (Lines 4–7), update the MBR of the minimum extend entry (Lines 8–9) and recursively call **insertInternal** algorithm to insert multi-dimensional object into the tree (Line 10). If the node is a leaf node, the multi-dimensional is added to the next column in the "Entries" family in node table (Lines 12–13), and the end column is increased by one (Line 14). Finally, it needs to split the node if needed (Line 15).

    split algorithm is shown in Algorithm 3. The start and end columns in the "Entries" family with specific version are got from the "Meta" family (Lines 2–3). Then if the node does not need to be split, it returns immediately (Lines 4–5). If the node needs to be split, the write version of this node and entire HMVR-tree are firstly increased to make the other insert operations work with the newest version (Lines 7–8). Then the entries are got and split into two groups

---

Algorithm 4. Range Query

Input: q: multi-dimensional range query;
Result: rs: the set of objects satisfies q;

1   **query(Query q)**
2   rootRow=get("MT", "Meta", "RootID");
3   version =get("MT", "Meta", "RV");
4      $queryInternal$(rootRow, query, version, rs);
5   **return** rs;

Algorithm 5. queryInternal

Input: *nodeID*: ID of the node in R-tree;
           q: multi-dimensional range query;
           version: the version of the node;
           rs: the set of objects satisfies q;

1   **queryInternal(long nodeID, Query q, long version, ResultSet rs)**
2   type = get(nodeID, "Type", version);
3   start = get(nodeID, "StartCol", version);
4   end = get(nodeID, "EndCol", version);
5   **if** *type!=LEAF* **then**
6   entries = $getEntries$(nodeID, "Entries", start, end);
7   **for** *each entry in entries* **do**
8   **if** *q.intersects(entry)* **then**
9                  $query$(entry.nodeID, q, version);

10   **else**
11   Objects =$getObjects$(nodeID, "Entries", start, end);
12   **for** *each object in objects* **do**
13   **if** *q.contain(object)* **then**
14   add object to rs;

(Lines 9–10). After that, two new nodes are allocated (Lines 11–12) and the two groups of entries are inserted into the newly allocated nodes respectively (Lines 13–14). The MBRs of the two groups are calculated (Lines 15–16) and inserted into the parent node (Lines 17–18). The read version of the node and the entire HMVR-tree are increased (Lines 19–20). Finally, it needs to split parent node if needed (Line 21).

3.4 Query Algorithm

The query algorithm of HMVR-tree is shown in Algorithm 4. First the root node ID is got from root information table (Line 2) and the read version of HMVR-tree is got from metadata table (Line 3). Then **queryInternal** algorithm is called to process the query (Line 4). Finally, the result set is returned (Line 5).

queryInternal algorithm is shown in Algorithm 5. The node type, start and end columns of the node are firstly got (Lines 2–4). If the node is not a leaf node, it searches the entries that intersect the query (Lines 6–9). If the node is a leaf node, the objects that are contained in the query range are added to candidate set (Lines 11–14).

4   Experiments

4.1   Experimental Setup

Hadoop versioned 2.3.0-cdh5.0.1 is used to provide HDFS for HBase and MapReduce framework for throughput evaluation. HBase versioned 0.96.1.1-cdh5.0.1 is used as experimental platform. Both the Hadoop cluster and the HBase cluster are deployed on 9 commodity PCs in a high speed Gigabit network, with one PC as Master node and the others as Slave nodes. Each PC has an Intel Quad Core 2.66 GHZ CPU, 4 GB memory and CentOS Linux 5.6 operating system. Each PC is set to hold maximum 4 Map or Reduce tasks running in parallel and the cluster is set to hold maximum 32 tasks running in parallel. MapReduce is used to simulate multiple clients that request server simultaneously.

We compared HMVR-tree with R-tree which uses HBase as storage (HR-tree). The parameters used in evaluation are summarized in Table 1. In the evaluations, all the parameters use default values unless otherwise specified.

4.2   Insertion Throughput Evaluation

We use one MapReduce job with different number of Map tasks running in parallel to simulate multiple concurrent access.

Figure 3(a) shows the throughput with regard to the number of clients. Compared with HR-tree, HMVR-tree has higher throughput. The reason is that the mechanisms in HMVR-tree make insertions among different nodes be executed in parallel.

It can also be found that the throughput of HMVR-tree increases as the number of clients increases while HR-tree keeps almost the same throughput. The reason is that the insertion operation can be executed in parallel among different nodes in HMVR-tree. This result also shows that HMVR-tree has good scalability.

Figure 3(b) shows the throughput with regard to the number of multi-dimensional objects. HMVR-tree has higher throughput than HR-tree. The

Table 1. Specifications of synthetic data

Parameter	Value range	Default value
#objects	10 k, 20 k, 40 k, 80 k, 160 k, 320 k	160 k
#dimensions	2	2
#clients	1, 2, 4, 8, 16, 32	32
Data distribution	Uniform	Uniform

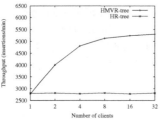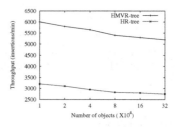

(a) Different number of clients.   (b) Different number of objects.

Fig. 3. Insert throughput evaluation

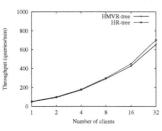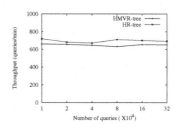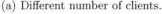

(a) Different number of clients.   (b) Different number of queries.

Fig. 4. Query throughput evaluation

throughputs of HMVR-tree and HR-tree both drop as the number of objects increases. The reason is that as the number of objects increases the depth of tree increases, so it needs to access to more nodes to complete insertion.

4.3 Query Throughput Evaluation

We use one MapReduce job with different number of Map tasks to simulate multiple clients that do range queries. The selectivity of each query is set to 0.01 %.

Figure 4(a) shows the query throughput with regard to different number of clients. The query throughput of HMVR-tree increases as the number of clients increases. This result shows that HMVR-tree has good scalability on processing queries. The throughput of HMVR-tree is a little lower than that of HR-tree. This is because HMVR-tree needs more operations to search different versions of nodes.

Figure 4(b) shows the query throughput with regard to different number of queries. It can be found in Fig. 4(b) that HMVR-tree has similarly throughput compared with HR-tree. The reason is that the newest version of HMVR-tree has similarly tree depth compared with HR-tree.

5   Conclusion

Designing a multi-dimensional index which supports multiple concurrent access for large scale data organization is a challenging problem. In this paper, we propose a multi-version R-tree based on HBase for concurrent access. HMVR-tree maintains the newest version of tree while keeping all the previous versions. HMVR-tree provides concurrent update and query access to different nodes of the tree. The evaluation results show that MHVR-tree has good scalability and has much higher update throughput and the same level query throughput compared to the original R-tree on HBase.

Acknowledgments. This research was partially supported by the National Natural Science Foundation of China under Grant nos. 61173030, 61272181, 61272182, 61173029, 61332014; and the Fundamental Research Funds for the Central Universities (N120816001).

References

1. HBase: Bigtable-like structured storage for Hadoop HDFS (2010). http://hadoop.apache.org/hbase/
2. ZooKeeper (2014). http://zookeeper.apache.org/
3. Borthakur, D.: The hadoop distributed file system: architecture and design. Hadoop Proj. Website **11**, 21 (2007)
4. Chang, F., Dean, J., Ghemawat, S., Hsieh, W.C., Wallach, D.A., Burrows, M., Chandra, T., Fikes, A., Gruber, R.E.: Bigtable: a distributed storage system for structured data. In: Proceedings of the 7th USENIX Symposium on Operating Systems Design and Implementation, OSDI 2006, vol. 7, p. 15. USENIX Association, Berkeley (2006)
5. Guttman, A.: R-trees: a dynamic index structure for spatial searching. SIGMOD Rec. **14**(2), 47–57 (1984)
6. Hsu, Y.T., Pan, Y.C., Wei, L.Y., Peng, W.C., Lee, W.C.: Key formulation schemes for spatial index in cloud data managements. In: 2012 IEEE 13th International Conference on Mobile Data Management (MDM), pp. 21–26, July 2012
7. Huang, S., Wang, B., Zhu, J., Wang, G., Yu, G.: R-HBase: a multi-dimensional indexing framework for cloud computing environment. In: 2014 IEEE International Conference on Data Mining Workshop, pp. 569–574. IEEE, December 2014
8. Nishimura, S., Das, S., Agrawal, D., El Abbadi, A.: $\mathcal{MD}$-HBase: design and implementation of an elastic data infrastructure for cloud-scale location services. Distrib. Parallel Databases **31**(2), 289–319 (2013)
9. Van, L.H., Takasu, A.: An efficient distributed index for geospatial databases. In: Chen, Q., Hameurlain, A., Toumani, F., Wagner, R., Decker, H. (eds.) DEXA 2015. LNCS, vol. 9261, pp. 28–42. Springer, Heidelberg (2015)
10. Wagner, R.E.: Indexing design considerations. IBM Syst. J. **12**(4), 351–367 (1973)
11. Wang, L., Chen, B., Liu, Y.: Distributed storage and index of vector spatial data based on HBase. In: 2013 21st International Conference on Geoinformatics, No. 2011, pp. 1–5. IEEE, June 2013
12. Zhou, X., Zhang, X., Wang, Y., Li, R., Wang, S.: Efficient distributed multi-dimensional index for big data management. In: Wang, J., Xiong, H., Ishikawa, Y., Xu, J., Zhou, J. (eds.) WAIM 2013. LNCS, vol. 7923, pp. 130–141. Springer, Heidelberg (2013)

Short- and Long-Distance Big Data Transmission: Tendency, Challenge Issues and Enabling Technologies

Weigang Hou[(✉)], Xu Zhang, Lei Guo, Yuyang Sun, Siqi Wang, and Ye Zhang

School of Computer Science and Engineering, Northeastern University, Shenyang 110819, China
houweigang@cse.neu.edu.cn

Abstract. Big data is playing an important role in daily life and has developed into a new subject. Especially, an efficient big data transmission is the foundation. This is because even with a high-efficient data analysis, a limited transmission speed still cannot satisfy the requirement of real-time big data. In this article, we first make an extensive analysis on the tendency of investing short- and long-distance big data transmission, and then summarize future challenge issues urgently to be solved: (1) in short-distance big data transmission, MapReduce well satisfies the requirement of big data processing, and it will be integrated with an optical-wireless hybrid data center network. The seamless convergence of wireless and optical subnets with different physical devices and protocols cannot be ignored; (2) to mitigate the pressures of data analysis and link capacity expansion caused by using traditional transparent-bit-rate transmission, the correlated data transmission should be considered. Some enabling technologies are proposed by us for solving the challenge issues above, along with simulation results that will guide the future work.

Keywords: Big data transmission · Virtual network embedding · Node placement

1 Introduction

The integration of man, machine and material gives rise to the explosive growth of data scales and high complexity of data patterns. The world has entered the era of networked big data. According to IDC forecast, the global data size will reach 40 ZB in 2020. Similar to natural and human resources, big data contains great social, economic and scientific values. How to effectively analyze enormous data and turn them into actionable knowledge has drawn great attentions all over the world. In the commercial field, lots of companies like IBM, Google, Amazon and Facebook are sparing no effort to develop their own big data processing technology. In academia, top international journals *"Nature"* and *"Science"* published special issues of *"Big data"* and *"Dealing with big data",* in order to discuss the challenges that big data face in terms of network economics and environmental science.

© Springer International Publishing Switzerland 2016
Y. Wang et al. (Eds.): BigCom 2016, LNCS 9784, pp. 78–87, 2016.
DOI: 10.1007/978-3-319-42553-5_7

Big data is playing an increasingly important role in daily life and has developed into a new subject direction, data science. To improve the ability of extracting knowledge from the vast amounts of data, USA started the project *"Big Data Research and Development Initiative"* in 2012, and EU also has research projects of the database in FP7 Call 8. In China, the topic of big data technology and application has been a major project for science foundation programs, mainly including data analysis based on cognitive computing, big-data-oriented grid computing, and the theory of an efficient transmission for networked big data. Among which, an efficient transmission is a foundation. This is because even with a high-efficient data analysis, a limited transmission speed still cannot satisfy the requirement of real-time big data.

2 Tendency of Big Data Transmission

2.1 Short-Distance Big Data Transmission

In the aspect of short-distance big data transmission within a data center (DC), MapReduce is an ideal framework [1–6] where the master node (one server) divides a raw chunk into data items that will be processed in parallel by the other servers functioned as mappers, and then these mappers shuffle, sort and merge intermediate results in the manner of all-to-all communication. With the mature of wireless technology supporting flexible all-to-all communication and simple deployment, a future MapReduce should be integrated with a wireless-optical hybrid intra-DC network where the servers from the same rack achieve all-to-all communication via wireless links while the communication among inter-rack servers is performed through reserved optical fiber cables [7]. According to the statistics result of related literature indexed by IEL and Elsevier databases from 2011 to 2015 in Figs. 1(a, b), the short-distance big data transmission is an emerging topic despite increasing concern on the future MapReduce under an optical-wireless hybrid intra-DC network.

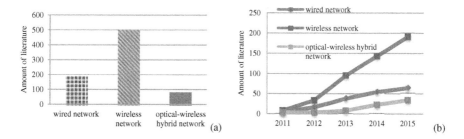

Fig. 1. Statistics result of literature focusing on data transmission based on MapReduce

2.2 Long-Distance Big Data Transmission

In the aspect of long-distance and inter-DC big data transmission [8], the transition from "transparent-bit-rate transmission" to "correlated data transmission" would be occurred so that the inherent advantages of big data analysis could be taken.

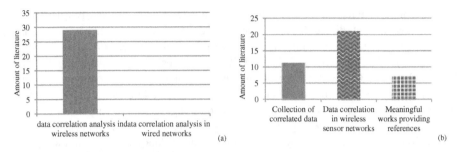

Fig. 2. Statistics result of literature focusing on data correlation analysis

In transparent-bit-rate transmission, the raw chunk generated from a DC is delivered hop-by-hop to another destination DC without in-path data fusion and simplifying. The delivery of unnecessary data items puts massive pressure on the expansion of link capacity and data analysis. In fact, there are different interest semantics, each of which corresponds to one group of data items within a chunk. Thus for the correlated data transmission, in-path computing nodes can be responsible for the analysis of data correlation within one chunk, in order to find a group of data items with the same interest semantic for each computing node. Only one local group of data items with the same interest semantic is retained as *"info"* and shall be switched as a single entity out from the current computing node until it has arrived at the destination DC. Since the destination handles small-size info rather than a big raw chunk, the pressures of data analysis and link capacity expansion are mitigated. According to the statistics result of related literature indexed by IEL and Elsevier databases from 2011 to 2015 in Figs. 2(a, b), some works focusing on analyzing data correlation in wireless networks [9–13] provide references though the research on correlated data transmission remains untouched in wired networks.

3 Challenge Issues of Big Data Transmission

3.1 Virtual Network Embedding for Short-Distance Big Data Transmission

In short-distance big data transmission, MapReduce well satisfies the requirement of big data processing, and it will be integrated with an optical-wireless hybrid intra-DC network in the future. The seamless convergence of wireless and optical subnets with different physical devices and protocols cannot be ignored. For tackling above problem, the network virtualization is a promising approach of decoupling big data processing services from the substrate network. Two different types (intra-rack and inter-rack) of big data processing services can be represented as virtual networks that will be embedded into the same substrate network according to a certain principle. As an example of the intra-rack virtual network owned by a big data processing service in Fig. 3(a), the nodes 2, 3, 4 and 5 will be embedded into substrate mappers, i.e., low-level servers each only with wireless interfaces, in a specific rack, and meanwhile,

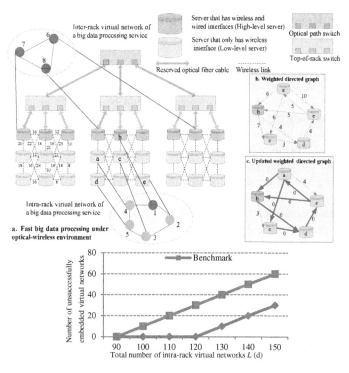

Fig. 3. Virtual network embedding for short-distance big data transmission (Color figure online)

the node 1 will be embedded into the substrate master node, i.e., a high-level server that has wireless and wireline interfaces. How to achieve the aforementioned intra-rack virtual network embedding with the least cost becomes a challenging issue.

3.2 Computing-Node Placement for Long-Distance Big Data Transmission

To mitigate the pressures of data analysis and link capacity expansion caused by using traditional transparent-bit-rate transmission, the correlated data transmission should be considered. The ability to analyze data correlation would be obtained by a reasonable computing-node placement. The network includes data sources (SNs) storing raw chunks and destination DCs (DNs) processing final data. The raw chunk initiated by a SN is transferred along in-path nodes to the specified DN. Due to the difference of territorial policy and economy, computing nodes (PNs) could obtain different levels of potential computing resources of analyzing data correlation at various locations. Thus, the PN placement is concerned with placing the least number of PNs in a subset of candidate locations with high potential computing resources, which is another challenging issue.

4 Possible Research Directions and Critical Technical Problems

In terms of challenge issues above, some possible research directions are summarized as follows. An intra-rack virtual network embedding algorithm with the objective of minimizing the transmission power of servers would be proposed to map the virtual networks of intra-rack big data processing services into the same substrate network via cutting the transmission-power-weighted graph. A PN-placement algorithm based on the weighted hybrid communication graph would be proposed to satisfy the minimum graph connectivity and guarantee considerable potential computing resources. An adaptive routing and bandwidth allocation of info and raw chunks are supposed to be realized using one SDN-based bandwidth customized strategy in a long-distance big data transmission network.

The corresponding critical technical problems to be solved are in the following. For the transmission-power-weighted graph cutting, we must consider how to mathematically represent the virtual networks of big data processing services, create one transmission-power-weighted graph for each rack, and select the final rack and its weighted graph as the substrate network to be mapped. PNs could obtain different levels of potential computing resources at various candidate locations, thus leading to the generation of diverse feasible solutions, each of which has one weighted hybrid communication graph for PN placement. Thus, it is necessary to determine the final weighted hybrid communication graph with the optimal feasible solution so that a considerable quantity of potential computing resources can be obtained.

5 Enabling Technologies

5.1 Intra-rack Virtual Network Embedding Algorithm for Short-Distance Big Data Transmission

Representation of Virtual Networks: For big data processing services, the corresponding intra-rack virtual network can be denoted as $vn(s, \phi, wb, c)$, s is the virtual node to be mapped to the substrate high-level server of a certain rack, ϕ denotes the set of virtual nodes to be mapped into substrate low-level servers in a specific rack. Assuming each virtual node has the same requirement of computing resources, i.e., c, and the virtual link between a pair of virtual nodes consumes the radio bandwidth wb.

Construction of a Transmission-Power-Weighted Graph: Due to the existence of radio communications in each rack, a transmission power $r(u)$ should be assigned to the server u. Therefore, we have the following definition of the weighted directed graph Γ representing the internal structure of a rack. In Γ, the weight $c(u, v)$ of the wireless link (u, v) is $Pu(v)$ which denotes the transmission power required to directly send data from server u to server v. The wireless link (u, v) exists if $r(u) \geq Pu(v)$.

Methodology: To minimize the total power cost $\Sigma u \in \Gamma\, r(u)$ in the weighted undirected graph Γ of one rack, we delete the vertexes with available computing capacity lower than c, and delete the wireless links with available radio bandwidth lower than wb. Thus, the updated graph Γ' is obtained, as an example in Fig. 3(b). In Γ', each node should be able to directly transmit data to the others. We then update the link weight of

Γ': $c(u, v) \rightarrow c(u, v) - min\{c(u, x), (u, x) \in \Gamma'\}$, here, $min\{c(u, x), (u, x) \in \Gamma'\}$ is the minimal weight among all outgoing links of the vertex u. As in Fig. 3(b), since the weights of the outgoing links (b, c) and (b, d) owned by the vertex b are 7 and 4, respectively, we have $min\{c(b, x), (b, x) \in \Gamma'\} = 4$. Correspondingly, we update the weights of (b, c) and (b, d) to 3 and 0, respectively, in Fig. 3(c). After updating all link weights, we only reserve the wireless links with none weight (such as the red arrows of Fig. 3(c)), so that the total power cost can be reduced. Because every rack may have a simplified graph, we utilize the following method to decide which graph is the final result. For the simplified Γ'_i of the ith rack, the sets of high- and low-level servers will be M'_i and P'_i, respectively. We let Ω^i_j record the available computing resources of the jth $(j \in M'_i)$ high-level server in Γ'_i, and Ω^i_k records the available computing resources of the kth $(k \in P'_i)$ low-level server in Γ'_i. The final graph should have the following properties: $\forall i: \left[\tau \Big/ \left(\sum_j \Omega^i_j + \sum_k \Omega^i_k\right)\right] \leq \Upsilon$, $\forall i: |P'_i| \geq |\phi|$, $|M'_i| \geq 1$, and each node is able to transmit data to the others with the least amount of relays. Here, Υ is the maximal delay of processing big data, and τ ($\tau > \Upsilon$) is the actual time duration of processing big data per unit of the computing resource. Next, let N_1 record the number of successfully embedded intra-rack virtual networks, then the residual $N_2 = (N - N_1)$ virtual networks will be changed into inter-rack ones that will be embedded into the same substrate network through reserved optical fiber cables.

Results: The test optical-wireless communication network with 3 racks each owns 3 high-level servers and 6 low-level servers is in Fig. 3(a), where the number beside every wireless link (u, v) is the pre-determined value of $Pu(v)$. For each intra-rack virtual network, $|\phi| = 2$, $c = 1$ and $wb = 1$. The initial capacity of computing resources owned by each low- and high-level server $SC_l = 10$, $SC_h = 20$. Finally, the wavelength capacity $ba = 6$. We compare the total number of unsuccessfully embedded virtual networks $\aleph$ between our design framework and benchmark neglecting virtual-network transformation [8], with the increasing number of intra-rack virtual networks L in Fig. 3(d). A small $\aleph$ means a good performance of virtual network embedding for big data processing. We can see that $\aleph = 0$ only when $L = 90$ for the benchmark, while for our design framework, $\aleph = 0$ when $L = \{90, 100, 110, 120\}$ because we can further change unsuccessfully intra-rack virtual networks into inter-rack ones that would be embedded into substrate high-level servers from different racks through reserved optical fiber cables. The improvement ratio of decreasing $\aleph$ is about 81 % over the benchmark.

5.2 PN Placement, Adaptive Routing and Bandwidth Allocation for Long-Distance Big Data Transmission

Construction of a Hybrid Communication Graph: We design the following hybrid communication graph (HCG), in order to ensure the algorithm has wide generality. Let χ be a set of SNs, B be a set of DNs, and Z be a set of candidate locations where PNs can be placed. Each node is assigned a weight that is related to its potential computing resources of analyzing data correlation. Since we are interested in the placement of PNs, for $y \in \chi \cup B$, the computing capacity $e_y = 0$, and the corresponding weight $C_y = 0$. For $z \in Z$, e_z ($0 \leq e_z \leq e_{max}$) is the computing capacity one PN placed at z can harvest, where e_{max} is the maximum computing capacity one PN can harvest. Correspondingly, the weight of a candidate location is given by:

$$C(z) = \frac{e_{max} - e_z}{e_{max}} + 1 \tag{1}$$

This weight function ensures that the locations with more computing capacity have lower weights, hence will be favored by our solution for PN placement. Based on the above conditions, we obtain the edge-weighted HCG($\chi \cup B \cup Z, w, E$) which is an edge-weighted undirected graph with the vertex set $V = \chi \cup B \cup Z$ and the edge set E. The weight of an edge $(u, v) \in E$ is given as:

$$w(u, v) = \frac{C(u) + C(v)}{2} \tag{2}$$

Figure 4(a) shows an example of HCG with $\chi = \{x_1, ..., x_6\}$, $B = \{b_1, b2\}$, and $Z = \{z_1, ..., z_{25}\}$. The numbers in parentheses are node weights, while the weights

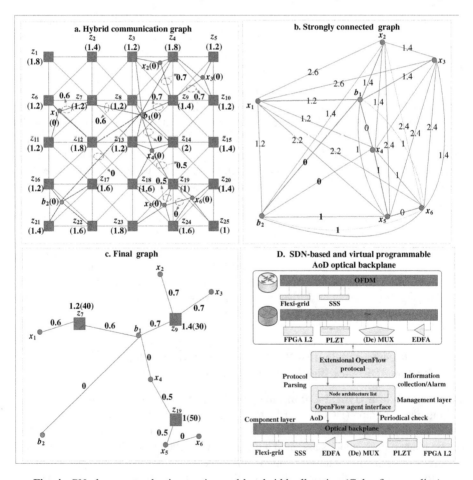

Fig. 4. PN placement, adaptive routing and bandwidth allocation (Color figure online)

(normal font numerals) of only the edges that form a part of the complete graph are listed in Fig. 4(a). The other edge weights are not shown to improve figure clarity. Figure 4(b) shows the complete graph converted from HCG in Fig. 4(a). This complete graph denoted by HCG($\chi \cup B \cup Y$, w, E) only includes DNs and SNs, meanwhile, every node is directly connected with others. The placement solution (a set of PNs $Y \subseteq Z$) is said to be feasible if HCG($\chi \cup B \cup Y$, w, E) has a high total computing capacity $\sum_{y \in \Upsilon} e_y$. Note that, the number of finally deployed PNs is $|\Upsilon|$, which is the size of the graph HCG($\chi \cup B \cup Y$, w, E). As in Fig. 4(b), the edge represents the determined the path between every pair of SN and DN, but we will have various results of the path under different feasible placement solutions. Obviously, the final solution Υ^* of our PN-placement problem is the graph HCG($\chi \cup B \cup \Upsilon^*$, w, E) with a high total computing capacity $\sum_{y \in \Upsilon^*} e_y$ and the smallest size $|\Upsilon^*|$.

Methodology: We first compute K ($K > 1$) paths between every pair of SN and DN since the total weight maybe not the optimal even if only the least-weighted path is determined for each pair of SN and DN. Here, the value of K is equal to the average node degree of the network. Next, we randomly select one of K paths as an edge between a pair of SN and DN, and together with SNs and DNs, these edges form a candidate HCG. Finally, we find the HCG with the highest total computing capacity and then merge the edges shared by paths into the final graph such as Fig. 4(c), where the number in parentheses is the computing capacity of PNs. The adaptive routing of info and raw chunks is conducted on the final graph. After achieving adaptive routing, we find that the switching of transmission functions between chunk and info is involved within every PN. As for a PN, the input is a raw chunk while the output is info. Correspondingly, the optical orthogonal frequency division multiplexing (OFDM) supports the transmission of raw chunks since a super channel can be established using OFDM; motivated by traffic grooming, the wavelength division multiplexing (WDM) is utilized to provide a fixed wavelength channel of aggregating info. We have achieved the function switching between OFDM and WDM-based on SDN and a virtual programmable architecture-on-demand (AoD) optical backplane, which can be seen in Fig. 4(d). The main idea of this approach is the recombination of components for the achievement of the desired transmission function in the manner of flow tables managed by a centralized controller NOX.

Results: The prototype system supporting the aforementioned switching of transmission functions is shown in Fig. 5, where we make the following expansion of Packet-In and Flow Mod messages: add a domain *"rate"* representing the size of info or a raw chunk into Packet-In message. The value of this domain is a random line rate and if it is within the scope [1–100], the WDM transmission function will be allocated for info, while the OFDM is allocated for a raw chunk with the line rate located in the scope [100–200]; on the other hand, we let the domain *"max_len"* of action_output denote a specific transmission function. For example, as shown in Fig. 4(d), the achievement of WDM transmission function involves components FPGA L2, PLZT, MUX, and EDFA on the virtual programmable optical backplane, which means max_len = 15, i.e., 0x000f, and the corresponding Wireshark of Flow Mod message is in Fig. 6; the achievement of OFDM transmission function involves SSS, FlexGridTx, and FlexGrid Rx on the virtual programmable optical backplane, which means max_len = 112, i.e., 0x0070.

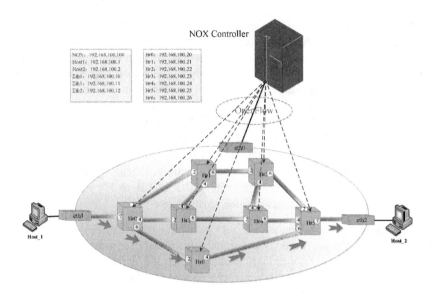

Fig. 5. Prototype system

Fig. 6. Wireshark of Flow Mod message when max_len = 15

6 Conclusion

In this article, we first made an analysis on the tendency of investigating short- and long-distance big data transmission. Though existing works have their advantages, they cannot well satisfy the requirement of big data transmission. Thus, we made a blueprint where some enabling technologies are executed to achieve virtual network embedding for short-distance big data transmission and node placement for long-distance correlated data transmission. Some simulation and experimental results demonstrated the effectiveness of our solutions. But in the near future, a series of algorithms and mechanisms will be investigated by us according to this blueprint.

Acknowledgements. This work was supported in part by Fundamental Research Funds for the Central Universities (Grant Nos. N130817002, N140405005), National Natural Science Foundation of China (Grant Nos. 61302070, 61401082, 61471109, 61502075).

References

1. Zhang, H., Zhang, Q., Zhou, Z.: Processing geo-dispersed big data in an advanced MapReduce framework. IEEE Netw. **29**(5), 29–30 (2015)
2. Suto, K., Nishiyama, H., Kato, N., et al.: Toward integrating overlay and physical networks for robust parallel processing architecture. IEEE Netw. **28**(4), 36–42 (2014)
3. Khan, A., Othman, M., Madani, S., et al.: A survey of mobile cloud computing application models. IEEE Commun. Surv. Tutor. **16**(2), 393–413 (2014)
4. Bari, M., Boutaba, R., Esteves, R.: Data center network virtualization: a survey. IEEE Commun. Surv. Tutor. **15**(2), 909–928 (2013)
5. Liu, J., Liu, F., Ansari, N.: Monitoring and analyzing big traffic data of a large-scale cellular network with Hadoop. IEEE Netw. **28**(27), 32–39 (2014)
6. Yi, X., Liu, F., Liu, J., et al.: Building a network highway for big data: architecture and challenges. IEEE Netw. **28**(27), 5–13 (2014)
7. Suto, K., Nishiyama, H., Katoi, N.: Context-aware task allocation for fast parallel big data processing in optical-wireless networks. In: Proceedings of the IWCMC, pp. 423–428 (2014)
8. Lu, P., Zhang, L., Liu, X., et al.: Highly efficient data migration and backup for big data applications in elastic optical inter-data-center networks. IEEE Netw. **29**(5), 36–42 (2015)
9. Tan, C., Zou, J., Wang, M., et al.: Correlated data gathering on dynamic network coding policy and opportunistic routing in wireless sensor network. In: Proceedings of the ICC, pp. 1–5 (2011)
10. Bandari, D., Pottie, G., Frossard, P.: Correlation-aware resource allocation in multi-cell networks. IEEE Trans. Wirel. Commun. **11**(12), 4438–4445 (2012)
11. Li, Y., Zou, J., Xiong, H.: Global correlated data gathering in wireless sensor networks with compressive sensing and randomized gossiping. In: Proceedings of the GLOBECOM, pp. 1–5 (2011)
12. Rashid, M., Gondal, I., Kamruzzaman, J.: Mining associated patterns from wireless sensor networks. IEEE Trans. Comput. **64**(7), 1998–2011 (2015)
13. Cheng, B., Xu, Z., Chen, C.: Spatial correlated data collection in wireless sensor networks with multiple sinks. In: Proceedings of the INFOCOM, pp. 578–583 (2011)

A Compact In-memory Index for Managing Set Membership Queries on Streaming Data

Yong Wang[1(✉)], Xiaochun Yun[2], Shupeng Wang[1], and Xi Wang[1]

[1] Institute of Information Engineering, CAS, Beijing, China
{wangyong, wangshupeng, wangxi}@iie.ac.cn
[2] CNCERT/CC, Beijing, China
yunxiaochun@cert.org.cn

Abstract. Membership query of dynamic sets is essential for applications which generate or process a continuous stream of data items. These applications often require to cache items dynamically and answer membership queries for duplicate detection on unbounded data streams. Three key challenges for the caching mechanism are the limited memory space, high precision requirement and different priority-levels related with items. In this paper, we propose a compact in-memory index, Bloom Filter Ring (BFR), which is more suitable for dynamic caching of items on unbounded data streams. We demonstrate the time complexity and precision of BFR in finite memory space, and theoretically prove that BFR has higher expectation of average capacity than Aging Bloom Filter, the current state of art. Furthermore, we propose Priority-aware BFR (PBFR) to support membership query scheme which takes into account priority levels of items. Experimental results show that our algorithms gain better performance in term of cache hit ratio and false negative rate.

Keywords: Membership query · Bloom filter · Priority · Hit ratio

1 Introduction

We are at the beginning of BIG DATA era [1], in which the data needed to be stored, computed and analyzed are incredibly fast accumulated. Many systems and applications involve a large volume of continuous data streams [2], which may contain a high degree of duplicate items. Thus, dynamic caching of items for membership queries of duplicate detection is particularly important to applications working on unbounded data streams. For instance, web crawlers which process a stream of web-links, rely on URL caching to avoid crawling massive duplicate web documents [3]. Cache of edge proxies in Content Distribution Networks rely on URL caching to locale target proxy of user request [4]. Obviously, an important factor that determines the efficacy of these applications, is the effective "Caching Mechanism".

Y. Wang—This work was supported by the National High Technology Research and Development Program of China (No. 013AA013205, No. 2012AA013001), the National Natural Science Foundation of China (No. 61271275, No. 61501457)

© Springer International Publishing Switzerland 2016
Y. Wang et al. (Eds.): BigCom 2016, LNCS 9784, pp. 88–98, 2016.
DOI: 10.1007/978-3-319-42553-5_8

Simple Web Crawler. Consider a simplistic web crawler which collects a set of web-links on web documents and then crawls those links recursively. Since some URLs may appear on multiple documents, it is important to identify duplicate URLs as accurately as possible and avoid crawling them multiple times. Thus, the crawler has to maintain a cache of URLs to record already crawled items previously. Besides, since there is a huge gap between costs of cache misses for URLs with different metadata (size, popularity, etc.), a further requirement for the caching mechanism is to maintain URLs according to its corresponding metadata.

Obviously, the key factor for solving the problem is the "Caching Mechanism", which should be memory-efficient and priority-aware. In this paper, we propose a compact in-memory index, Bloom Filter Ring (BFR), which is more suitable for dynamic caching of items on unbounded data streams. The proposed scheme, BFR, utilizes the memory space more efficiently than previous schemes. Furthermore, we propose an improved scheme for BFR, Priority-aware BFR (PBFR), to support membership query scheme which takes into account priority levels of data items.

Our contributions can be concluded as follows.

(1) We propose Bloom Filter Ring (BFR), a highly space efficient data structure for indexing and querying items on an unbounded data stream. Furthermore, we propose PBFR to support query scheme which takes into account priority levels.
(2) Via theoretical analysis, we prove that BFR have higher expectation of average capacity than Aging Bloom Filter, the current state of art. Besides, we demonstrate the time complexity and precision of our algorithms in finite memory.
(3) Our experimental evaluation for synthetic as well as real datasets shows that, our algorithms gain better performance in term of cache hit ratio and false negative rate.

2 Related Work

The bloom filter [5] is a space-efficient probabilistic data structure that supports set membership queries. Recently, bloom filters are popularly used in the area of high-speed network processing [6–8]. It consists of a bit array and a set of hash functions to index item. When an item is inserted, the corresponding bits are set to *one*. Meanwhile, we can probe every bit to give the answer of item existence.

Since standard bloom filter does not support element deletion operation, a bulk of studies focus on the bloom filter variants on dynamic sets. Decaying-based schemes, such as Stable Bloom Filter (SBF) [9], block Decaying Bloom Filter (b_DBF) [10], explicitly or implicitly delete stale data by decreasing the values of counters while item inserting. However, because of selecting cells randomly, false negative may exist in the membership query of other items. Besides, the setting of maximum of a cell is also a problem. There may be memory waste if the value is too large. Extending-based schemes, which assume the memory size is not restricted, such as Multi Dimension Dynamic Bloom Filter (MDDBF) [11], Bloom Filter Chain [12], add a new bit or unit when all the previous units are full. Buffering-based schemes, such as Double Buffering [13], Aging Bloom Filter [14] cache elements in SRAM and simulate cache replacement algorithms (LRU etc.) to delete stale data. Decaying-based and buffering-based schemes assume that the total memory size is already fixed. However, extending-based schemes may not be suitable for the memory-tight scenario.

Besides, plenty of previous works focus on the area of priority-aware bloom filters. L-priorities bloom filter (LPBF) [15] explicitly introduces priorities into bloom filters. LPBF keeps high space efficiency of standard bloom filter at the expense of time and space complexity. Aging Bloom Filter [14] assumes items in a data stream are time-sensitive. We do not make such assumption. We believe that the priority, which guides the insertion and deletion of items, should be assigned by user. Importance-aware Bloom Filter (IBF) [3] differs from previous works in its consideration of user-defined importance values. Experiments show that IBF has lower false positives and false negatives for important data items compared to SBF [9].

In this paper, we assume that the total memory size m and the allowed false positive rate f are already fixed. We propose an improved buffering scheme for bloom filter. Our goal of the proposed scheme is to maximize the number of data programmed into the bloom filter. We will mainly compare with IBF [3], SBF [9] and Aging Bloom Filter [14] respectively.

3 Algorithm and Analysis

In this section, we first describe design of Bloom Filter Ring (BFR), which is a highly space efficient data structure for indexing and querying items on an unbounded data stream. Compared to Aging Bloom Filter [14], BFR uses multiple bloom filter units organized in ring manner and reinserts duplicate items selectively. Afterwards, we extend BFR to priority-aware scenario and introduce PBFR algorithm. Then we will demonstrate the time complexity and precision of both algorithms. The notations used for our algorithms are listed in the Table 1 for quick reference.

Table 1. Notations

Parameter	Comment
m	Total available memory size
f	Allowed false positive rate
ni	Number of individual bloom filter units in BFR
mri	Minimum reinsert interval between item and its nearest duplicate in BFR
f_{single}	Allowed false positive rate of single bloom filter unit
N_{single}	Number of distinct data programmed into single bloom filter unit in BFR
N_b	Total number of distinct data programmed into BFR
H_b	Expected hit ratio of BFR
C	Number of priority categories in PBFR
P_i	number of items with priority i in single unit in PBFR. $0 \le i \le C - 1$
R	Initial clearing ratio of the lowest priority in PBFR
AWR	The average weighted priority of single unit in PBFR
z_{single}	The number of bits needed to be cleared in single unit in PBFR

3.1   Bloom Filter Ring

BFR (Bloom Filter Ring) consists of multiple bloom filter units organized in queue and a set of hash functions. We denote them by $BF[i](0 \leq i \leq ni - 1)$ and $H = (h_1, h_2, \ldots, h_k)$. Here ni is total number of units in the queue and k is the total number of hash functions. The bloom filter units in BFR work in round-robin manner that items are always inserted into the front unit of BFR, *BF[0]*. If *BF[0]* is full, then the tail of BFR, *BF[ni − 1]* is cleared and added to the front of queue as new *BF[0]*. We say a unit is full when the total number of inserted items is larger than its expected capacity.

We introduce an important parameter mri in the algorithm. When an item x is inserted, the algorithm first locate its nearest duplicate. If the interval is larger than mri, then item x will be reinserted into the current bloom filter unit of BFR. Otherwise, the item x will be ignored. The detailed algorithm of BFR is shown in Fig. 1.

```
Bloom Filter Ring(x)
1.   result := false
2.   for idx 0 to ni-1
3.     if x is in the BF[idx] then
4.         result := true
5.         break for
6.   end for
7.   if result is false or INTERVAL is larger than mri
then
8.     if the BF[0] is full then
9.       clean BF[ni-1], add to the front as new BF[0]
10.    insert x into BF[0]
11.  return result
```

Fig. 1. pseudo-code of Bloom Filter Ring algorithm

The BFR algorithm has some features that make it more suitable for the scenario of item aging. First, BFR consists of multiple bloom filter units, which makes it more smooth while item insertion and deletion. Since only one unit may not be filled with items at any given time, the average capacity is enlarged, resulting in better lower bound of capacity. Second, because of parameter *mri*, BFR does not always reinsert duplicate items, which utilizes the memory space more efficiently.

Theorem 1 (Average Capacity). *Given that {f,m} are constants, the average capacity of BFR is larger than or equal to that of Aging Bloom Filter.*

Proof: According to the principle of standard bloom filter, we can derive optimal k an N with given false positive rate f and memory size m.

$$k_{single} = \lfloor \log_2 \frac{1}{f_{single}} \rfloor \tag{1}$$

$$N_{single} = \lfloor \frac{m * \ln 2}{ni * k_{single}} \rfloor \tag{2}$$

After all the parameters are fixed, the average capacity of BFR is shown in formula (3), which is obviously larger than or equal to that of Aging Bloom Filter.

$$N_b = \frac{1}{2}(ni \bullet N_{single} + (ni - 1) \bullet N_{single} + 1) = \frac{1}{2} + (1 - \frac{1}{2 * ni}) \bullet \lfloor \frac{m \bullet \ln 2}{k_{single}} \rfloor \tag{3}$$

Furthermore, we assume the probability of duplicates in the latest dynamic sets with range X is $P(X)$, then the hit ratio can be represented in formula (4). Obviously, we can calculate the optimal ni when all the running parameters $\{f, m\}$ are already fixed. Experimental results also prove the correctness of theoretical analysis.

$$H_b = f + (1 - f) \bullet P(\frac{1}{2} + (ni - \frac{1}{2}) \bullet \lfloor \frac{m \bullet \ln 2}{ni \bullet \lfloor \log_2 \frac{1}{1 - \sqrt[ni]{1-f}} \rfloor} \rfloor) \tag{4}$$

3.2 Priority-Aware Bloom Filter Ring

PBFR (Priority-aware BFR) maintains the number of elements with different priorities in SRAM, and calculate the average weighted priority of single bloom filter unit when it is full accordingly. Meanwhile, we set different clearing ratio to different priority, R for the lowest priority. Afterwards, the number of bits needed to be cleared in single unit z_{single} can be calculated, which is used to clear bits randomly in corresponding unit. Obviously, this is useful for decreasing the false positive rate of items with higher priority. The structure of PBFR algorithm is shown in Fig. 2.

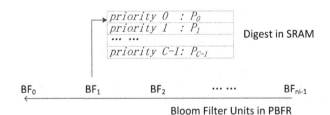

Fig. 2. Structure of PBFR

Theorem 2 (False Positive Rate). *False positive rate of PBFR is lower than that of BFR.*

Proof: Our goal is to analyze how the false positive rate behaves when we clear bits in single bloom filter. At that time, the rate of zero bits in bit array is 1/2. According to the statistic result of elements with differentiated priorities in single bloom filter unit, the number of bits needed to be cleared can be represented as follows.

$$z_{single} = \frac{1}{2} * m_{single} * AWR = \frac{m_{single}}{2N_{single}} * \sum_{i=0}^{C-1} \frac{P_i * R * (C-i)}{C} \qquad (5)$$

Afterwards, we can calculate the new false positive rate of single unit in PBFR. The value is represented in formula (6), which is obviously lower than that of BFR.

$$f'_{single} = f_{single} * (1 - \frac{2z_{single}}{m_{single}})^k \qquad (6)$$

3.3   Complexity Analysis

Theorem 3 (Time Complexity). *Given that $\{k,C\}$ are constants, the processing of each data element in the input stream in BFR and PBFR take constant time, independent of the length of the stream.*

Proof: The time cost of BFR for handling each element is dominated by k. Within each iteration, we firstly probe k cells simultaneously to detect duplicates, and then reinsert the element into the front unit in the worst case. Besides, when current bloom filter unit is full, we has to clear new unit. Since $\{k\}$ are all constants, the time complexity is $O(2k + \frac{k}{\ln 2})$, which is also constant.

In addition to clearing new bloom filter unit, PBFR also needs to clear some bits by average weighted priority for current bloom filter unit, So the time cost of PBFR is a little bit larger than that of BFR. However, since clearing operation is only done once when current bloom filter unit is full, the time complexity of PBFR is also constant, which is independent of the length of the stream.

4   Experimental Evaluation

In this section, we evaluate the proposed schemes. The synthetic dataset is generated under specific rule, where its duplication probability of items according with normal distribution. The real dataset is DNS traffic traces captured from the backbone network. Both of these datasets contain one million data items.

4.1   Cache Hit Ratio in BFR

In this section, We implement four schemes: BFR scheme with *mri* configured 1/16, BFR with *mri* configured 15/16, Aging Bloom Filter [14] and Stable Bloom Filter [9].

(1) *Experiment Parameters*

Setting f and m. All the schemes are given the same memory size m and allowed false positive rate f. The default value for m and f are 4 KB and 10^{-6}, respectively.
Setting K and N. Given that $\{f,m\}$ are constants, we can conclude optimal number of hash functions K and maximum capacity N.

(2) **Performance Metrics**

   HR (Hit Ratio). Hit Ratio is an important metric for effectiveness of caching algorithm, because it can reflect the memory utilization rate more closely.

   AHR (Actual Hit Ratio). We remove false positive rate from HR as AHR. Obviously, AHR can reflects the effectiveness of caching algorithm more precisely.

(3) **Results and Analysis**

   HR (Hit Ratio). Figure 3(a) shows how the hit ratio varies as f increases. We vary the false positive rate f from 10^{-9} to 10^{-3} and reach four conclusions. First, the hit ratio of all schemes increases with f since larger f always means larger capacity. Second, since BFR has larger capacity with given f and m, the cache hit ratio is comparatively higher than other schemes. Third, as f increases, the hit ratio of aging bloom filter gradually catch up with that of BFR since the minimum capacity is already enough to contain the major range of duplicates. Fourth, BFR has better hit ratio with lower false positive rate f and memory size m. The result shows that hit ratio of BFR has 19.7 % increment compared to Aging Bloom Filter while false positive rate f equals 10^{-9}, higher than that of other values. Figure 3(b) shows that how the hit ratio varies as m increases while f fixed. The hit ratio of BFR is also higher than that of other schemes.

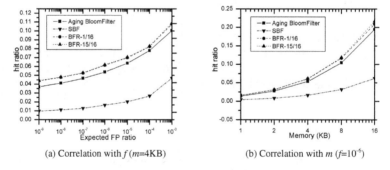

(a) Correlation with f (m=4KB)   (b) Correlation with m (f=10^{-6})

Fig. 3. Average hit ratio using synthetic dataset

The result using real dataset shown in Fig. 4 almost conforms with the previous one. Since the real dataset contains more duplicate items, the hit ratios of all schemes are all higher than using synthetic dataset. Among all schemes, BFR with *mri* configured 15/16 gains best hit ratio. This is mainly because with bigger value of *mri*, BFR has more opportunity to ignore duplicate items, resulting in better memory utilization rate.

   AHR (Actual Hit Ratio). Figure 5 shows the actual hit ratio with f varying from 10^{-9} to 10^{-3}. The default value for m is 4 KB. Since BFR with *mri* configured 15/16 has larger expectation of capacity and smaller fluctuation in capacity, it gains the best actual hit ratio. The results indicate the effectiveness of BFR algorithm heavily.

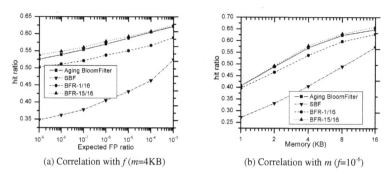

(a) Correlation with f (m=4KB)   (b) Correlation with m (f=10^{-6})

Fig. 4. Average hit ratio using real dataset

4.2 Optimal NI in BFR

Now we analyze what will happen when the number of bloom filter units (ni) in BFR grows. We assume the value of total memory size m and false positive rate f is 4 KB and 10^{-6}, respectively. It is obvious from Fig. 6 that with ni ranging from 1 to 32, the cache hit ratio reaches the maximum while ni equals 8, which is almost consistent with our theoretical analysis where the optimal ni is 8.476. However, we need to notice that, since the optimal value of formula (4) is related with data distribution, the optimal NI may be not consistent for different dataset. Besides, the parameter mri may also has some influence on the result.

4.3 Priority-Aware Bloom Filter Ring

In this section, we compare PBFR with BFR and Importance-aware Bloom Filter (IBF) [3]. Our overall goal is to see how these variants behave when different data items have different priorities.

(1) *Experiment Parameters*
Setting K and C. Given fixed memory size m and false positive ratio f, we can derive optimal number of hash functions K and maximum capacity N. Since IBF uses multiple bits for a cell to represent the value of priority, we set C to 8 for simplicity.

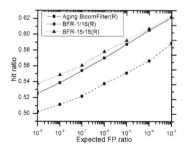   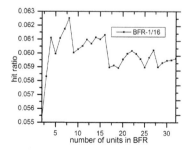

Fig. 5. Actual hit ratio of BFR algorithm   **Fig. 6.** Hit ratio with respect to ni

Setting ni and R in PBFR. After previous experiments, we use the optimal *ni* of BFR here. We set the value of *R* in PBFR to 0.5, which means that half of *non-zero* bits will be cleared if the unit is filled with elements with the lowest priority. **Setting P in IBF.** For fairness consideration, we set $P = K*C$ in IBF-MC, where P means No. of cells to delete. This is because that we need to balance the number of bits caused by element insertion and deletion. While element insertion, the values of bit vector will be increased by $K*C/2$. Considering that there is only half probability to choose *non-zero* cells while random deletion, the value of *P* will be set to $K*C$

(2) *Performance Metrics*

FP/FN Against Priority. Since FP may be included in HR, the answer to the existence is not necessarily correct. We give the false positive FP and false negative ratio FN on every category of priority to refine the impact of this factor.

(3) *Results and Analysis*

During the experiments, the real datasets are marked priorities ranging from 0 to 7 randomly. Figure 7(a) gives the distribution of items.

HR Against Priority. As shown in Fig. 7(b), IBF has the biggest increment between priority 0 and 7 among all schemes, which reflects its effectiveness in retaining items with higher priority. However, hit ratio of items with priority 7 in IBF is still lower than that of BFR and PBFR, indicating its lower memory utilization ratio relatively.

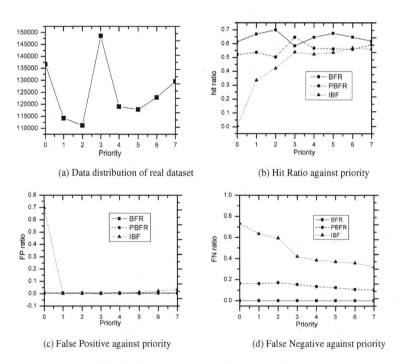

(a) Data distribution of real dataset   (b) Hit Ratio against priority

(c) False Positive against priority   (d) False Negative against priority

Fig. 7. Priority-aware results of real dataset

FP/FN Against Priority. Figure 7(c, d) show how FP and FN varies with priority ranging from 0 to 7. We can reach a series of conclusions from the result. First, false positive rate of PBFR is slightly lower than that of BFR, which is consistent with our theoretical analysis. Second, while the false positive of PBFR and IBF are almost the same, false negative rate of PBFR is almost 2 times lower than that of IBF. This is because IBF clears more bits than PBFR, causing more negative answers for elements in the cache. Third, elements with higher priority (priority 7) in PBFR gains less false positive rate and false negative rate than that with lower priority (priority 0).

5   Conclusion

Dynamic caching of items for membership query is of great importance for applications working on unbounded data streams, such as web crawlers [3], proxy caches [4]. The key challenge is the "Caching Mechanism", which should be able to maintain data items dynamically and efficiently. In this paper, we propose two aging schemes for bloom filter, BFR and its Priority-aware variant, which are more suitable for dynamic caching of items on unbounded streams. Experimental results show that our algorithms gain better performance in term of hit ratio and false negative rate.

In the practical aspect, how to design a flexible adjustment algorithm that can change the running parameters of BFR and PBFR, is a significant work in future. Besides, the average weighted priority may not be a best choice to distinguish differentiated priorities clearly in PBFR. The strategy of clearing non-zero bits may be further improved, which is another important work for us in future.

References

1. Lynch, C.: Big data: how do your data grow? Nature **455**, 28–29 (2008)
2. Asadi, N., Lin, J.: Fast candidate generation for real-time tweet search with bloom filter chains. ACM Trans. Inf. Syst. (TOIS) **31**, 13 (2013). ACM
3. Bhoraskar, R., Gabale, V., Kulkarni, P., et al.: Importance-aware bloom filter for managing set membership queries on streaming data. In: 5th International Conference on Communication Systems and Networks (COMSNETS), pp. 1–10. IEEE (2013)
4. Fan, L., Cao, P., Almeida, J., et al.: A scalable wide-area web cache sharing protocol. ACM SIGCOMM Comput. Commun. Rev. **28**(4), 254–265 (1998)
5. Bloom, B.H.: Space/time trade-offs in hash coding with allowable errors. Commun. ACM **13**(7), 422–426 (1970)
6. Jin, J., Ahn, S., Oh, H.: A multipath routing protocol based on bloom filter for multi-hop wireless networks. Mob. Inf. Syst. **2016**, 1–10 (2016)
7. Yang, T., Liu, A.X., Shahzad, M., et al.: A shifting bloom filter framework for set queries. Proc. VLDB Endow. **9**(5), 408–419 (2015)
8. Liu, W., Qu, W., Gong, J., et al.: Detection of superpoints using a vector bloom filter. IEEE Trans. Inf. Forensics Secur. **11**(3), 514–527 (2016)

9. Deng, F., Rafiei, D.: Approximately detecting duplicates for streaming data using stable bloom filters. In: Proceedings of the 2006 ACM SIGMOD International Conference on Management of Data, pp. 25–36. ACM (2006)

10. Shen, H., Zhang, Y.: Improved approximate detection of duplicates for data streams over sliding windows. J. Comput. Sci. Technol. **23**(6), 973–987 (2008)

11. Guo, D., Wu, J., Chen, H., et al.: Theory and network applications of dynamic bloom filters. In: INFOCOM, pp. 1–12. IEEE (2006)

12. Asadi, N., Lin, J.: Fast candidate generation for real-time tweet search with bloom filter chains. ACM Trans. Inf. Syst. (TOIS) **31**(3), 13 (2013)

13. Feng, W., Shin, K.G., Kandlur, D.D., et al.: The BLUE active queue management algorithms. IEEE/ACM Trans. Netw. (ToN) **10**(4), 513–528 (2002)

14. Yoon, M.K.: Aging bloom filter with two active buffers for dynamic sets. IEEE Trans. Knowl. Data Eng. **22**(1), 134–138 (2010). IEEE

15. Hu, H.S., Zhao, H.W., Mi, F.: L-priorities bloom filter: a new member of the bloom filter family. Int. J. Autom. Comput. **9**(2), 171–176 (2012)

Smart Phone and Sensing Application

Accurate Identification of Low-Level Radiation Sources with Crowd-Sensing Networks

Chaocan Xiang[1], Panlong Yang[2]([envelope]), Wanru Xu[3], Zhendong Yang[1], and Xin Shen[1]

[1] Logistic Engineering University, Chongqing, China
xiang.chaocan@gmail.com, {xcc123dbs,sxfrank0216}@163.com
[2] University of Science and Technology of China, Hefei, China
panlongyang@gmail.com
[3] PLA University of Science and Technology, Nanjing, China
xwr88023@gmail.com

Abstract. The use of crowd-sensing networks is a promising and low-cost way for identifying low-level radiation sources, which is greatly important for the security protection of modern cities. However, it is challenging to identify radiation sources based on the inaccurate crowd-sensing measurements with unknown sensor efficiency, due to uncontrollable nature of users. Existing methods mainly concentrate on wireless sensor network, where the sensor efficiency is available. To address this problem, inspired by EM (Expectation Maximization) method, we propose an iterative truthful-source identification algorithm. It alternately iterates between sensor efficiency estimation and truthful-source identification, gradually improving the identification accuracy. The extensive simulations and theoretical analysis show that, our method can converge into the maximum likelihood of crowd-sensing measurements, and achieve much higher identification accuracy than the existing methods.

Keywords: Crowd-sensing networks · EM (Expectation Maximization) method · Low-level radiation source

1 Introduction

With the rapid development of urbanization and increasing population, more and more attentions are paid to the identification of low-level radiation sources [2]. For example, RFTrax RAD-CZT sensors are used to detect the gamma radiation from the sources of dirty bombs and controlled aerosol injections *etc.* [4,13]. Although wireless sensor networks are proposed to identify the low-level radiation sources [2,13], its deployment and maintenance consume large quantities of money in a large-scale city [10]. As sensor technologies mature and drive down costs, the smartphones are equipped with rich set of sensors, such as accelerator, GPS and microphone [9]. We believe that the sensors of detecting radiation sources will also be embed in the future [7,9]. With the wide usages of smartphones, the smartphone users unintentionally form a dense, large-scale sensor

© Springer International Publishing Switzerland 2016
Y. Wang et al. (Eds.): BigCom 2016, LNCS 9784, pp. 101–110, 2016.
DOI: 10.1007/978-3-319-42553-5_9

network, called crowd-sensing networks [6,10]. It is low-cost and promising to identify low-level radiation sources based on crowd-sensing networks. However, it is non-trivial to build such systems with two main challenges as follows.

- First, the radiation measurements are random variables, following Poisson distribution [4]. Also, the intensity of the low-level radiation sources could be low enough to be appeared as "normal" background radiation.
- Even worse, the low-cost sensors of users have measurement errors, character-ized by the sensor efficiency [3]. The sensor efficiencies of users are unknown previously due to the uncontrollable nature of users.

The existing methods [2,4] are based on a ratio of the measurement likelihood under the assumption the source is truthful and that it is false. As these meth-ods focus on wireless sensor networks, they need to know the sensor efficiency previously. Moreover, their identification accuracy is greatly dependent on the identification threshold, which is extremely hard to be determined [11,17].

To address the drawbacks of status quo methods, we study how to identify the low-level radiation sources based on crowd-sensing networks. Inspired by EM (Expectation Maximization) method [5], we propose an iterative truthful-source identification algorithm, which alternately iterates between the sensor efficiency estimation of users and the truthful probability estimation of sources. This algorithm leverages the intermediate estimation results as feedbacks for the new estimations of the next iteration, gradually improving the estimation accu-racy of both the sensor efficiency and the truthful probability. Finally, we make extensive simulations to evaluate the identification performance of our method.

The major contribution of this paper is three-folds:

1. To the best of knowledge, we are the first work for identifying truthful low-level radiation sources based on crowd-sensing networks, where the sensor efficiency of users are unknown previously.
2. Inspired by EM method, we propose an iterative truthful-source identification algorithm. The sensor efficiency of users is estimated based on the estimations for the truthful probability of radiation sources. These estimation results are feeding back to re-estimate the truthful probability.
3. Theoretical analysis and simulation results show that, our method can con-verge into the optimal estimations of both the sensor efficiency and the truthful probability through limited iterations, where the likelihood of crowd-sensing measurements is maximized.

2   Related Work

With the development of the cities, it is greatly important to detect the low-level radiation sources, such as the defense strategy against dirty bomb [2,3]. As a simple way of identifying the radiation sources, Mean Detector is presented in [8], which exploits the mean of the measurements as the detector. If the detector is above the threshold, the assumption $H1$ (*i.e.* the radiation source is truthful) is decided; otherwise, the assumption $H0$ (*i.e.* it is false) is decided. Although this method is easy to use in practice, the identification accuracy is poor since the intensity of low-level radiation sources is too low to distinguish them from the background radiation.

To address the drawback of Mean Detector, the likelihood ratio is employed for identification. For example, Sundaresan *et al.* [14] use the Likelihood Ratio Test to identify the truthful radiation sources. Specifically, the ratio of the maximum likelihood under the assumption $H1$ to that under the assumption $H0$ is considered as the detector. If the likelihood ratio is above the identification threshold, the radiation source is considered as the truthful one, and vice versa. Moreover, they propose a distributed identification method, considering the limited bandwidth of wireless sensor network. Specifically, each sensor uses Likelihood Ratio Test for truthful identification based on the local measurements. And then, the local results of identification for each user are fused in the center, greatly decreasing the communication bandwidth. Similar to Sundaresan *et al.* [14], Chin [2,12] propose Sequential Probability Ratio Test (SPRT) method to identify the low-level radiation sources. They sequentially use multiple times of likelihood ratio test to identify the truthful sources, increasing the identification accuracy. Despite their high identification accuracy, the performance of these likelihood ratio test methods is tightly coupled with the identification threshold, however, which is extremely difficult to be determined [11]. Thus, these methods are difficult to be applied in practice. Further, these methods mainly consider wireless sensor networks, where the sensors can be calibrated. Nevertheless, this paper focuses on crowd-sensing networks, where the sensors of users can not be calibrated and the sensor efficiency are unknown due to the uncontrollable nature of users [9,16]. Thus, these methods cannot solve the problem of truthful radiation sources in crowd-sensing networks. In contrast, we propose an iterative truthful-source identification algorithm to alternately estimate between the truthful provability of sources and the sensor efficiency of users, increasing the likelihood of measurements to the maximum. Moreover, our identification threshold is determined easily, as its change makes a slight influence on the identification accuracy.

3 System Model and Problem Description

3.1 System Model

In this system model, we consider that, N users join in the crowd-sensing networks and measure the radiation counts about M candidates of low-level radiation sources. Let A_j and $\mathbb{X}_j$ denote the intensity and the location of the j-th source, respectively, $j = 1, 2 \ldots M$. According to the radiation intensity decay model [2,4], the radiation intensity of the j-th radiation source at the location $\mathbb{X}_{ij}$ is:

$$I_{ij} = \frac{A_j}{||\mathbb{X}_j - \mathbb{X}_{ij}||^2} \tag{1}$$

where $\| \bullet \|$ represents the Euclidean distance between the two locations.

Ideally, the radiation counts per unit time measured at the location $\mathbb{X}_{ij}$ follow a Poisson distribution with the parameter I_{ij} [14]. In addition, the background radiation is universal, which is characterized by a Poisson distribution with the parameter B_j. Also, the low-cost sensor of each user has measurement errors, characterized by the sensor efficiency e_i [3]. Let c_{ij} denote the radiation counts measured by the i-th user at the location $\mathbb{X}_{ij}$ for the j-th source. Note that, the radiation counts indicate the radiation counts per unit time unless otherwise specified. As a result, the measurement model is given by:

$$\begin{cases} H_0 : & c_{ij} \backsim \pi\big(e_i \cdot B_j\big) \\ H_1 : & c_{ij} \backsim \pi\big(e_i \cdot (I_{ij} + B_j)\big) \end{cases} \tag{2}$$

where H_1 and H_0 denote the assumption the source is truthful and that it is false, respectively. $\pi(\bullet)$ denotes the Poisson distribution. It is worth noting that, the above measurement model is widely used and validated in [2,4].

According to Eq. 2, the conditional probability of the radiation counts c_{ij} measrued by the i-th user about the j-th radiation source is given by:

$$p(c_{ij}|S_j^f) = \phi\big(e_i \cdot B_j\big) \tag{3}$$

$$p(c_{ij}|S_j^t) = \phi\big(e_i \cdot (I_{ij} + B_j)\big) \tag{4}$$

where S_j^t and S_j^f denote the j-th radiation source is truthful and false, respectively. $\phi(\bullet)$ is the probability function for the Poisson distribution, i.e. $\phi(\lambda) = \frac{\lambda^{c_{ij}}}{c_{ij}!} \exp(-\lambda)$ [1].

3.2 Problem Description

In the crowd-sensing networks, each user uses the available devices (such as smartphone) to make measurements about the radiation source, including the radiation counts (i.e. c_{ij}) and the measured location (i.e. $\mathcal{X}_{ij}$). Simultaneously, large amounts of crowd-sensing measurements are send to the central server by the available communication network, such as WiFi and cellular network [10]. As a result, the server acquires the measurement set of crowd-sensing users as:

$$Z = \{z_{ij}|z_{ij} = (c_{ij}, \mathbb{X}_{ij}), j = 1, 2 \cdots M, i \in \mathbb{U}_j\} \tag{5}$$

where $\mathbb{U}_j$ is the subset of the users, measuring the j-th radiation source. Note that, each radiation source is only sensed by parts of users, due to the roaming behavior of the crowd-sensing users. Thus, we can get $0 \leq \| \mathbb{U}_j \| \leq N$.

The crowd-sensing measurements of the users are susceptible to unknown measurement errors with unknown sensor efficiency. Further, these errors is extremely difficult to be calibrated by the users, due to the uncontrollable nature of users in crowd-sensing networks [9,16]. As a result, it is vitally important to identify the truthful radiation sources based on these inaccurate crowd-sensing measurements. In this paper, we study how to solve this problem, which is described as: *there are M candidates of low-level radiation sources with the known intensity at known locations, how to identify the truthful sources based on the measurement set Z of crowd-sensing users, whose sensor efficiency is unknown in prior.*

4   Iterative Truthful Source Identification Algorithm

4.1   Algorithm Design

We first formulate the truthful-source identification problem as a Maximum Likelihood Estimation problem, where the likelihood function is given by:

$$L(Z) = \prod_{j=1}^{M} \prod_{i \in \mathbb{U}_j} \log \left\{ p(c_{ij}|S_j^t)p(S_j^t) + p(c_{ij}|S_j^f)p(S_j^f) \right\} \tag{6}$$

According to Eq. 6, this Maximum Likelihood Estimation problem has incomplete data, *i.e.* the truthfulness status of the radiation sources, *e.g.* whether the source is truthful. In this paper, we leverage the EM method to solve this problem. Specifically, let V denote the truthfulness of the sources, *i.e.* $V = \{v_j, 1, 2 \cdots M\}$, where $v_j = 1(0)$ denotes the j-th source is truthful (or false). We choose V as the latent variables. Then, the likelihood function is given by:

$$L(Z|V) = \prod_{j=1}^{M} \prod_{i \in \mathbb{U}_j} \left\{ v_j \cdot \log \left[p(c_{ij}|S_j^t) \right] + (1 - v_j) \cdot \log \left[p(c_{ij}|S_j^f) \right] \right\} \tag{7}$$

EM method is a classic estimation method in Mathematics Statistics [5]. It iterates between E-step and M-step until convergence, increasing the likelihood value of measurements incrementally into the maximum. Inspired by EM method, we propose an iterative truthful-source identification algorithm, which iterates between the truthful probability estimation and sensor efficiency estimation, as shown in Fig. 1. Through iterations, the estimation accuracy of both the truthful probability and the sensor efficiency increases step by step until the likelihood of measurements converges. Finally, the truthful probability estimations of sources are used for truthful source identification according to the identification threshold.

   In the following, we take the $(k+1)$-th iteration as an example, and specify the truthful probability estimation and the sensor efficiency estimation.

Truthful Probability Estimation: We use the posterior probability of truthful probability based on the new estimations of sensor efficiency as the estimations of truthful probability. More specifically, let $\mathcal{E}^{(k)}$ denote the estimations of sensor efficiency in the k-th iteration, *i.e.* $\mathcal{E}^{(k)} = \{e_i^{(k)}, i = 1, \cdots N\}$, where $e_i^{(k)}$ denotes the estimation of e_i in the k-th iteration. Let $V(j, k+1)$ denote the truthful probability estimation of the j-th source in the $(k+1)$-th iteration. Then, deriving from Eqs. 1, 3, and 4, the truthful probability estimation

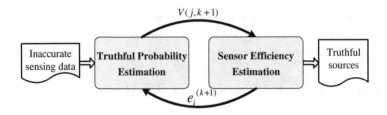

Fig. 1. Framework of iterative truthful-source identification algorithm. $V(j, k+1)$ and $e_i^{(k+1)}$ denote the estimations of truthful probability and sensor efficiency in the $(k+1)$-th iteration, respectively.

$V(j, k+1)$ is given by:

$$
\begin{aligned}
V(j, k+1) &= p(v_j = 1 | Z, \mathcal{E}^{(k)}) \\
&= \frac{p(Z, \mathcal{E}^{(k)} | v_j = 1) p(v_j = 1)}{\sum\limits_{\tau=0}^{\tau=1} p(Z, \mathcal{E}^{(k)} | v_j = \tau) p(v_j = \tau)} \\
&= \left\{ 1 + F(j, k) \left(\frac{1}{V(j, k)} - 1 \right) \right\}^{-1}
\end{aligned}
\tag{8}
$$

where $F(j, k) = \prod_{i \in \mathbb{U}_j} \left\{ \left[\frac{B_j}{I_{ij} + B_j} \right]^{c_{ij}} \cdot \exp(e_i^{(k)} \cdot I_{ij}) \right\}$.

Sensor Efficiency Estimation: Firstly, according to Eqs. 7 and 8, based on the new estimations of truthful probability, we get the expected likelihood function as:

$$
\begin{aligned}
Q(Z|V) &= E_{V|Z, \mathcal{E}^{(k)}} \left[L(Z|V) \right] \\
&= \prod_{j=1}^{M} \prod_{i \in \mathbb{U}_j} \left\{ V(j, k+1) \cdot \log \left[p(c_{ij} | S_j^t) \right] \right. \\
&\quad \left. + \left(1 - V(j, k+1) \right) \cdot \log \left[p(c_{ij} | S_j^f) \right] \right\}
\end{aligned}
\tag{9}
$$

And then, we compute the new estimations of sensor efficiency (*i.e.* $e_i^{(k+1)}$), so as to maximize the expected likelihood function in Eq. 9. Thus, we have

$$
\frac{\partial Q(Z|V)}{\partial e_i} = 0, i = 1, \dots N
\tag{10}
$$

At last, according to Eqs. 9 and 10, we can derive the sensor efficiency estimations $e_i^{(k+1)}$ as: $(i = 1, \cdots N)$

$$
e_i^{(k+1)} = \frac{\sum_{j \in \mathbb{S}_i} c_{ij}}{\sum_{j \in \mathbb{S}_i} \left[B_j + I_{ij} \cdot V(j, k+1) \right]}
\tag{11}
$$

where $\mathbb{S}_i$ denotes the set of sources measured by the i-th user.

4.2 Algorithm Description and Analysis

Based on the algorithm design of previous section, we describe the iterative truthful-source identification algorithm as Algorithm 1. Our algorithm is very simple, and the time complexity is extremely low. The time complexity is $O(N \cdot M \cdot K)$, where N, M and K denote the number of the users, the radiation sources and the iterations, respectively. As a result, our algorithm has a polynomial time complexity.

According to the convergence property [15] of EM method, our algorithm can converge into the maximum likelihood of crowd-sensing measurements with limited iterations, achieving the optimal estimation of the truthful probability. The proofs of the convergence are presented in the literature [15], and we specify them no more.

Algorithm 1. Iterative Truthful-source Identification Algorithm

---

1: Initialize $e_i^{(0)}$ and $V(j, 0)$, $i = 1, 2..N, j = 1, 2..M$;
2: $k = 0$;
3: **while** $Q(Z|V)$ does not converge **do**
4:    **for** $(j = 1; j \leq M; j++)$ **do**
5:       Compute $V(j, k+1)$ based on $V(j, k)$ and $e_i^{(k)}$, $i = 1, 2 \ldots, N$, according to Eq. 8.
6:    **end for**
7:    **for** $(i - 1; i \leq N; i++)$ **do**
8:       Compute $e_i^{(k+1)}$ based on $V(j, k+1), j = 1, 2 \ldots, M$, according to Eq. 11.
9:    **end for**
10:    $k = k + 1$;
11: **end while**
12: Let e_i^c = the converged value of $e_i^{(k)}$, $i = 1, 2 \ldots, N$;
13: $\hat{e}_i = e_i^c$, $i = 1, 2 \ldots, N$;
14: Let t_j^c = the converged value of $V(j, k)$, $j = 1, 2 \ldots, M$;
15: **for** $(j = 1; j \leq M; j++)$ **do**
16:    **if** $t_j^c \geq \tau$ **then**
17:       $\hat{t}_j = 1$;
18:    **else**
19:       $\hat{t}_j = 0$;
20:    **end if**
21: **end for**
22: **return** $\hat{e}_i$ and $\hat{t}_j$, $i = 1, 2 \ldots, N, j = 1, 2 \ldots, M$;

---

5 Experimental Evaluations

We conduct extensive simulations to evaluate our method in this section. First, we introduce the methodology and settings of these simulations. And then, we evaluate the identification performance of our method, *i.e.* the convergence of our algorithm.

5.1   Simulation Methodology and Settings

We simulate a medium-scale crowd-sensing networks to identify the low-level radiation sources. Specifically, 100 low-level radiation sources are randomly distributed in the square region of 2000m × 2000m. Each radiation source is present with the probability 0.4. The intensity of these sources changes randomly from 2×10^5 to 6×10^5 CPM (Counts-Per-Minute). The background radiation and the sensor efficiency randomly vary from 10 to 100 CPM and from 0.3 to 0.9, respectively. This settings is consistent with the real experiments [2,4]. N users participate this crowd-sensing networks. Each user makes measurements for a source with the probability 0.3. The identification threshold is set to 0.5 for our method unless otherwise specified. The simulation programs are written in Matlab, and run in a personal computer with Win7 Intel Core i5 processor and 4 GB RAM. All the simulations are executed for 100 times and we get the average values.

In addition, we compare our method with existing approaches based on the following two metrics:

– *False positive rate*: it denotes the ratio of the actually false sources in all the identified truthful sources, called as *false positive* concisely.
– *False negative rate*: it denotes the ratio of the actually truthful sources in all the identified false sources, called as *false negative* precisely.

5.2   Performance Evaluations

In this section, we evaluate the convergence of our algorithm. The number of users N is set to 100. We analyze the performance of our method in different iterations, in terms of the likelihood values and the identification accuracy, which includes the false positive rate and the false negative rate. Note that, the likelihood values denote the values of the expected likelihood function in Eq. 9.

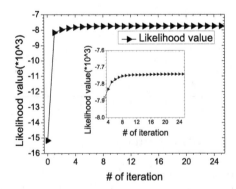

Fig. 2. Likelihood values versus the number of iterations. Our method converges only after 10 times of iterations.

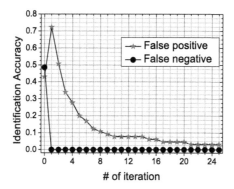

Fig. 3. The identification accuracy versus the number of iterations, including the false positive and false negative.

As shown in Fig. 2, the likelihood values increase with the number of iterations rapidly until convergence. Our method converges only after 10 times of iterations. Furthermore, as illustrated in Fig. 3, the identification errors decrease with the number of iterations until convergence, in terms of both the false positive rate and false negative rate. In addition, the false positive rate increases singularly in the first two times of iterations, as shown in Fig. 3. The reasons are as follows. The false negative rate decreases rapidly in these two iterations, leading to the increasing number of the identified truthful sources which are yet false. Thus, the false positive rate increases rapidly at the beginning.

In conclusion, the above experimental results indicate that, our method can achieve the maximum likelihood of measurements after limited iterations. These results are consistent with the theoretical analysis in Sect. 4.2.

6   Conclusion

In this paper, we propose an EM-based iterative truthful-source identification method, accurately identifying the low-level radiation sources based on inaccurate crowd-sensing measurements with unknown sensor efficiency. The sensor efficiency of users and the truthful probability of sources are iterated to be estimated alternatively, gradually increasing the likelihood values of crowd-sensing measurements.

Acknowledgment. This research is partially supported by Jiangsu Distinguished Young Scholar Awards, NSF China under Grants No. 61502520, 61272487, 61232018, and BK20150030.

References

1. Bickel, P.J., Li, B.: Mathematical statistics. Test 15 (1977)
2. Chin, J.C., Rao, N.S.V., Yau, D.K.Y., Shankar, M., Yang, Y., Hou, J.C., Srivathsan, S., Iyengar, S.: Identification of low-level point radioactive sources using a sensor network. ACM Trans. Sens. Netw. **7**(3), 1–35 (2010)
3. Chin, J.C., Yau, D.K.Y., Rao, N.S.V.: Efficient and robust localization of multiple radiation sources in complex environments. In: ICDCS, pp. 780–789. IEEE (2011)
4. Chin, J.C., Yau, D.K.Y., Rao, N.S.V., Yang, Y., Ma, C.Y.T., Shankar, M.: Accurate localization of low-level radioactive source under noise and measurement errors. In: SenSys (2008)
5. Dempster, A., Laird, N., Rubin, D.: Maximum likelihood from incomplete data via the em algorithm. J. R. Stat. Soc. Ser. B **39**(1), 1–38 (1977)
6. Ganti, R.K., Ye, F., Lei, H.: Mobile crowdsensing: current state and future challenges. IEEE Commun. Mag. **49**(11), 32–39 (2011)
7. Hasenfratz, D., Saukh, O., Sturzenegger, S., Thiele, L.: Participatory air pollution monitoring using smartphones. In: International Workshop on Mobile Sensing, Beijing, China (2012)
8. Jeremic, A., Nehorai, A.: Landmine detection and localization using chemical sensor array processing. IEEE Trans. Sig. Process. **48**(5), 1295–1305 (2000)
9. Lane, N.D., Miluzzo, E., Lu, H., Peebles, D., Choudhury, T., Campbell, A.T.: A survey of mobile phone sensing. IEEE Commun. Mag. **48**(9), 140–150 (2010)
10. Ma, H., Zhao, D., Yuan, P.: Opportunities in mobile crowd sensing. IEEE Commun. Mag. **52**(8), 29–35 (2014)
11. Nehorai, A., Porat, B., Paldi, E.: Detection and localization of vapor-emitting sources. IEEE Trans. Sig. Process. **43**(1), 243–253 (1995)
12. Rao, N.S.V., Shankar, M., Chin, J.C., Yau, D.K.Y., Srivathsan, S., Iyengar, S.S., Yang, Y., Hou, J.C.: Identification of low-level point radiation sources using a sensor network. In: IPSN, pp. 493–504. IEEE (2008)
13. Rao, N.S., Shankar, M., Chin, J.C., Yau, D.K., Ma, C.Y., Yang, Y., Hou, J.C., Xu, X., Sahni, S.: Localization under random measurements with application to radiation sources. In: International Conference on Information Fusion, pp. 1–8. IEEE (2008)
14. Sundaresan, A., Varshney, P.K., Rao, N.S.: Distributed detection of a nuclear radioactive source using fusion of correlated decisions. In: International Conference on Information Fusion, pp. 1–7. IEEE (2007)
15. Wu, C.F.J.: On the convergence properties of the em algorithm. Ann. Stat. **11**(1), 95–103 (1983)
16. Xiang, C., Yang, P., Tian, C., Zhang, L., Lin, H., Xiao, F., Zhang, M., Liu, Y.: CARM: crowd-sensing accurate outdoor RSS maps with error-prone smartphone measurements. IEEE Trans. Mobile Comput. pp. 99 (2016)
17. Zhao, T., Nehorai, A.: Detecting and estimating biochemical dispersion of a moving source in a semi infinite medium. IEEE Trans. Sig. Process. **54**(6), 2213–2225 (2006)

Rotate and Guide: Accurate and Lightweight Indoor Direction Finding Using Smartphones

Xiaopu Wang, Yan Xiong, and Wenchao Huang$^{(\boxtimes)}$

University of Science and Technology of China, Hefei, China
wangxp88@mail.ustc.edu.cn, {yxiong,huangwc}@ustc.edu.cn

Abstract. Today's localization technologies are multitudinous. Resear chers solve the indoor localization problems using diverse methods and equipments. Nowadays, we are still seeking the solutions to the indoor localization problems which have to be precise, efficient and lightweight. Unlike most localization techniques that require either specialized devices or extensive preparations, we propose a novel scheme to find the direction of target anchor points using common smartphones. Our method is derived from a key insight: by moving a smartphone in regular patterns, we can effectively emulate the sensitivity and functionality of an Uniform Circular Array to estimate angle of arrival of target signal. In other words, a user only needs to hold his/her smartphone still in front of him/her, and rotate his/her body around 360° duration with the smartphone. Then our system will provide accurate directional guidance and leads the user to their destinations (normal loudspeakers we preset in the indoor environment transmitting the high frequency acoustic signals) after a few measurements. Major challenges in implementing our system are not only imitating a virtual antenna array by ordinary smartphone but also overcoming the complex indoor environment. We propose rigorous algorithms to address these challenges, and then design and deploy our system in an underground parking lot and a shopping mall. Extensive comparative experiments show that our system is efficient and accurate under various circumstances.

Keywords: Indoor direction finding · Antenna array simulation · Multiple signal classification

1 Introduction

Localization technology is attractive in mobile social networks today for friending and sharing such as Weixin's Friendshake and Weibo's neighborhood microblog. However, most of these functions are based on the Global Positioning System (GPS) and cannot apply to the complex indoor environment. Many prior indoor

W. Huang—The research is supported by National Natural Science Foundation of China under Grant No. 61572453, No. 61202404, No. 61520106007, No. 61170233, No. 61232018, No. 61572454 Anhui Provincial Natural Science Foundation, No. 1508085SQF215.

© Springer International Publishing Switzerland 2016
Y. Wang et al. (Eds.): BigCom 2016, LNCS 9784, pp. 111–122, 2016.
DOI: 10.1007/978-3-319-42553-5_10

direction finding systems measure the direction of signal source using antenna array. They steer the arrays beam to determine the direction of maximum energy using multiple signal classification. This direction corresponds to the signals spatial angle of arrival. And these solutions are accurate and efficient. In order to gain the narrow beam and hence achieve a good resolution, one needs a large antenna array with a number of antenna elements. And this would result in a cumbersome and expensive device and impose restrictions on regular users in daily life.

To capture the benefits of an antenna array while avoiding its disadvantages, we simply utilize the movement of our smartphone to emulate an antenna array instead. Simply put, as the smartphone moves, it samples the received signal at successive locations in space, as if we had a receive antenna at each of these points. By treating consecutive time samples as spatial samples, we can imitate an antenna array and leverage it to determine signal's spatial angle of arrival. We propose an accurate and lightweight indoor direction finding scheme by treating high-frequency narrow-band acoustic signals as research subjects. Assume there is a loudspeaker emitting acoustic signals in indoor environment and the user moves the smartphone horizontally and steady in some regular patterns for a period of time with a approximate constant velocity. During this sampling period, we gather acoustic samples from the microphone of the smartphone. Then, after we applied the noise reduction (BPF) and signal optimizing (AGC), we imitate a virtual antenna array to process the received signals. Eventually, we leverage multiple signal classification (MUSIC) algorithm to estimate the direction of arrival of the target signals.

Speaking of antenna arrays, the Uniform Linear Arrays (ULA) are widely studied. We already did a lot of pre-studies about imitating a Virtual Uniform Linear Array (VULA) by moving the smartphone in front of the user's body horizontally and steady to determine the direction of received signals [11]. However, through abundant experiments, we discover that the accuracy of the VULA system is not only limited by the azimuth angle of the target signal but also affected by the elevation angle between the user and acoustic source. In practice, the smartphone and the signal source are not always at the same height. And during direction finding, when the user turn his/her back on the signal source will cause massive errors on the experiment results. In a word, the system based on the VULA is invalid under several circumstances.

To the best of our knowledge, the following properties of Uniform Circular Arrays (UCA) make them attractive to our case. The UCA provides 360° azimuthal coverage and also provide the information on source elevation angles. ULA, in contrast, provide only 180° azimuthal coverage, and no results of the elevation angles. Moreover, the signal resolution processing by ULA is high at some particular arrival angles but low at others. But the UCA has the same high signal resolution around 360° azimuth. And these advantages of UCA can solve the above problems perfectly. In Fig. 1, we hold the smartphone still and rotate our body around for 360° during sampling to imitate a Virtual Uniform Circular Array (VUCA). And we implement the UCA-RB-MUSIC algorithm to calculate the direction of the target signals and solve the multipath effect problem as well.

We designed, deployed, and evaluated our scheme of direction finding under diverse circumstances. Our extensive experiment results show that our theory supports high accuracy of direction finding. The flowchart of our systems are shown in Fig. 2. For phone to speaker direction finding, the mean error and the standard deviation of the measured angle is 3.4° and 3.9° respectively within the range of 20 m.

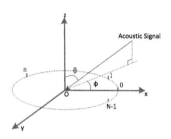

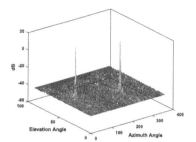

Fig. 1. VUCA direction finding   **Fig. 2.** Systems flowchart

2   Direction Finding Using VUCA System

2.1   Uniform Circular Array Simulation

We assume the user holds his/her smartphone still and rotates around his/her body for 360°. During the sampling period, we captures a single measurement in a particular sampling interval T as if we had a receive antenna array at each of these sampling points. These points are uniformly distributed on the moving circular trajectory.

According the VUCA geometry in Fig. 3 we regard the first sample point during rotating as antenna element 0. Assume the user rotates in constant angular velocity ω, the antenna elements are uniformly distributed over the circumference of a circle of radius r. In our case, the radius stands for the distance between users' hand and body (our default is $r = 0.3$ m for humanbeings in average height). And the x axis lies on the line which connect the antenna element 0 with the circle center O. $\theta \in [0, \frac{\pi}{2}]$ is the source elevation angle which is measured down from the z axis. And the azimuth angle $\phi \in [0, 2\pi]$ is measured from the x axis. Since we choose the first sample point as the element 0, the ground truth of our system is easy to detect. Because the user start rotating right in front of his/her body in most cases. We treat a single measurement we capture as antenna element n and there are N elements in total during sampling. We believe if the N is large enough, we can assume the trajectory of the smartphone during the whole sampling period is a closed circle. Hence, the array element can be displaced by angle γ_n from the x axis:

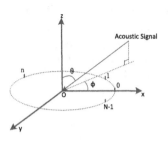

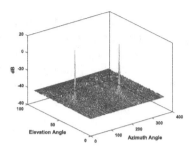

Fig. 3. VUCA geometry analysis

Fig. 4. An example of direction finding using VUCA in ideal environment

$$\gamma_n = n\omega T \approx \frac{2\pi n}{N}; \quad n = 0, 1, \cdots, (N-1) \tag{1}$$

However, assume the user rotates 360° in constant angular velocity ω, we can represent γ_n using only N and n approximatively and refrain from the fact that we do not know the exact velocity of the smartphone. Then the position vector of element n is:

$$\vec{p_n} = (r\cos\gamma_n, r\sin\gamma_n, 0) \tag{2}$$

And the unit vector of the incoming acoustic signal which is defined by elevation angle θ and azimuth angle ϕ has this form:

$$\hat{\gamma} = (\sin\theta\cos\phi, \sin\theta\sin\phi, \cos\theta) \tag{3}$$

For the purpose of calculating the phase difference between the signals received at the origin and at element n, we need to represent the time required for the signals to travel from these two points τ_n.

$$\tau_n = \frac{\hat{\gamma}\vec{p_n}}{c} = \frac{r}{c}\sin\theta\cos(\phi - \gamma) \tag{4}$$

The calculation of direction vector is similarly with the Uniform Linear Arrays processing above. Let vector $\vec{\theta} = (\beta, \phi)$ represent signal arrival direction. It can be expressed in the following equation:

$$A(\vec{\theta}) = \begin{bmatrix} e^{j\beta\cos(\phi-\gamma_0)} \\ e^{j\beta\cos(\phi-\gamma_1)} \\ \cdots \\ e^{j\beta\cos(\phi-\gamma_{N-1})} \end{bmatrix} \tag{5}$$

β is a parameter we introduce to define the value of elevation angle θ and c is the velocity of acoustic signals:

$$\beta = \frac{2\pi f_a}{c} r\sin\theta \tag{6}$$

where f_a is the center frequency of the target acoustic signal.

2.2 Phase Mode Excitation of Continuous Circular Aperture

Unfortunately, the calculated direction vector is not a Vandermonde matrix. In order to leverage MUSIC algorithm to determine the direction of acoustic source, we need to construct a preprocessing matrix for $A(\vec{\theta})$ via the phase mode excitation technique.

First we can consider the case of a continuous circular aperture. The excitation functions are periodic with period 2π and can be represented in terms of a Fourier series. To a arbitrary excitation function $w(\gamma)$ is determined by following formula:

$$w(\gamma) = \sum_{m=-\infty}^{+\infty} c_m e^{jm\gamma} \tag{7}$$

where the mth phase mode $w_m(\gamma) = e^{jm\gamma}$ is a spatial harmonic of the array excitation and c_m is the corresponding Fourier series coefficient. As the result of aperture exciting with the mth phase mode, the normalized far field pattern is:

$$f_m^c(\vec{\theta}) = \frac{1}{2\pi} \int_0^{2\pi} w_m(\gamma) e^{j\beta \cos(\phi-\gamma)} \, d\gamma \tag{8}$$

where the superscript c represents the continuous aperture. According to $w_m(\gamma)$, the far field pattern can be express as:

$$f_m^c(\vec{\theta}) = j^m J_m(\beta) e^{jm\phi} \tag{9}$$

where $J_m(\beta)$ is the Bessel function of the first kind of order m. It contains the information of the elevation angle and the amplitude. And thanks to the Automatic Gain Control (AGC) we utilize, the amplitude of the acoustic signal is replaced by another one that is close to constant. And also we can easily detect that the far field signal pattern and the excitation function share the same azimuthal angle change $e^{jm\phi}$.

But the number of modes can be excited is limited. Now we let M denote the highest order mode that can be excited by the aperture at a reasonable strength ($m < M$). We can say that visible region $\theta \in [\frac{\pi}{2}]$ translates into $\beta = \frac{2\pi f_a}{c} r \sin\theta \in [0, \frac{2\pi f_a r}{c}]$. The mode amplitude $J_m(\beta)$ is small when the Bessel function order m exceeds its argument β. If $m \geq M$, $f_m^c(\vec{\theta})$ will be small over the entire visible region. So

$$M \approx \left\lfloor \frac{2\pi f_a}{c} r \right\rfloor \tag{10}$$

2.3 Phase Mode Excitation of Uniform Circular Array

Now we consider phase mode excitation of an N elements virtual uniform circular array (VUCA) in our case. The normalized beamforming weight vector that excites the array can be express as:

$$w_m^{\mathrm{H}} = \frac{1}{N} \left[e^{jm\gamma_0}, \cdots, e^{jm\gamma_{N-1}} \right] \tag{11}$$

Then we can get the resulting array pattern $f_m^s(\theta)$:

$$f_m^s(\vec{\theta}) = w_m^{\mathrm{H}} A(\vec{\theta}) = \frac{1}{N} \sum_{n=0}^{N-1} e^{jm\gamma_n} e^{j\beta\cos(\phi-\gamma_n)} \tag{12}$$

where the superscript s denotes the sampled aperture which is discrete. As a result of $|m| < N$,

$$f_m^s(\vec{\theta}) = j^m J_m(\beta) e^{jm\phi} + \sum_{q=1}^{+\infty} [(j)^g J_g(\beta) e^{ig\phi} + (j)^h J_h(\beta) e^{jh\phi}] \tag{13}$$

In above equation, $g = Nq - m$ and $h = Nq + m$. The first term in this equation, the principal term, is the same with the far-field pattern of Eq. 9 corresponding to the continuous aperture case. The remaining terms are caused by the sampling of the continuous aperture. And they are the residual terms to our case. After setting the perspective from Eq. 13, we come to the conclusion that the residual terms can be ignored if $N > 2M$. Due to the attribute of $J_{-m}(\beta) = (-1)^m J_m(\beta)$, the UCA array pattern for mode m is:

$$f_m^s(\vec{\theta}) \approx (j)^{|m|} J_{|m|}(\beta) e^{jm\phi} \tag{14}$$

2.4   Beamforming Matrix and Direction Vector Construction

With this background on phase mode excitation of circular arrays, we can introduce UCA-RB-MUSIC algorithm to solve the direction finding problem. For the purpose of making the transformation of direction vector $A(\vec{\theta})$ from element space to beamspace, we need to introduce the beamformer F_r^{H}:

$$B(\vec{\theta}) = F_r^{\mathrm{H}} \cdot A(\vec{\theta}) \tag{15}$$

For clarity of calculation we also present F_e^{H} which is a intermediate quantity.

$$F_e^{\mathrm{H}} = C_v V^{\mathrm{H}} \tag{16}$$

where

$$C_v = diag\{j^{-M}, \cdots, j^{-1}, j^0, j^{-1}, \cdots, j^{-M}\} \tag{17}$$

and

$$V = \sqrt{N}[w_{-M}, \cdots, w_M] \tag{18}$$

Equation 17 helps to eliminate the term $(j)^{|m|}$ in Eq. 14. In Eq. 11, the column vector w_m^{H} is already defined. According to the above discussion, we can get:

$$F_e^{\mathrm{H}} A(\vec{\theta}) = C_v V^{\mathrm{H}} A(\vec{\theta}) = \sqrt{N} J(\beta) v(\phi) \tag{19}$$

The information of the azimuthal angle ϕ is only in the vector $v(\phi)$.

$$v(\phi) = [e^{-jM\phi}, \cdots, e^{-j\phi}, 1, e^{j\phi}, \cdots, e^{jM\phi}]^{\mathrm{H}} \tag{20}$$

Through observation, this is similar in Vandermonde form to VULA direction vector. And $J(\beta)$ contains the information of elevation angle θ:

$$J(\beta)=diag[J_M(\beta), J_{M-1}(\beta), \cdots, J_1(\beta), J_0(\beta), J_1(\beta), \cdots, J_M(\beta)] \tag{21}$$

Now we introduce W^H that has centro-Hermitian rows. The F_r^H is constructed by premultiplying F_e^H by W^H. The beamformer F_r^H can be express like this:

$$F_r^H = W^H F_e^H = W^H C_v V^H \tag{22}$$

So the beamspace manifold vector $B(\vec{\theta})$ will be:

$$B(\vec{\theta}) = F_r^H A(\vec{\theta}) = \sqrt{N} W^H J(\beta) v(\phi) \tag{23}$$

The centro-Hermitian vector multiply another one can construct a real-valued beamspace manifold vector. So W must satisfy $\tilde{I}W = W^*$.

$$W = \frac{1}{\sqrt{M'}}[v(\alpha_{-M}), \cdots, v(\alpha_0), \cdots, v(\alpha_M)] \tag{24}$$

where M' represents the total number of M which is $M' = 2M + 1$ and $\alpha_i = \frac{2\pi i}{M'}(i \in [-M, M])$.

Through observation, we learn that the during the progress of constructing a real-valued beamspace manifold vector is also a progress of smoothing in matter of fact. It helps the algorithm to eliminate the adverse impact of coherent signal in the environment.

2.5   Estimating Direction of Arrival by MUSIC Algorithm

Assume the smartphone receives the acoustic signals at sampling point n is $x[t_n] = A(\vec{\theta})S(t_n) + \sigma(t_n)$. And thanks to the BPF we leverage, the noise $\sigma(t_n)$ is eliminated. Now the UCA-RB-MUSIC algorithm utilize the beamformer F_r^H to make the transformation from element space to beamspace:

$$y[t_n] = F_r^H x[t_n] = B(\vec{\theta})S(t_n) \tag{25}$$

So the corresponding beamspace covariance matrix is:

$$R_y = E[y[t_n]y[t_n]^H] \tag{26}$$

Next step is the eigenvalue decomposition of covariance matrix $R = Re\{R_y\}$, and we introduce the signal-subspace and noise-subspace. We use $U_n = (v_2, \cdots, v_{M'})$ to represent noise eigenvectors of noise-subspace listed in descending order.

Eventually, the UCA-MUSIC spectrum has this form:

$$P(\vec{\theta}) = \frac{1}{B^T(\vec{\theta})U_n U_n^T B(\vec{\theta})} \tag{27}$$

We can estimate the direction of target signal depends on the 2-D search for peaks in the spectrum $P(\vec{\theta}) = P(\beta, \phi)$. The elevation angle which affect the spectrum through the parameter $\beta = \frac{2\pi f_a}{c} r \sin\theta$. And the azimuth angle $\phi(\in 0, 2\pi)$, which means that our system of indoor direction finding is omni-directional. An example of VUCA direction finding results under ideal circumstances is shown in Fig. 4.

3   Experiment

Our scheme is deployed on Sumsung NOTE2 with Android system. And several ordinary digital loudspeakers are chose to be the acoustic sources. We set them in various indoor environment as anchor points for us to locate. The acoustic signals' frequency in the experiments are selected to be 17000 Hz to 19500 Hz.

Experiment Design: The sketch of experiment design is shown in Fig. 5. The distance between the smartphone and the acoustic source is L. ϕ is the azimuth angle, θ is the elevation angle and the orientation angle of the acoustic source is β which is shown in Fig. 6.

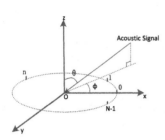

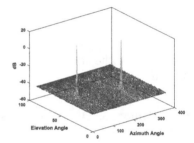

Fig. 5. Sketch of experiment design

Fig. 6. Orientation angle β of acoustic source

The main method of evaluating performance of our scheme is to vary L, ϕ, θ and β by deploying the loudspeakers and smartphones at different positions. We also did a lot of contrast experiment to Virtual Uniform Linear Array direction finding and Virtual Uniform Circular Array direction finding in the same environment to verify the superiority of VUCA system. We measure ϕ and θ 50 times for each circumstance with both VULA and VCLA.

3.1   Indoor Environment with Single High Frequency Acoustic Wave

Effected by the Distance and Azimuth Angle: We deploy our system in a large underground parking lot where there is only one acoustic source in the environment. The direction finding accuracy of different distance L is a significant evaluation to our system. Hence, we set $L = 5\,\text{m}, 10\,\text{m}, 20\,\text{m}, 30\,\text{m}$, $\phi = 30°, 90°, 240°$ and $\theta = 0°$. In matter of fact we also test the angular errors when $L > 30\,\text{m}$, but the results become unstable for both the VULA and VUCA since the signal is too weak. So we do not show the results of this case. Now we plot the mean angular errors on different distance between the smartphone and the speaker using both VULA and VUCA and the cumulative distribution function (CDF) of the angular errors of the VUCA system in Fig. 7.

First, we notice that the mean error of the VUCA system is less than $4°$ when $L < 20\,\text{m}$. And it is still acceptable when $L = 30\,\text{m}$. Then through observation, there are not much differences of the direction finding performance between the VULA system and the VUCA system when $\phi = 90°$. But when $\phi = 30°$ the VUCA performs better than VULA obviously. We believe the reason to that phenomenon is the VULA system's resolution to the acoustic signal is changing and it related to the rate of change of the direction vector. The resolution reaches the highest when the directions of the arrived signal are perpendicular to the axial line and gets lower and lower when it come close to the same direction along the axial line of VULA. But the VUCA system's resolution remains the same for $360°$ duration.

Eventually, we do not show the mean error of the VULA system when $\phi = 240°$. Because the VULA is very unstable when the user turns his back on the acoustic source. When $\phi_1 = 2\pi - \phi_2$, the direction of vectors of these two arrival signals are the same. It causes the fuzzy phenomenon of the VULA system and it affects our direction finding accuracy extremely.

Effected by the Elevation and the Orientation Angle: In this section, we test the angular errors when the speaker and the smartphone are not at the same height. We set $L = 8\,\text{m}$, $\phi = 45°$ and $\theta = 0°; 10°; 20°$ and $\beta = 0°$. We can find the different performances of the VULA system and the VUCA system in different scenarios in Fig. 8(a). We detect that the VULA is affected when the elevation angle θ grows. On the other hand, the VUCA retain almost the same accuracy with different elevation angles. We believe the main reason to these results is only the VUCA system take the elevation angle of the target signals θ into consideration.

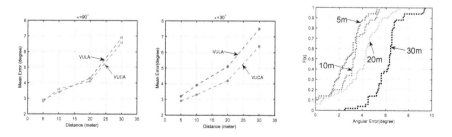

Fig. 7. (a)(b) Mean error of direction finding when $\phi = 90°$ or $30°$ with different distances L; (c) CDF of the angular errors when using VUCA and $L = 5\,\text{m}, 10\,\text{m}, 20\,\text{m}, 30\,\text{m}$

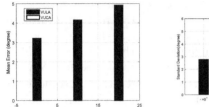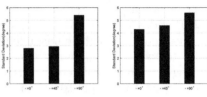

Fig. 8. (a) Mean error of VULA and VUCA when $\theta = 0°; 10°; 20°$ and $L = 8$ m; (b)(c) Standard division of angular error when $L \leq 6$ m and $L = 24$ m

The Orientation Angle of the Acoustic Source: In the experiments, we find that the different orientation angle β of the acoustic source will also affect the results. We now evaluate the VUCA system with different β. Figure 8(b), (c) show the standard division of angular error when $\beta = 0°, 45°, 90°$, $L \leq 6$ m, $L = 24$ m, $\theta = 0°$ and $\phi = 45°$. We learn that the closer we get to the acoustic source the easier direction finding accuracy is affected by the orientation angle β. We believe the reason to this phenomenon is that the acoustic source we choose is not omni-directional, and when we are near the acoustic source, the signals reflected from the wall sometimes are stronger than those directly goes to the smartphone. But when $L = 24$ m, the signals reflected from the wall becomes much weaker than those directly from the acoustic source. So the orientation angle has less influence to our results.

3.2 Indoor Environment with Multiple High Frequency Acoustic Waves

Our system is built on the assumption that a person in a library or a hospital can leverage their smartphone to locate the loudspeakers in the environment transmitting high frequency acoustic signals using our system. But in daily life, these speakers are used for other purposes half the time, i.e. playing music or announcements. So we need to detect the robustness of our system when the same acoustic source transmitting multiple frequencies acoustic signal.

We set $\beta = 0°, \phi = 45°$ and $\theta = 10°$. In Fig. 9(a), we can detect that when $L \leq 20$ m, the VUCA system is stable for the acoustic source transmitting both single and multiple acoustic signals. But when $L > 20$ m, the results have been affected. We believe that is because when the speaker sends multiple signals, the signal strength of each component becomes weaker. Fortunately, in the indoor application scenario such as a shopping mall or a hospital, there are high power speaker in a passageway or a conference room in most cases.

And we also have another assumption that the different loudspeakers transmitting various high frequency acoustic signals to distinguish different locations in indoor environment. If the user knows a specific frequency of his/her target acoustic signal. Our system can guide the user to his/her destination after

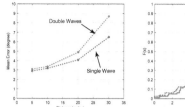 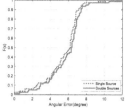 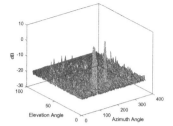

Fig. 9. (a) The same acoustic source with single and multiple waves (b) The CDF of the angular error in the noisy environment (c) An experiment result with different acoustic sources and signals in noisy environment (Color figure online)

he/she rotates 360°. So we also need to verify the direction finding ability of the VUCA system when the multiple acoustic sources transmitting different high frequency acoustic signals in the environment. And the experiment results show that our system is stable when there are multiple different high frequency acoustic signals in the environment. Figure 9(c) shows an example of experiment results when there are two different frequency acoustic sources transmitting by two loudspeakers in the noisy environment.

Noisy Environment: We deploy our VUCA system in a big shopping mall called WANDA Plaza where it is noisy and many people waking around and blocking the line connect from the acoustic sources (the digital loudspeakers we set on shelves or on the ground) and user. We also let the speakers send multiple signals. And the results of experiment show that almost all errors are less than 12 degrees for $L <= 30M$ which is acceptable for daily use. The CDF of the angular error in the noisy environment shows in Fig. 9(b).

4   Conclusion

In this paper, we propose a novel scheme to estimate the direction of the high frequency acoustic source in indoor environment. By rotating a common smartphone around the user's body for 360 degrees, our system can imitate a virtual uniform circular array (VUCA) to detect the direction of the user's destination. Comparing to other direction finding scheme, our method is lightweight and also accurate. In contrast to our previous work of virtual uniform linear array (VULA) system, we solve the Blind-zone problem and reduce the impact of elevation angle between the acoustic source and smartphone to the accuracy of direction finding. By getting rid of the multipath effect using UCA-RB-MUSIC algorithm, the extensive experiments show that our scheme works well under various circumstances. In addition, there are still some future works to do. For example, the calculation of VUCA system is more complex than the VULA system. We can optimize the algorithm of VUCA system in order to obtain faster response speed of our system. And also we can try to develop an indoor localization system which is based on our direction finding technique.

References

1. Huang, W., Xiong Y., Li, X. Y., Lin, H., Mao, X., Yang, P., Liu, Y.: Accurate indoor localization using acoustic direction finding via smart phones (2013). arXiv preprint arxiv:1306.1651
2. Zhang, Z., Zhou, X., Zhang, W., Zhang, Y., Wang, G., Zhao, B.Y., Zheng, H.: I am the antenna: accurate outdoor AP location using smartphones. In: Proceedings of the 17th Annual International Conference on Mobile Computing and Networking, pp. 109–120. ACM, September 2011
3. Tarzia, S.P., Dinda, P.A., Dick, R.P., Memik, G.: Indoor localization without infrastructure using the acoustic background spectrum. In: Proceedings of the 9th International Conference on Mobile Systems, Applications, and Services, pp. 155–168. ACM, June 2011
4. Xiong, J., Jamieson, K.: ArrayTrack: a fine grained indoor location system. In: NSDI, pp. 71–84, April 2013
5. Adib, F., Katabi, D.: See through walls with wifi!, vol. 43, no. 4, pp. 75–86. ACM (2013)
6. Peng, C., Shen, G., Zhang, Y., Li, Y., Tan, K. Beepbeep : a high accuracy acoustic ranging system using cots mobile devices. In: SenSys (2007)
7. Schmidt, R.O.: Multiple emitter location and signal parameter estimation. IEEE Trans. Antennas Propag. **34**(3), 276–280 (1986)
8. Mathews, C.P., Zoltowski, M.D.: Eigenstructure techniques for 2-D angle estimation with uniform circular arrays. IEEE Trans. Sig. Process. **42**(9), 2395–2407 (1994)
9. Bahl, P., Padmanabhan, V.N.: Radar: an in-building RF-based user location and tracking system. In: INFOCOM (2000)
10. Chandrasekaran, G., Ergin, M., Yang, J., Liu, S., Chen, Y., Gruteser, M., Martin, R.: Empirical evaluation of the limits on localization using signal strength. In: SECON (2009)
11. Wang, X., Xiong, Y., Huang, W.: Anti-multipath indoor direction finding using acoustic signal via smartphones. In: Wang, Y., Xiong, H., Argamon, S., Li, X.Y., Li, J.Z. (eds.) BigCom 2015. LNCS, vol. 9196, pp. 126–140. Springer, Heidelberg (2015)
12. Constandache, I., Bao, X., Azizyan, M., Choudhury, R.R.: Did you see bob?: human localization using mobile phones. In: MobiCom (2010)
13. Johnson, C.R., Sethares, W.A.: Telecommunication Breakdown; Concepts of Communication Transmitted via Software-Defined Radio. Prentice Hall, Englewood Cliffs (2003)
14. Kulakowski, P., Vales-Alonso, J., Egea-Lpez, E., Ludwin, W., Garca-Haro, J.: Angle-of-arrival localization based on antenna arrays for wireless sensor networks. Comput. Electr. Eng. **36**, 1181–1186 (2010)
15. Liu, H., Darabi, H., Banerjee, P.P., Liu, J.: Survey of wireless indoor positioning techniques and systems. IEEE Trans. Syst. Man Cybern. Part C **37**, 1067–1080 (2007)
16. Niculescu, D., Nath, B.: Vor base stations for indoor 802.11 positioning. In: MobiCom (2004)
17. Nishimura, Y., Imai, N., Yoshihara, K.: A proposal on direction estimation between devices using acoustic waves. In: MobiQuitous (2012)
18. Peng, C., Shen, G., Zhang, Y., Lu, S.: Point connect: intention-based device pairing for mobile phone users. In: MobiSys (2009)
19. Priyantha, N.B., Chakraborty, A., Balakrishnan, H.: The cricket location-support system. In: MobiCom (2000)

LaP: Landmark-Aided PDR on Smartphones for Indoor Mobile Positioning

Xi Wang[1], Mingxing Jiang[2], Zhongwen Guo[1(✉)], Naijun Hu[3],
Zhongwei Sun[1], and Jing Liu[1]

[1] Department of Computer Science and Technology, Ocean University of China,
Qingdao 266100, Shandong, China
`guozhw@ouc.edu.cn`
[2] Department of Computer Foundation, Ocean University of China,
Qingdao 266100, Shandong, China
`jiangmx@ouc.edu.cn`
[3] Qingdao Administration Bureau for Industry and Commerce,
Qingdao 266071, Shandong, China

Abstract. Location based service (LBS) becomes increasingly popular in indoor environments recently. Among these indoor positioning
techniques providing LBS, a fusion approach combining WiFi-based and
pedestrian dead reckoning (PDR) techniques is drawing more and more
attention of researchers. Although this fusion method performs well in
some cases, it still has some limiting problems. In this work, we study
map information of a given indoor environment, analyze variations of
WiFi received signal strength (RSS), define several kinds of indoor landmarks, and then utilize these landmarks to correct accumulated errors
derived from PDR. This fusion scheme, called Landmark-aided PDR
(LaP), is proved to be light-weighted and suitable for real-time implementation by running an Android app designed for experiment. A comparison has been made between LaP and PDR. Experimental results
show that the proposed scheme can achieve a significant improvement
with an average accuracy of 1.68 m.

Keywords: Indoor positioning · PDR · Landmarks · Fusion

1 Introduction

Recently the location based service (LBS) is becoming increasingly popular, in
indoor environments, because massive wireless networks are built according to
the IEEE 802.11 wireless Ethernet standard. Indoor mobile positioning techniques are the backbone of LBS. These techniques can be generally divided into
two categories according to the nature of measurements: (1) pedestrian dead
reckoning (PDR) based on inertial sensors such as accelerometers, gyroscopes,
etc. [1]; (2) received signal strength (RSS) of WiFi as a metric for location determination [2].

© Springer International Publishing Switzerland 2016
Y. Wang et al. (Eds.): BigCom 2016, LNCS 9784, pp. 123–134, 2016.
DOI: 10.1007/978-3-319-42553-5_11

PDR is a self-contained approach but will produce a growing drift as walking distance increases [14]. It relies on readings of inertial sensors embedded in smartphones to detect steps, calculate step length and determine walking direction. RSS-based positioning mainly includes model-based approach and fingerprinting method. Because of background interference, non-uniform spreading, signal fading and reflections in WiFi signal propagation [15], accurate path-loss model is hard to obtain, thus leading to an inevitable distinct error. Fingerprinting method has a higher accuracy, but requires tedious manual collection of data for training before positioning. In short, these RSS-based approaches are not suitable to implement on smartphones, either because of their low accuracy, or because of complicated preprocessing. Recent research tends to combine both PDR and RSS-based techniques to achieve a better performance [9–11]. Indoor map information is also taken into consideration among some of these studies [16,19].

Through observations, we find human behaviors, like turning, going upstairs or downstairs, can be easily recognized by reading value variations of inertial sensors on smartphones, such as gyroscope, altimeter sensor, and accelerometer, *etc.* In addition, we also notice that obvious fluctuation of WiFi RSS will take place when pedestrians pass by doors, or across projection points of WiFi Access Points (AP) in their walking paths. Such locations of turns, doors, and AP projection points can be obtained when map information is available, and they can be used to determine locations of the pedestrians. These locations are regarded as landmarks, which are considered as new initial points of a PDR algorithm to eliminate system cumulative errors. In this paper, we study the map information, analyze variations of WiFi RSS, redefine the conventional term landmark, and then propose an efficient, feasible fusion scheme for combining landmarks and PDR on smartphones, called Landmark-aided PDR (LaP). A comparison has been made between LaP and PDR. Experimental results show the proposed scheme can improve overall performance significantly with an average accuracy of 1.68 m.

The rest of the paper is organized as follows: some related works in the literature are introduced in Sect. 2. In Sect. 3, we present a conventional PDR and methods of identifying landmarks, as well as the fusion scheme. Section 4 is an evaluation and discussion of the experimental results. We make a conclusion of the paper and reveal some potential future works in Sect. 5.

2   Related Works

A conventional PDR mainly contains three parts: step detection, step length estimation and walking direction estimation. For step detection, there is a common method called peak detection [3,4], which can be used to analyze acceleration signals. The authors in [5] gave a dynamic step length estimation method based on proportional relationship between hip bounce and step length. An experimental equation representing a relation between step length and average acceleration during a step was proposed in [3]. For the walking direction estimation, some of the recent researches focus on combining gyroscope with other inertial sensors such as geomagnetic sensor [6–8].

There are accumulated errors in PDR due to the drift of inertial sensors. To integrate PDR with other positioning methods is a better solution to achieve high positioning accuracy. Recent research tends to fuse RSS-based localization technique and PDR together to navigate the pedestrian in indoor environments [9–11]. Most of the existing fusion methods adopt the Kalman filter or particle filter.

Floor plan is also of valuable reference in indoor mobile positioning and can be combined with PDR. *Lan et al.* transformed the floor plan into a link model, based on which a trajectory-based map matching algorithm was proposed in [12]. *Davidson et al.* put the focus on the influences of walls and obstacles, and proposed a particle filter-based fusion approach in [13].

3   Methodology

All localization techniques have their own strengths and drawbacks, including the PDR approach: providing high accuracy within a short range but leading to an inevitable drift during a pedestrian walk. In this section, we will give an introduction of conventional PDR algorithm, redefine the term 'landmarks', and then correct the drift error with these landmarks. The flow chart of the proposed LaP is shown in Fig. 1.

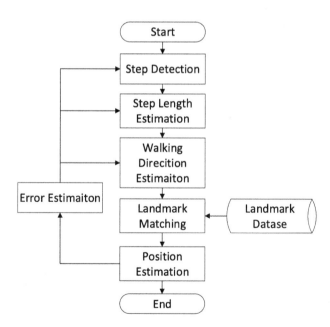

Fig. 1. Flow chart of LaP

3.1   Pedestrian Dead Reckoning

PDR is a pedestrian positioning solution which determines the next position of a pedestrian by adding travelled distance to the previous position, as Eq. (1) shows:

$$P_t = P_{t-1} + D_t \begin{pmatrix} \sin(\varphi_t) \\ \cos(\varphi_t) \end{pmatrix} \qquad (1)$$

Where P_t is the position at time stamp t, D_t is the step length and φ_t is the walking direction at time stamp t.

Current off-the-shelf inertial sensors, such as accelerometers, magnetometers and gyroscopes, become more trustworthy and are widely embedded in smartphones, so a PDR system can be implemented on these intelligent terminals more reliably. A classic PDR mainly contains three parts: step detection, step length estimation and walking direction estimation.

Step Detection. When the pedestrian walks horizontally, periodical variations can be detected from accelerometer readings, as shown in Fig. 2. It appears to be an approximate sinusoidal curve. By performing peak detection with a given threshold, pedestrian steps can be recognized in real time [3].

Step Length Estimation. There are two ways to estimate step length: one is to set a fixed step length during walking process according to the characteristic of pedestrian's body; the other is to establish a dynamic calculation formula of step length based on humans walking features. The former is easier to be implemented but has a larger error while the latter is more complicated with a higher accuracy. The widely used dynamic approaches are listed as follows, Scarlet approach is adopted and k is set to 0.81 in our paper, according to the experimental results in [17].

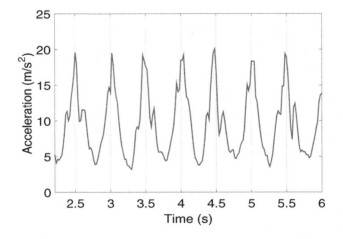

Fig. 2. Recordings from accelerometer during pedestrian walk

(1) Weinberg approach, the authors found that hip displacement in the vertical direction was proportional with step length to some degree [5]. Step length can be calculated as Eq. (2) illustrates:

$$L_{winberg} = k * \sqrt[4]{a_{max} - a_{min}} \tag{2}$$

where, a_{max} and a_{min} are the maximum and minimum value of the acceleration in vertical direction during a step, k is a constant.

(2) Kim approach, proposed an experimental equation as which was representing a relation between step length and average acceleration which occurred during a step [3]. The step length is calculated as Eq. (3):

$$L_{kim} = k * \sqrt[3]{\frac{\sum_{i=1}^{N} |a_i|}{N}} \tag{3}$$

where, N represents the number of acceleration sampling points during a step, a_i is the acceleration in one sampling process, k is a constant.

(3) Scarlet approach, improved the Weinberg approach, solved the variation problem deriving from different pedestrians or different paces and stride lengths of a same pedestrian [18]. The step length is calculated as Eq. (4):

$$L_{Scarlet} = k * \frac{\frac{\sum_{i=1}^{N} |a_i|}{N} - a_{min}}{a_{max} - a_{min}} \tag{4}$$

where, N, a_i represent the same as in Eq. (3), a_{max} and a_{min} have the same meaning of these in Eq. (2), k is a constant.

Walking Direction Estimation. Gyroscope is the most frequently used inertial sensor in identifying walking direction, because it can precisely measure the angular velocity of a moving object and is independent of interference from surroundings. By integrating gyroscope data, the turning angle Φ during a step can be obtained as Eq. (5):

$$\Phi = \sum_{i=1}^{N} \omega_i t \tag{5}$$

where, N represents the number of sampling points during a step, ω_i is the angle velocity in one sampling, t is the sampling interval.

By adding the turning angle at each step to the previous walking direction, new direction is determined. But due to an inherent drift error of gyroscope, accuracy of walking direction will decay if this error is not eliminated.

3.2 Definition and Identification of Landmarks

In this paper, we make the following assumptions about indoor environment:

① APs are placed inside the rooms or above the corridors, and the WiFi signal can cover the pedestrian area.

② Angles of indoor corners are all right angles; between every two adjacent corners is a straight path.

On the basis of above assumptions, certain location, such as building entrance, is picked as the origin to build a coordinate frame. Some other special locations with definite position information are defined as 'landmarks' which can be used to calibrate PDR positioning. Detailed definitions and identification procedures of theses landmarks are described as follows:

AP Within Visual Range. APs have been widely deployed in the indoor environments. Theoretically the distance between pedestrian and AP can be estimated by RSS measurement on the premise that accurate wireless signal transmission model is established. Indoor environment is much complex, the existence of reflection, refraction, scattering and a variety of segmentation loss make it difficult to realize accurate RSS measurement. But when a pedestrian is approaching an AP within visual range, the variation of RSS readings become relatively stable.

Suppose that a pedestrian is walking along a path under the visual range of an AP, RSS readings will present an obvious trend with a peak. For the RSS peak detection, we use a moving average filter to eliminate the indoor noise. The original RSS readings are smoothed with Eq. (6):

$$y_k' = \frac{1}{m} \sum_{i=0}^{m-1} y_{k+i} \qquad k = 1, 2, 3... \tag{6}$$

where y is the original reading, y' is the result after filtering, m is the filtering step.

Obtained from a smartphone when we walk past an AP above the corridor, all RSS readings are drawn in form of a curve in Fig. 3. According to this phenomenon, we can take the projection point of the AP on pedestrians walking path as a landmark.

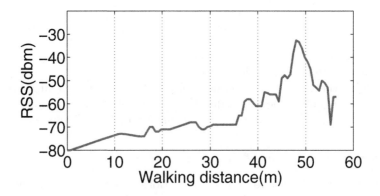

Fig. 3. RSS variations when passing by an AP (The AP is at 48)

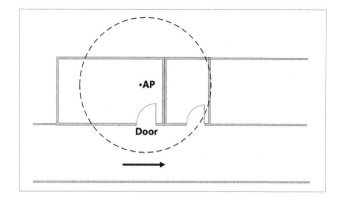

Fig. 4. Door with an AP inside

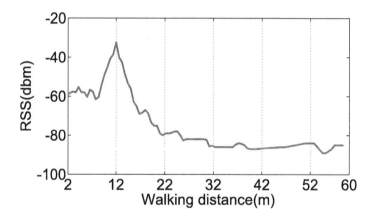

Fig. 5. RSS variations when passing by a door (The door is at 12)

Door with an AP Inside. As Fig. 4 shows, when a pedestrian walks past a door with an AP inside, measured RSS also presents an obvious trend with a peak because the shadowing effects caused by doors and walls are different. We carried out an experiment to collect RSS readings when passing by a door, the RSS curve is shown in Fig. 5. So a door with an AP inside can also be regarded as a kind of landmark.

Indoor Corner. Indoor corners contain explicit position and direction information, and can be regarded as another kind of landmark. To identify the corner on floor plan, the first step is to recognize turning actions of pedestrians. Considering that gyroscope can only provide relative directions, we use a slide window and a threshold to determine whether a turn is made.

When a turning action is recognized, the following step is corner matching. In this step, we compare the current position estimated by PDR to all corner positions in landmark database. If the deviation is under a certain threshold, we consider it as a successful matching.

3.3   Combination of Landmarks and PDR

After constructing a landmark database, we can make combination of landmarks and PDR for indoor positioning. The combination includes two parts: position calibration and error correction. When a pedestrian passes by a landmark, the position calibration of PDR can be made; when a pedestrian walks past two adjacent landmarks, the error correction of PDR is capable of being implemented.

Position Calibration. Position calibration procedure varies with landmarks, the details are as follows:

(1) When a pedestrian walks past an AP or door kind of landmark L, the position of L is P_L, the position derived from PDR is P', the position to update is P. If match succeeds, then $P = P_L$.

(2) When a pedestrian walks past a corner kind of landmark L, the position of L is P_L, the position derived from PDR is P', the position to update is P, then $P = P_L$. Besides, L contains direction information Φ', the direction to update is Φ, then $\Phi = \Phi'$.

Error Correction. When a pedestrian walks past two adjacent landmarks L_1, L_2, with positions marked as P_1, P_2, D' is the distance between the two landmarks, and D is the walking distance calculated by PDR, suppose the system error of PDR is E_{PDR}, then

$$E_{PDR} = \frac{D' - D}{D} \qquad (7)$$

Once obtaining the PDR system error, we can apply it to the coming positioning process to revise position estimation in real time. The equation we use is as follows:

$$P_t = P_{t-1} + D_t \begin{pmatrix} \sin(\varphi_t) \\ \cos(\varphi_t) \end{pmatrix} * (1 - E_{PDR}) \qquad (8)$$

4   Evaluation

In this section, real experiments are conducted to evaluate the performance of LaP. Experiment results are illustrated and analyzed, a comparison is made between PDR and LaP.

4.1   Experiment Setup

We develop an Android app to collect location data during the experiments and then analyze the data with MATLAB. The device involved in the experiments is a Hongmi 2 running the Android 4.4 operating system. The experiments are performed on the third floor in college of information science and engineering of our university, the flat size of the building is about 66 m by 80 m. Figure 6 shows the floor plan of the third floor. During the experiments, a pedestrian is supposed to walk along a pre-decided trajectory with the smartphone in hand. Treating the floorboard as a reference, we record the pedestrian's real position.

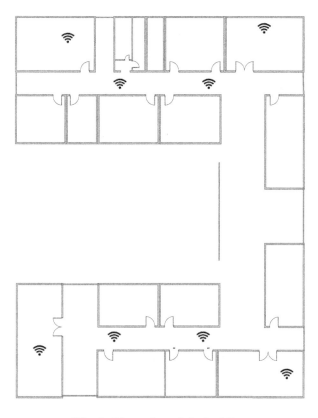

Fig. 6. Floor plan of the building

4.2   Experimental Results and Discussions

Figure 7 shows the true path, comparing with the trajectories of PDR only and LaP from one experiment. As the experiment goes on, PDR produces a large accumulated error on both distance and direction. In the first straight path, the trajectory of PDR only is obvious longer than the true path. Moreover, there is a great angle drift in clock-wise direction of PDR only. On the contrary, the trajectory of LaP is closer to the true path. When a pedestrian passes by landmarks, accumulated errors of the accelerometer and the gyroscope can be well corrected.

A comparison of positioning accuracy is demonstrated in Figs. 8 and 9. The mean localization error of PDR only and LaP is 4.92 m and 1.68 m respectively. LaP reduces the localization errors by 65.9 % compared with PDR only approach. The experimental results show that LaP effectively improves the localization accuracy.

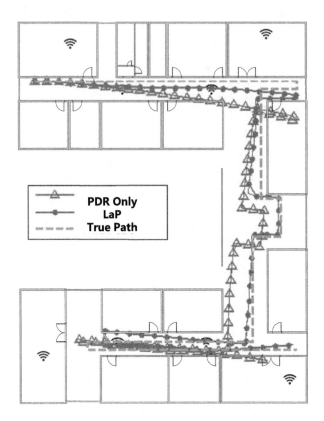

Fig. 7. The true path, the trajectories of PDR and LaP

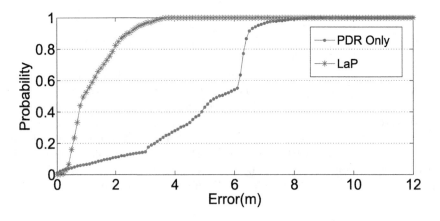

Fig. 8. Localization error CDF

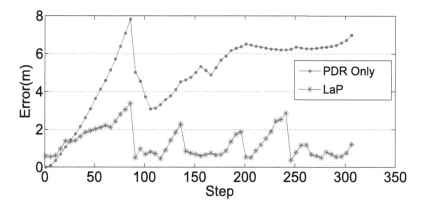

Fig. 9. Location error of each step

5   Conclusion

In this work, we have proposed a novel approach, LaP, for indoor positioning. LaP explores some special locations of indoor environments, which can be recognized by observing value variations of inertial sensors on smartphones. These special locations, called landmarks, are exploited to correct system cumulative errors. Finally, we develop an Android app for real experiments in a designate testbed to compare LaP with a PDR only approach. Experiment results show LaP effectively improved localization accuracy. Furthermore, LaP is a light-weighted approach that can be easily implemented in real time on smartphones.

In future works, we will focus on identifying more kinds of landmarks in indoor environment, such as stairs, elevators and so on, to support a better correction of PDR errors. Besides, we also find performance of PDR shows a distinct difference between different placements to smartphones during a pedestrian walk, motivating us to utilize this potential indicator for further improvement.

Acknowledgments. This work was supported by the National Natural Science Foundation of China (NSFC) under Grant Nos. 61572448, 61170258, 61379127, 61103196, 61379128, and by the Shandong Provincial Natural Science Foundation, China under Grant No. ZR2014JL043. Xi Wang and Mingxing Jiang contributed equally to this work and should be regarded as co-first authors. The corresponding author is Zhongwen Guo.

References

1. Harle, R.: A survey of indoor inertial positioning systems for pedestrians. IEEE Commun. Surv. Tutor. **15**(3), 1281–1293 (2013)
2. Gu, Y., Lo, A., Niemegeers, I.: A survey of indoor positioning systems for wireless personal networks. IEEE Commun. Surv. Tutor. **11**(1), 13–32 (2009)

3. Kim, J.W., Jang, H.J., Hwang, D.H., et al.: A step, stride and heading determination for the pedestrian navigation system. Positioning **3**(1&2), 273–279 (2004)
4. Godha, S., Lachapelle, G.: Foot mounted inertial system for pedestrian navigation. Meas. Sci. Technol. **19**(7), 697–703 (2008)
5. Weinberg, H.: Using the ADXL202 in pedometer and personal navigation applications. In: Analog Devices AN-602 application note, vol. 2, no.2, pp. 1–6 (2002)
6. Kang, W., Nam, S., Han, Y., Lee, S.: Improved heading estimation for smartphone-based indoor positioning systems. In: 2012 IEEE 23rd International Symposium Personal Indoor and Mobile Radio Communications (PIMRC), pp. 2449–2453. IEEE (2012)
7. Afzal, M.H., Renaudin, V., Lachapelle, G.: Magnetic field based heading estimation for pedestrian navigation environments. In: 2011 International Conference Indoor Positioning and Indoor Navigation (IPIN), pp. 1–10. IEEE (2011)
8. Chen, W., Chen, R., Chen, Y., Kuusniemi, H., Wang, J.: An effective pedestrian dead reckoning algorithm using a unified heading error model. In: 2010 IEEE/ION Position Location and Navigation Symposium (PLANS), pp. 340–347. IEEE (2010)
9. Li, W.W.L., Iltis, R.A., Win, M.Z.: A smartphone localization algorithm using RSSI and inertial sensor measurement fusion. In: 2013 IEEE Global Communications Conference (GLOBECOM), pp. 3335–3340. IEEE (2013)
10. Malyavej, V., Kumkeaw, W., Aorpimai, M.: Indoor robot localization by RSSI/IMU sensor fusion. In: 2013 10th International Conference Electrical Engineering/Electronics, Computer, Telecommunications and Information Technology (ECTI-CON), pp. 1–6. IEEE (2013)
11. Radu, V., Marina, M.K.: HiMLoc: indoor smartphone localization via activity aware pedestrian dead reckoning with selective crowdsourced wifi fingerprinting. In: 2013 International Conference Indoor Positioning and Indoor Navigation (IPIN), pp. 1–10. IEEE (2013)
12. Lan, K.C., Shih, W.Y.: Using smart-phones and floor plans for indoor location tracking-withdrawn. IEEE Trans. Hum. Mach. Syst. **44**(2), 211–221 (2014)
13. Davidson, P., Collin, J., Takala, J.: Application of particle filters for indoor positioning using floor plans. In: Ubiquitous Positioning Indoor Navigation and Location Based Service (UPINLBS), pp. 1–4. IEEE (2010)
14. Chen, Z., Zou, H., Jiang, H., et al.: Fusion of WiFi, smartphone sensors and landmarks using the Kalman filter for indoor localization. Sensors **15**(1), 715–732 (2015)
15. Chintalapudi, K., Padmanabha Iyer, A., Padmanabhan, V.N.: Indoor localization without the pain. In: Proceedings of the Sixteenth Annual International Conference on Mobile Computing and Networking, pp. 173–184. ACM (2010)
16. Leppäkoski, H., Collin, J., Takala, J.: Pedestrian navigation based on inertial sensors, indoor map, and WLAN signals. J. Sig. Process. Syst. **71**(3), 287–296 (2013)
17. Pratama, A.R., Hidayat, R.: Smartphone-based pedestrian dead reckoning as an indoor positioning system. In: 2012 International Conference on System Engineering and Technology (ICSET), pp. 1–6. IEEE (2012)
18. Scarlett, J.: Enhancing the performance of pedometers using a single accelerometer. In: Application Note, Analog Devices (2007)
19. Hong, F., Zhang, Y., Zhang, Z., Wei, M., Feng, Y., Guo, Z.: WaP: indoor localization and tracking using WiFi-assisted particle filter. In: 2014 IEEE 39th Conference on Local Computer Networks (LCN), pp. 210–217. IEEE (2014)

WhozDriving: Abnormal Driving Trajectory Detection by Studying Multi-faceted Driving Behavior Features

Meng He[1], Bin Guo[1(✉)], Huihui Chen[1], Alvin Chin[2], Jilei Tian[2], and Zhiwen Yu[1]

[1] Northwestern Polytechnical University, Xi'an, Shaanxi, China
{guob,zhiwenyu}@nwpu.edu.cn
[2] BMW Technology Corporation, BMW Group,
100 N Riverside Plaza, Suite 1900, Chicago, IL, USA

Abstract. Vehicles have become essential tools of transport, offering a great opportunity to exploit the relationship between people and the car. This paper aims to solve an interesting problem, recognizing who the person is through their driving behaviors. Driver identification is useful for quite a few situations, such as car usage authentication, context-based recommendation, and determination of auto-insurance compensation. In this work, we propose WhozDriving, an approach that analyzes drivers' driving behavior data and extract some sudden changes of driver behaviors as features which can be applied to distinguish different drivers. We propose a supervised learning method to detect anomaly driving trajectory from driving data. Experimental results on driving datasets show that our proposed approach is effective in terms of anomaly detection rate and misclassification anomaly rate.

Keywords: Driver identification · Anomaly detection · GPS trajectory · Driver behavior patterns · KNN

1 Introduction

In recent years, several anomaly detection studies have been carried out in different fields, e.g. intrusion detection, fraud detection, medical and health detection, text data anomaly detection and sensor network detection. The anomaly detection is intended to recognize patterns in data which do not match expected or normal behavior [1]. The anomaly in the data can be significant and crucial in different occasions. While different occasions have to consider different anomaly detection techniques since the definition of anomaly and the data feature are not the same. In this paper, we concentrate on anomaly detection of driving trajectory data.

For automobile insurers, telematics represents a growing and valuable way to quantify driver risk. Instead of pricing decisions on vehicle and driver characteristics, telematics gives the opportunity to measure the quantity and quality of a driver's behavior. Although there are some studies on human behavior, which define anomaly as significant changes in the activity level of a user not expected according to his usual activity level [2, 3], the experimental environment is indoor and the experimental subject

© Springer International Publishing Switzerland 2016
Y. Wang et al. (Eds.): BigCom 2016, LNCS 9784, pp. 135–144, 2016.
DOI: 10.1007/978-3-319-42553-5_12

is the single human without interacting with the physical world. In other words, these works only focus on human behavior changes in a given space. Particularly, detecting abnormal trajectories is very important since some automobile insurances are restricted to a specific driver. When a driver has an accident on the road, but applying for insurance claims is later than the accident, how to ensure that the accident driver is the applicant? So the definition of abnormal driving trajectory is an unmatched driver driving in an applicant's vehicle. What's more, the driving behavior is indirectly characterized by the movement trajectories of vehicles.

Therefore, we propose WhozDriving, an anomaly detection method based on supervised machine learning to facilitate this problem. WhozDriving tries to select optimal feature combination from original data to profile the driver and then uses a supervised learning method to recognize anomaly driving trajectory in a probabilistic sense. And we can correctly detect 90.5 % of abnormal driving trajectories from driver's trajectory data.

The remainder of this paper is structured as follows. We first review related work in Sect. 2, then formally define the problem in Sect. 3. We explain the detailed design of WhozDriving in Sect. 4, followed by experimental results in Sect. 5. Finally, we con-clude our work in Sect. 6 and discuss possible avenues for future work.

2 Related Work

We briefly review related work, which can be divided into the following three areas.

The first area is research on analyzing human behavior by ambient sensors or wearable sensors [4]. Several works have studied human behaviors in smart homes with different sensors embedded in the environment [5], such as RFID (radio-frequency identification) sensors placed on furniture [6], electricity usage detectors [7], cameras [8], and motion sensors [9] which can be used to measure human behavior and to detect anomaly in a smart home environment. In this work, vehicle driving coordinates are used to assess human behavior when driving in a vehicle. We can regard vehicle and sensor in the vehicle as our monitoring sensors.

The second one includes research into driving behavior. A smartphone –based model was used to detect aggressive reactions in senior drivers [10]. Driver performance was classified to improve safety [11]. Even only data provided by vehicle trackers was applied to classify driver behavior [12]. In the example above, each driving trajectory belongs to a specific driver by default. Nevertheless, there have always been some abnormal driving trajectories in the driver trajectory dataset. In this paper, we use driving data to detect abnormal driving trajectory.

The third one focuses on anomaly detection techniques, which vary with different application and data [1]. The anomaly detection techniques are mainly based on classification [13], clustering, [14] nearest neighbor [15] or statistics [16]. In this paper, we choose a supervised learning method in consideration of semi-labeled data for anomaly detection.

3 Problem Statement

In this section, we formulate the abnormal driving trajectory detection problem and show the key challenges in this work.

Set $D = \{d_1, d_2, d_3, \ldots, d_n\}$ denote n drivers, $A_i = \{a_{i,1}, a_{i,2}, a_{i,3} \ldots, a_{i,m}\}$ denote m driving trajectories of driver d_i. There are r abnormal driving trajectories in A_i which do not belong to d_i. Each trajectory $a_{i,j}$ is composed of driver d_i's 2D position coordinates (in meters) at every second, and the start point of every trajectory is $(0, 0)$ and $a_{i,j} = \{(x_{i,j,0}, y_{i,j,0}), (x_{i,j,1}, y_{i,j,1}), (x_{i,j,2}, y_{i,j,2}), \ldots, (x_{i,j,z}, y_{i,j,z})\}$. The abnormal trajectory detection problem is defined as follows.

Problem: Given one driver's trajectory data A_i with r abnormal trajectories, how can we recognize the r abnormal driving trajectories in A_i?

To address this problem, the key challenges are listed as follows:

- How to form an aggregate profile that potentially makes each driver unique?
- How to evaluate different features and extract an optimal combination of these features?
- How to know the detection result is close to the ground truth?

4   Detailed Design of WhozDriving

In this section, we describe the method for processing original data from the raw position coordinates and selecting the optimal feature combination, then we introduce our approach of detecting abnormal driving trajectories.

4.1   The Framework of WhozDriving

As a driving trajectory is too simple to profile a unique driver, the data processing module mainly calculates raw features from rotated position coordinates. The feature selecting part tries to extract the most valuable features from a mess of immature features. After all the preparations are completed, we utilize the KNN algorithm to identify the intentionally inserted abnormal driving trajectories. According to the analysis, a model is presented as shown in Fig. 1.

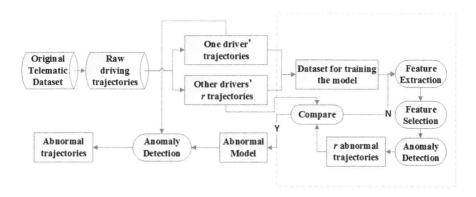

Fig. 1. The framework of WhozDriving

4.2   Feature Extraction

When a driver drives his vehicle on the road, he usually brakes due to traffic light or accelerates because of overtaking another vehicle. During the velocity changes, drivers' driving reaction may differ by their driving habits, particularly sudden velocity change. Thus we first calculate the velocity and acceleration using the following formulations, then divide the trajectory into many segments by the starting point of acceleration or deceleration.

Given a driver d_i's trajectory $a_{i,j}$, the velocity denoted by $v_{i,j,t}$ and the acceleration denoted by $a_{i,j,t}$ at time point t are calculated by Eqs. (1) and (2) respectively. Units of them are m/s and m/s^2 respectively and $v_{i,j,0} = 0$, $a_{i,j,0} = 0$.

$$v_{i,j,t} = \sqrt{\left(x_{i,j,t} - x_{i,j,t-1}\right)^2 + \left(y_{i,j,t} - y_{i,j,t-1}\right)^2} \tag{1}$$

$$a_{i,j,t} = v_{i,j,t} - v_{i,j,t-1} \tag{2}$$

Where t denotes time and $t > 0$.

As we are mainly concerned about the sudden change of velocity, we select those segments that continue one or two seconds in the same state of acceleration or deceleration. Now we have four different types of trajectory segment, they are one-second-acceleration, one-second-deceleration, two-second-acceleration and two–second-deceleration. Then we can calculate the statistic of characteristics of velocity and acceleration for every segment.

For each two-second-acceleration segment, the average value of velocity is calculated by $M(v_{i,j,t}) = (v_{i,j,t} + v_{i,j,t+1})/2$. Maximum of velocity is $Max(v_{i,j,t})$ minimum of velocity is $Min(v_{i,j,t})$, the average value of acceleration is calculated by $M(a_{i,j,t}) = (a_{i,j,t} + a_{i,j,t+1})/2$, variant of acceleration is $V(a_{i,j,t}) = ((a_{i,j,t} - M(a_{i,j,t}))^2 + (a_{i,j,t+1} - M(a_{i,j,t}))^2)/2$, maximum of acceleration is $Max(a_{i,j,t})$, and minimum of acceleration is $Min(a_{i,j,t})$. For each type segment, we compute the mathematical expectation and variance of previous seven statistics once again. Finally, we get 56 features. For the two-second- acceleration type segments, the features are shown in Table 1. The other three type segments are similar to this table.

Table 1. Raw features of two-second-acceleration segment

Category	$M(v_{i,j})$	$Max(v_{i,j})$	$Min(v_{i,j})$	$M(a_{i,j})$	$V(a_{i,j})$	$Max(a_{i,j})$	$Min(a_{i,j})$
Average	F_1	F_2	F_3	F_4	F_5	F_6	F_7
Variant	F_8	F_9	F_{10}	F_{11}	F_{12}	F_{13}	F_{14}

4.3   Feature Selection

The CfsSubsetEval[1] feature selection method evaluates the worth of a subset of attributes by considering the individual predictive ability of each feature along with the

---

[1] http://weka.sourceforge.net/doc.stable/weka/attributeSelection/CfsSubsetEval.html.

degree of redundancy between them. Subsets of features that are highly correlated with the class while having low intercorrelation are preferred. So we can use the CfsSubsetEval algorithm with the BestFirst search method in Weka to select the optimal features from a mess of features.

4.4 Algorithm Design

We propose an anomaly detection algorithm which includes two stages. In Phase 1, we use the CfsSubsetEval attribute selection algorithm to extract the optimal combination of features to profile drivers in a specific training set. After that, in Phase 2, we adopt the KNN algorithm to train the classifier from the training set.

KNN is the most elementary and most classic classification algorithm, and the basic idea is: if most of k neighborhoods of a data object o belongs to one class, then the data object o also belongs to the same class. Firstly, KNN utilizes labeled training to build the classifier. Then we randomly select some trajectories from driver d_m, put them into the trajectory set of driver d_n, change the selected trajectories' label to d_n, then get the test set of driver trajectories. If we can use the trained classifier to identify original trajectories of driver d_m from the new dataset, the algorithm would be useful to detect abnormal driver trajectories from a specific driver's trajectory set A_i.

The algorithm designed in this work is used for anomaly detection for driving trajectories. As the driving data is dynamic, it is necessary to update the detection model for different drivers to ensure its efficiency.

5 Experiments

5.1 The Dataset

AXA[2] provided a dataset of 547,200 driving trajectories of 2,736 anonymized drivers. Every driver has 200 driver trajectories. The trajectory is composed of the car's position coordinates (in meters) at every second. In order to protect the privacy of the drivers' location, the start point of every trajectory is the origin (0, 0), and all trajectories are randomly rotated, and short lengths of trajectory data were removed from the start/end of the trajectory. What's more, a small and random number of false trajectories (trajectories that were not driven by the driver of interest) are planted in each driver's trajectory (Fig. 2).

As mentioned in Sect. 4, in order to detect anomaly trajectories, we randomly insert other driver's trajectories to one driver's raw trajectories. The dataset for training the detection model is created by the following method. Given a driver d_m, we randomly insert r abnormal trajectories from other drivers. The sample data is selected from two drivers' trajectories (d_m and d_n) and different combinations of drivers need to randomly build different anomaly detection model. The original trajectories from driver d_m are assigned label d_m, the same as trajectories from driver d_n. We choose 10 % of two

---

[2] https://www.kaggle.com/c/axa-driver-telematics-analysis.

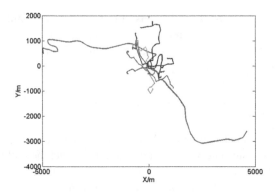

Fig. 2. Some trajectories of driver d_l

drives' randomly selected 400 trajectories as the test set. The test set includes p trajectories randomly selected from driver d_m and changed label from d_m to d_n which are regarded as abnormal trajectories for driver d_n. The remaining q trajectories in the test set are directly selected from driver d_n. p plus q is 40. The other 90 % of two drivers' trajectories constitute the training set. Thus, the number of abnormal trajectories is dynamic. It can help us to validate if our algorithm can adapt to different realistic data. The training data and test data are as shown in Table 2.

Table 2. Allocation situation of experiment data

Data	All	Driver d_m	Driver d_n
Training set	360	200-p	200-q
Test set	40	p	q

5.2 Metrics

There are two metrics used in our abnormal detection algorithm: detection rate (DR) and false alarm rate (FR). The algorithm with higher DR and lower FR are considered to be better. The confusion matrix is shown in Table 3, and the DR and FR and are used to evaluate our algorithm.

$$DR = \frac{TN}{FP + TN} \tag{3}$$

$$FR = \frac{FN}{FN + TN} \tag{4}$$

Table 3. Confusion matrix

Category	Classified as d_n	Classified as d_m
Driver d_n	TP	FN
Driver d_m (abnormal)	FP	TN

5.3   Experimental Results

We have implemented all the experiments in Python and Java, and have compared our algorithm with other anomaly detection approaches, including naive Bayes, Bayes Net, J48 and random forest.

After the data processing, we get 56 features. Then we use the CfsSubsetEval attribute selection algorithm to extract the optimal combination of features to profile drivers in a specific training set and we get 17 features in this experiment.

Secondly, we analyze the DR and FR of our algorithm in different experiment data to choose the optimal parameter for our approach and explain the relationship between FR (DR) and data distribution; and lastly we compare our algorithm with other algorithm by examining the DR and FR.

In the first stage, the CfsSubsetEval algorithm is adopted to extract appropriate features from the original unshaped features set. The 17 filtered features are highly correlated with the class while having low intercorrelation.

Parameter Selection. In the second stage, after we have synthesized all the experimental results, we finally adopt the KNN algorithm to solve this anomaly detection problem. The comparison between our algorithm and others is presented in the last stage. Different value for parameter K can contribute to different performance of the KNN algorithm. The detection results for DR and FR using different value for parameter K are respectively shown in Fig. 3.

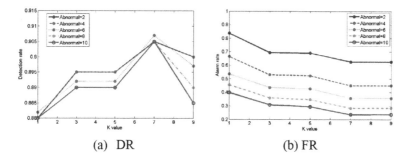

(a) DR   (b) FR

Fig. 3. Detection results for DR and FR using different value of K.

From the results of Fig. 3, we can see that KNN for K = 7 has the best performance with the highest DR and relatively low FR. When the parameter K is set as 7, the distribution of test data is still dynamic with the different abnormal trajectory number. So we display the relationship between DR (FR) and abnormal trajectory number in Fig. 4.

From the results of Fig. 4, we can find that abnormal trajectory number has almost no impact on DR, while the FR decreases with the abnormal trajectory number. We can easily comprehend these results. On the one hand, our algorithm is robust to different test data for the stable DR. On the other hand, when the abnormal trajectory number increases, the test set tends to be more balanced, which are fit for the KNN algorithm and we can find that FR gets lower and lower.

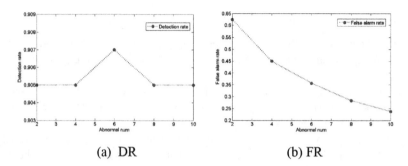

(a) DR   (b) FR

Fig. 4. Detection results of different abnormal number

Algorithm Comparison. In the last stage, we compared our algorithm with other anomaly detection methods by DR and FR, and the result is shown in Fig. 5.

The result which is depicted in Fig. 5 shows that KNN performs better than other algorithms, with the highest DR and lowest FR. In conclusion, our algorithm's detection rate (DR) is up to 90.5 %, and the false alarm rate (FR) is least down to 28.4 %. Our algorithm is also robust to different number of abnormal trajectories for the stable DR and the smaller and smaller FR. Therefore, WhozDriving is adequate for handling with dynamic real data.

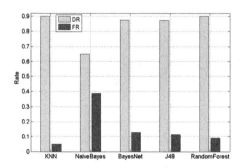

Fig. 5. Detection results of different algorithms

6   Conclusion and Future Work

In this paper, we have focused on the challenging issues of detecting abnormal driving trajectory in driver's history trajectories. We have proposed WhozDriving to solve this problem. Our experiment results indicated that WhozDriving is adequate for anomaly detection.

Although the experimental results suggest that WhozDriving is effective at anomaly detection, the results only based on a specific driving data and the data is poor for only rotated coordinates. Therefore, for future work, we will expand our algorithm to other drivers' more diversified driving trajectories, i.e., OBD (On-Board Diagnostic) data.

Furthermore, based on the detection of abnormal trajectory, we also want to describe the anomaly and even find some patterns. Our work is crucial for automobile insurance and claims settlement that will help drivers and insurance companies.

Acknowledgement. This work was partially supported by the National Basic Research Program of China (No. 2015CB352400), the National Natural Science Foundation of China (No. 61332005, 61373119), the Fundamental Research Funds for the Central Universities (3102015ZY095).

References

1. Chandola, V., Banerjee, A., Kumar, V.: Anomaly detection: a survey. ACM Comput. Surv. (CSUR) **41**(3), 15 (2009)
2. Lühr, S., West, G., Venkatesh, S.: Recognition of emergent human behaviour in a smart home: a data mining approach. Pervasive Mob. Comput. **3**(2), 95–116 (2007)
3. Candás, J.L.C., Peláez, V., López, G., et al.: An automatic data mining method to detect abnormal human behaviour using physical activity measurements. Pervasive Mob. Comput. **15**, 228–241 (2014)
4. Guo, B., Zhang, D., Yu, Z., Liang, Y., Wang, Z., Zhou, X.: From the internet of things to embedded intelligence. World Wide Web J. (WWWJ) **16**(4), 399–420 (2013)
5. Chikhaoui, B., Wang, S., Pigot, H.: ADR-SPLDA: activity discovery and recognition by combining sequential patterns and latent Dirichlet allocation. Pervasive Mob. Comput. **8**(6), 845–862 (2012)
6. Wang, L., Gu, T., Tao, X., Chen, H., Lu, J.: Recognizing multi-user activities using wearable sensors in a smart home. Pervasive Mob. Comput. **7**(3), 287–298 (2011)
7. Chen, C., Cook, D., Crandall, A.: The user side of sustainability: modeling behavior and energy usage in the home. Pervasive Mob. Comput. **9**(1), 161–175 (2013)
8. Khan, W.A., Hussain, M., Afzal, M., Amin, M.B., Lee, S.: Healthcare standards based sensory data exchange for home healthcare monitoring system. In: Engineering in Medicine and Biology Society (EMBC), pp. 1274–1277 (2012)
9. Virone, G.: Assessing everyday life behavioral rhythms for the older generation. Pervasive Mob. Comput. **5**(5), 606–622 (2009)
10. Koh, D.W., Kang, H.B.: Smartphone-based modeling and detection of aggressiveness reactions in senior drivers. In: 2015 IEEE Intelligent Vehicles Symposium (IV), pp. 12–17. IEEE (2015)
11. Jensen, M., Wagner, J., Alexander, K.: Analysis of in-vehicle driver behaviour data for improved safety. Int. J. Veh. Saf. **5**(3), 197–212 (2011)
12. Rigolli, M., Williams, Q., Gooding, M.J., et al.: Driver behavioural classification from trajectory data. In: Proceedings of the 2005 IEEE Intelligent Transportation Systems, pp. 889–894. IEEE (2005)
13. Mascaro, S., Nicholso, A.E., Korb, K.B.: Anomaly detection in vessel tracks using Bayesian networks. Int. J. Approximate Reasoning **55**(1), 84–98 (2014)
14. Muniyandi, A.P., Rajeswari, R., Rajaram, R.: Network anomaly detection by cascading k-means clustering and C4. 5 decision tree algorithm. Procedia Eng. **30**, 174–182 (2012)

15. Amer, M., Goldstein, M.: Nearest-neighbor and clustering based anomaly detection algorithms for rapidminer. In: Proceedings of the 3rd RapidMiner Community Meeting and Conference (RCOMM 2012), pp. 1–12 (2012)
16. Saligrama, V., Chen, Z.: Video anomaly detection based on local statistical aggregates. In: 2012 IEEE Conference on Computer Vision and Pattern Recognition (CVPR), pp. 2112–2119. IEEE (2012)

Trajectory Prediction in Campus Based on Markov Chains

Bonan Wang[✉], Yihong Hu, Guochu Shou, and Zhigang Guo

Beijing Key Laboratory of Network System Architecture and Convergence,
Beijing University of Posts and Telecommunications, Beijing 100876, China
{bnwang,yhhu,gcshou,gzgang}@bupt.edu.cn

Abstract. In this paper, we present a model of predicting the next location of a student in campus based on Markov chains. Since the activity of a student in campus is closely related to the time at which the activity occurs, we consider the notion of time in the prediction algorithm that we coined as Trajectory Prediction Algorithm (TPA). In order to evaluate the efficiency of our prediction model, we use our wireless data analysis system to collect real spatio-temporal trajectory data in campus for more than seven months. Experimental results show that our TPA has increased the accuracy of prediction for over 30 % than the original Markov chain.

Keywords: Wireless data analysis system · Trajectory prediction · Activity regularity · Markov chain

1 Introduction

With the rapid development of radio access technologies, it provides much convenience for us to collect a large number of user location information. An individual carrying the mobile phone unintentionally generates many spatio-temporal trajectories that are represented by a sequence of detection device IDs with corresponding access times [1]. When the individual does not know that his movements are recorded, these trajectory information can reflect the individual's actual activity regularity. Individual trajectory prediction plays a very important role in nowadays such as the traffic planning, urban planning and control of influenza problem.

In this paper, we established a model for predicting the student's trajectory in campus. Since the location-based service is based on the location of its user, predicting the next location of an individual can provide the recommendations of the corresponding surrounding restaurants, supermarkets or gas stations. In traffic planning, predicting activities of track traffic participants can inform possible future traffic conditions, which can further help the implementation of traffic control. In network optimization, predicting the trajectory of an individual can help the SDN controller to prepare the relevant cells before the individual arrives to guarantee seamless handover authentication, and then ensure seamless user experience during mobility [2]. On the basis of Markov process, we consider the notion of the time with student activity regularity, model for the student's trajectories and predict the next location of the

© Springer International Publishing Switzerland 2016
Y. Wang et al. (Eds.): BigCom 2016, LNCS 9784, pp. 145–154, 2016.
DOI: 10.1007/978-3-319-42553-5_13

student. We also calculate the accuracy and the predictability for the prediction of the next location to evaluate our forecast model.

The remainder of this paper is organized as follows. First, we introduce the related work in Sect. 2. Then we describe the trajectory prediction model, the Trajectory Prediction Algorithm (TPA) for the trajectory prediction in campus and the evaluation method of TPA in Sect. 3. Afterwards, we present the experiment analysis and evaluation results with the data of campus students in Sect. 4. Finally, this work is concluded in Sect. 5.

2 Related Work

For individual trajectory prediction, plenty of researchers have paid attention to Markov models. Markov chain represents the mobility behavior of an individual and predicts the next location based on the matrix of transition probability and the current location. For example, Ashbrook and Starner [3] have built a Markov model for predicting user future movements and extracted the Points Of Interest (POIs), which are frequently visited by an individual, before building the Markov model. POIs are extracted using a variant of the k-means clustering algorithm on the individual's mobility trajectories. In [4], a mobility Markov chain was built where they used a clustering algorithm called DJ-cluster to discover the POIs. Since different buildings in campus have their own functions, we extracted a student's POIs on the basis of the student's activity regularity and buildings' function.

A variant of Markov model called the Mixed Markov-chain Model (MMM) [5] has been proposed for predicting pedestrian movement. This approach clusters individuals into groups based on their mobility trajectories and then generates a specific Markov model for each group. This approach was evaluated experimentally on tracking data collected in the field and shows a model that takes into account the unknown factors for improving the accuracy of prediction. In [6], multiple order Markov chains were built to predict vehicle trajectories. The transition probabilities are computed on an individual vehicle's basis. Since different students possesses different activity regularities, a student's transition probabilities are based on the student's historical trajectories in the campus.

The trajectory prediction of mobile nodes is a part of the human mobility research. Trajectory data representing human mobility can help build a better social network and travel recommendation. Spyropoulos et al. [7] propose a model called "Community-based Mobility Model" to well simulate real nodes' movement. In his research, the model consists of two states: "local" state and "roaming" state, where the local state is a Random Direction movement restricted inside local community and the roaming state is a Random Direction movement outside local community. The "Community-based Mobility Model" is represented by using the two-state Markov Chain. Ekman et al. [8] have studied the human daily behavior, where human movement model has been divided into several sub-models in the time dimension. The model intuitively depicted the movement pattern of people. For instance, the model presents the everyday life that people go to work in the morning, spend their day at work, and commute back to their homes at evenings.

Song et al. [9] have compared the prediction accuracy of four major families of location predictors that have been tested on Dartmouth's campus-wide WiFi wireless network. The four major families of location predictors are respectively Markov-based, compression-based, PPM and SPM predictors. They proposed that low-order Markov predictors performed as well or even better than the more complex and more space-consuming compression-based predictors. On the theoretical side, Barabasi et al. [10] have analyzed the predictability of human mobility by studying the mobility patterns of anonymized mobile phone users. Their approach constructs a graph in which each node is associated with the percentage of time spent in the cell. Afterwards, the probability distributions of the three entropy measures are computed in order to characterize the predictability. Finally, a predictability score is computed, which represents the degree of predictability of the user's whereabouts. From the combination of the empirically measured user entropy and the Fano's inequality, the authors conclude that there is a potential 93 % average predictability in the human mobility.

3 Trajectory Prediction in Campus

3.1 Trajectory Prediction Model

An individual's next location can be predicted by using the Markov chain and their previous spatio-temporal trajectories. The spatio-temporal trajectory is a trace generated by a moving individual in geographical spaces, where each point consists of a location and timestamp such as $p = (x, t)$. A Markov chain is a stochastic process with the Markov property, which is widely used in discrete time states prediction. In a Markov chain, the probability of moving to a state (i.e., POI) depends on the current state and the probability matrix of the transitions between states. More precisely, a Markov chain is composed of:

- Each state, such as $x_1, x_2, x_3, \ldots$, corresponds to a POI. These states generally have an intrinsic semantic meaning, therefore semantic labels such as "dormitory" or "laboratory building" can often be attached to them. Since the Markov chain is a sequence of random that satisfies the Markov property, the future state only depends on the current state and is independent of the past states.
- The transition, such as $p_{i,j}$, represents the probability of moving from state x_i to state x_j. A transition from one state to itself can occur if the student has a probability of moving from one state to an occasional location before coming back to this state. For instance, a student can leave his "dormitory" to go shopping outside school before coming back to "dormitory".

A Markov chain can be represented either as graph (see Fig. 1) or a transition probability matrix. In the graph representation, nodes represent POIs while arrows symbolize the transitions between POIs. The transition probability that represents the transition between two states is described in corresponding line. In the matrix representation, the row corresponds to the POI of origin while the column corresponds to the destination POI. The cell stores the probability that represents the transition from origin location to destination.

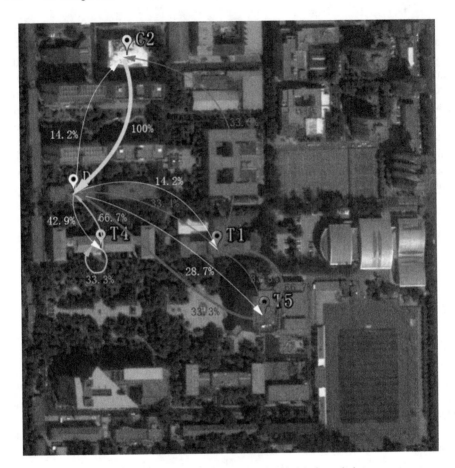

Fig. 1. Trajectory prediction model with Markov chain

The feature of Markov chain is that the probability model is based on the historical data, and forecast is determined only by the current POI. If different times in a same POI share the same prediction result, it may cause a large accuracy bias especially for people whose activity period has effects of their movement patterns, such as students in the campus. To address this issue, we divided the time domain to construct Markov Chain sub-models in our TPA.

3.2   Trajectory Prediction Algorithm

Thereafter, we describe the Trajectory Prediction Algorithm (TPA) for predicting students' next POI, which is decomposed in three steps (Algorithm 1). During the first step, we extract the student's POIs based on his activity regularity in campus. Afterwards, during the second step, we consider students' activity regularity to divide the time domain. Finally, the transition probability matrix of each time domain is computed.

Those four regions that students frequently visit are the dormitories, canteens, teaching building areas and laboratory buildings. Those canteens, teaching building areas, laboratory buildings and the student dormitory that the student has visited in the period regard as the student's POIs in corresponding sub-model. After the POIs are discovered, the transitions and their associated probabilities can be computed. The transitions between those POIs can represent the transition probability matrix.

The daily location transition of a student in campus is closely related to the time at which the transition occurs, because of the special social attribute of student in campus. Students depart from the dormitory to the teaching building area or laboratory on weekdays and they may not go to teaching building or laboratory on vacation. In addition, students have different courses on different days, then they may go to different teaching buildings on different days. At the same time, students have different mobility regularities even on different period of one day. For instance, that a student moves from dormitory to teaching building occurs much more frequently in day than in night. Therefore, taking the movement time into account will have some contributions to the prediction of student next location.

In this paper, we consider six kinds of dates, including Monday, Tuesday, Wednesday, Thursday, Friday, and vacation (including weekends, holidays, winter vacation and summer vacation). At the same time, one day's time is divided into three parts, including [08:00-12:00], [12:00-18:00], and [18:00-24:00]. Once the activity cycle is divided into sub-parts by time dimension and the POIs of every sub-parts are discovered, we separately calculate the transition probability matrixes for the eighteen sub-chains.

Algorithm 1 Construction of TPA

Requires: the student's original training trajectory data
Preprocess the original training trajectory data *TD* by deleting redundant trajectories thus producing *TD'* whose dwell time is greater than zero.
divide *TD'* into eighteen sub-trajectory data *STDs'* based on the time dimension
for each sub-trajectory data *STD'* in *STDs'* **do**
  for each record *R* in *STD'* **do**
    extract the location *L* from the record *R*
    put the *L* into *POIs* Set dataset
  end for
  compute the N-th sub-matrix of transition probability *nTPM* for *STD'*
end for
Return the eighteen sub-chains

The prediction algorithm (Algorithm 2) needs to input the current states (including timestamp and location) and all transition probability matrixes of the student's Trajectory Prediction Model, and then will output the prediction result. For instance, the input could be current timestamp that corresponds to the transition probability matrix such as Table 2 and the current location on T5. The algorithm finds the corresponding row and searches the most probable transition. In our example, as the current location is T5 at corresponding time, the prediction is T1 with a probability of 66.7 %.

Algorithm 2 Prediction using TPA

Require: Current timestamp and location, all transition probability matrixes of the student's TPA.

Transform the timestamp into date and time, then find corresponding transition probability matrix *TPM'*.

Search the row r in *TPM'* corresponding to the current location, let the maximum probability of transition $p_{max} = 0$

for each probability p_{rj} for the row r in *TPM'* **do**

    if the maximum probability of transition p_{max} is less than the p_{rj} **then**

        update p_{max} to p_{rj} and update the prediction location to the column with p_{rj}

    end if

end for

Return the POI corresponding to the column with p_{max}

3.3 Evaluation for TPA

In order to evaluate the efficiency of our prediction method, we compute two metrics: the *accuracy* and the *predictability*. The accuracy A_{cc} is the ratio between the number of correct predictions $p_{correct}$ over the total number of predictions p_{total}.

$$A_{cc} = P_{correct}/P_{total} \qquad (1)$$

The predictability P_{red} is a theoretical measure representing the degree that the mobility of an individual is predictable based on his corresponding Markov chain (in the same spirit as the work of Barabasi and co-authors [10]). For instance, if the predictor knows the student current location T5 with the corresponding sub-model (see Fig. 1), the probability of making a successful guess is theoretically equal to the maximal outgoing probability transition, which is 66.7 % for this particular example. More formally, the predictability P_{red} of a particular Markov chain is computed as the sum of the product between each element of the stationary vector π of the corresponding Markov chain, which corresponds to the probability of being in a particular state (for l, the total number of states of the Markov chain) and the maximum outgoing probability ($P_{max-out}$) of the kth state:

$$P_{red} = \sum\nolimits_{k=1}^{l} \left(\pi(k) \times P_{max-out}(k, *) \right) \qquad (2)$$

In this paper, we split the original trajectory data into two sets: the training set, which is used to build the prediction model, and the test set, which is used to evaluate the accuracy of the predictor. We compute the average predictability for each dataset category based on the students' Markov chain of corresponding category from training dataset. The average accuracy of each dataset category is computed by putting test dataset into corresponding sub-chains. We computed the accuracy of our prediction model and the theoretical predictability of student trajectories using the students' spatio-temporal data that are collected by the wireless data analysis system in the campus.

4 Experiment and Analysis

4.1 Data Acquisition

The experiment data in this paper are collected in campus by the wireless data analysis system, named WiCloud [11], which can provide edge networking, proximate computing and data acquisition for innovative services. We used OpenWrt system transforming the wireless router to develop the new WiFi access point. Our WiFi access point can detect the beacon frames that are sent by intelligent terminals and transmit the parsed beacon frames information to the cloud server over the network. We have deployed forty WiFi access points covering nineteen different places in the campus of BUPT, including dormitories, canteens, teaching buildings and laboratory buildings. In order to make the significance of prediction, we extracted more than two hundred million records from June 10, 2015 to January 31, 2016.

The students' mobility trajectory data are collected in real time by WiCloud in campus. When the subscriber who carries the smart terminal whose WiFi is open appears within the coverage area of the WiFi access point, smart terminal's MAC address and other spatio-temporal trajectory information will be recorded by WiCloud. Those detection data are collected per second, with the location information of the students. Finally, the students' trajectory information are transmitted to the cloud server for storage and processing.

4.2 Data Preprocess

In the data preprocessing progress, we need to handle hundreds of millions records collected from the WiFi access points to suitable format. In each piece of the original record, there are the MAC address of the smart terminal, radio signal strength, and the detected timestamp. The original data are like: 581F28382B53|-68|1441756631. Every WiFi access point also has a MAC address, and the original data are stored in a folder named with the MAC address in server. Then we can get students' spatio-temporal trajectories. The format of the original spatio-temproal trajectory data consists of five parts. They are the MAC address of the smart terminal, the student's arrival timestamp, the student's departure timestamp, the student's dwell time, and the name of detection point. The original spatio-temporal trajectory data are like: 80717A883D60|143978 2861|1439783625|764|student canteen.

We divide the total dataset into six different datasets, whose characteristics are summarized in Table 1. We selected these students whose spatio-temporal trajectory

Table 1. Characteristics of datasets

Char. (average)	Mon	Tue	Wed	Thu	Fri	Vac
Visit locations per student per day	10	10	10	10	10	7
POIs per student	4	4	4	4	4	3

records are relatively much in campus. Divide the preliminary processed trajectory data into training set and test set for every sub-model. The "visit locations per student per day" reflects the average number of students' transition location per day, while the "POIs per student" reflects the average number that students appeared in different locations per day. Table 1 shows student's activity is more frequently on workday than on vacation.

4.3 TPA Training

The transition probability matrix contains up to nine different states: "student dormitory" (D), "teaching building 1" (T1), "teaching building 2" (T2), "teaching building 3" (T3), "teaching building 4" (T4), "main teaching building" (T5), "laboratory" (L), "student canteen" (C1), "general canteen" (C2). Our goal is to predict the student next location based on his all transition probability matrixes of TPA. Thus, the rows of the transition probability matrix denote all possible current locations while a column represents the next position in the Markov chain. For instance, if the current position is D, the prediction of the next location will be T4 and a transition will occur from position D to position T4.

To illustrate the concept of prediction based on the Markov chains, Table 2 shows the transition probability matrix and the mobility trajectories are taken from a student of BUPT whom we simply name as Tom to preserve his anonymity. In our experiment, if the previous location is T4, the prediction will be D with a probability of 66.7 %.

Table 2. Transition probability matrix of Tom

Source/dest.	D	T1	T4	T5	C2
D	0.0	0.142	0.429	0.287	0.142
T1	0.334	0.0	0.0	0.333	0.333
T4	0.667	0.0	0.333	0.0	0.0
T5	0.333	0.667	0.0	0.0	0.0
C2	1.0	0.0	0.0	0.0	0.0

4.4 Experiment Evaluation

In our experiments, we split the trajectory data into two sets: the training set, which is used to build Markov chains, and the testing set, which is used to evaluate the accuracy of the prediction model. We extract two days data as the student's test set in every sub-model, and the others as training set. And we selected one hundred students'

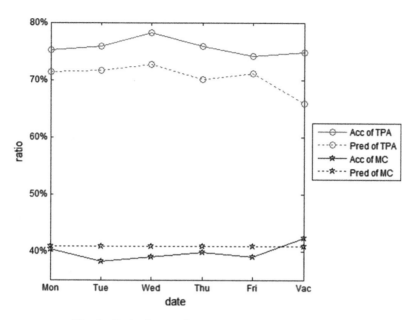

Fig. 2. Evaluation results on accuracy and predictability

spatio-temporal trajectories for the experiment evaluation. Figure 2 shows the evaluation results of the TPA and original Markov chain where the time domain is not divided.

Figure 2 shows that the accuracy of TPA ranges from 74.13 % to 78.25 % and the predictability ranges from 65.85 % to 72.71 %. While the accuracy of original Markov chain only ranges from 38.28 % to 42.24 % and the predictability is 40.82 %. The experimental results show that the TPA gives us a satisfying prediction result.

5 Conclusion

In this work, we have presented an algorithm for next location prediction in campus called Trajectory Prediction Algorithm (TPA) that considers the notion of time in the process of prediction. We divided the time domain into several sub-parts and respectively computed the corresponding transition probability matrix. Experiment results on wireless data analysis system show that the accuracy of TPA ranges from 74.13 % to 78.25 %. We concluded that the TPA did much better in forecasting the students' trajectory than original Markov chain.

Acknowledgment. This work is supported by National Natural Science Foundation of China (Grant No. 61471053).

References

1. Zheng, Y.: Trajectory data mining: an overview. ACM Trans. Intell. Syst. Technology. **6**(3), 1–41 (2015)
2. Duan, X., Wang, X.: Authentication handover and privacy protection in 5G hetnets using software-defined networking. IEEE Commun. Mag. **53**(4), 28–35 (2015)
3. Ashbrook, D.: Learning significant locations and predicting user movement with GPS. In: International Symposium on Wearable Computers IEEE, pp. 101–108 (2002)
4. Gambs, S., Killijian, M.O., et al.: Next place prediction using mobility Markov chains. In: Proceedings of EuroSys 2012 Workshop on Measurement, Privacy, and Mobility (MPM), pp. 1–6 (2012)
5. Asahara, A., Maruyama, K., Sato, A., et al.: Pedestrian-movement prediction based on mixed Markov-chain model. In: Proceedings of the 19th ACM SIGSPATIAL International Symposium on Advances in Geographic Information Systems (ACM-GIS 2011), Chicago, USA, pp. 25–33, November 2011
6. Zhu, Y., Wu, Y., Li, B.: Trajectory improves data delivery in urban vehicular networks. IEEE Trans. Parallel Distrib. Syst. **25**(4), 2183–2191 (2011)
7. Spyropoulos, T., Psounis, K., Raghavendra, C.S.: Performance analysis of mobility-assisted routing. In: Proceedings of the 7th ACM International Symposium on Mobile Ad Hoc Networking and Computing (MobiHoc), pp. 49–60 (2006)
8. Ekman, F., Keränen, A., Karvo, J., et al.: Working day movement model. In: Proceedings of the 1st AMC SIGMOBILE Workshop on Mobility Models, pp. 33–40, May 2008
9. Song, L., Kotz, D., Jain, R., et al.: Evaluating next-cell predictors with extensive wi-fi mobility data. IEEE Trans. Mob. Comput. **5**(12), 1633–1649 (2007)
10. Song, C., Qu, Z., Blumn, N., Barabási, A.L.: Limits of predictability in human mobility. Science **327**(5968), 1018–1021 (2010)
11. Li, H., Shou, G., Hu, Y., Guo, Z.: Mobile edge computing : progress and challenges. In: 2016 4th IEEE International Conference on Mobile Cloud Computing, Services, and Engineering, Oxford, United Kingdom, pp. 83–84 (2016)

Sensor Networks and RFID

Soil Moisture Content Detection Based on Sensor Networks

Zhan Huan$^{(\boxtimes)}$, Li Chen, LianTao Wang$^{(\boxtimes)}$, and CaiYan Wan

School of Information Science and Engineering, Changzhou University,
Wujin 213164, Jiangsu, China
hzh@cczu.edu.cn

Abstract. With rapidly development of wireless communications and electronics, precision agriculture turns into a promising application of the sensor networks. In this paper, the measurement of volumetric moisture content for soil is explored with the sensor networks. The method of high-frequency capacitance is applied to the moisture content detection for three kinds of arable soil: red soil, moisture soil and paddy soil. First of all, the measuring principle is analyzed: high-frequency equivalent electronic model of soil test plate is serially connected with constant inductor, so as to obtain the relation between the equivalent capacitance and resonance. Then we measure the correspondence between resonance frequency and soil volumetric moisture content through experimental methods, in addition, the impact of resonance frequency range and environmental temperature is analyzed. To the best of our knowledge, this is the first study on soil moisture content detection based on high-frequency capacitance covering circuit theory, hardware simulation, resonance-frequency selection, temperature compensation and sensor networks. The experimental results validate the effectiveness of our method, thus, our method possesses significant application value.

Keywords: Soil volumetric moisture content · Sensor networks · High-frequency capacitance · Dielectric constant · Series connection resonance

1 Introduction

Nowadays, due to rapidly development of wireless communications and electronics, the sensor networks are widely used for various application areas. Precision agriculture has become one of these application areas, which possesses a powerful trend in the field of agriculture.[1] Soil moisture content turns to be an important parameter in water-saving irrigation of precision agriculture [1]. Real-time monitoring of soil moisture content is able to help us understand the growth rhythm of crops, and has a significant meaning to provide a suitable growth environment for crops [2].

Methods based on dielectric constant are commonly used to measure soil moisture content. It utilizes the dielectric property of soil to determine the moisture content. The changes of the dielectric constant ε of soil fully reflects the changes of volumetric moisture content θ_v in soil. Several research results [3, 4] have been achieved based on

---

[1] Jiangsu Province, research joint innovation funds – BY2014037-07.

© Springer International Publishing Switzerland 2016
Y. Wang et al. (Eds.): BigCom 2016, LNCS 9784, pp. 157–171, 2016.
DOI: 10.1007/978-3-319-42553-5_14

this property in recent years. Refer to the relationship between ε and θ_v, the fully empirical formula of Topp et al. [5] and the half theoretical half empirical formula of Herkelrath et al. [6] are the most frequently employed. The formula of Topp et al. is a cubic polynomial equation describing the correspondence between θ_v and ε, which is determined through various kinds of soil test, as shown in Eq. (1):

$$\begin{aligned} \theta_v &= -5.3 \times 10^{-2} + 2.92 \times 10^{-4}\varepsilon \\ &- 5.5 \times 10^{-4}\varepsilon^2 + 4.3 \times 10^{-6}\varepsilon^3 \end{aligned} \tag{1}$$

We only need one parameter ε to get θ_v. The half theoretical half empirical formula of Herkelrath et al. has been used widely because of its better accuracy of measurement on soil moisture, as shown in Eq. (2):

$$\theta_v = a\sqrt{\varepsilon} + b \tag{2}$$

where both a and b are the calibration parameter, and they need to be calibrated according to different types of soil.

Zhu et al. [7] conduct research on the relationship between ε and θ_v in four types of soil in China by using time domain reflectometer (TDR). It has shown that Herkelrath's fitting equation is better than Topp's, and the RMSE value is smaller, so it can be considered as the first choice in corresponding applications. However, the measuring circuit of TDR method is difficult to design. We cannot measure accurately when the depth of soil is small, because reflection condition is complex, and the error is large, especially when the depth is less than 10 cm. Capacitance sensor method is considered as a substitute for TDR [8] because it has better precision with repeatability.

In contrast, we first analyse the changes of the soil volumetric moisture content θ_v and high-frequency series resonance frequency f_0 in Chinese three common kinds of arable soil from the aspects of circuit theory and simulation method. Then we determine the correspondence between soil volumetric moisture content and resonance frequency, using experimental approaches for the three kinds of soil respectively. We also present theoretical analysis for the selection of the resonance frequency range and temperature compensation.

2   Circuit Principle and Resonant Frequency Selection

The basic test principle of the high-frequency capacitor method is to use the LC resonance principle: a sensor is considered as an equivalent capacitor in the LC series resonance by making a series resonant circuit with a fixed inductor L_f on the outside of the sensor. With the change of soil moisture content between plates, the soil dielectric constant changes as well, which can lead to LC series resonance frequency change. Figure 1 below is the high-frequency electronic model of capacitive moisture sensor.

In Fig. 1, L_P represents the parasitic inductance between the plates. R_P and C_P stand for the parasitic resistance and the parasitic capacitance. R represents the soil resistance between the plates, Cx represents equivalent capacitance of the sensor. Parasitic L_P, R_P

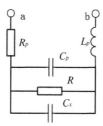

Fig. 1. High-frequency electronic model

and C_P are related to the shape and size of the measuring plate. The total complex impedance of the circuit is shown in Eq. (3):

$$Z = R_P + j\omega(L_f + L_P) + \frac{R}{j\omega(C_P + C_x)}$$
$$\times \frac{R \cdot j\omega(C_P + C_x)}{R^2 \cdot j\omega(C_P + C_x) + R} \tag{3}$$

which can be rewritten as Eq. (4):

$$Z = R_P + \frac{R}{1 + \omega^2 R^2 (C_P + C_x)^2}$$
$$+ j\left[\omega(L_f + L_P) - \frac{\omega R^2 (C_P + C_x)}{1 + \omega^2 R^2 (C_P + C_x)^2}\right]. \tag{4}$$

Through Eq. (5), we can get circuit resonance condition:

$$\omega(L_f + L_P) = \frac{\omega R^2 (C_P + C_x)}{1 + \omega^2 R^2 (C_P + C_x)^2}. \tag{5}$$

Denote $L = L_f + L_p$, $C = C_P + C_x$ in Eq. (5), we obtain resonant angular frequency w_0:

$$\omega_0 = \sqrt{(\frac{1}{LC} - \frac{1}{R^2 C^2})},$$
$$\text{where } \frac{1}{LC} > \frac{1}{R^2 C^2}. \tag{6}$$

Finally we are able to get the expression of resonance frequency:

$$f_0 = \frac{\sqrt{(\frac{1}{LC} - \frac{1}{R^2 C^2})}}{2\pi}$$

$$\text{with } \quad \frac{1}{LC} > \frac{1}{R^2C^2}, \tag{7}$$

where L represents the sum of the constant resonant inductance value L_f and the parasitic inductance of the capacitor L_P. L_P is related to the shape and size of the capacitor itself. C represents the sum of the parasitic capacitance C_P and the capacitor equivalent capacitance C_x. The value of C_P is related to the resonant frequency. R represents the resistance of the soil probe between plates. The entire measuring circuit is a series resonant circuit and the resonant quality factor Q is shown in Eq. (8):

$$Q = \frac{1}{R_P}\sqrt{\frac{L}{C}}. \tag{8}$$

3   Theoretical Calculation and Results

3.1   The Selection of the Test Frequency

Through the analysis of the basic testing principle, we get the basic expression of the resonance frequency f_0. In the expression, parasitic quantity L_P, R_P and C_P is associated with the probe's structure shape. Probes with different shapes and sizes have different parasitic values.

The capacity of sensor probes' equivalent capacitance is related to the surrounding media and its own parasitic capacitance C_P [11]. It is the function of dielectric constant ε of soil and geometric factor delta δ as shown in Eq. (9):

$$C_x = \delta\varepsilon, \tag{9}$$

Where δ represents the sensor probe plate geometric factor, and ε represents the dielectric constant of the soil.

Refer to Eq. (9), the equivalent capacitance of the sensor probe has a linear relation with the surrounding soil dielectric constant. Dry the Red soil up completely and put it into a container, then insert the sensor probe fully into the soil. We use high-precision capacitance meter to measure the capacitance value and it is about 18 pf in completely dry red soil. Through looking it after in the table [10], we can learn that the theoretical value of the dielectric constant of the red soil is 2.07. According to the theory, we obtain the geometric factor coefficient of the delta δ for probe with the shape, the size of it is 8.7×10^{12}. Similarly, it can be concluded that the geometric factor of the sensor probe plate for tide sandy clay soil and paddy soil are 11.2×10^{12} and 10×10^{12} respectively.

Herkelrath et al. [6] use TDR method to validate that Herkelrath's half theoretical half empirical formula can be used as the priority, and it gives the value of correction parameters a, b for different types of soil. According to the experiments, for red sandy soils, $a = 0.1098$, $b = 0.1568$. The RMSE of the curve fitted by this set of a, b values and the measured values $0.005\text{cm}^3\text{cm}^{-3}$. Similarly, we can choose a, b values for tide sandy clay soil and paddy soil correction respectively: $a = 0.1134$, $b = 0.2194$ and $a = 0.1117$, $b = 0.1626$.

After substituting Eq. (9) into Herkelrath's half theoretical half empirical formula, the relationship of equivalent capacitance C_x to soil volumetric moisture content and the equivalent capacitance are analyzed, as shown in Eq. (10):

$$C_x = k(\theta_v - b)^2$$

$$\text{where } k = \frac{\delta}{a^2}. \tag{10}$$

After substituting the formula (10) into the formula (8), we can examine the relationship between the soil volumetric moisture content and the circuit resonance frequency f_0:

$$f_0 = \frac{\sqrt{(\frac{1}{LC} - \frac{1}{R^2 C^2})}}{2\pi}$$

where

$$\frac{1}{LC} > \frac{1}{R^2 C^2} \text{ and } C = C_P + k(\theta_v - b)^2. \tag{11}$$

3.2 Relation Function Fitting

We can get corresponding moisture content of soil moisture volume through the sensor probe equivalent capacitance. The increase of soil moisture content can lead to the increase of dielectric constant and the probe plates. Suppose that the capacitance value increases by 15 pF, and 11 points are selected and substituted into Herkelrath's equation [6]. When the ambient temperature for experiment is 25 °C, we analyze the theoretical correspondence between the equivalent capacitance of C_x and soil volume number θ_v as shown in Fig. 2.

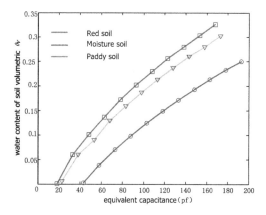

Fig. 2. The corresponding relationship between moisture content and the equivalent capacitance (Color figure online)

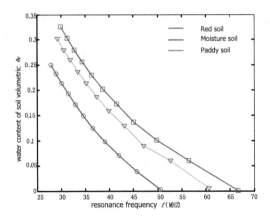

Fig. 3. Relation between moisture content and the resonance frequency (Color figure online)

Parasitic L_P, R_P and C_P are related to the shape and size of the plate. For the test probe, the magnitudes of parasitic L_P, R_P and C_P are nH, Ω, pF respectively. The soil resistance R between plates changes along with the moisture content of the soil. Compounding experimental soil into samples with different moisture content, we determine its order of magnitude under the condition of 25 °C. Finally it can be concluded that soil resistance between the plates ranges from 10 kΩ to hundreds of kΩ. Taking the value of parasitic inductance L_P as 10 nH, parasitic resistance R_P as 1 Ω, parasitic capacitance C_P ranging from 1 pF to 5 pF, then the soil resistance R ranges from 60 kΩ to 150 kΩ, along with moisture content changes.

We select winding patch inductance as the constant inductance, the value is set as 150 nH. According to the formula (8), we can calculate that in the ideal condition, quality factor of series resonance ranges from 30 to 90, and it has good resonance conditions. But in the practical measurement, the soil resistance R paralleled with the resonant capacitance in the equivalent circuit has the effect of reducing the Q value. In addition, the parasitic parameters of the test circuit and components will also reduce the Q value. After determining the order of magnitude and the value of parameters, we can use circuit simulation tool Multisim to simulate the soil electrical model. According to the size of the assumptive equivalent capacitance, we can obtain the circuit resonance frequency f_0 by simulation. The theoretic moisture content of soil volumetric can be calculated through the size of corresponding equivalent capacitance, and then we can get the relation between soil volumetric moisture content θ_v and resonance frequency f_0, as shown in Fig. 3.

4   Experimental Demonstration

4.1   The Experimental Process

We dry the red soil, moisture soil and paddy soil respectively to ensure that the moisture content of soil is close to 0, and the prepare experimental soil samples according to the definition of soil volumetric moisture content, as shown in formula (12):

$$\theta_v = \frac{v_w}{v_s} \times 100\,\%. \tag{12}$$

In the formula, θ_v represents soil volumetric moisture content, v_w represents water volume and v_s represents soil volume.

Compound the experimental soil into several test samples which respectively accounts for 5 %, 10 %, 15 %, 20 %, 25 %, 30 %, where each should be fully mixed and standing.

After configuring test samples, we can carry out the experiments. The hardware circuit for test mainly contains the sensor probe plate, voltage-controlled oscillation circuit, and oscilloscope. We also give metallic shield to the hardware circuit board. The voltage-controlled oscillator chip SiT3808 is selected for the Voltage-controlled oscillation circuit, the output of which is connected to the LC equivalent circuit. The input voltage V_{in} can be adjusted by the slide rheostat, and it will cause changes of the frequency on LC. We can use the oscilloscope to observe the output wave form amplitude, when the measured amplitude is the largest, the frequency represents the resonance frequency f_0. After measuring each soil sample for 10 times, we analyze the average value from several similar data sets. Then we can get the correspondence relationship between volume moisture content of the sample soil and the measured frequency.

4.2 Selection of Resonance Frequency Spectrum

The dielectric properties of the soil is influenced by many factors, of which the test frequency is the largest. When soil test frequency is lower than 1 MHz, soil dielectric constant is extremely unstable in a discrete state. It is even higher than that of water; When the test frequency is higher than 1 MHz, the dielectric constant of the soil is relatively stable [11]. Generally speaking, in order to avoid the electrode polarization effect, the frequency of testing should be at least 20 MHz.

Taking configured soil samples with 20 % moisture content; Adjusting the constant inductance; Changing their resonant inductance to change their resonance frequency. The adjusted frequencies are respectively about 10 kHz, 100 kHz, 1 MHz, 10 MHz, and 100 MHz. According to the formula (11), we can calculate the capacitance value of the moment, soil moisture can be obtained by compared to Fig. 2, as shown in Fig. 4.

It can be seen from Fig. 4 that we get more accurate measurement of soil volumetric moisture content with the frequency becomes higher. Therefore, considering the implementation of high frequency circuit hardware and the specific situation of the difficult actual test, we chose the patch winding inductance as the constant inductance, and set the value as 150 nH, thus the resonance frequency of the experimental circuit ranges 20–75 MHz.

4.3 Experimental Results at 25 °C

When the environment temperature is 25 °C, the patch winding inductance is 150 nH, the moisture content of experimental soil is 0, 5 %, 10 %, 15 %, 20 %, 25 %, 30 %, after taking repeated measurements, the experimental results are shown in Table 1.

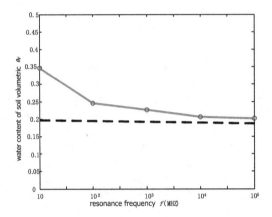

Fig. 4. Measured results under different frequency when moisture content is 20 %

In Table 1, θ_v is the moisture content, R denotes the measured frequency for red soil, M measured frequency for moisture soil, P measured frequency for paddy soil. When the experimental environment temperature is 25 °C, the correspondence curves of measured values and theoretical values for these three kinds of soils are shown in Figs. 5, 6 and 7 respectively. Measurement error is from −0.05 to +0.02.

Table 1. Correspondence of measured resonance frequency and moisture content

θ_v	0	0.05	0.10	0.15	0.20	0.25	0.30
R	72.3	56.7	51.2	45.3	36.3	32.6	28.4
M	54.6	44.6	38.2	31.4	27.6	23.8	21.4
P	64.0	56.4	46.2	37.2	32.7	28.1	27.2

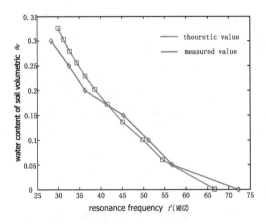

Fig. 5. Comparison of theoretical values and measured values at 25 °C for red soil (Color figure online)

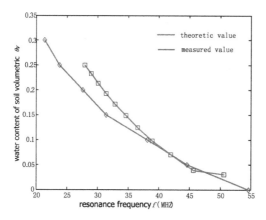

Fig. 6. Comparison of theoretical values and measured values at 25 °C for moisture soil (Color figure online)

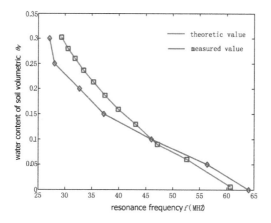

Fig. 7. Comparison of theoretical values and measured values at 25 °C for paddy soil (Color figure online)

5 Temperature Compensation

5.1 Improvement of Experimental Equipment

Considering that the sensor is mainly used in outdoor environment, and outdoor temperature cannot be maintained at 25 °C constantly, so we need to make temperature compensation to the sensor. We place the sensor at two different environments where temperatures are respectively 0 °C and 40 °C. In order to get more reliable test results, we have improved test device.

The entire test system consists of single-chip microcomputer control module, sampling module, D/A voltage-controlled oscillator module, sensor test module, data storage module, and temperature test module. 16-bit high-precision AD5660 is adopted

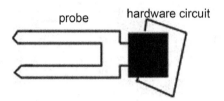

Fig. 8. Improved test device

for D/A sampling chip, MSP430F2012 with 10-bit precision AD sampling ports is adopted for single-chip, SIT3808 chip is adopted for voltage-controlled oscillation. Oscillation frequency ranges from 1 MHz to 80 MHz. MCU I/O port transforms digital signals into analog signals through D/A conversion chip which are used to control the output frequency of VCO. When the resonance of the constant inductance and soil equivalent capacitance occurs, the AD sampling value from the I/O port becomes maximum. We store both the AD sampling value and the soil temperature that is measured by the temperature module into the EEPROM through the storage module. After the EEPROM value is taken out, we can calculate the frequency when the circuit resonance occurs. The structure diagram of the test device is shown in Fig. 8:

5.2   Experimental Results

Topp [5] gives not only fully empirical formula of soil moisture content, but also presents the change formula of water dielectric constant with the temperature changes:

$$\varepsilon_w = 78.5(1 - 4.60 \times 10^{-3}(T - 25)$$
$$+ 8.8 \times 10^{-6}(T - 25)^2)$$

$$(13)$$

From the formula (13) we can know that the dielectric constant changes along with the temperature of the water.

After configuring the tested soil, we should place it in the high and low temperature alternating test chamber, set the temperature as 0 °C and 40 °C respectively and make a test on the soil every 2 h. Calculate the value in the EEPROM and take a length of the temperature date that relatively stable, and take the mean value as shown in Figs. 9, 10 and 11:

Through the figure above, we can find that environment temperature has a significant influence on the measured results when the temperature is unequal to 25 °C. In order to further improve the test precision of the sensor, we need to make a temperature compensation to it [12].

Place the configured soil with 20 % moisture content respectively into the test environment where the temperature ranges from 0 °C to 40 °C, and seal the test device to prevent the evaporation of water, then we can get the relationship curve between the measured values and the environment temperature [13], as shown in Fig. 12.

In order to get the compensation expression of the impact of temperature T to the measured value, we use the values measured at different temperature to minus the

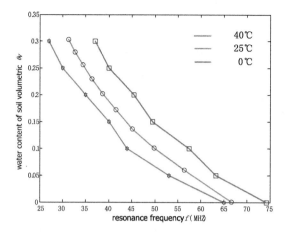

Fig. 9. Test results for red soil (Color figure online)

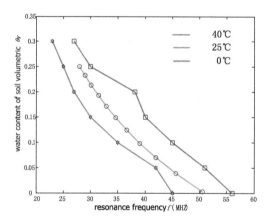

Fig. 10. Test results for moisture soil (Color figure online)

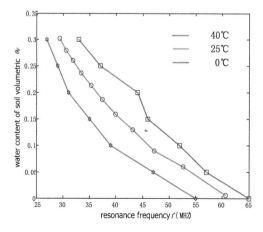

Fig. 11. Test results for paddy soil (Color figure online)

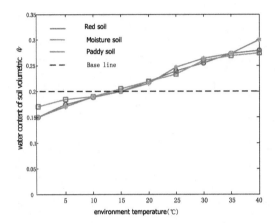

Fig. 12. Moisture content results for various soil under different temperatures (Color figure online)

moisture content (20 %) measured at indoor samples temperature, then we can obtain the error value Δy. We can get the function expression by Δy curve fitting, and write the fitting function into the single-chip. Note that real-time calculation will need high computational cost, so we need to get as many as possible corresponding error values, and put them into the program to check value processing.

Refer to formula 14 to 16 with error functions for red soil, moisture soil and paddy soil respectively.

$$\Delta y = -6.1279 \times 10^{-5} T^3 + 0.0026 T^2$$
$$+ 0.3173T - 4.6828 \tag{14}$$
$$R^2 = 0.9923$$

$$\Delta y = -0.0002 T^3 + 0.012747 T^2$$
$$+ 0.069428T - 2.702 \tag{15}$$
$$R^2 = 0.9885$$

$$\Delta y = -1.7508 \times 10^{-5} T^3 + 0.0018 T^2$$
$$+ 0.3246T - 4.8414 \tag{16}$$
$$R^2 = 0.9913$$

We set the revised test device into an environment with 20 % water volume content and range the temperature from 0 °C to 40 °C. Take the mean value of multiple tests, as shown in Figs. 13, 14 and 15.

From Table 2, T is denoted as environment temperature, R means results of red soil, M represents results of moisture soil, and P means results of paddy soil.

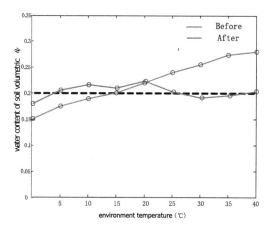

Fig. 13. Revised moisture content test results of red soil. (Color figure online)

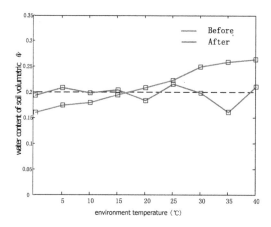

Fig. 14. Revised moisture content test results of moisture soil. (Color figure online)

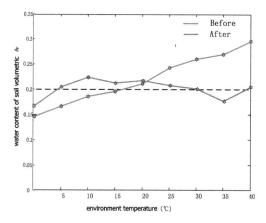

Fig. 15. Revised moisture content test results of paddy soil. (Color figure online)

Table 2. The revised error comparison table

$T_{(°C)}$	0	5	10	15
R	−2.5	1.2	1.5	1.2
M	−1.0	1.2	0.1	0.5
p	−3.0	0.9	2.5	1.7
$T_{(°C)}$	20	25	30	35
R	2	0.2	−0.5	−0.3
M	−2.3	1.6	−0.2	−5
p	1.7	0.5	0.2	−3.0

6   Conclusion

In this paper, by utilizing sensor networks, we obtained the relation expression between the resonance frequency and the equivalent capacitance by analyzing the capacitance soil moisture high-frequency electronic model. In addition, through the theoretical analysis and calculation, we analyzed the correspondence curves between resonance frequency and soil volumetric moisture content for three kinds of soils respectively. We used the measured method to get correspondence curve between the frequency values and the soil volumetric moisture content. Through temperature compensation, we made the correction to the test results of sensors. According to the experimental results, we summarized the following conclusions:

(1) The changes of the frequency with the soil volumetric moisture content have the same trend, and the measured frequency value can distinguish the range of soil volumetric moisture content. We completed the soil moisture content test by using the high frequency capacitance method to replace the TDR method.
(2) Test errors exist due to some external factors. However, for arable soil, the errors can be accepted because moisture measurement accuracy meets the requirements of crop moisture.
(3) Through temperature compensation, the influence of environment temperature to the sensor can be eliminated. Hence, we further improved the test precision and stability of the sensor.

References

1. Schieffer, J., Dillon, C.: Precision agriculture and agro-environmental policy. In: Precision Agriculture 2013, pp. 755–760. Wageningen Academic Publishers (2013)
2. Wang, X., Hu, J., Jiang, M., Zhao, X., Hu, J., Zhao, Y.: The experiment of additional resistance method to measure the percentage of moisture quickly. J. Agric. Eng. **25**(10), 76–81 (2009)
3. Wagner, N., Daschner, F., Scheuermann, A., et al.: Estimation of the soil water characteristics from dielectric relaxation spectra. In: 2014 IEEE Sensors Applications Symposium (SAS), pp. 242–247. IEEE (2014)

4. Mizuguchi, J., Piai, J.C., de França, J.A., et al.: Fringing field capacitive sensor for measuring soil moisture content: design, manufacture, and testing. IEEE Trans. Instrum. Meas. **64**, 212–220 (2015)
5. Topp, G.C., Davis, J.L., Annan, A.P.: Electromagnetic determination of soil moisture content: measurements in coaxial transmission lines. Water Resour. Res. **16**(3), 574–582 (1980)
6. Herkelrath, W.N., Hamburg, S.P., Murphy, F.: Automatic, real-time monitoring of soil moisture in a remote field area with time domain reflectometry. Water Resour. Res. **27**(5), 857–864 (1991)
7. Zhu, A., Ji, L., Zhang, J., Xin, X., Liu, J., Liu, H.: The study on the experiential relationship between dielectric constant and the volumetric moisture content in different types of soil. J. Soil **48**(2), 263–268 (2011)
8. Axel, R., Carlos, M.R.: Corrections for simultaneous measurements of soil moisture content and salinity using a capacitance sensor. In: Minneapolis ASABE Annual International Meeting, USA, pp. 1–10 (2007)
9. Kelleners, T.J., Soppe, R.W.O., Robinson, D.A., et al.: Calibration of capacitance probe sensors using electric circuit theory. Soil Sci. Soc. Am. J. **68**(2), 430–439 (2004)
10. Ju, Z.: The relationship between dielectric constant and the volumetric moisture content in Chinese several types of typical soil. Resource and Environment College, Chinese Agricultural University, Beijing (2005)
11. Ma, X., Ma, J.: The analysis on upper limit of dielectric measurement of soil moisture. Study Soil Water Conserv. **9**(2), 82–86 (2002)
12. Liu, F.: The study of soil profile moisture sensor which based on the principle of high frequency capacitance. Jiangsu University (2012)
13. Zhang, Y., Ma, Y., Jiang, Z., et al.: The development of portable soil moisture measuring instrument which including the temperature compensate. Sens. Micro Syst. **05**, 73–76 (2014)

Missing Value Imputation for Wireless Sensory Soil Data: A Comparative Study

Guodong Sun$^{(\boxtimes)}$, Jia Shao, Hui Han, and Xingjian Ding

School of Information Science and Technology, Beijing Forestry University,
Beijing 100083, China
sungd@bjfu.edu.cn

Abstract. Soil data is indispensable in hydrology or other environmental sciences. In present, the soil data is often collected by unattended wireless sensing system and then inevitably involves continuous missing values due to the unreliability of system, while in traditional commercial or manually-collected datasets, the data losses are sparsely distributed. time-series dataset, aimed at answering such a question: whether or not existing methods suit for wireless sensory soil dataset with continuous missing values, and how well they perform. With a real-world soil dataset involving two-month complete samples as the benchmark, we evaluate these six missing value infilling methods, compare their performance, and analyze the possible reasons behind. This study provides insights for designing new methods that can effectively deal with the missing values in wireless sensory soil dataset.

Keywords: Wireless sensory data · Soil dataset · Missing value imputation · Performance evaluation

1 Introduction

The existence of missing data makes it very difficult to realize accurate data analyzing and modeling. In fact the data missing is not only common in industry, commerce, and scientific research fields [18,22] but also inevitable in those scenarios. Generally data missing happens due to the errors or the failures of instrument or operation. Without careful considerations of missing data, domain experts cannot efficiently and precisely understand what their data really indicates [8]. For the hydrology, the agriculture, or other ecological fields, the ecological dataset is generally obtained by either human-operating devices or remotely automatic devices [14,19,29,30]. Nowadays, a popular methodology of implementing large-scale, micro-level ecosystem monitoring is to deploy wireless sensor networks [4,21] in the sites concerned by scientists. It benefits much—decreasing

---

Jia Shao and Xingjian Ding are master candidates of computer science at Beijing Forestry University Information School. Guodong Sun is an associate professor of computer science at Beijing Forestry University Information School; and Hui Han is an assistant professor in Beijing Forestry University Information School.

© Springer International Publishing Switzerland 2016
Y. Wang et al. (Eds.): BigCom 2016, LNCS 9784, pp. 172–184, 2016.
DOI: 10.1007/978-3-319-42553-5_15

the costs of human resources and maintenance, realizing real-time observations across geographically distributed regions [5,9,23,24]. In practice, however, the use of wireless sensor network in ecosystem monitoring poses new challenges—the dataset collected by wireless systems, often called wireless sensory dataset, often experiences more significant data losses than datasets of traditional fields, such like the bank and the medical study.

First, wireless ecology sensing systems are usually left unattended in outdoor environments, say, tropical forests, cold regions, wetlands, desserts, and riversides, and are expected to operate for a long term, say, a few weeks or even months. These systems are very prone to be accidentally damaged by extreme weather conditions, such as storms, rains, or lightening, and therefore cannot always record ecological events in time. Moreover, limited labor resources or unpredictable harsh weathers sometimes lead to infeasible visits to remotely deployed devices, and consequently, the damage or the failure of devices often cannot be discovered until the next routine checking, which aggravates the data loss so much that the missing values or even records in the dataset occur one after another—forming large gaps in the dataset.

Second, the low-power low-rate wireless links used to form ecological sensors into a network are unreliable and rendered dynamics sometimes [15,25], and consequently cannot deliver all the obtained data to end-users—also leading to non-ignorable data missing. Different than traditional datasets in which missing values are very sparsely scattered, therefore, the wireless sensory dataset inevitably suffers missing values that occur continuously in a larger range and considerably undermine the completeness of dataset. Also, it is worth noting that strictly speaking, repeating the operations of obtaining ecological data does not make sense because of the ceaseless temporal-spatial dynamics of natural environment. Figure 1 indicates the incompleteness in the dataset obtained by a small-scale wireless sensor network we use to monitor the hydrology in forests. Clearly we can see the continuous data missing due to the failed data communication through wireless links (at sensor 2) and the unattended battery depletion (at sensor 3).

Until now, however, researchers have not yet payed attention to infill the continuous missing values in wireless sensory time-series datasets, and have little knowledge about which existing methods are possibly effective under such a case. This study investigates several typical approaches of infilling missing data designed for traditional time-series dataset and examines their performances in

Fig. 1. Illustration of the continuous data missing in a dataset whose data points are returned by two wireless sensors

dealing with large-scale continuous data missing in the dataset of soil moisture, in hope of analyzing and determining which approaches will be more potential for this new task and giving some insights for designing new data missing infilling policies for wireless sensory ecological dataset. Our work is based on the soil moisture dataset because as a critical environmental factor [16], the soil moisture data is a common input to hydrologic and agricultural models in the soil and water management activities [1,2,7,11,20].

Recently, there have been more attempts which study the missing values infilling methods for soil moisture datasets. Wang et al. [27] present a three-dimensional method, based on the discrete cosine transforms, for filling the missing values of the satellite images dataset of soil moisture. Dumedah et al. [6] treat the soil moisture dataset to be a time-series and investigate the effectiveness of six methods, including the multiple linear regression, the weighted Pearson correlation coefficient, the station relative difference, the soil layer relative difference, the monthly average, and the merged method. In their subsequent work [7], they further evaluate nine neural network based infilling methods; they find that the nonlinear autoregressive neural network, the rough set method, and the monthly replacement can achieve better accuracy in comparison with the methods in their previous paper. Kornelsen et al. [13] examine the effectiveness of the monthly average, the soil layer relative difference, the linear and cubic interpolation, the artificial neural networks, and the evolutionary polynomial regression infilling methods; the evaluation results show that the interpolation and the artificial neural network methods are more effective, yet only for infilling small gaps in dataset. However, these methods all assume small gaps in the datasets and then are unable to be effectively applied to infill continuous missing data inherently existing in the wireless sensory datasets. In this paper we test six typical methods to evaluate their performance, which are the Linear Interpolation (LI), the Soil Layer Relative Difference (SLRD), the Autoregressive Integrated Moving Average (ARIMA), the Vertical Multiple Linear Regression (VMLR), the Horizontal Multiple Linear Regression (HMLR), and the Weighted K-Nearest Neighbors (WKNN). To thoroughly investigate these methods, we examine their performances with different gaps of continuous data missing, based on a soil moisture dataset involving unsteady records.

The rest of this paper is organized as follows. Section 2 describes the background of our study and some observations of soil moisture data in the real world. Section 3 presents six typical methods of infilling missing data and how to apply them in our dataset. Section 4 analyzes and evaluates these six methods in terms of accuracy. Finally, Sect. 5 concludes this study.

2   Soil Dataset

The dataset used in this paper is collected by a soil monitoring system deployed in the Jiufeng National Forestry Park, Beijing, China; this system is shown in Fig. 2, and it locates at 115.7°E and 39.4°N (marked with a red point). Beijing is of dry and monsoon-influenced humid continental climate, where the daily

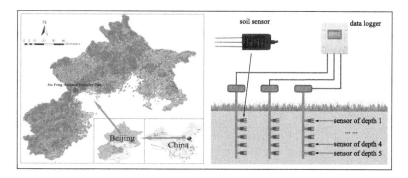

Fig. 2. Deployment of the soil monitoring site (Color figure online)

average temperature is only $-3.7\,^\circ$C in January and the precipitation from June to August is about three-fourths of the total yearly precipitation. In this system, there are three soil-monitoring stations around ten meters away from each other; and they report their data to a data logger which buffers the collected the data in local SD card. Every week, an operator manually pulled out the soil data file from the SD card. Each station is equipped with five soil sensing probes arranged at five top-bottom layers (depths): 2 cm, 5 cm, 10 cm, 15 cm, and 20 cm, respectively; and each probe simultaneously captures three attributes with an interval of 15 min: the soil moisture, the soil temperature, and the soil electrical conductivity. Also, the logger associates a timestamp with each record.

3   Description of Infilling Methods

This section will introduce six widely-used methods for infilling missing values in the soil moisture dataset. We develop programs based on the R language to implement those methods.

3.1   Linear Interpolation (LI)

Based on the curve fitting with linear polynomials, the linear interpolation (LI) is a simple but effective method in practice [17]. The LI fills the missing values of time series by Eq. (1), where y_0 and y_1 are the soil moisture values on time t_0 and $t_1 (t_1 > t_0)$, respectively, and then y will be the missing value on time t which ranges from t_0 to t_1.

$$y = y_0 + (y_1 - y_0)\frac{t - t_0}{t_1 - t_0} \tag{1}$$

3.2   Soil Layer Relative Difference (SLRD)

Field experts often resort to the SLRD method [26] to infill missing data and they usually employ the parametric test of relative difference among soil moisture data. Equation (2) shows how to impute the missing soil moisture data. Suppose that there are n soil-monitoring stations in a given region, each of which reports a time-series soil records including samples returned by the probes of different depths (layers). For a given sampling depth j, in Eq. (2), $\theta_{i,j}(t)$ represents the soil moisture of depth j at station i at time t, and $\bar{\theta}_j(t)$ represents the average over the depth-j soil moisture values reported by all the n stations at time t. And, $\delta_{i,j}$, called the relative difference, is calculated by the first equation of Eq. (2).

$$\delta_{i,j}(t) = \frac{\theta_{i,j}(t) - \bar{\theta}_j(t)}{\bar{\theta}_j(t)} \tag{2}$$

$$\bar{\theta}_j(t) = \frac{1}{n} \sum_{i=1}^{n} \theta_{i,j}(t)$$

Note that the SLRD method only takes into consideration the data with as the same depth as the missing data, because it assumes that across different stations, the soil moisture data with an identical depth is relatively correlated [6]. When soil moisture is missing at depth j of station i at time t, $\bar{\theta}_j(t)$ is computed by the available depth-j data of all the other stations, while $\bar{\delta}_{i,j}$ is estimated by the mean of all the values of the j-th depth at station i. The estimated soil moisture θ_{est} can be expressed with Eq. (3).

$$\theta_{est}(t) = \bar{\theta}_j(t) + \bar{\theta}_j(t) \times \bar{\delta}_{i,j} \tag{3}$$

3.3   Autoregressive Integrated Moving Average (ARIMA)

Typical for statistics, the ARIMA model is widely used to analyze the time-series data [12]. In fact ARIMA involves three types of models: the autoregressive model (AR), the moving average model (MA), and the model (ARMA) combining MA and AR. To process a non-stationary data series, like the soil data we use, ARIMA has to difference this data series to make it stationary for the const statistical properties. We do not consider the seasonal effect and then use the non-seasonal ARIMA(p, d, q) model [10] to predict (infill) the missing values, in which p is the number of autoregressive term, d, the number of nonseasonal differences for keep stationary, and q, the number of lagged forecast errors. The general ARIMA model is given together in Eqs. (4) and (5).

$$y_t = \begin{cases} Y_t & d = 0 \\ Y_t - Y_{t-1} & d = 1 \\ (Y_t - Y_{t-1}) - (Y_{t-1} - Y_{t-2}) & d = 2 \\ \cdots & \cdots \end{cases} \tag{4}$$

$$\hat{y}_t = \mu + \phi_1 y_{t-1} + \cdots \phi_p y_{t-p} - \theta_1 e_{t-1} - \cdots \theta_q t_{t-q} \tag{5}$$

In Eq. (4), Y_t is the observed data series until time t, y_t is d-th difference of Y_t, and generally, that $d \in [0, 4]$ is adequate to lead to a stationary series. For the general forecasting given by Eq. (5), $\phi_i (1 \leq i \leq p)$ and $\theta_i (1 \leq i \leq q)$ are model parameters, while p and q are the model orders. The parameters ϕ_i and θ_i are often estimated according to the least square or the maximum likelihood methods.

When a missing value is of sequence k in the whole data, ARIMA first chooses a sub-series of length L_k before the k-th data point. In this paper, we plot the original soil moisture data and find its non-stationarity. After empirically differencing the non-stationary soil data of length L_k with a proper d, we can determine a desirable pair of p and q by examining the auto-correlation and the partial-correlation of y_t. Finally we mainly use the `arima` function provided by the R language to complete the missing value imputation.

3.4   Vertical Multiple Linear Regression (VMLR)

Each sensing probe attached to the station can sample not only the soil moisture but also the soil temperature and the electrical conductivity data. The VMLR method assumes that for a given depth k, the soil moisture data of depth k correlates both with the soil moisture values of other depths and with the temperature and the electrical conductivity of depth k.

$$\hat{y}_k = a_1 \times t_k + a_2 \times c_k + \sum_{i=1, i \neq k}^{m} b_i \, y_i \tag{6}$$

If there are m layers, the VMLR model is expressed in Eq. (6) where t_k and c_k represent the temperature and the electrical conductivity of depth k, respectively, and y_i, the soil moisture value of depth $i (i \neq k)$. Therefore the task of the VMLR is to find parameters a_1, a_2, and b_i.

3.5   Horizontal Multiple Linear Regression (HMLR)

Similar to the VMLR method, the HMLR method also uses the multiple linear regression to infill the missing soil moisture values. Yet the HMLR method focuses on the correlation of data points at the same depth from different stations; in other words, for a given station s, the soil moisture data of depth k at s correlates both with the soil moisture values of depth k of other stations and with the temperature and the electrical conductivity of depth k at station s. The correlation of sensing attributes from nearby sensors are often employed to predict the missing data due to faulty devices [3,28].

$$\hat{y}_{s,k} = a_1 \times t_{s,k} + a_2 \times c_{s,k} + \sum_{i=1, i \neq s}^{m} b_i \cdot y_{i,k} \tag{7}$$

The HMLR model is given by Eq. (7) where m denotes the number of stations, $t_{s,k}$ and $c_{s,k}$ are the temperature and the electrical conductivity values of depth k at station s.

3.6   Weighted K-Nearest Neighbours (WKNN)

The WKNN resorts to K similar observations to impute missing values. The Euclidean distance is commonly used to determine the similarity between two

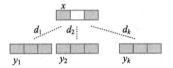

Fig. 3. Illustration for the WKNN method (the white block is the missing value)

data points. For the simplicity, suppose that data point x has a missing value at attribute a, denoted by $x^{(a)}$, and that there are n data points, $y_1, y_2, \ldots y_n$ in the training dataset. The similarity between x and $y_i (1 \leq i \leq n)$ can be calculated by Eq. (8) where m is the number of attributes of x or y_i.

$$d(x, y_i) = \sqrt{\sum_{j=1, j \neq a}^{m} \left(x^{(j)} - y_i^{(j)} \right)^2} \tag{8}$$

After obtaining all the distances between x to y_i, we can determine the k nearest neighbors. For instance, if the k nearest neighbors of x are shown in Fig. 3 and the distance from x to y_i is equal to d_i, we can infill $x^{(a)}$ with $\hat{x}^{(a)}$ calculated by Eqs. (9) and (10), both of which together express an implementation of a K-nearest neighbors model with a weighted function.

$$\hat{x}^{(a)} = \sum_{i=1}^{k} y_i^{(a)} w(d_i) \tag{9}$$

$$w(d_i) = e^{-d_i} \tag{10}$$

4   Analysis

4.1   Setup

The monitoring system in our study site operated from October 2010 to October 2012. In the whole dataset of two years there are a large amount of irregularly distributed data losses. We elaborately find that the set of records obtained from October 2010 to January 2011 involves only one missing soil moisture value; therefore this set of records can be reasonably reckoned to be a complete dataset; specifically, we we choose the data—returned by the sensing probe of depth 5 cm at a station— as the benchmark dataset to evaluate the six infilling methods. The benchmark has 6060 records of three soil attributes (the soil moisture, the soil temperature, and the soil conductivity). Figure 4 shows the distribution of all the soil moisture values in the benchmark dataset.

To simulate the continuous missing characteristics of soil dataset returned by wireless sensing system, we artificially specify various missing segments with different ratios. We first remove the missing segment from the benchmark dataset and then apply the six imputation methods to infill the values in this missing segment. Table 1 gives the missing ratios used in this paper. The choices of five

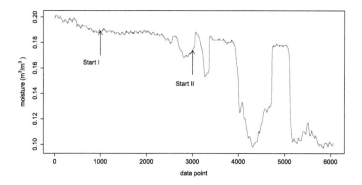

Fig. 4. Soil moisture data from the sensing probe of depth 5 cm at a station

Table 1. Configuration of the missing records in evaluation

Missing segment	Missing range	Missing ratio (%)	Duration (days)
Seg. 1	1001~1048	0.79	0.5
Seg. 2	1001~1192	3.17	2
Seg. 3	1001~1672	11.09	7
Seg. 4	1001~2344	22.18	14
Seg. 5	1001~3688	44.36	28
Seg. 6	3001~3048	0.79	0.5
Seg. 7	3001~3192	3.17	2
Seg. 8	3001~3672	11.09	7
Seg. 9	3001~4344	22.18	14
Seg. 10	3001~5688	44.36	28

missing ratios are determined by the inspection (physical visit) period in practice, which is usually half a day, one day, one week, or one month (four weeks). It
is clear, in Fig. 4, that the moisture varies steadily before the 2500-th data point,
but drastically after the 3000-th data point. So, to evaluate the performance of
the six methods under steady and dynamic time-series data, we specify two data
points in the benchmark dataset: Start I, the 1001-th data point and Start II, the
3001-th data point, as labeled in Fig. 4. In Table 1, missing segments 1~5 all start
from Start I and missing segments 6~10 all start from Start II.

$$RMSE = \sqrt{\frac{1}{n} \times \sum_{i=1}^{n}(\hat{y}_i - y_i)^2} \qquad (11)$$

In this study, we use the root-mean-square error (RMSE), widely-adopted
in the community [7], to evaluate the six methods of infilling the missing soil
moisture data. In detail, as shown in Eq. (11), RMSE is the root of the average

squared differences between the predicted value $(\hat{y}_i)$ and the original one (y_i). In general, the smaller the RSME derived by a method is, the better the effectiveness of this method.

4.2 Results

This section compares the performance of the six infilling methods with different missing scales and different fluctuations. Figure 5 plots the data points infilled by the six methods and the real data points. Note that the observed soil moisture values are marked by empty black circle, and the predicted values of the six methods are marked by different colors shown as the legend in Fig. 5(a). For the shortest missing segment over the steady dataset (Fig. 5(a)), these infilling methods except for the SLRD all works well; for the longest missing segment over the fluctuating dataset (Fig. 5(j)), the six methods differentiate much in performance. For each given missing rate, the performances of the LI, the ARIMA and the WKNN under unsteady dataset all decrease obviously, in comparison with their performances under steady dataset. Interestingly, the VLMR and the HLMR fits better with most of the missing segments starting from Start II, especially the VLMR with larger missing rates. For both the steady and the unsteady datasets, as the missing rate increases, the accuracy of the VLMR and WKNN does not change obviously, while the accuracies of all other methods degrade significantly. Noticeably, for infilling the significantly fluctuating dataset with more continuos missing values, the WKNN can also well predict the variation trend of dataset, like the VLMR and the HLMR, although its accuracy is lower than that of the VLMR. From Fig. 5, it can be seen that for the shortest missing segment over the steady dataset, the ARIMA, the WKNN and the LI have great accurate prediction, but the VMLR demonstrates the most steady and precise prediction as the dataset becomes unsteady and the missing ratio is larger.

The six methods are further compared in Fig. 6. It is worth mentioning that the imputation performances of the LI and the ARIMA become very poor for the missing segments beginning from the Start II, after which the soil moisture values varies drastically; when the missing segments are chosen from here, the LI method, only using two reference points, does not work well for infilling the large-scale continuous missing. The ARIMA just uses a segment of steady data before the missing values (Start II), which does not contain sufficient information (large or periodic dataset is preferable for ARIMA), and consequently results in lower performance. Both the VMLR and the HMLR employ the multiple linear regression to infill the missing soil moisture values, but the VMLR is preferred to the HMLR—suggesting that for a given station, the different soil layers (depths) for the VMLR can profile the temporal correlation of soil moisture with more accuracy, i.e., the data from vertically arranged layers at the same station render closer correlation, in comparison with the same layers at different stations.

A comprehensively numerical comparison in terms of RMSE is given in Table 2. For the missing segment beginning at Start I, in average, the WKNN is the best predictor, followed by the VMLR, the LI, and the ARIMA, the fifth is the HMLR, five of which are similar; and the worst is the SLRD. For the missing

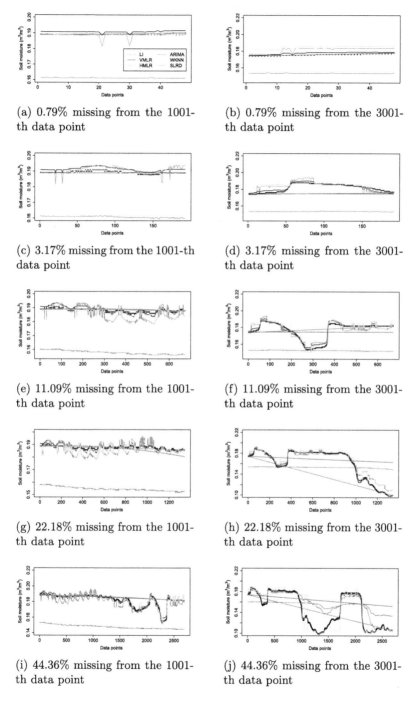

(a) 0.79% missing from the 1001-th data point

(b) 0.79% missing from the 3001-th data point

(c) 3.17% missing from the 1001-th data point

(d) 3.17% missing from the 3001-th data point

(e) 11.09% missing from the 1001-th data point

(f) 11.09% missing from the 3001-th data point

(g) 22.18% missing from the 1001-th data point

(h) 22.18% missing from the 3001-th data point

(i) 44.36% missing from the 1001-th data point

(j) 44.36% missing from the 3001-th data point

Fig. 5. Comparisons of the six methods with five different missing ratios. The legend in Fig. 5(a) works for all the other sub-figures. (Color figure online)

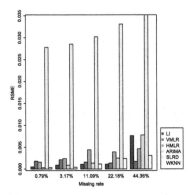
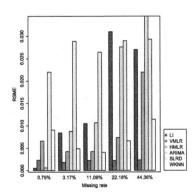

(a) missing segments starting from the 1001-th data point

(b) missing segments starting from the 3001-th data point

Fig. 6. Comparisons of the six methods with different missing ratios (Color figure online)

segment beginning at Start II, the VMLR performs the best and the SLRD still is the worst. It is noticeable that when being applied to infill the dataset with significant fluctuation, the performances of the LI, the ARIMA, and the WKNN all decrease, but the VMLR and the HMLR show slight promotion of performance. Based on the short-term time-series dataset used in this paper, the evaluation results show that the VMLR, the WKNN, the LI, the ARIMA, and the HMLR are all preferred to the SLRD which is commonly used by field experts. In particular, the VMLR method, with the average RMSE of 0.217 % over the first five missing segments, seems more suitable to infill unsteady dataset.

Table 2. RSMEs of six methods with different missing ratios

Method	RMSE at different missing segments (%)										
	Seg. 1	Seg. 2	Seg. 3	Seg. 4	Seg. 5	Avg. (seg. 1~5)	Seg.6	Seg. 7	Seg. 8	Seg. 9	Seg. 10	Avg. (seg. 6~10)
LI	.050	.089	.109	.110	.765	.225	.053	.843	1.049	3.098	2.703	1.549
SLRD	2.779	2.855	3.020	3.309	3.520	3.097	2.201	2.889	2.645	2.899	2.932	2.713
VMLR	.181	.211	.157	.138	.172	.172	.228	.181	.222	.220	.234	.217
HMLR	.159	.238	.444	.393	.465	.340	.662	.427	.424	.738	2.198	.890
ARIMA	.030	.089	.136	.249	.779	.257	.060	.876	1.068	2.760	3.444	1.642
WKNN	.035	.041	.116	.238	.309	.148	.905	.490	.407	.662	1.144	.722

5   Conclusions

Ecological time-series dataset collected by wireless sensing systems often experiences continuous data losses which pose new challenges for missing data processing. Researchers now have little knowledge about effective approaches to address this issue. This paper has investigated six typical methods that are used to infill missing data in a soil time-series dataset and compared their performances under different scenarios. We find that totally, the VMLR and the WKNN methods can achieve better accuracy in infilling continuous missing soil moisture data. In detail, to infill short missing segments of steady soil dataset, the ARIMA, the LI, and the WKNN perform desirably. To infill missing values in unsteady soil dataset with large continuous missing values, the VMLR overwhelms all the other methods, and the accuracy of the WKNN is slightly lower than that of the VMLR. For all the specified missing segments, the VMLR is almost always preferred to the HMLR, indicating that the data from different layers of a given station is more strongly correlated than the data from different stations at the same layer. Thus, taking into account the correlation among multiple factors will be a promising start to design effective missing value infilling methods.

Acknowledgements. This study was supported, in part, by the NSF of China with Grant no. 61300180 and the Fundamental Research Funds for the Central Universities of China with Grant no. TD2014-01.

References

1. Charoenhirunyingyosa, S., Hondaa, K., Kamthonkiatb, D., Inesc, A.: Soil moisture estimation from inverse modeling using multiple criteria functions. Comput. Electron. Agric. **75**(2), 278–287 (2011)
2. Coopersmith, E., Minsker, B., Wenzel, C., Gilmore, B.: Machine learning assessments of soil drying for agricultural planning. Comput. Electron. Agric. **104**, 93–104 (2014)
3. Coopersmitha, E., Minskera, B., Wenzelb, C., Gilmoreb, B.: Machine learning assessments of soil drying for agricultural planning. Comput. Electron. Agric. **104**, 93–104 (2014)
4. Culler, D., Estrin, D., Srivastava, M.: Overview of sensor networks. IEEE Comput. Mag. **37**(8), 41–49 (2004)
5. Dan, L., Sun, L., Dai, W.: Wireless sensor networks system of forest habitat factors collection. J. Harbin Inst. Technol. **46**(7), 123–128 (2014)
6. Dumedah, G., Coulibaly, P.: Evaluation of statistical methods for infilling missing values in high-resolution soil moisture data. J. Hydrol. **400**, 95–102 (2011)
7. Dumedah, G., Walker, J., Chik, L.: Assessing artificial neural networks and statistical methods for infilling missing soil moisture records. J. Hydrol. **515**(16), 330–344 (2014)
8. Farhangfar, A., Kurgan, L., Dy, J.: Impact of imputation of missing values on classification error for discrete data. Pattern Recogn. **41**, 3692–3705 (2008)
9. Gong, J., Geng, J., Chen, Z.: Real-time gis data model and sensor web service platform for environmental data management. Int. J. Health Geographics **14**(2) (2015)
10. Han, P., Wang, P., Zhang, S., Zhu, D.: Drought forecasting based on the remote sensing data using ARIMA models. Math. Comput. Model. **51**(11–12), 1398–1403 (2010)

11. Hardy, A., Barr, S., Mills, J., Miller, P.: Characterising soil moisture in transport corridor environments using airborne LIDAR and CASI data. Hydrol. Process. **26**(13), 1925–1936 (2012)
12. Kohn, R., Ansley, C.: Estimation, prediction, and interpolation for arima models with missing data. J. Am. Stat. Assoc. **81**(395), 751–761 (1986)
13. Kornelsen, K., Coulibaly, P.: Comparison of interpolation, statistical, and data-driven methods for imputation of missing values in a distributed soil moisture dataset. J. Hydrol. Eng. **19**(1), 26–43 (2014)
14. Lee, W., Alchanatis, V., Yang, C., Hirafuji, M., Moshou, D., Li, C.: Sensing technologies for precision specialty crop production. Comput. Electron. Agric. **74**(1), 2–33 (2010)
15. Li, J., Gao, H.: Survey on sensor network research. J. Softw. **45**(1), 1–15 (2008). (in Chinese)
16. Lindenmayer, D., Likens, G.: The science and application of ecological monitoring. Biol. Conserv. **143**, 1317–1328 (2010)
17. Meijering, E.: A chronology of interpolation: from ancient astronomy to modern signal and image processing. Proc. IEEE **90**, 319–342 (2002)
18. Moorthy, K., Mohamad, M.S., Deris, S.: A review on missing value imputation algorithms for microarray gene expression data. Current Bioinform. **9**, 18–22 (2014)
19. Mukhopadhyay, S., Jiang, J. (eds.): Wireless Sensor Networks and Ecological Monitoring (Smart Sensors, Measurement and Instrumentation). Springer, Heidelberg (2013)
20. Nemes, A., Wosten, J., Varallyay, G., Bouma, J.: Soil water balance scenariostudies using predicted soil hydraulic parameters. Hydrol. Process. **20**(5), 1075–1094 (2006)
21. Ojha, T., Misraa, S., Raghuwanshib, N.: Wireless sensor networks for agriculture: the state-of-the-art in practice and future challenges. Comput. Electron. Agric. **118**, 66–84 (2015)
22. Pigott, T.: A review of methods for missing data. Educ. Res. Eval. Int. J. Theory Pract. **7**, 353–383 (2001)
23. Pomati, F., Jokela, J., Simora, M., Veronesi, M., Ibelings, B.: An automated platform for phytoplankton ecology and aquatic ecosystem monitoring. Environ. Sci. Technol. **45**(22), 9658–9665 (2011)
24. Schneider, A.: Monitoring land cover change in urban and peri-urban areas using dense time stacks of landsat satellite data and a data mining approach. Remote Sens. Environ. **124**, 689–704 (2012)
25. Sun, G., Xu, B.: Drag: a priority-guaranteed routing for sensor network with low duty-cycles. Ad Hoc Sens. Wirel. Netw. **13**(1–2), 39–58 (2011)
26. Vachaud, G., Silans, A.P.D., Balabanis, P., Vauclin, M.: Temporal stability of spatially measured soil water probability density function. Soil Sci. Soc. Am. J. **49**(49), 822–828 (1985)
27. Wang, G., Garciab, D., Liu, Y., Jeua, R., Dolmana, A.: A three-dimensional gap filling method for large geophysical datasets: application to global satellite soil moisture observations. Environ. Model. Softw. **30**, 139–142 (2012)
28. Wang, J., Damevski, K., Chen, H.: Sensor data modeling and validating for wireless soil sensor network. Comput. Electron. Agric. **112**, 75–82 (2015)
29. Wang, N., Zhang, N., Wang, M.: Wireless sensors in agriculture and food industryrecent development and future perspective. Comput. Electron. Agric. **50**(1), 1–14 (2006)
30. Yang, J., Zhang, C., Li, X.: Integration of wireless sensor networks in environmental monitoring cyber infrastructure. Wirel. Netw. **16**(4), 1091–1108 (2010)

Redundancy Elimination of Big Sensor Data Using Bayesian Networks

Sai Xie, Zhe Chen$^{(\boxtimes)}$, Chong Fu, and Fangfang Li

School of Computer Science and Engineering, Northeastern University,
Shenyang, China
neuxs666@163.com, {chenzhe,fuchong,lifangfang}@mail.neu.edu.cn

Abstract. In the era of big data and Internet of things, massive sensor data are gathered with Internet of things. Quantity of data captured by sensor network are considered to contain highly useful and valuable information. However, since sensor data are usually correlated in time and space, not all the gathered data are valuable for further processing and analysis. Preprocessing is necessary for eliminating the redundancy in gathered massive sensor data. In this paper, approaches based on static Bayesian network (SBN) and dynamic Bayesian network (DBN) are proposed for preprocessing big sensor data, especially for redundancy elimination. Static sensor data redundancy detection algorithm (SSDRDA) for eliminating redundant data in static data sets and real-time sensor data redundancy detection algorithm (RSDRDA) for eliminating redundant sensor data in real-time are proposed. Experimental results show that the proposed algorithms are feasible and effective.

1 Introduction

Networks of thousands of sensors present a feasible and economic solution to some of our most challenging problems, such as environment monitoring, military sensing and tracking [1]. Since sensor data streams are measurements of continuous physical phenomenon, spatial and temporal correlations within data streams are inherent. Thus the probability that the data sampled by a node is highly correlated or repetitious over time is quite high [2].

Singular-value-qr decomposition (SVDQR) has been proposed in [3] to reduce the redundancy in wireless sensor networks. But this algorithm just select the principal data sets from particular sensor nodes to represent all the sensor nodes in the neighborhood, so the accuracy of redundant node detection is not very good. Extending an adaptive information filtering system to make decisions about the novelty and redundancy of relevant documents is addressed in [4]. [5] presents a simple and inexpensive on-line method to detect duplicates in the response set. [6] described a formulation of partial redundancy elimination based on a cost-benefits analysis of the flow graph. Costs and benefits are measured by the number of evaluations of an expression. But most of those methods mentioned above are used to process the redundancy of non-numeric data, such as text file. And these methods are hard to be used to process redundant data

© Springer International Publishing Switzerland 2016
Y. Wang et al. (Eds.): BigCom 2016, LNCS 9784, pp. 185–197, 2016.
DOI: 10.1007/978-3-319-42553-5_16

in realtime. Among the numerous tools designed for the analysis of temporal sequences, dynamic Bayesian networks has been the most successful one [7]. A dynamic Bayesian network (DBN) is an extension of static Bayesian network (SBN) to temporal domain, in which condition dependencies are modeled between random variables both within and across time slots [8]. In this paper, we present two redundancy elimination approaches based on SBN and DBN, respectively, i.e., static sensor data redundancy detection algorithm (SSDRDA) for eliminating redundant data in static data sets and real-time sensor data redundancy detection algorithm (RSDRDA) for eliminating redundant sensor data in real-time.

This paper is organized as follows: a brief literature survey related to Bayesian networks is described in Sects. 2. Then, in Sects. 3 and 4, the algorithm of static sensor data redundancy detection and real-time sensor data redundancy detection are presented with detailed description. Section 5 discusses the performance analysis and evaluation of our methods.

2   Problem Formulation

SBN represents a set of random variables in form of nodes on a directed acyclic graph. It indicates the conditional dependencies of the random variables. In a SBN, random variables are defined as a sequence $X=\{x_1, x_2, \cdots x_n\}$ and x_i is conditional dependent of its non-descendants given its parents. Therefore, the joint distribution of random variable x_i can be written as $P(x_1, x_2, \cdots, x_n) = \prod_{i=1}^{n} P(x_i|pa(x_i))$, where $pa(x_i)$ is the parent of x_i. A DBN is an extension of SBN to time domain, it is suitable for dealing with real-time problems. However, building a DBN with lots of random variables is a complex project. In practice, the structure of a Bayesian network will not change sharply in limited time, in order to simplify this problem, we make some reasonable assumptions [9]:

* the variation of condition probability is stable at a specific time.
* a dynamic process can be modeled by a first-order-Markovian:

$$P(x[t + 1]|x[1], x[2], \cdots, x[t]) = P(x[t + 1]|x[t])$$

* the transition probability $P(x[t + 1]|x[t])$ is stable in a time slot t

A DBN is formed with two parts $(B_0, B_\rightarrow)$, B_0 is an initial network which defines the prior $P(x[0])$, $B_\rightarrow$ is a transition network that defines a two slice temporal Bayes net [10]. Regardless it is initial network or transition network, the essence of learning the structure of DBN is to find the parents of a specific node. For initial network, it describes the relationship of nodes at current time, thus, the parents of typical node is at current time. For transition network, it describes the relationship of nodes between two slots, so the parents of one node in transition network is in its former time. The joint distribution of the model of DBN can be obtained by unrolling two slots temporal Bayes net until the network has T slots and multiplying together all of the conditional probability distributions:

$$P_{DBN}(x[0], x[1], \cdots, x[T]) = P_{B_0} \prod_{t=0}^{T-1} P_{B_{\rightarrow}}(x[t+1]|x[t]) \tag{1}$$

2.1 Learning the Structure of Bayesian Network

Building a specific Bayesian network can be described as finding a suitable structure of network while a training data set D is given. And a Bayesian network is represented as $B = (S, \theta)$, where S is the structure of network (i.e., determining what depends on what) and θ is the parameters (i.e., the strength of these dependencies) [11]. In order to build the Bayesian network, we divide the sensor data set into several random variables through cluster algorithm and get transition probability matrix through statistics approach [12]. In this paper, we use k-means algorithm to divide the sensor data, and the number of groups is dynamically determined by the degree of dispersion of sensor data. We use a score metrics to get the degree of matching between training sets D and the structure S, the probability of structure S while data set D is given can be written as:

$$P(S|D) = \frac{P(S)P(D|S)}{P(D)} = \frac{P(S) \int_\theta P(D|S, \theta)P(\theta|S)\, d\theta}{P(D)} \tag{2}$$

Thus, we can depend on the score metrics to search for the best Bayesian network. As we mentioned above, the main point of learning the structure of a network is to get the parent nodes of one specific node. From Eq. (2) we can get $P(S|D) \propto P(S)P(D|S)$, so we define a simplify score metrics:

$$Score = \log P(D|S, \theta_s) \tag{3}$$

where θ_s is the estimate optimal parameter which maximizes the likelihood function. For a dynamic network we give the following definition:

$$\theta^0_{i,j,k} = P(X_i[0] = k|pa(X_i[0]) = j), \theta^{\rightarrow}_{i,j,k} = P(X_i[t] = k|pa(X_i[t-1]) = j) \tag{4}$$

where $\theta^0_{i,j,k}$ is the conditional probability of X_i being in its kth value given that its parents $pa(X_i[0])$ in state j. $\theta^{\rightarrow}_{i,j,k}$ denotes in the transition network the conditional probability of X_i in its kth state at time t given that its parents $pa(X_i[t-1])$ in state j. We can get those conditional probabilities through statistical methods. Initial network describes the dependencies among the nodes at current time, and transition network describes the dependencies of the nodes between two temporal slots. So we define a counting rule for initial and transition networks as follows. If in initial network $T = t$, else if in transition network $T = t - 1$:

$$C(X_i[t] = k, pa(X_i[T]) = j) = \begin{cases} 1 & X_i[t] = k, pa(X_i[T]) = j \\ 0 & otherwise \end{cases} \tag{5}$$

According to the counting rule above, it is easy to get the number of specific state appeared in initial and transition network:

$$N^0_{i,j,k} = \sum_l C_0((X_i[0] = k, pa(X_i[0]) = j); X^l)$$

$$N^\rightarrow_{i,j,k} = \sum_l C_\rightarrow((X_i[t] = k, pa(X_i[t-1]) = j); X^l) \tag{6}$$

where ℓ denotes the number of training sequence, and in the training sequence $N_{i,j,k}$ denotes the number of X_i being in its kth state given that its parents in state j.

According to the methods mentioned above, we can get the conditional probability in initial network and transition network:

$$\theta^0_{i,j,k} = \frac{N^0_{i,j,k}}{\sum_k N^0_{i,j,k}}, \theta^\rightarrow_{i,j,k} = \frac{N^0_{i,j,k}}{\sum_k N^\rightarrow_{i,j,k}} \tag{7}$$

Consider the joint probability distribution of DBN, the likelihood function of a specific training data set given a possible network structure can be expressed as:

$$P(D|S, \theta_s) = \prod_i \prod_j \prod_k (\theta^0_{i,j,k})^{N^0_{i,j,k}} \times \prod_i \prod_j \prod_k (\theta^\rightarrow_{i,j,k})^{N^\rightarrow_{i,j,k}} \tag{8}$$

thus, the score metrics can be expressed as:

$$Score = \log P(D|S, \theta_s) = \sum_i \sum_j \sum_k N^0_{i,j,k} \times \log \theta^0_{i,j,k} + \sum_i \sum_j \sum_k N^\rightarrow_{i,j,k} \times \log \theta^\rightarrow_{i,j,k} \tag{9}$$

From the score metrics we can learn that the function is formed with two parts, one is the parameters in initial network, the other is the parameters in transition network. It denotes that the structure of initial and transition network can be learned separately. One of the most used algorithm for learning the structure of Bayesian network is k2 algorithm [13]. We combine the score metrics which was mentioned above with K2 algorithm, and K2 is like a greedy algorithm which maximizes the score of metrics. Because the structure of Bayesian network is directed acyclic graph (DAG) [14], in order to avoid cyclic graph in network, the K2 algorithm assumes an initial ordering of the nodes such that, if X_j proceeds X_i in order, an arc from X_j to X_i is not allowed. But the disadvantage is that the initial ordering should be based on prior expert knowledge, and in fact it is difficult to get the prior knowledge in practical environment. Thus, in the following algorithm we do not consider the initial ordering. First of all, we use K2 to get the dependencies of each node, and then modify the cyclic graph part in the network.

Algorithm 1. K2 algorithm

Input: - A set of nodes $X = \{X_1, X_2 \cdots, X_N\}$
       - A data set D
       - M is the maximum in the degree of node
Output: For each node, a printout of the parents of the node
1: **for** $i = 1$ to N **do**
2:     $\pi_i = \phi$
3:     $ScoreOld = score(D, pi_i, X_i)$
4:     $okToProceed = true$
5:     **while** okToProceed && $|\pi_i| < M$ **do**
6:       Let X_j be the node in $X - pi_i$ that maximizes $((D, pi_i, X_i)unionX_j)$
7:       $ScoreNew = Score((D, pi_i, X_i)unionX_j)$
8:       **if** $ScoreNew > ScoreOld$ **then**
9:         $ScoreOld = ScoreNew$
10:        $pi_i = pi_i unionX_j$
11:      **else**
12:        okToProceed=false
13:      **end if**
14:    **end while**
15: **end for**

3   Static Sensor Data Redundancy Detection

In a sensor network, there are many factors which cause data redundancy. For example, the gap among each node is close, the type of collecting data is similar. The sensor data stored in database is regarded as static data. We propose a static sensor data redundancy detection algorithm (SSDRDA) by building the SBN of the sensor nodes. According to the dependencies reflect in the SBN, the inference of redundant node can be figured out.

In the process of learning the structure of Bayesian network which mentioned above, we must first get the state transition probability matrix. Figure 1(a) shows an example of a Bayesian network structure for a four nodes problem. We can get the parents nodes of one specific node in the network. Figure 1(b) shows the transition probability matrix between current node and its dependent nodes. The row of the matrix denotes the number of state of parents nodes, and the column of the matrix denotes the number of state of current node. For each row $\sum_{i=1}^{n} P_{ki} = 1$, where $k = 1 \cdots m$. With the dependencies of each node, a specific node can form a subnet with its parent nodes. And according to the data sets those sensor nodes collected, we can get a state transition probability matrix of each subnet through statistical methods. If the conditional probability of X_t^i being in state s_{ik} approach to 1 given that its parents are in state s_i^{pa}, it indicates that we can inference the state of X_t^i by its parents node. And it is defined as:

$$P(X_t^i = s_{ik} | Pa(X_t^i) = s_i^{pa}) \longrightarrow 1 \tag{10}$$

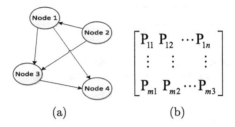

$$\begin{bmatrix} P_{11} & P_{12} & \cdots P_{1n} \\ \vdots & \vdots & \vdots \\ P_{m1} & P_{m2} & \cdots P_{m3} \end{bmatrix}$$

(a)   (b)

Fig. 1. A example of Bayesian network with four sensor nodes and transition probability matrix

---

Algorithm 2. Static Sensor Data Redundancy Detection Algorithm

---

Input: - A set of nodes $X = \{X_1, X_2 \cdots, X_N\}$
        - The Bayesian network of N nodes
Output: A printout of node redundancy
1: **for** $i = 1$ to N **do**
2:    isRedundancy=false
3:    set Pa_i to empty:$Pa_i = \phi$
4:    initialize the transition probability between X_i and its parents
       $transMatrix = \phi$
5:    $Pa_i = findTheParent(X_i)$
6:    $transMatrix = createTransMatrix(X_i, Pa_i)$
7:    **if** $\sum_{h=1}^{H} max(P(X_t^i = s_{ik} | Pa(X_t^i) = s_{ih}^{pa})) \longrightarrow H$ **then**
8:      $isRedundancy = true$
9:    **end if**
10: **end for**

Thus, if the state of current node can be inferred by parents nodes, we regard current node as redundant node. The conditional probability define as:

$$\sum_{h=1}^{H} max(P(X_t^i = s_{ik} | Pa(X_t^i) = s_{ih}^{pa})) \longrightarrow H \tag{11}$$

where X_t^i denotes node i at time t,s_{ik} denotes node i in its kth state, $Pa(X_t^i)$ denotes the parents nodes of node i at time t, s_{ih}^{pa} denotes the parents nodes in its hth state, H denotes the number of the state of parents nodes.

4   Real-Time Sensor Data Redundancy Detection

In Sect. 3, we have proposed an algorithm for static sensor data redundancy detection. Is there a way that we could detect the redundant node while it is working? If a specific node is detected as redundant node at time t, the node does not need to work at this time. A DBN is an extension of SBN to temporal domain, in which conditional dependencies are modeled between random variables both within and across time slots [7]. The varying dependencies of each node in DBN

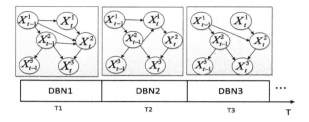

Fig. 2. The model of variable structure DBN

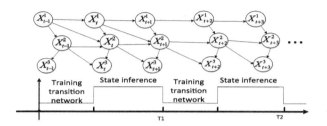

Fig. 3. The process of real-time redundancy detection

reflects the real-time characteristic of a sensor network. The main point of real-time data redundancy detection is that the state of a specific node at time t can be inferred by its dependent nodes at time $t-1$. The dependencies in a sensor network will not change sharply in limited time [15]. Figure 2 shows a model of variable structure DBN. If we unroll the DBN in $\{T_1, T_2 \cdots, T_n\}$ slices, the transition structure in each slice is invariable. Figure 3 shows that we split each time slice into two parts, in the former part all of the nodes are in waking state, and with the data collected in this part, we can learn the structure of Bayesian network in current time slice. As mentioned above, the structure of Bayesian network will not change sharply within a limited time. Thus, in the second part of the time slice, we use the structure which is trained in former part to predict the state of each node. Based on this mechanism, the sensor network is in a cycle of collecting data, learning transition network, and state inference.

Bayesian inference in SBN can be extended to DBN, and DBN mainly focus on the dependencies across two time slots [15,16]. Suppose the state sequence of node X is $\{X_1, X_2 \cdots, X_n\}$, if the conditional probability of node X in a specific states is approach to 1 given that the state of its parent nodes at previous time, it denotes that the state of current node X can be inferred by its parents nodes at previous time. If node X is working at this time the data collected by it can be regarded as redundant data. Node X in any states can be described as the confidence level of node X given that the state of its parent nodes as evidence.

Algorithm 3. Real-time Sensor Data Redundancy Detection

Input: - A set of nodes $X = \{X_1, X_2 \cdots, X_N\}$
           - The transition network for all nodes
           - The transition probability matrix for each node
           - A data set which was collected at $t - 1$ for all nodes
Output: A printout of state for each node
1: **for** $i = 1$ to N **do**
2:    $Sensor\_state = working$
3:    set Pa_i to empty: $Pa_i = \phi$
4:    initialize the transition probability between X_i and its parents
      $transMatrix = \phi$
5:    Find the parents of X_i according to the Bayesian network
      $Pa_i = findTheParent(X_i)$
6:    Get the states probability table of the parent of X_i at $t - 1$, elements in this
      table is like $P(X = states_i), i = 1, 2 \cdots$
7:    $transMatrix = createTransMatrix(X_i, Pa_i)$
8:    **for** $i = 1$ to $|state|$ **do**
9:        $P(X_s|e^{pa}) = \sum_{i,j \cdots k} P(X_s|pa_{1i}, pa_{2j}, \cdots, pa_{|pa|k}) \times \prod_{m=1}^{|pa|} P(pa_m|e_{pa_m})$
10:   **end for**
11:   **if** $max(P(X_s|e^{pa})) \to 1$ **then**
12:       $Sensor\_state = sleeping$
13:   **end if**
14: **end for**

For the inference list as follows:

$$P(X|e^{pa}) = P(X|e_{pa_1}, \cdots, e_{pa_i}, \cdots, e_{pa_{|pa|}})$$

$$= \sum_{i,j,\cdots k} P(X|pa_{1i}, \cdots, pa_{|pa|k})P(pa_{1i}, \cdots, pa_{|pa|k}|e_{pa_1}, e_{pa_2} \cdots e_{pa_{|pa|}})$$

$$= \sum_{i,j \cdots k} P(X|pa_{1i}, \cdots, pa_{|pa|k})P(pa_{1i}|e_{pa_1}) \cdots P(pa_{|pa|k}|e_{pa_{|pa|}}) \quad (12)$$

where pa_i denotes i^{th} parent node; e_{pa_i} denotes the probability of the state of parent node; $|pa|$ denotes the number of parent nodes; pa_{mn} denotes the value of parent node pa_i in state n. Thus, according to the evidence of parent nodes, the inference of current node in a specific state is defined as:

$$P(X_s|e^{pa}) = \sum_{i,j \cdots k} P(X_s|pa_{1i}, pa_{2j}, \cdots, pa_{|pa|k}) \prod_{m=1}^{|pa|} P(pa_{mn}|e_{pa_m}) \quad (13)$$

where s denotes the state of node X.

From Eq. (13) we can learn that the probability of current node in a specific state is the sum of the prior probability of the parents nodes in all state combination and the sum of conditional probability given that the state of its parents nodes. We can get the prior probability of the states of parents nodes in previous time through training data sets. Put the values of transition and state probability into Eq. (13), we can infer the specific state of current node. And the algorithm of real-time sensor data redundancy detection is shown above.

5 Experimental Results and Discussion

In this section, several experiments are conducted to validate the feasibility of the proposed algorithms on sensor data redundancy detection. Our test data comes from 25 sensor motes which use Arduino Leonardo boards, XBee radios, and a handful of off-the-shelf parts, including a temperature and humidity sensor, and an electret microphone amplifier. These motes were distributed around the conference venue, and reported back during the conference. The data were made publicly available online [17]. These sensor nodes collected temperature, humidity, and microphone values once every one minute. With the data collected by sensor nodes, we can learn the structure of dependencies among these nodes using the method described in Sect. 2.

Figure 4 shows the dependencies of each sensor node, in Fig. 4(a, b, c) horizontal axis denotes current node, and the star which are marked in vertical axis denotes its parent nodes. And in a static data set, if a specific node is detected as redundant node, it denotes the data collected by this node is redundancy and we can get those data by its parents nodes. Based on this mechanism, we can weigh

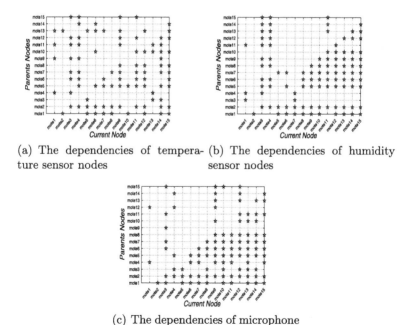

(a) The dependencies of temperature sensor nodes

(b) The dependencies of humidity
sensor nodes

(c) The dependencies of microphone
sensor nodes

Fig. 4. The dependencies of each sensor node in the data sets of temperature, humidity, and microphone

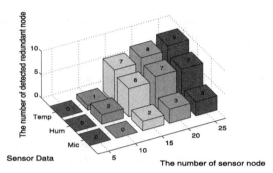

Fig. 5. The number of detected redundant nodes in different number of sensor nodes

the performance of our algorithm by the accuracy of estimating the redundant data. The root-mean-square-error (RMSE) between real and estimated values of redundant data can be regarded as metrics.

$$RMSE = \sqrt{mean[(y_{it} - \overline{y_{it}})^2]}, mean(RMSE) = \frac{\sum_{n=1}^{N} RMSE_n}{N} \quad (14)$$

where y_{it} is real value of node i at time t, $\overline{y_{it}}$ is predict value of node i at time t, mean(RMSE) is the mean RMSE of all redundant nodes, N is the number of redundant node.

For the static sensor data sets, we have proposed the SSDRDA to detect redundant nodes, and prior to the SSDRDA we have built a SBN (Fig. 4) of the 15 sensor nodes. Figure 5 shows the number of detected redundant nodes in different total number of sensor nodes. And we can learn that the number of redundant nodes in temperature and humidity data sets is more than microphone data set. The reason is that the temperature and humidity is gradually changed, and sensor nodes at different position may collect similar data. But the data of microphone sensor nodes collect is closely relevant to the position of the nodes and its data fluctuation is higher than that of temperature and humidity. Thus, the number of redundant nodes in temperature and humidity is more than microphone.

In our data sets there is no prior knowledge to clearly divide the set into redundant and non-redundant parts, so the effectiveness of the detected redundant sensor nodes is hard to be conducted in terms of recall and precision. In order to get the effectiveness of the algorithm, we estimate the data which is detected as redundant and the RMSE of estimating result can reflect the accuracy of our algorithm. Considering the purpose of estimating redundant data is just to validate the feasible of SSDRDA, we use the most common and simple method which named weight method for missing data estimation. In this method we put different weight on the parents of redundant nodes as Eq. (15), and the weight is base on the similarity between current node and its parent, d_k is the weight.

$$R = \frac{1}{W}[\sum_{k=1}^{N} (d_k X_k)] \quad (15)$$

where $W = \sum_{k=1}^{N} d_k$.

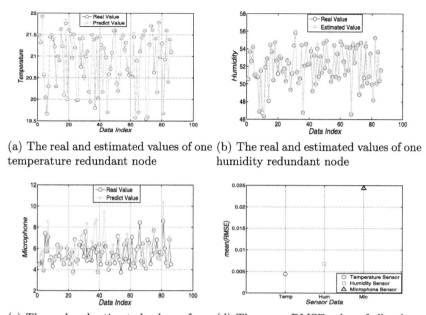

(a) The real and estimated values of one temperature redundant node

(b) The real and estimated values of one humidity redundant node

(c) The real and estimated values of one microphone redundant node

(d) The mean RMSE value of all redundant data in SSDRDA

Fig. 6. The results of estimating the data of redundant nodes in static data sets

Figure 6 shows the result of estimating the data of redundant node by its parents nodes. And Fig. 6(d) shows the mean RMSE of estimated and real value, because of the fluctuation of the data collected by microphone mote is higher than those of temperature and humidity, we can learn that the error rate of microphone data is higher than those of temperature and humidity.

Figure 3 shows the process of real-time redundancy detection. We define 100 min as one time slice, and in the first 60 min of a slice all of sensor nodes stay in waking, then use the data sets collected in first 60 min to build the transition network. Figure 7(a)-(c) shows the predicted state of the sensor nodes in the last 40 min. If the predicted state of one sensor node is "sleeping"at a specific time, it means if the node stay in waking at this time then it will generate redundant data and the node can sleep at this time. Otherwise, if the predicted state of one sensor node is "waking", then the node need to wake at this time. In order to validate the accuracy of the predicted state, we recover the redundant data. And Fig. 7(d) shows the mean RMSE of real and estimated data of all redundant node data. From Fig. 7(d) we can learn that the RSDRDA is good at real-time redundancy detection.

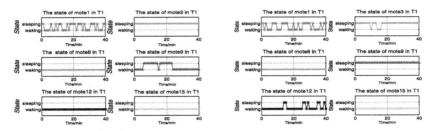

(a) The predicted state of sensor nodes using temperature data sets

(b) The predicted state of sensor nodes using humidity data sets

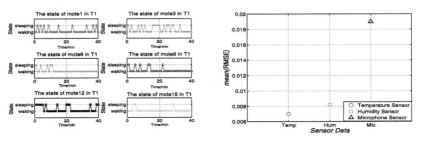

(c) The predicted state of sensor nodes using microphone data sets

(d) The mean RMSE value of all redundant data in RSDRDA

Fig. 7. The predicted state of parts of the sensor nodes using RSDRDA

6   Conclusion

This paper aims to big sensor data redundancy elimination. In this paper, approaches based on SBN and DBN are proposed for big sensor data elimination. We have proposed SSDRD to eliminate redundant data in a static data set and RSDRDA to eliminate redundant sensor data in real-time. And the RSDRDA is based on a new time varying DBN model that is capable of describing the evolution of nonstationary temporal sequences. In order to validate the accuracy of the proposed algorithms, we use a common method to recover redundant data, and the result of RMSE shows that the proposed algorithms are feasible and effective.

Acknowledgment. This work is supported by the Fundamental Research Funds for the Central Universities (N140404015, N150402004, and N140404013) and the National Natural Science Foundation of China (61271350).

References

1. Tsai, C.W., Lai, C.F., Chiang, M.C., Yang, L.T.: Data mining for internet of things: a survey. IEEE Commun. Surv. Tutorials **16**(1), 77–97 (2014)

2. Fateh, B., Govindarasu, M.: Energy minimization by exploiting data redundancy in real-time wireless sensor networks. Ad Hoc Netw. **11**(6), 1715–1731 (2013)
3. Liang, Q., Wang, L.: Redundancy reduction in wireless sensor networks using SVD-QR. In: Military Communications Conference, MILCOM 2005, vol. 3, pp. 1857–1861. IEEE (2005)
4. Zhang, Y., Callan, J., Minka, T.: Novelty and redundancy detection in adaptive filtering. In: Proceedings of the 25th Annual International ACM SIGIR Conference on Research and Development in Information Retrieval, pp. 81–88 (2002)
5. Dittrich, J.P., Seeger, B.: Data redundancy and duplicate detection in spatial join processing. In: International Conference on Data Engineering, pp. 535–546 (2000)
6. Horspool, R.N., Ho, H.: Partial redundancy elimination driven by a cost-benefit analysis. In: Proceedings of the Eighth Israeli Conference on Computer Systems and Software Engineering, pp. 111–118 (1997)
7. Wang, Z., Kuruoglu, E.E., Yang, X., Xu, Y.: Time varying dynamic Bayesian network for nonstationary events modeling and online inference. IEEE Trans. Sig. Process. **59**(4), 1553–1568 (2011)
8. Nielsen, S.H., Nielsen, T.D.: Adapting Bayes network structures to non-stationary domains. Int. J. Approximate Reasoning **49**(2), 379–397 (2008)
9. Ghanmy, N., Mahjoub, M.A., Amara, N.E.B.: Characterization of dynamic Bayesian network. Int. J. Adv. Comput. Sci. Appl. **2**(7), 53–60 (2011)
10. Sun, J., Sun, J.: A dynamic Bayesian network model for real-time crash prediction using traffic speed conditions data. Transp. Res. Part C Emerg. Technol. **54**, 176–186 (2015)
11. Larrañaga, P., Karshenas, H., Bielza, C., Santana, R.: A review on evolutionary algorithms in Bayesian network learning and inference tasks. Inf. Sci. **233**, 109–125 (2013)
12. Song, L., Kolar, M., Xing, E.P.: Time-varying dynamic Bayesian networks. Adv. Neural Inf. Process. Syst. **22**, 1732–1740 (2009)
13. Bouchaala, L., Masmoudi, A., Gargouri, F., Rebai, A.: Improving algorithms for structure learning in Bayesian networks using a new implicit score. Expert Syst. Appl. **37**(7), 5470–5475 (2010)
14. Cheng, J., Greiner, R., Kelly, J., Bell, D., Liu, W.: Learning Bayesian networks from data: an information-theory based approach. Artif. Intell. **137**(1), 43–90 (2002)
15. Murphy, K.P.: Dynamic Bayesian networks: representation, inference and learning. Probab. Graph. Models **13**, 303–306 (2002)
16. Robinson, J.W., Hartemink, A.J.: Non-stationary dynamic Bayesian networks. Adv. Neural Inf. Process. Syst. **11**(18), 1369–1376 (2008)
17. Hardware hacking for data scientists (2012). http://datasensinglab.com

IoT Sensing Parameters Adaptive Matching Algorithm

Zhijin Qiu[1], Naijun Hu[2], Zhongwen Guo[1(✉)], Like Qiu[1], Shuai Guo[1], and Xi Wang[1]

[1] Department of Computer Science and Technology, Ocean University of China, Qingdao, China
qzjouc@163.com, guozhw@ouc.edu.cn
[2] Information Center, Administration for Industry and Commerce of Qingdao, Qingdao, China

Abstract. As the 'Industry 4.0' and 'Made in China 2025' has been put forward, the need of the large-scale system integration for Internet of Things (IoT) has been more and more urgent. At present, different IoT systems have different database types, table structures and denominating rules for sensing parameters. So for the existing IoT system integration, there are such as sensing parameter's conversion difficulty, complex matching process, low integrating efficiency issues. To solve these problems, we propose a novel model for IoT sensing parameter automatically matching which can achieve the IoT system integration on a large-scale. Meanwhile combining KNN thought, using a weighted method to improve the KNN algorithm, we put forward the automatic IoT sensing parameters matching algorithm. By the multiple practical IoT system integration cases, we validate the rationality and efficiency of the model and the algorithm. The result shows that the model and the algorithm are feasible and efficient. They realize the rapid automatic matching for the heterogeneous IoT sensing parameters, improving the IoT system's integration efficiency. It is conducive to the large-scale heterogeneous IoT system quick integration and has great significance to promote the IoT's application in large scale.

Keywords: Internet of Things · KNN · System integration · Parameter matching

1 Introduction

With the development of Internet of Things (IoTs) technology, IoT begins to be applied in the areas of production and life. A typical IoT architecture, through the front sensors collecting the external physical information changes, it converts the acquired information into electrical signal according to a certain rule. Then it transmits, processes, analyze, and store the information through network and computer. The acquired sensing data and the analyzed results can be visually display in the form of curve, data list, etc. Currently, the IoT has been widely

© Springer International Publishing Switzerland 2016
Y. Wang et al. (Eds.): BigCom 2016, LNCS 9784, pp. 198–211, 2016.
DOI: 10.1007/978-3-319-42553-5_17

applied in the meteorology, medicine, environment and industrial production and other fields [1–5].

In the 'Industry 4.0' and 'Made in China 2025' plan, it mentions that the development of industrial enterprises needs to integrate lots of IoTs to form large data storage and data accumulation in order to process and analyze big data to improve the management and decision-making in the modern enterprises and promote the enterprises' transforming and upgrading [6,7]. At present, a lot of IoT systems are isolated from each other. For the sake of quick IoTs' integration, achieving the big data's process, analysis and application, it needs to come together the monitoring data collected by the existing IoTs [8–10]. So it needs to process the monitoring data which is stored in the different IoTs' database with the unified format, then store these data into the standard database of the integration platform and publish the external standard interfaces. As the different manufacturers use different IoTs' database, different table structure and different sensing parameter denominating methods [11–13], so in the data conversion, different data storage format requires different data converting process. In this process, it needs to configure the mapping relationship for the sensing parameters. Due to so many IoT's monitoring data, the mapping configuration is so complex, heavy workload and low efficiency.

Early IoT's research mainly focuses on the system's underlying algorithm design [14–16], the specific system implementation [17,18], and how to improve the efficiency of system's development [19,20], etc. There are few of research on IoT integration. In the paper [21], the author proposed an object-oriented architecture for IoT development to achieve modularity, reusability and independent design of hardware. In the literature [22], it studied the methods for IoTs' data acquisition and put forward a data collection method with high efficiency and low energy. In [23], it described a IoT's framework based on service and proposed the integration method of IoT. In the reference [24], it studied to standardize data interfaces after information system integration. The above researches have a very in-depth study on the IoT's architecture, data acquisition and so on. But for the large-scale IoTs' integration, it needs to research how to match data in the integrating process for the heterogeneous IoT systems. For the aforementioned problems, we summary and abstract the method for large-scale IoTs' integration, through the analysis of historical data, adopting the improved KNN algorithm to achieve the fast and automatic sensing parameters' matching between IoTs' database and integration platform's database, shorten the sensor parameters' mapping time and improve the efficiency of IoTs' integration. In order to ensure the effectiveness of the algorithm, it validates the rationality and efficiency of the model and the algorithm through the multiple IoTs' application cases.

2 Sensing Parameters' Matching Algorithm

2.1 Sensing Parameters' Matching Model

As shown in Fig. 1, when IoTs are integrated, the main work is the mapping for sensing parameters between the IoTs' database and integration platform's

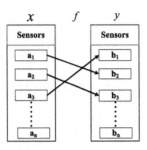

Fig. 1. Sensing parameters' mapping

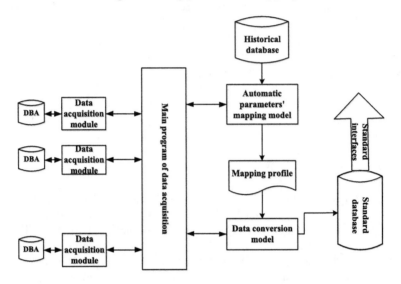

Fig. 2. Model of sensing parameters' matching

database. Currently, when integrating the sensing data, the developer needs to analyze the storage structure of database and sensing parameter x for the new IoT's integration, then configure these parameters as y in the integrated IoT's database according to the analysis. They implement the mapping relationship f between databases to convert the time-serial sensing data which is transmitted into the integrated platform's database in real-time. Due to the specific scenarios, there are masses of sensing parameters need to map, so the configuration is complicated and so high erroneous rate.

According to the same features of the IoT system's monitoring parameters in the specific application environment, based on there has been a lot of historical data in the integrated database and through the appropriate machine learning algorithms, we compare and analyze every sensing parameter between acquired parameters and historical parameters, completing to establish the sensing parameters' mapping relationship automatically. The model for sensing parameters' automatic matching as shown Fig. 2.

Data acquisition module: the data acquisition model corresponds to every IoT's database and connects to the accessing database directly. The model's function completes analyzing database's content based on the different databases' storing structures to extract the names and the values of sensing parameters.

Main program of data acquisition: the main program of data acquisition calls each data acquisition model dynamically and collects the acquired sensing parameters.

Automatic parameters' mapping model: through matching the sensing parameters in the historical database with the parameters in the IoT's database, it establishes the mapping relationship for the sensing parameters and formulates the sensing parameters' mapping profile.

Mapping profile: it describes the standard of the sensing parameters' mapping relationship which is established by the automatic parameters' mapping model.

Data conversion model: by loading and analyzing the mapping profile, it analyzes, maps and converts the sensing parameters acquired by the main program of data acquisition. Then it will store these converted parameters into the standard database according to the standard data format.

Standard interfaces: it publishes and shares the integrated data based on the standard data interfaces.

2.2   Improved KNN Algorithm

k-Nearest Neighbor algorithm (KNN) is one of the best algorithms for the classifying algorithm in data mining. KNN is the non-parametric estimating method which calculates objects' different eigenvalues to classify [25]. KNN algorithm extracts historical data's features based on the chosen features. The training parameters are formatted as feature vectors T.

The specific implementing procedures as follows:

Step 1. Depending on the choice of the features, acquiring the historical data's features' values in order to get the training set T of feature values vector. Among them, m represents the number of the training set, n represents the dimensions of the features.

$$T = \begin{pmatrix} t_{1,1} & \cdots & t_{1,n} \\ \vdots & \ddots & \vdots \\ t_{m,1} & \cdots & t_{m,n} \end{pmatrix} \tag{1}$$

S represents the vector of the training set and its corresponding parameters' type. Among them, p is the sensing parameters' category.

$$S = (T, Y) = \begin{pmatrix} t_{1,1} & \cdots & t_{1,n} & y_1 \\ t_{2,1} & \cdots & t_{2,n} & y_1 \\ t_{3,1} & \cdots & t_{3,n} & y_2 \\ \vdots & \ddots & \vdots \\ t_{m,1} & \cdots & t_{m,n} & y_p \end{pmatrix} \tag{2}$$

Step 2. Given testing parameter objects, according to the selected features, generating the testing set T'.

$$T' = (t'_1, t'_2, \cdots, t'_n) \tag{3}$$

Step 3. Calculate the Euclidean distance of each row vector in T' and T.

$$l_i(t'_j, t_{i,j}) = \sqrt{\sum_{j=1}^{n}(t'_j - t_{i,j})^2} \quad (i = 1, 2, \cdots, m) \tag{4}$$

Step 4. Sort the l_i, select the first K smallest distance values.

Step 5. According to the chosen K neighboring main categories, classify the testing parameter objects.

KNN has the traits of simple procedures, easy to understand, easy to implement, without training, high accuracy, and low outliers interference. But its disadvantages are the high computational complexity, large memory overhead. This paper gives good solutions for computing efficiency and space taking through optimizing and improving the KNN algorithm.

Grouping Fast Searching KNN Algorithm. KNN classification algorithm is the lazy one, testing set needs to calculate the Euclidean distance for each parameter in the training set, there are shortcomings of computing intensive, low efficient classification. Meanwhile, because it needs to calculate the Euclidean distance between each parameter, thereby it will produce a temporary boundary training set which will have a negative effect on the testing results and reduce the classifying accuracy. By using grouping fast searching KNN algorithm, it will optimize the KNN algorithm's large computation, low classifying efficiency and accuracy.

KNN grouping fast searching algorithm breaks the training set down into groups according to the category, calculates each group's center position which can represent this group. Testing set calculates the distance with every group's center position. Then select several nearest groups to apply the KNN algorithm to calculate the distances between the testing set and every training sets in the chosen groups. Sort the calculating distances and chose the $pre - K$ minimum values, then based on these K nearest neighboring main categories to classify the testing parameter objects. By KNN grouping fast searching algorithm, on the basis of ensuring the matching accuracy for sensing parameters, reduces the calculation and improves the classifying efficiency. The experiments show that the algorithm is suitable for sensing parameters' automatic matching in the large amount.

KNN Weighted Algorithm. When performing KNN algorithm to calculate the Euclidean distance of each row vector in the testing set and the training set, according to the same calculation for every weighted feature has the same contribution to the final outcome. But for the procedure for sensing parameters' automatic matching, every same weighted feature can't meet the actual needs. Equal weight has different distance between the feature vectors or cosine after calculation. There by the in accurate calculation affects the classifying accuracy. When matching sensing parameters, the greater dispersion features have, the more data can represent the features of different sensing parameters and the larger contribution on sensing parameters' matching. The small discrimination illustrates the small dispersion of different sensing parameters on this feature. For different contribution to each feature, the large dispersion sets higher weight, the small dispersion has small one. The variance is just a measure which can weigh the difference between sensing parameters and expectations on the different features and the fluctuation of sensing parameters.

KNN weighted algorithm uses the features' variance as the weight of this feature when calculating the Euclidean distance. The improved calculating method is as follows:

$$l_i(t'_j, t_{i,j}) = \sqrt{\sum_{j=1}^{n} \omega_j (t'_j - t_{i,j})^2} \quad (i = 1, 2, \cdots, m) \tag{5}$$

Among them, m is the amount of the training sets, n is the feature's dimension, ω is the variance of each feature.

2.3 Automatic Matching Algorithm for Sensing Parameters

On the basis of the proposed sensing parameters' adaptive matching model and the improved KNN algorithm, we propose the algorithm for sensing parameters' automatic matching which can reduce the calculation and achieve more accurately matching sensing parameters. The procedures of algorithm as below:

Step 1. Establish the connection between data acquisition module and IoT's database, analyze data and extract sensing parameters of the database.

Step 2. The main program of data acquisition calls data acquisition model to realize collecting the contents of sensing parameters.

Step 3. Parameters' automatic mapping model acquires historical data's eigenvalues according to the chosen features to get the feature vector set T of the training set (See formula 1). Among them, m is the amount of the training sets, n is the feature's dimension. Then solving the features' center coordinate C_p of every sensing parameter.

Step 4. Given testing parameter objects, according to the extracted features to generate test vectors T' (See formula 3). Calculate the distance l_p between testing vector and every feature's center coordinate C. Among them, p is the amount of sensing parameters' category.

$$l_p(t'_j, C_p) = \sqrt{\sum_{j=1}^{n} (t'_j - C_{k,j})^2} \quad (k = 1, 2, \cdots, p) \tag{6}$$

Sort the l_p in ascending order, chose the first $\hat{m}$ sensing parameters' categories and adopt the selected sensing parameters' feature vector to generate the new feature vector $\hat{T}$ of the training set.

$$\hat{T} = \begin{pmatrix} \hat{t}_{1,1} & \cdots & \hat{t}_{1,n} \\ \vdots & \ddots & \vdots \\ \hat{t}_{\hat{m},1} & \cdots & \hat{t}_{\hat{m},n} \end{pmatrix} \tag{7}$$

Step 5. Calculate every eigenvalue's mean μ_j and variance D_j.

$$\mu_j = E_j = \sum_{i=1}^{m} \hat{t}_{i,j}/\hat{m} \tag{8}$$

$$D_j = \sum_{j=1}^{m} (\hat{t}_{i,j} - \mu_j)^2/\hat{m} \tag{9}$$

Normalize each feature's variance to get D'_j.

$$D'_j = \frac{D_j - \min(D_j)}{\max(D_j) - \min(D_j)} \tag{10}$$

According to KNN weighted algorithm, take D'_j as the weight ω_j of each feature, that is $\omega_j = D'_j$. Calculate the Euclidean distance l_i of each row in testing sets and vector sets.

$$l_i(t'_j, \hat{t}_{i,j}) = \sqrt{\sum_{j=1}^{n} \omega_j(t'_j - \hat{t}_{i,j})^2} \quad (i = 1, 2, \cdots, \hat{m}) \tag{11}$$

Step 6. Sort l_i and chose $pre - K$ smallest values.

Step 7. According to these K neighboring main categories Y, sort testing parameter objects and generates the mapping profile.

Step 8. Data conversion model analyzes and maps the sensing parameters acquired by the main program of data acquisition by loading sensing parameters' mapping profile and convert these parameters to the standard data format stored in the standard database.

Step 9. Complete the sensing parameter's automatic matching procedures.

3   Algorithm Validation

3.1   Validating Environment

In order to verify the feasibility and the efficiency of the sensing parameters' automatic matching algorithm, we validate the algorithm on the basis of the existing data and the integrating database structure in refrigerator product test.

Fridge in the developing and testing period needs to be sampled to test its refrigerating capacity. The testing method firstly falls the freezing chamber to $-18\,^{\circ}$C, then places the freezing chamber to the Ballast load M package in the room temperature to start continuing cooling. In 24 h, the refrigerator's freezing load descends from $25\,^{\circ}$C to $-18\,^{\circ}$C, meanwhile, the freezing chamber's temperature keeps from $0\,°C$ to $12\,°C$. In order to describe the temperature and electrical parameters in the testing procedure, the parameters needed to be tested includes the temperature of cold closet, freezing chamber and refrigerating load M package as well as room temperature, voltage, current, power and power consumption.

For the sake of ensuring the scientific verification for the algorithm, by analyzing the sensing parameters in the historical database, we analyze the testing data accumulated in the recent two years. These parameters are collected by 156 tests, every test last 24 h, the acquiring interval is 2 s. At last 6,739,200 records have been got and every record contains 8 sensing parameters. We select 30 times testing data to validate in the accessing database.

3.2   Algorithm Implementation

Features' Selection. By analyzing the product testing method and the features of testing data, choose the features which can describe each category of sensing parameters completely.

Firstly, choose the features of the cold closet's temperature, the freezing chamber's temperature, the temperature of freezing load M package and the room temperature. In the time-serial data, the extreme points generally are of great significance. Through analyzing, we found that the temperatures of cold closet, freezing chamber, room are quite different, so the maximum, minimum, average of the testing data can be selected as the features. The freezing chamber's temperature and the temperature of the freezing load M package have the similar value in the numerical range, but both temperatures' changing trend are different, so the maximum and minimum slope need to be added in the features. The temperature's trend of the freezing load M package change from above freezing to subzero, so whether crossing the zero can be used as one of the features. Meanwhile, variance can measure the dispersion of the testing parameters well, so it can be a feature. Secondly, about voltage, current, electrical parameters of power and power consumption, the voltage remains substantially stable status, the value range is relatively stable around the rated voltage, current and power variation is consistent, but the value range is very different. Power consumption feature parameter keeps increasing in the testing process.

According to the above analysis, the selected features includes maximum, minimum, mean, variance, zero-passing point or not, the maximum positive and negative slopes.

Automatic Parameters' Matching. Data acquisition module establishes the connection with the IoT's database, then analyzes the data's contents and extracts the sensing parameters. The main program of data acquisition calls each data acquisition model dynamically and collects the acquired sensing values. Then the parameters' automatic mapping model obtains sensing values to do the format. The formatted data will be stored in Excel. Parameter's automatic mapping model reads the stored unified sensing data, obtains the historical data's features according to the selected features and gets the training set T. The recorded every sensor's name is to be as a label Y. Among them, the amount of the training set m is $156 * 8 = 1248$, the feature's dimension n is 7 and the solved center points of every sensor's feature C (See formula 12).

$$
C = \begin{pmatrix}
6.26 & 2.71 & 3.35 & 0.37 & 0 & 0.82 & -0.5 \\
-11.19 & -30.05 & -21.24 & 25.6 & 0 & 4.2 & -2.1 \\
28.73 & -24.6 & 5.09 & 398.83 & 1 & 19.5 & -21.92 \\
28.84 & 24.62 & 28.19 & 0.68 & 0 & 2.98 & -3.05 \\
220.11 & 219.8 & 219.96 & 0.35 & 0 & 0.23 & -0.15 \\
0.68 & 0 & 0.22 & 0.02 & 0 & 1 & -1 \\
149 & 0 & 43.81 & 952.96 & 0 & 2 & -1 \\
7.39 & 0 & 4.19 & 4.61 & 0 & 0.01 & 0
\end{pmatrix}
\tag{12}
$$

Give the testing parameter objects, choose the testing data in the accessing database, according to the selected features to generate the testing vector T' and record every testing sensor's name as the label Y'. Among them, the amount of testing sets is 30, the feature's dimension is 7.

Calculate the distance l between each testing set in the testing vector and each row vector in C. Sort the l in ascending order, choose the first 3 types of sensing parameters. Generate the feature vector $\hat{T}$ for the selected sensing parameters. Among them, the amount of the training sets is $156 * 3 = 468$ changing from m to $\hat{m}$, the feature's dimension is 7. Calculate the mean μ_j and the variance D_j of each eigenvalue's dimension and normalize every feature's variance D_j to get D'_j, the results is shown in Table 1.

According to KNN weighted algorithm, take D'_j as every feature's weight w_j. Calculate the Euclidean distance l_i between the testing set and each row vector in vector sets $\hat{T}$, now $n = 7$, $\hat{m} = 468$.

Sort the 468 calculated distances l in ascending order, select the K smallest values, according to the $pre - K$ neighboring main sensors' name label Y, establish the mapping relationship with the sensor's labels Y' in the testing sample and generate the both mapping profile. Data conversion model loads the sensing parameter's mapping profile to analyze and map the sensing parameters acquired

Table 1. The result of data processing

Feature	Average	Variance	Normalization
Maximum	53.73	329.61	0.00996
Minimum	24.06	397.88	0.01203
Mean	35.45	296.30	0.00895
Variance	172.93	33073.39	1
Zero-passing point or not	0.125	0.22	0
Maximum positive slopes	3.72	72.20	0.00218
Maximum negative slopes	−3.18	101.32	0.00306

by the main program of data acquisition. Then it converts these parameters to the standard data format stored into the standard database, and completes the parameter's automatic matching process.

K Value Choice. In order to ensure the accuracy of the sensing parameter's automatic matching algorithm, the appropriate K value will affect the label's mapping result directly. If the K value is too small, although the low computing complexity, it is susceptible by the noisy point and has the low accuracy. If the K value is too large, the computing complexity will increase and the accuracy is not guaranteed. In the existing validating environments for the algorithm, we do the comparative analysis for the accuracy of the label Y and Y' mapping relationship for different K values. K value typically is lower than the square root of the number of the training samples, different K values have different accuracy as shown in Table 2. As can be seen in Fig. 3, when the K value is 11, the accuracy is the highest.

Implementation of Sensing Parameter's Matching System. As shown in Fig. 4, according to the proposed sensing parameter's matching model, we design and implement the sensing parameter's matching system. The main implementing functions include the data acquisition model, the main program of data acquisition and automatic parameters' mapping model. Among them, it includes database connecting wizard which can guide the connecting parameters' configuration of the accessing database visually to realize accessing to different types of databases. In order to ensure the accuracy of the generated mapping profile,

Table 2. Accuracy of different K values

K	1	3	5	7	9	11	13	15	17	19	21	23
Accuracy %	85.12	85.20	86.12	89.11	91.86	92.80	92.65	91.52	91.41	91.32	91.26	91.25

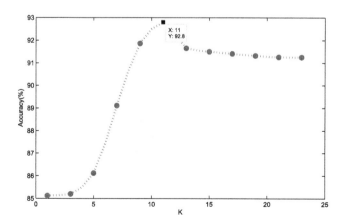

Fig. 3. Accuracy of different K values

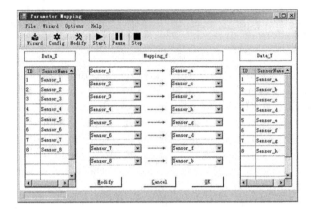

Fig. 4. The GUI of sensing parameters' matching system

it will not only display the results after automatically matching sensing parameters but also support the modification for the error mapping relationship. And it supports to save and import the parameter's mapping profile.

3.3   Performing Analysis of Algorithm

Analysis of Algorithm's Accuracy. According to different features have different effects on the classification, when using the sensing parameter's adaptive matching algorithm to calculate the feature's distance, KNN weighted algorithm is used to improve the matching accuracy.

According to the validating environment, select 30 times of testing data and obtain the variances of different features through using Table 1 to compare these two algorithms. The compared result as shown in Table 3, it can greatly improve the matching accuracy of sensing parameters through KNN weighted algorithm.

Table 3. Comparison of different algorithms accuracy

Parameter	KNN (average)		Weighted KNN (average)	
	Value	Rate	Value	Rate
Cold closet's temperature	25	83.3	29	96.7
Freezing chamber's temperature	26	86.7	30	100
Freezing load M package's temperature	25	83.3	30	100
Room temperature	27	90.0	29	96.7
Voltage	30	100.0	30	100.0
Current	29	96.7	30	100.0
Power	29	96.7	30	100.0
Power consumption	30	100.0	30	100.0

Through the above theory and verification, it can be proved that selecting variance as the distance to calculate the weight is right and effective. The classifying result's accuracy of the weighted KNN algorithm depends on the chosen weight. As can be seen in Table 1, whether zero-crossing feature weight is 0 which indicates this feature is similar in different tests. In the process of sensing parameter's matching, this feature is the redundant item, the weight is 0 indicates the feature's dimension decreases from 7 to 6. As can be seen, weighting KNN is also a method of selecting the features.

Analysis of Algorithm's Executing Efficiency. KNN classification algorithm is the lazy one, sensing parameter's adaptive matching algorithm improves the algorithm through the grouping fast searching method. Firstly, calculate the distances m between testing sets and the center point of each type of sensor's parameters. Sort the calculated distances in ascending order, select the first $\hat{m}$ types of sensors' parameters. Then use the selected feature vectors of sensor's parameters to generate the new feature vectors of the training sets. Through the grouping fast searching method, the efficiency of the algorithm is improved $m/\hat{m}$ times. In the algorithm's validation of this paper, ensuring the algorithm's accuracy, the efficiency of the algorithm is improved $m/\hat{m} = 1248/468 \approx 2.67$ times.

4 Conclusion

In this paper, we propose a sensing parameters matching algorithm, which realized sensing parameters adaptive matching between different IoT systems. Through improving and optimizing KNN algorithm, we improve the accuracy and reduce the computing complexity of the algorithm. We use the existing test environment to validate our model and algorithm. The result shows that our algorithm is more stable and more efficient. Our algorithm reduced the sensor parameter's mapping process between IoT systems and improved the efficiency of the IoT system integration. Our contributions as follows:

(1) Through putting forward the model for matching sensing parameters automatically, we define the sensor parameter adaptive mapping process between IoT systems.

(2) For solving the shortcomings of KNN algorithm's high computing complexity and large amount of data. etc., the improved grouping fast searching KNN algorithm reduced the computing complexity and improved the efficiency of the algorithm.

(3) According to different characteristics of different effects on the final classification result, we selected characteristic of variance as calculating the weights of KNN algorithm, which improved the classification accuracy and reduce the dimension of feature.

(4) Through the existing validating environment, we implement the sensing parameters adaptive matching model and validate the rationality and feasibility of aforesaid algorithm in the K value selection, algorithm's complexity

and accuracy. The results show that the algorithm can quickly establish sensing parameter's mapping relationship between different IoT systems and can achieve adaptive fast matching of the sensing parameters, at the same time, the improved algorithm can reduce the complexity of the original algorithm.

Our future work will try to use other classification algorithms and study the algorithm's computing complexity, accuracy and efficiency. Meanwhile, we are going to study the data's transmitting security for the IoT system integration and apply the sensing parameters adaptive matching model in wider areas and do the further study and validation.

Acknowledgment. Zhijin Qiu and Naijun Hu contributed equally to this work and should be regarded as co-first authors. This work is supported by the National Natural Science Foundation of China (Grant No. 61379127, No. 61572448 and No. 61170258), and Natural Science Foundation of Shandong ZR2014JL043. I would like to express my sincere gratitude to Yingjian Liu for her encouragement and constructive feedback.

References

1. Girish, S., Prakash, R.: Real-time remote monitoring of indoor air quality using internet of things (IoT) and GSM connectivity. In: Dash, S.S., Arun Bhaskar, M., Panigrahi, B.K., Das, S. (eds.) ICAIECES 2015. AISC, vol. 394, pp. 527–533. Springer, Heidelberg (2016)
2. Atzori, L., Iera, A.: The internet of things: a survey. Comput. Netw. **54**(15), 2787–2805 (2010)
3. Jara, A.J., Zamora, M.A.: An architecture based on internet of things to support mobility and security in medical environments. In: 2010 7th IEEE Consumer Communications and Networking Conference (CCNC), pp. 1–5. IEEE (2010)
4. Luo, J., Chen, Y.: Remote monitoring information system and its applications based on the internet of things. In: International Conference on Future BioMedical Information Engineering, FBIE 2009, pp. 482–485. IEEE (2009)
5. Bandyopadhyay, D., Sen, J.: Internet of things: applications and challenges in technology and standardization. Wirel. Pers. Commun. **58**(1), 49–69 (2011)
6. Lee, J., Kao, H.A.: Service innovation and smart analytics for industry 4.0 and big data environment. Procedia CIRP **16**, 3–8 (2014)
7. Spiess, P., Karnouskos, S.: SOA-based integration of the internet of things in enterprise services. In: IEEE International Conference on Web Services, ICWS 2009, pp. 968–975 (2009)
8. Bernardo, M., Casadesus, M.: Do integration difficulties influence management system integration levels? J. Clean. Prod. **21**(1), 23–33 (2012)
9. Tummala, R.R.: SOP: what is it and why? A new microsystem-integration technology paradigm-Moore's law for system integration of miniaturized convergent systems of the next decade. IEEE Trans. Adv. Packag. **27**(2), 241–249 (2004)
10. Chapman, C.S., Kihn, L.A.: Information system integration, enabling control and performance. Account. Organ. Soc. **34**(2), 151–169 (2009)
11. Chao, L., Qingsong, Y.: Component-based cloud computing service architecture for measurement system. In: 2013 IEEE International Conference on Green Computing and Communications and IEEE Internet of Things and IEEE Cyber, Physical and Social Computing, pp. 1650–1655. IEEE (2013)

12. Zhou, L., Chao, H.C.: Multimedia traffic security architecture for the internet of things. IEEE Netw. **25**(3), 35–40 (2011)
13. Riedel, T., Fantana, N.: Using web service gateways and code generation for sustainable IoT system development. In: Internet of Things (IOT), pp. 1–8. IEEE (2010)
14. Gubbi, J., Buyya, R.: Internet of things (IoT): a vision, architectural elements, and future directions. Future Gener. Comput. Syst. **29**(7), 1645–1660 (2013)
15. Kortuem, G., Kawsar, F., Fitton, D., et al.: Smart objects as building blocks for the internet of things. IEEE Internet Comput. **14**(1), 44–51 (2010)
16. Atzori, L., Iera, A.: SIoT: giving a social structure to the internet of things. IEEE Commun. Lett. **15**(11), 1193–1195 (2011)
17. Ning, H., Wang, Z.: Future internet of things architecture: like mankind neural system or social organization framework? IEEE Commun. Lett. **15**(4), 461–463 (2011)
18. Zorzi, M., Gluhak, A.: From today's intranet of things to a future internet of things: a wireless-and mobility-related view. IEEE Wirel. Commun. **17**(6), 44–51 (2010)
19. Wei, C., Li, Y.: Design of energy consumption monitoring and energy-saving management system of intelligent building based on the internet of things. In: 2011 International Conference on Electronics, Communications and Control (ICECC), pp. 3650–3652. IEEE (2011)
20. Chen, P., Guo, Z.W.: An advanced platform to develop test software for domestic appliances based on hybrid architecture. In: IEEE Instrumentation and Measurement Technology Conference, I2MTC 2009, pp. 743–748. IEEE (2009)
21. Daponte, P., Grimaldi, D.: Distributed measurement systems: an object-oriented architecture and a case study. Comput. Stand. Interfaces **18**(5), 383–395 (1997)
22. Qiu, Z.J., Guo, Z.W.: Adaptive high-speed data acquisition algorithm in sensor network nodes. J. Southeast Univ. Nat. Sci. Ed. **42**, 238–244 (2012)
23. Guo, Z.W., Chen, P.: IMA: an integrated monitoring architecture with sensor networks. IEEE Trans. Instrum. Meas. **61**(5), 1287–1295 (2012)
24. Guo, Z.W., Chen, P.: ISDP: interactive software development platform for household appliance testing industry. IEEE Trans. Instrum. Meas. **59**(5), 1439 (2010)
25. Keller, J.M., Gray, M.R.: A fuzzy k-nearest neighbor algorithm. IEEE Trans. Syst. Man Cybern. **4**, 580–585 (1985)

Big Data in Ocean Observation: Opportunities and Challenges

Yingjian Liu[✉], Meng Qiu, Chao Liu, and Zhongwen Guo

Department of Computer Science and Technology, Ocean University of China,
Qingdao 266100, China
liuyj@ouc.edu.cn

Abstract. Ocean observation plays an essential role in ocean exploration. Ocean science is entering into big data era with the exponentially growth of information technology and advances in ocean observatories. Ocean observatories are collections of platforms capable of carrying sensors to sample the ocean over appropriate spatio-temporal scales. Data collected by these platforms help answer a range of fundamental and applied research questions. Given the huge volume, diverse types, sustained measurement and potential uses of ocean observing data, it is a typical kind of big data, namely marine big data. The traditional data-centric infrastructure is insufficient to deal with new challenges arising in ocean science. This paper discusses some possible new strategies to solve marine big data challenges in the phases of data storage, data computing and analysis. A geological example illustrates the significant use of marine big data. Finally, we highlight some challenges and key issues in marine big data.

Keywords: Big data · Ocean observation · Marine big data · Infrastructure

1 Introduction

The ocean covers more than 2/3 of Earth's surface. Phytoplankton in the surface ocean produces half of the oxygen from photosynthesis on Earth. Ninety percent of heat from global warming has been absorbed by the ocean. No matter where we live, the ocean affects our life. However, 95 % of the ocean remains unexplored and under-appreciated by humans [1]. This calls for understanding all facets of the ocean as well as its complex connections with Earth's atmosphere, land, ice, seafloor, and life—including humanity. It is essential not only to advance knowledge about our planet, but also to ensure society's long-term welfare and to help guide human stewardship of the environment.

Oceanography is evolving from a ship-based expeditionary science to a distributed, observatory-based approach, facilitating data collection of long-term time series and providing an interactive capability to conduct experiments using data streaming in real time [2]. Multi-source ocean observing data are collected and stored at an unprecedented scale and speed [3]. Based upon Gartner's definition of big data [4], ocean observing data do have the 3Vs (Volume, Velocity and Variety) characteristics. Therefore, ocean observing data can be regarded as a typical kind of big data, i.e. marine big data.

© Springer International Publishing Switzerland 2016
Y. Wang et al. (Eds.): BigCom 2016, LNCS 9784, pp. 212–222, 2016.
DOI: 10.1007/978-3-319-42553-5_18

These data must be stored in raw format, parsed, calibrated and processed for quality control, then analyzed, and further derived into other products such as visualizations [5]. Due to the unique characteristics of marine big data, they exceed the processing and analysis capacities of conventional systems. This situation has caused new challenges for the traditional technologies such as relational databases and scale-up infrastructures [6]. Current researches involving big data primarily concern with how to discover and make sense of such high amounts of data more effectively and efficiently [7]. Key issues investigated include infrastructure [8], storage [9], analysis [10], security [11], etc.

The rest of this paper is organized as follows. In Sect. 2, we introduce some important ocean observatories and ocean observing programs for data acquisition. In Sects. 3 and 4, we discuss some possible strategies to resolve key issues in marine big data storage, computing and analysis, respectively. Applications in Sect. 5 illustrate the significance of marine big data, followed by the conclusion and future work in Sect. 6.

2 Data Acquisition

During data acquisition phase, ocean observatories equipped with various sensors are utilized to collect raw data from the ocean. This section will introduce some representative ocean observing platforms and projects for marine data acquisition.

2.1 Ocean Observing Platforms

The ocean observatories are collections of platforms capable of carrying sensors to collect data over certain spatio-temporal scales. These platforms include ships, satellites, and a range of Eulerian and Lagrangian systems [12].

- *Ships* have been the primary tool for oceanographers for centuries and will remain a central piece of infrastructure in the foreseeable future. The capabilities of the ships have improved significantly in the station holding and dynamic positioning, multi-beam and side-scan sonar systems.

- *Satellites* constitute the most essential oceanographic technology innovation in modern times. They are the new tools for understanding various ocean processes and land-air-sea interactions over decadal time scales. Satellite data have revealed new phenomena which were previously inaccessible using only in-situ observing data.

- *Seafloor electro-optic cables* with high bandwidth and sustained power offer potential means for providing sustained observation in the ocean. Seafloor cables have successfully been used to study a wide range of topics such as seafloor seismicity, tsunamis, seafloor dynamics, coastal upwelling ecosystem productivity, etc.

- *Drifters and Floats* are passive, battery powered Lagrangian platforms used in creating surface and subsurface maps of ocean currents and ocean properties, respectively.

- *Moorings* provide the means to deploy sensors at fixed depths between the seafloor and the sea surface. They provide high frequency fixed location subsurface data to supplement the spatial data collected by ships, autonomous underwater vehicles, and satellite remote sensing.

- *Gliders* are a type of autonomous underwater vehicle using buoyancy-based propulsion to convert vertical motion to horizontal motion. Due to very low-power consumption, gliders provide data over large spatio-temporal scales.

- *Autonomous Underwater Vehicles (AUVs)*, provide much-needed flexibility in ocean observations as they allow for the movement of sensors through the water in three-dimensions. They can systematically and synoptically survey particular lines, areas, and/or volumes. Like gliders, AUVs relay data and mission information to shore via satellite.

2.2   Ocean Observing Projects

The dream of long-term observation in the ocean has explored for more than twenty years. Many countries and organizations have given their contributions to establish global, regional or local ocean observing systems by using various platforms with multiple sensors onboard. Next, we introduce several national or international projects for long-term ocean observation.

- *Argo* [13] is a global array of more than 3000 free-drifting profiling floats that collect high-quality temperature and salinity profiles from the upper 2000 m of the ice-free global ocean and currents from intermediate depths. This allows, for the first time, continuous monitoring of the temperature, salinity, and velocity of the upper ocean. Deployments began in 2000 and national programs need to provide about 800 floats per year to maintain the Argo array. The broad-scale global array has already grown to be a major component of the ocean observing system. It builds on other upper-ocean ocean observing networks. It is the sole source of global subsurface datasets used in all ocean data assimilation models and analyses.

- *Ocean Networks Canada (ONC)* [14], an initiative of the University of Victoria, operates the world-leading NEPTUNE and VENUS cabled ocean observatories in the northeast Pacific Ocean off Canada's west coast. Its goals are to deliver science and information for good ocean management and responsible ocean use for the benefit of Canadians. ONC cabled observatories collect data that help scientists and leaders make informed decisions about coastal earthquakes and tsunamis, climate change, coastal management, conservation and marine safety.

- *Ocean Observatories Initiative (OOI)* [15] is a National Science Foundation-funded integrated infrastructure project composed of science-driven platforms and sensor systems that measure physical, chemical, geological and biological properties and processes from the seafloor to the air-sea interface. The OOI has transformed research of the oceans by establishing a network of interactive, globally distributed sensors with near real-time data access, enhancing our capabilities to address critical issues such as climate change, ecosystem variability, ocean acidification, and carbon cycling.

3   Data Storage

The collected marine data will be transferred to a data storage infrastructure for further processing and analysis. Long-term sustained and multi-source data acquisition leads to the rapid expansion and complexity of data. It raises huge challenges in storage and processing of these data [16]. The datasets stored at the data center come from many different sensors hosted on remote sensing or in-situ platforms. To optimize the system and considering storage capability, and speed response, the metadata and some types of data are stored in relational databases, and some other types of data are stored in files [17]. Normally, data types with a wide range of parameters but not too much data, such as nutrients, pollutants and any other sample measurements, are stored in relational databases. However, data types with few parameters but huge volume of data, such as CTD, ADCP and imagery sensors, are stored in binary, ASCII, or image files.

3.1 Storage Foundation

File systems, the bottom level in storage mechanisms, are the foundation of the applications at upper levels. Many companies and researchers have their solutions to meet the different demands for storage of big data. For example, Google's GFS is an expandable distributed file system to support large-scale, distributed, data-intensive applications [18]. HDFS [19] and Kosmosfs are derivatives of open source codes of GFS. Microsoft developed Cosmos to support its search and advertisement business [20]. Facebook utilizes Haystack to store the large amount of small-sized photos [21].

3.2 NoSQL Databases

Traditional relational databases cannot meet the challenges on categories and scales brought about by marine big data. NoSQL databases are becoming the core technology for big data storage. NoSQL databases feature flexible modes, support for simple and easy copy, simple API, eventual consistency, and support of large volume data [22]. This section will introduce three main NoSQL databases based on different data models: key-value databases, column-oriented databases, and document-oriented databases.

Key-value Databases. Key-value databases are constituted on a simple data model and data are stored corresponding to key-values. Every key is unique and customers may input queried values according to the keys. Such databases feature a simple structure and the modern key-value databases have higher expandability and shorter query response time than relational databases. Over the past few years, many key-value databases have appeared as motivated by Amazon's *Dynamo* [23] system.

Column-Oriented Databases. Column-oriented databases store and process data according to columns other than rows. Both columns and rows are segmented in multiple nodes to realize expandability. Many column-oriented databases are mainly inspired by Google's *BigTable* [24]. The basic data structure of BigTable is a multi-dimension sequenced mapping with sparse, distributed, and persistent storage. Indexes of mapping are row key, column key, and timestamps, and every value in mapping is an unanalyzed byte array.

Document-Oriented Databases. Compared with key-value storage, document storage can support more complex data forms. Since documents do not follow strict modes, there is no need to conduct mode migration. In addition, key-value pairs can still be saved. MongoDB, SimpleDB, and CouchDB are three important representatives of document storage systems [22]. *MongoDB* [25] stores documents as Binary JSON (BSON) objects. Every document has an ID field as the primary key. Data in *SimpleDB* [26] is organized into various domains in which data may be stored, acquired, and queried. Domains include different properties and name/value pair sets of projects. Data in *Apache CouchDB* [27] is organized into documents consisting of fields named by keys/names and values, which are stored and accessed as JSON objects. Every document is provided with a unique identifier.

3.3   In-memory Databases

To optimize the application performance, data centers not only scale their sizes but also change system architectures with a particular focus on storing and retrieving large datasets more quickly. Accessing data stored in secondary devices is time-consuming. Therefore, it is highly unlikely that a high-performance application would be able to perform jobs efficiently using disk-based system architectures, such as Hadoop and GFS. Notable trends are the growth of in-memory databases and the widespread adoption of flash SSDs in data centers [28]. In-memory databases primarily rely on DRAM main memory for data storage. They are orders of faster than disk-optimized databases in typical data analytics queries. New databases with simpler data models (often referred to as "NoSQL" or "NewSQL") become popular for applications that do not require rich RDBMS functionalities. These systems offer superior scalability and a low response time. Ever increasing main memory capacities have fostered the development of in-memory database systems [29]. For example, CedCom caches data in main memory [30], which combines the power of Cache-Only Memory Architecture (COMA) and the structural principle of Hadoop. Stanford University's RAMClouds aim to build a cluster scale storage system entirely with DRAM [31].

4   Data Computing and Analysis

Due to the multi-source, massive, heterogeneous, and dynamic characteristics of application data involved in a distributed environment, one of the most important characteristics of big data is to carry out computing on the petabyte (PB), even the exabyte (EB)-level data with a complex computing process [32]. Therefore, utilizing a parallel computing infrastructure to efficiently analyze and mine the distributed data are the critical goals for big data processing. In this section, we introduce some representative computing infrastructures, methods and tools for big data analysis.

4.1   Computational Model

Big data are generally stored in hundreds and even thousands of commercial servers. Thus, the traditional parallel models, such as Message Passing Interface (MPI) and Open Multi-processing (OpenMP), may not be adequate to support such large-scale parallel programs. Recently, some proposed parallel programming models effectively improve the performance of NoSQL and reduce the performance gap to relational databases. Therefore, these models have become the cornerstone for the analysis of massive data [22].

- *MapReduce* [33] is a simple but powerful programming model for large-scale computing using a large number of clusters of commercial PCs to achieve automatic parallel processing and distribution. In MapReduce, computing model only has two functions, i.e., Map and Reduce. The Map function processes input key-value pairs and generates intermediate key-value pairs. Then, MapReduce will combine all the intermediate values related to the same key and transmit them to the Reduce function. The user only needs to program the two functions to develop a parallel application.

- *Dryad* [34] is a general-purpose distributed execution engine for processing parallel applications of coarse-grained data. The operational structure of Dryad is a directed acyclic graph, in which vertexes represent programs and edges represent data channels. Dryad executes operations on the vertexes in clusters and transmits data via data channels. During operation, resources in a logic operation graph are automatically map to physical resources. Dryad allows vertexes to use any amount of input and output data, while MapReduce supports only one input and output set.

- *Pregel* [35] facilitates the processing of large-sized graphs, e.g., analysis of network graphs and social networking services. A computational task is expressed by a directed graph constituted by vertexes and directed edges. When the graph is built, the program conducts iterative calculations, which is called supersteps among which global synchronization points are set until algorithm completion and output completion.

4.2   Data Analysis

Data analysis is the final and the most important phase in the value chain of big data, with the purposes of extracting potential useful values and providing suggestions or decisions. However, data analysis is a broad area, which frequently changes and is extremely complex. Many traditional data analysis methods may still be utilized for big data analysis, such as Cluster Analysis, Factor Analysis, Correlation Analysis, Regression Analysis, A/B Testing, Statistical Analysis, Data Mining, etc. Some big data analysis methods can be used to speed up the extraction of key information from massive data. At present, the main processing methods of big data include Bloom Filter, Hashing, Index, Triel, Parallel Computing, etc.

For marine data analysis applications, data mining is an essential method to extract hidden, unknown, but potentially useful information and knowledge from massive, incomplete, noisy, fuzzy, and random data. In 2006, The IEEE International Conference on Data Mining Series (ICDM) identified ten most influential data mining algorithms [36], including C4.5, k-means, SVM, Apriori, EM, PageRank, AdaBoost, kNN, Naive Bayes, and CART. These ten algorithms cover classification, clustering, regression, statistical learning, association analysis, and linking mining, all of which are the most important topics in data mining research and development. To adapt to the multi-source, uncertain, dynamic marine big data, existing data mining methods should be expanded in many ways [37, 38].

Parallel processing has been the mainstream of designing efficient data-processing platforms so that data could be processed in a distributed and parallel manner, improving the throughput of data processing [39]. MapReduce is the most representative paradigm. Modern research on big data analysis has focused mostly on employing the MapReduce programming paradigm and the Hadoop Ecosystem, giving rise to a number of DBMSs that can be deployed in a distributed cloud-based environment [40], such as Pig [41] and Hive [42].

After algorithm parallelization, the traditional analysis software tools will have the ability of big data processing. Das et al. [43] integrated R, an open source statistical analysis tool, and Hadoop to improve the weak scalability of traditional analysis tool and poor analysis capabilities of Hadoop. The in-depth integration pushes data computation to parallel processing, which enables powerful deep analysis capabilities for Hadoop. Standard Weka, an open-source machine learning and data mining tool, can only run on a single machine with a limitation of 1-GB memory. Wegener et al. [44] integrated Weka and MapReduce to break through the limitations, taking the advantage of parallel computing to handle more than 100-GB data on MapReduce clusters. In recent years, extracting valuable information and insightful knowledge from big data has become an urgent need in many disciplines. Due to its high impact in many areas, more systems and analytical tools have been developed for big data analysis, such as Apache Mahout, MOA, SAMOA and Vowpal Wabbit [45].

5 Applications of Marine Big Data

Marine big data are fundamental to a variety of research fields in biology, earth science, and ocean and atmospheric science. This section will give an example of geological application to demonstrate the potential use of marine big data.

Tsunami is a massive, fast-moving wave created by an underwater earthquake or landslide. The large volume of water displaced by a sudden movement of the seafloor creates a pulse in the ocean that races out from its source at a speed of up to 500 miles per hour and extends thousands of feet below the surface. Although rare, tsunamis like those that occurred in March 2011 in Japan and December 2004 around the Indian Ocean were tragic reminders of the destructive power of the ocean. As a result, governments of countries surrounding the Pacific and Indian Oceans, with help from scientists from around the world, continuously monitor the ocean bottom for possible tsunami-producing seismic activity and the fast-moving signs of tsunamis in the open ocean. Even a few minutes' warning can mean the difference between wide scale catastrophe and saving hundreds or thousands of lives.

On April 1 at 4:46:45 PM Pacific Daylight Time (23:46:45 UTC), a magnitude 8.2 earthquake occurred off Chile's Pacific coastline, according to the US Geological Survey. Ocean Networks Canada instrumentation captured both ground shaking and a very small tsunami as they crossed the northeast Pacific (shown in Fig. 1).

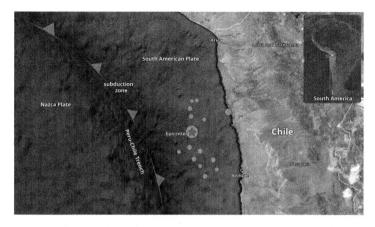

Fig. 1. Map of the epicentre and 16 aftershocks along the subduction zone between the Nazsca and South American plates, 1 April 2014 (Source: http://www.oceannetworks.ca/tsunami-alert-follows-82-quake-chile)

6 Conclusion and Future Work

Ocean science is entering into big data era with the exponentially growth of information technology and advances in ocean observatories. However, marine big data is still in its infancy. Many key technical issues, such as big data storage, computing model, analysis method, and application system supporting decision-making should be fully investigated. Some challenges need to be resolved in the future work.

- *Infrastructure:* Various ocean observatories are collecting and transmitting data continuously. Data quantity reaches to an unprecedented scale that will surpass the storage and processing capacities of existing infrastructures. A traditional data-centric infrastructure, in which a central data management system ingests data and serves them to users on a query basis, is insufficient to accomplish the range of scientific tasks, e.g. collecting real-time data, analyzing data and modeling the ocean on multiple scales and enabling adaptive experimentation within the ocean. The increasingly growing data and its real-time requirement cause problems of how to store and manage such huge heterogeneous datasets with moderate requirements on hardware and software infrastructure.

- *Data transfer:* Marine big data are often acquired and stored at different locations. Meanwhile, data volumes are continuously growing. PB or EB level data transfer may be involved in data acquisition, transmission, storage, and other spatial transformations. Data transfer usually incurs high costs, which is the bottleneck for big data computing. For example, typical data mining algorithms require all data to be loaded into the main memory. Even if we do have a super large main memory to hold all data for computing, moving such a huge amount of data across different locations is too expensive due to intensive network communication and other I/O costs. Data transfer time is far greater than its computing time. So improving the transfer efficiency is a key issue to improve computing in big data applications.

- *Ocean analytics:* Ocean Analytics is an exciting new way to distill and exploit the vast amount of marine data available from in-situ or remote sensing observatories. It can be designed for modeling and forecasting of both short-term high-impact events, such as earthquakes and tsunamis, and long-term large-area events, such as ocean acidification and global warming. It can also be applied to a multitude of different decision support applications that use large amounts of data and require complex calculations. Many existing data mining algorithms do not scale beyond datasets of a few million elements or cannot tolerate the statistical noise and gaps in marine data. New developed analytical algorithms should strengthen scalability, effectiveness, fault-tolerance, and parallelization.

The ocean affects our life. In turn, human activities affect the ocean. We need observe, measure, assess, protect, and manage the ocean. Researches on marine big data provide new tools and forecasts of decision making to improve safety, enhance the economy, and protect our environment. Marine big data pave the way for sustainable development and better life.

Acknowledgements. This work was supported by the National Natural Science Foundation of China (NSFC) under Grant No. 61572448, No. 61379127, and by the Shandong Provincial Natural Science Foundation, China under Grant No. ZR2014JL043.

References

1. Hole Oceanographic Institution. http://www.whoi.edu/Woods
2. Schofield, O., et al.: Automated sensor network to advance ocean science. EOS Trans. Am. Geophys. Union **91**(39), 345–346 (2010)
3. Chave, A.D., et al.: Cyberinfrastructure for the US Ocean Observatories Initiative: enabling interactive observation in the ocean. In: OCEANS 2009 – EUROPE, Bremen. IEEE (2009)
4. Beyer, M.A., Laney, D.: The Importance of 'Big Data': A Definition. Gartner Inc., Stamford (2012)
5. Farcas, C., et al.: Ocean Observatories Initiative scientific data model. In: OCEANS 2011, Waikoloa, HI. IEEE (2011)
6. Park, K., Nguyen, M.C., Won, H.: Web-based collaborative big data analytics on big data as a service platform. In: 2015 17th International Conference on Advanced Communication Technology (ICACT), Seoul. IEEE (2015)
7. Bellatreche, L., Furtado, P., Mohania, M.K.: Guest editorial: a special issue in physical design for big data warehousing and mining. Distrib. Parallel Databases **34**(3), 289–292 (2015)
8. Demchenko, Y., Laat, C., Membrey, P.: Defining architecture components of the Big Data Ecosystem. In: 2014 International Conference on Collaboration Technologies and Systems (CTS), Minneapolis, MN. IEEE (2014)
9. Du, Y., et al.: Study of migration model based on the massive marine data hybrid cloud storage. In: 2012 First International Conference on Agro-Geoinformatics (Agro-Geoinformatics), Shanghai. IEEE (2012)
10. Huang, D., et al.: Modeling and analysis in marine big data: advances and challenges. Math. Probl. Eng. **2015**, 1–13 (2015)

11. Yang, K., et al.: Enabling efficient access control with dynamic policy updating for big data in the cloud. In: 2014 Proceedings IEEE INFOCOM, Toronto, ON. IEEE (2014)
12. Schofield, O., et al.: Ocean observatories and information: building a global ocean observing network. In: Orcutt, J. (ed.) Earth System Monitoring: Selected Entries from the Encyclopedia of Sustainability Science and Technology, pp. 319–336. Springer, New York (2013)
13. Argo. http://www.argo.net/
14. Ocean Networks Canada. http://www.oceannetworks.ca/
15. Ocean Observatories Initiative. http://oceanobservatories.org/
16. Siriweera, T.H.A.S., et al.: Intelligent big data analysis architecture based on automatic service composition. In: 2015 IEEE International Congress on Big Data (BigData Congress), New York. IEEE (2015)
17. Antonia, C., Andrei, N., María-Jesús, G.: DAMAR: information management system for marine data. In: 2011 IEEE – Spain OCEANS, Santander. IEEE (2011)
18. Ghemawat, S., Gobioff, H., Leung, S.-T.: The Google file system. SIGOPS Oper. Syst. Rev. **37**(5), 29–43 (2003)
19. Shvachko, K., et al.: The Hadoop distributed file system. In: 2010 IEEE 26th Symposium on Mass Storage Systems and Technologies (MSST), Incline Village, NV. IEEE (2010)
20. Chaiken, R., et al.: SCOPE: easy and efficient parallel processing of massive data sets. Proc. VLDB Endow. **1**(2), 1265–1276 (2008)
21. Beaver, D., et al.: Finding a needle in Haystack: Facebook's photo storage. In: Proceedings of the 9th USENIX Conference on Operating Systems Design and Implementation, Vancouver, BC, Canada, pp. 1–8. USENIX Association (2010)
22. Chen, M., Mao, S., Liu, Y.: Big data: a survey. Mob. Netw. Appl. **19**(2), 171–209 (2014)
23. DeCandia, G., et al.: Dynamo: amazon's highly available key-value store. SIGOPS Oper. Syst. Rev. **41**(6), 205–220 (2007)
24. Chang, F., et al.: Bigtable: a distributed storage system for structured data. ACM Trans. Comput. Syst. **26**(2), 1–26 (2008)
25. Chodorow, K.: MongoDB: The Definitive Guide, 2nd edn. O'Reilly Media, Sebastopol (2013)
26. Murty, J.: Programming Amazon Web Services: S3, EC2, SQS, FPS, and SimpleDB. O'Reilly Media, Sebastopol (2008)
27. Anderson, J.C., Lehnardt, J., Slater, N.: CouchDB: The Definitive Guide. O'Reilly Media, Sebastopol (2010)
28. Cho, S.: Fast memory and storage architectures for the big data era. In: 2015 IEEE Asian Solid-State Circuits Conference (A-SSCC), Xiamen. IEEE (2015)
29. Mühlbauer, T., et al.: Instant loading for main memory databases. Proc. VLDB Endow. **6**(14), 1702–1713 (2013)
30. Raynaud, T., Haque, R., Aït-kaci, H.: CedCom: a high-performance architecture for Big Data applications. In: 2014 IEEE/ACS 11th International Conference on Computer Systems and Applications (AICCSA), Doha. IEEE (2014)
31. Ousterhout, J., et al.: The case for RAMClouds: scalable high-performance storage entirely in DRAM. SIGOPS Oper. Syst. Rev. **43**(4), 92–105 (2010)
32. Wu, X., et al.: Data mining with big data. IEEE Trans. Knowl. Data Eng. **26**(1), 97–107 (2014)
33. Dean, J., Ghemawat, S.: MapReduce: simplified data processing on large clusters. Commun. ACM **51**(1), 107–113 (2008)
34. Isard, M., et al.: Dryad: distributed data-parallel programs from sequential building blocks. In: Proceedings of the 2nd ACM SIGOPS/EuroSys European Conference on Computer Systems 2007, Lisbon, Portugal, pp. 59–72. ACM (2007)

35. Malewicz, G., et al.: Pregel: a system for large-scale graph processing. In: Proceedings of the 2010 ACM SIGMOD International Conference on Management of Data, Indianapolis, Indiana, USA, pp. 135–146. ACM (2010)
36. Wu, X.D., et al.: Top 10 algorithms in data mining. Knowl. Inf. Syst. **14**(1), 1–37 (2008)
37. Leung, C.K.S., MacKinnon, R.K., Jiang, F.: Reducing the search space for big data mining for interesting patterns from uncertain data. In: 2014 IEEE International Congress on Big Data (BigData Congress), Anchorage, AK. IEEE (2014)
38. Wu, X., Zhang, S.: Synthesizing high-frequency rules from different data sources. IEEE Trans. Knowl. Data Eng. **15**(2), 353–367 (2003)
39. Zhu, W., et al.: Multimedia big data computing. IEEE Multimedia **22**(3), 96-c3 (2015)
40. Kantere, V.: A holistic framework for big scientific data management. In: 2014 IEEE International Congress on Big Data (BigData Congress), Anchorage, AK. IEEE (2014)
41. Olston, C., et al.: Pig latin: a not-so-foreign language for data processing. In: Proceedings of the 2008 ACM SIGMOD International Conference on Management of Data, Vancouver, Canada, pp. 1099–1110. ACM (2008)
42. Thusoo, A., et al.: Hive - a petabyte scale data warehouse using Hadoop. In: 2010 IEEE 26th International Conference on Data Engineering (ICDE), Long Beach, CA. IEEE (2010)
43. Das, S., et al.: Ricardo: integrating R and Hadoop. In: Proceedings of the 2010 ACM SIGMOD International Conference on Management of data, Indianapolis, Indiana, USA, pp. 987–998. ACM (2010)
44. Wegener, D., et al.: Toolkit-based high-performance data mining of large data on MapReduce clusters. In: IEEE International Conference on Data Mining Workshops. ICDMW 2009, Miami, FL. IEEE (2009)
45. Lin, Y.C., Wu, C.-W., Tseng, V.S.: Mining high utility itemsets in big data. In: Cao, T., Lim, E.-P., Zhou, Z.-H., Ho, T.-B., Cheung, D., Motoda, H. (eds.) PAKDD 2015. LNCS, vol. 9078, pp. 649–661. Springer, Heidelberg (2015)

Machine Learning and Algorithm

MR-Similarity: Parallel Algorithm of Vessel Mobility Pattern Detection

Chao Liu$^{(\boxtimes)}$, Yingjian Liu$^{(\boxtimes)}$, Zhongwen Guo, Xi Wang, and Shuai Guo

Department of Computer Science and Technology, Ocean University of China,
Qingdao 266100, China
{liuchao,liuyj}@ouc.edu.cn

Abstract. The mobility pattern of vessel is one of the key metrics on ocean MDTN network. Because of the high cost, little experiment has focused on research of vessel mobility pattern for the moment. In this paper, we study the traces of thousands of vessels. Firstly, after studying the traces of vessels, we observe that the vessel's traces is confined by invisible boundary. Second, through defining the distance between traces, we design MR-Similarity algorithm to find the mobility pattern of vessels. Finally, we realize our algorithm on cluster and evaluate the performance and accuracy. Our results can provide the guidelines on design of data routing protocols on ocean MDTN.

Keywords: Ocean delay tolerant network · MapReduce · Mobility pattern · Trace similarity · Vessel data analysis

1 Introduction

The sparse network coverage on the ocean is a big problem, which make it hard to realize low cost communication in ocean area. Based on the knowledge of MDTN, the mobility of vessels can create the chances of end-to-end communication [1], which can realize a low cost communication networks structure.

In terrestrial MDTN, vehicles or humans are equipped with wireless devices which can communicate with each other as well as stationary infrastructure. The efficiency of the routing algorithm strongly depends on the mobility pattern of the node. In order to improve the delivery radio and reduce average delay, the researchers has paid much attention on studying the mobility pattern of humans [2–5] and vehicles [6–10]. In [4], the author provided a human mobility model based on the human inter-contact time pattern. Musolesi designed a human mobility model based on human's social features. In [8], Luo constructed SUVnet vehicle mobility model which is more realistic than the random waypoint model. In [10], Zhu used the historical vehicles' data to build a trajectory prediction model by using multiple order Markov chains.

However, unlike the mobility pattern of human and vehicle, the vessels in the ocean has different characteristics and challenges. First, unlike human, the vessel does not have social attribute, which makes the human mobility pattern cannot

© Springer International Publishing Switzerland 2016
Y. Wang et al. (Eds.): BigCom 2016, LNCS 9784, pp. 225–235, 2016.
DOI: 10.1007/978-3-319-42553-5_19

directly apply to the ocean area. Second, there are no roads in the ocean. The moving vehicles on the street are confined by roads. Different vehicles surely have the same trace when they pass through the same road. However, the vessel on the ocean may move freely. So, we need to find the mobility pattern of the vessels.

In order to investigate the mobility pattern of vessels, we use the vessels' trace datasets of Bohai Sea and Donghai Sea. We collected the data of over 4000 vessels for three months (from 2015-09-01 to 2015-12-01). In this paper, we provide MR-Similarity algorithm to detect the mobility pattern of vessels. To the best of our knowledge, it is the first paper report on vessel mobility pattern of vessels with real GPS data at this scale. Our main contributions are as follows:

1. We have detected that there are invisible boundary which confine the vessels during their sailing process.

2. We provide a new definition of distance between traces which can detect the similarity of two traces. By calculate the even trace of these similar traces, we detect the mobility pattern of most vessels. The pattern can be used to design data routing algorithm.

3. We use MapReduce model to realize the algorithm to increase the concurrency. We evaluate the performance and accuracy by conduct the experiment on the cluster.

The paper is organized as follows. In Sect. 2, we survey the related work of mobility pattern of human and vehicles. In Sect. 3, we design of MR-Similarity. In Sect. 4, we evaluate the performance of MR-Similarity. Finally, conclusions are presented and suggestions are made for future research in Sect. 5.

2   Related Work

In this section, we introduce some researches related to our paper. The nodes mobility pattern has a great effect on the network performance, so the research on mobility pattern has draw amounts of attentions. In general, these studies can be classified into two categories: the human mobility pattern and vehicle mobility pattern.

Human's social attribute and living habits result in the different inter-contact time and duration. Authors in [11–13] distribute special devices to volunteers to collect the inter-contact time, inter-contact duration, inter-contact locations and MAC address data. The researchers utilize these dataset to discover the mobility pattern of human. In [2], the author processes the dataset and put the inter-contact time's Cumulative Distribution Function (CDF) on logarithmic coordinate. He draws the conclusion that the inter-contact time obeys the power law distribution in 10 min to 24 h period. In [14], the author find that the CDF of inter-contact time obey the power law distribution in the short term and exponential decay in the long term. The authors utilize the social attribute of human and discover the human mobility pattern which can simulate humans' walking traces [3,4].

Vehicular Network are fundamental application of MDTN. To improve the delivery radio and reduce the delay. Authors in [15] collect the traces of 40 buses for nearly two months. By analyzing the data, the author discover the periodicity features of bus mobility. Authors in [16] design ShanghaiGrid project to collect the traces of 6850 taxies and 3620 buses. Zhu find that the taxies inter-contact time CDF obeys light tail distribution [6]. Authors in [8] utilize these traces to create the SUVnet mobility pattern which performs better than Random Waypoint model. In [10], the author find the mobility pattern from the historical data and use multiple order Markov chain to predict the future traces. He utilize the model to design a routing algorithm. The result shows that the pattern is effective.

However, the prior researches are all focus on the terrestrial network. In this paper, we will summarize the mobility pattern of vessels on the ocean.

3 MR-Similarity Design

In this section, we will provide the MR-Similarity algorithm that can be used to detect the mobility pattern of vessels. We first graphically analyze the vessels data. Then we provide a new definition called "distance between traces" to detect the similarity of different traces. We use MapReduce model to increased algorithm parallelism.

3.1 Vessel Trace Analysis

In Sect. 1, we mentioned that there is no road on the ocean to confine the vessels. After analyzing the trace data of 4000 vessels for three months, although the vessels' traces are all different, we have noticed that most traces are confined by invisible boundary as shown in Fig. 1. So we could treat these boundary as the overland road. Apparently, none of these similar traces could represent for others. We need to design an algorithm to detect these similar traces and find the "road" on the ocean.

3.2 Distance Between Traces

In this section, we provide a new definition called "distance between traces" to be the metric of traces' similarity.

Figure 2 shows two traces r_a and r_b. The points on traces r_a is denoted by

$$L_a = \{l_{a1}, l_{a2}, \ldots, l_{an}, \ldots\} \tag{1}$$

For each element in L_a, we can calculate the minimum distance from l_{ak} ($k = 1, 2, \ldots, n, \ldots$) to r_b. S in figure is the accurate distance between two points. The minimum distance set S_{ab} is denoted by

$$S_{ab} = \{S_{ab,1}. S_{ab,2}, \ldots, S_{ab,n}, \ldots\} \tag{2}$$

The distance from r_a to r_b is give by

$$d_{ab} = max(S_{ab}) \tag{3}$$

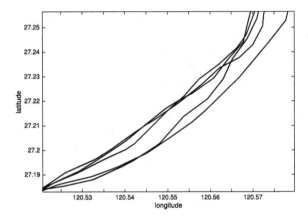

Fig. 1. Example of trace

Consider the condition of Fig. 3, the distance from r_a to r_b is $max(S_{ab})$. However the distance from r_b to r_a is $max(S_{ba})$. So $d_{ab} \neq d_{ba}$. So the distance between trace r_a and r_b is given by

$$D_{ab} = max(d_{ab}, d_{ba}) \tag{4}$$

The $s_{ab,i}$ in Fig. 2 and $max(s_{ba})$ in Fig. 3 is the distance between traces.

Based on the definition, we know that the distance between traces is strongly affected by each point on traces. The GPS signal is easy interfered by the environment that results in the data exception problem. We take S_{ab} as an example to show the detail process of delete exception data.

We first need to calculate the the average value of S_{ab}, $\overline{S_{ab}}$ is given by

$$\overline{S_{ab}} = \frac{s_{ab,1} + s_{ab,2} + \ldots + s_{ab,n} + \ldots}{S_{ab}.count} \tag{5}$$

The standard deviation σ_{ab} of S_{ab} is given by

$$\sigma_{ab} = \sqrt{\frac{\sum_{i=1}^{S_{ab}.count}(s_{ab,i} - \overline{S_{ab}})^2}{S_{ab}.count}} \tag{6}$$

Based on statistics knowledge, we take the data out of the range of $(\overline{S_{ab}} \pm 2\sigma_{ab})$ as exception data.

3.3 Algorithm Design

In this subsection, we will give the detailed description of MR-Similarity. The algorithm is divided into two phases: similarity detection and trace fusion. We use MapReduce model to design the algorithm to increase the parallelism.

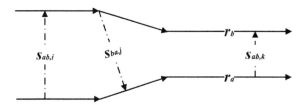

Fig. 2. Distance between trace a and b

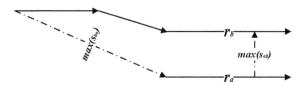

Fig. 3. Distance between trace a and b

Similarity Detection. Similarity detection phase is designed to detect the similar traces. Each trace needs to maintain a dataset called *nearTraceIDs* which is created to store the unique identifier of similar traces. We let *commRadius* be the threshold of of similarity. If the distance between two traces are less than *commRadius*, we treat them as the similar trace and put the trace's identifier in each *nearTraceIDs* set. The commRadius means the communication radius of vessel. We usually set the commRadius from 500 m to 1000 m.

Because there are infinite number of points on a trace, we need to even discretize the trace into $m - 1$ (m is big enough) pieces to make the algorithm runnable. According to MapReduce model, all the inputs and outputs should be the key-value pairs.

Algorithm 1 shows the Mapper of similarity detection phase. The input is the $< traceID, points >$ key-values pairs. The *traceID* is the unique identifier of a trace, the value *points* is the m length array of discretized points.

The functions calculateDistance can be used to calculate the distance and the parameters are two points.

The loop is designed to find each points' minimum distance to all other traces. As we discussed in Subsect. 3.2, the distance between two traces is calculated as Eq. (4). According to the MapReduce, the reducer function can easily process the data with same *interKey*. To ease the procedure, the Mapper of similarity detection needs to emit proper $< interKey, interValue >$. Before emitting the key-value pairs, we judge the value of *traceID*, and put the smaller one in front. So the reducer can find the maximum distance in one time.

Trace Fusion. Algorithm 2 shows the Reducer of similarity detection phase. Thanks to the Mapper, all the minimum distances from each points in each traces are all existing and the all the minimum distance between each two traces have the same *interKey*.

```
Input  :<traceID, points>;
Output:<interKey, interValue>;
for i from 0 to (m − 1) do
    for each tempTrace in trace do
        distance = infinity;
        for j from 0 to (m-1) do
            tempValue = calculateDistance(trace[traceID].points[i],
                    tempTrace.points[j]);
            if tempValue < distance then
            |   distance = tempvalue;
            end
        end
        if traceID <tempTrace.traceID then
        |   EmitIntermediate(traceID+':'+
        |           tempTrace.traceID, distance);
        else
        |   EmitIntermediate(tempTrace.traceID+':'+
        |           traceID, distance);
        end
    end
end
```

Algorithm 1. Mapper of similarity detection

The Reducer uses the loop to find the maximum distance that can be treated as the distance between two traces. Then it judge whether the distance is less than *commRadius*. If so, it parses the *interKey* by special character ':', and add the traceID into each other's *nearTraceIDs* dataset. To avoid the changing of *commRadius*, we also need to emit the distance key-value pairs.

As we mentioned in Subsect. 3.2. None of these similar traces could represent for others. In this phase, we will provide a trace fusion algorithm based on MapReduce to find the "road" on the ocean.

The idea of trace fusion is very simple. We discretize each similar trace into $(M − 1)$ pieces from same side and sequentially number the points from 0 to $(M − 1)$. For the points of same number, calculate the average of latitude and longitude. The fusion trace needs to maintain an attribute called *weight*, which represent the vessel's passing probability. It is the amount of fused traces.

Algorithm 3 shows the Mapper of trace fusion phase's preparation step. It is designed to group these similar traces. The fusion trace have four element. *fTraceID* is the fusion trace unique identifier. *coordinates* stores the average latitude and longitude pairs. *weight* stores the weight of fusion trace. *fusedTraceIds* stores the grouped *traceID*. *fTraceID* is the hash number of the sum of fused traces' traceID plus the character 'f' in front. Also each trace will add an element *fTraceID* which indicates the trace is belong to which fusion trace group.

Input :<$interKey, interValues$>;
Output:<$interKey, distance$>;
distance = interValues[0];
for *each interValue in interValues* **do**
    if *interValue > distance* **then**
        | distance = interValue;
    end
end
if *distance < commRadius* **then**
    tempID[] = **parse**(interKey,':');
    trace[tempID[0]].nearTraceIDs.**add**(tempID[1]);
    trace[tempID[1]].nearTraceIDs.**add**(tempID[0]);
end
Emit(interKey,distance);

Algorithm 2. Reducer of similarity detection

Input :<$traceID, nearTraceIDs$>;
if *nearTraceIDs == null* **then**
    fTraceID = 'f'+ **hash**(traceID);
    fTrace[fTraceID].fusedTraceIds.add(traceID);
    fTrace[fTraceID].weight = 1;
else
    sumID = 0;
    for *each nearTraceID in nearTraceIDs* **do**
        | sumID += nearTraceID;
    end
    fTraceID = 'f' + **hash**(sumID);
    fTrace[fTraceID].fusedTraceIds.**union**(traceID,
            trace[traceID].nearTraceIDs);
    fTrace[fTraceID].weight = fTrace[fTraceID].fusedTraceIds.length;
end
trace[traceID].fTraceID = fTraceID;

Algorithm 3. Mapper of group traces

Algorithm 4 shows the Mapper of trace fusion phase. It is designed to discretize each trace into (M-1) pieces. The input is the < $traceID$, $processedData$ > key-values pairs. The $processedData$ is the data processed by interpolation.

Input :<$traceID, processedData$>;
Output:<$interKey, interValue$>;
coordinates = **discretize**(processedData, M);
for *i from 0 to (M-1)* **do**
    | EmitIntermediate(traceID.fTraceID + ':' + i, coordinates[i]);
end

Algorithm 4. Mapper of trace fusion

The *interKey* is combined by fTraceID and the coordinate's sequence number on the trace. The reason why we deal with the data in this method is shown as Fig. 7. Figure 7 have five traces. Trace 1, 2 and 3 are similar traces. Their fTraceID is "f1". Trace 4 is "f2" and trace 5 is "f3". Because *interKey* is combined by fTraceID and the coordinate's sequence number, the same relative coordinate of similar traces has same *interKey*. For example, the first coordinate of trace 1,2 and 3's *interKey* are all "f1:0". So the Reducer could easily calculate the average coordinate. The Reducer of trace fusion is shown as Algorithm 5.

Input :$<interKey, interValues>$;
fTraceID = **parse**(interKey,':');
if *interValues.length > 1* **then**
> sumX = sumY = 0;
> **for** *each coordinate in interValues* **do**
>> sumX += coordinate.x;
>> sumY += coordinate.y;
>
> **end**
> aveX = sumX / interValues.length;
> aveY = sumY / interValues.length;
> fTrace[fTraceID[0]].**add**((aveX, aveY));

else
> fTrace[fTraceID[0]].**add**(interValues[0]);

end

Algorithm 5. Reducer of trace fusion

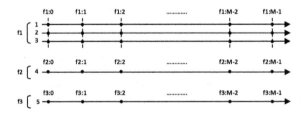

Fig. 4. Demonstration of trace fusion

So far, the whole procedure of MR-Similarity is finished. The simple example result of MR-Similarity is shown as Fig. 5. The red trace in Fig. 5 is the real vessel traces. The upper four traces are in the same group. The lower ten are in the same group. The blue trace is the fusion trace which indicate the mobility pattern of vessels in this monitoring area (Fig. 5).

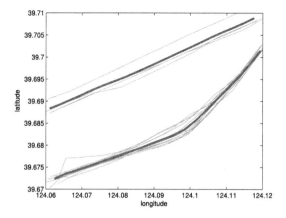

Fig. 5. Example result of MR-Similarity (Color figure online)

4   Performance Evaluation

In this section, we will evaluate the performance of MR-Similarity. We use real trace data to do the experiment.

4.1   Experiment Design

The MR-Similarity is running on normal PCs. We use three same computers to form the experiment environment. Each PC has 8 GB memory. The CPU is intel i5 4570 Quad-Core Processor(3.2 GHz). The operating system is Linux centOS 6.5. The Hadoop version is 2.3.0. All the PCs can be treated as Mapper and we use only one reducer in this experiment.

Firstly, we fixed m, M on 300 and amount of traces on 150. Change the Mapper from one to five, and record the running time of similarity detection phase and trace fusion phase.

Secondly, we fixed the Mapper number on five and m, M on 300. Increase the amount of traces with same increment from 50 to 250, and record the running time of similarity detection phase and trace fusion phase.

Finally, we fixed the Mapper number on five and amount of traces on 150. Increase the m and M with same increment from 100 to 500, and record the running time of similarity detection phase and trace fusion phase.

4.2   Result Analysis

Figure 6 illustrates the performance evaluation result of similarity detection phase. Figure 6(a) shows the time cost on different Mapper number. With the increasing of Mapper, the time cost of similarity detection is decreased like power function. Figure 6(b) shows the time cost on different amount of traces. With the increasing of traces, the time cost of similarity detection is increased by

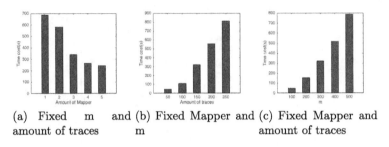

(a) Fixed m and (b) Fixed Mapper and (c) Fixed Mapper and
amount of traces   m   amount of traces

Fig. 6. Performance evaluation of similarity detection

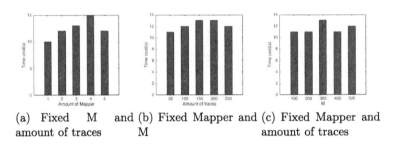

(a) Fixed M and (b) Fixed Mapper and (c) Fixed Mapper and
amount of traces   M   amount of traces

Fig. 7. Performance evaluation of trace fusion

square rule. Figure 6(c) shows the time cost on different m. With the increasing of traces, the time cost of similarity detection is increased by square rule. The user can choose proper parameters based on different situation.

Figure 7 illustrates the performance evaluation result of trace fusion phase. Figure 7(a) shows the time cost on different Mapper number. With the increasing of Mapper, the time cost of trace fusion is not decreased. Figure 7(b) shows the time cost on different amount of traces and Fig. 7(c) shows the time cost on different m. The time cost of the trace fusion is almost the same on different situations. By analyzing the log of Hadoop, we find that the mainly time cost of the algorithm is on the data reading and node schedule. We suggest use one node to running the algorithm to save resources.

5   Conclusion

In this paper, we collected the real trace of about 4000 vessels for three months. By analyzing the data, we find that the vessels' traces are confined by invisible boundary. According to this, we present a mobility pattern detection algorithm called MR-Similarity to find the "road" on the ocean. The mobility pattern could be used to help data routing algorithm design in ocean MDTN.

Nevertheless, many issues still remain to be explored. Our ongoing works are: (1) Find out the inter-contact pattern of vessels; (2) Design data routing algorithm based on this pattern; (3) Design a trace generating model for vessels.

Acknowledgment. This work was supported by the National Natural Science Foundation of China grant 61379127, 61379128, 61572448 and Natural Science Foundation of Shandong ZR2014JL043. C. Liu and Y. Liu contributed equally to this work and should be regarded as co-first authors. The corresponding author is Yingjian Liu.

References

1. Liu, C., Guo, Z., Hong, F., Wu, K.: DCEP: data collection strategy with the estimated paths in ocean delay tolerant network. Int. J. Distrib. Sens. Netw. **2014**, 155–184 (2014)
2. Chaintreau, A., Hui, P., Crowcroft, J., et al.: Impact of Human mobility on the design of opportunistic forwarding algorithms. In: Proceedings of IEEE INFO-COM, pp. 1–13 (2006)
3. Karagiannis, T., Boudec, J.Y.L., Vojnovic, M.: Power law and exponential decay of intercontact times between mobile devices. IEEE Trans. Mob. Comput. **9**(10), 1377–1390 (2010)
4. Lee, K., Hong, S., Kim, S.J., Rhee, I.: SLAW: a new mobility model for human walks. In: IEEE INFOCOM 2009, pp. 855–863. IEEE (2009)
5. Musolesi, M., Mascolo, C.: Designing mobility models based on social network theory. ACM SIGMOBILE Mob. Comput. Commun. Rev. **11**(3), 59–70 (2007)
6. Zhu, H., Fu, L., Xue, G., Zhu, Y., Li, M., Ni, L.M.: Recognizing exponential inter-contact time in VANETs. In: 2010 Proceedings IEEE INFOCOM, pp. 1–5. IEEE (2010)
7. Karnadi, F.K., Mo, Z.H., Lan, K.: Rapid generation of realistic mobility models for VANET. In: IEEE Wireless Communications and Networking Conference, WCNC 2007, pp. 2506–2511. IEEE (2007)
8. Luo, P., Huang, H., Shu, W., Li, M., Wu, M.Y.: Performance evaluation of vehicular DTN routing under realistic mobility models. In: IEEE Wireless Communications and Networking Conference, WCNC 2008, pp. 2206–2211. IEEE (2008)
9. Saha, A.K., Johnson, D.B.: Modeling mobility for vehicular ad-hoc networks. In: Proceedings of the 1st ACM International Workshop on Vehicular Ad Hoc Networks, pp. 91–92. ACM (2004)
10. Zhu, Y., Wu, Y., Li, B.: Trajectory improves data delivery in urban vehicular networks. IEEE Trans. Parallel Distrib. Syst. **25**(4), 1089–1100 (2014)
11. Hui, P., Chaintreau, A., Gass, R., Scott, J., Crowcroft, J., Diot, C.: Pocket switched networks and human mobility in conference environments. In: Proceedings of the 2005 ACM SIGCOMM Workshop on Delay-Tolerant Networking. ACM (2005)
12. Eagle, N., Pentland, A.: Reality mining: sensing complex social systems. Pers. Ubiquit. Comput. **10**(4), 255–268 (2006)
13. Henderson, T., Kotz, D., Abyzov, I.: The changing usage of a mature campus-wide wireless network. Comput. Netw. **52**(14), 2690–2712 (2008)
14. Karagiannis, T., Boudec, J.Y.L., Vojnovi, M.: Power law and exponential decay of intercontact times between mobile devices. IEEE Trans. Mob. Comput. **9**(10), 1377–1390 (2010)
15. Burgess, J., Gallagher, B., Jensen, D., Levine, B.N.: MaxProp: routing for vehicle-based disruption-tolerant networks. In: Proceedings of 25th IEEE International Conference on Computer Communications, INFOCOM 2006, pp. 1–11. IEEE (2006)
16. Zhu, H.Z., Li, M., Zhu, Y.M., Ni, L.M.: HERO: online real-time vehicle tracking in Shanghai. In: The 27th Conference on Computer Communications, INFOCOM 2008 (2008)

Knowledge Graph Completion for Hyper-relational Data

Miao Zhou[1]([⊠]), Chunhong Zhang[1], Xiao Han[1], Yang Ji[1], Zheng Hu[1], and Xiaofeng Qiu[2]

[1] State Key Laboratory of Networking and Switching Technology,
School of Information and Communication Engineering, BUPT, Beijing, China
{zm10211060,zhangch,hanxiao1007,jiyang,huzheng}@bupt.edu.cn
[2] Beijing Laboratory of Advanced Information Networks,
School of Information and Communication Engineering, BUPT, Beijing, China
qiuxiaofeng@bupt.edu.cn

Abstract. Knowledge graph completion aims to predict missing relations between known entities. In this paper, we consider the method of knowledge graph embedding for hyper-relational data, which is common in knowledge graphs. Previous models such as Trans(E, H, R) and CTransR either are insufficient to embed hyper-relational data or focus on projecting an entity into multiple embeddings, which might not be plausible for generalization and might not ideally reflect the real knowledge. To overcome the issues, we propose a novel model named TransHR, which transforms the vectors of hyper-relations between a pair of entities into an individual vector acting as a translation between them. We experimentally evaluate our model on two typical tasks including link prediction and triple classification. The results demonstrate that TransHR significantly outperforms Trans(E, H, R) and CTransR especially for hyper-relational data.

Keywords: Knowledge graph · Embedding · Distributed learning

1 Introduction

Knowledge graphs, such as WordNet [16], Freebase [1] and Yago [8], represent rich factual information and play an increasingly important role by facilitating various applications. However, the inherent complexity of real-world makes the knowledge graphs far from complete even if they usually contain huge amounts of entities and relations. Hence, it is meaningful to mine the potential knowledge rules from the large-scale knowledge graphs, thus attempt to complete them. In fact, many methods are proposed for knowledge graph completion by predicting missing relation facts among known entities under the supervision of a given knowledge graph.

An elementary fact of a knowledge graph is represented in the form of a triple by two entities and a relation, i.e., (*head, relation, tail*) denoted by (h, r, t). For example, (*Obama, born here, USA*) corresponds to the knowledge that *Obama was*

© Springer International Publishing Switzerland 2016
Y. Wang et al. (Eds.): BigCom 2016, LNCS 9784, pp. 236–246, 2016.
DOI: 10.1007/978-3-319-42553-5_20

born in USA. The basic idea behind knowledge graph completion in literature is to regard intuitively the triple as a computable equation when it is encoded into a metric space [4], that is, $\mathbf{h} + \mathbf{r} \approx \mathbf{t}$ holds for triple (h, r, t). This assumption results in the relation completion by finding a r^* such that it corresponds to one of the nearest neighbors of $\mathbf{r}$, that is, $\mathbf{h} + \mathbf{r}^* \approx \mathbf{t}$ for a given pair (h, t).

Difficulties arise when there are multiple relations between a pair of entities, since only one legal $\mathbf{r}$ is allowed by the equation in the metric space and multi-metric space based mechanisms are then proposed. For example, TransR [15] embeds entities and relations into distinct spaces, and project entities from entity space into relation spaces by relation-specific matrices. However, the separate projections disconnect the diverse aspects of the same entities which might have been highly semantically related. For an instance extracted from FB40K [14] as shown in Table 1, there are totally 14 relations between head entity *Judy Law* and tail entity *Sienna Miller*, which indicate the changing relationship of the celebrity couple in different periods of time. Obviously in order to reflect the real knowledge, it is more reasonable to model the multi-relations as an individual one rather than breaking one person into 14 different parts.

Motivated by above observation, we propose a translation-based schema, named **TransHR**, to especially address the issues of embedding multi-relations between entity pairs. First of all, to clearly distinguish our approach, it is necessary to re-define the relation patterns. In general, the relations in knowledge

Table 1. A case of hyper-relation in FB40K. There are 14 relations between the person entity *Judy Law* and the person entity *Sienna Miller*. For example, the relation "/people/person/spouse_s" indicates Jude Law spouses Sienna Miller.

Head	Relation	Tail
Jude Law[a]	/people/person/spouse_s	Sienna Miller[b]
	/celebrities/celebrity/sexual_relationships	
	/base/popstra/infidelity/perpetrator	
	/base/popstra/celebrity/insult_perpetrator	
	/base/popstra/celebrity/breakup	.
	/base/popstra/celebrity/infidelity_perpetrator	
	/base/popstra/celebrity/insult_victim	
	/people/marriage/spouse	
	/base/popstra/celebrity/dated	
	/base/popstra/public_insult/perpetrator	
	/base/popstra/public_insult/victim	
	/base/popstra/breakup/participant	
	/base/popstra/dated/participant	
	/celebrities/romantic_relationship/celebrity	

[a] https://en.wikipedia.org/wiki/Jude_Law
[b] https://en.wikipedia.org/wiki/Sienna_Miller

graphes are classified into four types by previous works in terms of the number of entities: 1-to-1, 1-to many, many-to-1, and many-to-many [4,15,23]. Although it is easily coincident with intuition, this straightforward relation classification is somewhat ambiguous and not efficient for our approach. We start from the view point of number of relations and classify them into two catalogues: **sole-relation** and **hyper-relation**. If there are multiple relations simultaneously between a pair of entities, then each of these relations is called a hyper-relation, as Fig. 1 shows an example. Hyper-relations are pretty common and the embedding accuracy of hyper-relations is of significance for knowledge graph completion. Following the definition of hyper-relation, the algorithm **TransHR** tries to learn the appropriate vector representations for both entities and relations, and then projects the relations from relation space into entity space by transition matrices. The advantages of **TransHR** are two folds. First, it is computationally efficient when compared to **TransR** and **CTransR** because the expensive operation of matrix projection is applied to individual relations rather than entities, whose number is usually order of magnitude smaller. Second, **TransHR** can capture the entity-independent properties, thus might be closer to the real knowledge.

The contributions of this paper are: (1) We propose a new relation category based on the topology of knowledge graphs, which provides a novel idea to embed triplets effectively; (2) We propose a new model called TransHR, which outperforms previous models including Trans(E, H, R) and CTransR in link prediction and triple classification, as lately shown in experiments.

The paper is organized as follows. We discuss related models in Sect. 2 and describe our model in Sect. 3. We detail an experimental study on Freebase in Sect. 4, comparing TransHR with many methods from the literature. Finally we give an conclusion in Sect. 5.

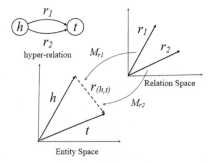

Fig. 1. Here shows an example of hyper-relational data at the top left corner. h, t represent entities and r_1, r_2 represent relations linking h and t. Entities h and t are embedded into entity space. Relations r_1 and r_2 are embedded into relation space. Two transition matrices $\mathbf{M_{r_1}}$ and $\mathbf{M_{r_2}}$ project the relation vectors $\mathbf{r_1}$ and $\mathbf{r_2}$ respectively from the relation space into a vector $\mathbf{r_{(h,t)}}$ in entity space such that $\mathbf{h}$, $\mathbf{t}$ and $\mathbf{r_{h,t}}$ can form a triangle, i.e., $\mathbf{r_{h,t}}$ performs as a translation from $\mathbf{h}$ to $\mathbf{t}$.

2   Related Work

We denote a triple by (h, r, t) and their embedding vectors by the same letters in boldface, $\mathbf{h}$, $\mathbf{r}$, $\mathbf{t}$. A relation-specific matrix is represented as $\mathbf{M_r}$ and the score function of a triple is expressed as $f_r(\mathbf{h}, \mathbf{t})$.

2.1   Translation-based Models

Translation-based models have a close connection with our model and some of them will be considered as baselines in experiments. As mentioned before, TransE [4] wants $\mathbf{h} + \mathbf{r} \approx \mathbf{t}$ when (h, r, t) holds, which indicates that $\mathbf{t}$ should be a nearest neighbor of $\mathbf{h} + \mathbf{r}$. The score function is $f_r(\mathbf{h}, \mathbf{t}) = \|\mathbf{h} + \mathbf{r} - \mathbf{t}\|_2^2$. But it has issues when modeling hyper-relational data.

To solve the issues of TransE, TransH [24] introduces the mechanism of projecting to the relation-specific hyperplane and enables an entity having different representations in different relations. Similar to TransE, TransH has the score function $f_r(\mathbf{h}, \mathbf{t}) = \|\mathbf{h}_\perp + \mathbf{r} - \mathbf{t}_\perp\|_2^2$. Though TransH embeds triplets by translating on hyperplane, it does not break the restraint of single space. Therefore, TransR [15] makes a meaningful adjustment, which models entities and relations in distinct spaces, i.e., **entity space** and multiple **relation spaces**, and performs translation in the corresponding relation space. The score function is obtained by $f_r(\mathbf{h}, \mathbf{t}) = \|\mathbf{h}\mathbf{M_r} + \mathbf{r} - \mathbf{t}\mathbf{M_r}\|_2^2$, where $\mathbf{M_r} \in \mathbb{R}^{k \times d}$, $\mathbf{h}, \mathbf{t} \in \mathbb{R}^k$ and $\mathbf{r} \in \mathbb{R}^d$. The motivation of TransR boils down to the multiple aspects of each entity and various relations focus on different aspects. However, head-tail entity pairs usually manifest diverse patterns under a specific relation. So CTransR is proposed as an extension of TransR, which clusters diverse head-tail entity pairs into groups and learns distinct relation vectors for each group. TransR and CTransR need two matrix-vector multiplications, which make them have large amount of calculation and can not apply on large-scale knowledge graphs.

Since the entities linked by a relation always contain various types and attributes, a more fine-grained model TransD [11] is proposed as an improvement of TransR and CTransR, which defines two vectors for each entity and relation, and uses them to generate an unique mapping matrix for every entity-relation pair. What's more, some other translation-based models inspired by other points also come out, such as PTransE [14], which considers relation paths as translations between entities for representation learning and TranSparse [12], which explores sparse projection matrices to deal with the issue that entities and relations are heterogeneous and unbalanced.

2.2   Compositional Representation based Models

Besides translation-based models, there are many other methods following the approaches of knowledge graph embedding, such as Bayesian clustering based models [13,17,22,25], neural network based models [2,3,5,7,21], circular correlation based on tensor product [10] as well as models based on matrix factorization [18–20] and gaussian distribution [10]. A major disadvantage of above approaches is that they usually require more parameters and are difficult to train.

3   Translating for Hyper-relational Data

To solve the problem of hyper-relation embeddings, we propose TransHR, which embeds entities and relations in entity space and relation space, respectively, and transforms the vectors of multiple relations between an entity pair into an individual vector acting as a translation in entity space. In addition, to simplify embedding problems, we categorize relations into two classes: sole-relation and hyper-relation.

3.1   Relation Category

Previous models usually adopt two kinds of relation category. One categorizes the relations into four classes: 1-to-1, 1-to-many, many-to-1 and many-to-many, according to the cardinalities of their *head* and *tail* arguments. For instance, if the average number of *tails* per *head* is greater than 1.5 and the average number of *heads* per *tail* is less than 1.5, the relation will be treated as 1-to-many. However, it might not always be consistent with the fact and might be somewhat complex. The other [12] categorizes relations into two classes: complex and simple relations, where the complexity of a relation is proportional to the number of triplets (or entities) linked by it. Though it reduces relation classes, sometimes it might be hard to distinguish due to its fuzzy definition.

In this paper, relations are categorized into sole-relation and hyper-relation. For all of the entity pairs linking by a relation r, if there does not exist any other relation between them, i.e., the relation r exist alone between those entity pairs, we call it sole-relation. Otherwise, it appears simultaneously with other relations between a pair of entities, so called hyper-relation. We denote all triples (h, r, t) in the knowledge graph as T, the whole relation set as R, sole-relation set as R_s and hyper-relation set as R_h. $R_{\bar{r}}$ denotes the whole relation set R eliminated the relation r. Then sole-relation and hyper-relation can be defined as

$$R_s = \{r | (h, r, t) \in T \ \& \ \forall r' \in R_{\bar{r}}, (h, r', t) \notin T\}$$

$$R_h = \{r | (h, r, t) \in T \ \& \ \exists r' \in R_{\bar{r}}, (h, r', t) \in T\}$$

It can be obtained by the above definitions that our relation category is definite and can always be consistent with the fact.

3.2   TransHR

When modeling hyper-relational data, previous models are either unable to distinguish the hyper-relations between a pair of entities or concentrated on breaking the entities into several parts, which can not easily catch the properties of entity-independence and might be bad for generalization. Intuitively, it is more reasonable to model the hyper-relations between a pair of entities as an individual vector rather than disconnecting the diverse aspects of them. Hence, we propose TransHR, which transforms vectors of the hyper-relations between a pair of entities from relation space into one vector performing as a translation in entity space. Since we do not destroy any independent entity or relation, our model might be closer to the real knowledge.

In TransHR, for each triple (h, r, t), entity embeddings are denoted by $\mathbf{h}, \mathbf{t} \in \mathbb{R}^k$ and relation embedding is denoted by $\mathbf{r} \in \mathbb{R}^d$. Note that, the dimension of entity embeddings is not necessarily equal to the dimension of relation embeddings, i.e., $k \neq d$.

Assume that there are n relations between a pair of entities and the ith relation is denoted by r_i $(i = 1, 2, ..., n)$. To project relation vectors from relation space to entity space, we denote a transition matrix $\mathbf{M_{r_i}} \in \mathbb{R}^{d \times k}$ for each relation r_i. With the transition matrices, the projected vectors can be obtained by

$$\mathbf{r_{(h,t)}} = \mathbf{r_i} \mathbf{M_{r_i}} (i = 1, 2, ..., n) \tag{1}$$

where $\mathbf{r_{(h,t)}} \in \mathbb{R}^k$. Therefore, each relation-specific matrix $\mathbf{M_{r_i}}$ transforms its corresponding d-dimensional vector $\mathbf{r_i}$ into an individual k-dimensional vector $\mathbf{r_{(h,t)}}$ which acts as a translation from the head entity vector $\mathbf{h}$ to tail entity vector $\mathbf{t}$. Then the score function can be correspondingly defined as follows

$$f_r(\mathbf{h}, \mathbf{t}) = \|\mathbf{h} + \mathbf{r_{(h,t)}} - \mathbf{t}\|_2^2 \tag{2}$$

where function f_r stands for a dissimilarity measure, which we take either L_1 or L_2-norm. Hence, $f_r(\mathbf{h}, \mathbf{t})$ indicates the dissimilarity of $\mathbf{h} + \mathbf{r_{(h,t)}}$ and $\mathbf{t}$. We assign a transition matrix for each relation between one entity pair, though those triplets have the same score, the relations in them can have different embedding vectors, and thus, TransHR achieves modeling hyper-relational data.

3.3   Training

To train the parameters of the score function $f_r(h, t)$, we follow [4] to minimize a margin-based score function as objective for training

$$L = \sum_{(h,r,t) \in S} \sum_{(h',r,t') \in S'} max(0, f_r(h, t) + \gamma - f_r(h', t')) \tag{3}$$

where $max(0, x)$ aims to get the maximum between 0 and x, $\gamma > 0$ is a margin hyperparameter (generally take the value 1) separating positive and negative triples, which is commonly used in many margin-based models such as SVMs [6]. As the embeddings of entities and relations are normalized, the margin γ can actually regularize the above objective and keep weights from collapsing or deviating. S denotes the set of positive triples and S' denotes the set of negative triples, which is generated by removing either the head or tail entity but not both and filling in with a randomly selecting entity. $f_r(h, t)$ is the score of the positive triple, while $f_r(h', t')$ denotes the score of corresponding negative triple. The loss function (3) prefers lower scores of positive triples than negative triples. The learning process is carried out by stochastic gradient descent(SGD). If $f_r(h, t) > f_r(h', t') - \gamma$, SGD is performed to minimize the objective function.

4   Experiments and Analysis

Experiments are conducted on data extracted from Freebase. Our task is to predict missing h or t for a correct triple (link prediction) and classify whether a triple is correct or not (triple classification). We first describe the data sets and then compare our model with current state-of-the-art methods on the above tasks.

4.1   Data Sets

We choose two data sets extracted from Freebase, which encodes general facts of the world. For example, the triple (*Obama, born_here, USA*) in Freebase builds a relation *born_here* as a translation from the name entity *Obama* to the location entity *USA*. In this paper, we employ FB15K used in [3] and download FB40K released by [14] and select the 607 relations which occur more than 10 times to create FB38K. Their statistics are displayed in Table 2.

4.2   Implementation

TransHR is obtained by modifying the codes in C++ downloaded from https://github.com/mrlyk423/relation_extraction and will be compared with Trans(E, H, R) and CTransR. The experiments are conducted on a Ubuntu server with Intel Xeon(R) CPU E5-26200 (2.00 GHz) and 12 GB RAM.

During the training phase, we use SGD for optimization. Following [4], entity and relation embeddings are initialized with the same random procedure proposed in [9]. To avoid overfitting, the transition matrix is initialized as an identity matrix. At each main iteration of the algorithm, we first randomly sample a triple from the training set, served as the positive triple, and sample a single corrupted triple as the negative triple. After that, the embedding vectors of the entities and relations are normalized. The parameters are updated by taking a gradient step with constant learning rate and the algorithm is stopped according to its performance on a validation set.

We select the learning rate α among $\{0.001, 0.005, 0.01\}$, the margin γ among $\{0.1, 0.5, 1, 2\}$, the dimension of entity vectors k and the dimension of relation vectors d among $\{20, 50, 80, 100\}$. The best configuration are: $\alpha = 0.001$, $\gamma = 1, m, n = 100$, and taking L_1 as dissimilarity. For both the two data sets, We traverse to training for 500 rounds.

Table 2. Data sets used in the experiments

Data Set	#Rel	#Ent	#Train	#Valid	#Test
FB15K	1345	14,951	483,142	50,000	59,071
FB38K	607	37516	322,696	8914	9,954

4.3   Link Prediction

Link prediction is to complete the missing h or t for a positive triple (h, r, t), i.e., complete t given (h, r) or complete h given (r, t). Instead of only giving one best result,we focus on ranking a set of candidate entities from the knowledge graph.

Evaluation Setup. We follow the same setup in [15]. For each test triple (h, r, t), h or t will be deleted and substituted by each entity in the knowledge graph in proper sequence. Scores of those corrupted triples are calculated by the models and ranked by ascending order, thus the rank of the correct entity will be recorded. Similar to [4], we report the *mean rank* of above predicted ranks and the *hits@10*, i.e., the ratio of ranks in the top10. This evaluation setting is named "Raw", which may be unfair to those models because the knowledge graph may contain corrupted triples and it should not be regarded as wrong to rank them before the original correct entity. Hence, before ranking we should eliminate these corrupted triples appeared in the knowledge graph and the new evaluation setting is named "Filter". For both settings, a lower *mean rank* and a higher *hits@10* is the mark of a better model.

Results Analysis. Table 3 shows the overall evaluation results on link prediction, from which, we conclude that TransHR consistently outperforms the counterparts on both FB15K and FB38K; TransR and CTransR are in the second place, while TransE and TransH acquire the worst results, which might validate that single space is insufficient to model hyper-relational data.

However, TransHR is primarily designed for modeling hyper-relational data and we hypothesis that the improvements are due to its advantage in modeling hyper-relational data. To confirm the point, we dig into the detailed results of the most frequently occurring 10 hyper-relations, shown in Table 4. We can observe that TransHR acquires significant improvements at most of the time. For instance, the relation "/location/location/contains" appears 20,597 times in the training set and TransHR can achieve an accuracy of 97.8 % (increased by 3 % points) predicting the head and 78.2 % (increased by 30 % points) predicting the tail.

Table 3. Evaluation results on link prediction. Mean Rank shows the average rank of correct entities and Hits@10 shows the proportion of correct entities ranked in top10. For Mean Rank, the lower, the better; while for Hits@10, the higher, the better. As observed, TransHR outperforms other models significantly.

DataSets	FB15K				FB38K			
Metric	Mean Rank		Hits@10(%)		Mean Rank		Hits@10(%)	
	Raw	Filter	Raw	Filter	Raw	Filter	Raw	Filter
TransE [4]	243	125	34.9	47.1	564	197	55.3	67.3
TransH [23]	211	84	42.5	58.5	560	190	54.6	66.1
TransR [15]	226	78	43.8	65.5	567	189	58.6	73.7
CTransR [15]	233	82	44	66.3	568	186	59.5	**76.7**
TransHR	**209**	**67**	**47.8**	**70.0**	**559**	**183**	**59.6**	76.5

Table 4. Hits@10 of Trans(E, H, R), CTransR and TransHR on top10 frequently occurring hyper-relations.The numbers in Frequency denote their occurrence number in training set.The improvements achieved by TransHR is very promising.

Relation	Frequency	Hits@10 (TransE/TransH/TransR/CTransR/TranHR)	
		Head	Tail
/people/person/nationality	21496	2.5 / 3.4 / 3.4 / 5.5 / 3.9	28.3 / 27.3 / 30.2 / 27.0 / 45.9
/location/location/contains	20597	95.0 / 94.4 / 96.0 / 95.9 /97.8	52.5 / 53.2 / 71.8 / 74.5 / 78.2
/location/location/containedby	20578	46.4 / 47.3 / 67.5 / 71.0 / 72.5	95.5 / 96.2 / 91.0 / 95.0 / 98.3
/people/person/place_lived	14146	47.5 / 42.2 / 53.7 / 53.9 / 61.1	86.6 / 86.4 / 92.0 / 94.5 / 93.8
/people/place_lived/location	14119	87.4 / 87.4 / 93.5 / 96.3 / 94.6	50.3 / 46.9 / 55.7 / 60.5 / 66.2
/location/location/people_born_here	13715	91.4 / 90.0 / 96.3 / 97.9 / 97.1	57.5 / 56.0 / 61.9 / 67.0 / 73.2
/people/person/place_of_birth	13607	57.5 / 58.2 / 62.0 / 68.9 / 69.6	91.9 / 91.3 / 96.6 / 97.8 / 96.9
/education/education/institution	11739	98.8 / 98.5 / 98.8 / 99.2 / 100	77.3 / 73.5 / 85.8 / 94.2 / 97.3
/education/educational_institution/students_graduates	11609	99.2 / 97.5 / 99.0 / 99.5 / 100	78.4 / 76.9 / 88.2 / 95.0 / 96.0
/education/education/student	11556	76.0 / 76.0 / 89.0 / 94.2 / 95.1	99.7 / 98.3 / 99.7 / 99.7 / 99.7

4.4   Triple Classification

This task is to identify whether a given triple (h, r, t) is correct or not, which is a binary classification researched in [21] for each triple. The metric is the accuracy based on how many triples are identified correctly.

Evaluation Setup. FB38K is used in this task and we follow the same settings in NTN [21]. As knowledge graphs only have positive triples and classification evaluation needs negative labels, we corrupt each positive triple in the selected testing set to create one corresponding negative triple resulting in a total of double testing triples with equal number of positive and negative examples. When generating the negative ones, we follow the approach in [21] that only the entities appeared in the same position of the replaced entity in the data set are qualified for the possible answer set.

Each relation is equipped with a relation-specific threshold δ_r. The decision rule for classification is simple: for a triple (h, r, t), if the dissimilarity score (by the score function f_r) is below δ_r, then predict positive; otherwise predict negative. The relation-specific threshold δ_r is determined by classification accuracy on the validation set.

We compare our model with the same models demonstrated in link prediction and also optimize with SGD. Note that the best settings of entity vector dimension k and relation vector dimension d here are 50.

Results Analysis. Table 5 shows the evaluation results of triples classification and TransHR outperforms all the other methods.

Table 5. Triple classification on FB38K

Dataset	FB38K
TransE [4]	80.6
TransH [23]	78.6
TransR [15]	80.2
CTransR [15]	70.4
TransHR	**81.8**

5   Conclusions and Acknowledgements

In this paper, we propose a novel knowledge graph embedding model TransHR for modeling hyper-relational data. TransHR transforms vectors of the hyper-relations between a pair of entities from relation space into an individual vector serving as a translation in entity space. Experiments on the task of link prediction and triple classification show that TransHR achieves promising improvements compared to Trans(E, H, R) and CTransR. In addition, the relation category introduced in this paper also turns out to be effective.

This work was supported by NSF Project (61302077) Social Search for Collaborative User Generated Services upon Online Social Networks and by 863 project (2014AA01A706).

References

1. Bollacker, K., Evans, C., Paritosh, P., Sturge, T., Taylor, J.: Freebase: a collaboratively created graph database for structuring human knowledge. In: Proceedings of the 2008 ACM SIGMOD International Conference on Management of Data, pp. 1247–1250 (2008)
2. Bordes, A., Glorot, X., Weston, J., Bengio, Y.: Joint learning of words and meaning representations for open-text semantic parsing. In: International Conference on Artificial Intelligence and Statistics, pp. 127–135 (2012)
3. Bordes, A., Glorot, X., Weston, J., Bengio, Y.: A semantic matching energy function for learning with multi-relational data. Mach. Learn. **94**(2), 233–259 (2014)
4. Bordes, A., Usunier, N., Garcia-Duran, A., Weston, J., Yakhnenko, O.: Translating embeddings for modeling multi-relational data. In: Burges, C., Bottou, L., Welling, M., Ghahramani, Z., Weinberger, K. (eds.) Advances in Neural Information Processing Systems 26, pp. 2787–2795. Curran Associates Inc., Red Hook (2013). http://papers.nips.cc/paper/5071-translating-embeddings-for-modeling-multi-relational-data.pdf
5. Bordes, A., Weston, J., Collobert, R., Bengio, Y.: Learning structured embeddings of knowledge bases. In: Conference on Artificial Intelligence, No. EPFL-CONF-192344 (2011)
6. Boser, B.E., Guyon, I.M., Vapnik, V.N.: A training algorithm for optimal margin classifiers. In: Proceedings of the Fifth Annual Workshop on Computational Learning Theory, pp. 144–152. ACM (1992)
7. Chen, D., Socher, R., Manning, C.D., Ng, A.Y.: Learning new facts from knowledge bases with neural tensor networks and semantic word vectors (2013). arXiv preprint arXiv:1301.3618
8. Fabian, M., Gjergji, K., Gerhard, W.: Yago: a core of semantic knowledge unifying wordnet and wikipedia. In: 16th International World Wide Web Conference, WWW, pp. 697–706 (2007)
9. Glorot, X., Bengio, Y.: Understanding the difficulty of training deep feedforward neural networks. In: International Conference on Artificial Intelligence and Statistics, pp. 249–256 (2010)
10. He, S., Liu, K., Ji, G., Zhao, J.: Learning to represent knowledge graphs with gaussian embedding. In: Proceedings of the 24th ACM International on Conference on Information and Knowledge Management, pp. 623–632. ACM (2015)

11. Ji, G., He, S., Xu, L., Liu, K., Zhao, J.: Knowledge graph embedding via dynamic mapping matrix
12. Ji, G., Liu, K., He, S., Zhao, J.: Knowledge graph completion with adaptive sparse transfer matrix (2016)
13. Kemp, C., Tenenbaum, J.B., Griffiths, T.L., Yamada, T., Ueda, N.: Learning systems of concepts with an infinite relational model. In: AAAI, vol. 3, p. 5 (2006)
14. Lin, Y., Liu, Z., Sun, M.: Modeling relation paths for representation learning of knowledge bases (2015). arXiv preprint arXiv:1506.00379
15. Lin, Y., Liu, Z., Sun, M., Liu, Y., Zhu, X.: Learning entity and relation embeddings for knowledge graph completion. In: Proceedings of AAAI (2015)
16. Miller, G.A.: Wordnet: a lexical database for english. Commun. ACM **38**(11), 39–41 (1995). http://doi.acm.org/10.1145/219717.219748
17. Miller, K., Jordan, M.I., Griffiths, T.L.: Nonparametric latent feature models for link prediction. In: Advances in Neural Information Processing Systems, pp. 1276–1284 (2009)
18. Nickel, M., Tresp, V., Kriegel, H.P.: A three-way model for collective learning on multi-relational data. In: Proceedings of the 28th International Conference on Machine Learning (ICML 2011), pp. 809–816 (2011)
19. Nickel, M., Tresp, V., Kriegel, H.P.: Factorizing yago: scalable machine learning for linked data. In: Proceedings of the 21st International Conference on World Wide Web, pp. 271–280. ACM (2012)
20. Singh, A.P., Gordon, G.J.: Relational learning via collective matrix factorization. In: Proceedings of the 14th ACM SIGKDD International Conference on Knowledge Discovery and Data Mining, pp. 650–658. ACM (2008)
21. Socher, R., Chen, D., Manning, C.D., Ng, A.: Reasoning with neural tensor networks for knowledge base completion. In: Advances in Neural Information Processing Systems, pp. 926–934 (2013)
22. Sutskever, I., Tenenbaum, J.B., Salakhutdinov, R.R.: Modelling relational data using Bayesian clustered tensor factorization. In: Advances in Neural Information Processing Systems, pp. 1821–1828 (2009)
23. Wang, Z., Zhang, J., Feng, J., Chen, Z.: Knowledge graph embedding by translating on hyperplanes. In: Proceedings of the Twenty-Eighth AAAI Conference on Artificial Intelligence, pp. 1112–1119. Citeseer (2014)
24. Wang, Z., Zhang, J., Feng, J., Chen, Z.: Knowledge graph embedding by translating on hyperplanes. In: AAAI - Association for the Advancement of Artificial Intelligence, July 2014. http://research.microsoft.com/apps/pubs/default.aspx?id=225161
25. Zhu, J.: Max-margin nonparametric latent feature models for link prediction (2012). arXiv preprint arXiv:1206.4659

Approximate Subgraph Matching Query over Large Graph

Yu Zhao[1]([✉]), Chunhong Zhang[1], Tingting Sun[1], Yang Ji[1], Zheng Hu[1], and Xiaofeng Qiu[2]

[1] State Key Laboratory of Networking and Switching Technology,
School of Information and Communication Engineering, BUPT, Beijing, China
{zhaoyuhaha,zhangch,suntingting,jiyang,huzheng}@bupt.edu.cn
[2] Beijing Laboratory of Advanced Information Networks,
School of Information and Communication Engineering, BUPT, Beijing, China
qiuxiaofeng@bupt.edu.cn

Abstract. Approximate subgraph matching query is increasingly adopted to retrieve labeled, heterogeneous networks with millions of vertices and edges. Those networks are usually noisy and lack of fixed schema. Previous exact subgraph matching query (such as subgraph isomorphism) and approximate matching aimed at small proprietary network are not practicable. Recently approximate subgraph matching over large graph usually reduces match accuracy to ensure query efficiency. In this paper, We present a novel approximate subgraph matching query method. We propose a similarity score function to measure the subgraph match quality. Based on it, we adopt a two-step-strategy in subgraph matching query processing: candidate selection and query processing. And we employ an indexing technique to improve query efficiency. We experimentally evaluate our method on query efficiency and effectiveness. The results demonstrate that our method outperforms state-of-the-art method NeMa especially on efficiency.

Keywords: Approaximate subgraph matching · Graph query · Large graph

1 Introduction

Subgraph matching query is widely adopted to retrieve information from emerging graph databases, e.g., knowledge graphs, social networks and genome databases. Given an attributed target network and a small query graph, how to efficiently identify a matched subgraph in the target network is a critical task for many graph applications, which has been widely studied in chemi-informatics, bioinformatics and Semantic Web, such as SPARQL [10] and XQuery [1]. However, many real-life graphs are noisy and incomplete with its topology and contend information, thus finding exact matches for a given query graph is not realistic, and approximate subgraph query is more appealing. There are also a variety of metrics to measure the quality of result subgraphs, such as subgraph

© Springer International Publishing Switzerland 2016
Y. Wang et al. (Eds.): BigCom 2016, LNCS 9784, pp. 247–256, 2016.
DOI: 10.1007/978-3-319-42553-5_21

isomorphism, maximum common subgraphs and graph edit distance. But unfortunately, those measures are suitable for biological and chemical structures, and not appropriate for real-life graphs. This motivates us to investigate approximate subgraph matching query techniques suitable for the above problem which can relax rigid label and topology matching constraints of subgraph isomorphism and other traditional graph similarity. The graph similarity metric must satisfy the following two observations: (a) if two vertices are close in a query graph, the corresponding vertices in the result subgraph must also be close. (b) There maybe some differences in labels of the matched vertices.

In this paper, we present a novel approximate subgraph matching query method ASMQ (Approximate Subgraph Matching Query), which adopts a two-step-strategy. The contributions are presented as follows. (1) We propose a similarity score function to measure the quality of the match, which aggregates the similarity of matching both individual vertices and graph structure (Sect. 3). (2) We employ an indexing technique that allows for quickly identifying the local topology and label information of each vertex (Sect. 4). (3) We adopt a two-step-strategy in the process of subgraph matching query (Sect. 5). (4) We experimentally evaluate our method on query efficiency and effectiveness to demonstrate that our method outperforms NeMa in some extend (Sect. 6).

2   Related Work

These days graph query has attracted great attention, which can be categorized into exact subgraph matching query and approximate subgraph matching query. Exact subgraph matching consists of C-Tree [3] and gCode [19], GraphQL [4] and SPath [17]. Those algorithms is too strict for real-life graphs which are complex and noisy. The approximate subgraph matching have been extensively studied in bioinformatics, such as PathBlast [5], NetAlign [8], SAGA [13], and IsoRank [11]. However, these algorithms target smaller biological networks. Others aimed at large graphs such as TALE [14] and SIGMA [9] utilize edge misses to measure the quality of a match, these techniques also cannot incorporate the concept of proximity among entities. There are other works on inexact subgraph matching, including belief propagation based net alignment [2], edge-edit-distance [16], subgraph matching in billion node graphs [12], regular expression based graph pattern matching [2], unbalanced ontology matching [18], SLQ [15], NESS [6], and NeMa [7]. Among them, NESS and NeMa is proposed for approximate subgraph matching query over large real-life graphs, which is close to us. But NESS only considers the proximity among vertices, asking for strict vertices label matching. NeMa considers both proximity among vertices and labels, but the vertex matching function in NeMa is a many to one function and the neighbourhood vector may not record all the topology information of the graph, So sometimes two vertices in query sometimes match to one vertex in the result subgraph.

3   Preliminaries

We start with a few definitions and then draw a mathematics description of our subgraph matching query problem. And then introduce the indexing technique adopted in ASMQ, which allows for quickly identifying vertices information when computing the matching score of a query graph with its matches.

3.1   Problem Definition

We use *target graph* and *query graph* to represent a heterogeneous network dataset and query graphs, respectively. Which denote as $G = (V_G, E_G, L_G)$ and $Q = (V_Q, E_Q, L_Q)$. [7] Given a target graph and a query graph. *Approximate subgraph matching* is that there exist a subgraph $X = (V_X, E_X, L_X)$ in G satisfy a function $f : V_Q \rightarrow V_X$, s.t., (1) $\forall v \in V_Q$, the similarity of $L(v)$ and $L(f(v))$, determined by a given label similarity function Δ_L, is more than or equal to a predefined threshold ϵ, and (2) $\forall (u, v) \in E_Q$, there is a path from $f(v)$ to $f(u)$ in E_X. Under these conditions, We call X a subgraph matching of Q in graph G. Furthermore, the vertex $f(v)$ in X is called the matching vertex w.r.t[1] vertex v in query Q, f is often referred to as a matching of Q in G and X=f(Q).

Definition 1 (Matching Score). *Given a query graph Q and a large data graph G, X is a matching of Q in graph G. The matching score of X is defined as:*

$$Score(X) = Score_v(X) + Score_e(X) \tag{1}$$

where

$$Score_v(X) = \sum_{i=1}^{|V_Q|} sim(v_i, f(v_i)), \tag{2}$$

$$Score_e(X) = \sum_{v_i, v_j \in Q} sim((v_i, v_j), (f(v_i), f(v_j))) \tag{3}$$

$Score_v(X)$ is the total similarity of all query vertices with its matched vertices. For a vertex v in query Q and a vertex u in target graph G, we use Jaccard similarity represented by $sim(v, u)$ to evaluate the semantic similarity between two entities connected to vertices u and v. The value range of Jaccard similarity is *0* to *1*, the more similar of the two label sets, the higher of $sim(v, u)$.

$Score_e(X)$ is a metric to valuate the similarity of proximity among vertex pairs in query graph and target graph, which can be called edge similarity. The consideration of value scope of edge similarity, we use the following function to compute it.

$$sim((v_i, v_j), (f(v_i), f(v_j))) = a^{|d(f(v_i), f(v_j)) - d(v_i, v_j)|} \tag{4}$$

Here, $d(v_i, v_j)$ is the distance between v_i and v_j, $d(f(v_i), f(v_j))$ is the distance between $f(v_i)$ and $f(v_j)$, which are the matching vertices of v_i and v_j respectively in G. We use the difference between the distance to measure edge similarity. Intuitively, if Q is subgraph isomorphism to G, the matching score is the

---

[1] w.r.t: with regard to.

upper bound score. So in this paper, we turn the problem of finding the most approximate match to identifying a match with highest matching score with the query graph.

3.2   Indexing

Neighborhood Domain. To capture the local topology information around a vertex, we introduced *k-Distance Set* and *Neighborhood Domain*, which decompose the graph into a distance-wise structure, thus reduce the space complexity to the linearity of the graph size. Given $u \in G$ and a distance k $(k \geq 0)$, the *k-distance set* of u, denoted as $N_k(u)$, is the set of vertices k hops away form u.

Definition 2 (Neighborhood Domain). *Given $u \in G$ and a non-negative neighborhood scope k_0, the neighborhood domain of u, denoted as $N(u)$, is defined as:*

$$N(u) = \{N_k(u) | k \leq k_0\} \tag{5}$$

$N(u)$ stores all k-distance sets of u from $k = 0$ (a singleton set with element u only) up to the neighborhood scope $k = k_0$. Therefore, all the topology information in the k_0-neighborhood subgraph of u is encoded in the neighborhood domain $N(u)$.

Hash Table Index. In ASMQ, we employ two hash tables, which are respectively named *NebhHT* and *LabHT*, as index for quickly identifying topology and labels information of vertices in target graph. A hash table is a kind of key-value structure (key-indexed) for storing data, as long as we input a key, we can find its corresponding value. *NebhHT* can preserve the local topology information around a vertex that as the key, using the vertices within its neighbourhood domain as values in the hash table. *LabHT* is corresponds to each label in graph, where we use single label as the key, and those vertices having the label are hashed as values. Utilizing the two hash tables, we can easily capture the information of a vertex in G, improving the query efficiency dramatically.

Here, we give a description of $list(v)$ used in ASMQ acquired through LabHT, where v is the query vertex. $list(v)$ is a set of vertices, which are the intersection of vertex sets in LabHT hashed by all the single label of v.

4   ASMQ Algorithm

The (sub)graph query problem is in general NP-hard, since the matching function is nondeterministic. That may be verified by subgraph isomorphism [3], a special case of graph query. So we resort to heuristic solution to the problem. We firstly identify *candidate set* for each query vertex according its semantic and neighbourhood domain. Then we adopt an inference technique to identify the optimal match. So ASMQ can be divided into two step, *Candidate Selection* and *Query Processing*.

4.1   Candidate Selection

We give the definition of *candidate set* as follows. Given a query vertex v_i, its candidate set $C(v_i)$ in target graph G must satisfy: (1) for all the u_i in $C(v_i)$, the vertex similarity $sim(v_i, u_i)$ is more than or equal to the predefined threshold ϵ, and (2) for all the v_j in *1-Distance Set* of v_i $N_1(v_i)$, there exists u_j in *neighbourhood domain* of u_i $N(u_i)$ satisfying that the labels similarity of v_j and u_j is more than or equal to ϵ. Algorithm 1 gives the pseudocode of candidate selection. For each vertex v in query graph, lines 1–2 quickly identify its $list(v)$ in G according to LabHT, which is introduced in Sect. 4.2. Intuitively, all the vertex u in $list(v)$ satisfy $L(v) \cap L(u) \neq \emptyset$. We only need to select candidate vertices from $list(v)$, because the other vertices in G don't have any similar labels with v. Then lines 3–9 select candidate vertices for each query vertex from $list(v)$ according to the definition of candidate set. Among it lines 4–6 choose vertices satisfy the first criterion in the definition, and further, lines 7–9 select vertices satisfy the second criterion. Finally we get candidate set $C(v)$ of each query vertex.

Algorithm 1. Candidate selection algorithm

Input: Target graph G, *Neighborhood domain* $N(u)$ of G, Query graph Q,
   1-Distance Set $N_1(v)$ of Q, similarity threshold ϵ
Output: Candidate set C(v)

1 **for** *each vertex* $v \in V_Q$ **do**
2 | identified $list(v)$ using LabHT;

3 **for** *each vertex* $v \in V_Q$ **do**
4 | **for** *each vertex* $u \in list(v)$ **do**
5 | | Compute $sim(v, u)$
6 | | **if** $sim(v, u) \geq \epsilon$ **then**
7 | | | **for** *all vertex* $v_1 \in N_1(v)$ **do**
8 | | | | **if** $\exists\, u_1 \in N(u)$ *satisfy* $sim(v_1, u_1) \geq \epsilon$ **then**
9 | | | | | put u into $C(v)$

4.2   Query Processing

ASMQ treat Q as a graphical model, where each vertex is a random variable with a set of matches as possible assignments [15]. It finds top matches that maximizes the joint probability for Q with highest matching scores.

Given a query graph Q, we identify a match X that maximizes $Score(X)$ by seeking $\max_{u_i} b(u_i)$. For each vertex $v_i \in V_Q$ and its match u_i, $b(u_i)$ is formulated as:

$$b^{(t)}(u_i) = \max_{u_i}(sim(v_i, u_i) + \sum\nolimits_{v_j \in N_1(v_i)} m_{ji}^{(t)}(u_i)), \tag{6}$$

for each match u_i of v_i and each v_j in the *1-distance set* $N_1(v_i)$ of v_i in Q. Here $m_{ji}^{(t)}(u_i)$ is a message (as a value) sent to u_i from the matches of $v_j \in N_1(v_i)$ at the tth iteration:

$$m_{ji}^{(t)}(u_i) = \max_{u_j}(sim(v_j, u_j) + sim((v_i, v_j)(u_i, u_j))$$

$$+ \sum_{v_k \in N_1(v_j)\backslash v_i} m_{kj}^{(t-1)}(u_j)), \tag{7}$$

for each match u_j of v_j. (u_j, u_i) represents the match of the query edge (v_j, v_i). Intuitively, the score $b^{(t)}(u_i)$ is determined by the quality of u_i as a vertex match to v_i ($sim(v)$), the quality of edge matches ($sim(e)$), and the match quality of its neighbors u_j as message ($m_{ji}^{(t)}(u_i)$).

In query graph, some vertices play more importance roles than others, which can be evaluate by its degree $deg(u)$ and candidate vertices numbers $|C(v)|$. We can use the function $rank(v) = \frac{|C(v)|}{deg(v)}$ to identify the most important one v_0 with littlest value. To improve the graph match precision, we choose v_0 as a start vertex and identify its match u_0 with highest $b(\cdot)$, then we find the match vertices with highest scores of the vertices in $N_1(v_0)$, and further, find the optimal matches of vertices connected to $N_1(v_0)$, and so on, until identifying the result subgraph.

Algorithm 2. Query Processing Algorithm

Input: Query graph Q, 1-Distance Set $N_1(v)$ of Q, candidate set $C(v)$.
Output: Maximum score matching of Q in G.

1 Choose start vertex v_i;
2 $t := 0$; $flag := true$.
3 Initialize the $m^0(\cdot) = 0$;
4 **while** $flag$ **do**
5     $i := i + 1$;
6   compute $b^{(t)}(u_i)$ using Eq. 7;
7   **for** each vertex $v_j \in N_1(v_i)$ **do**
8   **for** each vertex $u_j \in C(v)$ **do**
9   compute $b^{(t)}(u_j)$ using Eq. 7;
10   **repeat**
11   choose $v_j \in N_1(v_i)$ and let $v_i := v_j$;
12   jump to step 6;
13   **until** all the vertex in Q has been computed;;
14   **if** more than a threshold number of query vertices v satisfy $b^{(t)}(u_i) = b^{(t-1)}(u_i)$. **then**
15      $flag := false$;

The pseudocode of our query processing algorithm is shown in Algorithm 2. Given a query graph, line 1 firstly computes its start vertex v_i using ranking function. Next, lines 2–3 initialize the messages of each vertex $m(\cdot) = 0$. Lines 5–9 iteratively compute $b(\cdot)$ of v_i following message propagation, identify a match of v_i. Lines 10–13 choose a neighbour vertex of v_i, then compute its matched vertex, and repeat this step until all the query vertex has its matched vertex. Lines 14–15 compares the acquired matched vertices of the final iteration with previous iteration, if the number of query vertices that satisfy $b^{(t)}(u_i) = b^{(t-1)}(u_i)$ is more than a threshold number, the iteration terminate and we acquire the optimal matched subgraph.

ASMQ firstly computes candidate set for each query vertex according to label similarity function and neighbourhood domain in candidate selection. Then identifies a match u_0 of start vertex with the highest score $b(\cdot)$, and induces an optimal match $f(Q)$ following the vertex matches with top $b(\cdot)$ scores connected to u. Denoting $|V_Q|$ is the number of vertices query graph vertices, L is the average number of $list(v)$, m_Q and d_Q are respectively the average number of candidates and 1-distance vertices for each query vertex. And d and m are the average degree of graph Q and G respectively. Then the total time complexity in candidate selection is $O(d \cdot m \cdot L \cdot |V_Q|)$. The computation of start vertex has time complexity $O(|V_Q|)$. The time required for each iteration is $O(|V_Q| \cdot m_Q \cdot d_Q)$. If the total iterations is I, the overall time complexity of ASMQ is $O(d \cdot m \cdot L \cdot |V_Q| + |V_Q| + I \cdot |V_Q| \cdot m_Q \cdot d_Q)$.

5   Experiments

In this section, we present the experimental results to demonstrate the efficiency and the effectiveness of our algorithm ASMQ on real-life graph datasets including YAGO and IMDB. In order to evaluate ASMQ, we compared it with NeMa. We acquired the source code of NeMa from its author, and write our source code based on it. All the experiments were implemented in C++ and run using a single core in a 1TB, 2.5 GHz linux server.

5.1   Experimental Setup

Graph DateSets. We present our experimental results over datasets IMDB[2] and YAGO[3]. The Internet Movie Database (IMDB) with 12,811,149 vertices represent the entities of TV series, movies, actors, producers, directors, among others, and their relationships and 18,282,215 edges. YAGO with 2,932,657 vertices and 11,040,263 edges is a large knowledge base of information harvested from many sources including Wikipedia, WordNet and GeoNames. All the vertices in YAGO and IMDB are annotated with labels containing semantic information.

Query Graphs. We extracted subgraphs randomly from the target graphs to generate query graphs, and then introduced two type of *noise* to each query graph: *structural noise* and *label noise*. (1) *Structural noise* is that we randomly delete and insert edges to the extracted subgraphs. (2) *Label noise* is that we insert randomly generated words to the extracted subgraph vertex labels. The queries were characterized by *diameter and node number*, denoted by D_Q and $|V_Q|$, respectively.

---

[2] http://www.imdb.com/interfaces♯plain.
[3] http://www.mpi-inf.mpg.de/yago-naga/yago/.

Evaluation Metrics. Since we extract query graphs from target graphs, we have already known the correct vertex matches. So we use precision(P) correctly top-1 query graph matches over all the query graphs.

5.2   Experiment Results

Performance Analysis. In these experiments, we evaluate the performance of our algorithm over two real-life graphs. For each graph, we randomly generate 50 query graphs for each of the three sets: (1) $|V_Q| = 7$, $D_Q = 4$ (2) $|V_Q| = 5$, $D_Q = 3$, and (3) $|V_Q| = 3$, $D_Q = 2$.

   If we construct the index NebhHT according to neighbourhood domain with neighborhood scope $k_0 = 1$, it is easy to reach that the final matches are subgraph isomorphism to query graph, which is not our intention. And our experiments show that the query results are relatively satisfactory with $k_0 = 2$. It is unnecessary to construct index with a higher k_0, whose time complexity is exponential growth. The time consumed on neighbourhood domain with the neighborhood scope $k_0 = 2$ over YAGO and IMDB is respectively 9272 s and 11042 s, which can be constructed off-line.

   Fixed the label similarity threshold ϵ as 50 %. The average query time with $|V_Q| = 7$ is shown in Table 1, we can draw: (a) ASMQ identify the optimal match subgraph is around 2.3 s for YAGO, and 0.34 s for IMDB, it can be observed that our algorithm is efficient for large graph datasets. (b) Compared with candidate selection time, the query processing time is very small and it can be ignored when compute the total time. (c) The query time for IMDB is small, due to its vertex type is considered.

   The total query time in different query sizes of NeMa and ASMQ over both YAGO and IMDB networks is shown in Table 2. We can observe that the con-

Table 1. Average query time with $|V_Q| = 7$: CS means candidate selection time, QP refers query processing time in the second step, and TT is the total average time on querying the graph.

Dataset	CS (ms)	QP (ms)	TT (s)
YAGO	2362.52	6.68	2.37
IMDB	335.6	3.30	0.34

Table 2. Total query time: the total query time of NeMa and ASMQ over two graphs (YAGO and IMDB). The second row represent query size displayed by query vertices number of each graph and the total query time is present in sec.

	YAGO			IMDB		
	$|V_Q| = 7$	$|V_Q| = 5$	$|V_Q| = 3$	$|V_Q| = 7$	$|V_Q| = 5$	$|V_Q| = 3$
NeMa	2.05	0.99	0.73	0.63	0.18	0.21
ASMQ	2.37	1.07	**0.59**	**0.34**	**0.17**	**0.13**

Table 3. Precision of graph match (YAGO): the subgraph match precision of ASMQ and NeMa with different label noises shown in the second column, where $|V_Q|$ is the number of query vertices.

P	$|V_Q| = 7$			$|V_Q| = 5$			$|V_Q| = 3$		
	0	30 %	50 %	0	30 %	50 %	0	30 %	50 %
NeMa	0.67	0.62	0.67	0.93	0.94	0.93	0.96	0.92	0.83
ASMQ	0.90	0.90	0.90	0.96	0.96	0.94	0.97	0.97	0.92

sumed query time of ASMQ is smaller than NeMa on IMDB. And when the vertices size of the query is 3 on YAGO, the query time of ASMQ is also smaller than NeMa. So we draw the conclusion that the efficiency of our subgraph matching query algorithm ASMQ outperforms NeMa.

Performance Against Noise. In this set of experiments, we investigate the impact of varying noises on the performance of ASMQ. Fixing the label similarity threshold as 50 %, We vary the label noise from 0 % to 50 %, and investigate the effectiveness of ASMQ. Table 3 illustrate both algorithms subgraph match precision of ASMQ and NeMa with different label noises over YAGO network. The precision of ASMQ was improved compared with NeMa, especially when vertex number is 7. It is because when identify the matched subgraph, we firstly identify the optimal start vertex according to characteristics of the query graph, rather than a arbitrary one.

In those experiments, we can conclude that our subgraph matching query algorithm ASMQ outperforms by 2/3 on efficiency than NeMa with 30 % label noise and added another one edge to each query graph as structural noise. And although there are not any distinct differences on individual vertex match precision between both algorithms, ASMQ has improved graph match precision with different label noises, especially when query in the size of $|V_Q| = 7$ and $D_Q = 4$.

6 Conclusions and Acknowledgements

In this paper, we have introduced a new approximate subgraph matching query method ASMQ, which can relax the rigid label and topology matching constraints of subgraph isomorphism and other traditional graph and is more suitable for real-life graphs. We propose a score function to evaluate the match quality, and then employ a two-step-strategy, candidate selection and inference algorithm to identify the optimal graph matches. Our experimental results over real-life datasets show that ASMQ efficiently finds high-quality matches, as compared to state-of-the-art work NeMa.

This work was supported by NSF Project (61302077) Social Search for Collaborative User Generated Services upon Online Social Networks and by 863 project (2014AA01A706).

References

1. Barcel, P., Libkin, L., Reutter, J.L.: Querying graph patterns. In: Proceedings of the Thirtieth ACM SIGMOD-SIGACT-SIGART Symposium on Principles of Database Systems, pp. 199–210 (2011)
2. Bayati, M., Gerritsen, M., Gleich, D.F., Saberi, A., Wang, Y.: Algorithms for large, sparse network alignment problems. In: Ninth IEEE International Conference on Data Mining, ICDM 2009, pp. 705–710. IEEE (2009)
3. Cordella, L.P., Foggia, P., Sansone, C., Vento, M.: A (sub)graph isomorphism algorithm for matching large graphs. IEEE Trans. Pattern Anal. Mach. Intell. **26**(10), 1367–1372 (2004)
4. He, H., Singh, A.K.: Graphs-at-a-time: query language and access methods for graph databases. In: Advances in Database Systems, pp. 405–418 (2008)
5. Kelley, B.P., Yuan, B., Lewitter, F., Sharan, R., Stockwell, B.R., Ideker, T.: Pathblast: a tool for alignment of protein interaction networks. Nucleic Acids Res. **32**(12), W83–W88 (2004)
6. Khan, A., Li, N., Yan, X., Guan, Z., Chakraborty, S., Tao, S.: Neighborhood based fast graph search in large networks. In: Proceedings of the 2011 ACM SIGMOD International Conference on Management of Data, pp. 901–912 (2011)
7. Khan, A., Wu, Y., Aggarwal, C.C., Yan, X.: Nema: fast graph search with label similarity. Proc. VLDB Endowment **6**, 181–192 (2013). VLDB Endowment
8. Liang, Z., Xu, M., Teng, M., Niu, L.: Netalign: a web-based tool for comparison of protein interaction networks. Bioinformatics **22**(17), 2175–2177 (2006)
9. Mongiovi, M., Di Natale, R., Giugno, R., Pulvirenti, A., Ferro, A., Sharan, R.: Sigma: a set-cover-based inexact graph matching algorithm. J. Bioinform. Comput. Biol. **8**(02), 199–218 (2010)
10. PrudHommeaux, E., Seaborne, A., et al.: Sparql query language for rdf. W3C Recommendation 15 (2008)
11. Rohit, S., Jinbo, X., Bonnie, B.: Global alignment of multiple protein interaction networks with application to functional orthology detection. Proc. Nat. Acad. Sci. **131**(6), 1037–1047 (2011)
12. Sun, Z., Wang, H., Wang, H., Shao, B., Li, J.: Efficient subgraph matching on billion node graphs. Proc. VLDB Endowment **5**(9), 788–799 (2012)
13. Tian, Y., Mceachin, R.C., Santos, C., States, D.J., Patel, J.M.: Saga: a subgraph matching tool for biological graphs. Bioinformatics **23**(2), 232–239 (2007)
14. Tian, Y., Patel, J.M.: Tale: a tool for approximate large graph matching. In: IEEE 24th International Conference on Data Engineering, ICDE 2008, pp. 963–972. IEEE (2008)
15. Yang, S., Wu, Y., Sun, H., Yan, X.: Schemaless and structureless graph querying. Proc. VLDB Endowment **7**(7), 565–576 (2014)
16. Zhang, S., Yang, J., Jin, W.: Sapper: subgraph indexing and approximate matching in large graphs. Proc. VLDB Endowment **3**(1–2), 1185–1194 (2010)
17. Zhao, P., Han, J.: On graph query optimization in large networks. Proc. VLDB Endowment **3**(1–2), 340–351 (2010)
18. Zhong, Q., Li, H., Li, J., Xie, G., Tang, J., Zhou, L., Pan, Y.: A gauss function based approach for unbalanced ontology matching. In: Proceedings of the 2009 ACM SIGMOD International Conference on Management of Data, pp. 669–680. ACM (2009)
19. Zou, L., Chen, L., Yu, J.X., Lu, Y.: A novel spectral coding in a large graph database. In: International Conference on Extending Database Technology, pp. 181–192 (2008)

A Novel High-Dimensional Index Method Based on the Mathematical Features

Yu Zhang, Jiayu Li$^{(\boxtimes)}$, and Ye Yuan$^{(\boxtimes)}$

Northeastern University, Shenyang, China
zytemb@163.com, lijiayu570@126.com, yuanye@mail.neu.edu.cn

Abstract. Nowadays the nearest neighbor (NN) search in the high dimensional space can be applied in many fields and it becomes the focus of information science. Usually, R-near neighbor that sets a fixed query range R is used in place of NN search. However, the traditional methods for R-near neighbor can not achieve the satisfactory performance in the high dimensional space due to the curse of dimensionality. Moreover, some methods is based on probabilistic guarantees so it does not provide the 100 % accuracy guarantee. To improve the problem, in this paper, we propose a novel idea to build the index structure. This method is based on the mathematical features of the coordinates of the data points. Specifically, we employ the mean value and the standard deviation of the coordinate to index the data point. This method can efficiently solve the R-NN search with the 100 % accuracy guarantee in the high dimensional space. Extensive experimental results demonstrate the effectiveness of the proposed methods.

Keywords: R-near neighbor · High-dimension · Multimedia

1 Introduction

Nowadays there are the increasingly growing scale of multimedia information. For the explosive scale of multimedia information, a fundamental problem is how to effectively store and retrieve them. And these information always are represented as multi-dimensional data. So the nearest neighbor (NN) search becomes the hotspot application for a lot of fields. Let D be a collection of objects, and $d(o_i, o_j)$ denotes the distance between o_i and o_j, where o_i and o_j are two arbitrary objects in the collection D. Given a query object q, o_1 is the nearest neighbor (NN) of q if and only if $d(o_1, q) \leq d(o_i, q)$, where $o_i \in D$ and $o_i \neq o_1$. The nearest neighbor search contains $top - k$ nearest neighbor (kNN) and R-near neighbor (R-NN). Given a query object Q and a fixed query range R, R-NN is to find out all objects whose difference from the query object Q is less than the query radius R. Usually, R-NN is used in place of the NN search in the multimedia application. In this paper, we propose a novel method to solve the R-NN problem with 100 % accuracy guarantee.

To address the problem of the R-NN search in high dimensional space, in this paper we propose a high dimensional index mechanism that guarantees 100 %

© Springer International Publishing Switzerland 2016
Y. Wang et al. (Eds.): BigCom 2016, LNCS 9784, pp. 257–271, 2016.
DOI: 10.1007/978-3-319-42553-5_22

accuracy with satisfactory efficiency for the R-NN search. Firstly, the high dimensional data are transformed into 2-dimensional metric space in terms of their mathematical features. Then we use existent multi-dimensional structure (such as R-tree) to index them. Furthermore, based on mathematical features of this 2-dimensional index method we present a novel single dimensional index method. Specifically, we organize this single dimensional index method as a tree structure and in this paper the B+ tree is used in this method. As for the search algorithm, we respectively present 2-dimensional and single dimensional pruning mechanisms for the corresponding index methods. Given a query point Q, as for the 2-dimensional index method, to begin with it is transformed into 2-dimensional metric space. Moreover, we employ the pruning rules and Q to filter out false data points and to obtain the candidate set. Additionally, the candidate set is retrieved to achieve the true nearest neighbors. With regard to the single dimensional method, the similar search process can be implemented to obtain the true nearest neighbors. Extensive experiments shows the efficiency and effectiveness of our method.

Our main contributions are: (1) a novel way to address the NN search in the high dimensional space. We originally use the mathematical features of data points to build the index structure. This idea broadens the horizon of solving the problem of NN search in the high dimensional space. (2) The index methods and search algorithms. We propose the effective methods to address the problem of nearest neighbor search. Concretely, we present different methods to index the high-dimensional data, and these methods complement each other. Moreover, we provide the pruning mechanisms for search algorithms in the corresponding methods. (3) Extensive experiments. We perform ample experiments to show the superiority of the proposed methods over the traditional ones.

The rest of this paper is organized as follows. Section 2 discusses the related work. And Sect. 3 details the high dimensional index methods. In Sect. 4 we provide the experiment results. And finally we conclude this paper and present the future works in Sect. 5.

2   Related Works

Generally speaking, the multi-dimension and high-dimension index can roughly be divided into two parties: data partition and space partition. In addition to them, VA-file and approximate search methods also are effective index structures.

As for data partition, R-tree firstly was proposed to solve multi-dimension R-NN search problem [1]. It employs the minimum bounding rectangle (MBR) to simulate $B+$ tree index structure in multi-dimensional space. Then R-tree were extended to some variants. R^*-tree [9] and R^+-tree [10] are both of its variants. They improve the way to split MBRs to reduce overlaps. Additionally, M-tree [8] introduces distance from the current node to its parent node into the current node as an entry to add an extra filter scheme. However, these methods can only effectively cope with multi-dimensional data. With regard to high dimensional ones, the overlaps in data partition become far heavier as the increase of the dimension. And the heavy overlaps deteriorate the searching performance.

The space partition methods are overlap-free, because it partitions the entire space no matter whether there exists objects. The pyramid technique is a well-known method to index high dimensional objects. It partitions the unit hyper-cube space into $2d$ pyramids [4]. The iMinMax method is similar to pyramid technique [5]. iDistance is a special index structure because it fuses the characteristic of data partition with the one of space partition [3]. Additionally, $k - d$ tree and its variants are the traditional space partition methods [12]. It partitions the space into the sub-spaces in terms of the different dimensions each time.

However, with respect to high dimensional data, theoretically the efficiency of tree-like index structures is lower than sequential scan because random disk access is more expensive than sequential scan of the disk [11]. Thus the VA-file based on sequential scan was proposed to handle high dimensional index [6]. It compresses each high dimensional data into a bit-string of length b. Meanwhile, space filling curves also is a efficient dimension reduction method [7].

In order to accelerate the high dimensional NN searching, locality sensitive hashing (LSH) has been proposed [2]. It sacrifices a little accuracy and space to obtain a sub-linear searching time. It has some variants to improve the performance of NN searching [13,14]. But it is the approximate method so it can not guarantee the exact answers.

3   Algorithm

Traditional methods of high dimensional index geometrically partitions the Euclidean space into a series of sub-space. They assign each data points into the fixed sub-space in terms of different rules. But we try to find out a new coordinate system so as to transform the coordinate of the high dimensional data point into a new low dimensional one. We consider the unit metric space as the data space. This is meaningful because other data space can be mapped into the unit metric space. When we analyze the mathematical features of coordinates of the data point in different dimensions, we find that they indicate the structure features of coordinates of the data point. Furthermore, we can employ them to build a new coordinate system so as to represent these data points.

3.1   Preliminaries

Consider a dataset D of N data points in a unit d-dimensional metric space R^d. Let $d(X, Y)$ denotes the distance between X and Y, where X and Y are two arbitrary points in the dataset D. $(x_1, x_2, ..., x_d)$ and $(y_1, y_2, ..., y_d)$ respectively are coordinate values in different dimensions of X and Y. Given a query point Q and a query radius R, the R-near neighbor (R-NN) of the query point Q is denoted as $Q(R)$. $Q(R)$ is to find out all data points whose distance from the query point Q is less than the query radius R in dataset D. Generally speaking, distance $d(X, Y)$ is measured in terms of the Euclidean metric. So it is denoted as $d(X, Y) = \sqrt{\sum(x_i - y_i)^2}$, where x_i and y_i respectively are the coordinate values of X and Y in ith dimension. Geometrically speaking, the R-NN of the query point Q is to find out all data points within the hyper sphere whose center is Q and the radius is R. The notations used in this paper is described in Table 1.

Table 1. The meaning of notations

Notation	Meaning
D	The dataset
N	Number of data points in the dataset
d	Dimension of the dataset
X	A data point with coordinate $(x_1, x_2, ..., x_d)$
Y	A data point with coordinate $(y_1, y_2, ..., y_d)$
Q	A query point with coordinate $(q_1, q_2, ..., q_d)$
$\overline{X}$	A data point with coordinate $\overline{x}, \overline{x}, ..., \overline{x}$
O	Origin point with coordinate $(0, 0, ..., 0)$
R	A query radius of Q
$d(X, Y)$	Distance between X and Y
$\overline{x}$	Mean value of the data point X
δ_x	Standard deviation of the data point X
OV	Straight line $v_1 = v_2 = v_3 = ... = v_d$

It is acknowledged that the diagonal line through the center is the longest straight line in the unit d-dimensional metric space. Thus if we map the data points onto this diagonal line, the answer is the sparsest distribution of these mapped points on the straight line. There are 2^{d-1} the diagonal line through the center. We choose the straight line equation: $v_1 = v_2 = v_3 = ... = v_d$ as the first dimension of the new coordinate system, where v_1, v_2, v_3, ..., v_d are variables in different dimension of the point V on the diagonal line. Furthermore, when we map the data points onto this diagonal straight line $v_1 = v_2 = v_3 = ... = v_d$, we can obtain that as for the arbitrary data point $X : (x_1, x_2, ..., x_d)$ its distance from this diagonal line is the $\sqrt{d}$ times of its standard deviation.

Lemma 1. *With respect to the data point $X:(x_1, x_2, ..., x_d)$ and the diagonal line $OV : v_1 = v_2 = v_3 = ... = v_d$ in the unit d-dimensional metric space, the distance from the point X to the diagonal straight line is the $\sqrt{d}$ times of the standard deviation δ_x of $(x_1, x_2, ..., x_d)$, where δ_x is the standard deviation of $(x_1, x_2, ..., x_d)$, namely, $\delta_x = \sqrt{\frac{1}{d} \sum_{i=1}^{d} (x_i - \overline{x})^2}$ and $\overline{x}$ is the mean value of $(x_1, x_2, ..., x_d)$, that is, $\overline{x} = \frac{1}{d} \sum_{i=1}^{d} x_i$. If we make a vertical line from X to the diagonal line, the foot point is the point $(\overline{x}, \overline{x}, ..., \overline{x})$ and its length is $\sqrt{d}\delta_x$.*

Proof. With regard to the data point $X : (x_1, x_2, ..., x_d$, the distance between X and the arbitrary point on the straight line $OV : v_1 = v_2 = v_3 = ... = v_d$ is presented as $d(X, V) = \sqrt{\sum\limits_{i=1}^{d} (x_i - v_i)^2}$. Because the distance between X and the straight line OV is the shortest length among the distances from X to arbitrary point on this straight line, we can transform the original question into the one, solving the minimum of the function $f(v_1, v_2, ..., v_d) = \sum\limits_{i=1}^{d} (x_i - v_i)^2$. We can obtain the simplified function $g(v) = \sum\limits_{i=1}^{d} (x_i - v)^2$, where $v = v_1 = v_2 = v_3 = ... = v_d$, because the point v is on this straight line: $v_1 = v_2 = v_3 = ... = v_d$.

$$g(v) = \sum_{i=1}^{d} (x_i - v)^2 = dv^2 - 2v \sum_{i=1}^{d} x_i + \sum_{i=1}^{d} (x_i)^2 \qquad (1)$$

Thus when $v = \frac{1}{d} \sum\limits_{i=1}^{d} x_i = \overline{x}$, we can obtain the minimum distance between X and the straight line according to the (1). Therefore, the point $(\overline{x}, \overline{x}, ..., \overline{x})$ is the foot point of the vertical line from X to the straight line OV. And the length of the vertical line is $\sqrt{d}\delta_x$, where $\delta_x = \sqrt{\frac{1}{d} \sum\limits_{i=1}^{d} (x_i - \overline{x})^2}$.

3.2   The Pruning Algorithm

Now we can represent the data point $X : (x_1, x_2, ..., x_d)$ as the 2-dimension form $(\overline{x}, \delta_x)$. However, this 2-dimensional form representation can not determine the exact location of X, because this form is geometrically a hyperplane. The point on this hyperplane meets the condition that its vertical line to the straight line $OV : v_1 = v_2 = v_3 = ... = v_d$ has the foot point $\overline{X} (\overline{x}, \overline{x}, ..., \overline{x})$ and the length of the vertical line is $\sqrt{d}\delta_x$. But in fact the point $X : (x_1, x_2, ..., x_d)$ has the fixed location. So the transformation from $(x_1, x_2, ..., x_d)$ to $(\overline{x}, \delta_x)$ loses a little location information. The aim for the transformation has two: On the one hand, reducing the volume of the storage of the data point in order to make its index; on the other hand, easily obtaining the range of the distance between the data point and the query point so as to prune the inappropriate data point instead of heavily computing its exact value.

Given a query point $Q : (q_1, q_2, ..., q_d)$, because the 2-dimensional representation of data points lies in the range of the plane space, we will determine a plane in the unit d-dimensional space so that all data points and the query point can be mapped into this plane so as to measure the range of their distance. We choose the plane that is determined by the straight line $OV : v_1 = v_2 = v_3 = ... = v_d$ and the query point Q. The location information about the query point Q is decided. We map the data point X into the point C in the plane OVQ as shown in the Fig. 1. And the point C has the coordinate of 2-dimensional form $(\overline{x}, \delta_x)$ in the same side with the query point Q as regard to the straight line OV in this plane in the Fig. 1. Furthermore, the distance between the mapped point C and the query point Q is CQ: $\sqrt{d*(\overline{x}-\overline{q})^2+d*(\delta_x-\delta_q)^2}$, because the distance between $\overline{X}$:$(\overline{x},\overline{x},...,\overline{x})$ and $\overline{Q}$: $(\overline{q},\overline{q},...,\overline{q})$ on the straight line OV is $\sqrt{d}*(\overline{x}-\overline{q})$, specifically as described in the Fig. 2. If the data point X is mapped in the plane on the opposite side with Q, the distance between them is $\sqrt{d*(\overline{x}-\overline{q})^2+d*(\delta_x+\delta_q)^2}$.

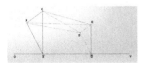
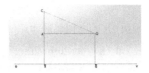
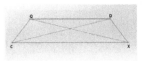

Fig. 1. The Query point Q, the data point X and their corresponding mapping points

Fig. 2. The Query point Q and the X's mapped point C in the plane OVQ

Fig. 3. The isosceles trapezoid $CXDQ$

Lemma 2. *Given a query point Q:$(q_1, q_2, ..., q_d)$, the distance between the data point X:$(x_1, x_2, ..., x_d)$ and Q is more than $\sqrt{d*(\overline{x}-\overline{q})^2+d*(\delta_x-\delta_q)^2}$ and this distance is less than $\sqrt{d*(\overline{x}-\overline{q})^2+d*(\delta_x+\delta_q)^2}$, where $\overline{x}$ and δ_x respectively are the mean value and the standard deviation of $(x_1, x_2, ..., x_d)$, and $\overline{q}$ and δ_q respectively are the mean value and the standard deviation of $(q_1, q_2, ..., q_d)$. The minimum of this distance is $\sqrt{d*(\overline{x}-\overline{q})^2+d*(\delta_x-\delta_q)^2}$ and its maximum is $\sqrt{d*(\overline{x}-\overline{q})^2+d*(\delta_x+\delta_q)^2}$.*

Proof. In the Fig. 1, the data point X is mapped into the point C in the plane that is determined by the point Q and the straight line OV. And similarly the query point Q is mapped into the point D in the plane that is determined by the point C and the straight line OV. So we can obtain that CX is parallel to QD and $QD = \frac{\delta_q}{\delta_x}CX$. So in the isosceles trapezoid $CXDQ$, according to the Ptolemy's theorem, we obtain that

$$CD \times QX = CX \times QD + CQ \times XD. \tag{2}$$

Moreover, $QX = CD$ and $CQ = XD$ because of the isosceles trapezoid $CXDQ$ as specifically described in the Fig. 3. Meanwhile, QX is the distance between the data point X and the query point Q. And $CQ = \sqrt{d*(\overline{x}-\overline{q})^2+d*(\delta_x-\delta_q)^2}$. So after substituting them into the Eq. (2), we can obtain the Eq. (3)

$$QX = \sqrt{d*(\overline{x}-\overline{q})^2+d*(\delta_x-\delta_q)^2+d*\frac{\delta_q}{\delta_x}*(CX)^2} \tag{3}$$

Because $0 \le CX \le 2\delta_x$, we can obtain the Eqs. (4) and (5) by substituting it into the Eq. (3)

$$QX \ge \sqrt{d*(\overline{x}-\overline{q})^2+d*(\delta_x-\delta_q)^2} \tag{4}$$

$$QX \le \sqrt{d*(\overline{x}-\overline{q})^2+d*(\delta_x+\delta_q)^2} \tag{5}$$

Furthermore, the difference between $(QX)^2$ and $(CQ)^2$ is $d * \frac{\delta_q}{\delta_x} * (CX)^2$ or $\frac{\delta_x}{\delta_q} * QD^2$, where $0 \leq CX \leq 2\delta_x$ and $0 \leq QD \leq 2\delta_q$.

Similarly, if we map Q in the plane which is determined by OV and X, we can make the same conclusion as the Eqs. (4) and (5). The difference is that we need map Q in different planes for different data points in every time.

Given a query point Q : $(q_1, q_2, ..., q_d)$ and a search radius R, the data point set $L_{\overline{x}\delta}$ contains the point X : $(x_1, x_2, ..., x_d)$ only if $\sqrt{d * (\overline{x} - \overline{q})^2 + d * (\delta_x - \delta_q)^2} \leq R$, where $\overline{x} = \frac{1}{d}\sum\limits_{i=1}^{d} x_i$ and $\delta_x = \sqrt{\frac{1}{d}\sum\limits_{i=1}^{d} (x_i - \overline{x})^2}$. Formally,

Definition 1 $(L_{\overline{x}\delta})$. *Given a query pointQ:$(q_1, q_2, ..., q_d)$ and a radius R, $L_{\overline{x}\delta}$ is a data point set. And the point X:$(x_1, x_2, ..., x_d)$ belongs to $L_{\overline{x}\delta}$ only if $\sqrt{d * (\overline{x} - \overline{q})^2 + d * (\delta_x - \delta_q)^2} \leq R$, where $\overline{x}$ and δ_x respectively are the mean value and the standard deviation of $(x_1, x_2, ..., x_d)$, and meanwhile, $\overline{q}$ and δ_q respectively are the mean value and the standard deviation of $(q_1, q_2, ..., q_d)$.*

Similarly, we can obtain the Definition of the data point set $U_{\overline{x}\delta}$ as follows.

Definition 2 $(U_{\overline{x}\delta})$. *Given a query point Q:$(q_1, q_2, ..., q_d)$ and a radius R, $U_{\overline{x}\delta}$ is a data point set. And the point X:$(x_1, x_2, ..., x_d)$ belongs to $U_{\overline{x}\delta}$ only if $\sqrt{d * (\overline{x} - \overline{q})^2 + d * (\delta_x + \delta_q)^2} \leq R$, where $\overline{x}$ and δ_x respectively are the mean value and the standard deviation of $(x_1, x_2, ..., x_d)$, and meanwhile, $\overline{q}$ and δ_q respectively are the mean value and the standard deviation of $(q_1, q_2, ..., q_d)$.*

Thus $L_{\overline{x}\delta}$ is the candidate set for the R-NN of Q and we can obtain $Q(R)$ from the candidate set $L_{\overline{x}\delta}$. Specifically,

Lemma 3. *That the point X:$(x_1, x_2, ..., x_d)$ belongs to $L_{\overline{x}\delta}$ is the necessary condition for that X belongs to the R-NN of Q. So $Q(R) \subseteq L_{\overline{x}\delta}$ and $L_{\overline{x}\delta} \subseteq D$.*

Proof. From the *Definition* 1 and *Lemma* 2, we can prove *Lemma* 3.

Moreover, if a point belongs to the data point set $U_{\overline{x}\delta}$, it must belong to R-NN of Q and $U_{\overline{x}\delta} \subseteq Q(R)$. Formally,

Lemma 4. *That the point X:$(x_1, x_2, ..., x_d)$ belongs to $U_{\overline{x}\delta}$ is the sufficient condition for that X belongs to the R-NN of Q. So $U_{\overline{x}\delta} \subseteq Q(R)$.*

Proof. We can prove this idea according to *Definition* 2 and *Lemma* 2.

3.3 The Extension of the Pruning Algorithm

Although we gain the 2-dimensional representation of the data point, we try to find some effective ways to transform 2-dimensional form into the 1-dimensional one. The relationship between $\overline{x}$ and δ_x can be deduced by the statistical theorem.

Lemma 5. *Given a point X:$(x_1, x_2, ..., x_d)$, its mean value is $\overline{x} = \frac{1}{d} \sum_{i=1}^{d} x_i$ and its standard deviation $\delta_x = \sqrt{\frac{1}{d} \sum_{i=1}^{d} (x_i - \overline{x})^2}$, so $\overline{x}^2 + \delta_x^2 = \frac{1}{d} \sum_{i=1}^{d} x_i^2$.*

Proof. We substitute $\overline{x}$ and δ_x into the statistical theorem $D^2(x) = E(x^2) - E^2(x)$, and the Eq. (6) can be inferred

$$\overline{x}^2 + \delta_x^2 = \frac{1}{d} \sum_{i=1}^{d} x_i^2 \tag{6}$$

Geometrically speaking, we can consider $\sum_{i=1}^{d} x_i^2$ as the distance between X and the origin point O : $(0, 0, ..., 0)$. Therefore, from Pythagoras theorem, we can also obtain the Eq. (6).

After analyzing the geometrical meanings of $L_{\overline{x}\delta}$ and the Eq. (6), we can find that $L_{\overline{x}\delta}$ represents the set of the data points inside a circle in the plane determined by OV and Q. This circle has the center Q : $(\overline{q}, \delta_q)$ and the radius $R/\sqrt{d}$. Also we can find that the Eq. (6) shows the points on the circle with the center O and the radius $\sqrt{\frac{1}{d} \sum_{i=1}^{d} x_i^2}$ in the same plane. In fact the Eq. (6) demonstrates that the point X : $(\overline{x}, \delta_x)$ is about $\sqrt{\frac{1}{d} \sum_{i=1}^{d} x_i^2}$ distant from O. Thus combining $L_{\overline{x}\delta}$ and the Eq. (6), if the point X : $(\overline{x}, \delta_x)$ lies inside the circle with the center $(\overline{q}, \delta_q)$ and the radius $R/\sqrt{d}$, it has to lie in the circular ring with the center O. The inner radius of this circular ring is $max(\sqrt{\frac{1}{d} \sum_{i=1}^{d} q_i^2} - R/\sqrt{d}, 0)$ and the outer radius of it is $\sqrt{\frac{1}{d} \sum_{i=1}^{d} q_i^2} + R/\sqrt{d}$, where $max(a, b)$ is a function whose value is the maximum between real numbers a and b. That is to say, The condition that the distance between X : $(\overline{x}, \delta_x)$ and O lies in the range from $max(\sqrt{\frac{1}{d} \sum_{i=1}^{d} q_i^2} - R/\sqrt{d}, 0)$ to $\sqrt{\frac{1}{d} \sum_{i=1}^{d} q_i^2} + R/\sqrt{d}$ is the necessary condition for that X belongs to $L_{\overline{x}\delta}$. More importantly, as for the same point X, the distance from $(x_1, x_2, ..., x_d)$ to O is $\sqrt{d}$ times of the distance from $(\overline{q}, \delta_q)$ to O. Although $(x_1, x_2, ..., x_d)$ and $(\overline{q}, \delta_q)$ are two different representations for the same point X, they have different distant from the origin O because they respectively belongs to two different coordinate systems.

Definition 3 *(S_r).* *Given a query point Q:$(\overline{q}, \delta_q)$ and a radius R, S_r is a data point set. Let $d(X, O)$ is the distance between X:$(\overline{x}, \delta_x)$ and O. And the* point $X{:}(\bar{x},\ \delta_x)$ belongs to S_r only if $max(\sqrt{\frac{1}{d}\sum_{i=1}^{d}q_i^2} - R/\sqrt{d}, 0) \leq d(X, O) \leq$

$\sqrt{\frac{1}{d}\sum_{i=1}^{d}q_i^2} + R/\sqrt{d}.$

Lemma 6. *That the point $X{:}(\bar{x},\ \delta_x)$ belongs to S_r is the necessary condition for that X belongs to $L_{\bar{x}\delta}$. So $L_{\bar{x}\delta} \subseteq S_r$ and $S_r \subseteq D$.*

Proof. As mentioned above, we can infer that the point X belongs to S_r from the condition that it belongs to $L_{\bar{x}\delta}$.

The set S_r is similar to the candidate set of iDistance in form, but essentially it is deduced as the extension from the 2-dimensional method. As a matter of fact, in the unit d-dimensional space, $\bar{x}$ and δ_x have the fixed bounds. Because OV is the diagonal line of the unit d-dimensional space, its length is $\sqrt{d}$. The maximum of $\bar{x}$ is $\sqrt{d}$. Moreover, according to the features of the unit hypercbe and the area of triangle, when d is the even number, the maximum of δ_x is $\frac{1}{2}\sqrt{d}$ and when d is the odd number the maximum of δ_x is $\frac{1}{2}\sqrt{(d+1)(d-1)/d}$. We denote the maximum of $\bar{x}$ as $MAX_{\bar{x}}$ and denote the maximum of δ_x as MAX_δ. Specifically, as for the arbitrary data point X, $\bar{x} \leq MAX_{\bar{x}}$ and $\delta_x \leq MAX_\delta$. So

$$MAX_{\bar{x}} = \sqrt{d} \qquad (7)$$

And when d is a event number

$$MAX_\delta = \frac{1}{2}\sqrt{d} \qquad (8)$$

or when d is a odd number

$$MAX_\delta = \frac{1}{2}\sqrt{(d+1)(d-1)/d} \qquad (9)$$

The Eq. (7) can be achieved in terms of the features of the diagonal line in the unit d-dimensional space. The Eqs. (8) and (9) can be obtained by the Eq. (7) and be obtained by the way to solve the maximum area of the triangle. Therefore, the query zone is like a rectangle with the length $MAX_{\bar{x}}$ and the width MAX_δ. However, it is strictly not a rectangle but a shape with a sawtooth in one side and a straight line in the other side, because as $\bar{x}$ of X lies in different places, some maximums of δ_x is less than MAX_δ. Even so, the values of δ_x is less than MAX_δ at all time. In this situation, we can transform 2-dimensional form $(\bar{x}, \delta_x)$ into one dimensional form by only considering $\bar{x}$ or δ_x as the coordinate. So we can acquire the candidate set for the index $\bar{x}$ or δ_x by the similar way as *Definition* 3. $min(a, b)$ is a function whose value is the minimum between real numbers a and b, and we have

Definition 4 *($S_{\bar{x}}$). Given a query point $Q{:}(\bar{q},\ \delta_q)$ and a radius R, $S_{\bar{x}}$ is a data point set. And the point $X{:}(\bar{x},\ \delta_x)$ belongs to $S_{\bar{x}}$ only if $max(\bar{q} - R/\sqrt{d}, 0) \leq \bar{x} \leq min(\bar{q} + R/\sqrt{d}, MAX_{\bar{x}})$.*

Definition 5 *(S_δ). Given a query point Q:$(\overline{q}, \delta_q)$ and a radius R, S_δ is a data point set. And the point X:$(\overline{x}, \delta_x)$ belongs to S_δ only if $max(\delta_q - R/\sqrt{d}, 0)0 \leq \overline{x} \leq min(\delta_q + R/\sqrt{d}, MAX_\delta)$.*

In fact, when $\overline{q} + R/\sqrt{d} \geq MAX_{\overline{x}}$, we can substitute $MAX_{\overline{x}}$ for $(\overline{q} + R/\sqrt{d})$, because $\overline{x}$ is always less than $MAX_{\overline{x}}$. Similarly, we can obtain the *Lemma* 7.

Lemma 7. *That the point X:$(\overline{x}, \delta_x)$ belongs to $S_{\overline{x}}$ is the necessary condition for that X belongs to $L_{\overline{x}\delta}$. So $L_{\overline{x}\delta} \subseteq S_{\overline{x}}$ and $S_{\overline{x}} \subseteq D$. And X belongs to S_δ is the necessary condition for that X belongs to $L_{\overline{x}\delta}$. So $L_{\overline{x}\delta} \subseteq S_\delta$ and $S_\delta \subseteq D$.*

Proof. The process of proving *Lemma* 7 is similar to that of proving *Lemma* 6.

Furthermore, given the query point Q and a radius R, the query zone determined by only δ_x is approximately twice of the query zone determined by only $\overline{x}$ from the *Definitions* 4, 5 and the Eqs. (7) and (8) when $\delta_q + R/\sqrt{d} \leq MAX_\delta$. Because the $MAX_{\overline{x}}$ is about twice of MAX_δ. That is to say, the number of points in S_δ is approximately twice of that in $S_{\overline{x}}$. If the data points have uniform distribution in the space, using $\overline{x}$ as the 1-dimensional form probably is better than using δ_x as that form. As for S_r under the uniform distribution, sometimes the points in S_r are more than that in $S_{\overline{x}}$, and at the other time they are less.

3.4   Index Structure

For the 2-dimensional form $(\overline{x}, \delta_x)$ of the data point X, we can employ the existent spatial index methods to build an efficient storage structure. For example, $k - d$ tree is an effective spatial index structure that partitions the space in terms of the different axis. Also R-tree is a convenient and efficient spatial index method that clusters the neighbor points instead of partitioning the space. Because the $(\overline{x}, \delta_x)$ is a very low dimensional representation of the space data, these existed spatial index methods are excellent tools.

With respect to one dimensional representation of the point X, we can exploit the classical B^+ tree method to index it. When $\frac{1}{d} \sum_{i=1}^{d} x_i^2$ are used for the index of B^+ tree, $\overline{x}$ and δ_x also are considered as the secondary index information to be stored in the leaf nodes. After obtaining the candidate set S_r, we can further determine whether each point in S_r belongs to $L_{\overline{x}\delta}$ and whether it belongs to $U_{\overline{x}\delta}$. If the point X does not belongs to $L_{\overline{x}\delta}$, it definitely does not belong to $Q(R)$. And if it belongs to $L_{\overline{x}\delta}$, $d(X, Q)$ is computed to make sure whether it belongs to $Q(R)$. On the other hand, $\overline{x}$ can be employed to index X in the B^+ tree. We firstly acquire the candidate set $S_{\overline{x}}$, namely all points in the interval $[max((\overline{q} - R/\sqrt{d}, 0), min((\overline{q} + R/\sqrt{d}), MAX_{\overline{x}})]$. Then we determine whether each point in $S_{\overline{x}}$ belongs to $L_{\overline{x}\delta}$ and whether it belongs to $U_{\overline{x}\delta}$. Furthermore, we obtain the set $Q(R)$ in the same way as the 2-dimensional method. Similarly, we deal with the index δ_x of X in the same way as doing $\overline{x}$.

4 Experiments

In this section, we study the performance of our proposed methods by comparing it with the traditional methods of high dimensional index.

4.1 The Experimental Environment and Performance Measurement

We implement our proposed methods and the traditional methods in $C + +$ environment of the $.Net$ framework. We use B+ tree to index transformed data in the single dimensional space, and employ R tree to index the data in the 2-dimensional space.

We use the 16-dimensional dataset with 400000, 450000, 500000, 600000 and 700000 uniform distributed points to measure the performance. Specifically, the 16-dimensional points in the dataset are scattered in terms of uniformity distribution into a unit metric space.

Additionally, we define some new performance measurements to analyze the performances of different methods.

(1) Because we obtain the candidate set by the query hyperrectangle intersecting with the nodes of R tree. In fact some data points in the candidate nodes of R tree does not meet the condition of the pruning rules and we define these points as the trifling points.
(2) We define the proportion of the numbers of IO of the single dimensional index method to that of the traditional one as the efficient proportion. It is used to analyze the change of the efficiency of our proposed methods.

The cost of query processing mainly consists of both disk I/O cost and CPU computation cost. The bottleneck of the performance of computing machinery is the disk storage device, so the disk I/O cost far overweigh the CPU computation cost in the query processing. Thus in the experiments, we only take into account the disk I/O cost as the factor to influence the performance. Because the scale of the candidate set is proportional to the I/O cost. So in this experiment, firstly we employ the scale of the candidate set to represent the cost. Furthermore, we measure the numbers of IO of different methods to compare their performances. In the addition, we analyze the change of the new performance measurements, the trifling points and the efficient proportion.

4.2 The Performance Comparison of the Index Methods

In this experiment, we compare the performance of the presented methods with that of the iDistance method. We respectively perform these methods on the 16-dimensional datasets with 400000, 450000, 500000, 600000 and 700000 uniform distributed points. We implement the R-NN query with 1000 query points on those datasets and choose the appropriate value of the range R.

The points in the dataset are randomly and uniformly distributed into the unit metric space, so we do not cluster these points into different partitions and only choose the mean values of different dimension coordinates as the virtual center for the iDistance method. This is expected, the virtual center is very close to but not coincident with the center of the unit hypercube because of the uniform distribution. Furthermore, partitioning the points into different clusters can be equivalently transformed into distributing these points into different the unit hypercubes. And we will extend the proposed methods to application for the different partitions in the future works. So we only focus on the single unit hypercube and choose only one virtual center point of our proposed methods and iDistance for the fair comparison.

Moreover, we use the R-tree to index the 2-dimensional method in this paper. And the representation, $(\overline{x}, \delta_x)$, is considered as the index key. With respect to the one dimension method in this paper, we employ the $B+$ tree as the index structure, and $\overline{x}$ is regarded as the index key because in this experiment δ_x has no pruning ability.

Table 2. Query in the dataset

The method	500000 Points		450000 Points		400000 Points	
	The number of candidates	The number of exact points	The number of candidates	The number of exact points	The number of candidates	The number of exact points
2-dimensional Method	413753	4.4	373307	4	332420	3.7
$\overline{x}$ Index structure	426952	4.4	385369	4	343288	3.7
iDistance	499500	4.4	449379	4	399333	3.7

Table 2 shows that the methods in this paper has better pruning ability than iDistance. Meanwhile, iDistance nearly lost the pruning ability without clustering preprocessing in the unit metric space. Furthermore, the 2-dimensional method in this paper has only a little better performance than the one-dimension one. So taking into account the computation and storage model, the one-dimension method is an efficient one.

The performance analysis of methods under the different scale of the dataset also is shown in Table 2. So we can find that as the scale of dataset expands, the pruning ability of the methods presented in this paper keep the effectiveness.

The Fig. 4 shows the comparison of the number of IO between the $\overline{x}$ index structure(The Mean Index structure) and the iDistance method, and the horizontal axis represents the scale of the dataset. For the sake of fairness, we use the same B^+ tree structure and datasets to count the number of IO. The 2-dimensional method employs R tree structure so it is passed over in the comparison for the fair. The numbers of IO, as expected, increases as the scale of the dataset increases, and the number of IO of the $\overline{x}$ index structure is less than that of the iDistance method so it has better performance. We consider the current capacity of the buffer as the original one and increase the capacity of the buffer to measure the performance.

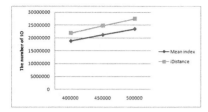

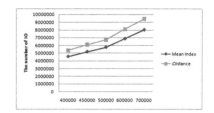

Fig. 4. The comparison of the numbers of IO

Fig. 5. The comparison of the numbers of IO under quadruple the original capacity of the buffer

Moreover, the Fig. 5 shows the comparison of the performance of the 2-dimensional method with that of the iDistance method under quadruple the original capacity of the buffer. On the one hand, we can find that there are the less numbers of IO of both methods in the Fig. 5 than that in the Fig. 4 because of the increase of the capacity of the buffer. On the other hand, the numbers of IO of both method increase as the dataset expands, and the $\bar{x}$ index structure always has the less number of IO than the iDistance method along with the increase of the scale of the dataset.

In the Fig. 6 we adjust the capacity of the buffer so as to measure the effect of the buffer on the number of IO. In the Fig. 6, the horizontal axis represents the times of the capacity of buffer to the original one. The Fig. 6 shows that the numbers of IO of both the $\bar{x}$ index structure and the iDistance method sharply diminish as the capacity of the buffer increases. On the other hand, the efficient proportion is the proportion of the numbers of IO of the $\bar{x}$ index structure to that of the iDistance. And we measure the response of the efficient proportion to the expansion of the capacity of the buffer. The Fig. 7 shows that the efficient proportion changes very little along with the expansion of the capacity of the buffer. However, in the Fig. 7 the numbers of IO of both methods similarly reduce to 49 percent, 24 percent and 12.5 percent of original one as the capacity of the buffer increases to twice, four times and eight times of the original capacity of the buffer. Thus we can achieve the appropriate numbers of IO by means of increasing the capacity of the buffer.

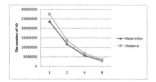

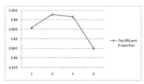

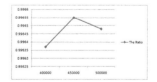

Fig. 6. The relation between the numbers of IO and the buffer

Fig. 7. The proportion of the numbers of IO of $\bar{x}$ index structure to that of iDistance

Fig. 8. The efficiency of R tree

With regard to the 2-dimensional method in this paper, we compute the ratio of the point number in the candidate without trifling points to that in the candidate set with trifling points. When the ratio is close 1, the 2-dimensional method has great efficiency. This ratio is shown in the Fig. 8 and the horizontal axis represents the scale of the dataset. The Fig. 8 demonstrates that the trifling points nearly are non-existent in the candidate set regardless of the scale of the dataset. Thus 2-dimensional method is excellently efficient.

5   Conclusion and Future Works

In this paper, we analyze the characteristics of high dimensional data and present the effective index methods in the unit metric space. In the future, we will apply these methods into the cluster dataset instead of the unit hypercube. Moreover, the cluster data can be assigned into different partitions and each partitions can be considered as one unit hypercube. And the methods in this paper can respectively be applied in each partitions to index high dimensional data.

References

1. Guttman, A.: R-trees: a dynamic index structure for spatial searching. In: Proceedings of the ACM Special Interest Group on Management of Data(SIGMOD), pp. 47–57 (1984)
2. Indyk, P., Motwani, R.: Approximate nearest neighbors: towards removing the curse of dimensionality. In: Proceedings of the Annual ACM Symposium on Theory of Computing, pp. 604–613 (1998)
3. Jagadish, H.V., Ooi, B.C., Tan, K.L., Yu, C., Zhang, R.: Idistance: an adaptive B^+-tree based Indexing method for nearest neighbor search. ACM Trans. Database Syst. 30(2), 364–397 (2005)
4. Berchtold, S., Bohm, C., Kriegel, H.-P.: The pyramid-technique: towards indexing beyond the curse of dimensionality. In: Proceedings of the ACM SIGMOD, pp. 142–153 (1998)
5. Zhuang, Y.T., Yang, Y., Wu, F.: Mining semantic correlation of heterogeneous multimedia data for cross-media retrieval. IEEE Trans. Multimedia 10(2), 221–229 (2008)
6. Weber, R., Schek, H.J., Blott, S.: A quantitative analysis and performance study for similarity-search methods in high-dimensional spaces. In: Proceedings of International Conference on Very Large Databases, pp. 194–205 (1998)
7. Lawder, J.K., King, P.J.H.: Using space-filling curves for multi-dimensional indexing. In: Jeffery, K., Lings, B. (eds.) BNCOD 2000. LNCS, vol. 1832, pp. 20–35. Springer, Heidelberg (2000)
8. Ciaccia, P., Patella, M., Zezula, P.: M-tree: an efficient access method for similarity search in metric spaces. In: Proceedings of International Conference on Very Large Databases, pp. 426–435 (1997)
9. Beckmann, N., Kriegel, R. Schneider Seeger, B.: The R^*-tree: an efficient and robust access method for points and rectangles. In: Proceedings of the ACM SIGMOD, pp. 322–331 (1990)

10. Sellis, T., Roussopoulos, N., Faloutsos, C.: The R^+-tree: a dynamic index for multidimensional objects. In: Proceedings of International Conference on Very Large Databases, pp. 507–518 (1987)
11. Bohm, C.: A cost model for query processing in high-dimensional data. ACM Trans. Database Syst. **25**, 129–178 (2000)
12. Robinson, J.: The K-D-B-tree: a search structure for large multidimensional dynamic indexes. In: Proceedings of the ACM SIGMOD, pp. 10–18 (1981)
13. Jinyang, H.V., Jagadish, W.L., Ooi, B.C.: DSH: data sensitive hashing for high-dimensional k-NN search. In: Proceedings of the ACM SIGMOD, pp. 1127–1138 (2014)
14. Tao, Y., Yi, K., Sheng, C., Kalnis, P.: Quality and efficiency in high dimensional nearest neighbor search. In: Proceedings of the ACM SIGMOD, pp. 563–576 (2009)

Architecture and Applications

Target Detection and Tracking in Big Surveillance Video Data

Aiyun Yan, Jingjiao Li[⊠], Zhenni Li, and Lan Yao

College of Information Science and Engineering, Northeastern University,
Shenyang, China
{yanaiyun,lijingjiao,lizhenni,yaolan}@ise.neu.edu.cn

Abstract. The big video data information has become widely used in many application areas such as video monitoring. Moving object detection and tracking is one of the most important and difficult problems. This paper puts forward an improved background difference method for moving target area, realizes the motion detection and uses an improved centroid tracking method for target tracking. In our solution, the parallel processing mechanism and powerful computing capability of FPGA platform is applied to improve processing speed and performance of the system. Altera FPGA is chosen as the master control chip, and Qsys setup test system is involved. After multiple tests, the system processes size 320×240 RGB image at 30 frames per second, achieving the moving target monitoring and real-time tracking, and the accuracy is above 90 %. This design increases the reliability of the detection and tracking system on the basis of ensuring the running speed.

Keywords: Big video data · Inter-frame difference · Centroid tracking

1 Introduction

Visual surveillance uses video cameras to monitor the activities of targets(humans, vehicles, etc.) in a scene. Video monitoring system is developing towards highly clear display, and intelligence. And Video monitoring and big data is combined more and more closely. Furthermore, with the requirement of larger storage, accurate recognition through detection algorithm, higher accuracy, Video monitoring of big data processing make the application more efficient. In order to classify, track or analyze activities of interested objects, it is necessary to extract the moving object from the scene. Moving target detection in video surveillance is to detect the foreground object moving relatively to the background in the video sequence by analyzing the motion state and image characteristics (such as color, edge, texture, etc.). The image segmentation and the main methods of moving object detection include: inter-frame difference, optical flow method and background subtraction method. Inter-frame difference method has small computation, fast detection and good real-time performance, which is suitable for hardware implementation. But in a complex environment inter-frame difference method can't extract moving objects except the contour in the whole area. At the same time, the choice of time interval between the frame is very important for the realization of the algorithm. Object with quick or slow motion is almost undetectable. Zhang [1] uses edge

© Springer International Publishing Switzerland 2016
Y. Wang et al. (Eds.): BigCom 2016, LNCS 9784, pp. 275–284, 2016.
DOI: 10.1007/978-3-319-42553-5_23

detection algorithm combining inter-frame difference to achieve moving target detection. This paper focuses on the improvement of traditional median filtering algorithm and classic sobel algorithm. Moving target was derived by the difference between two adjacent frames. It is possible to accurately detect moving objects appearing in the video. Compared to traditional method, the frame difference algorithm consumed fewer hardware resources and fully meets the real-time requirements. Gujrathi, et al. [2] have used the FPGA to achieve a moving target detection basing on background subtraction method. The design first use a background image as a reference image which was stored in the SDRAM. Then video stream was transferred to frames. Each frame (pixels) subtracts the background image to detect the motion area. Background difference method is a simple and effective method [3], which is good for moving object detection under the complicated environmental. Small amount of calculation of this method make it suitable for hardware implementation. While background tend to change, resulting in the detection effect is not obvious. So this design uses an improved algorithm based on background difference. The improved algorithm can make the background image update adaptively, reduce the influence of background changes on the testing results.

Tracking algorithm based on feature matching include edge tracking algorithm, correlation tracking algorithm and centroid tracking algorithm [4]. The basic principle of Centroid tracking algorithm [5] is that the position coordinates of the moving object in which the grayscale value corresponds to the target point represents itself. Then the energy of the target is calculated. Thereby the target trajectory is obtained. Centroid is the center of the moving target gray value. Because the movement target gray values will not change while the movement of the target form changes, which have a strong inhibition to noise and clutter. So the target tracking algorithm is more stable [6]. The advantages of centroid tracking algorithm is a small amount of computation, fast, simple, and can meet the requirements of the real-time system, especially the FPGA implementation.

The remaining of the paper is organized as follows. The moving object detection algorithm is briefly described in Sect. 2. Centroid tracking algorithm is introduced in Sect. 3. Implementation course is explained in Sect. 4. Experimental results is presented to validate the robustness of proposal in Sect. 5. Conclusions are drawn in the last Section.

2   Moving Object Detection

This design uses an improved background subtraction and establish background model prior to the detection and updates the background real-time. Then the current frame and the background image of the video make the difference. Finally, the dynamic threshold is used to and extract moving target.

2.1   Background Update

Adaptive background update of pixel level detection can solve the slow-moving and fast-moving object detection problems. First, the N frame image data of initial acquisition is to average as the initial image. The collected image is very close to the real image of the background image, avoiding the environmental impact of mutations on the background image. The design selects the first eight frame in order to reduce the amount of computation and save hardware resources. Equation (1) is below.

$$B_0 = \frac{1}{N} \sum_{k=1}^{N} I_k(x, y) \tag{1}$$

After obtaining the initial background B_0, the design use the Formula (2) iterative update.

$$B_i(x, y) = \begin{cases} B_{i-1}(x, y) & I_k(x, y) \geq T \\ aI_k(x, y) + (1 - a)B_{i-1}(x, y) & I_k(x, y) < T \end{cases} \tag{2}$$

The resulting equation $B_i(x, y)$ represents the current background, $B_{i-1}(x, y)$ represents the background before the current moment, $I_k(x, y)$ represents the current frame image, a represents the update rate, T represents the threshold. The update rate a generally ranges from 0 to 1. A value of 0 is for the traditional background subtraction, and the value of 1 is for the inter-frame difference method. If the value is too small, it is not likely to keep up with the speed of updating of the background. If the value is too large, the non-background image is likely to be detected as the background, which can produce hollow phenomenon. So the value is experimentally set as 0.25. Either fractional treatment can be finished through the right, or decimal multiplication process can be achieved through reusing adder summing. This algorithm saves multipliers.

2.2 Dynamic Threshold

If the threshold T is artificially defined, some of the changing light and complex environment does not apply. It is necessary for the threshold to be updated. Taking into account the complexity of the hardware implementation, the design uses the mean gray value of a maximum and minimum gray value images as the threshold segmentation. The following formula is

$$T = \frac{\max I_k(x, y) + \min I_k(x, y)}{2} \tag{3}$$

2.3 Moving Target Detection

The improved background subtraction for motion detecting is to extract moving target in the current frame image. This is because in most cases, there is a big difference between the gray value of the background and the gray value of moving target. And the gray values of moving object itself generally do not have great changes, occasional minor changes is negligible. Suppose the previous frame image be $I_i(x, y)$, the background image is $B_i(x, y)$, the difference image after binarization is shown by Formula (4).

$$DB_i(x, y) = \begin{cases} 1 & I_i(x, y) - B_i(x, y) \geq T \\ 0 & I_i(x, y) - B_i(x, y) < T \end{cases} \qquad (4)$$

From the formula we found that after the binary image point of value 1 can be seen as moving targets.

2.4 Morphological Processing

Morphological processing includes opening operation and closing operation. The opening operation that is designed in this paper to preclude the use of corrosion after the first expansion of the background difference binarized data input module morphological filtering process, starting by etching operation to remove the binarized image isolated noise point, and then by the expansion of the operation crack repair part of the target. After morphological processing of the image area is the moving target area.

3 Target Tracking Implementation

After gradation conversion, median filtering, filtered by the improved background subtraction and morphological, the target area is the area corresponding to pixel gray value of 1 in the obtained binary image. Then, moving target is tracked and, the whole process is to extract the moving target parameters, target parameters and use them to model. Whereby the actual spatial relationship between the moving objects can be achieved.

The adaptive centroid tracking algorithm [7] is applied in this design. We firstly set up tracking window, which traces the outline of the selected target motion and, shields outside part of the local area of the moving target. If the tracking window does not change with the size of the window and position of a moving object, it is called a fixed window; if the size of the tracking window in the process of tracking the target changes with the target size or position varies, it is called adaptive window. This design uses an adaptive window, so the attitude change goals can be effectively tracked. Schematic-based centroid tracking method of tracking window is shown in Fig. 1.

Wherein the frame is adaptive tracking window frame, "+" is the centroid position of the target.

The design selects the centroid length and width of the moving target image as the tracking feature of the sport aspect. In the video surveillance scenario, the centroid

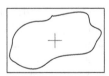

Fig. 1. Tracking diagram based on windows and centroid

position of the moving target and the length width of the border are extracted. The designed tracking module uses green filled squares to identify the centroid position, and the red rectangle identifies the length and width of the border.

3.1   Extraction Boundary

The length and width of the boundary is Extracted. Border vertex position of the movement target area extraction formula is as follows:
minimum coordinate of X direction boundary:

$$MinX = \min(f(x_i, y_j) \cdot x_i) \tag{5}$$

maximum coordinate of X direction boundary:

$$MaxX = \max(f(x_i, y_j) \cdot x_i) \tag{6}$$

minimum coordinate of Y direction boundary::

$$MinY = \min(f(x_i, y_j) \cdot y_j) \tag{7}$$

maximum coordinate of Y direction boundary:

$$MaxY = \max(f(x_i, y_j) \cdot y_j) \tag{8}$$

3.2   Centroid Position Extraction

Then, the local regionalization where moving object within the window is divided into a matrix, which was divided target cells in wave gate. The target centroid is calculated based on the total number of points according to the target cell location data and the target cell [8]. In one window of $M \times N$, the target centroid coordinates is assumed to be (X_e, Y_e), then the moving target area image gray centroid extraction formula is as follows:

$$X_c = \frac{\sum\limits_{i=0}^{N}\sum\limits_{j=0}^{M} f(x_i, y_j) \cdot x_i}{\sum\limits_{i=0}^{N}\sum\limits_{j=0}^{M} f(x_i, y_j)} \tag{9}$$

$$Y_c = \frac{\sum\limits_{i=0}^{N}\sum\limits_{j=0}^{M} f(x_i, y_j) \cdot y_j}{\sum\limits_{i=0}^{N}\sum\limits_{j=0}^{M} f(x_i, y_j)} \tag{10}$$

Where $f(x, y)$ is the pixel value of binary image after the morphological filtering, M, N are the number of pixels of the x and y directions in the tracking window. According to the results mentioned above, if the result of background difference is 1, then the pixel is moving target, the result is 0 for background. A 16-bit counter cnt with value "1" pixel in the function $f(x, y)$ is used as the counter, the cross with two 25-bit registers cntx and cnty is designed to store accumulate value of pixel ordinate for pixel value of "1", with two counters x and y coordinates of the current pixel to represent the point. When the read-out value of $f(x_i, y_i)$ is 1, calculation is based on the following formula:

$$cnt = cnt + 1 \qquad (11)$$

$$cntx = cntx + x \qquad (12)$$

$$cnty = cnty + y \qquad (13)$$

When scanning complete images, you can get the center of the current image by the following formula:

$$CenterX = \frac{cntx}{cnt} \qquad (14)$$

$$CenterY = \frac{cnty}{cnt} \qquad (15)$$

In the moving target tracking module, the pixel value is read first. A pixel horizontal and vertical coordinates were achieved. Then determine whether the pixel value is "1". If it is "1", that point pixel is proved to be moving target, otherwise it is the background image and continue to read the next pixel without any processing. And finally according to Formulas (14) and (15) calculate the coordinates of the center of mass. The latter frame image in the image transfer is completed with green squares to indicate the location of the center of mass. Because the calculation of the centroid is an average statistical process, the results of the tracking point obtained is not the individual brightest point, but the gray of weighted average position of each image pixel. Thus, using the centroid of the target image as a tracking point has small error on the track to give effect, anti-interference ability and high accuracy [9, 10].

Selecting a target centroid as a tracking feature has the following characteristics: target centroid obtained is the determined point after a statistical average. When the target size or posture changes, the centroid position changes little; the position of the center of mass is not affected by the target area of the size; target centroid calculation of the algorithm is with respect to the binary image of the target area normalized basis, which does not restricted by the distribution of binary image, so the target intensity distribution is not limited, there is a little affect of the little noise in the window to the position of the centroid. When voids and break occur within the moving target region, the deviation of centroid location extracted is not large.

4   Algorithm Implementation

After the system design is completed, the design requires Quartus II to compile system project. System resource utilization was obtained. DE2-115 board FPGA resource usage is shown in Fig. 2.

Flow Summary	
Flow Status	Successful - Mon Jun 08 11:45:28 2015
Quartus II 64-Bit Version	13.0.1 Build 232 06/12/2013 SP 1 SJ Full Version
Revision Name	DE2_115_CAMERA
Top-level Entity Name	DE2_115_CAMERA
Family	Cyclone IV E
Device	EP4CE115F29C7
Timing Models	Final
Total logic elements	27,090 / 114,480 (24 %)
Total combinational functions	18,607 / 114,480 (16 %)
Dedicated logic registers	17,943 / 114,480 (16 %)
Total registers	17943
Total pins	428 / 529 (81 %)
Total virtual pins	0
Total memory bits	2,895,608 / 3,981,312 (73 %)
Embedded Multiplier 9-bit elements	100 / 532 (19 %)
Total PLLs	2 / 4 (50 %)

Fig. 2. FPGA resource consumption

Before the power cable was downloaded to the PC. The development board was connected to monitor via VGA interface. Then the system was powered and the SOF file was downloaded to the development board, the SW19 was appropriated RUN, and the system starts operating. SW0 switch is turned on, and the camera began collecting data to track the real-time display of images on the display. The key KEY2 was pressed to pause VGA display, and LED light shows the total number of image frames acquired.

Test 1: A simple background unobstructed tracking

After SW0 was turned on, the tracking results were displayed real-time in VGA, as shown in Fig. 3. Under bright light conditions the background is very complex. Moving objects can still be tracked when the color of moving objects approaches with light.

Fig. 3. Results displayed on VGA

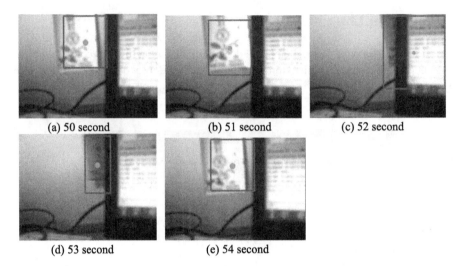

(a) 50 second   (b) 51 second   (c) 52 second

(d) 53 second   (e) 54 second

Fig. 4. Tracking results of occlusions under a simple background (Color figure online)

Running test.avi, the time of video is 1 min 21 s with a frame rate of 30 frames/sec. The background is white walls, and blocking objects is the computer. The background is relatively simple, and the goal to track is the yogurt box which is similar to the background in color. Figure 4 is the tracking results of the images in the video file for 50 s, 51 s, 52 s, 53 s, 54 s respectively.

Test III: the complex environments with cover background

The background is the laboratory environment (similar to environment), and the tracking target is pedestrians, and the blocking object is a laboratory seat.

5   Experimental Results

The video frame is processed by the 24-bit true color image system with size of 320 × 240. According to the results shown in Figs. 4 and 5, it can be drawn that the system can track a moving object. The system selects 30 s with a total of 900 frame to analysis the results. The result meets the requirements of real-time processing.

When the background is relatively simple, the tracking accuracy of the system is high. In the test, the tracking accuracy is shown in Table 1.

In more complex context, the tracking accuracy of the system decreases relatively, which is shown in Fig. 5. The tracking process will be inaccurate, but the overall accuracy rate is still high. Throughout the video, the tracking accuracy is shown in Table 2. As can be seen from the experimental result, the system can be a good method for real-time motion target detection and tracking.

By two typical tests of different complexity backgrounds, the tracking algorithm of this system has good robustness, high accuracy tracking with average tracking accuracy rate of 93.00 %. The comparison test results show that the tracking accuracy of first video test is higher. This is mainly because the background in first video test is simple,

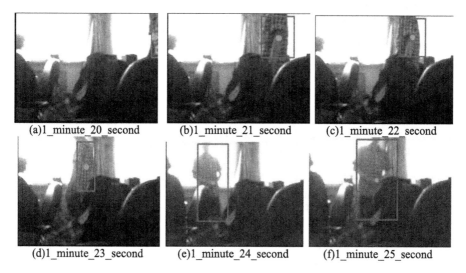

(a)1_minute_20_second   (b)1_minute_21_second   (c)1_minute_22_second

(d)1_minute_23_second   (e)1_minute_24_second   (f)1_minute_25_second

Fig. 5. Occlusion tracking results under a complex background (Color figure online)

Table 1. The data statistics of simple background

The total number of frames for tracking	The number of frames including moving object	The frames of right tracking	Tracking accuracy
900	898	890	98.9 %

Table 2. The data statistics of complex background

The total number of frames for tracking	The number of frames including moving object	The frames of right tracking	Tracking accuracy
900	860	840	93.3 %

and objectives and background colors differences are significant. And the background in second video test is complex, objectives and background colors are closer to each other. So tracking target is more difficult.

6 Conclusions

This paper addresses an adaptive background subtraction method in which the average frame updates within a certain time in the case of adaptive background image. This method is more efficient than the general methods because in this case the frequent moving objects and temporarily stationary objects, etc., will not become part of the background image. Therefore the proposed method, effectively solves the problem of the effect on tracking results from background diversity. The experiments indicate the robust and advanced performance of this method.

Acknowledgements. This research is supported by the National Natural Science Foundation of China under Grant No. 61173027 and the Fundamental Research Funds for the Central Universities (N140404006, N130316001).

References

1. Zhang, C.: The Design and Reaearch of FPGA-based Video Moving Target Detection System (D). Wuhan University of Technology, WuHan (2014)
2. Gujrathi, P., Arokia Priya, R., Malathi, P.: Detecting moving object using background subtraction algorithm in FPGA. In: 2014 Fourth International Conference on Advances in Computing and Communications (ICACC), pp. 117–120. IEEE (2014)
3. Kaixuan, Z., Dongjian, H.: Target detection method for moving cows based on background subtraction. Int. J. Agric. Biol. Eng. **8**(1), 42–49 (2015)
4. Han, Z.X., Zhang, B.H.: Research of tracking algorithm for moving object based on video sequence. Appl. Mech. Mater. **556**, 3088–3092 (2014)
5. Xiabin, D., Xinsheng, H., Yongbin, Z., et al.: A novel infrared small moving target detection method based on tracking interest points under complicated background. Infrared Phys. Technol. **65**, 36–42 (2014)
6. Rao, V.M.S., Natarajan, A., Moorthi, S., et al: Real-time object tracking in a video stream using Field Programmable Gate Array. In: 2012 Annual IEEE India Conference (INDICON) 48(11), pp. 167–170(2012)
7. Yin, T.H., Bing, C.T., Yu, T.P., et al.: Feature points based video object tracking for dynamic scenes and its FPGA system prototyping. In: 2014 Tenth International Conference on Intelligent Information Hiding and Multimedia Signal Processing (IIH-MSP), pp. 325–328. IEEE (2014)
8. Amali, T.J.R., Akila, C., Kavitha, V.: Rapid background subtraction from video sequences. In: 2012 International Conference on Computing, Electronics and Electrical Technologies (ICCEET), pp. 1077–1086. IEEE (2012)
9. Hu, G., Lian, H., Wang, P.: Design and research on the motion target detection and tracking algorithm. In: 2010 2nd International Conference on Information Science and Engineering (ICISE), pp. 1114–1117. IEEE (2010)
10. The Video and Embedded Evaluation Kit - Multi-touch on Cyclone® V SoC Development Board[EB] (2014). http://www.terasic.com.tw

SGraph: A Distributed Streaming System for Processing Big Graphs

Cheng Chen[1,2], Hejun Wu[1,2(✉)], Dyce Jing Zhao[3], Da Yan[4],
and James Cheng[4]

[1] Guangdong Province Key Laboratory of Big Data Analysis and Processing,
Sun Yat-Sen University, Guangzhou, China
[2] SYSU-CMU Shunde International Joint Research Institute (JRI), Foshan, China
chench48@mail2.sysu.edu.cn, wuhejun@mail.sysu.edu.cn
[3] BNU-HKBU United International College, Zhuhai, Hong Kong
jzhao@uic.edu.hk
[4] Department of Computer Science and Engineering,
The Chinese University of Hong Kong, Shatin, Hong Kong
{yanda,jcheng}@cse.cuhk.edu.hk

Abstract. Big graph processing has been widely used in various computational domains, ranging from language modeling to social networks. Graph-parallel systems have been proposed to process such big graphs on clusters with up to hundreds of nodes. However, the size of a big graph often exceeds the available main memories in a small cluster. As a consequence, task failures happen frequently. To address this problem, we propose SGraph, a distributed streaming graph processing system built on top of Spark. SGraph introduces a streaming data model to avoid loading all of the graph data which may exceed the available RAM space. In addition, SGraph leverages an edge-centric scatter-gather computing model that can be used to conveniently implement graph algorithms. Experiments demonstrate that SGraph can process graphs with up to 1.5 billion edges on small clusters with several low-cost commodity PCs, whereas existing systems may require up to tens or hundreds of high-end machines. Furthermore, SGraph is up to 2.3 times faster than existing systems.

Keywords: Distributed computing · Graph processing · Streaming

1 Introduction

Graph structure offers enormous flexibility for describing the complex relationships between discrete objects in various domains, such as social networks, web graphs and communication networks. For instance, in a social network, people are naturally mapped to vertices and the relationships between people are denoted by edges. The size of graphs can be extremely large, for example, Facebook reached 1 billion users and 140.3 billion friendship connections [1] in October 2012.

© Springer International Publishing Switzerland 2016
Y. Wang et al. (Eds.): BigCom 2016, LNCS 9784, pp. 285–294, 2016.
DOI: 10.1007/978-3-319-42553-5_24

Researchers have proposed distributed frameworks to process the big graph. Apache Spark [11] is initially designed for general large-scale data, using an abstract data structure called *resilient distributed dataset* (RDD) with a group of useful operators. Spark is later adopted for distributed graph processing.

There are also distributed systems specifically for graph computation. Graph-Builder [5] introduces a scalable ETL graph framework using the MapReduce model, which offloads complexities of graph construction. Pregel [7] uses a *vertex-centric* message passing model, in which each vertex can send messages to other vertices, receive messages sent in previous *super-steps* and modify attribute of itself. Giraph [3] is a distributed graph computing system built on Apache Hadoop and implements the computing model of Pregel. PowerGraph [4] proposes a *GAS* model to divide the vertex-program into edge-parallel and vertex-parallel stages, so as to reduce network communication and storage costs. GraphX [10] is a graph computing system built on top of Spark and abstracts graph RDDs, VertexRDD and EdgeRDD. GraphX enhances Pregel [7] computing model with the GraphX APIs. However, if the cluster has insufficient main memories to load a large graph, computation failures and task re-executions may happen.

In this paper, we present SGraph, a streaming cluster computing system that is also based on Spark and takes a trade-off between computing resources and job runtime. SGraph compresses the EdgeRDD to reduce I/O communication costs. In addition, SGraph contributes to the abstraction of graph data with new auxiliary RDDs, including SourceVertexRDD and UpdateVertexRDD. SGraph co-locates partitions of SourceVertexRDD and corresponding partitions of EdgeRDD with worker nodes to obtain data locality and implements the streaming model. The edge-centric scatter-gather model is a general computing model that can implement many graph algorithms. SGraph supports both in-memory and out-of-core workloads, and the source code is released on https://github.com/zixicc/SGraph. We summarize our main contributions with SGraph as follows:

- We improve the RDD abstraction of graph data to achieve more scalable and efficient graph processing.
- With the new RDD abstraction, we integrate a streaming computation model with the edge-centric computing model on distributed clusters.
- Experimental results show that SGraph performs well even in small clusters. In addition, SGraph achieves comparable or even better performance than *Pregel-like* systems with much less RAM consumption.

This paper is organized as follows. Section 2 introduces the preliminaries. Section 3 overviews the SGraph abstraction. Section 4 presents the system implementation of SGraph and the performances are evaluated in Sect. 5. Finally, Sect. 6 concludes this paper and discusses future works.

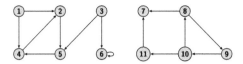

Fig. 1: A graph example

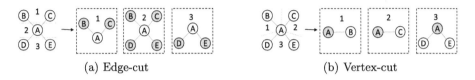

(a) Edge-cut   (b) Vertex-cut

Fig. 2: A 3-way edge-cut and a 3-way vertex-cut.

2 Preliminaries

2.1 Graph Data

A graph $G = (V, E)$ is represented by V, a nonempty set of vertices, and E, a set of edges. Directed graphs contain direction in each edge. In Fig. 1, we show an example of a directed graph of 11 vertices and 14 edges. This example graph will be used in the following sections.

2.2 Partitioning

Edge-cuts and vertex-cuts [4] are two common approaches to deliver graph data to a distributed cluster. Figure 2(a) and (b) shows a 3-way edge-cut and 3-way vertex-cut respectively, in which shaded vertices are ghosts vertices (local replicas) of the graph. We can see that the edge-cut method produces more vertex replicas than vertex-cut.

2.3 Graph-Parallel Computation

In data-parallel computation, each data record is processed independently. However, the parallelism is limited by graph structure, as vertices may be connected and need to be processed iteratively. For example, PageRank [8] computes the rank value of each vertex by iteratively aggregating the rank values of its neighbor vertices until convergency.

3 SGraph Abstraction

3.1 SGraph Architecture

Figure 3 shows the architecture of SGraph. SGraph uses Spark [11] as the fundamental computing framework to take advantage of the abstractive RDD data

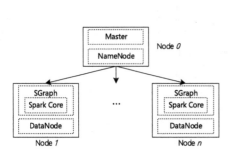

Fig. 3: The SGraph architecture.

SCATTER
1   edge_scatter(edge e)
2   generate update(dstId, value) from e.srcId

GATHER
1   update_gather(update u)
2   apply update u to u.dstId

EDGE-CENTRIC LOOP
1   while not done
2   for all e ∈ edges
3   edge_scatter(e)
4   for all u ∈ updates
5   update_gather(u)

Fig. 4: Edge-centric scatter-gather model.

structure and its corresponding operators. The Hadoop cluster is used to provides storage infrastructure. The deployment of DataNodes of Hadoop and Workers of Spark on the same machines allows Spark to take advantage of the data locality of HDFS.

3.2   SGraph Computing Model

SGraph adopts the *edge-centric scatter-gather* computing model [9]. The pseudocode of Fig. 4 illustrates such an edge-centric model. The *edge_scatter* procedure generates update from source vertex of an edge and gets an update key-value pair (dstId, value). The *update_gather* procedure applies an update to its destination vertex. Each edge is processed in the *edge_scatter* procedure. Then, each update is processed in the *update_gather* procedure. This model makes SGraph iterate over all edges and updates rather than vertices. As the edge set is much larger than the vertex set in most graphs, edges dominates the memory. Hence, we can reduce the memory usage by streaming so as to process a very big graph on a small commodity cluster.

```
def PageRank(graph: Graph, numIters: Int, resetProb: Double) {
    // Initialize vertex attributes
    val pagerankGraph = graph.mapVertices((vtxId, attr) => 1.0)
    // Define the PageRank vertex program
    def vtxProgram(vtxId: VertexId, attr: Double, valueSum: Double):
        Double = resetProb + (1.0 - resetProb) * valueSum
    def scatter(vtxId: VertexId, attr: Double, outDegree: Int): Double =
        (vtxId, attr / outDegree)
    def gather(a: Double, b: Double): Double = a + b
    ScatterGather(pagerankGraph, numIters)(vtxProgram, scatter, gather)
}
```

Listing 1.1: PageRank implementation of the computing model

Listing 1.1 shows a PageRank implementation of the computing model in SGraph. The program firstly initializes attributes of vertices, and then defines a *vtxProgram* function that aggregates rank values from neighbor vertices. The *scatter* and *gather* function correspond to *scatter* and *gather* procedure in Fig. 4, and the *ScatterGrather* function represents the *edge-centric loop*.

3.3   Graph Data Abstraction

In SGraph, edges can be expressed by EdgeRDD because of the immutability of RDD; vertices can be expressed by VertexRDD as new RDDs will be generated from old RDDs via the operators. When an algorithm needs to modify attributes of edges, there are also operators in EdgeRDD that help to generate a new one. We decompose SourceVertexRDD from EdgeRDD to support our edge-streaming model in SGraph. In addition, SGraph introduces UpdateVertexRDD as the intermediate data structure for updating vertex attributes. We now details these RDDs used in SGraph as follows.

An *EdgeRDD* contains all the edges of a graph file. A partition strategy (partitioner) distributes an edge to a target edge partition. In Fig. 6, the *edges* part shows that edges of the example graph are partitioned by a 3-way random vertex-cut and grouped by source vertices. The *source vertices* part contains information of all the source vertices. In the EdgeRDD, edges and their attributes use columnar store.

An *SourceVertexRDD* is extracted from the EdgeRDD and has the same partitioner and the same partition number as the EdgeRDD. For each partition of the SourceVertexRDD, a *hash table* is used to store the source vertex set and an array is used to store attributes of these vertices. The functionality of the SourceVertexRDD is to send attributes of source vertices over edges in the *scatter* stage of the computing model.

An *VertexRDD* has the same partitioner as the EdgeRDD and contains all the vertices of the graph. In Fig. 6, the *vertices* part shows the vertex set of the example graph. The vertex set of the VertexRDD is the superset of the vertex set of the SourceVertexRDD.

An *UpdateVertexRDD* is an intermediate RDD generated in the computing process. During computation stages, the SourceVertexRDD scatters its updates via the EdgeRDD and these updates are shuffled to destination machines to form update vertex partitions, which constitute an UpdateVertexRDD.

4   System Implementation

4.1   Preprocessing ETL

The ETL process contains three stages: *extract, transform* and *load*. The process in SGraph is responsible for fetching data out from the storage infrastructure and delivering graph data to target location. Figure 6 shows the ETL result of the graph example, and Fig. 5 presents the whole ETL process from HDFS file to graph RDDs. The process is described as follows:

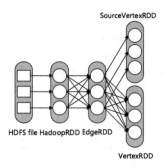

Fig. 5: The ETL process.

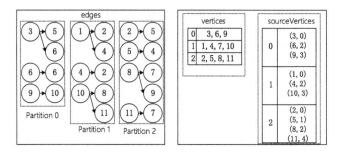

Fig. 6: A process from the example graph to graph RDDs.

Extract. A raw graph file has many lines of strings, each of which represents an edge and consists of source vertex ID and destination vertex ID. In this stage, SGraph transfers data blocks in HDFS to partitions, which constitute a HadoopRDD. Also, during the *extract* process, SGraph assigns initial value to edge attributes, thus transfers each line to an edge triple.

Transform. First of all, the HadoopRDD needs to be repartitioned, so a partition strategy should be specified. SGraph adopts a random vertex-cut approach. A hash function is applied to each source vertex ID as well as the edges that include the source vertex. Then a shuffle is performed to distributes edges to different worker nodes. To further compact the edge RDD and subsequently the overhead, we replace the source vertex array in each edge partition by a *tuple vector*. A tuple vector includes a source vertex ID and its index. Figure 6, shows that the right part, *source vertices*, contains the *tuple vector*. The left part of the figure, *edges*, stores one source vertex ID for edges that share the same source vertex.

The SourceVertexRDD can be directly extracted from the EdgeRDD, as shown in Fig. 5. The process is to get source vertices from each edge partition, assign initial value to source vertices and finally constitute source vertex partitions. It is obvious that a source vertex partition has the same placement with the corresponding edge partition, thus SGraph can finish the *scatter* phase without shuffling data among machines.

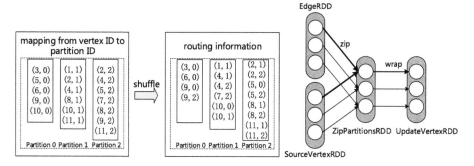

Fig. 7: The process to get routing information

Fig. 8: Streaming model.

The VertexRDD takes the EdgeRDD's partitioner, through which each vertex gets a partition ID. A mapping from vertex ID to partition ID is built first, and then the mapping information are shuffled to target partitions to get the *routing information*, which is used to trace each vertex. Figure 7 shows the process to get routing information of the example graph. Vertex partitions can be built by leveraging routing information, which is stored in the corresponding vertex partitions. Finally we can get the VertexRDD.

We further propose an *UpdateVertexRDD* to store update information. During one scatter-gather stage, an UpdateVertexRDD is generated as intermediate data and used to update attributes of the SourceVertexRDD and VertexRDD. **Load.** RDDs generated in the *transform* stage are references to the real data, which are managed by the *BlockManager*. These RDDs contain mappings of each partition to each real data block. The *load* phase materializes RDDs that are *cached* or *persisted*, and delivers data blocks of graph data to target machines, storing these blocks with specific *StorageLevels*.

4.2 Streaming Data Model

Figure 8 shows that partitions of the EdgeRDD zips with partitions of the SourceVertexRDD, and an UpdateVertexRDD is wrapped from the zipped RDD in SGraph. According to the *ETL* process, each partition of the EdgeRDD has a corresponding partition of the SourceVertexRDD. SGraph regards the data as partition instances and takes partition instances as instance stream. Then it loads the data blocks instance by instance to memory for processing. After processing the partitions in memory, partitions on disk will be loaded continuously. Since the edge set is always much larger than the source vertex set, the memory size of each node is predictable.

5 Evaluation

We choose Spark-0.9.1 as the infrastructure and evaluate the performance of SGraph comparing with GraphX [10] integrated with Spark and Giraph-1.1 [3].

Table 1: Graph data

Dataset	Edges	Vertices	Diameter
LiveJournal [2]	68,993,773	4,847,571	16
Twitter [6]	1,468,365,182	41,652,230	18

Table 2: Cluster setup

Cluster	Node	Node number
Tiny cluster 1 (TC1)	4 cores, 8G memory	1 + 3
Small cluster (SC)	4 cores, 8G memory	1 + 6
Tiny cluster 2 (TC2)	8 cores, 10G memory	1 + 3

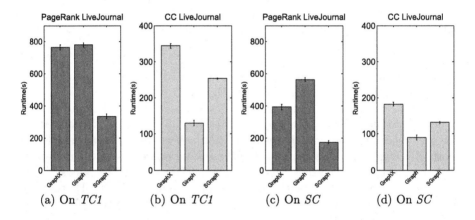

(a) On *TC1*   (b) On *TC1*   (c) On *SC*   (d) On *SC*

Fig. 9: Evaluation on different clusters

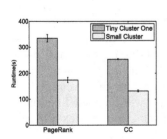

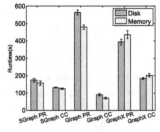

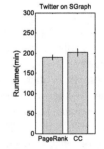

Fig. 10: Migrating from 3 workers to 6 workers

Fig. 11: Different storage media

Fig. 12: Performance of SGraph on Twitter

The datasets are shown in Table 1 and the *diameter* means *longest shortest path*. The experiment setup is as Table 2.

In the evaluation, SGraph and GraphX are specified the same partition strategy, and Giraph uses an edge-cut partition strategy. All the experiments are conducted on commodity PCs and all the clusters are running on 64-bit Linux. We use Hadoop-1.0.4 to store the datasets: all the 3 clusters use the same architecture as in Fig. 3. For cluster *TC1* and *SC*, we assign 4G memory to each Worker, and for cluster *TC2*, we assign 8G memory to each Worker. For Giraph, we run out-of-core graph. The rest memory of each node is for operating system and Hadoop cluster. While launching GraphX, we set *spark.storage.memoryFraction* to 0.6.

The performances of SGraph, GraphX and Giraph are evaluated on two simple and typical graph algorithms, PageRank and Connected Components. For each system, we run both the algorithms on *LiveJournal*, however, for our clusters, *Twitter* is too big to be processed in GraphX and Giraph. We run the PageRank algorithms 15 iterations and Connected Components until the convergence. Each experiment is plotted the mean and standard deviation for 10 times. The StorageLevel of RDDs in SGraph is configurable, however, if RDDs in GraphX are to be persisted on disk, we should modify the source code.

Figure 9 shows the performances of PageRank and Connected Components of LiveJournal on *TC1* and *SC*, both using *DISK_ONLY* StorageLevel. We can see that SGraph outperforms GraphX on the LiveJournal graph of both the two algorithms. The reason is that the combination of the computing model and streaming model works well and the compression of EdgeRDD reduces communication cost. However, Giraph outperforms SGraph while running Connected Components. We think this is on account of three aspects: the vertex-centric computing model of Giraph, the property of Connected Component algorithm and the size of LiveJournal work together and reduce the runtime.

Figure 10 presents a comparison of *TC1* and *SC* on SGraph with *DISK_ONLY* StorageLevel. It can be seen that SGraph scales out well for both the two algorithms when migrating from clusters of three Workers to clusters of six Workers. Figure 11 presents a comparison of both the two graph processing systems of Spark on *SC* with *DISK_ONLY* and *MEMORY_ONLY* StorageLevel, and Giraph with in-memory and out-of-core graph. There is only slight improvement of runtime on SGraph. However, runtime on GraphX increases when using *MEMORY_ONLY* instead of *DISK_ONLY* StorageLevel. In SGraph, the total size of data is less than the memory. As a result, the memory caches data when using the *DISK_ONLY* StorageLevel and its performance is slightly improved. In Giraph, the Hadoop MapReduce for resource scheduling benefits the runtime improvement. As for GraphX, there are other RDDs such as *Replicated-VertexView* except graph RDDs. These RDDs occupy a lot of memory spaces, leading to data size exceeding memory size according to our observation. We conjecture that a worse performance of GraphX with *MEMORY_ONLY* StorageLevel is due to trashing, which exchanges data in memory from data on disk.

Figure 12, shows the performance of *Twitter* on *TC2* with *DISK_ONLY* StorageLevel. Because of the other data structures and their in-memory storage,

GraphX is not able to process Twitter on our small clusters. The reason that SGraph is able to complete algorithms on such a big graph is the combination of streaming data model and edge-centric programming model of SGraph.

6   Conclusion and Future Work

SGraph provides a general purpose model that can express many graph algorithms. The experiment evaluation demonstrate that SGraph is capable to handle graph computation, both on disk and in memory. SGraph can also achieve a good performance on big clusters. In the future, we will tune the implementation details and apply our system to more practical problems.

Acknowledgement. We appreciate the reviewers's comments and the efforts of open-source contributors. This paper is supported by National Natural Science Foundation of China-Guangdong Government Joint Funding (2nd) for Super Computer Application Research and the Hong Kong GRF 2150851.

References

1. http://newsroom.fb.com/News/457/One-Billion-People-on-Facebook
2. http://snap.stanford.edu/data/soc-LiveJournal1.html
3. Avery, C.: Giraph: large-scale graph processing infrastructure on Hadoop. In: Proceedings of the Hadoop Summit, Santa Clara (2011)
4. Gonzalez, J.E., Low, Y., Gu, H., Bickson, D., Guestrin, C.: Powergraph: distributed graph-parallel computation on natural graphs. In: OSDI, vol. 12, p. 2 (2012)
5. Jain, N., Liao, G., Willke, T.L.: Graphbuilder: scalable graph ETL framework. In: First International Workshop on Graph Data Management Experiences and Systems, p. 4. ACM (2013)
6. Kwak, H., Lee, C., Park, H., Moon, S.: What is Twitter, a social network or a news media? In: Proceedings of the 19th International Conference on World Wide Web, pp. 591–600. ACM (2010)
7. Malewicz, G., Austern, M.H., Bik, A.J., Dehnert, J.C., Horn, I., Leiser, N., Czajkowski, G.: Pregel: a system for large-scale graph processing. In: Proceedings of the 2010 ACM SIGMOD International Conference on Management of Data, pp. 135–146. ACM (2010)
8. Page, L., Brin, S., Motwani, R., Winograd, T.: The Pagerank Citation Ranking: Bringing Order to the Web (1999)
9. Roy, A., Mihailovic, I., Zwaenepoel, W.: X-stream: edge-centric graph processing using streaming partitions. In: Proceedings of the Twenty-Fourth ACM Symposium on Operating Systems Principles, pp. 472–488. ACM (2013)
10. Xin, R.S., Crankshaw, D., Dave, A., Gonzalez, J.E., Franklin, M.J., Stoica, I.: GraphX: Unifying Data-Parallel and Graph-Parallel Analytics (2014). arXiv preprint arXiv:1402.2394
11. Zaharia, M., Chowdhury, M., Das, T., Dave, A., Ma, J., McCauley, M., Franklin, M.J., Shenker, S., Stoica, I.: Resilient distributed datasets: a fault-tolerant abstraction for in-memory cluster computing. In: Proceedings of the 9th USENIX Conference on Networked Systems Design and Implementation, p. 2. USENIX Association (2012)

Towards Semantic Web of Things: From Manual to Semi-automatic Semantic Annotation on Web of Things

Zhenyu Wu$^{(\boxtimes)}$, Yuan Xu, Chunhong Zhang, Yunong Yang, and Yang Ji

School of Information and Communication Engineering, Beijing University of Posts and Telecommunications (BUPT), Beijing, People's Republic of China
{shower0512, zhangch, yangyunong, jiyang}@bupt.edu.cn,
xyuanu2011@gmail.com

Abstract. Web of Things (WoT) unifies the syntactic representations of physical objects via web pattern, which facilitates the integrations and mashups of heterogeneous data and web services. However, the lack of unified representation markup tools and methods at semantic layer hinders the interoperability, integration and scalable search of things. This paper proposes a Semantic Web of Things Framework to improve the interoperability among domain-specific Web of Things applications by providing a unified WoT Knowledge Base construction framework. For this purpose, a Microdata vocabulary extended from Semantic Sensor Network ontology is proposed to facilitate manual annotation on HTML-based WoT representations. Moreover, to improve the scalability of extraction of semantics of structured Web of Things resources, a semi-automatic semantic annotation method based on entity linking model is also proposed. To testify the technical feasibility of the framework, a reference implementation and quantitative evaluation on annotation results are illustrated.

Keywords: Semantic annotation · Web-of-Things · Microdata · Lined open data · Semantic sensor network · Entity linking · Probabilistic graph model

1 Introduction

Web of Things [1] aims at reusing Web patterns and protocols to make networked physical objects first-class citizens of the World Wide Web. Typically, application developers and open platform vendors, such as Thingspeak, Yeelink and etc., could define their own data model and web APIs to mashup with other services. Obviously, the openness lowers the barriers of developing IoT application, however, it also results in heterogeneity and isolation of data from different domain-specific data sources. Accordingly, bridging semantic technology to the Web of Things facilitates the creation of a networked knowledge infrastructure [2] with more interoperable data from both physical and cyber world. Hence, the semantic WoT applications allow user to get the high-level details of the sensory observation and infer and query additional

© Springer International Publishing Switzerland 2016
Y. Wang et al. (Eds.): BigCom 2016, LNCS 9784, pp. 295–308, 2016.
DOI: 10.1007/978-3-319-42553-5_25

knowledge to gain more contextual and intuitive NL-based (Natural Language) inter-actions. According to the vision of the semantic Web of Things, annotation, processing and reasoning thing data on a large-scale will be a challenging task for applications that publish and utilize these data from various sources.

There are several efforts to integrate semantic web with web-based Internet of Things (IoT) platform including SENSEI, Semantic Sensor Web [3], SPITFIRE [4], as well as work by the Kno.e.sis Center, CSIRO, and the Spanish Meteorological Agency. By annotating sensor-related features such as the network, deployment, data formats, etc., with machine-understandable vocabulary, i.e., Semantic Sensor Network (SSN) ontology [5], it becomes possible to automate further tasks, e.g., deployment, maintenance, and integration. However, these efforts have limitations: things are modeled using domain-specific vocabularies without considering general approach compatible with growing body of semantic global knowledge base (KB)/Linked Open Data (LOD) such as DBpedia, Yago, GeoNames, FOAF and etc.; the frameworks do not support (semi-) automatically annotation on raw metadata of things, which is not scalable for large-scale deployment of WoT applications.

In this paper, our proposed Semantic Web of Things (SWoT) framework addresses these limitations by providing (1) a SWoT vocabularies to integrate descriptive meta-data of WoT resource with the external vocabularies and ontologies, as well as a Microdata markup template with this SWoT vocabularies; (2) an entity-linking (EL)-based methodology to annotate and extract semantics from domain-specific represen-tations of WoT resource to facilitate semi-automatic construction of WoT KB.

The remainder of this paper is structured as follows. In Sect. 2, we describe a typical use case to illustrate our goal and requirements of designing SWoT, as well as challenges. Section 3 mainly presents the architecture of the SWoT system, along with the manual and semi-automatic annotation models and methods respectively. In Sect. 4, we propose a reference implementation to testify the feasibility of the SWoT framework. The previous work related to semantic sensor web and KB construction are summed up in Sect. 5. Section 6 concludes the paper with summary and outline of the remaining steps as future work.

2   Motivating Scenario and Requirements

Current web-based IoT platforms, such as Thingspeak [6], Yeelink [7] and etc., provide open APIs for sensors and things to integrate to the Internet with global access. Each APIs of these platforms could be considered as WoT resources, and they could be integrated and mashuped across each other and other web services, as well as searched by search engines on the Web. The APIs in each of these platform both contains (1) resources with raw data stream or controller without descriptive metadata; (2) re-sources with data steam described by platform-specific metadata. To regulate the definition used in our framework, we firstly define the terminology as Table 1 shown.

In general, our goal could be summarized as constructing WoT KB by designing a semantic linked data model with manual and semi-automatic annotation framework:

- **Unified semantic representation model for WoT.** According to features of IoT applications, we formalize that typical semantic triples in IoT scenarios as: *Sensor-observes-Observation, Observation-generates-Event, Actuator-triggers-Action, Action-changes-Observation (State), Objectlocates-Location and Owner-owns-Object*.
- **Manual and (semi-) automatic KB Construction for WoT.** It is to annotate, extract semantics from the Plain/Domain-specific WoT resources and link them to the global background KB.

Table 1. Terminology of Plain WoT and Domain-specific WoT resources.

Plain WoT (P-WoT)	Following the basic designing principles of WoT (RESTified) without rich structured meta-data information (description and contextual information). It is a Web abstraction of plain data stream or controller inherently generated by devices. Plain WoT could be regarded as the most atomic resources which is able to be manually mashuped in WoT applications by Web developers
Domain-specific WoT (D-WoT)	Using domain-specific meta-data structure to markup and represent physical object. The meta-data structures are following domain-specific schemas, vocabularies or ontologies, which syntactically or semantically describe the contextual information of objects. It is also formatted as key-value structures, such as XML or JSON, in which schema represents the key and type of the value

According to the use cases and research goals, the requirements and technical challenges could be summarized from perspectives of P-WoT and D-WoT respectively:

P-WoT Manual Annotation: (1) how to annotate P-WoT in WoT mashup application with HTML5 representations (Microdata [8] is a candidate that is naturally compatible with HTML5) via reusable linked vocabularies and ontologies from schema.org, GeoNames and FOAF, as well as DBpedia and Yago; (2) a skeleton and markup template should be modeled or inherited from existing pattern, e.g., SSN, which could be linked to reusable LOD vocabularies and ontologies.; (3) extract semantics from the instance/facts of the annotated data by linking them to entities in the background KB to generate a linked open WoT data.

D-WoT Semi-automatic Annotation: (1) How to extract schema type from domain-specific D-WoT data according to given background KB; (2) how to generate and rank candidate entities for each value instance from given KB; (3) how to extract relation between schemas of a D-WoT (4) how to model the EL problem for D-WoT, and how to choose the inference algorithms.

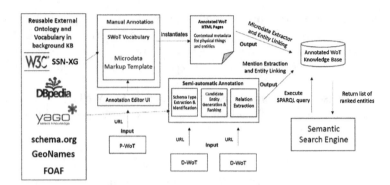

Fig. 1. Overall architecture of semantic WoT framework including manual annotator, semi-automatic annotator and semantic search engine

3   Semantic Web of Things Framework

3.1   System Architecture

An overview of the SWoT system architecture is depicted in Fig. 1. The whole system is composed of three main components: Manual Annotator, Semi-automatic Annotator and Semantic Search Engine.

- **Manual Annotator:** This building block is designed for annotating representations of P-WoT resources with SWoT vocabulary and Microdata markup template. The input of this module is the P-WoT and the output is an instance of annotated HTML-based WoT page with Microdata markups and semantic vocabularies. The instantiation process is edited by WoT application developers with Annotation Editor UI and the generated WoT application could be published to the Web. A Microdata extractor will extract the RDF triple tuples, e.g. *(ssn:temperature_sensor swot:hasLocation gn:BUPT),* and *(swot:hasLocation rdfs:subPropertyOf DUL:hasLocation)* from the annotated WoT HTML pages, and an EL process will be performed to link the instance value (e.g., *BUPT*) to the entity (e.g. *Beijing Youdian Daxue*) in the GeoNames KB.

- **Semi-automatic annotator:** This building block is designed for (semi-) automatically extracting semantics and annotating LOD from D-WoT according to background KB. The input of this module is the D-WoT with different schema format, and the output is the annotated and linked D-WoT data with semantics and relations mapped to given KBs. The subtasks of the extraction and annotation is Schema Type Extraction & Identification, Candidate Entity Generation & Ranking and Relation Extraction, which is based on EL [9] framework that is usually used in NLP system for information extraction on relational data.

- **Semantic Search Engine:** This building block is the typical application for SWoT which aims at providing a semantic search capability based on the constructed WoT KB. The query is based on a SPARQL language, and a list of ranked entities that matches the query are returned. The detail of the semantic search framework and related algorithms, e.g., ranking and reasoning, is not the main focus in this paper.

3.2   An Unified WoT Data Model and Upper Base Ontology for P-WoT

According to the requirements mentioned in Sect. 2, some key relational triples should be annotated to describe the meta-data of WoT resources. The SWoT base ontology skeleton (seen in Fig. 2) is referred to and extended from SSN structure.

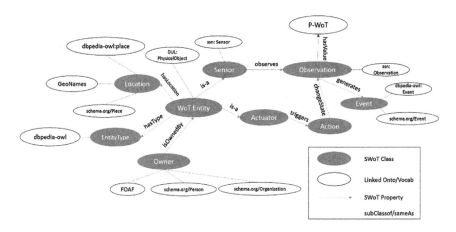

Fig. 2. WoT data model and SWoT base ontology by reusing external vocabularies

We should map the classes and properties that describe the meta-data of WoT resource to the existing common reusable linked vocabularies and ontologies. Location, Entity Type, Owner, as well as other thematic information (Type) are basic meta-data that should be specifically annotated. While Event, Observation and Action are senior contextual information that could be optionally annotated. To guarantee a better quality of KB construction for reasoning, searching and mashup, we still recommend to annotate these contextual data manually as complete as possible.

Location: Location-specific information for WoT Entity could include very specific geo-locations defined as altitude and latitude and/or high level information that describe the location in the high-level terms. Considering the location could refer to endless relative location data (e.g., *on* Table 1 *of Room 10 in Building 3*), while current vocabulary and instance could not totally cover, we limit the granularity or resolution to a high-level (a specific building, or a street) with GPS coordinates. Therefore, schema.org/Place, GeoNames and dbpedia-owl:place could be alternatives to map to the *Location* and its properties.

Entity Type: Type-specific information for WoT Entity describes the type of sensor, actuator or physical objects, e.g. temperature, occupation and etc. For this purpose, we use DBpedia for Sensor Types (general types). It also worth mentioning that in many applications relying on only general sensor type definitions by community-driven vocabularies such as DBpedia will not be sufficient; however, in this example we only demonstrate how linked-sensor-data can benefit from existing resources and at the same type contribute to the extension of linked-data.

Owner: Owner information of WoT Entity could include the ownership of deployed physical objects which could be personal or organizational, e.g., a wearable bracelet belongs to an individual and a parking occupation sensor belongs to a University. Thus, FOAF or shcema.org/Person vocabulary could be used for personal ownership, and schema.org/Organization or dbpedia-owl:organization could be used for organizational ownership.

Observation-Event-Action: The raw data of sensors are a set of data stream of sequential literal values which could not be directly represent the state changes or happening events. It is usually transformed to high-level state of observations by rule-based approaches [10], e.g., if the temperature of Room#1 is lower than 10°, the Room#1 is at a "Cold" state. Moreover, the action triggered by actuator could change the state of an observation by controlling physical object, e.g., the action of opening the HVAC in Room#1 will gradually change the state of it into "Warm" state. Thus, SWRL [11] could be used to markup the "*generates*" property for rule-based inference of an event, and schema.org/Event or dbpedia-owl:Event could be used for Event class.

To annotate the P-WoT in WoT mashup applications with this linked SWoT vocabulary, we leverage Microdata to embed into HTML5 representations. As an example, Fig. 3 presents parts of a markup representation of a temperature sensor embedded in a web page. This shows how the P-WoT could be annotated with unambiguous machine-understandable descriptions.

```
<!-- Name of WoT Sensor-->
<div itemscope itemtype="http://example.org/swot/sensor">
<a itemprop="url" href="http://exmaple.org/temperature_sensor/1/datastream">
<div>BUPTTempSensor</div>
<!-- EntityType: mapped to Concept in DBpedia-->
<div itemscope itemtype="http://example.org/swot/entity_type">
<div itemprop="hasType">Temperature Sensor</div>
</div>
<!--Location: owl:sameAs  http://www.geonames.org/ontology/ -->
<div itemscope itemtype="http://example.org/swot/location">
<meta itemprop="locates" value="http://www.geonames.org/ontology/">
<div itemprop="name">BUPT</div>
</div>
<!-- Owner: owl:sameAs http://xmlns.com/foaf/0.1/Person/-->
<div itemscope itemtype="http://example.org/swot/owner">
<meta itemprop="isOwnedBy" value="http://xmlns.com/foaf/0.1/Person /">
<div itemprop="name">Zhenyu Wu</div>
</div>
<!-- Observation by sensors with value link and rules for high-level state inference->
<div itemscope itemtype="http://example.org/swot/observation">
<div itemprop="observes">Comfort in Room 818 at BUPT</div>
<meta itemprop="hasValue" val-
ue="http://exmaple.org/temperature_sensor/1/datastream">
<meta itemprop="generates" val-
ue="http://exmaple.org/temperature_sensor/1/event_rule">
</div>
</div>
```

Fig. 3. Exemplary Microdata markup of a temperature sensor with SWoT vocabulary

3.3   Semi-automatic Annotation on D-WoT Resource via Entity Linking

3.3.1   Approach and Model

Some previous work have proposed methods to annotate entities, types and relations from web tables or relational data [14, 15]. Similar to these research, the D-WoT are structured hierarchical data which could also be modeled as web tables with headers and cell values (Fig. 4 shown).

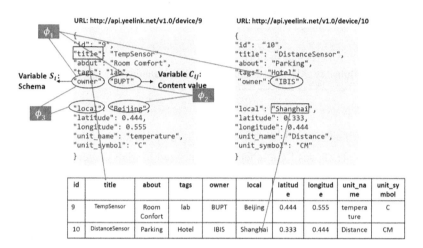

id	title	about	tags	owner	local	latitud e	longitud e	unit_na me	unit_sy mbol
9	TempSensor	Room Confort	lab	BUPT	Beijing	0.444	0.555	tempera ture	C
10	DistanceSensor	Parking	Hotel	IBIS	Shanghai	0.333	0.444	Distance	CM

Fig. 4. Modeling the annotating of D-WoT as EL task on relational data with key-value pairs. And using a probabilistic graphical model to jointly inference the linking and mapping.

The system queries the background KB sources to generate initial ranked lists of candidate assignments for schemas, content values and relations between schemas. Once candidate assignments are generated, the joint inference component uses a probabilistic graphical model to capture the correlation between schemas, content values and schema relations to make class, entity and relation assignments. After the mapping is complete, linked data triples are produced. DBpedia, Yago, GeoNames and FOAF are used as the referent KB that these knowledge sources provide good coverage for most of the D-WoT. Figure 4 presents an example of linking sensors of Yeelink platform to DBpedia.

- Candidate entity generation and ranking for content value

We generate an initial set of candidate entities for each content value using given KB. The content of schema and content values of other schemas are used as context when querying given KB. The query for temperature from DBpedia, for example, consists of the query string "humidity". The DBpedia returns the lists of candidate entities "Humidity", "Aboslute_Humidity", "Relative_Humidity" and etc. An entity ranker then re-ranks a content value's candidates entities using a supervised machine-learning approach adapted from [16] and features from [17] to return a measure of how likely the given entity is the correct assignment for the string mention.

```
Input: sparql statement
select DISTINCT ?s1
  ( sql:rnk_scale ( <LONG::IRI_RANK> ( ?s1 ) ) ) as ?rank
    where
    {
      ?s1 rdfs:label ?o1 .
      ?o1 bif:contains "( QueryString)" .( e.g.  Humidity )
        Filter regex (str(?s1),"resource").
    }
Output: All matching instance from KB
(e.g. Humidity ,Absolute_Humidity,Relative_Humidity...)
```

- Candidate type generation for schema type

Initial candidate classes for a schema are generated from its content values, each of which has a set of candidate entities, which in turn have sets of DBpedia classes (annotated by *rdf:type*). The schema's potential classes is just the union of the classes from its content values. If no candidate entities are generated for the reason that literal constant have no mapping entities in the given KBs, the candidate type for schema type will be generated according to the syntactic similarities of the words.

```
Input: sparql statement
PREFIX rdf:<http://www.w3.org/1999/02/22-rdf-syntax-ns#>
      SELECT DISTINCT ?type
      WHERE {
      <Current candidate> rdf:type ?type.
      }
Output: All matching types under rdf:type from KB
```

- Generating candidate relation between schemas

Identifying relations between schemas is an important part of structure data understanding and is modeled by finding appropriate predicates from the reference LOD's ontologies (e.g., DBpedia). We generate candidate relations for every pair of schemas in a structural file, based on the content value pairs in the same D-WoT files with different schemas. Each content value has a set of candidate entities, which in turn may be linked to other entities in the reference LOD resources. We use the links between pairs of entities to generate candidate relations. For a pair of content values in the same D-WoT file between the two schemas, the candidate entity sets for both content values are obtained. The candidate relation set for the schema pair is generated by taking a union of the set of candidate relations between individual pairs of content values. However, according to the domain-specific features of IoT, most common relations for IoT and sensor network data is difficult to be directly found in current given KB, e.g. DBpedia, hence, we could use the upper types' (or class's) relations of candidate entities as the candidate relations of schemas to extend the sets of possible candidate relations.

```
Input: sparql statement
SELECT DISTINCT ?relation
WHERE {
<Row1_Current candidate> ?relation <Row2_Current candidate>.
                    (or converse)
    }
Output: All matching relations between this entity pair from KB
```

3.3.2   Joint Inference Model

Once the initial sets of candidate assignments are generated, the joint inference module assigns values to schemas and content values and identifies relations between the schemas. The result is a representation of the meaning of the D-WoT as a whole. Probabilistic graphical models [18] provide a powerful and convenient framework for expressing a joint probability over a set of variables and performing inference or joint assignment of values to the variables. We represent a set of D-WoT data with the same domain-specific structures as an undirected Markov network graph in which the schemas and content values represent the variable nodes and the edges between them represent their interactions.

- Schema and content value

Figure 5 shows the interaction between schema and content values (represented by S_i, where $i = 1, 2, 3, \ldots, |S|$) and content values (represented by C_{ij}, where $i, j = 1, 2, 3, \ldots |C|$). The schema contains string data of a single syntactic type (e.g., *locatedArea*) that represent entities or content values of a common type (e.g., *place*), and the content value (e.g., *BUPT, Haidian, Beijing*) are instances of that type. Thus, knowing the type of the schemas, influences the decision of the assignment to the content value of that schema and vice-versa. To capture this interaction, we insert an edge between the schema variable and each of the content values of that column. And we define a factor node ϕ_1 (shown in Fig. 5) to compute the agreement between the class assigned to schema and entities linked to the content values in that schema;

- Content values across the schemas in a D-WoT file

Content values across a given D-WoT file are also related that the interpretation of each content value is influenced by the interpretation of the other one in the same D-WoT representation file. This co-relation when considered between pairs of content

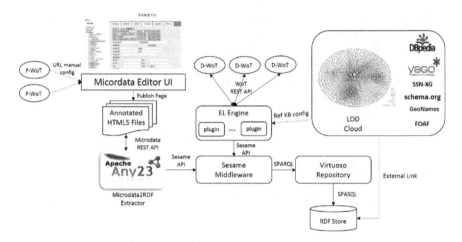

Fig. 5. A reference implementation of SWoT system based on Any23, Sesame and Virtuoso

values between two schemas can also be used to identify relations between schemas. To capture this context, we insert edges between all the content value variables in a given D-WoT file. And we define a factor node ϕ_2 (shown in Fig. 5) between content values for a given pair of schemas.

- Relation between pair schemas

Similar interactions exist between schemas. The schema *owner* suggests that content values might refer to organizational instances, e.g. *BUPT*. However, if the other schemas appear to refer to Location, Coordinates, we can infer that the owner schema refers to a deployed organization's location as well. This interaction is captured by inserting edges between schema variables. And we define a factor node ϕ_3 (shown in Fig. 5) between schemas.

After modeling the problem as a factor graph, the inference process will use a Iterative Messaging Passing (IMP) algorithm, referred to previous work on web table annotation [13], to iteratively update the entity and relation annotations until the graph converges. Due to the limitation of the paper, we only illustrate the inference model and framework, and the detail of the inference algorithm will be not presented here. Some quantitative evaluation on this framework will analyzed in Sect. 4.

4   Reference Implementation and Evaluation

Reference Implementation. To demonstrate the feasibility of the proposed architecture, we propose a reference implementation of the SWoT platform prototype based on open source projects (Fig. 5 shown). Any23 is used for the RDF Extractor from Microdata-annotated HTML5 files; Sesame and Virtuoso are used for RDF triple processing and storage via sesame API and SPARQL quires. A WoT open platform developed by us in previous work is also leveraged to explore and configure the WoT resources via Web UI, and it could be extended as the Microdata annotator for manual annotation task, as well as providing P-WoT and D-WoT original resources for EL tasks.

Evaluation on Entity Linking for D-WoT Resource. The D-WoT test dataset is based on randomly defined domain-specific metadata according to an upper-level data model for sensors and actuator. The device type, location, organization, measurement unit and observation are randomly composed as the property of a D-WoT resource. We generated 120 copies of D-WoT resource which contains the same schemas. Before the IMP process, the SVM re-rank model is trained based on fixedWebTable dataset from [15].

After convergence iterations, every element in D-WoT is assigned to an entity in knowledge base or to a string "no-annotation" which mean there is no appropriate entity to link. As our algorithm cannot annotate an inexistent entity to a text, we drop the entities that missing ground truth in DBpedia. Then we compare the entity links generated by our system to the ground truth we have manually labeled before. If the assignment generated from our joint inference model comply with the ground truth, we consider it as a correct prediction. Otherwise, it is wrong. We present the result about accuracy of our algorithm in entity annotations in Table 2, we also present accuracy without re-rank module in contrast to show how important re-rank is.

Table 2. The accuracy of entity annotations

	IMP only	IMP + Re-rank
User generated datasets	57.2 %	74.2 %

As our input table have several schema elements, we evaluate entity linking accuracy in each column and present the result in Table 3, in which we can obviously find the column of unit has an extraordinary low accuracy, far below the other columns.

Lower accuracy for entity linking is likely due to the lack of relevant data in DBpedia. Although our system might have discovered the correct assignments for column header and relation, if the entity does not have the same type and relation information in DBpedia, our system will miss this correct assignment.

For instance, the column of unit is annotated as DBpedia class "UnitOfMeasurement113583724". Some of our input text are "ms" which means millisecond, "kpH" which means kilometres per Hour. Both of them has ground truth in DBpedia, but none of them has "rdf:type" label. It means they lack type information so that the correct assignment is filtered by our column joint inference. Lower accuracy also stem from the size of the candidate entity set. We restricted the size of the candidate entities set to 10 in joint inference module.

Table 3. The entity annotation accuracy comparison between IMP & re-rank and IMP only in different column

	Schema DeviceType	Schema unit	Schema organization	Schema location	Schema observation
IMP + Re-rank	91.3 %	26.1 %	93.3 %	88 %	81.8 %
IMP only	60.8 %	21.7 %	66.7 %	76 %	66.7 %

5 Previous Work

In this section we provide an overview of related work on Semantic Sensor Web and Linked Sensor data. We also describe the KB construction methods and techniques, e.g. EL, for extracting linked semantics from (semi-) structured relational data.

A. Semantic Sensor Web and Linked Sensor data

There are some notable work that try to build semantic model and link semantic annotation for IoT. The Semantic Sensor Web (SSW) proposes annotating sensor data with spatial, temporal, and thematic semantic metadata [3]. This approach uses the current OGC and SWE specifications and attempts to extend them with semantic web technologies to provide enhanced descriptions to facilitate access to sensor data. W3C Semantic Sensor Networks Incubator Group (SSN-XG) [5] is also working on developing an ontology for describing sensors. Effective description of sensor, observation and measurement data and utilising semantic Web technologies for this purpose, are fundamental steps to construct semantic sensor network. However, associating this data to the existing concepts on the Web and reasoning the data is also an important task to make this information widely available for different application, front-end services and data consumers.

Linked Sensor Middleware (LSM) [19] provides many functionalities such as: (i) wrappers for real time data collection and publishing; (ii) a web interface for data annotation and visualization; and (iii) a SPARQL endpoint for querying unified Linked Stream Data and Linked Data. It facilitates the integration of sensed data with data from other sources, both sensor stream sources and data are being enriched with semantic descriptions, creating Linked Stream Data. SPRITE [4] is a Semantic Web of Things framework which provides abstractions for things, fundamental services for search and annotation, as well as by integrating sensors and things into the LOD cloud using Linked Data principles. Moreover, SPRITE also provides a semi-automatic creation of semantic sensor descriptions by calculating the similarities and correlations of the sensing patterns between sensors. Nevertheless, the linking and correlating the representations of things to the existing KBs automatically are seldomly researched.

B. KB Construction and EL on relational data

KB construction and Lined Data extraction usually are an EL tasks. Several EL research on web tables, web lists and other relational data are highly related to the automatic annotation task on WoT. Limaye et al. [14] proposed to simultaneously annotate table cells with entities, table columns with types and pairs of table columns with relations in a knowledge base. They modeled the table annotation problem using a number of interrelated random variables following a suitable joint distribution, and represented them using a probabilistic graphical model. The inference of this task is to search for an assignment of values to variables that maximizes the joint probability, which is NP-hard. They resorted to an approximate algorithm called message-passing [18] to solve this problem. Mulwad et al. [13] also jointly model entity linking, column type identification and relation extraction using a graphical model. And a semantic message passing algorithm is proposed. TabEL [15] uses a collective classification technique to collectively disambiguate all mentions in a given table. Instead of using a strict mapping of types and relations into a reference Knowledge Base, TabEL uses soft constraints in its graphical model to sidestep errors introduced by an incomplete or noisy KB. Xu et al. [20] propose an upper-ontology-based approach for automatically generate IoT ontology. The method propose an end-end framework for ontology construction based on calculating semantic similarity with input schemas with existing IoT ontologies, e.g. SSN.

6 Conclusion

In this paper we introduce a Semantic Web of Things framework which aims at creating linked data from WoT by providing a semantic descriptive vocabulary and associating their attributes to existing KB on the Web in both manual and (semi-) automatic method. The requirements and technical challenges are analyzed according to two typical WoT application use cases. Then, the Manual Annotator is proposed to provide a Microdata markup template with SWoT vocabulary for P-WoT when manually creating web mashup applications, along with a semantic extraction and linking process with given KB by collective disambiguation method. To facilitate the (semi-) automatic annotation on D-WoT resources, an EL framework for relational data is proposed based on a probabilistic graph model. The inference of the model is based on ML and message passing algorithm to calculate the joint probability of contexts inside the representation of D-WoT. To testify the feasibility, a practical reference implementation is proposed and a quantitative evaluation on semi-automatic annotation engine is analyzed.

Future steps of our framework will focus on implementation of the typical end-end use cases described in Sect. 2. Moreover, the validation and optimization of the algorithms of EL for D-WoT based on high-quality data sets are also important future work, as well as trying other algorithms, e.g. unsupervised ML method on structural data or stream data semantic mining methods.

Acknowledgements. This work was supported by the Chinese Megaproject under grant No. 2015ZX03003012.

References

1. Guinard, D., Trifa, V., Mattern, F., Wilde, E.: From the internet of things to the web of things: resource oriented architecture and best practices. In: Uckelmann, D., Harrison, M., Michahelles, F. (eds.) Architecting the Internet of Things, pp. 97–129. Springer, Germany (2011)
2. Hauswirth, M., Decker, S.: Semantic reality - connecting the real and the virtual world. In: Microsoft SemGrail Workshop, pp. 21–22, June 2007
3. Sheth, A., Henson, C., Sahoo, S.: Semantic sensor web. In: IEEE Internet Computing, July/August 2008, pp. 78–83 (2008)

4. Pfisterer, D., et al.: SPITFIRE: toward a semantic web of things. IEEE Commun. Mag. **49**(11), 40–48 (2011)
5. Lefort, L., Henson, C., Taylor, K., Barnaghi, P., Compton, M., Corcho, O., Castro, R., Graybeal, J., Herzog, A., Janowicz, K., Neuhaus, H., Nikolov, A., Page, K.: Semantic sensor network XG final report. In: W3C Incubator Group Report, 28 June 2011
6. Thingspeak. http://thingspeak.com
7. Yeelink. http://yeelink.net
8. Hickson, I.: HTML Microdata, 29 October 2013. W3C Note. http://www.w3.org/TR/microdata/
9. Shen, W., Wang, J., Han, J.: Entity linking with a knowledge base: issues, techniques, and solutions. IEEE Trans. Knowl. Data Eng. **27**(2), 443–460 (2015)
10. Ganz, F., Barnaghi, P., Carrez, F.: Automated semantic knowledge acquisition from sensor data. IEEE Syst. J. 1–12 (2014)
11. Horrocks, I., Patel-Schneider, P.F., Boley, H., Tabet, S., Grosof, B., Dean, M., et al.: SWRL: a semantic web rule language combining OWL and RuleML. W3C Member Submission, vol. 21, p. 79 (2004)
12. Kellogg, G., Hickson, I., Kellogg, G., Tenniso, J., Herman, I.: Microdata to RDF – Second Edition, 16 December 2014. W3C Interest Group Note. http://www.w3.org/TR/microdata-rdf/
13. Mulwad, V., Finin, T., Joshi, A.: Semantic message passing for generating linked data from tables. In: Alani, H., et al. (eds.) ISWC 2013, Part I. LNCS, vol. 8218, pp. 363–378. Springer, Heidelberg (2013)
14. Limaye, G., Sarawagi, S., Chakrabarti, S.: Annotating and searching web tables using entities, types and relationships. In: Proceedings of the VLDB, pp. 1338–1347 (2010)
15. Bhagavatula, C.S., Noraset, T., Downey, D.: TabEL: entity linking in web tables. In: Arenas, M., et al. (eds.) ISWC 2015, Part I. LNCS, vol. 9366, pp. 425–441. Springer, Heidelberg (2015)
16. Dredze, M., McNamee, P., Rao, D., Gerber, A., Finin, T.: Entity disambiguation for knowledge base population. In: COLING. pp. 277–285 (2010)
17. Mulwad, V., Finin, T., Syed, Z., Joshi, A.: Using linked data to interpret tables. In: Proceedings of the 1st International Workshop on Consuming Linked Data, Shanghai (2010)
18. Koller, D., Friedman, N.: Probabilistic Graphical Models: Principles and Techniques. MIT Press, Cambridge (2009)
19. Le-Phuoc, D., Quoc, H., Parreira, J., Hauswirth, M.: The linked sensor middleware–connecting the real world and the semantic web. Technical report, Semantic Web Challenge 2011 (2011)
20. Xu, Y., Zhang, C., Ji, Y.: An upper-ontology-based approach for automatic construction of IOT ontology. Int. J. Distrib. Sens. Netw. **2014**(5), 1–17 (2014)

Efficient Online Surveillance Video Processing Based on Spark Framework

Haitao Zhang, Jin Yan[(✉)], and Yue Kou

Beijing Key Lab of Intelligent Telecommunication Software and Multimedia, Beijing
University of Posts and Telecommunications, Beijing 100876, China
{zht,2011213221}@bupt.edu.cn, zivacore@gmail.com

Abstract. In the current surveillance video processing systems, the video processing algorithms and the physical resources are highly coupled, and a video stream is usually used as a basic task scheduling unit. With the expansion of the scale of the system, the traditional systems will cause the large resource fragments that cannot be utilized adequately. In this paper, we propose a novel online surveillance video processing system architecture that combines the distributed Kafka message queue and Spark computing framework. Our system decouples the video stream collection and the video stream processing, and further decouples the video processing tasks and the physical resources. This loosely coupled architecture can quickly recover the failed tasks without data loss for the large-scale video surveillance, and can provide the more scalable distributed computing ability. In addition, a fine-grained online video task management method, which uses the cached video data blocks as the scheduling units, is proposed to increase the resource utilization. Experimental results show that our system has the higher resource utilization and the higher task capacity compared with the traditional systems.

Keywords: Video surveillance · Distributed video processing · Spark · Message queue

1 Introduction

Nowadays, Video Surveillance Systems (VSSs) are ubiquitously deployed and continuously generate huge amount of video data. Though the widespread deployment of VSSs offers enormous opportunity in many useful applications, it is inefficient and unpractical to find the interesting objects or events from the huge supply of video streams in real time by human monitoring. Consequently, computer vision and pattern recognition techniques are increasingly used to provide intelligent video analysis and automatic event-based realtime alerts, such as intrusion detection, traffic flow analysis, traffic violation detection, and abandoned object detection, to enhance city management [1,2]. However, digging information from the large-scale video streams is a challenging task, and it can be further exacerbated by the existing predicaments of multiplatform, multi-format, multi-codec on video processing [3]. Therefore, designing

© Springer International Publishing Switzerland 2016
Y. Wang et al. (Eds.): BigCom 2016, LNCS 9784, pp. 309–318, 2016.
DOI: 10.1007/978-3-319-42553-5_26

and implementing an efficient, reliable and scalable video processing system is an important issue for the large-scale intelligent video surveillance applications.

There are many effective video processing technologies used for handling the surveillance video, such as multi-target tracking [4], and pedestrian detection [5], and these surveillance video processing methods are data-intensive and computing-intensive. Cloud computing can provide the low-cost and elastic computing resources with near-infinite amount of resource capacity. So some recent work focuses on using cloud computing technologies to alleviate the problems of the traditional surveillance video processing [2,3,6,7]. Generally, the current online surveillance video processing systems use a video stream as a basic scheduling unit, and the video processing ability and the physical resources are highly coupled [2]. Because each video stream processing task can cause the enormous resource consumption of one server, the traditional coarse-grained task scheduling scheme will lead to the large resource fragments that cannot be utilized adequately. Though some other fine-grained resource planning approaches are proposed for improving the cloud resource utilization [8,9], they usually do not consider the features of the continuous video stream processing tasks and cannot improve the video task processing efficiency.

Currently, some efficient distributed computing frameworks are widely used for processing video big data, such as MapReduce [10], Storm [11], and Spark [12]. Zhao et al. designed and implemented the video precessing interfaces based on Hadoop [7]. Ryu et al. proposed an extensible video processing framework in Hadoop [13]. Wang et al. used Spark framework to perform large-scale human action recognition [14]. However, all above work focuses on the efficient batch processing of large-scale video files, and cannot be integrated with video surveillance system directly.

In this paper, we propose a novel online surveillance video processing system architecture that combines the distributed Kafka message queue [15] and Spark computing framework. Our system decouples the video stream collection and the video stream processing, and further decouples the video processing tasks and the physical resources. Kafka distributed message queue is used for the reliable data aggregation of the large-scale video stream, and Spark distributed computing framework is then used for providing the efficient processing of video data. This loosely coupled architecture can quickly recover the failed tasks without data loss for the large-scale video surveillance, and can provide the more scalable distributed computing ability. In addition, a fine-grained online video stream task management method, which uses the cached video data block as a scheduling unit, is proposed to increase the resource utilization and the task capacity. We implement the proposed online video processing system, and conduct the extensive experiments. The experimental results show that our system outperforms the traditional online surveillance video processing schemes significantly.

The rest of this paper is organized as follows. Section 2 describes the system architecture. Section 3 explains the designing principles of data collection queue. Section 4 describes the designing principles of Spark Streaming based distributed video processing. We show the experimental results in Sect. 5. Section 6 concludes this paper.

2 System Architecture

In this section, we present the architecture of the distributed online surveillance video processing system. Our system can support the whole operating process of the online surveillance video analysis, including data collection, data processing, and data storage. As shown in Fig. 1, our system contains the following main components.

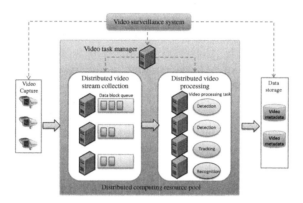

Fig. 1. System architecture.

(1) *Video capture* component consists of the IP cameras that capture the surveillance video data from the monitoring region and send the live video streams to other system components through broadband networks.
(2) *Distributed video stream collection* component aggregates the massive live video streams based on the Kafka message queue cluster. It works as a large-scale data buffer between the data capture component and the distributed data processing component. By using the distributed message queue, we can decouple the video stream collection and the video stream processing, and deal with the mismatch of the processing rates between the video stream producer and the video stream consumer.
(3) *Distributed video processing* component performs the distributed video stream processing functions based on Spark Streaming computing cluster. It firstly extracts the data blocks from the distributed video collection component, and then converts the data format from the video stream to the series of video frames. Finally, it implements the adaptive distributed image processing.
(4) *Video task manager* is responsible for managing the video stream processing tasks. Its main tasks include: Receive and analyze the task request from the video surveillance system. Schedule the video tasks in the distributed computing resource pool. Collect the video processing results and send the results back to the video surveillance system.

(5) *Data storage* component is used for persistent storage of the video metadata generated by the previous video processing component.

(6) *Video surveillance system* is a centralized video surveillance management unit, which is used to friendly interact with end user. Furthermore, it can send the video processing requests to the distributed computing resource pool.

In the traditional intelligent video surveillance system, one video analysis server collects and processes the video streams each of which is the basic task scheduling unit. If the server fails, the stream data will be lost. In addition, the coarse-grained task scheduling can produce the large resource fragmentation which cannot be used sufficiently. However, in our system, we decouple the video stream receiving function and the video analysis function in processing module by deploying an independent distributed data collection component before the video processing component. The distributed data collection component offers the buffer and backup mechanism for the massive continuous video streams. Consequently, the system can reschedule the video data from the collection component and recovers the video tasks efficiently once some video processing servers crash or cannot process the continuous data stream in real time. It will improve the reliability of the online system.

3   Data Collection Based on Distributed Message Queue

This section introduces the design principles of Kafka-based distributed video stream collection queue. Apache Kafka provides the high-throughput data processing capability, and can deal with the stateful data flow and low-latency distributed queries. However, Kafka message queue is mainly used to process the text data. Therefore, we firstly design a new unified message format for encapsulating the video data, and then present the message parsing process from the unified message format to the video frames.

The system is required to deal with kinds of video streams which may vary widely in data rate, data format and transmission protocol. In addition, a stateful video task should continuously process a specific video stream, and it requires the system can identify and distinguish the sources of the video messages. To solve these issues, we define a unified message data structure KVM for aggregating the different kinds of surveillance video streams through the Kafka customized message, where $KVM = [MagicByte(\text{int8}), Attributes(\text{int16}), Key(\text{int16}), Value(\text{bytes}), CRC(\text{int32})]$. In KVM message structure, $MagicByte$ field represents the version of the message format, $Attributes$ field represents the metadata of the message including the identification number, the encoding format, and the message length, Key field is a flag to represent the metadata of the message $Value$ block, $Value$ field storages the message content, and CRC field is used for the data verification. For identifying and distinguishing the video streams from different data sources, Key field is actually used for the unique camera ID storage.

Before the distributed processing component analyzes the video content, the Kafka messages need to be parsed and be converted to the image frames which are actually the input of the video processing algorithms. Algorithm 1 illustrates the Kafka message parsing process. Firstly, each receiver of the distributed processing component reads the Kafka video messages from the task-related message queue. The system uses the list structure $ListCam(cameraID, encoder)$ to map a specific encoder for the video messages from a given camera. Then, the system will check if the key of an obtained message exists in the set of the camera ID of the list $ListCam$ (line 3). If it exists, the system will connect to the corresponding decoder. The receiver applies Xuggler open source library [16] as the codec to parse the video messages (line 5). Or else, the system will analyze the encoding information of this video message, and creates a new codec and saves it in $ListCam$ (line 7). Finally, the decoded video frames will be kept in the current buffer of the distributed processing component through ($CameraID$-$Timestamp, videoFrame$) key-value pair mode (line 12), and form the Resilient Distributed Datasets (RDD) [17] in Spark framework.

Algorithm 1. Kafka message parsing

Input:

   Encapsulated Kafka message set M; $ListCam(cameraID, encoder)$;

Output:

   $ListFrame(cameraID$-$Timestamp, videoFrame)$;

 1: $Keys \leftarrow M.getKey()$;
 2: **for** Each $Key \in Keys$ **do**
 3:   **if** $Key \in ListCam.getCamID()$ **then**
 4:     $V \leftarrow M.getValue(Key)$;
 5:     $ListFrame(cameraID$-$Timestamp, videoFrame) \leftarrow Xuggle.parse(V)$;
 6:   **else**
 7:     Create a new element in $ListCam$;
 8:     $V \leftarrow M.getValue(Key)$;
 9:     $ListFrame(cameraID$-$Timestamp, videoFrame) \leftarrow Xuggle.parse(V)$;
10:   **end if**
11: **end for**
12: Save $ListFrame$ in the current buffer;
13: **return** $ListFrame$.

---

4 Distributed Video Processing Based on Spark Streaming

In this section, we present the distributed video processing method used in our system, which is based on Spark Streaming framework with a stateful data computing scheme. It works as a consumer of the previous Kafka message queue.

We propose a distributed video task management method to support the fine-grained online video stream task scheduling. Our objective is to appropriately schedule the computing resources in order to increase the resource utilization and the task capacity.

To model the process of the distributed video task scheduling in our system, we assume that there exist K different video streams captured from K network cameras, and each video stream is marked with a unique $cameraID \in \{1, 2, \ldots, K\}$. And there exist N partitions in the Kafka message queue cluster. So each video message of the video stream K will be encapsulated in the $(K \bmod N)$th partition with the key K. The distributed video task management method is given by Algorithm 2, and it describes the message scheduling process from the Kafka queue to the Spark framework.

Algorithm 2. Distributed video task management

Input:
    Encapsulated Kafka message queue;
Output:
    Results of video processing;
1: **for** Each $node \in Spark_{Receiver}$ **do**
2:   **if** $node$ doesn't overflow **then**
3:     $node_K \leftarrow nodesInKafka.getNode()$;
4:     $node.buildConnection(node_K)$;
5:     $M \leftarrow copyFrom(ZooKeeper.getLocation(node))$;
6:     $ListFrame(cameraID\text{-}Timestamp, videoFrame)$
       $\leftarrow KafkaMessageParsing(M, currentListCam)$;
7:   **end if**
8: **end for**
9: **for** Each $node \in Spark_{processing}$ **do**
10:   $elements \leftarrow node.get(ListFrame)$;
11:   $frames \leftarrow elements.getKey().sort()$;
12:   $results \leftarrow videoProcessing(frames)$;
13: **end for**
14: **return** results.

Our algorithm schedules and processes the video messages obtained from the distributed Kafka queue in the Spark computing framework, and then gives the results of the video processing. In detail, each receiver node of the Spark cluster builds the connection to the Kafka message queue, and pulls the video messages (line 1–4). We use the distributed system configuration maintaining service ZooKeeper [18] to manage the offset of the received video messages in the Kafka queue. Therefore, the receiver nodes of the Spark cluster can continuously copy the messages from the last task break point (line 5). Next, the algorithm calls the Kafka message parsing process (given in Algorithm 1) to convert the message format into the video frames which can be processed by the video processing algorithms (line 6). Consequently, the parsed video frames are stored in the value field of $ListFrame$. Meanwhile, the processing nodes in the Spark cluster get the elements from part of $ListFrame$ following the Spark scheduling strategy (line 10). Then, the video frames of the obtained list elements are sorted according to $cameraID$ and $Timestamp$, and the video frames from the same video stream are arranged orderly (line 11). Finally, the orderly video frames are processed continuously, and the obtained results are returned to the user (line 12–14).

5 System Implementation and Experimental Results

5.1 System Implementation Method

In this subsection, we introduce the implemented core classes and methods of Kafka queue and Spark Streaming framework in our system, including `KafkaVideoUtil` class, `VideoReceiver` class, and `ParallelParitioner` class.

`KafkaVideoUtil` tool class can implement the deserialization of the messages in Kafka message queue. It decodes the video data and encapsulates them into our defined message format that can be processed by Spark Streaming framework. `KafkaVideoUtil` class provides two main interfaces which are respectively `getPartition` and `creatStream`. The first interface `getPartition` plays a visitor role of the Kafka cluster and obtains the queued data partition information on a specific topic or key. The second interface `creatStream` is responsible for receiving the video messages from a certain partition of a given topic or key and then converting the messages into $ListFrame(cameraID\text{-}Timestamp, videoFrame)$.

Spark Streaming framework provides an abstract class `Receiver` for user to customize data receiving function. `VideoReceiver` class is inherited from `Receiver` class, and rewrites `onStart()` and `onStop()` methods. In our system, the message offset in each Kafka queue partition is managed by ZooKeeper [18]. When some video task crash, the corresponding Spark processing node is restarted but has missed the received video data permanently. To solve this problem, our system records and updates the message offset in each Kafka queue partition, and periodically reports it to ZooKeeper.

`ParallelParitioner` class is inherited from Spark `Partitioner` abstract class. It rewrites `numPartitions()` method that is used to set the number of the message queue partitions, and rewrites `getPartitions()` method that is used for getting the partition data received from `VideoReceiver` class.

5.2 Experimental Results

In this section, we compare our system with the traditional online surveillance video processing system in terms of the resource utilization and the task rejection rate.

Experiment Setup. Table 1 shows the hardware configuration in our experiment. Following the architecture of the traditional video surveillance system, the master node is used as the video task management unit, and 4 slave nodes are used as the video processing units. Specifically, node 1 and node 2 implement

Table 1. Experimental hardware environment

Server type	Hardware
Master node	Intel Xeon E5620 Dual-core, 12G DDR2
Slave nodes (Node1, Node2, Node3, Node4)	Intel Pentium E5800 Dual-core, 4G DDR2
Kafka nodes (Node5, Node6)	Intel Pentium E5800 Dual-core, 4G DDR2

the license plate extraction algorithm, and node 3 and node 4 implement the human density analysis algorithm. Based on the same hardware environment, we deploy a Spark computing cluster with 1 master node and 4 computing nodes using Spark 1.5.1, and the video task can be scheduled on any computing node. In addition, we deploy a 2-node Kafka distributed message system using Kafka 0.8.1.1r. For assessing the system performance, we conduct our experiments using the different types of the task configuration which is shown in Table 2. The input video streams are collected from a real video surveillance system online.

Table 2. Task configuration types

Task name	Algorithm type	Number of streams
Job1	License plate extraction	4
Job2	License plate extraction	6
Job3	License plate extraction	8
Job4	Human density analysis	20
Job5	Human density analysis	30
Job6	Human density analysis	40

Test Case 1. We run (job1 + job4), (job1 + job5), and (job3 + job4) in the two video processing systems respectively, and collect CPU utilization state of each of sever. Figure 2 shows the experimental results of the traditional system and our system. As shown in the figure, our system outperforms the traditional system in terms of the load balancing ability. Because our system can reduce the large resource fragments, it can utilize the cluster computing resources more adequately. Specifically, in Fig. 2(a), though the resource requirement of (job1 + job5) exceeds the processing ability of node3 and node4, the idle resources of node1 and node2 cannot be borrowed to process the overload tasks of node3 and node4. Similarly, the idle resources of node3 and node4 are wasted when the system runs (job3 + job4). However, as shown in Fig. 2(b), our system can balance the CPU utilization of every node, and make full use of the entire cluster computing resources.

Test Case 2. We run (job1 + job2), (job1 + job5), (job3 + job5), and (job3 + job6) in the two video processing systems respectively, and then collect and calculate the average task rejection rate of the two systems. As shown in Fig. 3, our system have the higher capacity of video tasks than the traditional system. Specifically, the traditional system generate the large resource fragments that cannot be utilized fully, and thus the average task rejection rate increases rapidly with the increase of task number. As for our system, because it can reassign the idle resource fragments, the average task rejection rate increases quit slowly compared with that of the traditional system.

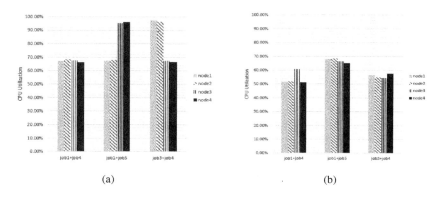

(a)   (b)

Fig. 2. CPU utilization of two systems. (a) Traditional system. (b) Our system

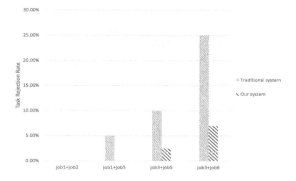

Fig. 3. Average task rejection rate of two systems

6 Conclusion

In this paper, we investigate the online distributed surveillance video processing solution based on Spark framework. Kafka message queue and Spark Streaming framework are integrated to eliminate the coupling between the video stream collection and the video stream processing, and further decouple the video processing tasks and the physical resources. Consequently, our solution can provide scalable, reliable and efficient surveillance video computing ability. Then, we present a fine-grained online video stream task management method that uses a cached video data block as a scheduling unit to improve the resource utilization. We implement the proposed system, and the experimental results show that our system outperforms the traditional online surveillance video processing systems significantly.

Acknowledgment. This work is supported by the National High Technology Research and Development Program of China (No. 2014AA015101); National Natural Science Foundation of China (No. 61300013); Doctoral Program Foundation of Institutions of Higher Education of China (No. 20130005120011); Asia Foresight Program under NSFC Grant No. 61411146001.

References

1. Zhao, X.M., Ma, H.D., Zhang, H.T., Tang, Y., Fu, G.P.: Metadata extraction and correction for large-scale traffic surveillance videos. In: Proceedings of IEEE Big Data 2014, pp. 412–420 (2014)
2. Yang, X., Zhang, H., Ma, H., Li, W., Fu, G., Tang, Y.: Multi-resource allocation for virtual machine placement in video surveillance cloud. In: Zu, Q., Hu, B. (eds.) HCC 2016. LNCS, vol. 9567, pp. 544–555. Springer, Heidelberg (2016). doi:10.1007/978-3-319-31854-7_49
3. Zhang, W., Xu, L., Duan, P., Gong, W., Liu, X., Lu, Q.: Towards a high speed video cloud based on batch processing integrated with fast processing. In: Proceedings of IIKI 2014, pp. 28–33 (2014)
4. Benfold, B., Reid, I.: Stable multi-target tracking in real-time surveillance video. In: Proceedings of CVPR 2011, pp. 3457–3464 (2011)
5. Chowdhury, A., Tripathy, S.: Detection of human presence in a surveillance video using fuzzy approach. In: Proceedings of SPIN 2014, pp. 216–219 (2014)
6. Hossain, M., Hassan, M., Qurishi, M., Alghamdi, A.: Resource allocation for service composition in cloud based video surveillance platform. In: Proceedings of IEEE ICME Workshops 2012, pp. 408–412 (2012)
7. Zhao, X.M., Ma, H.D., Zhang, H.T., Tang, Y., Kou, Y.: HVPI: extending Hadoop to support video analytic applications. In: Proceedings of IEEE Cloud 2015, pp. 789–796 (2015)
8. Hu, R., Jiang, J., Liu, G., Wang, L.: KSwSVR: a new load forecasting method for efficient resources provisioning in cloud. In: Proceedings of IEEE 10th SCC, pp. 120–127 (2013)
9. Zhao, H., Pan, M., Liu, X., Li, X., Fang, Y.: Exploring fine-grained resource rental planning in cloud computing. IEEE Trans. Cloud Comput. **3**(3), 304–317 (2015)
10. Dean, J., Ghemawat, S.: MapReduce: simplified data processing on large clusters. Commun. ACM **51**(1), 107–113 (2008)
11. Apache Storm. http://storm.apache.org/
12. Zaharia, M., Chowdhury, M., Franklin, M., Shenker, S., Stoica, I.: Spark: cluster computing with working sets. In: Proceedings of HotCloud 2010 (2010)
13. Ryu, C., Lee, D., Jang, M., Kim, C., Seo, E.: Extensible video processing framework in Apache Hadoop. In: Proceedings of IEEE 5th CloudCom 2013, vol. 2, pp. 305–310 (2013)
14. Wang, H., Zheng, X., Bo, X.: Large-scale human action recognition with Spark. In: Proceedings of MMSP 2015 (2015)
15. Apache Kafka: A high-throughput distributed messaging system. http://Kafka.apache.org/
16. Xuggler. http://www.xuggle.com/xuggler/
17. Zaharia, M., Chowdhury, M., Das, T., et al.: Resilient distributed datasets: a fault-tolerant abstraction for in-memory cluster computing. In: Proceedings of NSDI 2012 (2012)
18. ZooKeeper. http://zookeeper.apache.org/

Routing and Resource Management

Improved PC Based Resource Scheduling Algorithm for Virtual Machines in Cloud Computing

Baiyou Qiao[✉], Muchuan Shen, Junhai Zhu, Yujie Zheng,
Xiaolong Li, Bin Tong, Donghai Chen, and Guoren Wang

School of Computer Science and Engineering, Northeastern University,
Shenyang, China
{qiaobaiyou,wangguoren}@mail.neu.edu.cn,
{617107459,672168505,123724667,1006524725,1481038266,
1046102779}@qq.com

Abstract. The existing resource scheduling algorithms for virtual machines usually use serial job deployment ways which easily lead to the job completion time overlong and the system load unbalance. To solve the problems, an Improved Potential Capacity (IPC) based resource scheduling algorithm for virtual machines is proposed, which comprehensively considers the overall job completion time and system load balancing, and applies a new metric to dynamically estimate the resource remaining capacities of virtual machines, and thus reduce the inexact matching between jobs and virtual machines. A batch job deployment method is also proposed to execute the batch job deployment. Many simulation experimental results show that the proposed algorithm can effectively decrease the overall job completion time and improve the load balancing of a cloud system.

Keywords: Cloud computing · Virtual machine · Resource scheduling

1 Introduction

In modern data center, virtualization technology [1] has played an important role in simplifying resource management, integrating server capability and improving resource utilization. It has become the key supporting technology in cloud computing systems. Virtual machine resource scheduling [2] is one of the core techniques in this field, how to design the resource scheduling algorithms for virtual machines and thus ensure the load balancing of system and improve the user experience has been a hot research topic. Most resource scheduling algorithms for virtual machines apply serial ways to deploy user jobs, which can cause the higher resource updating frequency, the longer of the overall job completion time and the poor user experience. Furthermore, serial job deployment usually uses greedy strategy and cannot achieve the global optimum. This may lead to the serious load imbalance and affect the overall system performance. To solve these problems, researchers have proposed many resource scheduling algorithms for virtual machines.

© Springer International Publishing Switzerland 2016
Y. Wang et al. (Eds.): BigCom 2016, LNCS 9784, pp. 321–331, 2016.
DOI: 10.1007/978-3-319-42553-5_27

Liu et al. [3] presented two new metrics, Balance Capacity (BC) and Potential Capacity (PC) for virtual machines and used greedy strategy to deploy batch jobs serially, although it makes virtual machines have better scalability, it also can lead to the overall job completion time longer and load imbalance of a cloud system. Zhang [4] proposed a resource scheduling approach for virtual machines based on OpenStack, which can reduce the unbalance of resource and the consumption of power, but the algorithm don't consider the dependencies of the virtual machines. Minarolli and Freisleben [5] presented a resource management algorithm based on artificial neural network which reduced the number of active servers, but this method mainly focuses on energy consumption, and do not consider load balance and user experience. [6] proposed a random resource scheduling algorithm which has good load balancing. But the state of the virtual machine is unknown, which may lead to the heavy load imbalance of virtual machines and long waiting time of the tasks. Qu et al. [7] proposed a CPU resource scheduling method based on workload-Aware, this algorithm is a cyclical algorithm, and each cycle should adjusts the weights, and it lead to the computational cost very expensive. Dong et al. [8] proposed a two-stage virtual machine scheduling model achieving a tradeoff between energy efficiency and network performance, but the method cannot accurately estimate the cost of dynamic migrating virtual machines. Aiming at the problem of uncertainties in the resource allocation, Umamageswari and Babu [9] proposed a dynamic resource allocation optimization method for virtual machines, which improved the cloud system load balancing in some extent, and reduced the expense cost, but this method used the static allocation algorithm and cannot adapt to requirements of dynamic job resource scheduling. Carril et al. [10] presented a fault-tolerant virtual cluster architecture, which mainly focused on the fault-tolerant issues of the virtual machine clusters in a cloud environment.

In summary, the existing resource scheduling algorithms for virtual machines consider only one or two factors; the overall job completion time is too long, and it may lead to the system load imbalance. To solve the problems, an improved PC based resource scheduling algorithm for virtual machines is proposed, which comprehensively considers the overall job completion time and load balance of a cloud platform, use an improve potential capacity (IPC) to accurately calculate resource remaining capacities for virtual machines, which can avoid inexact match between jobs and servers, and a batch job deployment way is proposed to reduce the update time and the serial deployment time. The experimental results show that the proposed algorithm can effectively reduce the overall job completion time, improve the load balance of a cloud system and has better performance.

2   The Improved PC Based Resource Scheduling Algorithm for Virtual Machines

2.1   The Measures of Virtual Machine Capacity

In cloud computing systems, virtual machines are basic units of dynamic deploying, sharing server's calculation capacity and facilitating management. How to exactly and dynamically measure the capacity of virtual machines is a very important problem in jobs scheduling. In this paper we made the deep research on the elastic new metrics, Balance Capacity (BC) and Potential Capacity (PC) for virtual machines which are proposed by Liu et al. [3], and did the necessary amendments to the calculation method to make it more reasonable. On this basis, we designed a new batch job scheduling algorithm. Usually the resource sharing model apples Min, Max and Share three parameters to describe the server resources occupied by a virtual machine, where the parameter Min represents the amount of the server resources occupied by a virtual machine without any load; Max represents the amount of the server resources occupied by a virtual machine with full loads; Share represents the share ratio of a virtual machine be allocated the competition resource. Next we will give the definitions of BC and PC and the corresponding calculation formulas.

Definition 1. Balance Capacity (BC) is the guarantee capacity to assign each virtual machine in the worst case. Considering a virtual machine set of $VM = \{vm_1, \ldots, vm_n\}$, vm_i is the i-th $(1 \leq i \leq n)$ virtual machine, $Min(Min > 0)$ is re minimum load of the virtual machine, $Max \leq pCap$ is the maximum load of the virtual machine, $pCap$ represents the total resource number of the physic machine containing the virtual machine. The BC of virtual machine i can be calculated as the following.

$$pCap' = pCap - \sum_{k=1}^{m} Min_k \tag{1}$$

$$BC'_i = Min_i + share_i / \sum_{k=1}^{m} share_k * pCap' \tag{2}$$

$$BC_i = \begin{cases} BC'_i & BC'_j < Max_i \\ Max_i & BC'_i \geq Max_i \end{cases} \tag{3}$$

Obviously, the BC of a virtual machine is independent of the dynamic system parameters of cloud systems, when the number of virtual machines on a physic node is fixed; the BCs of the virtual machines on the physic node are fixed and become constant values, so it do not reflect the system dynamic characters.

Definition 2. Potential Capacity (PC) is the maximum available capacity of a virtual machine in some system state.

PC of a virtual machine relies on the current remaining resource of physic node in the cloud platform. The current resource utilization of vm_i is U_i. When there are N + 1 virtual machines running on a physic node, the computation of PC_B for a virtual machine B is as shown in formula (4).

$$PC_B = \begin{cases} min\{pCap - \sum_{i=1}^{N} U_i, Max_B\} & \sum_{i=1}^{N} U_i \leq \sum_{i=1}^{N} BC_i \\ pCap - \sum_{i=1}^{N} U_i & otherwise \end{cases} \tag{4}$$

Obviously, with the change of utilization of other virtual machines, and the value of PC is dynamic changes, it is possible to truly reflect the virtual machines available capacity. $PC - U_i$ (U_i is the resource utilization of i-th virtual machine) represents the current resource remaining capacity for every virtual machine in the cloud platform, when the current resource utilization ratio of a virtual machine increases, resource remaining capacity should decrease, which is reasonable. In summary, as the value of PC increase, the value of $PC - U_i$ increase, it indicates that the greater the ability of the remaining resource of the virtual machines, the more of available resource.

According to the formula (4), we can get the value of PC for various resource of virtual machines such as CPU, memory, network, I/O and etc. The current resource remaining capacity of the i-th virtual machine can be represented by a set $VM_i = \{vm_{i1}, vm_{i2}, \ldots, vm_{im}\}$, $vm_{ij} = pc_{ij} - u_{ij}$, vm_{ij} is the remaining amount of the j-th resource on the i-th virtual machine.

2.2   Measures of Job Resource Requirements

Jobs are divided into independent jobs and collaboration jobs in Cloud Computing systems [11], we only consider scheduling strategy and deployment strategy of independent jobs in this paper. It assumes that a set of batch jobs $Job = \{job_1, \ldots, job_n\}$, job_i ($0 \leq i \leq n$) represents the i-th jobs in job queue submitted by a user. In order to express various VM resource requirements of jobs, we use the job requirement vector to express various resources requirements. The job requirement vector of the i-th job is $Re_i = \{e_{i1}, e_{i2}, \ldots, e_{im}\}$, e_{ij} is the value of the j-th ($0 \leq j \leq m$) resource requirement of the i-th job.

In order to calculate and measure the various resources requirements of jobs conveniently, these resources value need to be normalized to between 0 and 1 ($0 \leq e_{ij} \leq 1$). It assumes that the maximum value of CPUs is Max_{cpu}, and the maximum value of memory is Max_{mem}, the maximum value of network is $Max_{network}$, the maximum value of I/O is $Max_{i/o}$ and the maximum value of other types of resources. The resource requirement value of the j-th resource on the i-th job can be normalized to $e_{ij} = e_{ij} / Max_{(cpu,mem,network,i/o)}$, and the resource requirements vector of job i can be expressed as $Re_i = \{e_{i1}, e_{i2}, \ldots, e_{im}\}, 0 \leq e_{ij} \leq 1$.

Job resource requirements cannot adequately reflect the importance of jobs requirement for various resource such as compute-intensive jobs [12], network-intensive jobs, I/O-intensive jobs and etc. So we need a vector $Weight_i$ to represents the weights of various resource in job i, which is called job resource weight vector, $Weight_i = \{w_{i1}, w_{i2}, \ldots, w_{im}\}$, w_{ij} is the weight value of the j-th resource for the i-th job, and $\sum_{k=1}^{m} w_{ik} = 1$.

2.3   Job Deployment Algorithm

A match matrix *value* is used to express the match degree between jobs requirement and resource remaining capacity of virtual machines, the matrix *value* can be computed by the formula (5).

$$Value = \begin{bmatrix} \sum_{i=1}^{m} \left(\frac{vm_{1i}}{e_{1i}} * w_{1i} \right) & \cdots & \sum_{i=1}^{m} \left(\frac{vm_{ni}}{e_{1i}} * w_{1i} \right) \\ \vdots & \ddots & \vdots \\ \sum_{i=1}^{m} \left(\frac{vm_{1i}}{e_{ni}} * w_{ni} \right) & \cdots & \sum_{i=1}^{m} \left(\frac{vm_{ni}}{e_{ni}} * w_{ni} \right) \end{bmatrix} \qquad (5)$$

The matrix *value* is consists of n rows and m columns, m is number of virtual machines (VMs) and n is the number of jobs, an element a_{ij} in the *value* represents the match degree between job i and VM j. if the value of a_{ij} is less than 1, it represents that the i-th job cannot deployed to the j-th VM; if the value of a_{ij} is greater than or equal to 1, it shows that the i-th job can be deployed to the j-th VM. Based on the above matrix, we proposed the cross elimination approach to deploy the jobs.

In the matrix *value*, if a_{ij} is the optimal match pair <job, VM> from a global perspective, then eliminates i-th row and j-th column, and the i-th job is deployed to the j-th virtual machine. Repeated do this process, we can realize the deployment of batch jobs in a short time. The proposed job deployment method selects match pairs <jobs, VMs> from a global perspective and deploys batch jobs as optimal as possible. Its basic idea is that trying to minimize the number of elements that their value are less than 1 in the matrix *value*, and makes the number of mismatch pairs <jobs, VMs> be minimum. There are two steps to choose a_{ij}, the first step is to select a_{ij} that is greater than or equal to 1 in the matrix; the second step is to count sum_i of the elements whose value are less than 1 in this row of the matrix, and sum_j which is the number of elements that its value are less than 1 in this column. If sum of sum_i and sum_j is greater than the sum of the number of row elements and the column elements which are less than 1, then the i-th job is dynamically deployed to the j-th virtual machine, and the row and column elements value in this element a_{ij} assigns to 0. This approach eliminates the elements of jobs and the virtual machine does not match elements from a global perspective. Repeated this process until there is no element can be eliminated.

Lastly the results have two cases. First, the matrix *value* is empty, it shows that all batch jobs which remove from the job queue have already been completed deployment; second, the matrix *value* is not empty, it shows that there are some jobs that cannot be completed deployment. In order to complete the jobs deployment of which cannot be successfully deployed as soon as possible, the jobs are inserted to the front of job queue to redeployment, so that they can be selected in next time. It may decrease the overall job completion time as soon as possible and reduce job QoS requirement impact for users, the deployment algorithm shown in Algorithm 1.

Algorithm 1. The resource scheduling algorithm based on improved PC for VMs

public void scheduling algorithm (List<Vm> vmsList, List<Cloudlet> CloudletList)

Input: utility[][],   pCap[][],   pCap[][],   bc[][],   pc[][],   job_resource_metrics[][],   value[][],
vmRes_remain[][];

    { Map<Host,List<Vm>>HostToVms_Map=HostToVms(vmsList);
    UpdateVmsPC(HostToVms_Map,vmsList);
    Double[][] vmRes_remain=new Double[vmsList.size()][4];
    vmRes_remain=GetVmRes_Remain(vmsList,4,vmRes_remain);
    Double[][] JR=new Double[CloudletList.size()][4];
    JR=GetJR_Remain(CloudletList,4,JR);
    Double[][] value=new Double[vmsList.size()][CloudletList.size()];
    value=GetValueMatrix(vmRes_remain,JR,value);
    for(int i=0;i<CloudletList.size();i++)
        value=CrossEliminationMethod(value,vmsList,CloudletList);}
    protected void submit Cloudlets() {
    int CloudletSum=getVmsCreatedList().size();//Get the amount of VMs
    List<Vm> vms=getVmsCreatedList();//Get the list of VMs
    List<Cloudlet> CloudletList=new ArrayList<Cloudlet>();
    int ctualCloudletListSum=CloudletSum>getCloudletList().size()?
        getCloudletList().size():CloudletSum;
    for(int i=0;i<actualCloudletListSum;i++)
        CloudletList.add(getCloudletList().get(i));
        if(CloudletList.size()>0)
        bindCloudletsToVmsTimeAwared_IPC(vms,CloudletList);
    for(Cloudlet cloudlet : getCloudletSubmittedList())
    getCloudletList().remove(cloudlet); //remove submitted cloudlets from waiting list
    }

3   Experimental Evaluation

To evaluate the performance of the improved algorithm, we setup the corresponding experiment environment and make a large number of experiments. The comparisons between the proposed algorithm and other algorithms are given in detail.

3.1   Experiment Environment

We designed and implemented the proposed algorithm based on the cloud simulation platform CloudSim3.0.1 [13], and then tested the performance of the proposed algorithm from the job completion time and load balancing capacity two aspects. Table 1 illustrates the experiment parameters including the experimental data size and its scope, where MIPS is the executing speed of VMs or jobs, and the job length represents the length of job executing time.

Table 1. Experimental parameters

Parameter	Number	MIPS	Memory	CPUs	Disk size	Bandwidth (BPS)	Job length (MIPS)
Servers	5	4200	4G	1	6T	1G	null
VMs	[20,35]	[500,700]	512 M	1	100G	1G	Null
jobs	[500,3500]	[50,150]	Null	null	null	null	[0,15000]

3.2   Minimum and Maximum Load of VMs and the Number of VMS

We tested the algorithm on our virtualization management cloud platform consists of five servers and created 20 to 35 VMs, each VM has and 1 CPU of 700 MIPS, 512 M RAM and 100G Disk. After launching the service of Xend and virtualization management, we use MPSTAT command to check the CPU loads. In Fig. 1, (a) is CPU loads of server before VM created; (b) is the CPU loads after create one virtual machine

```
Linux  3.1.2 (yum)      06/09/2015      _x86_64_      (2 CPU)

04:25:07 AM  CPU   %usr   %nice   %sys %iowait   %irq   %soft   %steal   %guest   %idle
04:25:07 AM  all   0.01    0.00   0.01    0.02   0.00    0.00     0.00     0.00   99.96
```
(a) CPU loads of server before VM created

```
09:11:00 PM  CPU   %usr   %nice   %sys %iowait   %irq   %soft   %steal   %guest   %idle
09:11:00 PM  all   0.02    0.00   0.01    0.08   0.00    0.00     0.00     0.00   99.88
```
(b) CPU loads of server when VM empty load

```
Linux  3.1.2 (yum)      06/09/2015      _x86_64_      (2 CPU)

06:16:42 AM  CPU   %usr   %nice   %sys %iowait   %irq   %soft   %steal   %guest   %idle
06:16:44 AM  all  33.33    0.00   0.00    0.00   0.00    0.00     0.00     0.00   66.67
```
(c) CPU loads of server when VM reaches full load

Fig. 1. The CPU load variation of a server with different VM loads

on the server; (c) is the CPU loads of the server when running CPU pressure test cases and VM reaches its full load state.

It can be concluded that the percentage of the minimum load of a VM on this server is $99.96-99.88 = 0.08$, while the maximum load is $99.96-66.67 = 33.29$. So the minimum CPU load of configuring virtual machine deployment on the server is 0.08 %, the maximum load is 33.29 %. So the number of VMs when all VMs running on a server node reached full load is 3 ($0.3329*3 = 0.9987$ is close to 1). On the other hand, when the VMs are running without any load, the number of VMs may be 12 ($0.08*12 = 0.96$ is close to 1). Therefore, the number of VMs on each server will be between 3 and 12. After reasonably calculation, the reasonable number of VMs on each server ranges from 4 to 7. Here the number of VMs on each server is set to 6.

3.3   Feasibility of Cross Elimination Method

For the *Value* matrix obtained, the cross elimination method is proposed to perform the batch job deployment, elements range from 0 to 2.5, and the scale is 100×100.

Experiments were repeated 100 times, 500 times and 1000 times respectively. The average success rate of the method is shown in Fig. 2.

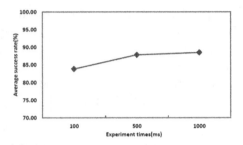

From the Fig. 2 we can see that when the experiments were repeated 100 times, 500 times and 1000 times, the average success rate of cross elimination method exceeds 0.84. We also analyzed the failure rate of the cross elimination method. When the matrix *value* is not

Fig. 2. The results of cross elimination

empty, the average remaining elements of the matrix is as shown in Table 2.

As the result shows that when the matrix *Value* is not empty, average remaining elements number of the matrix ranges from 1.80 to 2.54, indicating that only 1 to 2 job failed to complete the deployment, which only has a slight impact on the job completion time, job throughput and load balance of cloud system. Therefore, we can use cross elimination method for matching jobs resource requirements and VMs remaining resources and implementing the job deployment. So the cross elimination method is suitable for batch job deployment.

Table 2. Average remaining elements number after cross elimination

Repeated times	Round1	Round2	Round3	Round4	Round5	Round6
100	1.85	2.54	2	1.95	2.09	1.84
500	1.92	2.01	2.45	1.68	2.38	2.542
1000	2.01	2.189	1.725	2.16	2.43	1.960

3.4 Performance Analysis of the Algorithm

When calculating the IPCs of VMs, the share value of each VM should be known. Assuming that the share is average value, if there are 5 VMs on a server, and the share value of each VM is $1/5 = 0.2$. We compared the algorithms from two aspects.

(1) The comparison of the overall job completion time. In CloudSim, We set the task instruction length (MI) to 2000 and MIPS of each VM to 1000, we use three groups of data for experiment. The range of instruction length of first group is (0, 5000], the second group is [5000, 10000], and the third group is [10000, 15000], the results of three groups are shown in Figs. 3, 4 and 5 respectively.

We can see from the figures that when the number of jobs is 3500 and the range of instruction length is (0, 5000], the overall time of the improved potential capacity (IPC) algorithm is reduced by about 500 ms; when the range of job length is [5000, 15000], the overall time of IPC algorithm is reduced by about 200 ms.We can concluded that IPC algorithm performed better than the greedy algorithm and CloudSim polling strategy as for the overall job completion time, especially when the range of job

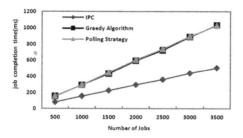

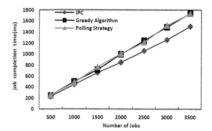

Fig. 3. Overall completion time of jobs (job length ∈ (0, 5000))

Fig. 4. Overall completion time of jobs (job length ∈ (5000, 10000))

length is (0, 5000]. That is because PC-U of VMs can dynamically represent the resource remaining capacity of the VMs, when the length of a job is shorter, PC-U can better meet the resource requirements of jobs.

(2) The comparison of the load balancing. To verify the load balance of computing system under different algorithms, the load balance degree is introduced to measure the load balance level of computing system, which is calculated by using the variance of each server at one time point, the calculation is as formula (6).

$$LoadDegree = \frac{1}{n}\sum\nolimits_{i=1}^{n} D_i \qquad (6)$$

Where D_i is the CPU load variance of all servers in computing system at the i-th time point, n is the times of collecting data for each server load on the cloud platform. The higher of LoadDegree means the worse of the load balancing, and the lower of LoadDegree means the better of load balancing. In the experiment, we set the number of time point is 10, the time points are uniformly distributed throughout the process of the experiments. When the total number of jobs submitted by user is 500 and job length is [5000, 10000], the results of three algorithms is shown as Fig. 6. When the total number of jobs is 1500 and job length is [5000, 10000] the results is show as Figs. 7 and 8 represents the results that the total number of jobs is 2500 and job length is [5000, 10000]. The results of Figs. 6, 7 and 8 show that the proposed algorithm IPC achieves better load balancing than any other algorithm.

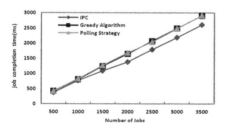

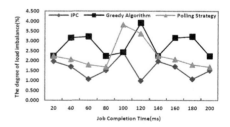

Fig. 5. Overall completion time of jobs (job length ∈ (10000, 15000))

Fig. 6. Load balance of cloud platform (the number of jobs = 500)

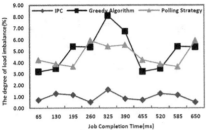
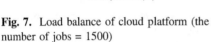
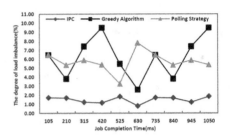

Fig. 7. Load balance of cloud platform (the number of jobs = 1500)

Fig. 8. Load balance of cloud platform (the number of jobs = 2500)

From the above two aspects, we can get a conclusion that the proposed resource scheduling algorithm IPC can decrease the overall job completion time and has better load balancing than the other algorithm.

4   Conclusions

In this paper, we deeply study the resource schedule algorithms for VMs, and propose an improved potential capacity (IPC) based resource schedule algorithm. The algorithm comprehensively considers the overall job completion time and system load balancing, and uses the IPC to dynamically compute the resource remaining capacities of VMs, so it can avoid the inexact matching between the jobs and the server resources, and greatly reduce the job deployment time and improve the load balancing of the system. The algorithm is compared with the greedy algorithm and the polling strategy based on CloudSim simulation software, the experimental results show that the proposed algorithm has a better performance in reducing overall job completion time and improving the load balance of cloud platform. Next we will further improve the performance of the proposed algorithm and apply it to real cloud systems for further test.

Acknowledgements. This research was supported by the National Natural Science Foundation of China (Nos. 61073063 and 61332006) and the Public Science and Technology Research Funds Projects of Ocean (No. 201105033).

References

1. Wang, Z.G., Wang, X.L., Jin, X.X., Wang, Z.L., Luo, Y.W.: MBalancer.: predictive dynamic memory balancing for virtual machines. J. Ruan Jian Xue Bao/J. Softw. **25**(10), 2206–2219 (2014). (in Chinese)
2. Qian, Q.F., Chun-Lin, L.I., Zhang, X.Q., et al.: Survey of virtual resource management in cloud data center. J. Appl. Res. Comput. **29**(7), 2411–2415 (2012)
3. Liu, Y., Bobroff, N., Fong, L., et al.: New metrics for scheduling jobs on cluster of virtual machines. In: IEEE International Symposium on Parallel and Distributed Processing Workshops and Ph.d. Forum (IPDPSW), pp. 1001–1008, Tokyo (2011)

4. Zhang, L.L.: The key technology research of virtual machine resource scheduling based on openstack. Beijing University of Posts and Telecommunication (2015). (in Chinese)
5. Minarolli, D., Freisleben, B.: Distributed resource allocation to virtual machines via artificial neural networks. In: 22nd Euromicro International Conference on Parallel, Distributed and Network-Based Processing (PDP), pp. 490–499, Torino (2014)
6. Atiewi, S., Yussof, S., Ezanee, M.: A comparative analysis of task scheduling algorithms of virtual machines in cloud environment. J. Comput. Sci. **11**(6), 804–812 (2015)
7. Qu, H.S., Liu, X.D., Xu, H.T.: A workload-aware resources scheduling method for virtual machine. Int. J. Grid Distrib. Comput. **8**(1), 247–258 (2015)
8. Dong, J., Wang, H., Cheng, S.: Energy-performance tradeoffs in IaaS cloud with virtual machine scheduling. J. Wirel. Commun. Over Zigbee Automot. Inclin. Meas. Chin. Commun. **12**(2), 155–166 (2015)
9. Umamageswari, S., Babu, M.C.: Cost optimization in dynamic resource allocation using virtual machines for cloud computing environment. J. Asia Pac. J. Res. **1**(11), 1–12 (2014)
10. Carril, L.M., Valin, R., Cotelo, C., et al.: Fault-tolerant virtual cluster experiments on federated sites using BonFIRE. J. Future Gener. Comput. Syst. **34**, 17–25 (2014)
11. Lu, G., Tan, W., Sun, Y., et al.: QoS constraint based workflow scheduling for cloud computing services. J. Softw. **9**(4), 926–930 (2014)
12. Negi, V., Kalra, M.: Optimizing battery utilization and reducing time consumption in smartphones exploiting the power of cloud computing. J. Adv. Intell. Syst. Comput. **236**, 865–872 (2014)
13. Calheiros, R.N., et al.: CloudSim: a novel framework for modeling and simulation of cloud computing infrastructures and services. Technical Report, arXiv preprint arXiv:0903.2525 (2009)

Resource Scheduling and Data Locality for Virtualized Hadoop on IaaS Cloud Platform

Dan Tao[1](✉), Bingxu Wang[1], Zhaowen Lin[2,3,4], and Tin-Yu Wu[5]

[1] School of Electronic and Information Engineering, Beijing Jiaotong University,
Beijing 100044, China
dtao@bjtu.edu.cn
[2] Network and Information Center, Institute of Network Technology,
Beijing University of Posts and Telecommunications, Beijing 100876, China
[3] Science and Technology on Information Transmission and Dissemination in
Communication Networks Laboratory, Beijing University of Posts and
Telecommunications, Beijing 100876, China
[4] National Engineering Laboratory for Mobile Network Security (No. [2013] 2685),
Beijing University of Posts and Telecommunications, Beijing 100876, China
[5] Department of Computer Science and Information Engineering,
National Ilan University, Yilan 26041, Taiwan

Abstract. With cloud computing technology becoming more mature, it is urgent to combine big data processing tool Hadoop with IaaS cloud platform. In this paper, we firstly propose a new Dynamic Hadoop Cluster on IaaS (DHCI) architecture, which includes four key modules: monitoring module, scheduling module, virtual machine management module and virtual machine migration module. The load of both physical hosts and virtual machines are collected by the monitoring module, and can be used for designing resource scheduling and data locality solutions. Secondly, we present a load feedback based resource scheduling scheme. The resource allocation can be avoided on overburdened physical hosts or the strong scalability of virtualized cluster can be achieved by fluctuating the amount of virtual machines (VMs). Thirdly, we reuse the method of VM migration and propose a dynamic migration based data locality scheme. We migrate computation nodes to different host(s) or rack(s) where the corresponding storage nodes are deployed to satisfy the requirement of data locality. We evaluate our solutions in a realistic scenario based on Openstack. Massive experimental results demonstrate the effectiveness of our solutions that contribute to balance workload and performance improvement, even under heavy-loaded cloud system conditions.

Keywords: Hadoop · Resource scheduling · Data locality · IaaS

1 Introduction

Cloud computing is one of the hottest areas of research at home and abroad, which integrates large-scale computing, storage and network resource via network and provides these resource for different users on demand [1]. As an open

© Springer International Publishing Switzerland 2016
Y. Wang et al. (Eds.): BigCom 2016, LNCS 9784, pp. 332–341, 2016.
DOI: 10.1007/978-3-319-42553-5_28

source framework for distributed system architecture, Hadoop can achieve large-scale data computation and storage, and is usually deployed on physical cluster. There are some drawbacks in traditional Hadoop clusters. Firstly, its deployment and configuration become tedious tasks. When Hadoop starts running, the real-time monitoring on Hadoop needs to spend plenty of manpower and financial resources. Secondly, the fluctuation of tasks will cause the imbalance of resource utilization. With the appearance of the peaks of task, resource bottlenecks may be encountered. In contrast, the valleys of task will bring idle resource. Hadoop cannot realize dynamic resource allocations. Thirdly, the utilization of high performance computers in physical clusters is insufficient, especially for computation and storage resource, which result in severe resource waste.

To solve the problems mentioned above, it is urgent to deploy Hadoop cluster on Openstack cloud as its service [2]. This paper adopts Openstack, which can provide Infrastructure as a Service (IaaS) solution in the form of VMs. Sahara, as an open source project, is developed to quickly deploy Hadoop cluster in Openstack cloud environment. Virtualized cluster which can simplify cluster management enables autonomic management of underlying hardware, facilitating cost-effective workload consolidation and dynamic resource allocations for better throughput and energy efficiency. However, virtualization in such cloud platform is known to cause performance overheads [3]. How to optimize the performance of Hadoop cluster increasingly attracts lots of attention. Researchers have accumulated a series of research achievements on resource scheduling and data locality in the related context.

Scheduling techniques for dynamic resource adjustment have been recently addressed. *Sharma et al.* [4] proposed MROrchestrator, a MapReduce resource Orchestrator framework, which dynamically identified resource bottlenecks, and resolved them through fine-grained, co-ordinated, and on-demand resource allocations. However, the studies mentioned above focused on resource scheduling based traditional Hadoop cluster. *Lama and Zhou* [5] studied automated resource allocation and configuration of MapReduce environment in the cloud without considering the load of physical hosts. *Corradi et al.* [6] investigated how to rebalance virtual resources. And they optimized load balancing by scheduling VMs but not Hadoop resource from stressed out physical hosts to less overtaxed ones.

For data locality, to address the conflict between locality and fairness, *Zaharia et al.* [7] proposed a simple delay scheduling algorithm, in which a job waited for a limited amount of time for a scheduling opportunity on a node that has data for it. Experimental results showed that waiting can achieve both high fairness and high data locality. *Jin et al.* [8] proposed an Availability-aware DAta PlacemenT strategy, and its basic idea was to dispatch data based on the availability of each node for reducing network traffic and improve data locality. Both of works were studied on traditional Hadoop cluster. *Thaha et al.* [9] presented a data-location aware virtual cluster provisioning strategy to identify the data location and provision the cluster near to the storage. However, multiple tasks might be executed on a same physical host, which negatively impacted system performance.

Motivated by this, we propose load feedback based resource scheduling and dynamic migration based data locality solutions based on a novel dynamic Hadoop cluster on IaaS (DHCI) architecture. The resource utilization can be improved by the load balance of physical hosts and the flexible scalability of virtual machines. Moreover, based on the separated deployment of computation VMs and storage VMs, computation VMs can be quickly migrated to match their corresponding storage VMs to guarantee the data locality effectively.

The rest of this paper is organized as follows In Sect. 2, we introduce a Dynamic Hadoop Cluster on IaaS architecture. Based on this architecture, load feedback based resource scheduling and dynamic migration based data locality solutions are explored in Sects. 3 and 4, respectively. In Sect. 5, we perform a comprehensive evaluation to validate our solutions. Finally, we conclude this paper in Sect. 6.

2   DHCI Architecture

There exists a big difference on Hadoop's running environment between physical cluster and IaaS cloud platform. In IaaS cloud environment, Hadoop is deployed on virtual machines provided by cloud platform. In this case, Hadoop cluster cannot know well about the resource usage of the underlying physical hosts, which will result in load imbalance and performance degradation. In addition, the scalability of Hadoop cluster is not good, by contrast, the virtualized Hadoop cluster on cloud platform is more convenient for the flexible adjustment of cluster scale.

Motivated by this, we integrate Hadoop onto IaaS cloud platform and propose a new Dynamic Hadoop Cluster on IaaS (DHCI) architecture. In DHCI architecture which is illustrated in Fig. 1, we introduce four kernel modules besides the original packages of private cloud and Hadoop.

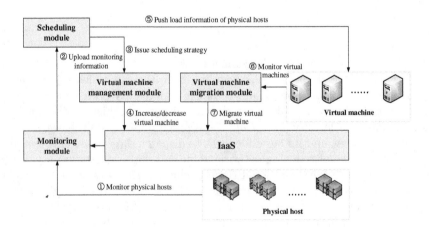

Fig. 1. DHCI architecture.

- *Monitoring Module:* Considering that different clusters in a virtualized environment are isolated, Hadoop cannot get the load of physical hosts at all. Monitoring module is introduced to periodically monitor the load on physical hosts as well as VMs. The load information collected can be used to provide the basis for resource scheduling.
- *Scheduling Module:* It is charge of two aspects: (i) periodically pushing the load information of physical hosts to scheduling node (*e.g.* ResourceManager) in Hadoop; (ii) issuing the corresponding scalability strategy to the VM management module according to the load of VM clusters.
- *Virtual Machine Management Module:* It achieves dynamic scale of VMs by adding or deleting operations. This is an execution module which takes order from the scheduling module and interacts with VMs on IaaS platform.
- *Virtual Machine Migration Module:* It is used to detect a task's data locality and execution process. Once this module finds (i) the execution progress of a task is slower than a given threshold; and (ii) its CN and SN doesn't meet data locality, it will migrate this task to the right physical host by the storage of data duplication.

In summary, DHCI architecture has two core features: (1) joint load monitoring, and (2) flexible resource scheduling. The monitoring module monitors physical and virtual resources with full awareness of current system load conditions. These necessary data can be utilized to optimize subsequent resource scheduling. By the scheduling module and the VM management module, the resource utilization can be optimized according to the load balance of physical hosts and the flexible scalability of VMs. Based on the idea of "mobile computing", the reuse of VMs migration achieved by the VM migration module in DHCI architecture can also reduce bandwidth consumption and improve system performance.

3   Load Feedback Based Resource Scheduling

The basic idea of our resource scheduling solution is to consider the load of physical hosts and VMs, and thus optimize resource scheduling. In our solution, the load of physical hosts can be described from two aspects: CPU utility rate and load average. Load average denotes the average utilization rate of run-queues. The more the values of CPU utility rate and load average are, the heavier the workload of a physical host will be. Here, their values can be collected using *top* command in Linux OS by every minute.

In DHCI architecture, for a physical host, its load information will be uploaded and fed back to the scheduling module periodically via the monitoring module. We adopt a single-level threshold method to compare the load information. Once the value of load is greater than a preset threshold, the physical host is considered as a stressed out one, and the resource application from it will be cancelled; otherwise, the resource application from it will be supported.

One of the most significant advantages of integrating Hadoop onto IaaS cloud platform is flexibility. That is, the scale of virtual cluster can dynamically adjust by their real-time workloads. Similarly, for virtualized Hadoop cluster made up of multiple VMs, the monitoring module in DHCI architecture collects its load information and feedbacks to the scheduling module. A double-level threshold method is used to distinguish between the lowest-load VM and highest-load one. If the value of load is greater than a ceiling, then the VM adding operation will be issued and a new VM will be created on the lowest-load physical host. Otherwise, if it is less than a floor, then the VM deleting operation will be issued and excessive VM(s) will be deleted on the highest-load one.

4   Dynamic Migration Based Data Locality

Data locality is a critical factor impacting on performance of a virtualized Hadoop system. In traditional Hadoop cluster made up of physical hosts, computation VMs (used for task computation, denoted by CNs) and storage VMs (used for data storage, denoted by SNs) are combined in a single VM. The advantage is CNs can directly acquire data from SNs while avoiding data transmission across a network. However, this deployment is no longer an effective method for a virtualized Hadoop system. The scalability of a virtualized Hadoop cluster can be achieved by dynamically adding or deleting VMs. The combination of CNs and SNs results in poor scalability. Therefore, in DHCI architecture, the separation of CNs and SNs is adopted to improve flexibility. Specifically, they are deployed as respective VMs. In this way, CNs can be migrated to "suitable" place based on the idea of "mobile computing".

Compared to that of in traditional Hadoop cluster, data locality in DHCI architecture can be classified into three categories [10]: host data locality (CNs and SNs are deployed on a same host), rack data locality (CNs and SNs are deployed on a same rack but different hosts) and across-Rack data locality (CNs and SNs are deployed on different racks). Experimental results have shown that the speeds of task execution for meeting different types of data locality are significantly different under the same conditions. In particular, the task completion time for meeting "Rack data locality" and "Across-Rack data locality" approaches three and four times as long as that for meeting "Host data locality", respectively [11]. Data transmission between co-located VMs is often as efficient as local data access mainly because inter-VM communication within a single host is optimized by hypervisor [12]. Hence, we consider to improve "Host data locality" in order to optimize the performance of DHCI architecture. Considering that the separation of CNs and SNs brings certain effect on data locality, we dynamically migrate CNs to any host(s) or rack(s) where the corresponding SNs stored data replication are deployed to guarantee data locality. During the migration process, a VM keeps on and the program executed in this VM keeps running state. Even if this VM is connected to a network, the network connection won't be affected. In fact, the cost of migrating VM is much less than that of reading/writing operations among different VMs [10].

Firstly, the initial resource allocation should be kept data locality. In Hadoop YARN adopted, ContainerAllocator is responsible for communicating with the ResourceManager and applying resource for tasks. Usually, there exist three backups for each task in HDFS. Considering the level difference of data locality, there will be multiple resource requests. VMs can be allocated resource, prioritized by "Host data locality", "Rack data locality", and "Across-Rack data locality". A resource request of task can be described as a tuple <Priority, Hostname, Capability, Containers>, where "Hostname" can represent the ID of host or rack.

Secondly, data locality should be optimized in the process of task execution. Hadoop monitors task execution and judges whether data locality is satisfied or not. If not, Hadoop continues to search whether there exist one or more hosts which can meet the requirement of data locality, and then CN will migrate to the right one.

To achieve a completed CN migration, three major issues ("2W1H") should be solved:

- *Which a CN needs to be migrated?* A CN needs to be migrated must satisfy two conditions: (i) the progress implemented on CN is slow; (ii) CN and its corresponding SN are on separated host or rack. In a virtualized Hadoop system, a metric named progress score which values between 0 and 1 is used to monitor the progress of each task and identify the stragglers. Here, we adopt a simple heuristic proposed in Ref. [13] to predict task remaining finish time, and thus find out the slowest task.
- *Where a CN should be migrated?* The destination host to which a CN is migrated, should include its corresponding SNs store data replication. In a virtualized Hadoop cluster, each task can is partitioned into a number of Map and Reduce tasks. Each Map task runs map functions processing one data block (128 MB by default in YARN). The data replication of each data block is three by default, and can be stored in different hosts even racks. Here, we choose the least-loaded host which satisfies the requirement of data locality as the destination one with the lowest cost.
- *How to migrate a CN?* OpenStack cloud platform selected can support VM migration very quickly. The whole migration process involves three kinds of physical hosts, and they are source host, destination host and control host. We mainly utilize python interface function in Libvirt tool to migrate VM, and data transmission can be realized by a tunneled way.

5   Simulation and Analysis

In this simulation, we choose Openstack as cloud platform and Hibench as Hadoop performance testing tool. Here, three benchmark test cases: WordCount, TeraSort and Sort are adopted to evaluate the performance of the DHCI architecture proposed. The hardware configuration for testing environment can be listed in Table 1.

5.1   Comparison on Running Time Under Same Load

Firstly, we make a comparison on the running times using three classic schedulers (FIFO Scheduler, Fair Scheduler and Capacity Scheduler) under traditional Hadoop cluster and DHCI architecture, respectively. The simulation results in

Table 1. The hardware configuration for testing environment.

Parameter	Configuration
CPU type	4-core 2.4 GHz Intel(R) Xeon (R)
Memory	32 GB
Network card	Three 2 Gbps LANs
OS	Linux 14.04

Fig. 2 show that the running time in DHCI architecture is less than that of in traditional Hadoop cluster with the same workload (data volume is 2 GB). Take fair scheduler as an example, for WordCount, TeraSort and Sort cases, the running time in DHCI architecture are respectively decreased by 14 %, 9 % and 8 %.

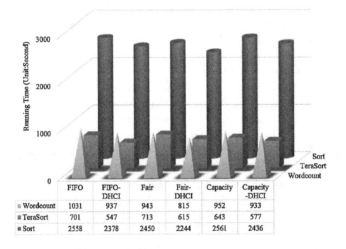

	FIFO	FIFO-DHCI	Fair	Fair-DHCI	Capacity	Capacity-DHCI
Wordcount	1031	937	943	815	952	933
TeraSort	701	547	713	615	643	577
Sort	2558	2378	2450	2244	2561	2436

Fig. 2. Comparison on running time for three schedulers under two architectures. (Color figure online)

5.2 Comparison on Running Time Under Load Pressure

To test the operation condition of Hadoop cluster under certain load pressure in a private cloud environment, new virtual cluster(s) will be added into the original virtual cluster(s). For example, only virtual cluster 1 runs on IaaS cloud platform originally, virtual cluster 2 is added later.

The workload of task (Sort) run on the new added virtual cluster 2 is 2 GB. And the original task (WordCount, TeraSort and Sort) is run on virtual cluster 1 at the same time. Through increasing the number of new virtual cluster(s) with certain computation resource of cloud platform, the effect on the operation efficiency of task under two architectures before and after load pressure can be illustrated in Fig. 3. There is no doubt that the new added task will

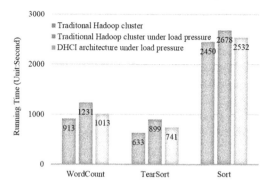

Fig. 3. Comparison on running time under two architectures before and after load pressure. (Color figure online)

result in more running time. The workload of the new added task is as relative as that of the original one. However, compared to the running time for traditional Hadoop cluster, that for traditional Hadoop cluster under load pressure respectively increases by 35 %, 40 % and 9 % for WordCount, TeraSort and Sort. This depicts that multiple tasks can be simultaneously operated on virtualized Hadoop cluster with relatively low cost.

5.3   Comparison on CPU Utility Rate and Load Average Between Two Architectures

In this section, we evaluate the performance parameters of each physical host when WordCount task is executed in DHCI architecture.

We take their averages for each physical host respectively, as are illustrated in Fig. 4. And then we calculate their variances to reflect the fluctuations in workload of multiple physical hosts. The variance of CPU utility rate in traditional Hadoop cluster and DHCI architecture are 0.196 and 0.1 respectively. The efficiency of cluster load balance in DHCI architecture is superior to that in traditional Hadoop cluster. From the perspective of load average, the similar conclusion can be drawn.

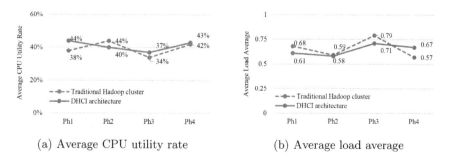

(a) Average CPU utility rate   (b) Average load average

Fig. 4. Performance parameters of each physical host in two architectures

5.4   Test on Data Locality Optimization

To verify the effectiveness of data locality optimization strategy, we also use benchmark test cases WordCount, TeraSort and Sort with 2 GB data volume. The data in Fig. 5 shows the difference of testing data from DHCI architecture without and with data locality optimization, respectively. We can draw a conclusion that the time it takes to execute these tasks with data locality optimization is less than that of without data locality optimization while under the same data volume condition.

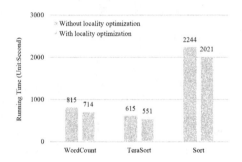

Fig. 5. Comparison on running time in DHCI architecture without and with data locality optimization. (Color figure online)

6   Conclusion

In this paper, we design a novel dynamic Hadoop cluster IaaS architecture by introducing four kernel modules. In particular, we propose resource scheduling and data locality solutions. We assess the efficiency of our solutions on the aforementioned virtualized Hadoop cluster. Massive experimental results show that our solutions can effectively balance load and improve system performance.

Acknowledgement. This work was supported by the National High Technology Research and Development Program of China (863 Program) No. 2013AA014702, Fundamental Research Funds for the Central Universities (2014PTB-00-04, 2014ZD03-03), the Fundamental Research Funds for the Central Universities under Grant No. 2016JBM011.

References

1. Wang, L., Tao, J., Ranjan, R., et al.: G-Hadoop: MapReduce across distributed data centers for data-intensive computing. Future Gener. Comput. Syst. **29**(3), 739–750 (2013)
2. Armbrust, M., Fox, A., Griffith, R., et al.: A view of cloud computing. Commun. ACM **53**(4), 50–58 (2010)

3. Kang, H., Chen, Y., Wong, J.L., Sion, R., Wu, J.: Enhancement of Xens scheduler for MapReduce workloads. In: ACM International Conference on High Performance Distributed Computing (HPDC), pp. 251–262 (2011)
4. Sharma, B., Prabhakar, R., Lim, S.H., et al.: MROrchestrator: a fine-grained resource orchestration framework for MapReduce clusters. In: IEEE 5th International Conference on Cloud Computing (CLOUD), pp. 1–8 (2012)
5. Lama, P., Zhou, X.: AROMA: automated resource allocation and configuration of MapReduce environment in the cloud. In: Proceedings of the 9th International Conference on Autonomic Computing (2012)
6. Corradi, A., Foschini, L., Pipolo, V., et al.: Elastic provisioning of virtual Hadoop clusters in OpenStack-based clouds. In: IEEE International Conference on Communication Workshop (ICCW), pp. 1914–1920 (2015)
7. Zaharia, M., Borthakur, D., Sen Sarma, J., et al.: Delay scheduling: a simple technique for achieving locality and fairness in cluster scheduling. In: ACM Proceedings of the 5th European Conference on Computer Systems, pp. 265–278 (2010)
8. Jin, H., Yang, X., Sun, X.H., et al.: ADAPT: availability-aware MapReduce data placement for non-dedicated distributed computing. In: IEEE International Conference on Distributed Computing Systems, pp. 516–525 (2012)
9. Thaha, A.F., Singh, M., Amin, A.H.M., et al.: Hadoop in OpenStack: data-location-aware cluster provisioning. In: 2014 IEEE the 4th World Congress on Information and Communication Technologies (WICT), pp. 296–301 (2014)
10. Sun, R., Yang, J., Gao, Z., He, Z.: A resource scheduling approach to improving data locality for virtualized Hadoop cluster. J. Comput. Res. Dev. 51(Suppl.), 189–198 (2014)
11. Bu, X., Rao, J., Xu, C.: Interference and locality-aware task scheduling for MapReduce applications in virtual clusters. In: ACM Proceedings of the 22nd International Symposium on High-Performance Parallel and Distributed Computing, pp. 227–238 (2013)
12. Zhang, Q., Liu, L., Ren, Y., et al.: Residency aware inter-VM communication in virtualized cloud performance measurement and analysis. In: Proceedings of the 6th IEEE International Conference on Cloud Computing, pp. 204–211 (2013)
13. Zaharia, M., Konwinski, A., Joseph, A., Katz, R., Stoica, I.: Improving MapReduce performance in heterogeneous environments. In: Proceedings of the 8th USENIX Symposium on Operating Systems Design and Implementation (OSDI), pp. 29–42 (2008)

An Asynchronous 2D-Torus Network-on-Chip Using Adaptive Routing Algorithm

Zhenni Li, Jingjiao Li$^{(\boxtimes)}$, Aiyun Yan, and Lan Yao

College of Information Science and Engineering, Northeastern University,
Shenyang, China
{lizhenni,lijingjiao,yanaiyun,yaolan}@ise.neu.edu.cn

Abstract. An asynchronous 2D-Torus Network-on-Chip (ATNoC) design based on System Verilog is implemented in this paper. A dynamic asynchronous XY routing algorithm DA-XY is proposed and designed as an Intellectual Property (IP) core and embedded to the ATNoC. Asynchronous circuit design methodology is used to design each routing node which could be divided into the following components, that is, receiving module, Hamming decoding module, routing analysis module, splitting module, arbiter module, Hamming encoding module and sending module. A test platform is built to analyze the function and the performance of the asynchronous NoC. The test result shows that the asynchronous NoC could support self-adaptive routing, multi-directional communication, and parallel multi-channel communications.

Keywords: NoC · Asynchronous design · 2D-Torus · Adaptive routing algorithm

1 Introduction

With the development of integrated circuits, the application of System on Chip (SoC) has become a tendency. Multi-cores, such as processors, DSPs, on-chip memories and etc. are integrated on a single chip. Traditional shared bus could not meet the multi-core communication requirement, therefore a Network-on-Chip (NoC) design diagram is proposed [1]. NoC based architectures have many advantages: high scalability, high throughput and good link performance [2]. It is often based on packet switching to provide dynamic communication possibilities. Although NoC architecture seems to be an appropriate solution for the communication of multiprocessors in high performance SoC, it also faces many challenges, like clock skew, and clock management when the multiprocessors work in different clock domain. In a synchronous NoC, the clock skew is a very important matter [3]. To obtain a minimum clock skew, the global clock has to be distributed among the chip, which requires the design of a large clock buffer tree that consume more than 40 % of the total power [4]. Globally Asynchronous Locally Synchronous (GALS) system is proposed to solve this problem [5, 6]. In GALS systems, the multi-cores are no longer required to use the same clock, and the communication between these processing elements is asynchronous [7, 8]. Moreover, a fully asynchronous NoC architecture is also one of the useful approaches to realize clock management and to meet the wide-bandwidth demands in large-scaled SoC. Besides,

© Springer International Publishing Switzerland 2016
Y. Wang et al. (Eds.): BigCom 2016, LNCS 9784, pp. 342–351, 2016.
DOI: 10.1007/978-3-319-42553-5_29

Asynchronous NoC (based on GALS systems or fully asynchronous) has the advantages of low dynamic energy dissipation, tolerance to delay variations, unified network interfaces, easy system integration and excellent electro-magnetic compatibility [9]. Therefore, it is a promising candidate for future high performance SoC. It is expected that half of the global signaling will be driven asynchronously by year 2024 [10].

Currently, the classical Asynchronous NoC could be listed as below: ANOC based on GALS system, uses virtual channel and provides low latency [11]. MANGO is an asynchronous NoC, uses 4-phase 32-bit bundled data and two Virtual Channel (VC) to provide guaranteed service and best effort [12]. SpiNNaker is based on GALS system, and it aims at simulating a billion spiking neurons in real time, and the tree topology is applied [13]. The NoC in [14] is a 2D-Mesh NoC where bi-synchronous FIFOs are used to connect routers at each node. ASPIN has the currently shortest transmission cycle, uses simple router architecture and 2D-Mesh topology [15]. The asynchronous NoC in [16] is designed for portable-battery devices, it uses efficient two-phase bundled-data links and four-phase routers, and has a efficient energy. The asynchronous NoC router in [17] uses level-encoded dual-rail encoding with 2D-Mesh topology, and could achieve high-throughput and delay-insensitive. Almost all the asynchronous NoC systems mentioned before use determined routing algorithm. When the routing congestion occurs, there will be a waste of routing resources, and finally results in the reduce of the data transmission efficiency. The asynchronous NoC mentioned in [18] has used adaptive routing mechanism, and Quasi Delay Insensitive (QDI) logic. However, the paper is focused on circuit design, and the routing algorithm is not specified in detail.

In this paper, we propose a fully asynchronous NoC architecture Asynchronous 2D-Torus NoC (ATNOC) which integrates Dynamic Asynchronous X-Y routing algorithm (DA-XY) for ATNOC and System Verilog development platform. The method of graphical representation is used to design the routing node in this ATNOC. Each routing node is composed of the following modules: receiving module, Hamming decoding module, routing analysis module, splitting module, arbiter module, Hamming encoding module and sending module. To specify the highly concurrent system, the petri net [19] is designed to describe the module interface behavior and the data flow between the modules. Asynchronous Burst-Mode (BM) Finite State Machine (FSM) [19, 20] is used to design the function and the behavior of each module.

The proposed architecture and its associated routing protocol are presented in Sect. 2. The design of the ATNOC router node is presented in Sect. 3. The experimental results are shown in Sects. 4. and 5 finally concludes this paper.

2 ATNOC: An Asynchronous 2D-Torus NoC

2.1 ATNOC Architecture Description

The ATNOC communication architecture is composed of routing nodes, IP cores, and links between nodes, which is shown in Fig. 1. The routing nodes are the basic elements of the ATNOC system, and they are connected by the point-to-point links using 2D-Torus topology. The routing nodes compute the transmission route of the incoming data according to the DA-XY routing algorithm, arbitrate between concurrent data and finally transmit the data on the chosen link.

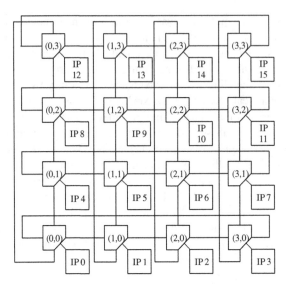

Fig. 1. ATNOC architecture

2.2   ATNOC DA-XY Routing Algorithm

A dynamic asynchronous routing algorithm named DA-XY routing algorithm is used to determine the output port of the data received from Hamming decoding module. And it is executed in the routing analysis module of the routing node. The basic principle of the algorithm is: the routing strategy is no longer performed statically, it could adjust the next-hop routing node dynamically according to the blocking information in the ATNOC architecture, while the shortest path strategy is also considered. Moreover, seriously blocking or malfunctioning routing nodes are avoided during the routing section, aimed to reduce the routing delay.

The ATNOC architecture uses 2D-Torus topology, therefore, during the routing section, the case of equidistance might happen. The length from the destination node to the current node might be the same no matter measured from the north or the south. In this case, direction north is judged preferentially. And the length from the destination node to the current node might be the same no matter measured from the west or the east. In this case, direction east is judged preferentially.

The DA-XY routing algorithm is specified as below: given the source node coordinate is $S(x\_s, y\_s)$, the destination node coordinate is $D(x\_dst, y\_dst)$, and the current node coordinate is $C(x,y)$. At the beginning of the routing, $C(x,y) = S(x\_s, y\_s)$. Besides, the paper takes the node $(0,0)$ as the lower left corner of the ATNOC architecture. The signal 'full' is used as the local blocking signal, it takes the logical value '0' when the specific direction is not blocked, while it takes the logical value '1' when the specific direction is blocked. And in order to represent the specific direction, several 'full' signals are used, namely, 'full_e', 'full_w', 'full_s', and 'full_n', which represent the blocking information of the east, the west, the south and the north respectively.

For a $N \times N$ ATNOC architecture, the DA-XY routing algorithm could be divided into two circumstances.

(i) If the destination node is in the south, the north, the west or the east of the current code, the blocking information is not considered. Three situations are listed as following:

- If $y\_dst = y$, $x\_dst = x$, the current node is the destination node, then the data will be sent to the IP core of the current routing node local port.
- If $y\_dst = y$, and whether $x\_dst = (x - i) \bmod (N)$, $i = 1, 2, \cdots, t$, t is an integer, and $t \le (N - 1)/2$. If yes, then the current node is in the west of the destination node, the data will be sent to the west port of the current node. If no, then the current node is in the east of the destination node, the data will be sent to the east of the current node.
- If $x\_dst = x$, and whether $y\_dst = (y - i) \bmod (N)$, $i = 1, 2, \cdots, t$, t is an integer, and $t \le (N - 1)/2$. If yes, then the current node is in the south of the destination node, the data will be sent to the south port of the current node. If no, then the current node is in the north of the destination node, the data will be sent to the north of the current node.

(ii) If the destination node is in the northeast, the southeast, the northwest or the southwest of the current code, the blocking information is considered.

Given P represents the direction east or west, and given Q represents the direction south or north. Then if there is no blocking either in direction P or in direction Q of the current node, the next-hop routing node is determined using the polling strategy. For example, if the last output direction is P, then the next output direction is Q. In this way, network congestion due to the continuous data transmission on one dimensional direction in a short period of time could be avoided on the one hand, and on the other hand, multi-way data transmission could make full use of the ATNOC, and the data load could be balanced. While if there is blocking in both direction P and in direction Q, then the data transmission is stopped until the blocking is removed. Moreover, if there is blocking either in direction P or in direction Q, the current node could get the blocking information from the signal 'full', and then adjust the routing path accordingly.

Four situations are listed as below:

- If $y\_dst = (y - i) \bmod (N)$, $x\_dst = (x - i) \bmod (N)$, $i = 1, 2, \cdots, t$, t is an integer, and $t \le (N - 1)/2$. Then the current node is in the southwest of the destination node, and the routing analysis module of the current node needs to judge the blocking situation of the south port and the west port of the current node. If full_w = 1, and full_s = 0, then the data is sent to the south port of the current node, else the data will be sent to the west port of the current node.
- If $y\_dst = (y - i) \bmod (N)$, $x\_dst = (x + j) \bmod (N)$, $i = 1, 2, \cdots, t$, t is an integer, and $t \le (N - 1)/2$, $j = 1, 2, \cdots, k$, and if N is odd number, then $k = (N - 1)/2$, else $k = N/2$. Then the current node is in the southeast of the destination node, and the routing analysis module of the current node needs to judge the blocking situation of the south port and the east port of the current node. If full_e = 1, and full_s = 0, then the data is sent to the south port of the current node, else the data will be sent to the east port of the current node.
- If $y\_dst = (y + j) \bmod (N)$, $x\_dst = (x - i) \bmod (N)$, $i = 1, 2, \cdots, t$, t is an integer, and $t \le (N - 1)/2$, $j = 1, 2, \cdots, k$, and if N is odd number, then $k = (N - 1)/2$, else

$k = N/2$. Then the current node is in the northwest of the destination node, and the routing analysis module of the current node needs to judge the blocking situation of the north port and the west port of the current node. If full_w = 1, and full_n = 0, then the data is sent to the north port of the current node, else the data will be sent to the west port of the current node.

- If $y\_dst = (y+j) \bmod (N)$, $x\_dst = (x+j) \bmod (N)$, $j = 1, 2, \cdots, k$, and if N is odd number, then $k=(N-1)/2$, else $k = N/2$. Then the current node is in the northeast of the destination node, and the routing analysis module of the current node needs to judge the blocking situation of the north port and the east port of the current node. If full_e = 1, and full_n = 0, then the data is sent to the north port of the current node, else the data will be sent to the east port of the current node.

3 Design of the ATNOC Routing Node

The ATNOC routing node is the main part of the ATNOC architecture. The DA-XY routing algorithm is performed in the routing node, aimed to calculate the transfer route of the data packet, while concurrent data could also be arbitrated.

3.1 The Overall Structure of ATNOC Routing Node

Each routing node is composed of five ports: east port, west port, south port, north port and local port. And each port contains the following modules: receiving module, hamming decoding module, routing analysis module, splitting module, arbiter module, hamming encoding module and sending module. Hamming encoding and hamming decoding modules are used to provide fault tolerance. Besides, the local port is connected to the IP core, where the data transferred is processed. For example, an asynchronous multiplier IP core could be attached to the local port of a certain routing node. The other four ports are connected to the adjacent asynchronous routing node. The data packet from upstream asynchronous routing node is received by these four ports, then the suitable output port is selected by the routing analysis module, splitting module and arbiter module, and finally, the data packet is passed to the downstream asynchronous routing node.

3.2 BM FSM Design of ATNOC Routing Node

Asynchronous BM state machine is used to design the modules in the ATNOC routing node. In the BM state machine, the arcs between the states are labeled with the input and output signal transitions. Only the design of the ATNOC crucial modules are listed down below, including the design of routing analysis module, and the design of splitting module.

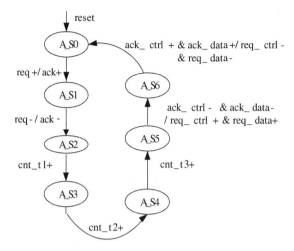

Fig. 2. The BM state machine of routing analysis module

Design of routing analysis module. The state variation of routing analysis module is described by BM state machine, which is shown in Fig. 2.

There are seven states in the BM state machine.

A_S0: The state machine enters into this state after reset, when the data request signal from hamming decoding module named 'req' is effective, that is, transfer from low level to high level, then the response signal to the hamming decoding module named 'ack' is set to be high level. Afterwards, the state machine goes to state A_S1;

A_S1: Data is received and stored, and the state machine waits for the invalid of req. When req is ineffective, then ack is set to be ineffective. Afterwards, the state machine goes to state A_S2;

A_S2: The destination address, the data transfer status of each port and block state information of neighboring nodes are stored. The time of the storage is controlled by the signal cnt_t1, when it is effective, then the state machine goes to state A_S3;

A_S3: The displacement information between destination node and current node is calculated in this state. The time of calculation is controlled by the signal cnt_t2, when it is effective, then the state machine goes to state A_S4;

A_S4: The DA-XY routing algorithm is performed in this state. The time of execution is controlled by cnt_t3, when it is effective, then the state machine goes to state A_S5;

A_S5: If the data and control response signal from splitting module ack_data and ack_ctrl is detected to be ineffective, then the data and control request signal to splitting module req_data and req_ctrl is set to be high level. Afterwards, the state machine goes to state A_S6;

A_S6: If ack_data and ack_ctrl is detected to be effective, then req_data and req_ctrl is set to be low level, and the state machine goes back to A_S0.

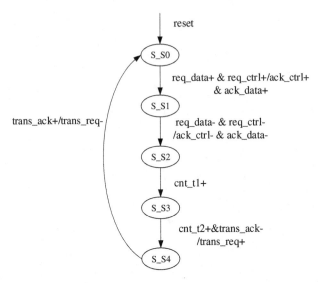

Fig. 3. The BM state machine of splitting module

Design of splitting module. The BM state machine of splitting module is described in Fig. 3.

There are five states in the BM state machine.

S_S0: The state machine enters into this state after reset, when the data and control request signal from routing analysis module req_data and req_ctrl is effective, then the data and control response signal to the routing analysis module ack_data and ack_ctrl is set to be high level. Afterwards, the state machine goes to state S_S1;

S_S1: Data is stored in the module, and the state machine waits for the invalid of req_data and req_ctrl. When they are ineffective, then ack_data and ack_ctrl is set to be ineffective. Afterwards, the state machine goes to state S_S2;

S_S2: The control signal is extracted, after the delay presented by the signal cnt_t1, the state machine goes to state S_S3;

S_S3: The output port for data transfer is chosen in this state, after the delay presented by the signal cnt_t2, if the response signal from arbiter module named 'trans_ack' is set to be low level, then the request signal to arbiter module named 'trans_req' is set to be high level. Afterwards, the state machine goes to state S_S4;

S_S4: The state machines waits for the effectiveness of trans_ack, if trans_ack is detected to be high level, then trans_req is set to be low level. Afterwards, the state machine goes back to S_S0.

4   Experiment Results

First and foremost, the DA-XY routing algorithm is simulated with OPNET modeler, in order to show the advantage of this routing algorithm. The ATNOC system is then realized by System Verilog, and is implemented in the environment of Modelsim 10.0.

A fully asynchronous multiplier IP core is designed and realized to test the communication performance of the ATNOC. Several tests are conducted, and parallel communication test is presented in this paper.

4.1 DA-XY Routing Algorithm Simulation Test

The DA-XY routing algorithm used in the ATNOC is simulated using OPNET modeler. Uniform flow pattern data model is used, and the average latency and the throughput rate of DA-XY routing algorithm, comparing with the classical XY routing algorithm is analyzed. The ATNOC network size is designed as 8×8, and an independent buffer is designed in the input port and output port of each routing node. The simulation result is presented in Fig. 4.

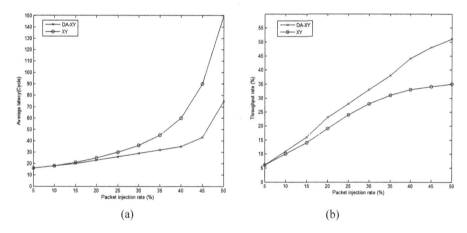

(a)   (b)

Fig. 4. Packet injection rate impact on network

From Fig. 4(a), the average latency is bigger with the increase of packet injection rate. When the packet injection rate reaches 35 %, the average delay of XY routing algorithm begins to increase continuously. While the packet injection rate gets to 45 %, the average latency of XY routing algorithm is almost two times of the average latency of DA-XY routing algorithm. The average delay of the two routing algorithm augments massively when the packet injection rate arrives at 50 %.

From Fig. 4(b), the throughput begins to increase slowly while the packet injection rate reaches 35 %. For the network using the XY routing algorithm, the throughput achieves nearly saturated state at 35 % packet injection rate. While for the DA-XY routing algorithm, the throughput achieves the saturated state at nearly 50 % packet injection rate.

It could be concluded that because of the adaptive routing strategy of the DA-XY routing algorithm, the throughput and average latency of the network is improved, compared with the network using XY routing algorithm.

4.2   Parallel Communication Test

In the test, nodes (0,0), (3,0), (0,3) and (3,3) are designed as the master nodes. Nodes (1,1), (2,2), (1,3) and (3,1) are designed as the slave nodes, where the 4 × 4 asynchronous multiplier IP core is embedded in. The master node sends data to the salve node, the slave node calls the asynchronous multiplier IP core and performs the multiplication, and finally the data calculated will be sent back to the master node. We take several samples, like 3*3, 4*6, 3*12 and 6*8. The simulation result indicates that the ATNOC could support multiple direction communication, and parallel multi-channel communications.

Besides, the DA-XY routing algorithm is also simulated in the ATNOC platform. And the result presents that the ATNOC could avoid seriously congested or malfunctioning routing nodes. And by detecting the busyness of the output port, the routing node could reasonably distribute the data to the suitable output port, and effectively decrease the routing delays.

5   Conclusions

A new asynchronous NoC architecture using dynamic asynchronous routing algorithm is proposed in this paper. Asynchronous circuit design methodology, including petri net and BM FSM, is used to design a 4 × 4 ATNOC. The DA-XY routing algorithm is designed as an IP core and embedded to the routing analysis module of the ATNOC. Compared with the XY routing algorithm that most asynchronous NoC used, DA-XY routing algorithm has better average latency and throughput. Besides, in each routing node, hamming encoding and decoding is used to provide fault tolerance. The experimental results show that the ATNOC could avoid seriously congested or malfunctioning routing nodes. Therefore could reduce the routing delays. Moreover, it could support self-adaptive routing, multiple direction communication, and parallel multi-channel communications.

Acknowledgements. This research is supported by the National Natural Science Foundation of China under Grant No. 61173027 and the Fundamental Research Funds for the Central Universities (N140404006, N130316001).

References

1. Jantsch, A., Tenhunen, H.: Network on Chip. Kluwer Academic Publishers, Berlin (2003)
2. Marculescu, R., Ogras, U., Peh, L.S., et al.: Outstanding research problems in NoC design: system, microarchitecture, and circuit perspectives. IEEE Trans. Comput. Aided Des. Integr. Circ. Syst. **28**(1), 3–21 (2009)
3. Amde, M., Felicijan, T., Efthymiou, A., et al.: Asynchronous on-chip networks. Comput. Digit. Tech. **152**(2), 273–283 (2005)
4. Vangal, S., Howard, J., Ruhl, G., Dighe, S., et al.: An 80-Tile 1.28TFLOPS Network-on-Chip in 65 nm CMOS. In: Proceedings of the 2007 Solid-State Circuits Conference, pp. 98–589 (2007)

5. Chapiro, D.: Globally asynchronous locally synchronous systems. Ph.D. dissertation, Department Computer Science, Stranford University (1984)
6. Hernandez, C., Roca, A., Silla, F., et al.: On the impact of within-die process variation in GALS-based NoC performance. IEEE Trans. Comput. Aided Des. Integr. Circ. Syst. **31**(2), 294–307 (2012)
7. Tran, A.T., Truong, D.N., Baas, B.: A reconfigurable source synchronous on-chip network for GALS many-core platforms. IEEE Trans. Comput. Aided Des. Integr. Circ. Syst. **29**(6), 897–910 (2010)
8. Horak, M., Nowick, S., Carlberg, M., et al.: A low-overhead asynchronous interconnection network for GALS chip multiprocessors. IEEE Trans. Comput. Aided Des. Integr. Circ. Syst. **30**(4), 494–507 (2011)
9. Wei, S., Edwards, D.: Survey of asynchronous Networks-on-Chip. J. Comput. Aided Des. Comput. Graph. **24**(6), 699–709 (2012)
10. International Technology Roadmap for semiconductor. Chapter design [OL] [10-10-2011]. http://www.itrs.net/Link/2009ITRs/Home2009.html
11. Belgne, E., clermidy, F., Vivet, P., et al.: An asynchronous NoC architecture providing low latency service and its multi-level design framework. In: Proceedings of the 11th International Symposium on Asynchronous Circuits and Systems, pp. 54–63 (2005)
12. Bjerregaard, T., Sparso, J.: A router architecture for connection-oriented service guarantees in the MANGO clockless Network-on-Chip. In: Proceedings of the conference on Design, Automation and Test in Europe, pp. 1226–1231 (2005)
13. Plana, L.A., Furber, S.B., Temple, S., et al.: A GALS infrastructure for a massively parallel multiprocessor. IEEE Des. Test Comput. **24**(5), 454–463 (2007)
14. Panades, I.M., Greiner, A.: Bi-synchronous FIFO for synchronous circuit communication well suited for Network-on-Chip in GALS architectures. In: Proceedings of the First International Symposium on Networks-on-Chip, pp. 83–94 (2007)
15. Sheibanyrad, A.: Asynchronous Implementation of a Distributed Network-on-Chip. University of Pierre et Marie Curie. Laboratory of Computer Sciences, Paris (2008)
16. Gebhardt, D., You, J.S., Stevens, K.: Design of an energy-efficient asynchronous NoC and its optimization tools for heterogeneous SoCs. IEEE Trans. Comput. Aided Des. Integr. Circ. Syst. **30**(9), 1387–1399 (2011)
17. Onizawa, N., Atsushi, M., Tomoyoshi, F.: High throughput compact delay-insensitive asynchronous NoC router. IEEE Trans. Comput. **63**(3), 637–649 (2014)
18. Alhussien, A., Wang, C.F., Bagherzadeh, N.: A scalable delay insensitive asynchronous NoC with adaptive routing. In: Proceedings of the 17th International Conference on Telecommunications, pp. 995–1002 (2010)
19. Chris, J.M.: Asynchronous Circuit Design, pp. 85–130. Wiley-Interscience, New York (2004)
20. Jens, S., Steve, F.: Principles of Asynchronous Circuit Design: A Systems Perspective. Kluwer Academic Publishers, London (2009)

Security and Privacy

Infringement of Individual Privacy via Mining Differentially Private GWAS Statistics

Yue Wang[1], Jia Wen[1], Xintao Wu[2], and Xinghua Shi[1(✉)]

[1] University of North Carolina at Charlotte, Charlotte, NC, USA
{ywang91,jwen6,x.shi}@uncc.edu
[2] University of Arkansas, Fayetteville, AR, USA
xintaowu@uark.edu

Abstract. Individual privacy in genomic era is becoming a growing concern as more individuals get their genomes sequenced or genotyped. Infringement of genetic privacy can be conducted even without raw genotypes or sequencing data. Studies have reported that summary statistics from Genome Wide Association Studies (GWAS) can be exploited to threat individual privacy. In this study, we show that even with differentially private GWAS statistics, there is still a risk for leaking individual privacy. Specifically, we constructed a Bayesian network through mining public GWAS statistics, and evaluated two attacks, namely trait inference attack and identity inference attack, for infringement of individual privacy not only for GWAS participants but also regular individuals. We used both simulation and real human genetic data from 1000 Genome Project to evaluate our methods. Our results demonstrated that unexpected privacy breaches could occur and attackers can derive identity information and private information by utilizing these algorithms. Hence, more methodological studies should be invested to understand the infringement and protection of genetic privacy.

1 Introduction

In the era of genomic medicine, it is critical to share genomic information with minimal worries about genetic privacy. To achieve this goal, we need to investigate human genetic data such as individual genotypes, and explore if and to what extent genetic privacy [1–4] can be breached. Human genotype data is sensitive by nature and belongs to the data type that should be dealt with scrutiny and specific restrictions. For example, the Health Insurance Portability and Accountability Act of 1996 (HIPAA) is deployed protects the privacy of individually identifiable health information in the USA [5]. In response to the HIPAA privacy rule, data collectors and supervisory organization must meet the requirements that ensure the data analysts agree with privacy restrictions according to USA Genetic Information Nondiscrimination Act of 2008 (GINA),

© Springer International Publishing Switzerland 2016
Y. Wang et al. (Eds.): BigCom 2016, LNCS 9784, pp. 355–366, 2016.
DOI: 10.1007/978-3-319-42553-5_30

and organizations should protect against all forms of genetic discrimination from using individuals' genetic information.

However, studies have shown that publicly available data not covered by HIPAA protection (e.g. allele frequency of genetic variants) can be used to infer identifiable personal information [1,6]. Taking Homer et al.(2008)'s research as an example, they developed a method that can identify straightforward whether a target with some known SNPs comes from an population with known allele frequency [7]. It attracted more and more attention on the privacy disclosure of the public dissemination of the genotype-related data and aggregate statistics from the genome-wide association studies (GWAS) [8–10]. Hence, the database of Genotypes and Phenotypes (dbGaP) was deployed to manage controlled access to genotype data. However, even without raw genotype or sequence data, summary statistics can be exploited by attackers where such public information is combined with health records and other online information [1,6]. One recent study [11] showed that full identities of personal genomes can be exposed via surname inference from recreational genetic genealogy databases followed by Internet searches. They considered a scenario in which the genomic data are available with the target's year of birth and state of residency, two identifiers not protected by HIPAA.

Our previous work [12] studied whether and to what extent the unperturbed GWAS statistics can be exploited to breach the privacy of regular individuals who are not GWAS participants. We introduced a framework based on Bayesian networks that captures the associations between SNPs and traits mined from public GWAS statistics in the GWAS catalog [13]. Two attacks, namely trait inference attack and identify inference attack, which can be exploited to breach genetic privacy of non-participant individuals, were formalized based on the Bayesian network inference and empirically evaluated.

Several research works [14,15] have been conducted for the safe release of aggregate GWAS statistics without compromising a participant's privacy. Their ideas were based on differential privacy [16]. According to [6,16,17], differential privacy is defined as a paradigm of post-processing the output and is agnostic to auxiliary information an adversary may possess, and provides guarantees against arbitrary attacks. A differentially private algorithm provides an assurance that the output cannot be exploited by the attacker to derive whether or not any individual's record is included.

In this paper, we focus on examining whether and to what extent the differentially private GWAS statistics can still be exploited by attackers to breach the privacy. As the differentially private GWAS statistics are perturbed with noise, one conjecture is that the perturbed GWAS statistics will do no harm to regular individuals. To examine this conjecture, we construct the Bayesian network using the differentially private GWAS statistics, develop efficient formulas to infer the probability of conducting these two attacks, and conduct empirical evaluations of our formulas and algorithms on simulation and real human genetic data. Our results reveal that these privacy protected statistics under differential privacy can still be employed by attackers to identity individuals or derive private information.

2   Differentially Private GWAS Statistics

2.1   Differential Privacy

We first revisit the formal definition and mechanism of differential privacy [17]. In prior work on differential privacy, a database is treated as a collection of *rows*, with each row corresponding to the data of an individual. Here we focus on how to compute GWAS statistics under differential privacy. The goal is to ensure that the inclusion or exclusion of an individual in the GWAS dataset makes no statistical difference to the results.

Definition 1 *(Differential Privacy). A GWAS algorithm Ψ that takes as input a GWAS dataset D, and outputs $\Psi(D)$, preserves (ϵ)-differential privacy if for all closed subsets S of the output space, and all pairs of neighboring datasets D and D' from $\Gamma(D)$,*

$$Pr[\Psi(D) \in S] \leq e^{\epsilon} \cdot Pr[\Psi(D') \in S], \tag{1}$$

where D and D' are two neighboring datasets that differ in only one record.

A general method for computing an approximation to any function f while preserving ϵ-differential privacy is given in [16]. The mechanism for achieving differential privacy computes the sum of the true answer and random noise generated from a Laplace distribution. The magnitude of the noise distribution is determined by the sensitivity of the computation and the privacy parameter specified by the data owner. The sensitivity of a computation bounds the possible change in the computation output over any two neighboring datasets (differing at most one individual's record).

Theorem 1 *(The Mechanism of Adding Laplace noise [16]). An algorithm A takes as input a dataset D, and some $\epsilon > 0$, a query Q with computing function $f : D \to \mathbf{R}^d$, and outputs*

$$\mathbf{A}(D) = f(D) + (Y_1, ..., Y_d) \tag{2}$$

where the Y_i are drawn i.i.d from $Lap(GS_f(D)/\epsilon)$ and $GS_f(D) := \max_{D, D' s.t. D' \in \Gamma(D)} \|f(D) - f(D')\|_1$ is the global sensitivity of a function f. The mechanism satisfies ϵ-differential privacy.

Differential privacy applies equally well to an interactive process, in which an adversary adaptively questions the system about the data. Differential privacy maintains composability, i.e., differential privacy guarantees can be provided even when multiple differentially private releases are available to an adversary.

2.2   GWAS Catalog and Statistics

Case-control studies under the GWAS framework are usually conducted by comparing the genotypes of two groups of participants: individual with the trait (case group) and matched individuals without the trait (control group). Dependent on genotyping platform, the number of SNPs genotyped in a GWAS setting typically ranges from tens of thousands to tens of millions. From genotype data, we can view that an SNP locus has two possible alleles, a risk allele and a non-risk allele. The risk allele is the allele that is more frequent in the case group comparing with the control group. The odds ratio, which is defined as the ratio of the proportion of individuals in the case group having a specific allele, and the proportion of individuals in the control group having the same allele, is often used to report the difference. When the allele frequency in the case group is higher than in the control group, the odds ratio will be higher than 1. Additionally, a p-value for the significance of the odds ratio is typically calculated using a simple chi-squared test. Those SNPs whose odds ratios are significantly different from 1, along with the statistics (e.g. p-value and odds ratio) are curated as the GWAS catalog [13].

Specifically, we can extract the following data from the GWAS catalog: a trait set $\mathcal{T}$, which contains m traits, and an SNP set $\mathcal{S}$, which contains n SNPs. For each specific trait $T_k \in \mathcal{T}$, we have a subset of associated SNPs. For each associated SNP S_j, we can extract its corresponding risk allele type $(rSNP_{kj})$ associated trait T_k, the odds ratio O_{kj} of the association test, and the risk allele frequency in the control group f_{kj}^t.

Though not directly given in the GWAS catalog, the risk allele frequency in the case group can be derived from the corresponding odds ratio and the risk allele frequency in the control group. For an SNP S_j associated with a trait T_k, with the released odds ratio (O_{kj}) and the risk allele frequency in the control group f_{kj}^t, the risk allele frequency in the case group f_{kj}^c can be derived as

$$f_{kj}^c = \frac{O_{kj} \cdot f_{kj}^t}{O_{kj} \cdot f_{kj}^t + 1 - f_{kj}^t}. \tag{3}$$

2.3   Differentially Private GWAS Statistics

Differential privacy has been significantly studied from a theoretical perspective [18–21]. Enforcing differential privacy in genomic data has been recently proposed [14,15], where classical GWAS statistics and models (e.g., the allele frequencies of cases and controls, chi-square statistic and p-values) were explored.

We use $\mathbf{x} = \{\mathbf{x}_1, \mathbf{x}_2, ..., \mathbf{x}_{n_c+n_t}\}$ to denote a GWAS data set that contains n_c cases and n_t controls. Each SNP profile $\mathbf{x}_i$ contains N SNPs. The purpose of a typical GWAS study is to identify K SNPs that are significantly associated with the trait under study. For each SNP, we can easily derive that the risk allele frequency in the case (control) group f^c (f^t) has a global sensitivity of $\frac{1}{n_c}$ ($\frac{1}{n_t}$) where $n_c(n_t)$ is the number of individuals in the case (control) group. The sensitivity of various statistics used for statistical tests between a given SNP and the trait can also be derived straightforwardly. For example, the sensitivity values of chi-square statistic and p-values were derived in [14] and those sensitivity values are small. For those statistics with large sensitivity values (e.g., the sensitivity of odds ratio is infinity), we can use perturbed risk allele frequencies to indirectly calculate them.

One naive approach for differentially private releasing K significant SNPs based on a given statistics Φ (e.g., chi-square statistic) is to add the Laplace noise $Lap(\frac{N}{\epsilon}GS_\Phi)$ to the true statistic value of each of N SNPs and then output K SNPs with most significant perturbed statistics values. However, this naive approach is infeasible in GWAS because the noise magnitude of $Lap(\frac{N}{\epsilon}GS_\Phi)$ is very large due to the large number of SNPs (N). In [18], the authors developed an effective differential privacy preserving method on how to release the most significant patterns together with their frequencies in the context of frequent pattern mining. The authors in [14] adapted this method to GWAS and aimed to release K most significant SNPs. This algorithm achieves ϵ differential privacy, with the magnitude of added noise proportional to K rather that to N. This is more efficient since that the number of significant SNPs (K) is much smaller than the number of total SNPs (N).

Here, we assume we are not able to access the raw SNP genotype data, while we have access to significant SNPs Γ associated with a trait via the released GWAS catalog. Thus we add the Laplace noise directly to the statistics of those SNPs Γ. In particular, for each significant SNP, we add the Laplace noise of mean zero and magnitude of $Lap(\frac{2K}{\epsilon n_c})$ ($Lap(\frac{2K}{\epsilon n_t})$) to the risk allele frequency in the case group f^c (in the control group f^t), and then use the perturbed frequencies to calculate the odds ratio. Recall that the risk allele frequency in the case (control) group f^c (f^t) has a global sensitivity of $\frac{1}{n_c}$ ($\frac{1}{n_t}$). Algorithm 1 shows our detailed algorithm. The perturbed odds ratio values are used to construct the two-layered Bayesian network.

Algorithm 1. *Differentially Private Genome-wide Association Study.*

Input: The genotype profile dataset $\mathbf{x} = \{\mathbf{x}_1, \mathbf{x}_2, ..., \mathbf{x}_{n_c+n_t}\}$ containing n_c cases and n_t controls in terms of a total number of N SNPs; the number of most relevant SNPs to be released K; the sufficient statistic function F; the privacy parameter ϵ_0, ϵ.

Output: The K most relevant SNPs with corresponding noisy statistics.

1: Compute the sufficient statistics $F(\mathbf{x})$ for each of the N SNPs and perturb each real value with the Laplace noise of mean zero and magnitude of $Lap(\frac{4K}{\epsilon}GS_F)$.

2: Pick K most relevant SNPs in terms of the noisy $F(\mathbf{x})$. Let this set be denoted as $\mathbf{S}$.

3: Perturb the true value $F(\mathbf{x})$ with the new Laplace noise with mean zero and magnitude of $Lap(\frac{2K}{\epsilon_0})GS_F$ and output $\mathbf{S}$.

4: Calculate and output other related statistics to be released for the SNPs in $\mathbf{S}$, for example risk allele frequency in control f^t and that in case f^c, under differential privacy with additional amount of privacy parameter ϵ based on their corresponding global sensitivity.

3   Attack Inference Based on a Bayesian Network

3.1   Constructing a Bayesian Network from Perturbed GWAS Statistics

A Bayesian network $G = (V, E)$ is a Directed Acyclic Graph (DAG), where the nodes in V represent the variables and the edges in E represent the dependence relationships among the variables. The dependence/independence relationships are graphically encoded by the presence or absence of direct connections between pairs of variables. Hence a Bayesian network shows the (in)dependencies between the variables qualitatively, by means of the edges, and quantitatively, by means of conditional probability distributions which specify the relationships.

In GWAS, we distinguish between two different sets of variables: the set $\mathcal{T}$ of the m traits, T_k, and the set $\mathcal{S}$ of the n SNPs, S_j. Each trait T_k is a binary random variable taking values in the set $\{1, 0\}$, where 1 stands for the presence of the trait of a participant and 0 stands for the absence. Similarly, each SNP S_j has its domain in the set $\{1, 0\}$, where 1 stands for the SNP has the risk allele and 0 otherwise. Throughout this paper, we use upper-case alphabets, e.g., X, to represent a variable; bold upper-case alphabets, e.g., $\mathbf{X}$, to represent a subset of variables. We use lower-case alphabets, e.g., x, to represent a value assignment of X; bold lower-case alphabets, e.g., $\mathbf{x}$ to represent a value assignment of $\mathbf{X}$.

We adopt the approach [12] to build a two-layered Bayesian network from the aforementioned perturbed GWAS statistics. The constructed network is composed of two layers, the trait layer and the SNP layer, with edges only going from trait nodes to SNP nodes. Each node at the top level denotes a specific trait; while each node at the second level denotes an SNP. If an SNP(S_j) is associated with a trait(T_k), a directed edge is added from T_k to S_j. The conditional probability table associated with each node is populated with the derived information from the perturbed GWAS statistics.

With the Bayesian network constructed from the perturbed GWAS statistics, we can calculate the joint probability for any desired assignment of values to variables sets $\mathbf{S}$ (SNPs), $\mathbf{T}$ (traits) by

$$P(\mathbf{s}, \mathbf{t}) = \sum_{\mathbf{T}'} \left(\prod_{S \in \mathbf{S}} P(s | Par(S)) \cdot \prod_{T \in \mathbf{T}} P(t) \cdot \prod_{T' \in \mathbf{T}'} P(t') \right) \qquad (4)$$

where lowercase $\mathbf{s}$ and $\mathbf{t}$ denote value assignment to variable sets $\mathbf{S}$ and $\mathbf{T}$, $\mathbf{T}'$ denotes the set of all the parent traits of the SNPs in $\mathbf{S}$ except for those already contained in $\mathbf{T}$, i.e., $\mathbf{T}' = Par(\mathbf{S}) \backslash \mathbf{T}$, and $\sum_{\mathbf{X}} f(\mathbf{x})$ means to sum up all $f(\mathbf{x})$ going through all instances of attributes $\mathbf{X}$ (i.e., all value combinations of attributes in $\mathbf{X}$).

Additionally, we can calculate the conditional joint probability for any *desired* assignment of values to variables sets $\mathbf{S}_x, \mathbf{T}_x$ given the *observed* assignment of variables sets $\mathbf{S}_y, \mathbf{T}_y$ by

$$P(\mathbf{s}_x, \mathbf{t}_x | \mathbf{s}_y, \mathbf{t}_y) = \frac{P(\mathbf{s}_x, \mathbf{t}_x, \mathbf{s}_y, \mathbf{t}_y)}{P(\mathbf{s}_y, \mathbf{t}_y)} \qquad (5)$$

where $\mathbf{S}_x$ and $\mathbf{S}_y$ denote the set of SNPs, $\mathbf{T}_x$, $\mathbf{T}_y$ denote the set of traits, and the joint probability $P(\mathbf{S}_x, \mathbf{T}_x, \mathbf{S}_y, \mathbf{T}_y)$ and $P(\mathbf{S}_y, \mathbf{T}_y)$ can be calculated Eq. 4.

Equations 4 and 5 are straightforwardly derived by following the marginalization strategy in the reasoning process of the Bayesian network. Note that we do not need to involve all variables in our summation to calculate $P(\mathbf{S}, \mathbf{T})$ and we can apply marginalization by summing out 'irrelevant' variables. In our two-layer Bayesian network, irrelevant variables include all nodes that are not in the ancestor subgraph for the set of variables of interest $(\mathbf{S}, \mathbf{T})$.

3.2 Inference Attacks Based on a Two-Layered Bayesian Network

The constructed Bayesian network, which captures the conditional dependency between SNPs and their associated traits, is used as background knowledge for two attacks.

Trait Inference Attack. We assume that an attacker has stolen genotype profile of the target and aims to derive the probability that the victim has a specific trait using the constructed Bayesian network. The probability of the prevalence of a specific trait, which is retrievable from the literature or the internet, is used as the prior probability that the target has the specific trait. The attacker can improve his/her guess by calculating the posterior probability of the target having the trait by inferring from with the target's genotypes. Formally, we represent the genotype of a target v as a vector, $\mathbf{r}_v = (r_{v1}, r_{v2}, \cdots, r_{vn})$, with each entry r_{vj} denoting the allele type of SNP j. The attacker aims to learn the posteriori probability $P(t_k|\mathbf{r}_v)$ that the target has a specific trait T_k given the target's genotype profile $\mathbf{r}_v$ using the constructed Bayesian network. The posteriori probability $P(t_k|\mathbf{r}_v)$ can be calculated by

$$P(t_k|\mathbf{r}_v) = P(t_k|Chd(T_k)) = \frac{P(t_k) \cdot \prod_{S \in Chd(T_k)} P(s|t_k)}{\sum_{T_k} P(t_k) \cdot \prod_{S \in Chd(T_k)} P(s|t_k)}, \tag{6}$$

where $Chd(T_k)$ denotes children SNP nodes of trait T_k.

Instead of conducting inference based on the whole Bayesian network G, the attacker can simply identify the subgraph G_k that contains all children SNPs of the target trait T_k, and then calculate the posterior probability following Eq. 6.

Identity Inference Attack. We assume that the attacker has access to an anonymized genotype dataset that contains the target's genotype record and the attacker knows a subset of traits the target has. Formally, we denote the anonymized genotype profile dataset as $\mathbf{R}$, where each record $\mathbf{r}_i = (r_{i1}, r_{i2}, \cdots, r_{in})$ represents the genotype profile of an anonymized individual i. We assume that the genotype profile of the target $\mathbf{r}_v$ is contained in $\mathbf{R}$, and the attacker knows $\mathbf{T}^*$, a subset of traits the target has. The attacker aims to learn the posteriori probability $P(\mathbf{r}_i = \mathbf{r}_v|\mathbf{t}^*)$ that the genotype record $\mathbf{r}_i$ corresponds to the target using the constructed Bayesian network.

For each genotype record $\mathbf{r}_i \in \mathbf{R}$, the posterior probability $P(\mathbf{r}_i|\mathbf{t}^\star)$ is

$$P(\mathbf{r}_i|\mathbf{t}^\star) = \sum_{\mathbf{T}'} \left(\prod_{j=1}^{|\mathbf{r}_i|} P(r_{ij}|Par(S_j)) \cdot \prod_{T' \in \mathbf{T}'} P(t') \right), \tag{7}$$

and the probability that $\mathbf{r}_i$ belongs to the target v is

$$P(\mathbf{r}_i = \mathbf{r}_v|\mathbf{t}^\star) = \frac{P(\mathbf{r}_v|\mathbf{t}^\star)}{\sum_{i=1}^{|\mathbf{R}|} P(\mathbf{r}_i|\mathbf{t}^\star)} = \frac{\sum_{\mathbf{T}'} \left(\prod_{j=1}^{|\mathbf{r}_v|} P(r_{vj}|Par(S_j)) \cdot \prod_{T' \in \mathbf{T}'} P(t') \right)}{\sum_{i=1}^{|\mathbf{R}|} \sum_{\mathbf{T}'} \left(\prod_{j=1}^{|\mathbf{r}_i|} P(r_{ij}|Par(S_j)) \cdot \prod_{T' \in \mathbf{T}'} P(t') \right)} \tag{8}$$

where $\mathbf{T}' = T \backslash \mathbf{T}^\star$.

Since the calculation of $P(\mathbf{r}_i = \mathbf{r}_v|\mathbf{t}^\star)$ shown in Eq. 8 involves summation over $\mathbf{T}'$. We present a simplified formula. For each genotype record, the probability that $\mathbf{r}_i$ belongs to the target v is

$$P(\mathbf{r}_i = \mathbf{r}_v|\mathbf{t}^\star) = \frac{\prod_{j=1}^{|\mathbf{r}_i|} P(r_{ij}|Par(S_j))}{\sum_{i=1}^{|\mathbf{R}|} \prod_{j=1}^{|\mathbf{r}_i|} P(r_{ij}|Par(S_j))}. \tag{9}$$

Identity inference attack describes a possible approach an attacker could take to identify the target individual's record in the dataset. Based on this attack, the attacker can also infer other private information of the target individual. For example, after deriving the probability that each record in the genotype dataset belongs to the target individual, the attacker can further derive any other trait that the target may have, based on the genotype information contained in the dataset. Assume the attacker also knows the target individual has a subset of traits, $\mathbf{T}_S$. The probability that the target has a new trait T_{new} can be derived as

$$P(t_{new}|\mathbf{r}_v \in \mathbf{R}, \mathbf{t}^\star) = \sum_{i=1}^{|\mathbf{R}|} P(\mathbf{r}_i = \mathbf{r}_v|\mathbf{r}_v \in \mathbf{R}, \mathbf{t}^\star) \times P(t_{new}|\mathbf{r}_i). \tag{10}$$

4   Evaluation

We conduct experiments to evaluate how the trait inference attack and the identity inference attack work based on the Bayesian network constructed from the differentially private statistics. Our evaluation is based on the 85 Utah residents with ancestry from northern and western Europe (CEU) from the 1000 Genomes Project. In our experiments, we choose two privacy threshold values, $\epsilon = 2$ and $\epsilon = 0.2$, which represent two settings for reasonable privacy preservation in GWAS. For each ϵ, we follow the procedure in Sect. 2.3 to derive the differential privacy preserving statistics and then construct the Bayesian network.

Table 1 shows the comparison of the trait inference attack. Column $P(t_k = 1)$ shows the prevalence of the trait in population. Columns $\overline{P}(t_k = 1|r_{ij} = 1)$, $\overline{P}(t_k = 1|r_{ij} = 1)(\epsilon = 2)$, and $\overline{P}(t_k = 1|r_{ij} = 1)(\epsilon = 0.2)$ show the average probability that the 85 CEU participants from the 1000 Genomes Project has each

Table 1. Differential private posterior probability of certain trait considering one SNP.

Index	$P(t_k = 1)$	$\overline{P}(t_k = 1\|r_{ij} = 1)$	$\overline{P}(t_k = 1\|r_{ij} = 1)(\epsilon = 2)$	$\overline{P}(t_k = 1\|r_{ij} = 1)(\epsilon = 0.2)$
1	0.05	0.0751	0.0749	0.0749
2		0.0701	0.0670	0.0679
3		0.0584	0.0581	0.0571
4	8E-5	$1.54E-4$	$1.59E-4$	$1.49E-4$
5	0.056	0.0923	0.0934	0.2637
6	0.036	0.023	0.023	0.023
7	0.10	0.2031	0.2054	0.2055
8		0.0303	0.0360	0.0360
9		0.0258	0.0300	0.0301
10	0.16	0.1991	0.1992	0.1986

trait under three compared scenarios, using directly released GWAS statistics, 2-differentially private statistics, and 0.2-differentially private statistics, respectively. The results from Table 1 shows that most of the average probabilities are significantly different than the corresponding prior probability of having a trait. We are interested in how the derived posterior probabilities using perturbed statistics are different from those using the original statistics. We define the average absolute relative error as $\gamma(\epsilon) = \frac{1}{K} \sum_{j=1}^{K} \frac{|\overline{P}(t_k=1|r_{ij}=1)-\overline{P}_\epsilon(t_k=1|r_{ij}=1)|}{\overline{P}(t_k=1|r_{ij}=1)}$. Our results show $\gamma(2) = 0.0408$ and $\gamma(0.2) = 0.2282$, which indicate the more rigorous privacy protection incurs more loss of attack performance in terms of accuracy.

We also use the differentially private statistics to run the identity inference attack again on 'CEU' dataset. In Table 2, each row corresponds to some certain number of traits the target individual has. The columns under label 'Original', '$\epsilon = 2$' and '$\epsilon = 0.2$' denote the average probability of correctly identifying

Table 2. Average probability of identity inference attack with different amount of background knowledge.

$\|\mathbf{T}^\star\|$	$\overline{P}(\mathbf{r}_i = \mathbf{r}_v\|\mathbf{T}^\star)$					
	Original		$\epsilon = 2$		$\epsilon = 0.2$	
	ave	std	ave	std	ave	std
1	0.0697	0.0321	0.0645	0.0275	0.0325	0.0075
2	0.1493	0.0312	0.1320	0.0576	0.0646	0.0229
3	0.2503	0.1138	0.2118	0.0916	0.0978	0.0497
4	0.3725	0.1578	0.3032	0.1348	0.1230	0.0923
5	0.5158	0.2047	0.4079	0.1911	0.1360	0.1484
6	0.6792	0.2565	0.5323	0.2657	0.1340	0.2200

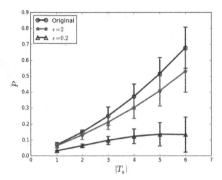

Fig. 1. Average Probability of Identity Inference Attack with Different Amount of Background Knowledge. (Color figure online)

the target individual $\overline{P}(\mathbf{r}_i = \mathbf{r}_v|\mathbf{t}^\star)$ calculated with original value of GWAS statistics, the 2-differentially private GWAS statistics, and the 0.2-differentially private GWAS statistics respectively. For each scenario, we use 'ave' and 'std' to denote the mean and the standard deviation. We can easily observe from Table 2 and Fig. 1 that the average probability of correctly identifying the target individual $\overline{P}(\mathbf{r}_i = \mathbf{r}_v|\mathbf{t}^\star)$ increases as the number of known traits increases under three scenarios. This observation shows that the more background knowledge the attacker has, the more likely the target individual can be identified. We are interested in how the performance of the identity inference attack is affected by the perturbed GWAS statistics. We can see that the attack performance is significantly decreased when GWAS statistics are distorted under rigorous privacy protection. For example, as the last row shows, when $|\mathbf{T}^\star| = 6$, the accuracy of the attack decreases from 0.6792 to 0.5323 ($\epsilon = 2$), and further to 0.1340 ($\epsilon = 0.2$). However, the probability (0.1340) that the target individual being correctly identified under $\epsilon = 0.2$ is still an order high than the probability of random guess (0.0116).

5   Conclusions and Future Work

In summary, we constructed a Bayesian network from perturbed GWAS catalog and explored whether an attacker can get the private information from public population and to what extent if so. We evaluated two types of attacks, trait inference attack and identity inference attack respectively. Both of these two attacks derive private information by using the GWAS public catalog data that capture the relationship between SNPs and their associated traits. Using both simulated and real human genetic data, we found that both of these two attacks can be real threat to the privacy of general population, even when the GWAS statistics are already perturbed under differential privacy. In our future work, we will further incorporate trait-trait relationships and/or SNP-SNP correlations into our perturbed Bayesian network and develop new inference algorithms on the network. We aim to develop methods that could protect data privacy or could release GWAS statistics with less threat for general population.

Acknowledgements. The work is supported in part by US National Science Foundation (DGE-1523115 and IIS-1502273 to XW, and DGE-1523154 and IIS-1502172 to XS).

References

1. Erlich, Y., Narayanan, A.: Routes for breaching and protecting genetic privacy. Nat. Rev. Genet. **15**(6), 409–421 (2014)
2. Greenbaum, D., Gerstein, M.: Genomic anonymity: have we already lost it? Am. J. Bioeth. **8**(10), 71–74 (2008)
3. Greenbaum, D., Gerstein, M.: Social networking and personal genomics: suggestions for optimizing the interaction. Am. J. Bioeth. **9**(6–7), 15–19 (2009)
4. Greenbaum, D., Sboner, A., Mu, X.J., Gerstein, M.: Genomics and privacy: implications of the new reality of closed data for the field. PLoS Comput. Biol. **7**(12), e1002278 (2011)
5. The Health Insurance Portability and Accountability Act of 1996 (HIPAA). http://www.hhs.gov/hipaa/
6. Shi, X., Wu, X.: Genetic privacy: risks, ethics, and protection techniques. In: The Workshop on Data Science Learning and Applications to Biomedical and Health Sciences, pp. 57–62, New York, NY (2016)
7. Homer, N., Szelinger, S., Redman, M., Duggan, D., Tembe, W., Muehling, J., Pearson, J.V., Stephan, D.A., Nelson, S.F., Craig, D.W.: Resolving individuals contributing trace amounts of DNA to highly complex mixtures using high-density SNP genotyping microarrays. PLoS Genet. **4**(8), e1000167 (2008)
8. Masca, N., Burton, P.R., Sheehan, N.A.: Participant identification in genetic association studies: improved methods and practical implications. Int. J. Epidemiol. **40**(6), 1629–1642 (2011)
9. Wang, R., Li, Y.F., Wang, X., Tang, H., Zhou, X.: Learning your identity and disease from research papers: information leaks in genome wide association study. In: 16th ACM Conference on Computer and Communications Security, pp. 534–544. ACM (2009)
10. Zhou, X., Peng, B., Li, Y.F., Chen, Y., Tang, H., Wang, X.F.: To release or not to release: evaluating information leaks in aggregate human-genome data. In: Atluri, V., Diaz, C. (eds.) ESORICS 2011. LNCS, vol. 6879, pp. 607–627. Springer, Heidelberg (2011)
11. Gymrek, M., McGuire, A.L., Golan, D., Halperin, E., Erlich, Y.: Identifying personal genomes by surname inference. Science **339**(6117), 321–324 (2013)
12. Wang, Y., Wu, X., Shi, X.: Using aggregate human genome data for individual identification. In,: IEEE International Conference on Bioinformatics and Biomedicine, pp. 410–415. IEEE, Shenzhen, China (2013)
13. Hindorff, L.A., MacArthur, J., Morales, J., Junkins, H.A., Hall, P.N., Klemm, A.K., Manolio, T.A.: A Catalog of Published Genome-wide Association Studies. http://www.genome.gov/gwastudies
14. Fienberg, S.E., Slavkovic, A., Uhler, C.: Privacy preserving GWAS data sharing. In: 11th International Conference on Data Mining Workshops, pp. 628–635. IEEE (2011)

15. Johnson, A., Shmatikov, V.: Privacy-preserving data exploration in genome-wide association studies. In: 19th ACM International Conference on Knowledge Discovery and Data Mining, pp. 1079–1087. ACM, Chicago, IL (2013)

16. Dwork, C., McSherry, F., Nissim, K., Smith, A.: Calibrating noise to sensitivity in private data analysis. In: Halevi, S., Rabin, T. (eds.) TCC 2006. LNCS, vol. 3876, pp. 265–284. Springer, Heidelberg (2006)

17. Dwork, C.: A firm foundation for private data analysis. Commun. ACM **54**(1), 86–95 (2011)

18. Bhaskar, R., Laxman, S., Smith, A., Thakurta, A.: Discovering frequent patterns in sensitive data. In: 16th ACM International Conference on Knowledge Discovery and Data Mining, pp. 503–512. ACM, Washington, DC (2010)

19. Chaudhuri, K., Monteleoni, C.: Privacy-preserving logistic regression. In: 23rd Annual Conference on Neural Information Processing Systems, pp. 289–296. Citeseer, Vancouver, B.C., Canada (2008)

20. Kifer, D., Machanavajjhala, A.: No free lunch in data privacy. In: 17th ACM International Conference on Knowledge Discovery and Data Mining, pp. 193–204. ACM, San Diego, CA (2011)

21. Lee, J., Clifton, C.: Differential identifiability. In: 18th ACM International Conference on Knowledge Discovery and Data Mining, pp. 1041–1049. ACM, Beijing, China (2012)

Privacy Preserving in the Publication
of Large-Scale Trajectory Databases

Fengyun Li[✉], Fuxiang Gao, Lan Yao, and Yu Pan

School of Computer Science and Engineering, Northeastern University,
Shenyang 110819, People's Republic of China
{lifengyun,gaofuxiang,yaolan}@mail.neu.edu.cn,
neu_py@163.com

Abstract. In recent years, preserving individual privacy when publishing trajectory data receives increasing attention. However, the existing trajectory data privacy preserving techniques cannot resolve the anonymous issues of large-scale trajectory databases. In traditional clustering constraint based trajectory privacy preserving algorithms, the anonymous groups lack of diversity and they cannot effectively prevent re-clustering attacks against the characteristics of publishing data. In this thesis, a segment clustering based privacy preserving algorithm is proposed. Firstly, the original database is divided into blocks and each block is treated as a separate database. Then, the trajectories in each block are partitioned into segments based on the minimum description length principle. Lastly, these segments are anonymized with cluster-constraint strategy. Experimental results show that the proposed algorithm can improve the safety and have good performance in data quality and anonymous efficiency.

Keywords: Privacy preserving · Large-scale databases · Trajectory data publishing · Segment clustering

1 Introduction

Privacy preserving issues for trajectory data publishing have a critical significance in its development, and have become a hot research topic [1]. Due to the characteristics of trajectory data such as large-scale, high-dimension, and rich-background, the research on privacy preserving issues is facing severe challenges [2, 3].

The existing privacy preserving methods for trajectory data publishing mainly transform the trajectory anonymous problem into the trajectory clustering constraint problem to protect user's privacy [4, 5]. In those methods, the trajectory data is clustered according to the similarity firstly. Then, the generated clustering groups are transformed into corresponding anonymous groups by using the constraint operations. Among them, the constraint operations include suppression, generalization, feature release technology and space translation technology. In traditional clustering constraints based trajectory privacy preserving method, the trajectory database exist the problem of lack of diversity in the anonymous group and is vulnerable to re-clustering attacks. Furthermore, the existing trajectory anonymous techniques are mainly applied to simple trajectory database. When they are used to the anonymous issues of

© Springer International Publishing Switzerland 2016
Y. Wang et al. (Eds.): BigCom 2016, LNCS 9784, pp. 367–376, 2016.
DOI: 10.1007/978-3-319-42553-5_31

large-scale trajectory databases directly, there are some problems such as more difficulty and lower data quality.

Aiming at the above problems, this paper mainly focuses on the privacy preserving issues in the publishing of large-scale trajectory databases, and using the trajectory blocking techniques to improve the anonymous time and enhance the anonymous quality. A trajectory privacy preserving algorithm based on segment clustering is proposed and implemented. In our algorithm, the raw database is partitioned into blocks firstly. And then, the blocks of the trajectories are partitioned into segments based on the minimum description length (MDL) principle. Then, these segments are anonymized based on the cluster-constraint strategy.

The rest of this paper is organized as follows. Section 2 describes the related work. Section 3 proposes a segment clustering based privacy preserving algorithm for trajectory data publishing. Section 4 reports the experimental results. Conclusions are drawn in Sect. 5.

2 Related Work

In recent years, people have done a lot of research on the privacy preserving issues for trajectory data publishing [6–10]. Most of these researches are major in disturbing trajectory data, generalizing or characterizing their release based on k-anonymity model [11]. Of all the schemes, k-anonymity technology is applied most commonly. The k-anonymity model is a kind of technology proposed by Sweeney for relational data privacy preserving. In k-anonymity model, the attributes in each tuple are divided in quasi-identifiers and sensitive attributes [12], and doing the anonymous process to the quasi-identifiers in each record to make there are at least k-1 records has the same quasi-identifiers in the database. For the k-anonymity processing on relational datasets, the researchers generally used generalization and inhibition technology to make the probability for an attacker to identify a specific user decreased to 1/k. However, since the trajectory data has high dimensions, temporal and spatial correlation, and the characteristics of background knowledge, so it will not be able to divide data into fixed quasi-identifiers and the sensitive attributes. These methods based on k-anonymity for relational data cannot effectively be used directly in the trajectory dataset.

Abul et al. are the first one to transform the anonymity problem into a constrained trajectory clustering problem to achieve privacy preserving [13]. And on the basis of k-anonymity, they propose the (k, δ)-anonymity model using the inherent uncertainty of positioning system [14]. Abul et al. cluster the trajectory with the same period of time according to Euclidean distance, and get the cluster group which is composed of the trajectories with similar distance. Then, they distort the trajectories in each clustering groups. After data processing, for any trajectory, it has at least k-1 the same trajectory under the uncertainty threshold k. Subsequently, Abul puts forward the improved algorithm of W4M [10], use EDR [12] instead of the Euclidean distance as the similarity function in trajectory clustering process. They improved of each trajectory requires at the same time interval in Euclidean distance, the trajectories in different time range can be clustered together to form a cluster group. Nergiz [9] also adopted the strategy of constraining after clustering, then generalizing each trajectory in a clustering group. Generalization refers each sampling point moment all covered with a rectangular area, and only released the generalized trajectories locate in the rectangular region. Although the privacy preserving degree of this kind of algorithm is high, but it can only support simple aggregation analysis, and could not be applied to other applications such as behavior pattern discovery and the mining of association rules.

In all the above clustering constraint based strategies in trajectory data privacy preserving, they regard the entire trajectory as the basic unit for clustering. Although, they can reduce the probability that the attackers can identify the user's particular location information to 1/k. However, they neglect the problem that take a trajectory as a whole while clustering will make the distortion degree very big in the constraint process and the trajectories lack of diversity in the clustering groups after constraints, so they cannot effectively prevent re-clustering attacks [16]. At the same time, once the existing research achievements are applied to large-scale trajectory databases, they will face the problem of a great difficulty in anonymity and the low data quality.

3   Segment Clustering Based Privacy Preserving Algorithm for Trajectory Data Publishing

3.1   Overall Design of SC-TDP Algorithm

Aiming at the difficulty in publishing large-scale trajectory data, and the lack of diversity in the anonymous group of traditional trajectory algorithm that cannot resist the re-clustering attacks, this paper presents a segment clustering based privacy preserving algorithm for trajectory data publishing(SC-TDP for short), see Algorithm 1.

Algorithm 1. SC-TDP Algorithm.

Input: D, k, δ, π
Output: D'
1: initialize(Max_Trash)
2: D'← $\emptyset$
3: D^c←SC-TDP_blocking(D)
4: for all $D^{cc} \in D^c$ do
5: D^{cc}← $SC - TDP\_part(D^c, \pi)$
6: for all $D_T \in D^{cc}$ do
7:   if ($|D_T| \geq$ k) do
8:     Trash_quota(T) ← $\left\lfloor \frac{|D_T|}{|D|} * Max\_Trash \right\rfloor$
9:     $\gamma \leftarrow SC - TDP\_clust(D_T, k, Trash\_quota(T))$
10:    D'← D' $\cup SC - TDP\_st(\gamma, \delta)$

In the trajectory privacy preserving algorithm SC-TDP, the raw database is partitioned into blocks firstly. And then, the blocks of the trajectories are partitioned into segments based on the MDL principle. Then, the segments of the trajectories are clustered by using linear time-tolerant distance function (LSTD for short). Finally, these segments are anonymized with cluster-constraint strategy. To adapt to large-scale database, the original database is partitioned into blocks by rough distance function (O (1)) before segment, clustering and anonymization in this algorithm. During clustering, this algorithm uses the modified LSTD function to clustering these trajectories. Unlike the existing algorithm, SC-TDP algorithm considers the trajectory's characteristics of space and time fully.

SC-TDP algorithm mainly contains the following four stages:

1. Database blocking: The algorithm partitions the similar trajectories in the original database into blocks by rough distance function (O(1)). Therefore, the similar trajectory are divided into the same block. For a given anonymous threshold value k, the size of the block should be 20 k and the last block contains 2*20 trajectories at most.
2. Trajectory segmenting: The algorithm segments each block according to the behavior characteristics of the trajectories, and based on MDL principle. To ensure the availability of segments, and considering trajectory's characteristics of space and time in the clustering stage, this algorithm introduces the concept of time π. The detailed trajectory segmenting algorithm will be introduced in Sect. 3.2.
3. Trajectory clustering: This stage uses clustering algorithm base on the Greedy strategy to clustering the segments of these trajectories. The k-1 trajectories those are closing to the central trajectory form a clustering group by using LSTD function. By deleting some abnormal trajectories, all trajectories in the clustering group are placed in a small cylinder.
4. Spatio-temporal editing perturbation: This stage use the technique of spatio-temporal editing perturbation based on the result of clustering stage. The position of minority trajectories are perturbed, by computing whether a matching point is within the scope of $\delta/2$ radius to the point in the center of trajectory. Finally, each clustering group is changed into a (k, δ)-anonymized set.

The SC-TDP algorithm's input is original trajectory database D, anonymous threshold value k, uncertainty threshold δ and time granularity π. Firstly, the original database is partitioned into blocks (line 3). The size of each block is 20 k. Secondly, each block is divided into segments based on the time granularity π (line 5). Then, for the equivalence classes whose segment number are greater than k, the algorithm make them clustering, and ensure that each cluster group has at least one k segments (line 9). Finally, each clustering group is handled with the technique of spatio-temporal editing perturbation. Then, these segments are re-compounded and published. The value of parameter Max_Trash is initialized automatically in the first line of the algorithm (the default size is ten percent of the original trajectory database). The value of Max_Trash specifies the maximum number of trajectory segments that can be deleted.

3.2   Trajectory Segmenting Algorithm

In order to solve the weighing problem of accuracy and simplicity, this paper introduced the MDL principle which is widely used in information theory. The trajectory segment problem is converted into a minimum description length problem to be solved, and use the least number of segments to describe the characteristics of the trajectory. The cost of MDL is mainly composed of two parts [17]: L(H) and L(D|H), where H is hypothesis, D is the data to be described. L(H) is the bit length required to describe hypothesis H, L(D|H) is the bit length to describe D when we use the hypothesis H to encode data D. For a given data D, the best hypothesis H is a hypothesis that can make the minimum sum of L(H) and L(D|H), namely

$$H = \arg \min_H (L(H) + L(D|H)) \tag{1}$$

In the above MDL, the hypothesis H corresponds to a trajectory segment result. For a trajectory, L(H) describes the number of bits required, it can effectively reflect the simplicity of the trajectory segment. When the value of L(H) is larger, the trajectory segment is less simplicity. L(D|H) is the number of bits required when describes the difference between the trajectory segments and the original trajectory. When the L(D|H) is larger, the accuracy is lower. Obviously, the hypothesis H that meets MDL is the segment result that can maximize the sum of simplicity and accuracy. Therefore, the optimal trajectory segment problem is equivalent to the use of MDL principle to find the optimal hypothesis that can represent a trajectory.

Since the high cost of obtain the optimal trajectory segment based on MDL principle, we use the greedy algorithm to find the closest optimal segmentation results. In our algorithm, $MDL_{par}(p_i, p_j)$ represents the MDL cost (L(H) + L(D|H)) when there are only two feature nodes p_i and p_j in a trajectory from p_i to p_j, that is to say, there is only one trajectory segment $p_i p_j$. $MDL_{nopar}(p_i, p_j)$ represents the MDL cost (L(H) + L(D|H)) when there are no trajectory segment in a trajectory from pi to p_j. Since the original trajectory is not divided into segments, the value of L(D|H) is equal to 0, and L(H) is the number of binary bits required when describes the original trajectory. In this case, to a longest trajectory segment $p_i p_j$, a local optimal result of the algorithm is $k \in [i, j]$ and it satisfy $MDL_{par}(p_i, p_k) \leq MDL_{nopar}(p_i, p_k)$. If $MDL_{par}(p_i, p_k)$ is lower than $MDL_{nopar}(p_i, p_k)$, it means the cost of choosing p_k as feature nodes is lower than not choosing them as feature nodes. In order to realize the simplicity of trajectory segment, the algorithm always tries to increase the length of the trajectory segment. The pseudo-code of trajectory segments algorithm (SC-TDP_part for short) can be seen in Algorithm 2.

In SC-TDP_part algorithm, the input is the original trajectory dataset D^c nd the time interval π. The output is the equivalence class D^{ec} which is composed of all the equivalence classes that meet the time interval π. In the algorithm, $\tau[i]$ means the sampling node of trajectory in time i. $\tau[i, j]$ means the part of trajectory τ which locates between time interval i and j $(i < j)$. $D_{[i,j]}$ means the equivalence class which is composed of trajectory segments, where i is the started time, and j is the finished time.

The algorithm starts from the nodes whose first sampling time is the integer multiple of π (line 3). For the sampling nodes locate at time interval π, our algorithm calculates the MDL cost of choosing it as feature node and not as a feature node separately (lines 7–8). Then, the trajectory segment between the two feature nodes is putted into corresponding equivalence classes (line 10). The algorithm abandons those parts of the trajectory locate besides the first feature node and the last feature node for simple. At last, all the trajectory segments are putted into corresponding equivalence classes (line 11).

Algorithm 2 SC-TDP_part segment algorithm

Input: D^c, π
Output: D^{ec}
1: for all $\tau \in D^c$ do
2: Let $[t_b, t_e]$ be the time span of τ
3:   $i \leftarrow \min\{t \mid t \geq t_b \cap t \bmod \pi = 0\}$
4:   length$\leftarrow 1$
5:   while ($i + \text{length}*\pi \leq t_e$) do
6:       $j \leftarrow i + \text{length}*\pi$
7:       cost_par$\leftarrow$MDL_par($\tau[i] + \tau[j]$)
8:       cost_nopar$\leftarrow$MDL_nopar($\tau[i] + \tau[j]$)
9:       if (cost_par>cost_nopar) then
10:           insert $\tau[i, j-\pi]$ in $D^c_{[i, j-\pi]}$
11:           $i \leftarrow j-\pi$, length$\leftarrow 1$
12:       else
13:           length$\leftarrow$length+1
14:   if($i!=j$) insert $\tau[i,j]$ in $D_{[i,j]}$
15: $D^{ec} \leftarrow \cup\{ D^c_{[i,j]} \mid i \bmod \pi = 0 \cap j \bmod \pi = 0\}$

4   Experimental Study

In this experimental study, we compare our proposed algorithm which is disposed by blocking and LSTD function with the traditional algorithm NWA, and test the performances in the aspects of running time and data quality.

4.1   Experimental Datasets and Setting

In this article, we use two moving object datasets to carry out experiments of anonymization. One is the real-word trajectory dataset, and the other one is generated using network-based generator of moving objects. The real-word trajectory dataset comes from GeoPKDD project. It contains a set of trajectories of moving cars which is obtained by GPS equips in the city of Milan (Italy) in April 2007. After simple preprocessing, this database contains 45 k trajectories and about 4.7 M spatio-temporal points. This dataset is manifested as Milian. The second database was generated by network-based generator of moving objects. This generator is provided by Brinkhoff in [15]. It contains 100,000 trajectories and manifests one day movement over the road network of Oldenburg (Germany). Since the traditional NWA algorithm cannot be used to the anonymization of large-scale trajectory databases, therefore, we only use SC-TDP algorithm to the anonymization of Milan dataset.

Table 1 shows the statistical information of the two datasets. Among them, radius (D) is the half-diagonal of the minimum bounding box, |D| is the number of trajectories, Points is the number of spatio-temporal points, Max length is the maximum number of points in one trajectory, and Avg.step manifest the average step.

Table 1. Statistics of moving objects database

Parameter name	Value1	Value2
D	Milan	Olden
Radius(D)	298328.6	35779.3
|D|	45639	100000
Points	4729613	4780954
Max length	287	141
Avg.step	2541.9	124.5

All the experiments were performed on a quad-core PC compatible machine with Intel(R) Core(TM) 2 Quad 2.83 GHz processor, 4 GB of RAM, and Windows 7 platform. The algorithm is implemented in C language. The parameter max_radius is set to 0.5 % of the diagonal of the minimum bounding box. The parameter Max_Trash is the maximum number of trajectories that can be suppressed, and is set to 10 % of the dataset. While using EDR in the stage of clustering, dx and dy are set to four times the uncertainty parameter δ, dt = 4*δ/average_speed, where average_speed is the average speed of all the moving objects in the dataset to be anonymized.

4.2   Running Time

Table 2 showed the running time comparison of using NWA and SC-TDP algorithm to the anonymization of Oldenburg dataset, where δ = 1000. From Table 2, we can see that the running time increases while the uncertainty threshold value of k increasing. Our proposed SC-TDP algorithm cost only one order of magnitude time than the traditional NWA in anonymizing the Oldenburg dataset, though our algorithm contains more process steps for privacy preserving than NWA.

Table 2. The runtime test for anonymous publication

k	NWA(seconds)	SC-TDP(seconds)
10	$0.5*10^3$	$0.25*10^3$
20	$0.6*10^3$	$0.7*10^3$
30	$0.7*10^3$	$0.05*10^4$
40	$0.75*10^3$	$0.17*10^4$
50	$0.8*10^3$	$0.25*10^4$
60	$0.85*10^3$	$0.3*10^4$
70	$0.89*10^3$	$0.39*10^4$
80	$0.9*10^3$	$0.49*10^4$
90	$0.91*10^3$	$0.6*10^4$
100	$0.92*10^3$	$0.6*10^4$

4.3   Distortion Degree of Range Query

We use the distortion degree of range query to compare the results between queries on the original dataset D and the anonymized version $D^{'}$. Since the location of a moving object τ changes continuously, we may ask if the condition that every possible motion curve $f_{PMC^{\tau}}$ is inside the region R(inside(R, t)) is satisfied sometime or always within a timestamp $[t_b, t_e]$. We focus only on the two extreme cases, Possibly_Sometime_Inside (PSI) and Definitely_Always_Inside (DAI), where

$$\text{Possibly\_Sometime\_Inside}(\tau, R, t_b, t_e) \equiv (\exists f_{PMC^{\tau}})(\exists t$$
$$\in [t_b, t_e] \text{inside}(R, f_{PMC^{\tau}}(t), t)$$

$$\text{Definitely\_Always\_Inside}(\tau, R, t_b, t_e) \equiv (\forall f_{PMC^{\tau}})(\forall t$$
$$\in [t_b, t_e] \text{inside}(R, f_{PMC^{\tau}}(t), t)$$

Since the large length of trajectories and the complexity of the city road, the traditional algorithm NWA cannot be used in the anonymization of large-scale Milan dataset. Thus, the experiment on the distortion degree of range query only used SC-TDP algorithm. The value of δ is set to different values to make comparison. In the experiment, we take different values of uncertainty value k and δ to compute the distortion degree of range query, and δ is set to 200, 400 and 600.

From Figs. 1 and 2, it can be seen that both the error rate of PSI and DAI grows up with the increase of value k. Possibly_Sometime_Inside range queries have a distortion below 1 for all values of k and δ. For Definitely_Always_Inside range queries, the distortion introduced grows to above 1 for all the different δ when k = 50. We can also see that, the error rate grows up for smaller value of δ.

From the experiments result of running time and the range query error rate, we can conclude that our proposed algorithm can gain in efficiency without paid in terms of the quality of anonymization.

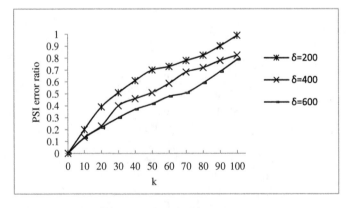

Fig. 1. Possibly_Sometime_Inside range query error rate

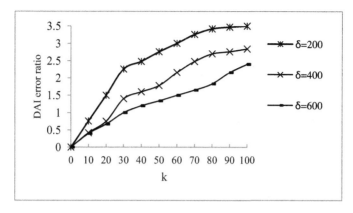

Fig. 2. Definitely_Always_Inside range query error rate

5 Conclusions

Nowadays, privacy preserving data publishing is receiving widespread attention. In this article, we addressed the anonymous problem of publishing large-scale trajectory database. We introduced the technique of dividing the original track database into blocks, and proposed a segment-clustering based privacy preserving algorithm which turned the trajectory segment problem into the optimization problem based MDL. Our proposed algorithm guaranteed the characteristic diversity of the trajectories by dividing the trajectories into segments before clustering them. To evaluate the performance of our proposed algorithm, we conducted the experimental study on both synthetic datasets and real datasets. The results demonstrated that our approach can ensure the quality of the data and the anonymous efficiency while preserving the privacy of the users.

Acknowledgement. This work is supported by Fundamental Research Funds for the Central Universities (N130316001, N140404006) and the National Natural Science Foundation of China under Grant No. 61173027.

References

1. Elahe, G.K., Mahdi, A., Fatemeh, D.: PPTD: preserving personalized privacy in trajectory data publishing by sensitive attribute generalization and trajectory local suppression. Knowl.-Based Syst. **94**, 43–59 (2016)
2. Huo, Z., Meng, X.F.: A survey of trajectory privacy preserving techniques. Chin. J. Comput. **34**(10), 1820–1830 (2011)
3. Chen, R., Xiao, Q., Zhang, Y.: Differentially private high-dimensional data publication via sampling-based inference. In: 21st ACM SIGKDD Conference on Knowledge Discovery and Data Mining (SIGKDD), pp. 129–138. ACM Press, Sydney (2015)
4. Parmar, S., Gupta, M.P.: A comparative study and literature survey on privacy preserving data mining techniques. Int. J. Comput. Sci. Mob. Comput. **4**(4), 480–486 (2015)

5. Zhang, L., Cormode, G., Procopiuc, C.M., Srivastava, D.: PrivBayes: private data release via Bayesian networks. In: ACM SIGMOD International Conference on Management of Data, pp. 1423–1434. ACM Press, Snowbird (2014)

6. Gidofalvi, G., Huang, X., Pedersen, T.B: Privacy-preserving data mining on moving object trajectories. In: International Conference on Mobile Data Management, pp. 60–68. IEEE Press, Mannheim (2007)

7. Yarovoy, R., Bonchi, F., Lakshmanan, L.V.S.: Anonymizing moving objects: how to hide a MOB in a crowd. In: 12th International Conference on Extending Database Technology, pp. 72–83. ACM Press, Saint Petersburg (2009)

8. Hoh, B., Gruteser, M., Xiong, H.: Achieving guaranteed anonymity in GPS Traces via uncertainty-aware path cloaking. IEEE Trans. Mob. Comput. **9**(8), 1089–1107 (2010)

9. Nergiz, M.E., Atzori, M., Saygin, Y.: Towards trajectory anonymization: a generalization-based approach. In: SIGSPATIAL ACM GIS 2008 International Workshop on Security and Privacy in GIS and LBS, pp. 52–61. ACM Press, Irvine (2008)

10. Abul, O., Bonchi, F., Nanni, M.: Anonymization of moving objects databases by clustering and perturbation. Inf. Syst. **35**(8), 884–910 (2010)

11. Sweeney, L.: k-anonymity: a model for protecting privacy. Int. J. Uncertainty Fuzziness Knowl.-Based Syst. **10**(5), 557–570 (2002)

12. Arunkuma, S., Srivatsac, M., Rajarajan, M.: A review paper on preserving privacy in mobile environments. J. Netw. Comput. Appl. **53**, 74–90 (2015)

13. Abul, O., Bonchim, F., Nanni, M.: Never walk alone: uncertainty for anonymity in moving objects databases. In: 24th IEEE International Conference on Data Engineering (ICDE 2008), pp. 376–385. IEEE Press, Cancún (2008)

14. Khalil, A.H., Benjamin, C.M.F., William, K.C.: Privacy-preserving trajectory stream publishing. Data Knowl. Eng. **94**, 89–109 (2014)

15. Sashi, G.R., Dan, L., Wei, J., Ali, H., Rui, Z.: Traffic information publication with privacy preservation. ACM Trans. Intell. Syst. Technol. **5**(3), 1–26 (2014)

16. Grunwald, P.D., Myung, I.J., Pitt, M.A.: Advances in Minimum Description Length: Theory and Applications, pp. 20–28. MIT Press, Cambridge (2005)

17. Brinkhoff, T.: Generating traffic data. IEEE Data Eng. Bull. **26**(2), 19–25 (2003)

A Trust System for Detecting Selective Forwarding Attacks in VANETs

Suwan Wang$^{(\boxtimes)}$ and Yuan He

School of Software and TNLIST, Tsinghua University, Beijing, China
suwan_wang@163.com, he@greenorbs.com

Abstract. Vehicular ad-hoc Networks (VANETs) have inherent high mobility and take data forwarding as a basic mechanism to share information among vehicles. Selective forwarding attack, in which malicious nodes deliberately drop data packets, destroys the integrity of data and hurts the validity of real VANETs applications. Because malicious nodes usually masquerade themselves as normal nodes and collude with each other whenever possible, it is hard to obtain clear and direct evidence of selective forwarding attacks. In this paper, we address the issue of detecting selective forwarding attacks by building a trust system. The proposed approach to maintain this system mainly includes (1) local and global detection of attacks based on mutual monitoring among all nodes, and (2) detection of abnormal driving patterns of malicious nodes. Since both in-band and out-band information is utilized, our approach is effective in relatively low-density road conditions and resilient to various scenarios, such as different rate of malicious occurrence or different road's range. The extensive simulations demonstrate that our approach achieves a high fault tolerance by choosing most reliable nodes for information delivery, while at the same time identify malicious nodes with relatively high accuracy.

Keywords: VANETs · Selective forwarding attack · Detection · Driving pattern

1 Introduction

With rapid progress in wireless communication and mobile network, Vehicular Ad-hoc Network (VANET) has become an important and basic part in modern intelligent transportation systems. In VANETs, important information, e.g. accidents, can be disseminated to all vehicular nodes through the ad-hoc networks [1], so as to ensure driving safety, to improve transportation efficiency, or to provide data communication services [2, 3]. Efficient data delivery is clearly a key technique for service provisioning in VANETs applications.

Due to the mobile ad-hoc nature of VANETs, the vehicular nodes usually rely on multi-hop forwarding [4] to transmit data. Note that the vehicular nodes usually move at a flexible context. The data forwarding among them is thus vulnerable to various network attacks.

© Springer International Publishing Switzerland 2016
Y. Wang et al. (Eds.): BigCom 2016, LNCS 9784, pp. 377–386, 2016.
DOI: 10.1007/978-3-319-42553-5_32

A typical attack is selective forwarding [6]. By masquerading itself as a normal node, a malicious node is able to hijack the forwarded data and then randomly or selectively drops the data packets. Therefore the downstream nodes of that malicious node cannot receive integrated data, probably causing not only unpredictable but serious consequences.

Because malicious nodes usually masquerade themselves as normal nodes and collude with each other whenever possible, it is hard to obtain clear and direct evidence of selective forwarding attacks. At the same time, the forwarded data traffic is highly dynamic and hard to control under network-wide inconsistence. As a result, general techniques to detect malicious attacks in VANETs often fail to identify the behavior of selective forwarding. The existing proposals to detect forwarding attacks usually require global information and incur intensive communication cost, which cannot be applied to real large-scale VANETs.

In order to address the above issue, we in this paper propose a trust-based system [7] for detecting selective forwarding attacks. The insight behind our design is that selective forwarding attack must have direct or indirect reflections in a VANETs. The direct reflection refers to the apparent gap between the outgoing and incoming data traffic on a malicious node, which can be detected by mutual monitoring among vehicular nodes or between vehicular nodes and Road Side Units (RSU). The indirect reflection refers to the abnormal driving patterns of a malicious node. Driven by the purpose of maximizing its destructive impact, a malicious node is always apt to stay longer in the less monitoring areas of VANETs, thus, they tend to reduce speed for longer remain. Such tendency can be punished by monitoring nodes' risks of making bad influence.

Aiming at above observations, we propose to utilize both in-band and out-band information for detecting selective forwarding attacks in VANETs. Our contributions can be summarized as follows.

1. We propose a trust system to detect forwarding attacks, in which both in-band and out-band information of vehicle nodes are utilized. This makes our proposal applicable in different real scenarios based on the assumption we propose later.
2. We propose to monitor the movements of nodes and detect malicious nodes according to their abnormal driving patterns. As far as we know, we are the first to propose such a behavior-based approach for detecting selective forwarding attacks in VANETs.
3. We carry out extensive simulations to evaluate our approach. The results demonstrate that our approach achieves a high fault tolerance for real practice, and reduce the chances for potential malicious nodes to make a wide influence.

The rest of this paper is organized as follows. In Sect. 1 we briefly introduce related works and discuss the difference between them and our work. Section 2 introduces models and assumptions used in this paper. Section 3 elaborates on our design in detail, followed the evaluation results in Sect. 4. We conclude our work and discuss the future work in Sect. 5.

2   Models and Assumptions

The work is based on three models, dissemination model, selective forwarding attack model and trust model. It makes use of the selective forwarding attack model in [5, 6] to identify how selective forwarding nodes really behave. And then it classifies all vehicles with the help of trust model in [7], It also illustrates monitoring process based on disseminating theory described in [8–10] to explain how packets are forwarded in a multi-hop forwarding manner.

2.1   Dissemination Model

In our proposal, every road is divided into several blocks, its length equaling to specific geographical radius that be set in advance. Therefore, every block is geographically localized. Then we regulate that the vehicle closest to the center of geographical block with the highest trust value is chosen as center sender, which disseminates messages to all nodes within its covering range (a cell) and noted by small circles in Fig. 1. For data centers, they could utilize their GPS localization method and beaconing messages to make sure whether they stay at the surroundings of the assigned center point while being monitored by neighbors. After receiving the information from neighboring block, it continuously forwards packets in broadcast way and chooses the farthest node who are highly reliable as the next hop, which could form a route to reach the center of next block.

2.2   Selective Forwarding Attack Model

In VANETs, It's important to disseminate data packets timely and accurately. However, communications across nodes could be easily interrupted by selective forwarding attack. Most of the selective forwarding nodes tend to randomly discard some packets.

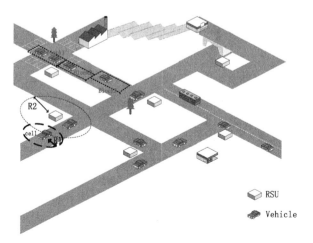

Fig. 1. Data propagation based on vehicle's cell model.

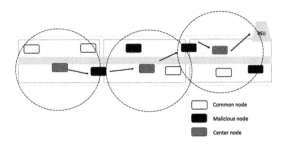

Fig. 2. Distribution features of malicious vehicles. (Color figure online)

Only a minority of nodes tend to discard all packets completely. Both behaviors above would risk the system stability and data integrity. Our work summarizes its definitions and behavior features of selective forwarding attacks as follows [6].

- The traffic a malicious node exports is always less than what they receive.
- The malicious tend to collude with each other by choosing a place to do the crime, which is shown in Fig. 2, malicious nodes are aggregate at the intersection point of two blocks.

2.3   Trust Model

According to [7], we use GTA to administer nodes' registration license, When a new vehicle firstly appears in the field administrated by GTA, it should report news to a nearest RSU, which help retransmits new coming news to GTA. After acquiring new vehicle's registration information, GTA will assign a specific ID number and storage space to save confidence value, which is usually initialed by a score 20 when a new-registration vehicle comes. GTA is what we rely on to update trust value, keep confidence records and eliminate nodes with low level scores.

As Table 1 shows, new coming vehicle belongs to C_2 level, C_1 level nodes with unreliable trust values should be eliminated from the system. C_6 level nodes have a static trust value which could sometimes replace RSU to broadcast reliable messages.

Table 1. Trust-based nodes' classification

Classification	Trust value range	Node description
C_1	$T_a < 0$	Malicious node
C_2	$0 < T_a \leq 20$	New coming vehicle node
C_3	$20 < T_a \leq 40$	Node with low trust value
C_4	$40 < T_a \leq 60$	Common node
C_5	$60 \leq T_a < 80$	Node with high trust value
C_6	$80 \leq T_a < 100$	Monitors with static trust

2.4 Assumptions

- According to [11], RSU could have highest efficiency for monitoring and recording by setting themselves on every crossing of the road. This arrangement could help realize a large coverage of monitoring.
- Considering that our work aims at area with low density, which means that the influence brought by congestion is modest.
- In the whole network system, the amount of malicious nodes are far less than that of common nodes.

3 Method Design

In this part, through taking collusion as consideration and enlarging the amount of monitoring vehicles, it intensify the monitoring strength and complement the short-comings of the original model.

3.1 Intensive Monitoring Detection

Block-Based Local Detection: Process Description. It's easy to find in Fig. 2 that when a node gets into covering range of the center node, selective forwarding attack become so difficult, since they are supervised by authorized center nodes and all pre-listener. However, when a node gets out of the center node's covering range, it may cause a great amount of data lost since nodes at the edge could possibly become a transmitting node and easily avoid being monitored, situation would become worse when malicious nodes collectively broadcast news to an unknown area, which may cause emergent messages losing its efficiency. Therefore, it is not realistic to depend on neighbors' reports alone. Therefore, some proposed strategies are listed as follows.

- When the forwarding messages are disseminated inside the covering range of center node. All nodes could receive the broadcast information coming from the center but only let the farthest node disseminate messages, while at the same time being monitored by its neighbors.
- When the messages' dissemination is out of the covering range of the center. The information coming from retransmitting nodes is validated by all its neighbors, if it cheats, all receivers on the edge broadcasting complete information heard from prior center.

Thus, when malicious nodes standing at the intersection of the geographical division try to collude with others to drop packets. Compulsive command of all broadcasting guarantees some correct messages could be disseminated.

Block-Based Local Detection: Calculation Principle. During calculation process, RSU and GTA are used for recording and calculating separately. RSU will distribute

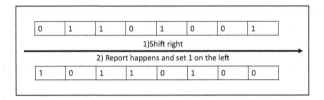

Fig. 3. Illustration of RSU's record process for report.

8-bit spaces for a node reported by others to record its history, while GTA will extract all information stored in RSUs after a certain period and calculates for nodes' trust value and decides whether they should stay or leave.

In RSU, when a node a_i announce a report for node a_j, most significant bit of a_i's reported space would be set a 1 (just as Fig. 3 shows). If it doesn't exist any report during certain period of time, the whole 8-bit will shift right and then set a 0 at most significant bit. What worth to emphasize here is that when this space value maintains 0 for a long time, RSU could cancel the assignment for a_j to save space. For nodes which had ever judged others, RSU still needs to assign 8-bit space to record history in order to reward judgment involved nodes, which shares the same recording approach with reported nodes.

In GTA, after a certain period of time, it will automatically abstract all records values from RSUs, and reduce trust value for every vehicle node which is reported based on Formulas (1) and (2), while increasing the trust value of monitoring nodes as rewards. Rewarding process is similar to the punishment, which is shown Formula (3), then corresponding scores would be add as a reward. (In this experiment, we treat a_i as a node was reported, a_j is a node proposing a report).

Transmitting RSU's record to a punishment rate:

$$rate(a_i) = \frac{(10011101)_2}{2^8} \tag{1}$$

Reducing trust value of a_i:

$$T_{a_i} = T_{a_i} - rate(a_i)^*35^*(T_{a_j}/100) \tag{2}$$

Transmitting RSU's record to a rewarding rate:

$$rate(a_j) = \frac{(00001000)_2}{2^8} \tag{3}$$

Here are two special points that should be further explained.

- The report given by C_6 level node or RSU should be taken as a highly trustable evidence and render fierce punishment.
- RSUs should upload their records every few minutes. The interval should be less than 8 times of right-shift interval to ensure timely and accurate calculation.

Risk-based Global Detection. We plan to improve the reliability of news by using multi-path rebroadcasting strategies. However, problems of collusion still risks the security of the system. Thus, we try to utilize the risky rate to judge whether a node is reliable or not.

For a node N_i monitored by nodes $\{N_1, N_2, \ldots, N_n\}$ sending news to nodes $\{M_1, M_2, \ldots, M_n\}$ at position *Pos*, $\{M_1, M_2, \ldots, M_n\}$ will document **where** this news coming from and **where** the position is in the form of a vector: *{pos, source, receive}*, here *pos* represents the position, *source* represents the source of the receiving news, and *receive* is a value equals to 2 which represents they are the nodes receiving some news from N_i. Besides, $\{N_1, N_2, \ldots, N_n\}$ will also document N_i 's behavior at the time when N_i is sending news, and they will judge N_i's behavior in the form of another vector: *{pos, monitor, judge}*, here *pos* represents the position, *monitor* documents the vehicle ID of the sender node that they were keeping watch on, and *judge* is a value which documents the judgment of N_i, which would be given a value 1 as a report, a value −1 for none malicious. Finally, RSU will collect all information of this road and store them in the form of a matrix.

3.2   Detection Method Based on Driving Patterns

According to the description of selective forwarding attacks, behaviors of malicious nodes is quite different with that of common nodes, which means they are likely to perform an abnormal driving pattern from aspects of traces or speeds.

Therefore, algorithm is designed here to describe the situation when a vehicle node N_i tends to retransmit a message from a prior hop at position *pos*. Firstly, all nodes nearby have to document some location information for N_i. For neighbors that are responsible for monitoring, they need to make judgment and make it deliver to RSU. But for neighbors who can only get the message from N_i, they need to memorize N_i as their information source and inform RSU. Besides, all neighbors at *pos* need to make a measurement about speeds for each other. When RSU gets all information, it synthesizes them and submits data to GTA periodically and get some feedback. Finally, N_i may get a certification that approves its reliability or be challenged to reduce its trust value.

4   Performance Evaluation

4.1   Introduction of Simulation Process

We use MATLAB to simulate vehicles' movement. The simulation regulates that roads only have directions of East-West and South-North with two-way paths. Each car is assigned to a special ID number and randomly distributed in different blocks. For reporting process, we design a reporting matrix with its row ID representing judgers and column ID representing nodes being judged. The judged node would be given a 1 if it is malicious, and given a 0 if is benign. The recording data is organized in a matrix structure which is suitable for speed monitoring and being collected by RSU.

There are some controllable parameters in our experiment:

- Numbers of methods which are taken into detection process (numbers are between 1 and 2).
- Inspection time period of Detection process.
- Numbers of vehicles in this field, number of streets and avenues.
- Occurrence probability and speed of malicious nodes.
- Intensity of GTA's punishment in each method.

4.2   Results Analysis

Firstly, we compare the difference between methods of using report only and method containing driving pattern detection. And then we try to find out whether slower speed pattern would be a considerable focus than any other features. The results are shown in Figs. 4, 5, and 6 successively. Through obeying the instructions described in Sect. 3.2 vehicles' trust values are updated according to the records.

As results shown in Fig. 4, the malicious represents a high probability to delivery packets at intersections. And for results of "monitoring risk rate" methods that are shown in Figs. 4, 5, and 6, malicious nodes' speed is purposely reduced or added, in order to find out whether an abnormal speed would influence the amount of transmitting packets. It's easy to find out packets amount increases a lot when vehicles were speeding up at the intersection of blocks than that when vehicles were slowing down. Therefore, it indicates that we should focus more on higher speed nodes than on slower speed nodes.

Figure 5 shows the results of nodes' average risks of different driving pattern. However, slower speed vehicles get a higher risk rate this time, which means slower vehicles are more dangerous when transmitting messages, since it would always affect a wide area while not being completely monitored. Figure 6 supports the assumption, higher speed nodes' trust values are highly decreased to a level similar to using report method alone. So risky rate detection is working for high-speed ones, but it still not good enough for slower ones.

4.3   Illustration of Other Parameters

After testing the effectiveness of proposed methods by experiments, we decide to change other controllable parameters in order to seek a best performance in different situations.

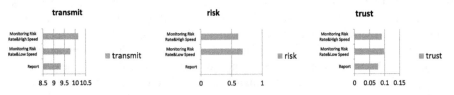

Fig. 4. Comparison of transmitting number

Fig. 5. Comparison of nodes' risk

Fig. 6. Comparison of trust value

(1) Firstly, increasing the coverage range of GTA management. The results are shown in Figs. 7 and 8;

(2) Next, increasing vehicles' number. It is aimed to test the support limit of the vehicles in the system. In our experiment, vehicle number rises tenfold;

(3) Lastly, detection period is extended from 1 h to 5 h.

As a real-time system, it should preferentially focus on how to ensure a high stability and sustain a peaceful environment rather than detect as many malicious nodes as possible. Therefore, in Fig. 8, we use malicious nodes' risk rate, trust value and transmitting number which are collected from 1 h detection to illustrate the difference. By comparing different conditions, trust value reduction and risky rate is intuitively used for judging whether a malicious node can do great harm to a system.

Results in Fig. 7 tell us that when detection area become larger, reporting rate and risks rate decrease a lot, it impacts the judgment between each other and cause a slight increase of malicious average trust value. And for a traffic-density area, for example, with 10000 on-road vehicles, malicious nodes get a chance to be highly risky since they get lots of chances to become transmitting nodes.

Figure 8 shows that our methods get a relatively high false positive rate since our methods treat slow-speed nodes as candidates of the malicious, however, it won't damage the trust system due to existence of the rewarding mechanism. When we compare the result of vehicle number equals to 10000 or the result of time equals to 300 min with comparison group, it is found that when detection area is denser, malicious nodes behavior is harder to be captured, which causes false positive rate to increase. However, the longer detection time performs better since it increases the probability for GTA to recognize the truth.

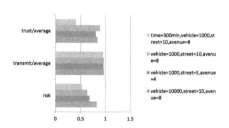

Fig. 7. Methods performance under different conditions (Color figure online)

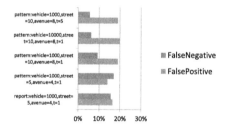

Fig. 8. False negative and false positive with different parameter (Color figure online)

5 Conclusion and Future Work

Selective forwarding is a critical challenge to real VANETs systems. Our work is aimed at solving present contradictions between detection accuracy and system's false tolerance. We take advantage of vehicles' behavior patterns, which could reveal their identities, namely normal vs. malicious. The simulation results demonstrate the effectiveness of our approach with respect to different performance metrics.

This work mainly focuses on real-time data packets' dissemination. Attacks to the general communication process is not fully addressed, and these issues will be included in our next step of study. In order to guarantee the security of whole network, protocols for packets dissemination [3] under attacks should also be redesigned, so as to satisfy the demand of keeping system's availability and robustness.

Acknowledgments. The authors would like to thank the anonymous reviewers for the helpful comments and suggestions. This work was supported in part by the NSF of China under grant No. 61422207, No. 61472382.

References

1. Lin, X., Lu, R., Zhang, C.: Security in vehicular ad hoc networks. In: Proceedings of the IEEE Communications Magazine, pp. 88–95 (2008)
2. Rahman, S.U., Hengartner, U.: Secure crash reporting in vehicular ad hoc networks. In: IEEE SecureComm, pp. 443–452 (2007)
3. Hartenstein, H., Laberteaux, K.P.: A tutorial survey on vehicular ad hoc networks. In: Proceedings of IEEE Communications Magazine, pp. 164–171 (2008)
4. Tseng, Y.T., Jan, R.H., Chen, C.: A vehicle-density-based forwarding scheme for emergency message broadcasts in VANETs. In: IEEE Mobile Adhoc and Sensor Systems (MASS), pp. 703–708, 8–12 2010
5. Wu, K., Li, H., Wang, L., et al.: hJam: attachment transmission in WLANs. In: IEEE Mobile Computing, pp. 2334–2345 (2013)
6. Yu, B., Xiao, B.: Detecting selective forwarding attacks in wireless sensor networks. In: IEEE IPDPS, pp. 25–29 (2006)
7. Monir, M.B., El Aziz, M.H.A., Hamid, A.A.A.: A trust-based message reporting scheme for VANET. In: Proceedings of International Journal of Emerging Technology and Advanced Engineering, pp. 276–394 (2013)
8. Yan, G., Olariu, S., Weigle, M.C.: Providing VANET security through active position detection. In: Proceedings of IEEE Computer Communications, pp. 2883–2897 (2008)
9. Raya, M., Aziz, A., Hubaux, J.P.: Efficient secure aggregation in VANETs. In: Proceedings of the 3rd International Workshop on Vehicular Ad Hoc Networks, pp. 67–75 (2006)
10. Wang, L., Wu, K., Xiao, J., et al.: Harnessing frequency domain for cooperative sensing and multi-channel contention in CRAHNs. In: IEEE Wireless Communications, pp. 440–449 (2014)
11. Sun, Y., Zhang, B., Zhao, B., et al.: Mix-zones optimal deployment for protecting location privacy in VANET. Peer-to-Peer Netw. Appl. **8**(6), 1108–1121 (2015)

Certificateless Key-Insulated Encryption: Cryptographic Primitive for Achieving Key-Escrow Free and Key-Exposure Resilience

Libo He[✉], Chen Yuan, Hu Xiong, and Zhiguang Qin

School of Information and Software Engineering,
University of Electronic Science and Technology of China,
Chengdu 610054, Sichuan, China
libowqrs@gmail.com, yuanchenincn@gmail.com, {xionghu,qinzg}@uestc.edu.cn

Abstract. Certificateless encryption (CLE) alleviates the heavy certificate management in traditional public key encryption and the key escrow problem in the ID-based encryption simultaneously. Current CLE schemes assumed that the user's secret key is absolutely secure. Unfortunately, this assumption is too strong in case the CLE is deployed in the hostile setting and the leakage of a secret key is inevitable. In this paper, we present a new concept called a certificateless key-insulated encryption scheme (CL-KIE). We argue that this is an important cryptographic primitive that can be used to achieve key-escrow free and key-exposure resilience. We also present an efficient CL-KIE scheme based on bilinear pairing. After that, the security of our scheme is proved under the Bilinear Diffie-Hellman assumption in the random oracle model.

Keywords: Bilinear pairing · Certificateless cryptography · Key-insulated

1 Introduction

1.1 Motivation and Related Work

In a traditional public key cryptosystem, every user owns a pair of a public key which will be published and publicly accessible and a private key which will be preserved by the user himself. In 1978, Rivest et al. [14], who first publicly published the RSA algorithm whose security is relied on practical difficulty of factoring the product of two large prime number. It is the first practical Public Key Encryption in nowadays. ElGama algorithm is another widely used public key cryptography which is based on the Diffie-Hellman key exchange. It was described by ElGamal [15] in 1985. The public key cryptosystem needs Public Key Infrastructure(PKI) to offer the authentication and validation for the public key. But PKI will encounter a lot of challenges on efficiency and scalability for its complicated structure. In 1984, the Identity-based Encryption has been proposed by Shamir [1]. By this approach, the private key generated in Key

© Springer International Publishing Switzerland 2016
Y. Wang et al. (Eds.): BigCom 2016, LNCS 9784, pp. 387–395, 2016.
DOI: 10.1007/978-3-319-42553-5_33

Generation Center(KGC) could be arbitrary characters related to users identity. So the certificate will not be necessary but the key escrow problem arises that the malicious authority can impersonate any users to get the corresponding private key. In 2001, Boneh and Franklin [16] proposed an identity-based encryption system based on Weil pairing over elliptic curves and finite fields. Based on the rapid calculation of the bilinear pairing, the identity-based encryption becomes a research hotspot since then. To solve the problem of key escrow in Identity-based Encryption and avoid the use of certificates to guarantee the authenticity of public keys in Public Key Encryption, the Certificateless Public Key Encryption(CL-PKE) has been introduced by Al-Riyami and Paterson [2] in 2003. In CL-PKE, the private key is separated into two parts: one partial private key is still generated in KGC, and the secret key is selected by the user himself. The malicious KGC only can get the partial private key, hence, the Certificateless Public Key Encryption solves the problems of key escrow. Since then, several other relevant certificateless schemes [4–9] have been developed.

The leakage of a private key is the devastating disaster for the public key cryptosystem since it means all security guarantees are lost. To avoid key exposure, Dodis et al. proposed the notion of key-insulated security in 2002 [3]. In their approach, the private key is composed of two parts: one part is generated by the master key and the other is created by the helper key from a physically-secure device. The lifetime of the private key is divided into N time periods and the private key is updated in every time period with the help of the helper key. Meanwhile, the public key is maintained during the whole key updating. By this approach, even the adversary who steals the private key in the present time period can not get the private key in the former or later period. It solves the problem of leakage of private key successfully to some extent.

Since then, key-insulated security has attracted much attentions and a lot of primitives for encryption [10–13] have been described. However, none of the prior key-insulated encryptions is constructed on CL-PKE. Current CL-PKE schemes assumed that the user's secret key is absolutely secure. Unfortunately, this assumption is too strong in case the CL-PKE is deployed in the hostile setting and the leakage of a secret key is inevitable. To alleviate this problem, we construct a new scheme which integrates CL-PKE and key-insulated notion. So this new scheme will not only prevent attacks from the malicious KGC but also avoid the leakage of the private key.

1.2 Contribution

In this paper, we present a new concept called a certificateless key-insulated encryption scheme (CL-KIE). We argue that this is an important cryptographic primitive that can be used to achieve key-escrow free and key-exposure resilience. We also present an efficient CL-KIE scheme based on bilinear pairing. After that, the security of our scheme is proved under the Bilinear Diffie-Hellman assumption in the random oracle model.

2   Formal Definition and Security Model

The proposed scheme is based on the bilinear pairing over the elliptic curve and finite field. The related security assumption is built on the Bilinear Diffie-Hellman problem. In this section, we formalize the definition of our new scheme CL-KIE and give a security model for the CL-KIE scheme.

2.1   Definition of CL-KIE

We formalize the CL-KIE (Certificateless Key Insulated Encryption) scheme, which consists of the following algorithms:

- **Setup:** The algorithm is given a security parameter k regarded as the security parameter, and returns $params$ (system parameters), a `master-key` and a `helper-key`. The system parameters include a description of a finite message space $\mathcal{M}$, a description of a finite ciphertext space $\mathcal{C}$ and a randomness space $\mathcal{R}$.
- **SecretValExtract:** The algorithm takes as input $params$ and an identity string ID_A and returns a random $x_A \in Z_q$ as the secret value associated with the entity A.
- **PartialKeyExtract:** The algorithm takes as input $params$, `master-key`, and an identity string $ID_A \in \{0,1\}^*$, and returns a partial private key D_A associated to ID_A.
- **HelperKeyUpdate:** The algorithm takes as input $params$, a time period i, `helper-key`, an identity string ID_A, and returns the helper key $HK_{A,i}$ at a time period i.
- **PrivateKeyUpdate:** The algorithm takes as input $params$, a time period i, the helper key $HK_{A,i}$, an identity string ID_A, the partial private key D_A and the secret value x_A, and outputs the private key $S_{A,i}$ at a time period i.
- **PublicKeyExtract:** The algorithm takes as input $params$, the secret value x_A and an identity string ID_A, and outputs a public key P_A of the entity A.
- **Encrypt:** The algorithm takes as input a time period i, $params$, ID_A, P_A and $M \in \mathcal{M}$. It returns a ciphertext $C \in \mathcal{C}$.
- **Decrypt:** The algorithm takes as input a time period i, $params$, $S_{A,i}$ and a ciphertext C. It returns the corresponding plaintext $M \in \mathcal{M}$.

2.2   Security Model

In this subsection, we give the the security model defined in Indistinguishability of Encryption Against Adaptive Chosen Ciphertext Attacker (IND-CCA2) game which is conducted between a challenger $\mathcal{S}$ and an adversary $\mathcal{A}$. In our scheme, we define two kind adversaries $TypeI$ adversary ($\mathcal{A}_I$) and $TypeII$ adversary ($\mathcal{A}_{II}$): $\mathcal{A}_I$ represents an external attacker, who can not access the *master-key* and *helper-key*. We allow $\mathcal{A}_I$ can replace the public key for any entity with a value of its choice since the lack of authentication for the public key in our scheme; $\mathcal{A}_{II}$ represents the malicious KGC, who can access the *master-key*.

We prohibit $\mathcal{A}_{II}$ from replacing the public key. First, we give a list of oracles that a general adversary in our scheme may carry out, then we define the IND-CCA2 game of the CL-KIE scheme for two kinds of adversaries respectively.

The list of oracles that a general adversary in CL-KIE may carry out:

– **Partial-Private-Key-Queries(PPK-Queries):** If necessary, $\mathcal{A}$ makes **PPK-Queries** on the identity ID_A, $\mathcal{S}$ returns the partial private key D_A associated with ID_A to $\mathcal{A}$.
– **Helper-Key-Queries(HK-Queries):** $\mathcal{A}$ makes **HK-Queries** on identity ID_A at a time period i, $\mathcal{S}$ returns the helper key $HK_{A,i}$ to $\mathcal{A}$.
– **Secret-Value-Queries(SV-Queries):** If necessary, $\mathcal{A}$ makes **SV-Queries** on the identity ID_A, $\mathcal{S}$ returns the secret value x_A associated with ID_A to $\mathcal{A}$.
– **Public-Key-Queries(PK-Queries):** $\mathcal{A}$ makes **PK-Queries** on the identity ID_A, $\mathcal{S}$ returns the helper key P_A to $\mathcal{A}$.
– **Public-Key-Replace(PK-Replace):** If necessary, $\mathcal{A}$ can repeatedly make **PK-Replace** to set the public key P_A for any value of its choice.
– **Decryption-Queries(Dec-Queries):** $\mathcal{A}$ makes **Dec-Queries** for a ciphertext C on identity ID_A at a time period i. If the recovered redundancy in M is valid, $\mathcal{S}$ returns the associated plaintext M to $\mathcal{A}$.

The IND-CCA2 game for the CL-KIE scheme can be defined between two different Adversaries ($\mathcal{A}_I$ and $\mathcal{A}_{II}$) and the challenger $\mathcal{S}$ as follows:

– **Chosen Ciphertext Security for CL-KIE on $\mathcal{A}_I$**
   • **Setup:** The challenger $\mathcal{S}$ takes as input a security parameter k and execute the **Setup** algorithm. It returns $params$ expect $master\text{-}key$ and $helper\text{-}key$ to $\mathcal{A}_I$.
   • **Phase 1:** $\mathcal{A}_I$ can access a sequence of oracles: **PPK-Queries, HK-Queries, SV-Queries, PK-Replace, Dec-Queries**. These queries may be requested adaptively, and restricted by the rule of adversary behavior.
   • **Challenge:** $\mathcal{A}_I$ outputs two equal-length plaintext $M_0^*, M_1^* \in M$, associated with the challenge identity ID_A^* and a time period i^*. The challenger $\mathcal{S}$ picks a random number $b \in \{0,1\}$, and generates C^* in relation to (i^*, M_b^*, ID^*). C^* is delivered to $\mathcal{A}_I$ as a target challenge.
   • **Phase 2:** $\mathcal{A}_I$ continues to access a sequence of oracles as in Phase 1, and $\int$ responds these queries as in Phase 1.
   • **Guess:** At the end, $\mathcal{A}_I$ outputs a guess $b' \in \{0,1\}$. The adversary wins the game if $b = b'$. We define $\mathcal{A}_I's$ advantage in this game to be $Adv(\mathcal{A}_\mathcal{I}) = 2(Pr[b = b'] - \frac{1}{2})$.
   There are a few restrictions on the $\mathcal{A}_I$ as follows:
   • $\mathcal{A}_I$ is not allowed to extract the private key on ID_A^*.
   • If the public key has been replaced, $\mathcal{A}_I$ is not allowed to request **PPK-Queries** and **HK-Queries** simultaneously.
   • $\mathcal{A}_I$ is not allowed to do the following concurrently: to replace the public key on ID_A^* in Phase 1 and request the **PPK-Queries** and **HK-Queries** on ID_A^* simultaneously at any moment.
   • In Phase 2, $\mathcal{A}_I$ is not allowed to request **Dec-Queries** on ID_A^*.

– **Chosen Ciphertext Security for CL-KIE on $\mathcal{A}_{II}$**
  - **Setup:** The challenger f takes as input a security parameter k and execute the **Setup** algorithm. It returns *params* to $\mathcal{A}_{II}$.
  - **Phase 1:** $\mathcal{A}_{II}$ can access a sequence of oracles: **PPK-Queries, HK-Queries, Dec-Queries**. These queries may be requested adaptively, and restricted by the rule of adversary behavior.
  - **Challenge:** $\mathcal{A}_{II}$ outputs two-equal length plaintext $M_0^*, M_1^* \in M$, associated with the challenge identity ID_A^* and a time period i^*. The challenge $\mathcal{S}$ picks a random number $b \in \{0,1\}$, and generate C^* in relation to (i^*, M_b^*, ID^*). C^* is delivered to $\mathcal{A}_{II}$ as a target challenge.
  - **Phase 2:** $\mathcal{A}_{II}$ continues to access a sequence of oracles as in Phase 1, and $\mathcal{S}$ responds these queries as in Phase 1.
  - **Guess:** At the end, $\mathcal{A}_{II}$ outputs a guess $b' \in \{0,1\}$. The adversary wins the game if $b = b'$. We define $\mathcal{A}_{II}'s$ advantage in this game to be $Adv(\mathcal{A}_{II}) = 2(Pr[b = b'] - \frac{1}{2})$.

There are a few restrictions on the $\mathcal{A}_{II}$ as follows:
  - $\mathcal{A}_{II}$ is not allowed to replace the public key.
  - $\mathcal{A}_{II}$ cannot extract the private key on ID_A^* at any moment.
  - In Phase 2, $\mathcal{A}_I$ is not allowed to request **Dec-Queries** on ID_A^*.

3   KI-CLPKE Scheme

3.1   Bilinear Pairing

– **Bilinear Pairing**
  Let $\mathbb{G}_1$ denotes a cyclic additive group of order q for some large prime q, let $\mathbb{G}_2$ be a cyclic multiplicative group of the same order q, We can make use of a bilinear map:$\hat{e} : \mathbb{G}_1 \times \mathbb{G}_1 \rightarrow \mathbb{G}_2$ above these two groups which must satisfy the following properties:
  - **Bilinearity**
    $\hat{e}(aP, bQ) = \hat{e}(P, Q)^{ab}$
    $\hat{e}(P_1 + P_2, Q) = \hat{e}(P_1, Q)\hat{e}(P_2, Q)$
    $\hat{e}(P, Q_1 + Q_2) = \hat{e}(P, Q_1)\hat{e}(P, Q_2)$
  - **Non-Degeneracy**
    If P is the generator for $\mathbb{G}_1$, $\hat{e}(P, P)$ is the generator for $\mathbb{G}_2$.
  - **Computability**
    For $\forall P, Q \in \mathbb{G}_1$, $\hat{e}(P, Q)$ can be computed through a efficient algorithm in a polynomial-time.
– **Bilinear Diffie-Hellman(BDH) Problem**
  BDHP is for $a, b, c \in \mathbb{Z}_q$, given $P, aP, bP, cP \in \mathbb{G}_1$, to compute abc which satisfies $\hat{e}(P, Q)^{abc} \in \mathbb{G}_2$.

3.2   Construction

- **Setup:** We can randomly select a security parameter $k \in \mathbb{Z}^+$, the Setup algorithm works as follows:

  Step1: Pick two groups $(\mathbb{G}_1, +)$ and $(\mathbb{G}_2, \times)$ of the same prime order q where $|q| = k$. Choose a generator P over $\mathbb{G}_1$ randomly, we can get a bilinear map $\hat{e} : G_1 \times G_1 \to \mathbb{G}_2$.

  Setp2: Choose a random $s \in \mathbb{Z}_q$ to compute $P_{pub} = sP$, the corresponding s can be regarded as the *master-key*: $M_{mk} = s$;

  Choose a random $w \in \mathbb{Z}_q$ to compute $P_{hk} = wP$, the corresponding w can be regarded as the *helper-key*: $M_{hk} = w$.

  Setp3: For some integer $n > 0$,we can select three cryptographic hash functions:
  - $H_1 : \{0,1\}^n \to \mathbb{G}_1$
  - $H_2 : \{0,1\}^n \times \mathbb{Z}^+ \to \mathbb{G}_1$
  - $H_3 : \mathbb{G}_1 \times \mathbb{G}_2 \to \{0,1\}^n$

  The system parameters $params = (\mathbb{G}_1, \mathbb{G}_2, p, \hat{e}, n, P, P_{pub}, P_{hp}, H_1, H_2, H_3)$. The master key $M_{mk} = s$ and the master helper key $M_{hk} = w$.

  The message space is $\mathcal{M} = \{0,1\}^n$, the ciphertext space is $\mathcal{C} = \{0,1\}^n \times \{0,1\}^n$, the randomness space is $\mathcal{R} = \{0,1\}^n$.

- **SecretValExtract**$(params, ID_A)$: Given an identity ID_A and $params$, the algorithm outputs a random $x_A \in Z_q$ as the secret value for the entity A.

- **PartialKeyExtrat**$(params, M_{mk}, ID_A)$: Given an identity $ID_A \in \{0,1\}^*$ of the entity A, $params$ and M_{sk}, the algorithm computes $D_A = sH_1(ID_A)$.

- **HelperKeyUpdate**$(i, ID_A, M_{hk}, params)$: Given an identity string ID_A and a time period $i \in \{0, \ldots, n-1\}$, the helper generates a helper key $HK_{A,i}$ which can help the private key to be updated at the time period $i \in \{0, \ldots, n-1\}$:

$$HK_{A,i} = wH_2(ID_A, i)$$

- **PrivateKeyExtract**$(i, ID_A, HK_{A,i}, params, D_A, x_A)$: Given an identity ID_A, At a time period $i \in \{0, \ldots, n-1\}$, the private key is generated as:

$$S_{A,i} = x_A H_1(ID_A) + D_A + HK_{A,i}$$
$$= x_A H_1(ID_A) + sH_1(ID_A) + wH_2(ID_A, i)$$

  the value $S_{A,i-1}$ will be deleted subsequently.

- **PublicKeyExtract**$(params, x_A, ID_A)$: Given $params$ and x_A, the algorithm outputs $P_A = \langle X_A, Y_A \rangle = \langle x_A P, x_A sP \rangle$.

- **Encrypt**$(i, params, ID_A, P_A, M)$: At a time period $i \in \{0, \ldots, n-1\}$, to encrypt a plaintext $M \in \{0,1\}^n$, the algorithm does:
  1. Check whether the equality $\hat{e}(X_A, sP) = \hat{e}(Y_A, P)$ holds or not. If not, output $\perp$ and abort encryption.
  2. Select a random $r \in Z_q$, $U = rP$.
  3. Compute $\xi = \hat{e}(X_A, rH_1(ID_A))\hat{e}(P_{pub}, rH_1(ID_A))\hat{e}(P_{hk}, rH_2(ID_A, i))$.
  4. Output the ciphertext: $C = \langle i, U, M \oplus H_3(U, \xi) \rangle$.

- **Decrypt**$(i, params, S_{A,i}, C)$: Received the ciphertext $C = \langle i, U, V \rangle$ at the time period $i \in \{0, \ldots, n-1\}$, the algorithm performs the following steps:

1. Compute $\xi' = \hat{e}(U, S_{A,i})$.
2. Compute $M' = V \oplus H_3(U, \xi')$.
3. If the recovered redundancy in M is valid, then accept M' the plaintext.

4   Analysis

4.1   Security Proof

Theorem 1. *Let hash functions H_1, H_2, H_3 be random oracles. In IND-CCA2 game, the CL-KIE scheme against chosen ciphertext attacks for TypeI adversary is secure in the random oracle model, considering the BDH assumption.*

Proof. We first deal with the $TypeI$ adversary A_I. For the first type adversary A_I adversary is an external attacker who can not get the *master-key* and *helper-key*, Given a BDH problem (P, aP, bP, cP), we can construct a challenger $\mathcal{S}$ to compute $\hat{e}(P, P)^{abc}$ by making use of A_I as an adversary. When games begin, $\mathcal{S}$ sets $P_{pub} = aP$ as an instance of BDH problem and simulates hash functions as random oracles. During the simulation, $\mathcal{S}$ needs to guess every bit in target plaintext M_1^* with a time period i^*. $\mathcal{S}$ will set $H_1(ID_A^*) = bP$, $H_2(ID_A^*, i^*) = (h^*,_{i^*} P)$, $V^* = H_3(U^*, \xi^*) = H_3(cP, \xi^*)$. In the challenge phase, $\mathcal{S}$ returns a simulated ciphertext $C^* = (i^*, U^*, V^*)$, which implies the parameter ξ^* is defined as:

$$\xi^* = \hat{e}(X_A, rH_1(ID_A^*))\hat{e}(P_{pub}, rH_1(ID_A^*))\hat{e}(P_{hk}, rH_2(ID_A^*, i^*))$$
$$= \hat{e}(x_A rP, bP)\hat{e}(bP, acP)\hat{e}(wP, r(h^*,_{i^*} P))$$
$$= \hat{e}(P, P)^{abc}\hat{e}(aP, cP)^{x_A}\hat{e}(wP, (h^*,_{i^*})cP)$$

Above all, $\mathcal{S}$ can get the solution to the BDH problem: $\hat{e}(P, P)^{abc} = \xi^*(\hat{e}(aP, cP)^{x_A} \hat{e}(wP, (h^*,_{i^*})cP))^{-1}$. So that,we can prove the security of the scheme for the $TypeI$ adversary through this reduction.

Theorem 2. *Let hash functions H_1, H_2, H_3 be random oracles. In IND-CCA2 game, the CL-KIE scheme against chosen ciphertext attacks for TypeII adversary is secure in the random oracle model, considering the BDH assumption.*

Proof. We secondly deal with the $TypeII$ adversary A_{II}. For the $TypeII$ adversary is a malicious KGC attacker, Given a BDH problem (P, aP, bP, cP), we can construct a challenger $\mathcal{S}$ to compute $\hat{e}(P, P)^{a,b,c}$ by making use of A_{II} as an adversary. When games begin, $\mathcal{S}$ sets $X_A = aP$ as an instance of the BDH problem and simulates hash functions as random oracles. During the simulation, $\mathcal{S}$ needs to guess every bit in target plaintext M_2^* with a time period i^*. $\mathcal{S}$ will set $H_1(ID_A^*) = bP$, $H_2(ID_A^*, i^*) = (h^*,_{i^*} P)$, $V^* = H_3(U^*, \xi^*) = H_3(cP, \xi^*)$. In the challenge phase, $\mathcal{S}$ returns a simulated ciphertext $C^* = (i^*, U^*, V^*)$, which implies the parameter ξ^* is defined as:

$$\xi^* = \hat{e}(X_A, rH_1(ID_A^*))\hat{e}(P_{pub}, rH_1(ID_A^*))\hat{e}(P_{hk}, rH_2(ID_A^*, i^*))$$
$$= \hat{e}(aP, bcP)\hat{e}(bP, cP)^s \hat{e}(wP, r(h^*,_{i^*} P))$$
$$= \hat{e}(P, P)^{abc}\hat{e}(bP, cP)^s \hat{e}(wP, (h^*,_{i^*})cP)$$

Above all, S can get the solution to the BDH problem: $\hat{e}(P,P)^{abc} = \xi^*(\hat{e}(bP,cP)^s \ \hat{e}(wP,(h^*,_{i^*})cP))^{-1}$. So that, we can prove the security of the scheme for the $TypeII$ adversary through this reduction.

4.2   Performance Comparison

We compare the major computational cost of our scheme with certificateless public key cryptography proposed by Al-Riyami and Paterson [2] in Table 1. We assume both the two schemes are implemented on $\mid \mathbb{G}_1 \mid = 160$ bits, $\mid \mathbb{G}_2 \mid = 1024$ bits, $\mid p \mid = 160$ bits and hash value $= 160$ bits. We denote by M the point multiplication in $\mathbb{G}_1$, E the exponentiation in $\mathbb{G}_2$ and P the pairing computation. The other computations are trivial so we can omit them.

Table 1. Performance comparison

	CL-PKE	CL-KIE
PartialKeyExtract	M	$3M$
PubilicKeyExtract	$2M$	$2M$
Encrypt	$M+P+E$	$4M+3P$
Decrypt	P	P

From Table 1, we can see that in the PublicKeyExtract and Decrypt phase our scheme has the same computational cost as the CL-PKE scheme; However in the PrivateKeyExtract and Encrypt phase our scheme is less efficient on executed time compared with the CL-PKE scheme. Because the private key consisting of three parts in our scheme is more complicated than it in CL-PKE. The additional composition of the private key in our scheme can be updated with the time period changed, so our scheme provides the extra security capability that it can alleviate the problem for leakage of private key in hostile practical environment. This is a trade-off between efficiency and security capability.

5   Conclusion

In this paper, we firstly formalized the definition of a CL-KIE scheme based on the bilinear pairing and constructed the security model of the CL-KIE scheme for two different adversaries in IND-CCA2 game respectively. Then we gave the concrete construction of the CL-KIE scheme. After that, we proved the security of our scheme against the IND-CCA2 attacks in the random oracle under the BDH assumption. Finally, we compared the CL-KIE scheme with the CL-PKE scheme both on the security capacity and efficiency. Our scheme can achieve key-escrow free and key-exposure resilience in hostile practical environments.

Acknowledgements. This work was supported in part by the National Natural Science Foundation of China under Grant 61003230, Grant 61370026, Grant 61133016 and Grant 61202445.

References

1. Youngblood, C.: An Introduction to Identity-Based Cryptography. CSEP 590TU (2005)
2. Al-Riyami, S.S., Paterson, K.G.: Certificateless public key cryptography. In: Laih, C.-S. (ed.) ASIACRYPT 2003. LNCS, vol. 2894, pp. 452–473. Springer, Heidelberg (2003)
3. Dodis, Y., Katz, J., Xu, S., Yung, M.: Key-insulated public key cryptosystems. In: Knudsen, L.R. (ed.) EUROCRYPT 2002. LNCS, vol. 2332, p. 65. Springer, Heidelberg (2002)
4. Baek, J., Safavi-Naini, R., Susilo, W.: Certificateless public key encryption without pairing. In: Zhou, J., López, J., Deng, R.H., Bao, F. (eds.) ISC 2005. LNCS, vol. 3650, pp. 134–148. Springer, Heidelberg (2005)
5. Dent, A.W., Libert, B., Paterson, K.G.: Certificateless encryption schemes strongly secure in the standard model. In: Cramer, R. (ed.) PKC 2008. LNCS, vol. 4939, pp. 344–359. Springer, Heidelberg (2008)
6. Libert, B., Quisquater, J.-J.: On constructing certificateless cryptosystems from identity based encryption. In: Yung, M., Dodis, Y., Kiayias, A., Malkin, T. (eds.) PKC 2006. LNCS, vol. 3958, pp. 474–490. Springer, Heidelberg (2006)
7. Liu, J.K., Au, M.H., Susilo, W.: Self-generated-certificate public key cryptography and certificateless signature/encryption scheme in the standard model. In: Proceedings of the 2nd ACM Symposium on Information, Computer and Communications Security (ASIACCS 2007), pp. 302–311. ACM, New York (2007)
8. Sun, Y., Li, H.: Short-ciphertext and BDH-based CCA2 secure certificateless encryption. Sci. China Inf. Sci. **53**(10), 2005–2015 (2010)
9. Yang, W., Zhang, F., Shen, L.: Efficient certificateless encryption withstanding attacks from malicious KGC without using random oracles. Secur. Commun. Netw. **7**(2), 445–454 (2014)
10. Bellare, M., Palacio, A.: Protecting against key exposure: strongly key-insulated encryption with optimal threshold. Appl. Algebra Eng. Commun. Comput. **16**(6), 379–396 (2006)
11. Hsu, C., Lin, H.: An identity-based key-insulated encryption with message linkages for peer-to-peer communication network. TIIS **7**(11), 2928–2940 (2013)
12. Hanaoka, Y., Hanaoka, G., Shikata, J., Imai, H.: Unconditionally secure key insulated cryptosystems: models, bounds and constructions. In: Deng, R.H., Qing, S., Bao, F., Zhou, J. (eds.) ICICS 2002. LNCS, vol. 2513, pp. 85–96. Springer, Heidelberg (2002)
13. Qiu, W., Zhou, Y., Zhu, B., Zheng, Y., Wen, M., Gong, Z.: Key-insulated encryption based key pre-distribution scheme for WSN. In: Park, J.H., Chen, H.-H., Atiquzzaman, M., Lee, C., Kim, T., Yeo, S.-S. (eds.) ISA 2009. LNCS, vol. 5576, pp. 200–209. Springer, Heidelberg (2009)
14. Rivestm, L.R., Shamir, A., Adleman, L.: A method for obtaining digital signatures and public-key cryptosystems. Commun. ACM **21**(2), 120–126 (1978)
15. El Gamal, T.: A public key cryptosystem and a signature scheme based on discrete logarithms. In: Blakely, G.R., Chaum, D. (eds.) CRYPTO 1984. LNCS, vol. 196, pp. 10–18. Springer, Heidelberg (1985)
16. Boneh, D., Franklin, M.: Identity-based encryption from the weil pairing. In: Kilian, J. (ed.) CRYPTO 2001. LNCS, vol. 2139, pp. 213–229. Springer, Heidelberg (2001)

Signal Processing
and Pattern Recognition

A Novel J wave Detection Method Based on Massive ECG Data and MapReduce

Dengao Li$^{(\boxtimes)}$, Wei Ma, and Jumin Zhao

College of Information Engineering, Taiyuan University of Technology,
Taiyuan 030024, China
{lidengao,zhaojumin}@tyut.edu.cn, mawei0203@link.tyut.edu.cn

Abstract. J wave is an ECG sign of many clinical syndrome and the accurate detection about it is conducive to the clinical diagnosis of J wave syndrome. Under the background of ECG big data, a novel J wave detection method based on massive ECG data and MapReduce is proposed, which use data mining technology to detect abnormal ECG signal, especially J wave. Firstly, the characteristic of ECG time and frequency domain signal are extracted, and the information gain of every feature is extracted; then, the decision tree is used to classify and recognize ECG signal; lastly, above process are implemented under the parallel programming model MapReduce so that the massive ECG data can be handled, to detect J wave accurately. In order to test and verify the validity of this method, all the ECG data of MIT-BIH are used to do the experiment, and the results demonstrated that, the accuracy and specificity of the proposed method are satisfactory, which provides a new research mentality for the detection of many clinical syndrome.

Keywords: J wave · Data mining · MapReduce · Decision tree

1 Introduction

The rapid development of Mobile Internet, Internet of Things, social media networks and other related technologies bring major changes to data technology, data applications and data value. Based on the user data, by expanding the datas transparency, sharing and mobility, more multiple correlation analysis was tapped to provide a new way for the various research areas. In terms of healthcare big data, in medical institutions and medical research institutions at home and abroad, the magnitude of accumulate data from bulk collect data in clinical trials is huge [1].

ECG reflects the electrical activity of the heart excited process, its has important reference value for heart basic function and cardiac pathology research [2]. ECG can analysis and identify various possible abnormal heart rhythm; it also reflect the extent and development process of myocardial damage and function structural condition of atrial and ventricular. By the method of signal processing, realize intelligent identification and classification for ECG signal is helpful to

© Springer International Publishing Switzerland 2016
Y. Wang et al. (Eds.): BigCom 2016, LNCS 9784, pp. 399–408, 2016.
DOI: 10.1007/978-3-319-42553-5_34

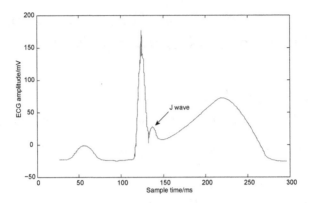

Fig. 1. ECG signal containing J wave

clinical diagnosis. J wave is the dome-shaped or hump-shaped potential changes between the QRS complex and ST segment in ECG. As shown in Fig. 1, the medicine has identified there is a certain relationship between the generate of J waves and some heart disease. J wave syndrome including Early Repolarization Syndrome (ERS), Brugada syndrome, and low-temperature resistance J waves, which may cause malignant ventricular arrhythmias, sudden cardiac death and other major diseases [3]. Currently, J-wave detection technology is still relatively little. Existing methods including Non-Negative Matrix Factorization (NMF) [4], Hidden Markov Model (HMM) [5] and Support Vector Machine (SVM) [6]. These algorithms to some extent realized the J wave detection and identification. However, these papers not combined ECG analysis with the background of big data, but also in terms of accuracy and specificity there is still much room for improvement.

Under the background of the ECG big datathis paper using the feature extraction method and the decision tree classification technology in the theory of data mining to achieve the classification of normal ECG signals and the heart rate abnormal ECG signal, and through the secondary classification of abnormal ECG signal, it can identify the ECG signal which contain the J wave [7]. In addition, to improve J wave recognition efficiency, this article uses the parallel programming model MapReduce to run J wave identification algorithm, with the mass of ECG data to achieve efficient detection of J wave.

2   J wave Detection Method

2.1   Methods Summary

In order to accurately detect the J wave, the paper processing vast amounts of ECG data, using feature extraction machine combine with learning algorithms to achieve classification of J wave, on the other hand, in order to improve the efficiency of data processing, the paper selected parallel programming model

Mapreduce to achieve the above feature extraction and the training process of machine learning algorithms [8], therefore, the flowchart of R-wave detection method proposed in this paper is shown in Fig. 2.

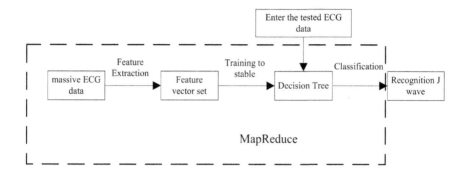

Fig. 2. J wave detection method system diagram

As can be seen from Fig. 2, J-wave detection method proposed in this paper can be divided into J wave detection algorithm based on feature extraction and decision tree, J wave detection algorithm based on Mapreduce parallel implementation of two parts, the proposed method will be described from two parts.

2.2 Detection Method

2.2.1 Feature Extraction

J point and the starting point of the T wave
This paper first interception point for S-T and refined to the point of J to starting point of T wave. The starting point of T wave is the first point of the left slope mutated in T-wave, we use local transformation method to detect T-wave starting point, the basic idea of local transformation method is to put the local start and end point in detection region together into a straight line, and then calculate the difference between the function value for each point and the amplitude value of the corresponding point on the line, Extreme difference is the slope change point of mutation detection zone [9].

Specific detection algorithm is as follows:

(1) Using quadratic spline wavelet decompose ECG signal, and on the basis of QRS complex and T wave is detected, take the area between the S-wave peak point of QRS complex and T wave peak point as S-T segment detection area.

(2) Connect the S-wave peak point and T wave peak point as a straight line, and find the equation of the line:

$$y(n) = x(S_{peak}) + (n - S_{peak}) \frac{x(T_{peak}) - x(S_{peak})}{T_{peak} - S_{peak}} \tag{1}$$

(3) Corresponding to the local transformation equation:

$$D(n) = |x(n) - y(n)| \tag{2}$$

where: $x(n)$ is the horizontal detection area corresponding to ECG signal voltage amplitude for point n, respectively, S_{peak} and T_{peak} corresponding to S-wave peak point and T wave peak point of abscissa.
(4) Find the extreme value of D (n), take extreme point that near S-wave peak as J point, which is the end point of the QRS complex; take extreme point near the peak of the T-wave peak as the starting point of the T-wave.

ECG characteristic points detection is shown in Fig. 3.

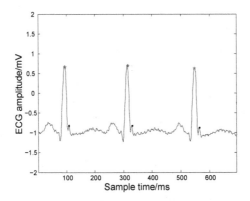

Fig. 3. ECG characteristic points detection

We chose two time domain features from the S-T segment: the amplitude value of the J point and the starting point of the T wave, S-T segment interval.

Extraction ECG power spectrum and cumulative probability
In addition to the above two feature, ECG power spectrum and the cumulative probability have been extracted in this paper. Through a large number of normal and abnormal ECG analysis, we found critical condition between two ECG can be used to distinguish them [10]. Shown in Fig. 4, selected two typical ECG from MIT-BIH database, Fig. 4(a) is the normal ECG, Fig. 4(b) is the abnormal ECG.

By short-time Fourier transformation calculating the power spectrum, and the results show in Fig. 5. We can see that Normal ECG amplitude ranged from −70 to −10, while the amplitude of the signal anomalies between −100 to 0. Secondly, in order to combine with the decision tree, we need to quantify the distribution, so the variance of the power spectrum is calculated, we can see that the variance of the abnormal signal is less than the abnormalities. Through a large number of experiments certification, the power spectrum variance threshold is defined as 153.

When an exception occurs, the ECG will be more uncertainty, so cumulative probability of ECG were also analyzed, as shown in Fig. 6.

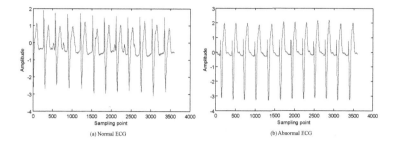

Fig. 4. Two typical ECG signals

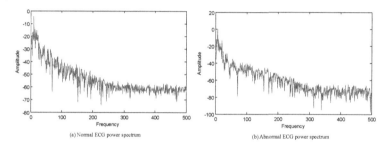

Fig. 5. The power spectrum of two typical ECG signals

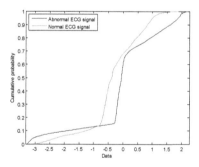

Fig. 6. The cumulative probability of two typical ECG signals (Color figure online)

When the signal amplitude is less than -0.7, the cumulative probability of abnormal ECG signal is greater than normal ECG; and when the amplitude is greater than -0.7, they just the opposite. From the cumulative probability of the trend, whether it is normal ECG or abnormalities, there will be a point mutations, by a large number of experiments, we get that cumulative probability point mutation of a normal ECG in the vicinity of -0.7, and abnormal around -0.2. Ultimately, the critical threshold is defined as -0.5.

2.2.2   C5.0 Decision Tree

C5.0 decision tree algorithm is based on the maximum information gain field to divide the sample data, and the leaves of the tree are cutted or merged to improve the classification accuracy, finally determine the optimal threshold of leaves [11].

C5.0 decision tree algorithm using the information gain of attribute to select attribute, calculated as follows:

Let T as dataset, classification set is $\{C_1, C_2, ..., C_k\}$, select a attribute V to divide T into a plurality of subsets.

Suppose V has n numerical values $\{v_1, v_2, ..., v_n\}$ which do not overlap each other, Then T is divided into n subsets $\{T_1, T_2, ..., T_n\}$, here the value of all instances in T_i are v_i.

Make: $|T|$ is the examples number of dataset T, $|T_i|$ is the examples number of $v = v_i$, $|C_j| = freq(C_j, T)$ is the examples number of class C_j, $|C_j v|$ is the examples number of example $v = v_i$ which is belong to class C_i. There are:

(1) The probability of occurrence for class C_j:

$$P(C_i) = \frac{|C_i|}{|T|} = \frac{freq(C_i, T)}{|T|} \tag{3}$$

(2) The probability of occurrence attribute:

$$P(v_i) = \frac{|T_i|}{|T|} \tag{4}$$

(3) For the examples of attribute $V = v_i$, the conditional probability of having class C_j is:

$$P(C_i \mid v_i) = \frac{|C_j v|}{|T_i|} \tag{5}$$

(4) Entropy of class is:

$$\begin{aligned} H(C) &= -\sum_j P(C_j) log_2(P(C_j)) \\ &= -\sum_j \frac{freq(C,T)}{|T|} \times log_2(\frac{freq(C_j,T)}{|T|}) = info(T) \end{aligned} \tag{6}$$

(5) Segmenting the set T according to the attribute V, then the entropy of class is:

$$\begin{aligned} H(C \mid V) &= -\sum P(v_i) \sum P(C_j \mid v_i) log_2 P(C_j \mid v_i) \\ &= \sum_{i=1}^{n} \frac{|T_i|}{|T|} \times info(T_i) = infov(T) \end{aligned} \tag{7}$$

(6) Information gain, namely mutual information:

$$I(C, V) = H(C) - (C \mid V) = into(T) - infov(T) = gain(V) \tag{8}$$

2.2.3   The Parallel Implementation of J wave Detection Algorithm in MapReduce

From the above we can know that there are use parallel programming model Mapreduce to achieve mass ECG data feature extraction and decision tree training two processes, shown in Fig. 2:

The core of this paradigm is two functions: map and reduce. The map function takes a key-value pair as input, performs the user specified function, and outputs a list of intermediate key-value pairs which may be different from the input. The runtime system groups all the values associated with the same key with shuffle function and forms the input to the reduce function automatically. The Reduce function takes a key-value pair as input, performs the Reduce function, and outputs a list of values. Note that the input values mean the list of all the values associated with the same key.

Considering the detection accuracy and efficiency, the paper set up a parallel procedure Mapreduce to achieve J wave detection algorithm which has been described before, shown in Fig. 7:

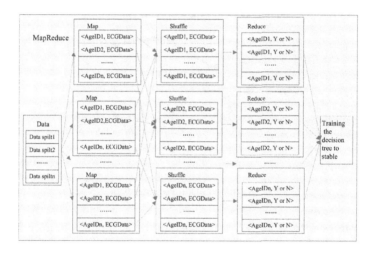

Fig. 7. Structure of MapReduce

In MapReduce, the ECG data acquired from the MIT-BIH database as inputs which are unordered, and when you enter it into blocks, data that come from the same block together into a map function, it is also enters into a compute node, in map function, Age number of individual data recording points in each block of ECG data is extracted, when the map function output, age numbered as <key, value> the key output, thus in the shuffle function process, the same age numbers of ECG was together, in order to be easy for reduce function extraction and train the decision tree in later [12]. Therefore Map function is defined as follows:

Map (data spilt) → <Age ID, ECG data>

In the Reduce function stage, the procession of each node, the same age of ECG data is first extracted, get massive multi-dimensional feature vector set which be used to train decision tree, and ultimately achieve use massive ECG data to train decision tree until its stable, therefore the Reduce function is defined as follows:

Reduce < Age ID, ECG data > → < Age ID, Y or N >

3   Experimental Results

3.1   Feature Information Gain Analysis

Since the decision tree is based on information gain of feature to determines priorities of detected, so, we first analysis the information gain of four feature (the amplitude of J point and T wave outset point (J-T point), S-T interval, power spectrum and cumulative probability), as the Fig. 8 shows.

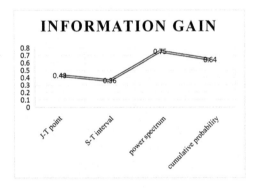

Fig. 8. Information gain analysis

As we can seen from Fig. 8, power spectrum has the maximum information gain, S-T interval has the smallest information gain. By results of the analysis we can build the decision tree for the J wave detection.

3.2   Assessment Detection Algorithm

In order to verify classification performance for the proposed method of this paper, we using three standard metrics: accuracy (AC), sensitivity (SN), specificity (SP).

To test the performance of Decision Tree classifier, all the ECG data of MIT-BIH database are used for training and test. Among them, 50 % of samples are used for training and rest are used for test. Test result of the proposed method is presented in Table 1. It can be seen that the proposed model computed an overall performance that is slightly higher 96 % for the AC, SN and SP measures of performance.

Table 1. The result of the proposed method for J wave detection

Beat type	Samples	Accuracy	Sensitivity	Specificity
Normal	69465	98.54 %	97.23 %	98.12 %
Abnormal	3478	96.14 %	95.27 %	96.51 %
J wave	86	96.23 %	93.14 %	96.75 %

Figure 9 shows a comparison among classification accuracies, sensitivities and specificities of the proposed method, Hidden Markova model (HMM) [5] and Support vector machine (SVM) [6]. As we can see from the results, the proposed method achieves a remarkable classification accuracy rate of 96 % and it is superior to other methods.

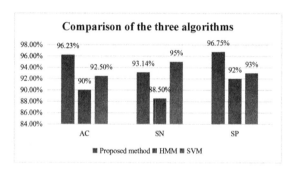

Fig. 9. Comparison of proposed expert system with the studies in the literature (Color figure online)

4   Conclusion

With the continuous development of social medical treatment, the massive data of ECG will face storage and processing problems. This paper in MapReduce platform using data mining decision tree algorithm realize the abnormal heart rhythm -J wave detection and identification at the background of massive data. Firstly, extract the frequency domain feature of ECG signal and set the critical point of classification; Secondly complete the construction of a decision tree by analyzing the information gain of each characteristic; Finally, make the decision tree stable through training, so as to realize the detection of the J wave of ECG signal. By experimental verification, the method of this article reached a very high accuracy. In the future, We will make efforts on the feature extraction and optimization the decision tree. In desirable to provide a more solid rely on clinical diagnosis.

Acknowledgment. This work was supported by National Natural Science Foundation of China (Grant No. 61371062); Scientific Research Project for Shanxi Scholarship Council of China (Grant No. 2013-032); International Cooperation Project of Shanxi Province (Grant No. 2014081029-01).

References

1. Bughin, J., Chui, M., Manyika, J.: Clouds, big data, and smart assets: ten tech-enabled business trends to watch. McKinsey Q. **56**(1), 75–86 (2010)
2. Jacobs, A.: The pathologies of big data. Commun. ACM **52**(8), 36–44 (2009)
3. Antzelevitch, C., Yan, G.X.: J-wave syndromes. From cell to bedside. J. Electro-cardiol. **44**(6), 656–661 (2011)
4. Li, D., Lv, J., Zhao, J., et al.: An effective way of J wave separation based on multilayer NMF. Comput. Math. Methods Med. 2014 (2014)
5. Li, D., Bai, Y., Zhao, J.: A method for automated J wave detection and characteri-sation based on feature extraction. In: Wang, Y., Xiong, H., Argamon, S., Li, X.Y., Li, J.Z. (eds.) BigCom 2015. LNCS, vol. 9196, pp. 421–433. Springer, Heidelberg (2015)
6. Li, D., Liu, X., Zhao, J.: An approach for J wave auto-detection based on support vector machine. In: Wang, Y., Xiong, H., Argamon, S., Li, X.Y., Li, J.Z. (eds.) BigCom 2015. LNCS, vol. 9196, pp. 453–461. Springer, Heidelberg (2015)
7. Tran, H.L., Pham, V.N., Vuong, H.N.: Multiple neural network integration using a binary decision tree to improve the ECG signal recognition accuracy. Int. J. Appl. Math. Comput. Sci. **24**(3), 647–655 (2014)
8. Dean, J., Ghemawat, S.: MapReduce: simplified data processing on large clusters. Commun. ACM **51**(1), 107–113 (2008)
9. Kim, K.H., Bang, S.W., Kim, S.R.: Emotion recognition system using short-term monitoring of physiological signals. Med. Biol. Eng. Comput. **42**(3), 419–427 (2004)
10. Koome, M.E., Bennet, L., Booth, L.C., et al.: Quantifying the power spectrum of fetal heart rate variability. Exp. Physiol. **99**(2), 468–468 (2014)
11. Bujlow, T., Riaz, T., Pedersen, J.M.: A method for classification of network traffic based on C5.0 machine learning algorithm. In: 2012 International Conference on Computing, Networking and Communications (ICNC), pp. 237–241. IEEE (2012)
12. McKenna, A., Hanna, M., Banks, E., et al.: The genome analysis toolkit: a MapRe-duce framework for analyzing next-generation DNA sequencing data. Genome Res. **20**(9), 1297–1303 (2010)

A Decision Level Fusion Algorithm for Time Series in Cyber Physical System

Jinshun Yang[1], Xu Zhang[1(⊠)], and Dongbin Wang[2,3,4]

[1] School of Network Education,
Beijing University of Posts and Telecommunications, Beijing 100876, China
{yangjinshun, selina_zhangx}@bupt.edu.cn
[2] School of Software Engineering,
Beijing University of Posts and Telecommunications, Beijing 100876, China
dbwang@bupt.edu.cn
[3] National Engineering Laboratory for Mobile Network Security,
Beijing University of Posts and Telecommunications, Beijing, China
[4] Key Laboratory of Trustworthy Distributed Computing and Service (BUPT),
Ministry of Education, Beijing, China

Abstract. Cyber-Physical Systems (CPS) is a new intelligent complex system that generates and processes large amounts of data. To improve the ability of information abstraction, data fusion is usually introduced in CPS. Since the characters of CPS are different from the existing system's such as close loop feedback and auto-control in a long term period, the decision level fusion method that has been proposed is hard to migrate to CPS directly. In this paper, a novel multiple decision trees weighting fusion algorithm for time series with internal feedback is proposed in view of the long-term valuable historical data of the CPS. Moreover, simulations using JAVA language are performed on mobile medical platform to validate the algorithm and the results show that the historical data have the ability to influence the decision fusion for making an overall judgment and the system can achieve a stable state.

Keywords: Cyber-Physical Systems (CPS) · Decision level fusion · Multiple decision trees · Time series · Feedback

1 Introduction

Nowadays, data fusion is widely used in all kinds of applications such as robotics, industrial manufacturing systems, smart buildings and healthcare [1, 2]. With the more maturity of low level fusion method, research on high level fusion has given more and more attention [2]. In addition, decision-level fusion has smaller amounts of data and computation overhead.

In recent years, Cyber-Physical Systems (CPS) has become a research hotspot. Since a large number of equipment elements such as sensors and actuators are involved, CPS will lead to producing large amounts of data as a kind of new intelligent complex system of multi-dimensional and heterogeneous. Applying data fusion technology to the CPS can improve the ability of information abstraction and reduce the

© Springer International Publishing Switzerland 2016
Y. Wang et al. (Eds.): BigCom 2016, LNCS 9784, pp. 409–420, 2016.
DOI: 10.1007/978-3-319-42553-5_35

network load. Moreover, considering the time attribute of CPS, CPS will accumulate a large number of valuable historical data with the passage of time. However, these historical data are not fully taken into account in most of the existing fusion methods related to time series, so it maybe affect the reliability of the fusion results.

In this paper, the sensor decision fusion theory is applied to the CPS. We study the problem of time sequences fusion for the long-term data generated from CPS system and explore decision fusion's influence on the accuracy of decision-making on the time dimension. On the one hand, the fusion of different time series data is helpful to the comprehensive analysis of the data, the accuracy of the decision-making and the reliability of the system. On the other hand, impact factor can be adjusted dynamically by the feedback of evaluation, to achieve the stability of the system.

The main contributions of our work are as follows:

- The sensor decision fusion theory is introduced into CPS for its heterogeneity, we use the multiple decision trees fusion algorithm that can overcome the deviation of the individual decision-making.
- Considering the time correlation, we use the weighted fusion algorithm with the weight for each time series undergo decay on a timescale. We analyze the data for time series in order to observe the accuracy of decision-making, which is relatively rare in the current data fusion studies. The basic idea is that the closer to present, the greater the impact.
- We take the following measures to guarantee the decision accuracy: the preprocessing of data entered can filter wrong data and realize the early warning function; Moreover, impact factor that we set can be adjusted by internal feedback, making the system reach to steady state gradually.
- A case study is given and validated on mobile medical projects, which can be extended to the similar scenario.

The paper is organized as follows. We describe related work in Sect. 2 and present problem definition in Sect. 3. A multiple decision trees weighting fusion algorithm for time series with feedback is described in Sect. 4. Simulations are presented in Sect. 5 to validate the proposed algorithm. Finally, we propose future work and conclude our work in Sect. 6.

2   Releated Work

Time attribute is an important problem for the performance requirement of feedback and control in CPS. In the aspect of fusion about time, Datcu et al. [3] proposed a bimodal system for emotion recognition, Hidden Markov Models (HMMs) are used for learning and describing the temporal dynamics of the emotion clues in the visual and acoustic channels. Jeon et al. [4] proposed a multi-temporal classification to use of context information of time properly, which makes the whole decision by summarizing the optimal local decisions. The proposed weighted majority decision fusion classifier can solve the reliability of data sets and improve the overall accuracy of classification. Here, multi-temporal fusion is actually equivalent to the traditional multi-source fusion. Besides, McCarty et al. [5] and Preden et al. [6] both considered spatio-temporal relation when building the architecture. Wang et al. [7] and Melgani et al. [8] used spatio-temporal context information for image classification. Liu et al. [9] presented a novel anchorperson detection algorithm based on spatio-temporal slice (STS).

The fusion methods mentioned above have not considered the long-term data of CPS, most of them are only considered current time (temporality). Swain et al. [10] indicated that the ideal model of classification is combining the current observation, historical observations and knowledge. Thus, the importance of historical data should not be overlook, to this, analysis and research for decision fusion with time as the dimension would be carried on in our work.

On the method of decision level fusion, weighted fusion has been widely used, Jung et al. [11] proposed a multi-source data fusion method based on affinity scores, experimental results showed the better space consistency compared with existing data. But, its error may be larger as the weight of each participant in data fusion was all same. To this, several paper about the adjustment and optimization of fusion weights have appeared like Wilkins et al. [12] for the fusion weights of medical image retrieval. Inspired by the improvement of generalization performance with "weight-decay" [13], we introduce it to our decision level fusion algorithm to achieve weight decay of each time series. This also conforms to ideal classification model with the involvement of historical observation in [10].

3 Problem Definition

Nodes in CPS can be classified into five types [14], which includes sensor, sink, controller, dispatch and actuator as illustrated in Fig. 1.

In order to full use of the long-term valuable data of CPS, we make a decision level fusion analysis on the time dimension. Assume $T = \{t | t \in Z^+\}$ is a set that consists of different time, $D = \{d_j | j = 1, 2, \ldots, M\}$ is a set that consists of different types of sensor nodes, and $H = \{h_k | k = 1, 2, \ldots, N\}$ is a set that consists of different types of sink nodes.

Sensor is responsible for data collection, and transmits the collected data to the corresponding sink node. Assume that each sensor outputs only one kind of type data, each sensor d_j needs to collect the raw data v_{t_j} at time t, and assume Sensor_output$(t) = \{d_j, h_k, v_{t_j} | t \in T, j = 1, 2, \ldots, M, k = 1, 2, \ldots, N\}$ as its output object.

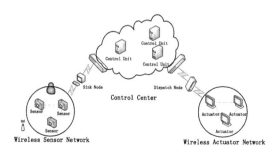

Fig. 1. System model

The contribution of sink can be described briefly as follows: Firstly, sink node determines whether to receive the data entered or not by the identity fields h_k. Next, it preprocesses the input data to detect exceptional events of input data which defined as $E = \{E_1, E_2, \ldots, E_m\}$. And then data without error can be fused according to certain rules, which is called local fusion. Finally, sink node outputs the object $\text{Sink\_output}(t) = \{h_k, s_{t_k}, \{v_{t_1}, v_{t_2}, \ldots, v_{t_j}, v_{t_M}\} | t \in T, j = 1, 2, \ldots, M, k = 1, 2, \ldots, N\}$ that contains local fusion results s_{t_k} and send it to controller.

Controller node uses the method to fuse the data from different types of sink in time t, which is called global fusion. The system will record the fusion result in t. We define the overall fused result of time t as $S_t = \sum_{k=1}^{N} W_k \times s_{t_k} (t \in T)$ based on weighted fusion algorithm, where W_k is the weight of h_k, which can be obtained by training methods or designated by expert. Thus, $\{S_t, t \in T\}$ forms a set of time series.

Then we need to resolve three problems as follows:

- How to integrate each time series to let historical data of the CPS have an effect on the overall decision fusion?
- How to grasp intensity of the impact of the above mentioned?
- How to guarantee the accuracy of fusion and the stability of the system?

Detailed discussion of these problem is conducted in Sect. 4.

4 Multiple Decision Trees Weighting Fusion Algorithm for Time Series with Feedback

As shown in Fig. 1, fusion happened in sink and controller node. Fusion in sink is called local fusion or sub-fusion, and in controller is called global decision fusion. Global decision fusion is the part that we are concerned.

4.1 Data Analysis

First, we need to analyze and process the data from sensor, as shown in Fig. 2.

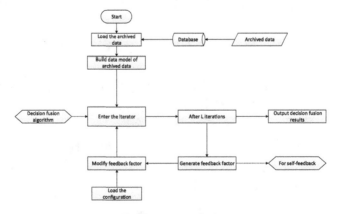

Fig. 2. Data analysis

The iterator in Fig. 2 is the fusion of different time series. Decision fusion algorithm is a data fusion in a time series, it can be used as a separate module and can be achieved by various ways such as neural network, Bayes theorem, genetic algorithm, decision tree, etc. What specific method can be used is associated with specific scenarios. The decision tree is selected in this paper for briefness and clearness of data structure and simplicity of realization. This detailed flow chart is given in Sect. 4.2.

Suppose P_t is the weight of time t, controller integrates the preliminary fused score S_t of different time. After the completion of the iteration L times, we define the final fused score as $S_{score} = \sum_{t=1}^{L} P_t \times S_t$ based on weighted fusion algorithm. Here, we define the fusion object with score, it can be divided by different level as required, such as O_1: [a, b], O_2: [c, d], a, b, c, d $\in R^+$. Decay is performed on the weight of each time series for the influence of different time series. This detailed design is given in Sect. 4.3.

In addition, internal closed-loop feedback is set to modification and adjustment of the next fused score. It outputs not only fusion results, but also feedback factor after the accomplishment of L iterations. The feedback can make the system into a stable state gradually. The reason and detailed design are given in Sect. 4.4.

4.2 Decision Fusion Model Design

For each time series, we present the decision fusion model diagram, as shown in Fig. 3 for time t. In order to overcome the one-sidedness of individual fusion, we adopt the method of multiple independent sub decision modules. Suppose the number of sub child decision modules is N. Each decision module outputs $S_{t_1}, S_{t_2}, \ldots, S_{t_k}, S_{t_N}$ corresponding to each sink output. According to Sect. 3, we can calculate fusion score: $S_t = \sum_{k=1}^{N} W_k \times S_{t_k}$, where S_{t_k} is the normalized value (local fusion score) of module K and W_k is the weight of module K. Finally, we can obtain the whole fused score on all the time series: $S_{score} = \sum_{t=1}^{L} P_t \times S_t$, where P_t is the weight of different time series.

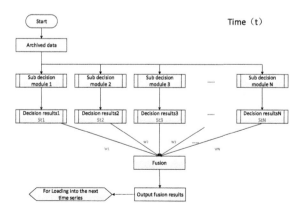

Fig. 3. The basic flow of decision fusion algorithm

4.3   Timestamp Decay Model Design

Because of time correlation, we consider the closer to the current time, the higher the weight of the time series is. Weight correction itself using decay function as auxiliary function to calculate, namely, the weight itself is a decay model. Firstly, we need to set step according to actual condition (e.g. a patient sees a doctor once a week) to divide each timestamp into corresponding section. We set section for unifying data granularity, because the probability distribution that we designed is only aimed at a granularity. Each section may have multiple internal timestamps (e.g. the patient tests several times a week), we think that the timestamps within a section obey uniform distribution.

Main design idea is as follows:

- Timestamp of the closest to the current time has the largest influence;
- The accumulated timestamp of the past can also have a big enough impact to balance the current timestamp;
- The more the number of timestamp is, the more balanced it is. The less the number of timestamp is, the more prone to large deviation.

The timestamp decay algorithm (pseudo code):

---

1. Sort Set<TimeStamp> Ascend // Ascending sort
2. For TimeStamp(i) in Set<TimeStamp> //Traverse the timestamp collection
2.1> ΔTimeStamp=0   // (i = 1)
*   ΔTimeStamp=TimeStamp(i)-TimeStamp(i-1) //(i > 1)*
2.2> if ΔTimeStamp >= step //Timestamp classification
*   New Section*
*   else*
*   Old Section*
Set<Section>
3. P(Average_Section)=1/Set<Section>.Count
*   // Calculate the probability distribution of sections*
4. For Section(i) in Set<Section> //Traversal section collection to calculate the probability of all segments of decay
4.1> P(i)=P(average)+P(remain)   // Superposition
4.2> P(i)=P(i)(1-rate) //Decay except the last timestamp*
*4.3> P(remain) = P(i)*rate   // For the next*
5. For Section(i) in Set<Section>
5.1> P(Average_TimeStamp)=P(i)/Section(i).Count

//calculate each timestamp probability in a section (uniform distribution)

4.4   Feedback Model Design

Impact factor prediction is the key of the feedback. Suppose F is impact factor, S_{score} is the total fusion score, which is also called the total standard score.

Main design idea is as follows:

- Impact factor can affect the next calculation result, the next standard score will be adjusted by $S_{score} \times (1 + F)$. If F < 0, called it "narrow feedback". If F > 0, called it "amplification feedback". F should be smaller and smaller, means that the system is more and more stable.
- Impact factor should have a limited range for itself and F will decrease gradually with the increase of iteration times (convergence limit), namely, generation $\rightarrow$ max, $\Delta F \rightarrow 0$.
- Using the regression method of mathematical statistics to predict impact factor.
- The rate of amplitude attenuation of impact factor can be changed by adjusting the regression formula and convergence function.

5 Case Study

5.1 Introduction

We used the project of mobile medical in our laboratory involved in pediatric chronic kidney disease (CKD) to verify the proposed algorithm. Management controller and three kinds of mobile clients of patient, doctor and administrator are included in this system. Our work is mainly in the part of management controller, providing multilevel exceptional alarm of health index of patients, informing three mobile clients of alarm and outputting the patients' condition with decision fusion to help doctors analysis patient's situation, and make system more intelligent. In fact, the diagnosis of the patient's condition not only decided by a laboratory sheet, but also combined with the analysis of previous medical records. This way can make diagnosis more accurate and reliable.

Management platform of this project holds various laboratory sheets of patients with a timestamp. Assume the indexes of different laboratory sheets are independent of each other and various laboratory sheets are also independent of each other. Data source can be classified as Table 1.

5.2 Description of Simulation Conditions

Simulation Times. Simulation on behalf of the patient's laboratory test records, so the number of simulation is equivalent to number of diagnosis. It can be set at random.

Table 1. Data classification

	Index	Remarks
Blood laboratory sheet	Blood_WBC	White blood cell (blood)
	Blood_Gran	Neutrophil
	Blood_HGB	Hemoglobin
	Blood_PLT	Blood platelet
Urine laboratory sheet	Urine_RBC	Red blood cell
	Urine_WBC	White blood cell (urine)
	Urine_PRO	Urine protein

There have the number of simulation increased contrast figure (5 times VS 10 times) in behind.

Simulation Step Size. It is used to divide the timestamp, and could be set by the actual diagnosis. In this paper, it was assumed to a week, namely, 604800000 ms.

Decay Constant. It is used for time series weight decay. We set 0.5 first, then compared the difference of different decay constant (0.1/0.7) to observe the effects of decay factor.

Laboratory Sheets Weight Distributions. We can obtain them by training study of previous diagnosis or acquisition of doctor evaluation criteria. In simulation, we supposed blood assay and urine assay sheet have the same weight, namely, both are 0.5.

Index Normalization. We used the method of the max - min normalization for knowing the range of related indexes values. The dependencies of different indexes are needed by the specification of related doctors or diagnoses. Since the research is just in the first stage, we only did the situation that indexes are independent of each other.

Exception Classification Setting. Combined with the actual situation, we divided index exceptions into three categories (normal, warning and error) based on preprocessing of sink in Sect. 3. Once the warning and error happens, reminder is given to doctor, patient and system as well as fusion calculation stops. If indexes are beyond normal range, the exceptions will give different levels.

Feedback Setting. Evaluation system can be used by the form of study, such as neural network or the form of assessment and feedback from doctors. We chose the latter in simulation and it could be improved in the future. After outputting the fusion results, doctor will compare this fusion results with his diagnosis and an evaluation that is comprised of overweight, appropriate and lack will be given for modifying impact factor in next round. If the evaluation is overweight, that is to say, the fusion score is high, we will use impact factor to reduce the fusion score next time with "narrow feedback" in Sect. 4.4; If the evaluation is lack, that is to say, the fusion score is low, we will use impact factor to magnify the fusion score next time with "amplification feedback" in Sect. 4.4.

5.3   Results and Discussion

Feedback Factor Variation. According to the above mentioned simulation conditions, the change rule of feedback factor with the number of simulation is shown in Fig. 4. From the figure, we can see the fluctuation of feedback factor becomes smaller gradually and its absolute value also tend to zero gradually. It shows that, the absolute value of factor became smaller with the increasing number of simulation. Thus, the adjustment of feedback correction is declined, which means that the system converges to a stable state gradually.

Probability Distribution of Time Series. The weight distribution of different time series is given in Table 2 when decay rate is 0.5, the number of time series is 1, 2, 3, 4, 5

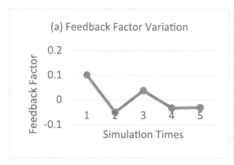 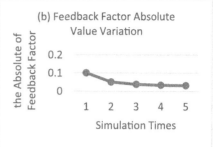

Fig. 4. The change rule of feedback factor with the number of simulation, where simulation times = {1, 2, 3, 4, 5}, simulation step size = 604800000 ms, decay constant = 0.5, laboratory sheets both have the same weight

respectively. We compared and analyzed the variation of the weight of each time series and the variation of accumulated weight of the past time series and current weight.

From the Table 2, we find that, with the increasing of the number of simulation, the weight of time series presents regular change: A single weight of historical time series is smaller, but the total weight of historical time series is bigger little by little. Actually, For the treatment, the influence of historical records should be smaller and smaller, but the cumulative effect should be able to have greater influence on the overall judgment.

Table 2. Time series weight distribution

Simulation count	Amount of time series	Iteration count	Time series weight	Historical weight	Current weight
1	1	1	1	0	1
2	2	1	0.25	0.25	0.75
		2	0.75		
3	3	1	0.166666667	0.416666667	0.583333333
		2	0.25		
		3	0.583333333		
4	4	1	0.125	0.53125	0.46875
		2	0.1875		
		3	0.21875		
		4	0.46875		
5	5	1	0.1	0.6125	0.3875
		2	0.15		
		3	0.175		
		4	0.1875		
		5	0.3875		

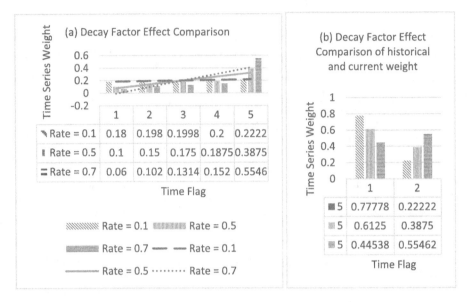

Fig. 5. The comparison of decay factor, where simulation step size = 604800000 ms, laboratory sheets both have the same weight, decay constant = 0.1, 0.5, 0.7, time series number = 5

We discuss 2 points in time series weight distribution as follows:

- Discussion about the impact of different decay rate

The Fig. 5(a) shows time series weight distribution comparison chart of different decay rate of 0.1, 0.5 and 0.7 respectively, where all the number of time series is 5. Here, x-axis represents the flag of time series (1 ~ 5) corresponding to each time series, and the last one (5) on behalf of the current time sequence. The y-axis shows the weight of each time series. The Fig. 5(b) compares the weight of all historical time series (1 ~ 4) and the current time series (5) corresponding to 1 and 2 in x-axis respectively.

From three different trend line about different decay rate as shown in Fig. 5(a), we can see that the higher rate produces a steeper curve. From the Fig. 5(b), it reflects the more weight of historical time series under the condition of the smaller decay rate, the less weight of historical time series under the condition of the bigger decay rate. Connecting with P(remain) in Sect. 4.3, the smaller decay rate means the smaller P(remain), namely, the smaller cross-entropy, so that historical data keeps more weight. As a matter of fact, the entropy of the latter time series is partial added by the entropy of the former time series, it belongs to the partial contains of entropy. Such weights have association relationships on the amount of information, it also complies with the doctor for diagnosis.

- Discussion about iterations of time series

Time series weight distribution with the number of simulation increased to 10 as shown in Fig. 6. The figure presents that with the increase of the number of iterations, the weight of history shows a trend of growth, the current weight shows a trend of

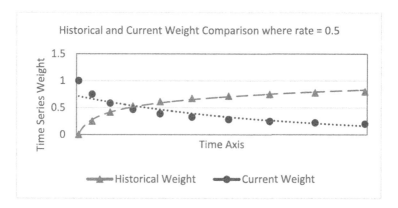

Fig. 6. Time series weight distribution trend of 10 iteration time, where simulation times = 10, simulation step size = 604800000 ms, laboratory sheets both have the same weight, decay constant = 0.5

decrease, and the proportion of current weight and history weight tends to a relatively stable value. At this time, we can think of the patient's condition state in a data volume enough stable state, that is to say, system can able to be a stable state gradually on the timeline.

6   Conclusion and Future Work

Considering long-term valuable historical data of the CPS, in this paper, a multiple decision trees weighting fusion algorithm for time series is presented. First, the input attributes that are come from history data and current data of the CPS will be fused together, providing the required system context and realizing the upper part of the profession functions according to the output results. Then, the function of exceptional detection of indexes are also added, to filter out erroneous data and present the early warning. Finally, the internal feedback is set to improve the system stability. Feedback factor and probability distribution of time series were mainly discussed in simulation, and the results show that the impact of a single historical weight became smaller along with the increasing of the number of time series, but the accumulated weight of history became larger and larger, which means that the historical data can have a greater impact on decision fusion. Moreover, our system could be gradually into a stable state. In the case study, feedback was coming from the assessment of experts, it is not reasonable for the CPS of the intelligent system. In future research, we will simulate diagnosis by machine learning to replace the expert evaluation, such as neural network and genetic algorithm.

Acknowledgments. This research is supported by National Science and Technology Major Project of the Ministry of Science and Technology of China (No. 2012BAH45B01) and Fundamental Research Funds for the Central Universities (No. 2014ZD03-03).

References

1. Hall, D.L., Llinas, J.: An introduction to multisensor data fusion. Proc. IEEE **85**(1), 6–23 (1997)
2. Khaleghi, B., Khamis, A., Karray, F.O., Razavi, S.N.: Multisensor data fusion: a review of the state-of-the-art. Inf. Fusion **14**(1), 28–44 (2013)
3. Datcu, D., Rothkrantz, L.J.M.: Emotion recognition using bimodal data fusion. In: Proceedings of the 12th International Conference on Computer Systems and Technologies, pp. 122–128 (2011)
4. Jeon, B., Landgrebe, D.A.: Decision fusion approach for multitemporal classification. IEEE Trans. Geosci. Remote Sens. **37**(3), 1227–1233 (1999)
5. McCarty, K., Manic, M., Cherry, S., McQueen, M.: A temporal-spatial data fusion architecture for monitoring complex systems. In: 2010 3rd Conference on Human System Interactions (HSI), Rzeszow, pp. 101–106 (2010)
6. Preden, J., Motus, L., Meriste, M., Riid, A.: Situation awareness for networked systems. In: 2011 IEEE First International Multi-Disciplinary Conference on Cognitive Methods in Situation Awareness and Decision Support (CogSIMA), Miami Beach, FL, pp. 123–130 (2011)
7. Wang, H.H., Lu, Y.S., Cai, A.P.: A method of contextual data fusion on multisensor image classification. In: 2006 International Conference on Machine Learning and Cybernetics, Dalian, China, pp. 3745–3750 (2006)
8. Melgani, F., Serpico, S.B.: A Markov random field approach to spatio-temporal contextual image classification. IEEE Trans. Geosci. Remote Sens. **41**(11), 2478–2487 (2003)
9. Liu, A., Tang, S., Zhang, Y.D., et al.: A novel anchorperson detection algorithm based on spatio-temporal slice. In: 14th International Conference on Image Analysis and Processing (ICIAP), Modena, pp. 371–375 (2007)
10. Swain, P.H.: Bayesian classification in a time-varying environment. IEEE Trans. Syst. Man Cybern. **8**(12), 879–883 (1978)
11. Jung, M., Henkel, K., Herold, M., et al.: Exploiting synergies of global land cover products for carbon cycle modeling. Remote Sens. Environ. **101**(4), 534–553 (2006)
12. Wilkins, P., Smeaton, A.F., Ferguson, P.: Properties of optimally weighted data fusion in CBMIR. In: Proceedings of the 33rd international ACM SIGIR Conference on Research and Development in Information Retrieval, pp. 643–650 (2010)
13. Hinton, G.E.: Learning translation invariant recognition in a massively parallel networks. In: Treleaven, P.C., de Bakker, J.W., Nijman, A.J. (eds.) PARLE 1987. LNCS, vol. 258, pp. 1–13. Springer, Heidelberg (1987)
14. Li, H., Zhang, X., Dong, Y., et al.: An optimal data aggregation algorithm STAC for cyber-physical system. Comput. Eng. Softw. **10**, 49–54 (2013). (in Chinese)

An Improved Image Classification Method Considering Rotation Based on Convolutional Neural Network

Jingyi Qu[(⊠)]

Tianjin Key Laboratory for Advanced Signal Processing,
Civil Aviation University of China, Tianjin 300300, China
jyqu@cauc.edu.cn

Abstract. Convolution Neural Network (CNN) is one of the most popular deep learning methods in recent years, which achieves great success in the field of image classification. In this paper, an improved image classification method considering rotation based on CNN is proposed. Essentially, convolution is only a method to smooth the image, which doesn't consider the effect of image rotation any more. It can be proven that after some images are rotated 180°, CNN can recognize them well while fail to recognize them before. So, rotation is one of the efficient ways to improve object recognition. Four kinds of typical CNN are adopted in this paper, which are CaffeNet, VGG16, VGG19 and GoolgcNct. It has been proven that the accurate rates are all increased no matter which one is adopted among these four CNN. This method proposed in this paper can recognize dangerous objects automatically with good performances.

Keywords: Convolution Neural Network · Object recognition · Rotation

1 Introduction

The feedforward neural network is one of the most popular methods for object recognition. However, as the depth and width of network increase, there are so many parameters to train. Compared with standard forward feedforward neural network, Convolutional Neural Networks (CNN) have much fewer connections and parameters and so they are easy to train (LeCun et al. 1990, 2004; Lee et al. 2009; Pinto et al. 2009; Jarrett et al. 2009; Turaga et al. 2010). ConvNets have recently achieved a great success in large-scale image and video recognition (Krizhevsky et al. 2012; Zeiler and Fergus 2014; Sermanet et al. 2014; Simonyan and Zisserman 2014) which has become possible due to the large public image repositories and high performance computing systems, such as GPUs or large-scale distributed clusters (Dean et al. 2012). With CaffeNet becoming more of a commodity, a number of attempts have been made to improve original architecture to achieve better accuracy. Simonyan et al. proposed a thorough

© Springer International Publishing Switzerland 2016
Y. Wang et al. (Eds.): BigCom 2016, LNCS 9784, pp. 421–429, 2016.
DOI: 10.1007/978-3-319-42553-5_36

evaluation of network of increasing depth using an architecture with very small convolution filters, which shows that a significant improvement on the prior-art configurations can be achieved by pushing the depth to 16–19 weight layers, called VGG net (Simonyan and Zisserman 2015). Google Inc. proposed a 22 layers deep convolutional neural network architecture for computer vision called GoogleNet. To optimize quality, the architectural decisions were based on the Hebbian principle and intuition of multi-scale processing (Szegedy et al. 2014).

To train typical deeper and wider CNN mentioned above, larger dataset is essential. Previous datasets of labeled images were relatively small, only tens of or thousands of images, such as BORB (LeCun et al. 2004), Caltech-101/256 (Fei et al. 2007; Griffin et al. 2007) and CIFAR-10/100 (Krizhevsky 2009). Simple recognition tasks can be solved quite well with datasets of this size. But, for difficult recognition task, larger training datasets should be prepared. The new larger datasets include LabelMe (Russell et al. 2008) and ImageNet (Deng et al. 2009). The ImageNet is a database of over 15 million labeled high-resolution images belonging to about 22000 categories. The images were collected from the web and labeled by human labelers. Starting in 2010, as part of the Pascal Visual Object Challenge, an annual competition called ImageNet Large-Scale Visual Recognition Challenge (ILSVRC) has been held. ILSVRC uses a subset of ImageNet with roughly 1000 images in each of 1000 categories. In all, there are about 1.2 million training images, 50000 validation images, and 150000 testing images (Krizhevsky et al. 2012). ImageNet consists of variable resolution images, while our system requires a constant input dimensionality. Therefore, we down-sampled the images to a fixed resolution of 256×256.

Dangerous goods of air transport refer to the explosive combustion, corrosive, radioactive substances, which can obviously harm personal safety in air transport process. In ILSVRC dataset, there are dangerous categories such as guns, can openers and so on. It is a good idea that using trained typical convolutional neural network to identify dangerous images.

In this paper, an improved image classification method considering rotation based on Convolutional Neural Network is proposed. Convolution is the most important and fundamental concept in signal processing and analysis, which is a formal mathematical operation, just as multiplication, addition, and integration. It is a method to smooth the signal. In image processing, the convolution of a template with an image means the origin of template is coincided with a point of the image firstly. Then, the pixels on the template multiplex the corresponding pixels on the image and sum. It is found that for some dangerous image, CNN can not identify it. But, if the image rotates 180°, CNN can recognize it well. Test results have proven that four popular convolutional neural networks, CaffeNet, VGG16, VGG19 and GoogleNet, can well identify dangerous images. Moreover, if considering image rotation, accurate rate will be improved obviously. The methodology description is provided in Sect. 2. Simulation results are presented in Sects. 3 and 4 is devoted to the discussion of the results and give the conclusion.

2   Methodology

Table 1 lists 27 kinds of dangerous goods belonging to the civil aviation transportation in 1000 categories of ILSVRC dataset. Figure 1 gives the method to identify these dangerous objects using CNN. The test images are directly input into one of the four trained CNN. If the output category belongs to Table 1, this image is classified as dangerous one. Compared with previous methods before deep learning, the accuracy rate of object recognition using deep convolutional neural networks has been greatly improved. However, there are still some kinds of test images which can not be correctly identified.

Table 1. The list of dangerous categories in ILSVRC dataset

Category ID	Description
413	Assault rifle, assault gun
465	Bulletproof vest
473	Can opener, tin opener
477	Carpenter's kit, tool kit
491	Chain saw, chainsaw
499	Cleaver, meat cleaver, chopper
512	Corkscrew, bottle screw
585	Hair spray
587	Hammer
596	Hatchet
597	Holster
623	Letter opener, paper knife, paperknife
626	Lighter, light, igniter, ignitor
631	Lotion
644	Matchstick
674	Mousetrap
677	Nail
710	Pencil sharpener
726	Plane, carpenter's plane, woodworking plane
740	Power drill
763	Revolver, six-gun, six-shooter
764	Rifle
772	Safety pin
783	Screw
784	Screwdriver
813	Spatula
845	Syringe

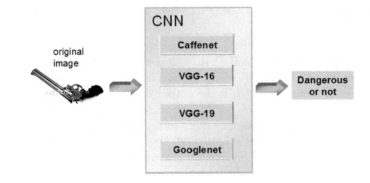

Fig. 1. The method to identify dangerous object using CNN

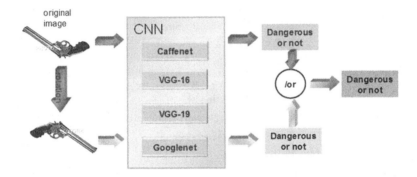

Fig. 2. The method to identify dangerous object using CNN considering rotation

Essentially, convolution operation is a smooth operation of the image, which doesn't consider the effect of rotation any more. If the image can not be correctly identified, after 180° rotation, sometimes it can be correctly identified. As shown in Fig. 2, both original image and 180° rotation image are input into neural network, as long as one of two outputs indicates that it is dangerous, then the image is classified as dangerous one.

3   Experiment Results

In this section, we present the dangerous object detection results achieved by the four CNN using ILSVRC-2012 dataset, respectively. The dataset includes images of 1000 classes, and is split into two sets: training set and test set. The training set include 1.3 M images as usual. Test images include all 27 dangerous categories, each category has 50 images. The classification performance is evaluated using top-5 accurate rate, which is the fraction of test images for which the correct label is among the five labels considered most probable by the model.

3.1   Classification Method Based on Four CNN

Figure 3 list some examples in test dataset that original dangerous images can not be recognized using CaffeNet while after 180° rotation, the same images can be recognized well. The five most probably categories are given. It can be proven that considering rotation will help to identify dangerous objects.

Figures 4, 5, 6 and 7 list the top-5 accurate rate of 27 categories using CaffeNet, VGG16 model, VGG19 model and GoogleNet, respectively. The results with rotation or not are compared. Horizontal ordinate is category ID and vertical coordinate is accurate rate. It can be seen that the GoogleNet has the highest accuracy rate for dangerous object recognition, while CaffeNet has the lowest accuracy. For example, for category 413, the accurate rate using CaffeNet is 0.66, that means 33 in 50 images can be identified correctly with rotation. The accurate rate will be improved to 0.84 with rotation by GoogleNet, that means 42 among 50 images can be recognized correctly.

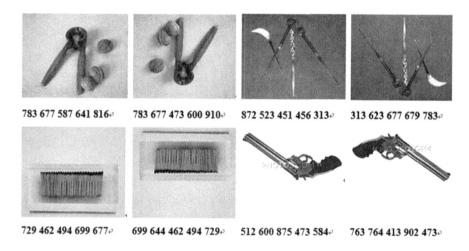

783 677 587 641 816   783 677 473 600 910   872 523 451 456 313   313 623 677 679 783

729 462 494 699 677   699 644 462 494 729   512 600 875 473 584   763 764 413 902 473

Fig. 3. Images examples that can be recognized considering rotation using top-5, which can not be correctly recognized by CaffeNet without considering rotation

It is obvious that with considering rotation, the accuracy rates of most categories are increased no matter which one of these four CNN is adopted. For instance, for category 473, if considering image rotation, the accurate rate will be improved 0.6, 0.4, 0.4, 0.4 adopting CaffeNet, VGG16, VGG19, GoogleNet, respectively. For CaffeNet, if considering rotation, the accurate rates of all categories are increased more or less. For VGG 16 and VGG 19, 22 and 20 categories are increased. Even if for the most efficient method Googlenet, if considering rotation, the accurate rates of 15 categories are still improved.

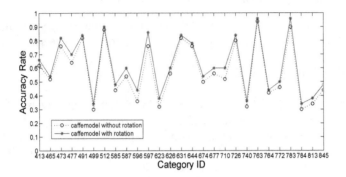

Fig. 4. The top-5 accurate rate of 27 categories by CaffeNet

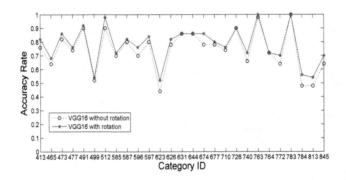

Fig. 5. The top-5 accurate rate of 27 categories by VGG 16

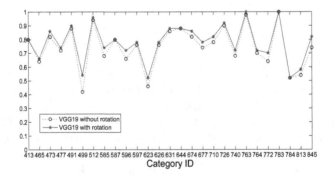

Fig. 6. The top-5 accurate rate of 27 categories by VGG 19

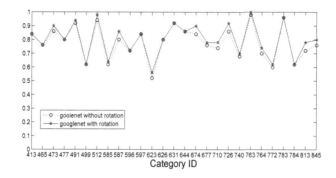

Fig. 7. The top-5 accurate rate of 27 categories by GoogleNet

3.2   Effects of Top-K

The classification performance is evaluated using top-K accurate rate, which is the fraction of test images for which the correct label is among the K labels considered most probable by the model. Figure 8 shows the accurate rates for 413 and 763 categories with $top - K$ for four CNN. 413 and 763 are two typical dangerous categories, 413 is difficult to be recognized while 763 is easy to be recognized. It can be seen that with the increasing of K, the accurate rate increases greatly at the beginning. As K values continue to increase, the accurate rate maintains almost unchanged. So, the value of K is generally set as five.

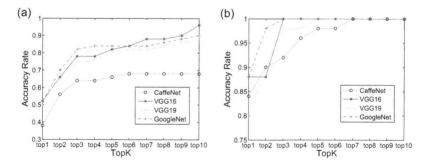

Fig. 8. The accurate rate with change of top K using four CNN. K from 1 to 10. (a) for 413 category, (b) for 763 category

4   Conclusion

In this paper, we improve a dangerous object recognition method considering rotation using four typical CNN, which are CaffeNet, VGG16, VGG19 and GoogleNet. Compared with previous methods, CNN has better performance. It is found that for some dangerous images failed to be recognized, if the image rotates 180°, CNN can recognize it well. The dataset is ILSVRC-2012 with 1000 categories, in which 27 categories are dangerous in civil aviation. During simulation, three conclusions are given. (1) Among four CNN, GoogleNet has the best performance while CaffeNet has the worst one. (2) Rotation is one of the efficient way to improve dangerous object recognition since with considering rotation, the accurate rate of most categories is increased no matter what kind of CNN is adopted. (3) The $top - K$ has effect on accurate rate, the value of K is generally set as modest. This method can recognize dangerous objects automatically.

Acknowledgements. The work is supported by National Natural Science Foundation of China (No. 11402294, No. 11502062) and Open Fund of Tianjin Key Lab for Advanced Signal Processing (No. 2015AFS03).

References

Jarrett, K., Kavukcuoglu, K., Ranzato, M.A., LeCun, Y.: What is the best multi-stage architecture for object recognition. In: International Conference on Computer Vision, ICCV 2009, pp. 2146–2153 (2009)

LeCun, Y., Boser, B., Denker, J.S., Henderson, D., Howard, R.E., Hubbard, W., Jackel, L.D., et al.: Handwritten digit recognition with a back-propagation network. In: Advances in Neural Information Processing Systems, NIPS 1989, pp. 396–404 (1990)

LeCun, Y., Huang, F.J., Bottou, L.: Learning methods for generic object recognition with invariance to pose and lighting. In: Proceedings Computer Vision and Pattern Recognition, CVPR 2004, pp. 97–104 (2004)

Lee, H., Grosse, R., Ranganath, R., Ng, A.Y.: Convolutional deep belief networks for scalable unsupervised learning of hierarchical representations. In: Proceedings of the 26th Annual International Conference on Machine Learning, pp. 609–616 (2009)

Pinto, N., Doukhan, D., DiCarlo, J.J., Cox, D.D.: A high-throughput screening approach to discovering good forms of biologically inspired visual representation. PLoS Comput. Biol. **5**(11), e1000579 (2009)

Turaga, S.C., Murray, J.F., Jain, V., Roth, F., Helmstaedter, M., Briggman, K., Denk, W., Seung, H.S.: Convolutional networks can learn to generate affinity graphs for image segmentation. Neural Comput. **22**(2), 511–538 (2010)

Krizhevsky, A., Sutskever, I., Hinton, G.E.: ImageNet classification with deep convolutional neural networks. In: Advances in Neural Information Processing Systems, vol. 25, NIPS 2012, pp. 1106–1114 (2012)

Zeiler, M.D., Fergus, R.: Visualizing and understanding convolutional networks. In: Fleet, D., Pajdla, T., Schiele, B., Tuytelaars, T. (eds.) ECCV 2014, Part I. LNCS, vol. 8689, pp. 818–833. Springer, Heidelberg (2014)

Sermanet, P., Eigen, D., Zhang, X., Mathieu, M., Fergus, R., LeCun, Y.: OverFeat: integrated recognition, localization and detection using convolutional networks. In: Proceedings of International Conference on Learning Representations, ICLR 2014, pp. 1–16 (2014)

Simonyan, K., Zisserman, A.: Two-stream convolutional networks for action recognition in videos. In: Advances in Neural Information Processing Systems, vol. 27, NIPS 2014, pp. 1–9 (2014)

Dean, J., Corrado, G., Monga, R., Chen, K., Devin, M., Mao, M., Ranzato, M., Senior, A., Tucker, P., Yang, K., Le, Q.V., Ng, A.Y.: Large scale distributed deep networks. In: Advances in Neural Information Processing Systems, vol. 25, NIPS 2012, pp. 1232–1240 (2012)

Simonyan, K., Zisserman, A.: Very deep convolutional networks for large-scale image recognition. In: Proceedings of International Conference on Learning Representations, ICLR 2015, pp. 1–10 (2015)

Szegedy, C., Liu, W., Jia, Y., et al.: Going deeper with convolutions. In: Proceedings of Conference on Computer Vision and Pattern Recognition, CVPR 2015, pp. 1–9 (2015)

Fei, L., Fergus, R., Perona, P.: Learning generative visual models from few training examples: an incremental Bayesian approach tested on 101 object categories. Comput. Vis. Image Underst. **106**(1), 59–70 (2007)

Griffin, G., Holub, A., Perona, P.: Caltech-256 object categorydataset. Technical report 7694, California Institute of Technology (2007). http://authors.library.caltech.edu/7694

Krizhevsky, A.: Learning multiple layers of features from tiny images. Masters thesis, Department of Computer Science, University of Toronto (2009)

Russell, B.C., Torralba, A., Murphy, K.P., Freeman, W.T.: LabelMe: a database and web-based tool for image annotation. Int. J. Comput. Vis. **77**(1), 157–173 (2008)

Deng, J., Dong, W., Socher, R., Li, L.J., Li, K., Fei-Fei, L.: ImageNet: a large-scale hierarchical image database. In: Proceedings of Conference on Computer Vision and Pattern Recognition, CVPR 2009, pp. 1–8 (2009)

Social Networks and Recommendation

Semantic Trajectories Based Social Relationships Discovery Using WiFi Monitors

Fengzi Wang[✉], Xinning Zhu, and Jiansong Miao

Beijing University of Posts and Telecommunications, Beijing, China
{wangfengzi,zhuxn,miaojiansong}@bupt.edu.cn

Abstract. Smart phones are configured to automatically send WiFi probe message transmissions (latter called WiFi probes) to surrounding environments to search for available networks. Prior studies have provided evidence that it is possible to uncover social relationships of mobile users by studying time and location information contained in these WiFi probes. However, their approaches miss information about transfer patterns between different locations. In this paper, we argue that places mobile users have been to should not be considered in isolation. We propose that semantic trajectory should be used to modeling mobile users and semantic trajectory patterns can well characterize users' transfer patterns between different locations. Then, we propose a novel semantic trajectory similarity measurement to estimate similarity among mobile users. We deploy WiFi detectors in a university to collect WiFi probes, through which we collect around 20G byte data containing hundreds of millions of records. Through experimental evaluation, we demonstrate that the proposed semantic trajectory similarity measurement is effective. What is more, we experimentally show that the trajectory similarity measurement can be used to exploit underlying social networks exist in the university.

Keywords: WiFi probes · Semantic trajectory similarity · Social networks

1 Introduction

Smart phones with WiFi enabled scan and connect to WiFi access points automatically. During this process, smart phones continuously transmit WiFi probes. WiFi probes contain a lot of information about devices, including media access control (MAC) addresses, associated received signal strength indicators (RSSI), timestamp, list of the names of the networks the user typically connects to (SSID), etc. Prior studies [1, 3, 4, 9, 10] have shown that it is possible to infer social relationships among mobile users by studying these information. In [1, 4], authors think

---

This study is supported by the Fundamental Research Funds for the Central Universities (2014ZD03-1).

© Springer International Publishing Switzerland 2016
Y. Wang et al. (Eds.): BigCom 2016, LNCS 9784, pp. 433–442, 2016.
DOI: 10.1007/978-3-319-42553-5_37

that if two users share more SSIDs in the Preferred Network List (PNL) than others, they are more likely to have a social relationship. In [3], authors focus on location and co-location history among users to uncover the presence and type of social relationships of users. These approaches can be used to uncover social relationships but miss information about transfer patterns between different locations. In fact, if two mobile users follow similar location movement pattern, which means they follow the same daily pattern to some degree. Then, they are more likely to have a relationship. Compared to the way of only considering locations, it will be more accurate to judge relationships in this way. In this paper, we try to uncover social relationships among mobile users based on semantic trajectory. Semantic trajectory refers to trajectories are tagged with a number of semantic labels such as School, Park, etc. Semantic trajectory patterns exist in semantic trajectories can well reflect users' transfer patterns between different locations. In our study, we use the locations where WiFi detectors are deployed and timestamps contained by WiFi transmissions to extract semantic trajectories of detected devices. To estimate similarity between two semantic trajectories, we propose a novel semantic trajectory similarity measurement. What is more, we add a variable ΔT, defined as a threshold of time difference between a pair of stops, to determine whether two stops (from two different semantic trajectories) are matched, which make the algorithm more flexible.

We deploy 19 WiFi detectors in a university to collect WiFi probes. After 6 months (from April 1, 2015 to September 30, 2015), we collect around 20G byte data containing hundreds of millions of records. Based on our proposed trajectory similarity measurement, we analyse underlying social networks constructed by the *resident population*[1] of 4 different kinds of buildings on campus including teaching building, canteen, research building and dormitory. In our work, we propose an algorithm named RPC (Resident Population Classification) to extract devices whose owners are *resident population* of a building. Then, community detection algorithm is used to find communities in the 4 social networks. The result shows that the networks constructed by resident population of different kinds of buildings have different structures.

The primary contributions of this paper are as follows:

- We use semantic trajectory to uncover social relationships of mobile users and propose a novel semantic trajectory similarity measurement to estimate the similarity among mobile users.
- We propose a algorithm named RPC to extract the resident population of a building. Based on the similarity estimation, we find that resident population of different kinds of buildings on campus constitute social networks with different structures.

The remainder of the paper is structured as follows: Data collection and preprocessing methodology, our proposed RPC Algorithm is introduced in Sect. 2.

---

[1] The *resident population* of a building refers to the people who take regular activities in the building. For different kinds of buildings, it has different meanings. For example, for a residential building, it indicates the people who living in this building. For a canteen, it refers to the people who often eat in this building, etc.

Section 3 describes the semantic trajectory generation approach, our proposed semantic trajectory similarity measurement, social network construction and community detection approach. We present the experimental results in Sect. 4 and review the related works in Sect. 5. Finally, we conclude the paper in Sect. 6.

2   Data Collection and Preprocessing

Data Collection: We conduct our research on a university campus using WiFi detectors to collect WiFi probes on the campus. The detector records MAC addresses, RSSI and timestamp contained in probes emitted by surrounding mobile phones. The MAC is regarded as the unique identity of a smart phone user. The RSSI refers to the signal intensity of received packets emitted by mobile phones. The timestamp indicates the time when WiFi detectors receive the packets. We deploy 19 WiFi detectors near the doors of 19 buildings in the university to collect users' WiFi probes. The buildings where the detectors deployed contain 4 teaching buildings, 2 scientific research buildings, 2 student canteens and 11 student dormitories, which cover most of the buildings on the campus.

After 6 months of data acquisition (from April 1, 2015 to September 30, 2015), we collect around 20G byte data containing around 8.9 billion records and 30 thousand unique devices are detected. Each record contains a 4-tuple (MAC,RSSI,Timestamp,LocId). The LocId is regarded as the unique identifier of each building since a detector corresponds to a building.

Resident Population Classification Algorithm: In our dataset, each WiFi detector detects hundreds of thousands of different devices, whose owners are divided into two types. One is the resident population of the building, which includes students, teachers or school staffs. These types of devices are detected by almost all detectors for a large number of times. The other is off campus population. These types of devices are detected by only one or few detectors for a few times. In this study, we take the resident population of buildings as analysis object. So, we propose a classification algorithm named RPC (Resident Population Classification) Algorithm to extract resident population of a building. The following is a brief introduction of the algorithm.

1. Find all devices detected by the WiFi detector deployed on the target building.
2. For each device, extract all of its records in the target building. Then, count the number of the device's records and the number of days it appeared in the target building. If the number of both records and days is small, which means the device owners only occasionally come to this building. So, exclude this device.
3. For each remaining device, extract timestamps in weekdays from its all records. Then, we use k-means clustering algorithm to cluster all its qualified time points. If its cluster centers follow the detection time pattern of the target building, the device will be regarded as resident population of the target building.

To obtain the detection time pattern of the 4 buildings, we count the total person flow in each hour for 6 months of each building, which is shown in Fig. 1(a).

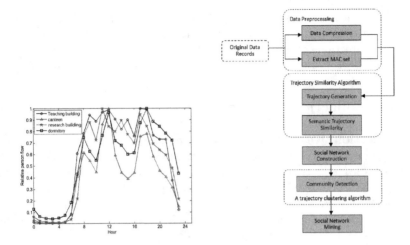

Fig. 1. (a) Detection time patterns of different kinds of buildings (b) Methodology for social relationship discovery

We argue that if a device is the resident population of a building, the time points its cluster centers corresponding to should be around the rush hour. For different kinds of buildings, the rules that the cluster centers meet should be adjusted according to Fig. 1(a). We apply the algorithm to a teaching building, a canteen, a dormitory and a research building. We survey the specific number of resident population of all buildings and calculate the correct rate. The number of resident population of each building and corresponding correct rate is listed as Table 1 where Teach indicates the teaching building and Research refers to the scientific research building.

Table 1. The number of resident population of each building and the corresponding correct rate

Buildings	Teach	Canteen	Research	Dormitory
Number	2399	9782	3862	1150
Correct rate	91.2 %	92.1 %	89.5 %	94.5 %

3   Relationship Discovery Methodology

In this section, we introduce our relationship inference methodology, as is shown in Fig. 1(b). For a set of devices, their semantic trajectories are firstly extracted from data. Secondly, our proposed semantic trajectory similarity measurement is used to estimate the similarity between each pair of device owners. Thirdly, analyse the social network constructed by the devices owners based on similarity value among them. Fourthly, the proposed semantic trajectory similarity measurement based hierarchical clustering algorithm is applied to detect communities in the network.

3.1 Semantic Trajectory Generation

Generally, a semantic trajectory is regarded as a sequence of locations with semantic tags to capture the landmarks passed by, which is defined as a sequence that composed of a starting location, a end location and all stops. Seen as: $tra_{sem} = \{begin, stop_1, stop_2, \cdots, stop_n, end\}$. In our study, mobile users' data we collected are coming from various WiFi detectors deployed in different buildings. These buildings can be regarded as *stops* because they involves mobile users' main activities, for example, taking lessons, doing research, having dinner, etc. Traditional semantic trajectory definition only considers locations of stops and lacks temporal information. Intuitively, if we consider both temporal and spatial information, it will be more beneficial to our study. Thus, we define a new representation of semantic trajectory based on the stops: Let $(stop_i, t_j)$ denote the object emerges at the $stop_i$ at the time t_j. Suppose that there are a total of m stops on a semantic trajectory, the new semantic trajectory is defined as: $tra_{sem} = \{(begin, t_0), (stop_i, t_1), (stop_i, t_2), (stop_i, t_3) \cdots, (stop_i, t_{n-1}), (end, t_n)\}$, where $stop_i \in \{stop_1, stop_2, \cdots stop_m\}$. For each device, its semantic trajectory is within 6 months, from April 1, 2015 to September 30, 2015. Details to obtain a semantic trajectory for a certain device are as follows:

1. Extract this device's all records from the dataset. The format of each record is $(MAC, timestamp, LocId)$.
2. Convert all records to stop points. The format of each stop point is $(LocId, t)$ where t refers to the time that the *timestamp* corresponding to.
3. Sort all the stop points according to timestamps.

3.2 Semantic Trajectory Similarity Calculation

In this section, we describe our proposed semantic trajectory similarity estimation. Then, we verify the effectiveness of the algorithm through experiments.

Definition 1. *Let tra_1 and tra_2 denote two trajectories, $|tra_1|$ and $|tra_2|$ represent the number of points in each trajectory. The similarity of these two trajectories is defined as*

$$Sim_{\Delta T}(tra_1, tra_2) = \frac{LCSS_{\Delta T}(tra_1, tra_2)}{(|tra_1| + |tra_2|)/2}$$

LCSS means the number of the Longest Common SubSequence. It represents the number of the longest common trajectory points sequences of two trajectories when it used in trajectory points sequences. ΔT is a threshold of time difference between a pair of stops, only if the stop points of trajectory $tra1$ and $tra2$ are the same as well as their time difference is within ΔT, we will match these two points.

So, if it is set to be large enough, which means we only consider spacial information of two trajectories when we try to match them. In this case, if the *LocIds* of two trajectory points on two tracks are the same, then these two points are matched.

Intuitively, if this kind of similarity value between two users is large, it indicates that the two users share a large number of common locations and follow similar transfer patterns between different locations.

Algorithm 1. Revised longest common subsequence

Input: two semantic trajectories tra_1, tra_2.
Output: Similarity of two trajectories.
1: $m \leftarrow |tra_1|, n \leftarrow |tra_2|$
2: Initialize $M[m][n] = 0$ //matrix to store the LCSS
3: **for** $i = 1; i < m; i{+}{+}$ **do**
4:     **for** $j = 1; j < n; j{+}{+}$ **do**
5:         **if** $tra_1[i].pos == tra_2[j].pos$&&
6: $abs(tra_1[i].time - tra_2[j].time) <= \Delta T$ **then**
7:             $M[i][j] = M[i-1][j-1] + 1$
8:         **else if** $M[i-1][j] >= M[i][j-1]$ **then**
9:             $M[i][j] = M[i-1][j]$
10:         **else**
11:             $M[i][j] = M[i][j-1]$
12:         **end if**
13:     **end for**
14: **end for**
15: Return $M[m][n]/avg(|tra_1|, |tra_2|)$

On the contrary, if we set ΔT to be small (3 min in the latter experiment), which means that we consider both spacial and temporal information of two trajectories points when we try to match them.

Each pair of matching trajectory points indicates that two users may take activities together. If the number of matched trajectory points pairs is large, it means the two users often take activities together. It can be expected that if two users are friends, roommates or classmates, they will take activities together more regularly and experience more frequent encounters than strangers. Furthermore, by observing the time and location features of matched trajectory points pairs, we can further infer the specific type of relationships of two users.

We use the dynamic programming approach to calculate the similarity above, as is shown in Algorithm 1.

3.3   Social Network Construction and Community Detection

Definition 2. *The undirected graph with trajectory similarity as weight is defined as $G(V, E, W, F)$, where V represents the node set; $E = \{< u, v > | u, v \in V\}$ represents the edge set and $< u, v >$ indicates the edge between node u and v; $W = \{w_{i,j} \in R \text{ and } < i, j > \in E\}$ stands for the weight set of edges; F is a mapping that assigns weights to edges: $F : sim(tra_i, tra_j) \rightarrow w_{i,j}$.*

A social network is composed of a finite set of elements and their interactions. The key of a social network is how to represent relationships. Based on the defined trajectory similarity estimation, we construct a social network where the nodes represent the detected mobile users, and the edges represent the relationship between the detected users. The social network, denoted by $G(V, E, W, F)$, is shown as Definiton 2. Based on the Definition 2, communities can be represented as subgraphs $\{C_i = (V_i, E_i, W, F)\}_{i=1}^N$, where $C_i \in G$ and N is the number of communities. Below, we introduce our community discovery method.

In society, people tend to organize themselves in social groups or communities, such as families, colleagues, and friends. As a result, most of social networks exhibit strong modular nature or community structure. Generally, a community consists of nodes having similar properties, so finding communities helps to mine some useful information of social networks. In this subsection, we describe our community detection method to further find communities in the social networks. We use the proposed semantic trajectory similarity estimation based hierarchical clustering algorithm to detect communities. Specific steps are as follows:

1. Initialize each trajectory as a cluster, and calculate distance between each pair of clusters.
2. Take out the minimum value of all the distances. If it is smaller than the set threshold value, we combine the corresponding clusters.
3. Delete the combined two clusters and their relevant distance. Then, calculate distance between the newly combined cluster and the others.
4. Repeat procedures 2 and 3 till the distance between each two clusters is larger than the threshold value.

4   Results

In this section, we conduct an experiment based on our proposed trajectory similarity estimation. For each kind of building, we set the ΔT in semantic trajectory estimation to be large enough (ignore temporal information), and use the proposed method to analyse the social network constructed by the resident population of the four buildings. The experimental result show that our method is effective.

Table 2. Structural properties of the social networks

AP location	$|V|$	$|E|$	$\bar{d}$	D	GD	C_c	M	L
Teaching building (T)	2399	8244	6.87	20	0.003	0.726	0.684	4.964
Scientific research building (S)	3862	20697	10.718	8	0.005	0.756	0.452	4.104
Student canteen (S)	3151	10040	6.373	19	0.002	0.745	0.736	4.361
Dormitory (D)	1150	5147	8.951	13	0.008	0.743	0.4	3.853

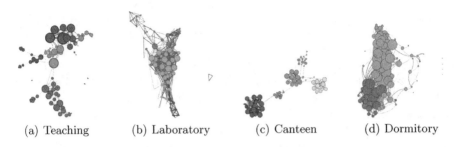

(a) Teaching   (b) Laboratory   (c) Canteen   (d) Dormitory

Fig. 2. The network graph of different types of buildings. (Color figure online)

4.1 Social Network Analysis

We take the resident population of each kind of building extracted above (Table 1) as experiment object. For resident population of each kind of building, we have operations on them successively according to methodology Fig. 1(b). In the end, we extract four different kinds of social networks. The properties and characteristics of these networks is shown in Table 2. For each of our social networks: we calculate the nodes number $|V|$, edges number $|E|$, average node degree $\bar{d}$, the diameter D, graph density GD, the clustering coefficient C_c, the modularity M [6], average path length L. For each of the social networks, we draw the thumbnail of it according to its structure using graph analysis software Gephi [2]. The output is shown in Fig. 2, in which a node represents a device or a phone user, a edge refers to relationships between the two users it links. The color of a node stands for the community that the node belongs to, and nodes with the same color belong to the same community. The size of a node is determined by its degree. The thickness of an edge is decided by similarity ranking size.

From Fig. 2 and Table 2, we can see that different kinds of buildings have social graphs with different structures. The analysis of these social networks is listed as below:

Teaching Building: As is shown in Table 2 and Fig. 2(a), resident population of a teaching building makes up this kind of network, which is characterized by follows: small average node degree, large network diameter and links among users are weak. Undergraduate students occupy most of the population, whose mobility is relatively large. Their activities cover most buildings on campus. As a result, there are a large number of different semantic trajectory patterns followed by this population.

Scientific Research Building: As is shown in Table 2 and Fig. 2(b), resident population of a laboratory building makes up this kind of network, which is characterized by follows: high average node degree and almost all of nodes are linked to build a large community. Graduate students occupy most of the population, whose mobility is poor. Their activities cover only several buildings on the campus. As a result, most of graduate students share similar semantic trajectory patterns.

Canteen: As is shown in Table 2 and Fig. 2(c), resident population of a canteen makes up this kind of network, which is characterized by follows: large modularity and large clustering coefficient. The reasons are that the resident population of a canteen come from various groups of people on campus. People in the same group share similar semantic trajectory patterns and belong to the same community. As is shown in Fig. 2(c), the red, green, yellow, blue and single red nodes stand for undergraduate group, graduate group, doctoral students, teachers group and school staffs respectively.

Dormitory: As is shown in Table 2 and Fig. 2(d), resident population of a dormitory makes up this kind of network. This kind of social network has highest average node degree compared to the three formers and members forming it are high connected. The reason is that most of members living in the same dormitory building follow similar semantic trajectory patterns.

5   Related Work

In this section, we describe the research status of related fields from 3 aspects: the application of WiFi data, the trajectory similarity estimation and community detection.

The use of WiFi probes as a way to discover user mobility patterns and uncover social relationships among mobile users has recently gained attention of the community. In [1], authors measure similarity of mobile users by taking into account both intersection of the PNLs (Preferred Network List) and the popularity of SSIDs. In [3], authors formalize the notion of encounter to captures a significant interaction between two users.

Past research about calculating distance between two trajectories mainly concentrate on two aspects: shape similarity and semantic similarity. DTW distance, EDR distance and ERP distance are all significant trajectory similarity measure method. However, they are only applicable to geographic information and thus can not be used to measure user similarity based on semantic trajectory. As to semantic trajectory similarity, Ying et al. [8] proposed MSTP-Similarity to measures semantic similarity between trajectories. In [5], author propose a revised LCSS algorithm to measures the semantic similarity.

For now, there are many algorithms having advantages and disadvantages for community detection. Based on graph theory, there are KernighanLin Algorithm and bisection of spectrum. Based on hierarchical clustering, there are aggregation algorithm including CNM Algorithm and Newman Fast Algorithm, splitting algorithm including GN Algorithm. In [7], authors envision the target network as an adaptive dynamical system and spots communities in a network by examining the changes of distances among nodes.

6   Conclusions

In this work, we use semantic trajectory to uncover social relationships among mobile users from WiFi probes. We extract mobile users' semantic trajectories from our dataset and propose a new trajectory similarity estimation to measure the similarity among mobile users. Then, we use the similarity measurement to discover social networks exist in a university and infer specific types of relationships between two mobile users. Our results show that resident population of different kinds of buildings on campus constitute social networks with different structures.

References

1. Barbera, M.V., Epasto, A., Mei, A., Perta, V.C., Stefa, J.: Signals from the crowd: uncovering social relationships through smartphone probes. In: Proceedings of the 2013 Conference on Internet Measurement Conference, pp. 265–276 (2013)
2. Bastian, M., Jacomy, M., Heymann, S.: Gephi: an open source software for exploring and manipulating networks. In: Third International AAAI Conference on Weblogs and Social Media (2009)
3. Bilogrevic, I., Huguenin, K., Jadliwala, M., Lopez, F., Hubaux, J.P., Ginzboorg, P., Niemi, V.: Inferring social ties in academic networks using short-range wireless communications. In: 12th Workshop on Privacy in the Electronic Society (WPES 2013), Co-located with ACM CCS, pp. 179–188 (2013)
4. Cheng, N., Mohapatra, P., Cunche, M., Kaafar, M.A., Boreli, R., Krishnamurthy, S.: Inferring user relationship from hidden information in WLANs. In: Military Communications Conference, MILCOM 2012, pp. 1–6 (2012)
5. Liu, H., Schneider, M.: Similarity measurement of moving object trajectories. In: Proceedings of the Third ACM SIGSPATIAL International Workshop on GeoStreaming, pp. 19–22 (2012)
6. Newman, M.E.: Modularity and community structure in networks. In: 2006 APS March Meeting, pp. 8577–8582 (2006)
7. Shao, J., Han, Z., Yang, Q., Zhou, T.: Community detection based on distance dynamics. In: The ACM SIGKDD International Conference, pp. 1075–1084 (2015)
8. Ying, J.C., Lu, H.C., Lee, W.C., Weng, T.C., Tseng, V.S.: Mining user similarity from semantic trajectories. In: LBSN (2010)
9. Yu, Z., Wang, H., Guo, B., Gu, T.: Supporting serendipitous social interaction using human mobility prediction. IEEE Trans. Hum. Mach. Syst. **45**(6), 1–8 (2015)
10. Yu, Z., Zhou, X., Zhang, D., Schiele, G., Becker, C.: Understanding social relationship evolution by using real-world sensing data. World Wide Web-Internet Web Inf. Syst. **16**(5–6), 749–762 (2013)

Improving Location Prediction Based on the Spatial-Temporal Trajectory

Ping Li[✉], Xinning Zhu, and Jiansong Miao

College of Information and Communication Engineering,
Beijing University of Posts and Telecommunications, Beijing, China
liping_bupt@126.com, {zhuxn,miaojiansong}@bupt.edu.cn

Abstract. The development of wireless technology enables collecting massive human movement data based on mobile terminals, due to the close relation between the mobile terminal and human. In this paper, we design a new data collection way which based on wireless detection to capture the smart phone's Wi-Fi signal in our campus, and according to the new data collection method, a location prediction model T-PST based on Probabilistic Suffix Tree (PST) is proposed. The prediction model considers not only the spatial historical trajectories but also the corresponding probabilities about the time when objects appear. To evaluate our proposed prediction algorithm, the experiment was conducted along several months, using data collected from thousands of users that freely moved inside the numerous buildings existent in our campus.

Keywords: Location prediction · Suffix tree · Trajectory

1 Introduction

Location prediction has attracted a significant amount of research effort conducted based on data collected using GPS receivers, data from the usage of GSM networks, or data from other sources (e.g. sensor tags attached to animals). Both these works have made great progress in prediction accuracy.

For our experiments, we used a dataset gathered by placing Wi-Fi monitors in our campus. Wi-Fi monitors can sense when Wi-Fi-enabled devices make a signal. It doesn't need moving object to access to the network. Every time one user is moving in a area covered by Wi-Fi monitor, he/she will be detected and a log is done as long as he/she opens Wi-Fi switch. Each log contains a MAC of the detected device, received signal strength indication and a time stamp. In this paper, we refer to a MAC address as a user, although a user may own more than one device with a wireless network interface. Each user's trace is a series of locations, that is, the MAC of Wi-Fi monitor. We started to collect data since December 2014. With deploying 40 Wi-Fi monitors in our campus, there are over 30000 unique macs detected each day. Since the members of the academic community are using more and more mobile devices, portable computers, tracking the use of these devices ends up to be a good way of collecting the trace of people.

Based on the dataset, we firstly makes a deep mining on the mobility of human beings which can betterly understand the learning pattern and the behavior

© Springer International Publishing Switzerland 2016
Y. Wang et al. (Eds.): BigCom 2016, LNCS 9784, pp. 443–452, 2016.
DOI: 10.1007/978-3-319-42553-5_38

characteristic of the campus students. Then we introduce a location prediction model T-PST to capture the spatio-temporal trajectory of user visits, which considers not only the spatial historical trajectories, but also the temporal appearing probability. We take into consider the visit frequency of each significant region in different periods to approach the time distribution of each significant region. The model we proposed is an efficient compression scheme that converts a large trajectory data into a compact but representative model which reduces the storage size of trajectory patterns compared to association rules proposed. We conduct extensive experiments using a real dataset and the results demonstrate the effectiveness of the proposed models.

2   Datasets and Processing

2.1   Data Collection

This paper is to collect users' mobile data with the Wi-Fi monitor in the campus. As we all know, smart phones with Wi-Fi enabled periodically transmit request signal, even when not associated to a network. In our experiment, we deploy 40 Wi-Fi monitors to detect the signal from moving objects. Each of the Wi-Fi monitors will generate a file of data records and every data record has three fields: MAC address, RSSI in dB and timestamp as shown in Table 1. For example, the first record in Table 1 means a device whose MAC address is "8853xxxx3334" is sending a probe request signal caught by the Wi-Fi monitor and the signal strength is −90 dB at time "1445044980" (2015/10/17 09:23:00).

These monitors are deployed in main buildings of the campus including teaching-buildings, dormitories, school gates, cafeterias and so on. Until now, the data has lasted 14 months, during which time about 300000 unique MACs were observed. Figure 1 shows the unique devices detected for each day over a two-month period. The number of detected devices varies from 14,000 to 50,100 per day due to the varied life patterns of the participants. The high number of observed devices indicates that the monitor has a great potential to estimate large-scale human mobility despite a small number of data collectors. Figure 2 shows the unique devices detected for five minutes. The result

Table 1. Samples of original data records

MAC	RSSI (dB)	TimeStamp
8853xxxx3334	−90	1445044980
8853xxxx3334	−78	1445044981
F8A4xxxxDC0B	−69	1445044980
F8A4xxxxDC0B	−72	1445044980
0024xxxx8773	−81	1445044982
1C4Bxxxx81A3	−76	1445044982
0024xxxx8773	−80	1445044983
...	...	...

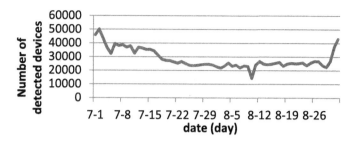

Fig. 1. Distribution of detected devices by WiFi monitors over a two-month period

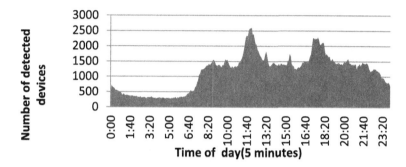

Fig. 2. Distribution of detected devices by WiFi monitors in a day

shows that the pedestrian flow curve, to a certain extend, can reflect the flow of people in the campus. For example, the peaks in the figure appear at the dinner time which can be explained that there are a large number of students.

2.2 The Feature of Datasets

To better obtain representative movement behavior analysis, we further explored the features of data sets, mainly for the following three conditions: 1. The interval of signal records; 2. The distribution of Received Signal Strength Indication (RSSI); 3. The distribution of the unknown devices.

We firstly introduce the distribution of the signal records interval as shown in Fig. 3. It can be seen from the figure, nearly 65 % data records interval time is 0 s. It means that when the user enter the area coverd by monitor, it will generate a plurality of monitoring records. And can be seen from the figure, a process generated record is continuous, only a few records of adjacent time interval will be greater than 100 s.

The signal intensity can reflect the distance between a user and a Wi-Fi monitor to a certain extent. When the signal strength is greater, it indicates that the user from the monitor is near, on the contrary, it is far distance. As shown in Fig. 4, it's the distri-bution of the RSSI. From the figure we can see that there are few records which signal

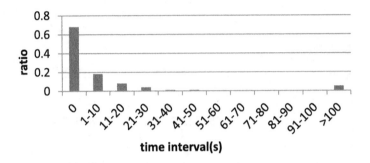

Fig. 3. The adjacent monitoring time interval ratio

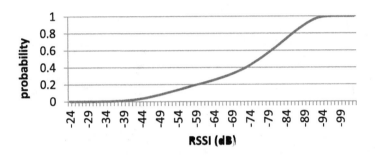

Fig. 4. The distribution of RSSI

strength is lower than −90 dB and higher than −50 dB recorded and about 80 % of the records signal strength in between −50 dB to −90 dB.

As we all know each wireless network card has a unique MAC address which will not change on the usual. In the actual monitoring, when we let each MAC correspond to the manufacturers, we found there are a lot of devices whose MAC address's prefix is not in the list of IEEE assigned to manufacturers, called the unknown devices. The blue line in Fig. 5 shows that the number of unknown devices detect ed each day, and the green line means the normal device that can find its manufacturer. From the figure

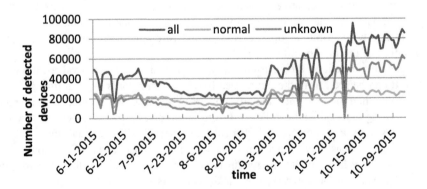

Fig. 5. The distribution of the number of detected devices (Color figure online)

we find that the number of normal devices is almost 20,000 which is the number of students in our campus. At present, we still not found the cause of the unknown MAC.

3 Model and Algorithm

3.1 Preliminaries

In this section, we will explain a few terms that are required for the subsequent discussion, and define the problem addressed in this paper.

Definition 1. A trace lists locations of Wi-Fi monitors by which the device was detected along with a time stamp. Mobility traces have the following form:

$$L = \{(l_1, t_1, r_1) \ldots \ldots (l_n, t_n, r_n)\} \tag{1}$$

Each of the three tuple consists of three elements: the position of the current access to the Wi-Fi monitor l, the current time t and the signal strength of being detected by the Wi-Fi monitor r. And n is the length of the trace. As the position of each Wi-Fi monitor is fixed, it's easy to extract user's mobility traces.

Definition 2. A spatio-temporal trajectory stands for the sequences of stay points with the arrival time and leaving time. A spatio-temporal trajectory of length n > 0 will be represented as follows:

$$T = (s_1, t_{s_1}, t_{e_1}) \rightarrow (s_2, t_{s_2}, t_{e_2}) \rightarrow \ldots \ldots \rightarrow (s_n, t_{s_n}, t_{e_n}) \tag{2}$$

where t_{s_i} represents the arrival time at stay point s_i, t_{e_i} represents the living time at stay point s_i.

Since these Wi-Fi monitors are fixed and easily identifiable from their globally unique MAC addresses, these stay points can be detected automatically from a user's mobility traces by seeking the Wi-Fi monitors where the user spends a period exceeding a certain threshold. Each stay point we extract contains information about the position of Wi-Fi monitor, arrival time and leaving time. Thus, a user's mobility traces can be transformed into the sequences of stay points.

3.2 Spatial Prior

In this section, we introduce how to compute spatial probability given the spatial historical trajectories. After a user's mobility traces are transformed into the spatial-temporal trajectory, we can calculate the transition probability between user's significant regions which a user frequently visited. It corresponds to the probability of the next location given the current spatial context without considering any temporal information. Thus, a probability suffix tree can be constructed. The essence of PST is a compact representation of a variable-order Markov chain. It uses suffix tree as the storage structure for efficient storage and retrieval. In this paper, a symbol means a Wi-Fi monitor to label each edge in this tree which indicates one movement from one Wi-Fi monitor to the other one. And each tree node is labeled by a sequence, which represents a path from the node to the root. To illustrate, Fig. 6 shows the second-order

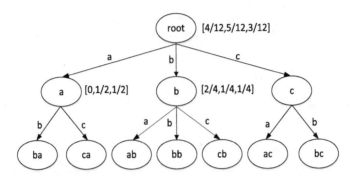

Fig. 6. The probability suffix tree of the depth L = 2

PST inferred from the sample "abacbcabacbbc". From the figure, we can see that each node has a probability vector of each possible next movement. The symbol with maximum probability will be the prediction result. For example, the probability vector [2/4,1/4,1/4] of node b in the tree represents the probability that the next location will be a, b, c is 2/4,1/4,1/4. The maximum probability 2/4 of the node a will be the prediction location when it doesn't consider the temporal probability.

Given a database of moving object history traces, the construction process of PST is divided into two steps. At beginning of the first step, we hold a PST consisting of a single root node with the counts of each frequent region in the trajectories. If the count of frequent region s_i is larger than the predefined MinSup, one tree node labeled as s_i will be created as a child node of the root. Then, tree node s_i will maintain the conditional probability of the frequent region s_{i+1} with the prefix segment of node s_i in the predictive table. For each sequence of frequent regions $s_1s_2...s_i$, if a frequent region s_{i+1} appears behind it, those statistical information of nodes labeled as all suffix of $s_1s_2...s_i$ should be updated accordingly.

In this paper, we adopt the algorithm to construct the probabilistic suffix tree which is proposed by the author in [1]. It can guarantee the time complexity and space complexity of the tree is O(n).

3.3   Temporal Constraints

In this section, we introduce how the time factor influence the accuracy of prediction. Then we introduce how to compute the temporal probability.

The movement patterns of moving objects tend to be from one time period to another (e.g., weekdays vs. weekends). In Fig. 7, we visualized the number of users visited a teaching building in our campus at weekdays and weekends. The lines separately represent the distribution of the number of macs detected by the monitor at weekdays and weekends. From the figure we can see that there are more peaks which appears mostly in class period in the weekdays. In contrast, during weekends, traffic starts somewhat later and remains relatively stable throughout the day, with a slight increase of traffic just at dinner time. These differences can obviously be explained by the fact that students have class during the week and use the weekend for spare-time

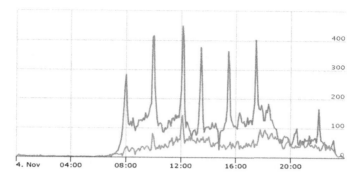

Fig. 7. Activity in weekends and weekdays

activities. In this paper, to enhance the accuracy of location prediction, we will consider the probability that the moving object visits one place at the query time.

After constructing probability suffix tree to represent the transition probability between user's significant locations, we need retrieve the temporal information of moving behavior. In our prediction model, the region with larger spatial probability and temporal probability has the greater chance that an object will move to. In [2], Gao et al. considered the user's visits frequency following Gaussian distribution over the day of week and the hour of the day. And the temporal information of the visit happening at a given location could be decomposed into "daily" and "hourly" information.

3.4   Prediction

PST represents the probability characteristic of sequence context. Given a series of historical visits in a previous time section, and a context of the latest visit location with the time of the next visit, we first encode the recent movements into a query sequence. Then the tree node of PST will be located by the best similar of its labeled pattern and the query sequence.

As we know, the location which was passed a long time ago has little influence on the prediction. Thus, we need to reverse the query sequence when search the best similar node. The search process will be repeated after removing the location with the farthest t query time when we cannot find the query sequence node in the PST.

After the best similar node is located, the moving potential of each next movement candidate is calculated to decide the next movement. The region with larger spatial probability and temporal probability in the predictive table has the greater chance that an object will move to.

4   Experimental Evaluation

In this section, we first introduce the dataset in the experiment, then extensive experiments are performed to evaluate the effectiveness and efficiency of our proposed location prediction method.

4.1 Datasets and Settings

In our traces, many users which are not accustomed to turning on their Wi-Fi switch appear in the traces only for a few days. As we want to find meaningful patterns of user mobility, we need to remove these users who are not frequently detected by Wi-Fi monitor. Figure 8 shows the distribution of the days which moving objects detected in during 52 days. This figure shows that there were almost eighty percent users who were detected by Wi-Fi monitor less than twenty-five days. Figure 9 shows the distribution of the numbers of monitors which moving objects visited in past three months. We can see that most users tend to turn on their Wi-Fi switch at fixed Wi-Fi monitor. The users who did not appear or did not connect to the wireless network frequently will be eliminated as their moving behavior are not apparent.

We select 50 users who are detected by more than 20 Wi-Fi monitors between Mar. 2015 and Aug. 2015. Then we divide the data into two parts: the 4 first months of data as the training data, the 2 last months as the testing data. We use prediction accuracy to evaluate our approach, which is the ratio of correctly predicted visits over the total number of predictions.

4.2 Experimental Results

In our experiment, we use prediction accuracy to evaluate our approach. It defined as the ration between the frequency of the correct predictions $p_{correct}$ over the total number of predictions p_{total}:

$$Acc = p_{correct}/p_{total} \qquad (3)$$

We firstly examine the effect of time factor to the prediction. Figure 10 shows the performances of both our method and the prediction without considering the temporal information. The experimental result shows that our prediction method is more precise than without considering the temporal information. And when the height of PST equals two, the performance will be the best. When the length of a query sequence is greater

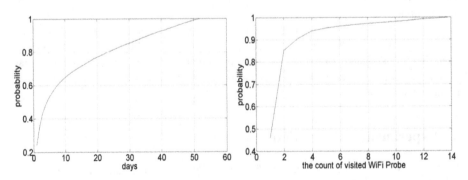

Fig. 8. The CDF of appearing days distribution

Fig. 9. The CDF of the count of visited WiFi monitor

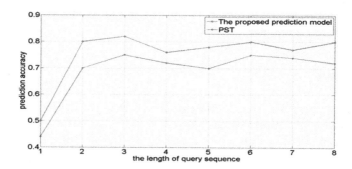

Fig. 10. Performance comparison of our prediction model and PST

than 2, the prediction effect of the our model is relatively constant, and the length of the adaptive sequence can be effectively predicted.

5 Related Work

The study of location prediction has attracted a lot of attentions in recent years. Generally, these approaches can be divided into three major categories based on the perspective from which the data is being considered: spatial, temporal, and joint spatio-temporal approaches.

Traditional location prediction approaches on mobile data make use of spatial trajectory pattern. Temporal information is considered as an order indicator when generating the location sequence in most of these approaches. Markov chain models have been used to predict the next movement of moving objects. In [3], the author extends a mobility model called Mobility Markov Chain (MMC) in order to incorporate the n previous visited locations and the author develops a novel algorithm for next location prediction based on this mobility model that we coined as n-MMC. In [4] the author predicts the future location with hidden Markov models. The center idea of these works is that user moving behavior is transformed into a series of discrete stochastic process, the prediction depends only on the transition probability from a state to another state. The prediction algorithm based on Markov model.

With the rise of data mining, many researches discussed the problems of predicting the next location based on sequential pattern mining [5, 6]. This type of predictors tend to mine frequent trajectory pattern represents the mobility behavior of an individual. Then they consider the support and confidence in selecting the association rules for making predictions.

Researchers have also investigated the user's temporal pattern on mobile data. In [7], the author propose WhereNext to predict the next location. The prediction uses previously extracted movement patterns named Trajectory Patterns, which are a concise representation of behaviors of moving objects as sequences of regions frequently visited with a typical travel time.

This paper presents a probability suffix tree model T-PST which is a principled and scalable implementation of a variable length Markov model. It also presents various models that are capable of dealing with situations when the user has no mobility history to use for inferring future locations.

6   Conclusion

In this paper, a new wireless detection method was used to obtain data. Compared with the wireless campus network log data adopted in previous similar research, firstly, it disengaged from the dependence on logging on the campus network; secondly, the collected data were outdoor data, reflecting users' mobility features but not indoor using features. These two features made our study better for the research of human mobility on campus. Based on the data set, we have explored the spatio-temporal trajectory pattern to predict the next sampling location that a moving object will arrive at. The prediction model considers not only the spatial historical trajectories but also the corresponding probabilities about the time when objects appear. In this paper, we utilize the probability suffix tree to represent the spatial transition probability. And the distributions of the visit times at each state are captured to describe the individual's movement habit. The evaluation over traces collected by Wi-Fi monitors deployed in our campus. Our prediction model is able to achieve reasonable accuracy with considering time factor. As part of future work, we plan to utilize social relationship to predict the next location.

Acknowledgements. This study is supported by the Fundamental Research Funds for the Central Universities (2014ZD03-01).

References

1. Lin, J., Jiang, Y., Adjeroh, D.: The virtual suffix tree. Int. J. Found. Comput. Sci. **6**, 1109–1133 (2012)
2. Thanh, N., Tu, M.P.: A Gaussian mixture model for mobile location prediction. In: IEEE International Conference on Research Innovation & Vision for the Future, vol. 2, pp. 914–919 (2007)
3. Goldbach, H.: Mobile location prediction in spatio-temporal context. In: Boron in Plant and Animal Nutrition. Springer, Berlin (2009)
4. Mathew, W., Raposo, R., Martins, B.: Predicting future locations with hidden Markov models. In: ACM Conference on Ubiquitous Computing, pp. 911–918. ACM Press, New York (2012)
5. Katsaros, D., Manolopoulos, Y.: Prediction in wireless networks by Markov chains. IEEE Wirel. Commun. **16**, 56–64 (2009)
6. Lei, P.R., Shen, T.J., Peng, W.C.: Exploring spatial-temporal trajectory model for location prediction. In: IEEE International Conference on Mobile Data Management, pp. 58–67. IEEE Press, Luleå (2011)
7. Monreale, A., Pinelli, F., Trasarti, R.: WhereNext: a location predictor on trajectory pattern mining. In: ACM SIGKDD International Conference on Knowledge Discovery and Data Mining, pp. 637–646. ACM Press, New York (2009)

Path Sampling Based Relevance Search in Heterogeneous Networks

Qiang Gu[1]([✉]), Chunhong Zhang[1], Tingting Sun[1], Yang Ji[1], Zheng Hu[1],
and Xiaofeng Qiu[2]

[1] State Key Laboratory of Networking and Switching Technology,
School of Information and Communication Engineering, BUPT,
Beijing, China
{guqiang,zhangch,suntingting,jiyang,huzheng}@bupt.edu.cn
[2] Beijing Laboratory of Advanced Information Networks,
School of Information and Communication Engineering,
BUPT, Beijing, China
qiuxiaofeng@bupt.edu.cn

Abstract. With the boom of study on heterogeneous network, searching relevant objects of different types has become a research focus. For example, people are interested in finding actors who cooperate with the famous director Steven Spielberg the most frequently in movie network. Considering the time and memory consuming drawbacks of traditional random walk models, this paper presents a random path sampling measure RSSim, where the tradeoff can be made between efficiency and estimating accuracy, to discover relevant objects in heterogeneous network. The key idea of this algorithm is that we use a Monte Carlo simulation to make an ε-approximation to our relevance measure defined on meta path, an important concept to catch up the semantic meaning of a search. The lightweight property and quickness of Monte Carlo simulation make the algorithm applicable to large scale networks. Moreover, we give the theoretical proofs for the error bound and confidence followed in the process of estimation. Experiments validate that RSSim is 100 times faster than several optional methods and can make a good ranking accuracy approximation to the baseline with a small sample size.

Keywords: Heterogeneous information networks · Relevance search · Random path sampling

1 Introduction

With the prosperity of study on Heterogeneous Information Network (HIN) [13], much works has been done to estimate the relevance among different-typed objects in such complex networks. Relevance search problem aims to discover target objects relevant to search object with some semantic meaning, and it is the foundation of many data mining tasks, such as clustering and recommendation.

© Springer International Publishing Switzerland 2016
Y. Wang et al. (Eds.): BigCom 2016, LNCS 9784, pp. 453–463, 2016.
DOI: 10.1007/978-3-319-42553-5_39

Some works have been done to find relevant objects in HIN [8,9,12,14]. As an abstraction of unique semantic characteristic in HIN, meta path [14], a sequence of relations connecting two objects, is widely used to catch sensitive semantic information in relevance search. Based on meta path constrained random walk models, Lao and Cohen [9] learn a combination of constrained paths to find target objects in information retrieval task. Sun et al. [14] present a path counting based measure, PathSim algorithm, to find similar peers using a symmetric meta path. Shi et al. [12] propose a pair-wise random walk based method, which measures relevance between different-typed objects. These works usually build full random walk models, which require matrix chain multiplication. That is, they take all objects involved in the process of random walk into consideration. However, the high computation cost of their algorithms results in a low efficiency problem, thus, they are not applicable to large scale networks. Though there are some strategies, such as truncation and dynamic programming [6,11], to reduce the computational complexity, they still have a bias to both meta path and the statistical property of the network.

It seems a good way to make an approximation to the full random walk models. Nevertheless, the challenges of approximating relevance between objects in large scale networks mainly lie in two aspects. (1) It's hard to efficiently estimate the relevance scores with low cost. (2) How to judge the accuracy of a relevance estimation?

In order to deal with the problems mentioned above, we contrive a useful random path sampling method, referred to as RSSim, which quickly estimates the relevance between objects in HIN. This idea is inspired from [16]. Generally speaking, we assign a number of walkers to walk randomly along the meta path. Consequently, we think that the search object is relevant to the objects where the walkers frequently arrive. From the aspect of sampling, our method can be viewed as a Monte Carlo solution over a domain of path instances defined by meta path, and we measure the relevance score by the normalized count of number of walkers visiting a target object. We give a theoretical proof for the sample size bounded by the error bound and confidence. Experiments on IMDB dataset validate the effectiveness of the proposed method compared to the conventional methods.

The main contributions of our work are listed as follows.

(1) We propose a novel Monte Carlo based path sampling method to simulate the relation propagation along meta path. This can greatly reduce storage space and computational complexity for top-k relevance search in HIN.
(2) We provide theoretical analysis on the accuracy and convergence of our algorithm. Extensive experiments on real-world large network show the superiority of our method and confirm our theoretical findings.

The rest of the paper is organized as below. We introduce the related work in Sect. 2. In Sect. 3, we present the RSSim measure. Extensive experiments are conducted to validate the effectiveness of RSSim in Sect. 4. Section 5 makes a conclusion of this paper and illustrate the future work.

2   Related Work

Relevance search in HIN and sampling method are key research areas closely to the study. Relevance search is derived from similarity search, which focuses on same-typed objects. And here we make a brief summary to these works. Many link based methods use link relations in a network: SimRank [3] follows the intuition that two nodes are similar if they are referenced by similar nodes. Personalized PageRank [4] uses the thought of unbiased random walk to find similar nodes recursively.

There are Monte Carlo or sampling based measures to reduce the time and space complexity on those methods [5,7,10]. Recently, Zhang et al. [16] propose a path sampling method Panther to measure node similarity in large scale homogeneous network. However, these approaches can not deal with networks that contain different-typed objects or links.

For studies in heterogeneous information networks, Lao and Cohen propose PCRW [9], mainly used in information retrieval task. The similarity in PCRW is defined by a learned combination of similarity through a constrained random walk. Sun et al. [14] first present the concept of meta path and PathSim algorithm, which only finds similar peers in HIN. Based on the model of pair-wise random walk, Shi et al. [12] propose HeteSim, which measures relevance between different-typed objects according to the probability of them walking at the same middle object. Similar to HeteSim, Meng et al. [8] propose the AvgSim measure that evaluates similarity score through two random walk processes along the original and reversed meta path, respectively.

However, they all have the defect that they suffer from high computation and memory demand. In RSSim, we view the relevance search as a probability estimation problem. The good merits (e.g. easy to paralleled and fast convergence) make it enable applications in large scale networks.

3   RSSim: A Path Sampling Based Top-K Relevance Search

3.1   Preliminaries and Problem Definition

In this part, we give some basic concepts related to our method and the problem definition.

An **information network** is defined as a directed graph $G = (V, E)$ with an object type mapping function $V \rightarrow A$ and a link type mapping function $E \rightarrow R$. Each object $v \in V$ belongs to one particular object type in object type set $\mathcal{A}$, and each link $e \in E$ belongs to one particular relation in relation type set $\mathcal{R}$. When $|\mathcal{A}| > 1$ or $|\mathcal{R}| > 1$, the network is called **heterogeneous information network**; otherwise, it is a homogeneous information network. And The **network schema** is a meta template for the heterogeneous network $G = (V, E)$, denoted as $T_G = (\mathcal{A}, \mathcal{R})$. Figure 1(a), (b) show an example of movie HIN and its network schema.

A **meta path** [14] P is a path defined on the network schema $T_G = (\mathcal{A}, \mathcal{R})$, and is denoted in the form of $P = A_1 \xrightarrow{R_1} A_2 \xrightarrow{R_2} \ldots \xrightarrow{R_l} A_{l+1}$, which defines a composite relation $R = R_1 \circ R_2 \circ \ldots \circ R_l$ between type A_1 and A_{l+1}, where $\circ$ denotes the composition operator on relations. The length of the meta path P is l. A **path instance** is a concrete path defined on the information network $G = (V, E)$. let $p = a_1 a_2 \ldots a_{l+1}$, where each link $e_i =< a_i, a_{i+1} >$ belongs to the relation R_i in P.

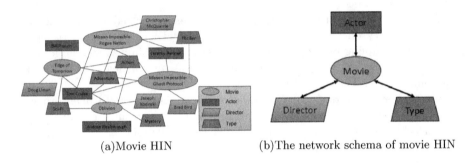

(a)Movie HIN   (b)The network schema of movie HIN

Fig. 1. An example of HIN and its network schema

The relevance search problem can be described in the following. Given a search object s and a related meta path $P = A_1 A_2 \ldots A_{l+1}$, find out a set of the top relevant target objects $X_{s,P}$ according to the semantic meaning from P.

To formulize the relevance of two objects, one can consider an approach of full random walk on HIN, whose probability distribution $rele_P(s, t)$ is as follows. If P is the empty path, i.e. $l = 0$, then

$$rele_P(s, t) = \begin{cases} 1, & \text{if } t = s \\ 0, & \text{otherwise} \end{cases} \tag{1}$$

If $P = R_1 R_2 \ldots R_l$ is nonempty, then let $P' = R_1 R_2 \ldots R_{l-1}$ and define

$$rele_P(s, t) = \sum_{t' \in I(t|R_l)} rele_{P'}(s, t') \cdot \frac{\delta(R_l(t', t))}{|O(t'|R_l)|} \tag{2}$$

where $R_l(t', t)$ indicates t and t' are linked by R_l, and $\delta(R_l(t', t))$ is an indicator function with the value 1 if $R_l(t', t)$ and 0 otherwise. $I(t|R_l)$ is the set of in-neighbors of t based on relation R_l, and $O(t'|R_l)$ is the set of out-neighbors of t' based on relation R_l. $|O(t'|R_l)|$ represents the set size.

Thus, the set $X_{s,P}$ is chosen from top-k $rele_P(s, t)$. We can see from Eq. (2) that $rele_P(s, t)$ is derived from the sum of all the in-neighbors related functions. However it is difficult for such model to scale up to large HIN because of its high time cost. One important idea is to obtain an approximate set $X_{s,P}^*$. From the perspective of approximation, we aim to minimize the difference between $X_{s,P}^*$

and $X_{s,P}$ so as to be bounded by a small constant, i.e., $\text{Diff}(X^*_{s,P}, X_{s,P}) \leqslant \varepsilon$, with a confidence $1 - \delta$. Next, we will define a relevance measure and introduce our method on how to approximate it. In short, we give an approach of probability estimation in the domain of all path instances determined by meta path.

3.2   Random Path Sampling

We reconsider the object relevance from the perspective of path. Let Π denotes all the path instances of l length meta path $P = A_1 \xrightarrow{R_1} A_2 \xrightarrow{R_2} \ldots \xrightarrow{R_l} A_{l+1}$. A path instance $p = a_1 a_2 \ldots a_{l+1}$, where a_i belongs to A_i, i from 1 to $l + 1$. Let $w(p)$ be the weight of a path p. Here we define it in the following formula.

$$w(p) = \prod_{i=1}^{l} \frac{1}{|O(a_i|R_i)|} \tag{3}$$

where $O(a_i|R_i)$ has the same meaning with Eq. (2) and the denominator indicates the out-degree of each object in p based on its forward relation. $w(p)$ actually is the accumulation of transition probabilities of the l relations based path p. Given this, the path relevance between s and t is defined as:

$$Rel_P(s,t) = \frac{\sum_{p \in P_{s,t}} w(p)}{\sum_{p \in P_s} w(p)} \tag{4}$$

where P_s is the subset of Π starting with s, and $P_{s,t}$ is the subset of Π that starts with s and ends with t. To use Eq. (4) to measure relevance, we have to calculate all the unique paths in the domain P_s. However, the time complexity is exponentially proportional to the path length l. Therefore, we propose a sampling method to estimate the path relevance Eq. (4). The key idea is that we randomly sample N path instances from P_s and recalculate Eq. (4).

$$RSSim_P(s,t) = \frac{\sum_{p \in P_{s,t}} w(p)}{\sum_{p \in S_s} w(p)} \tag{5}$$

Here S_s is the set of sampled path instances from P_s. We notice from Eq. (3) that $w(p)$ also represents the probability that a path p is sampled from P_s, thus, by substituting it into Eq. (5), we can rewrite $RSSim_P(s,t)$ as below:

$$RSSim_P(s,t) = \frac{|P_{s,t}|}{N} \tag{6}$$

In fact, the proposed method RSSim can be viewed as a Monte Carlo algorithm. In ranking problem, Fogaras and Rácz [1] show that using this algorithm and a small number of trials is sufficient to distinguish between the high and low ranked objects in Personalized PageRank. For our top-k relevance search, we care more about high ranked objects in the ranking list. Therefore, RSSim, the Monte Carlo based method, is expected to seek out the high ranked objects using a small number of samplers.

Algorithm 1. RSSim

Input: A network G, meta path P, parameters ε, δ, search object s and k.
Output: top-k relevant objects to s.
1: Calculate sample size $N = \frac{1}{\varepsilon^2}(1 + ln\frac{1}{\delta})$;
2: Initialize all elements in $Trails$ as 0; /*$Trails$ is a map that counts the numbers
   of trails arriving at the end of a path*/
3: GenerateRandomPaths(G,N,s);
4: **for all** p_i in P_s **do**
5:     $Trails[p_i.PathEnd] + +$;
6: **end for**
7: $Relevance \leftarrow$ Top-k reversed sort on $Trails$;
8: **for all** $j \in [1, k]$ **do**
9:     Set $Relevance[j] = Relevance[j]/N$;
10: **end for**
11: Return top-k similar objects according to $Relevance$;

Now we illustrate the process of RSSim algorithm. First, we generate the entire sampled path instances. As we are interested in the recurrent frequency of target objects, then we make a top-k sorted word-frequency counting, and output the normalized relevance scores. The algorithm is formalized as Algorithm 1.

The time complexity of RSSim includes two parts: Random path generating and Top-k similarity search. The former is $O(Nlog\bar{d})$, where $\bar{d}$ is the average degree w.r.t. meta path. And the later is $O(N + Mlogk)$, where M is the number of ending objects involved.

3.3 Theoretical Analysis

We aim to establish the relationship between sample size N and its effect factors: error ε, confidence $1 - \delta$. The path relevance can be viewed as a probability measure defined over all path instances, thus, we adopt the results from VC learning theory [15] to analyze the relationship. One important result of VC theory is that if we can bound the VC-dimension of a range set, it is possible to build an ε-approximation by randomly sampling points from a domain. Actually, in our context, VC-dimension controls the required sample size in ε-approximation. This is summarized in the following theorem.

Theorem 1. *Let $\mathcal{F}$ be a range set on a domain $\mathcal{G}$, with $VC(\mathcal{F}) \leqslant d$.*

$$|S| = \frac{c}{\varepsilon^2}(d + ln\frac{1}{\delta}), \tag{7}$$

where c is a universal positive constant. Then S is an ε-approximation to $(\mathcal{F}, \phi)$ with probability of at least $1 - \delta$.

In our context, we give an upper bound of the VC-dimension of $\mathcal{F}$ in Lemma: $VC(\mathcal{F}) = 1$, where $\mathcal{F}$ denotes range set of paths starting from source and ending at some target. The lemma can be proved by contradiction [16]. So, we derive sample size $N = \frac{c}{\varepsilon^2}(1 + ln\frac{1}{\delta})$.

4   Experiments

In the section, we use IMDB dataset to show the effectiveness of the proposed method in efficiency and accuracy, by doing various experiments. We make a parameter sensitivity analysis to further discuss the adaption of our method to the complexity of heterogeneity. We also present two case studies as the qualitative analysis and in the end. The codes are implemented in C++ and experiments are conducted on a Ubuntu server with four Intel Xeon(R) CPU (2.5 GHz) and 16 G RAM.

4.1   Dataset

The IMDB dataset is HIN structured and contains movie, actor, director and type objects. The dataset we use is crawled from IMDB site. It contains $87K$ movies identified by titles, $103K$ actors, $39K$ directors and 27 types. Our movie network are built according to the network schema introduced in Fig. 1(b).

4.2   Accuracy Performance

We evaluate the accuracy performance of proposed method on object ranking based on meta path. We choose the full path relevance measure as our baseline and use nDCG score [2] as the ranking accuracy. In the next, we reveal the relation between our error bound ε and this accuracy.

In our RSSim, the value of ε controls the ranking accuracy. However, it is hard to establish the precise relation between them. Experiments show that we would get a higher ranking accuracy score when setting $\frac{1}{\varepsilon^2} = |M|$, where M indicates the range size of target objects. So we derive $\varepsilon = c\sqrt{\frac{1}{|M|}}$, where c is a constant, set 1. Table 1 shows the ranking accuracy measured by nDCG on different meta paths with the derived ε.

Table 1. The ranking accuracy measured by nDCG on different meta paths

Meta path	TMAMT	TMDMT	DMAMD	DMTMD	AMDMA	AMTMA	MAMAM
nDCG score	0.989	0.978	0.910	0.869	0.938	0.815	0.980

4.3   Efficiency Performance

We evaluate the computational time of our method using the derived ε. Table 2 lists the efficiency performance of RSSim as well as alternative methods on 7 common different meta paths. We fix $k = 10$ and $\varepsilon = c\sqrt{\frac{1}{|M|}}$. Clearly, RSSim is much faster than the competing methods.

Table 2. Efficiency performance (CPU time) of relevance search on different meta paths. "—" indicates that the corresponding method cannot finish the computation within a reasonable memory.

Methods	Running time (seconds)						
	TMAMT	TMDMT	DMAMD	DMTMD	AMDMA	AMTMA	MAMAM
PCRW	1.811	1.740	1.803	1.732	1.868	1.783	1.788
PathCount	1.859	1.904	2.060	–	2.172	–	7.429
PathSim	1.876	2.223	–	–	–	–	–
HeteSim	1.901	1.924	2.075	1.914	1.917	2.183	2.121
Baseline	0.298	0.139	**0.000178**	0.157	**0.00249**	0.558	0.00299
RSSim	**0.00462**	**0.00191**	0.000761	**0.129**	0.00452	**0.481**	**0.00233**

4.4   Parameter Sensitivity Analysis

Our method has multiple input and output parameters, including meta-path P, path length l and error-bound ε. Since they are sensitive to the performance of our method, we analyze the sensitivity of the above parameters.

Effect of path length l. Figure 2(a) shows the accuracy performance of RSSim on three meta paths of different length, where l is a positive integer varies from 1 to 5. Figure 2(b) shows the accuracy on AMA^l with variable k. We reach the conclusion that a longer meta path can result in a lower accuracy score under a certain ε. This is reasonable since a longer meta path requires longer path instances to sample, making a wider range of target objects.

Effect of meta path P. Figure 3 shows how different meta paths alone would affect the ranking accuracy measured by RSSim. Comparing Fig. 3(a), (b), and (c), we see that to reach a certain ranking accuracy, different meta paths need different ε to control, and it always varies a lot according to meta paths. Details about effect factor will be discussed in the effect of ε.

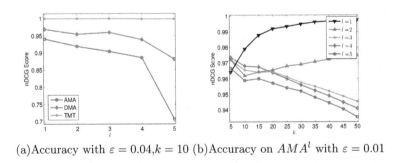

(a) Accuracy with $\varepsilon = 0.04, k = 10$ (b) Accuracy on AMA^l with $\varepsilon = 0.01$

Fig. 2. Accuracy on different length of meta path

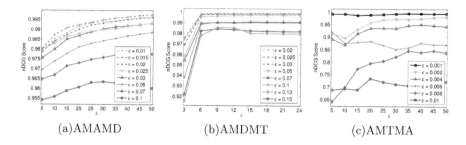

(a)AMAMD   (b)AMDMT   (c)AMTMA

Fig. 3. Effect of meta path and ε

Effect of error-bound ε. Fig. 3 shows the accuracy performance of RSSim by varying ε on different meta paths. They reflect the fact that when the error bound ε reaches down a critical point, accuracy scores of RSSim are almost convergent to 1. This experiment validates that a small sample size is enough to make an accurate similarity ranking. Also, Fig. 3 qualitatively shows a negative correlation between critical point and the average range size of target objects.

4.5   Case Study

In this section, we demonstrate the traits of RSSim through case study in other two tasks: automatic object profiling and celebrity discovering.

Automatic Object Profiling. We first study the effectiveness of our approach on different-typed relevance measurement in the automatic object profiling task. If we want to discover the profile description of an object in some type, we can compute the top k relevance of the object to objects from other types respectfully. For example, as to object *JackieChan* in actor type, relevance searches are finished on three paths AMA, AMD and AMT, denoting the stars who play with him the most frequently, the directors who cooperate with him most and the most possible movie types of the movies that he plays in. Table 3 shows top 5 relevant objects in various types.

Table 3. Automatic object profiling task on type "Jackie Chan" on IMDB dataset.

Path	AMA	AMD	AMT
Rank	Actors	Directors	Types
1	Jackie Chan	Jackie Chan	Action
2	Sammo Kam-Bo Hung	Stanley Tong	Comedy
3	Chris Tucker	Wei Lo	Drama
4	Maggie Cheung	Sammo Kam-Bo Hung	Crime
5	Siu Tin Yuen	Brett Ratner	Thriller

Table 4. Relatedness values of actors and types measured by RSSim on IMDB dataset.

Action		Adventure		Romance	
Actors	Scores	Actors	Scores	Actors	Scores
Sammo Kam-Bo Hung	0.00142	Lex Barker	0.00157	John Wayne	0.00141
Akshay Kumar	0.00142	William Boyd	0.00150	Salman Khan	0.00127
Sunny Deol	0.00137	Andy Clyde	0.00130	RiShi Kapoor	0.00126

Celebrity Discovering. Suppose we know the celebrities in one domain, the celebrity discovering task is to find celebrities in other domains through their relative importance. Specifically, based on a domain-celebrity path, two celebrities share the same status if the distance is short between the relevance of the new celebrity-new domain and that of the known celebrity-known domain. Table 4 shows the relevance scores returned by different approaches on six "type-actor" pairs on IMDB dataset. Comparing RSSim scores, we can find $AkshayKumar$, $AndyClyde$ and $JohnWayne$ should be famous actors in Comedy, Adventure and Romance, respectively, since they have very close RSSim score to $SunnyDeol$, a famous Action Star.

5   Conclusion and Acknowledgements

This paper presents a novel random path sampling measure RSSim, which aims to discover relevant objects in large scale heterogeneous networks. We evaluate the efficiency and accuracy performances of RSSim on IMDB dataset. We also give a formula to choose error bound ε in different meta paths so that to obtain a high ranking accuracy. Moreover, we make a parameter sensitivity analysis about meta path, path length and ε.

This work was supported by NSF Project(61302077) Social Search for Collaborative User Generated Services upon Online Social Networks and by 863 project(2014AA01A706).

References

1. Fogaras, D., Rácz, B.: Towards scaling fully personalized PageRank. In: Leonardi, S. (ed.) WAW 2004. LNCS, vol. 3243, pp. 105–117. Springer, Heidelberg (2004)
2. Jarrelin, B.K., Kekalainen, J.: (2002) cumulated gain based evaluation of ir techniques. In: ACM Transactions on Information system (2010)
3. Jeh, G., Widom, J.: Simrank: a measure of structural-context similarity. In: Proceedings of the Eighth ACM SIGKDD International Conference on Knowledge Discovery and Data Mining, pp. 538–543 (2002)
4. Jeh, G., Widom, J.: Scaling personalized web search. In: Proceedings of the 12th International Conference on World Wide Web, pp. 271–279 (2003)
5. Kusumoto, M., Maehara, T., Kawarabayashi, K.i.: Scalable similarity search for simrank. In: Proceedings of the 2014 ACM SIGMOD International Conference on Management of Data, pp. 325–336. ACM (2014)

6. Lao, N., Cohen, W.W.: Fast query execution for retrieval models based on path-constrained random walks. In: Proceedings of the 16th ACM SIGKDD International Conference on Knowledge Discovery and Data Mining, pp. 881–888 (2010)
7. Li, Z., Fang, Y., Liu, Q., Cheng, J., Cheng, R., Lui, J.: Walking in the cloud: parallel simrank at scale. Proc. VLDB Endowment 9(1), 24–35 (2015)
8. Meng, X., Shi, C., Li, Y., Zhang, L., Wu, B.: Relevance measure in large-scale heterogeneous networks. In: Chen, L., Jia, Y., Sellis, T., Liu, G. (eds.) APWeb 2014. LNCS, vol. 8709, pp. 636–643. Springer, Heidelberg (2014)
9. Lao, N.: W.W.C.: relational retrieval using a combination of path-constrained random walks. Mach. Learn. 81, 53–67 (2010)
10. Shao, Y., Cui, B., Chen, L., Liu, M., Xie, X.: An efficient similarity search framework for simrank over large dynamic graphs. Proc. VLDB Endowment 8(8), 838–849 (2015)
11. Shi, C., Kong, X., Huang, Y., Yu, P.S.: Hetesim: a general framework for relevance measure in heterogeneous networks. IEEE Trans. Knowl. Data Eng. 26(10), 2479–2492 (2014)
12. Shi, C., Kong, X., Yu, P.S., Xie, S., Wu, B.: Relevance search in heterogeneous networks. In. In Proceedings of 2012 International Conference on Extending Database Technology (EDBT 2012), pp. 180–191 (2012)
13. Shi, C., Li, Y., Zhang, J., Sun, Y., Yu, P.S.: A survey of heterogeneous information network analysis. CoRR abs/1511.04854 (2015). http://arxiv.org/abs/1511.04854
14. Sun, Y., Han, J., Yan, X., Yu, P.S., Wu, T.: Pathsim: meta path-based top-k similarity search in heterogeneous information networks. In: VLDB 2011 (2011)
15. Vapnik, V.N., Chervonenkis, A.Y.: On the uniform convergence of relative frequencies of events to their probabilities. Theor. Probab. Appl. 17(2), 264–280 (1971)
16. Zhang, J., Tang, J., Ma, C., Tong, H., Jing, Y., Li, J.: Panther: fast top-k similarity search in large networks. CoRR abs/1504.02577 (2015). http://arxiv.org/abs/1504.02577

Author Index